T0373187

THE SECOND CREATION

The Second Creation

Fixing the American Constitution in the Founding Era

JONATHAN GIENAPP

THE BELKNAP PRESS OF
HARVARD UNIVERSITY PRESS
Cambridge, Massachusetts
London, England
2018

Second printing

Library of Congress Cataloging-in-Publication Data

Names: Gienapp, Jonathan, 1983– author.
Title: The second creation : fixing the American Constitution in the
Founding era / Jonathan Gienapp.
Description: Cambridge, Massachusetts : The Belknap Press of Harvard University
Press, 2018. | Includes bibliographical references and index.
Identifiers: LCCN 2018008168 | ISBN 9780674185043 (alk. paper)
Subjects: LCSH: Constitutional history—United States. | United States.
Constitution. | Constitutional law—United States.
Classification: LCC KF4541 .G54 2018 | DDC 342.7302/9—dc23
LC record available at https://lccn.loc.gov/2018008168

For Annie

Contents

THE SECOND CREATION

Introduction

Reimagining the Creation of the American Constitution

This epoch will be . . . a third revolution in the United States.
—Comte de Moustier to Comte de Montmorin, June 9, 1789

Nearly two years after the United States Constitution had been written, James Jackson took to the floor of the First Congress to draw attention to the amorphous, inchoate character of the nation's founding instrument. "Our constitution," he stressed, "is like a vessel just launched, and lying at the wharf, she is untried, you can hardly discover any one of her properties." The Georgia representative was emphasizing something that was inescapably clear at the time but has since proved difficult to see—that when the Constitution first appeared, it was shrouded in uncertainty. People were unclear about not only what the Constitution meant but, far more fundamentally, what the Constitution itself actually *was*. Over the course of the next decade, many openly wondered about its defining makeup—about the constitution of the Constitution. As Representative John Vining of Delaware remarked two years after Jackson, "On some occasions the constitution is like the sensitive plant, which shrinks from the smallest touch; on others, it is like the sturdy oak which braves the force of thunder." Such vivid attempts at imagining the Constitution's constitutive identity speak volumes. Before it could have meaning, command authority, or regulate life, the Constitution first had to be conceived in the mind and given fundamental characteristics. This book is about those imaginings—their development, their transformation, their consequences, and, above all, the struggle over their legitimacy. In turn, it is about how grasping the significance of

I

these imaginings forces us to reimagine the conventional story of the Constitution's creation.[1]

THERE HAS been no shortage of attention lavished on the Constitution's birth. Much of this interest emanates from its obvious historical importance. Drafted during the summer of 1787 and ratified by the American people over the course of the following year, the Constitution was the culmination of the Revolutionary struggle against Great Britain that gave birth to the United States, and it has often seemed to neatly capture the ideals and the contradictions of the American Revolution itself. Obsession with the Constitution's beginnings, however, stems at least as much from the present, for to live in the United States is to feel the relevance of the Constitution's origins. One of the most venerated symbols of the nation's founding, the Constitution has acquired almost mythic status in American culture, inspiring reverence for the occasion of its construction and the wisdom of its authors. Battling over the Constitution's framers—in books, on Broadway, and at political rallies—has been an enduring American pursuit that is not likely to abate. Many observers treat the original Constitution as a blueprint for the kind of society America is or ought to be. To some, it was the paradigmatic expression of Enlightenment political science, limiting and balancing government in the name of individual liberty; to others, it mandated moral and economic progress; and to others yet, it bore the worst marks of eighteenth-century inequality and dispossession, nowhere more striking than in its complicity with slavery. Whether viewed as an engine of freedom or of inequality, the Constitution is tethered to the story of its origins.[2]

The Constitution's outsized role in shaping American identity has likewise made it an object of fascination and debate. Lacking the ethnic or political foundations of other nations, the United States has been uniquely yoked to its constitutional order. In no small measure, the "people" identified in the preamble's ringing opening—"We the People"—were created and have been sustained by the very Constitution that announced their presence. Much the same could be said of the Declaration of Independence, which has endured as an important national touchstone because it articulates aspirational creeds and values that define national identity. Yet, unlike the Declaration, the Constitution is commanding because of its distinctive function as the nation's highest juridical authority. All Americans, citizens and officeholders alike, are subject to its directives. Embodying Thomas

Paine's paean to American republicanism, the Constitution is king. Because it is used to adjudicate specific disputes and regulate and even overturn controversial government actions, the Constitution has a concrete presence in modern life—a status that breathes recurring life into the search for its original purpose.[3]

The contemporary importance of the Constitution's origins has intensified in recent years as the theory of constitutional originalism has surged in popularity. Its swelling cadre of champions—spread across the federal judiciary, law school faculties, high-profile think tanks, and powerful political officeholders—maintains that the Constitution must be interpreted today in accordance with its original meaning at the time of its inception. But originalism did not inaugurate our preoccupation with the Constitution's distant origins. Rather, it sprung from it, taking shape as it has in a culture that perpetually litigates the Founders' vision, where the Constitution's origins are fundamental to the shared, if not mutual, understanding of America.[4]

Yet, notwithstanding this endless fixation on the Constitution's creation, essential features of that story have long been obscured, not least because virtually all accounts of the Constitution's construction privilege the events and debates of 1787 and 1788—when the document was written and ratified. While this eighteen-month period of intense deliberation has been the subject of many indispensable historical works and will always merit essential study, this emphatic focus has tended to draw a categorical line between the pre- and post-1788 periods. What comes before is the story of making, inventing, and authoring, while what comes after is the essentially different story of implementing, construing, and fleshing out. Whatever else might have been true in 1788, the thinking goes, the Constitution thereafter existed, and even though it has been formally amended since, and many aspects of American politics and society have changed, the same words that the drafters wrote in Philadelphia still govern the republic to this day. Through ratification, Americans *created* a constitution; thereafter they merely *interpreted* it.[5]

Appearances can be deceiving, however. When the Constitution was born, it was unclear what kind of thing it was. Accordingly, it was not fully created when it was written or ratified. That the document approved in 1788 still largely remains in operation does not mean that the Constitution as we know it had already come into existence by that point. For the Constitution has been defined not simply by its words or its structure, but by a set of core characteristics that—by delineating what kind of object it is and, from there, what kind of contents it possesses and what kind of authority it wields—afford it definitive shape and substance. The Constitution was born without many of its defining attributes; these had to be provided through acts of imagination. And it acquired them primarily after 1788, especially during the tumultuous decade that followed ratification, a period that did as much to mold the Constitution into what it became as anything that came before.

The Second Creation tells this largely unknown story of how the American Constitution was made. It is a story of imagining and reimagining a profoundly uncertain Constitution that turned on the basic ambiguities embedded in the idea and activity of "fixing"—a concept that late eighteenth-century Americans repeatedly invoked in different ways in the context of constitutionalism. During the formative period following ratification, American leaders struggled to *fix* the Constitution—to resolve the uncertainties latent in an amorphous and unknown system. But, in so doing, they unwittingly helped imagine the Constitution as *fixed* rigidly in place. They did so by remaking the very idea of a fixed constitution, which they came to understand as an authoritative text circumscribed in historical time. Recovering the origins of this enduring feature of American constitutional imagination helps correct our modern understanding of the original Constitution by casting many of its supposedly essential features in a new light— as the optional, later additions that they were. If they were imagined in a historically contingent way, they can be reimagined differently. And if the Constitution is broken and needs fixing in the present, as many have suggested, then a clearer understanding of the complex circumstances of its creation is in order.[6]

REIMAGINING the conventional story of constitutional creation requires first reimagining the original Constitution. It necessitates bracketing present assumptions and returning to a time when the American Constitution was breathtakingly novel and, because of that, a profound unknown—when not only its meaning but also its core characteristics were deeply uncertain. This point cannot be overstated, in part because it can seem so counterintuitive. It might seem obvious that, in 1787, the federal Constitution was a fundamental charter of government, comprising seven articles, written on four sheets of parchment, which collectively structured and distributed powers within a new federal polity. In a certain sense, this basic description is obviously correct. But in another, no less important sense, it is highly misleading, immediately begging all the critical questions. When it first appeared, the new Constitution was a completely unprecedented kind of object; as a result, describing and interpreting it was an entirely novel exercise. With respect to its character, was the Constitution a finished document, capable of addressing all potential issues, or was it necessarily unfinished and incomplete either by design or because of the limitations of its human authors? If it was unfinished, how was it to be completed, and by whom? In terms of its defining makeup, was it to be considered, all at once, a "machine," "instrument," "frame," "fabrick," "system," "engine," "order of things," "compact," "charter of incorporation," "fundamental law," "structure," and "text," or was it better captured by some of these favored contemporary descriptors than others? When interpreting the Constitution, did it have any credible analogues (such as other constitutions, compacts, or legal instruments)? Or was it something entirely novel, equipped with its own logic and requirements? With regard to enforcing the Constitution, did anything about its defining characteristics afford one group or entity—be it Congress, the president, the judiciary, or perhaps just the people—special responsibility? And when put to work, did it come with any built-in rules? If not, were any external rules available? Was it governed by any existing protocols at all? Interpretive questions that center on the Constitution's meaning (which have been the subject of sustained scholarly attention) presuppose answers to these more basic ontological questions about the Constitution's fundamental character (which have been largely ignored). But these deeper questions were unanswered when the inaugural federal government gathered under the Constitution's auspices in the spring of 1789. This is why James Madison declared, "We are in a wilderness without a single footstep to guide us."[7]

Few have appreciated just how deeply in flux the original Constitution itself was at this critical juncture. Given the thrust of the best scholarship on early American constitutionalism, this is perhaps surprising, for the signature, and pathbreaking, contribution has been to illuminate the incredible dynamism that defined American constitutional thinking and development between colonial Americans' fateful decision to declare independence from Britain in 1776 and the calling of the Constitutional Convention barely over a decade later. During this formative period—when the newly independent states wrote their first constitutions and national leaders hammered together a confederacy through the Articles of Confederation—constitutional assumptions were pushed and pulled in numerous competing directions under the strain of the exigencies of war and fierce debate. At a time when constitutional disputants were in limbo, caught between assumptions that had been ingrained under the British constitution and the new realities of American republicanism, the breathless rapidity of change far outpaced any stability that could take root. But as skillfully as historians have portrayed the changing landscape of this period, they have tended to tell an enclosed story, one that neatly confines creative constitutional creation and rapid constitutional transformation to the years between 1776 and 1788. The implication has been that those forces that so fundamentally transformed constitutionalism during the 1770s and 1780s did not spill over into the 1790s (at least not in quite the same form), presumably because ratification of the federal Constitution erected the walls necessary to contain further constitutional revolution.[8]

Hence, in even the best portraits, ratification of the federal Constitution marks the culmination of one kind of constitutional story and the inauguration of another. That so many have stressed how swiftly the Constitution was sanctified as an authoritative standard of political life—including, especially, how quickly opponents of the Constitution's ratification resigned themselves to the document's existence and instead devoted their energies to controlling its implementation—has only reinforced the point. The story of the Constitution's origins—and the constitutional revolution from which it issued—recedes from view, and the much different story of the Constitution's implementation takes center stage. But just because Americans pivoted from arguing over whether to accept the Constitution to arguing under its established authority does not mean there was immediate clarity on the Constitution's character. The Constitution was quickly accepted as a kind of authoritative arbiter, but that did not eliminate the uncertainty that surrounded its defining features. No matter what had been settled by 1788, the sheer novelty of interpreting an unprecedented object like the American Constitution remained. So while there is a mountain of scholarship dedicated to the early decades of the Constitution's existence, almost all of it explores how a Constitution we would readily recognize was debated, interpreted, and enforced in the early republic rather than explaining how such a recognizable Constitution emerged in the first place. The more basic problem has gone largely unnoticed.[9]

This blind spot reflects a pervasive set of assumptions that infect constitutional study—a presentism that presupposes that the American Constitution's essential attributes have been with it since birth. Most of these assumptions cluster under two popular descriptions. The first is that the Constitution is fundamentally a written text. This idea signals something beyond the mere recognition that the Constitution was enumerated on parchment and is thus, ostensibly enough, a textual artifact. It gestures toward the much stronger belief that the Constitution is enclosed within its words; that language limns its boundaries and defines its contents; that the Constitution is defined by its textuality. Few assumptions have been more foundational to the study of American constitutional law. As Akhil Reed Amar has put it, "the very concept of a written Constitution forms part of our national language and lies at the heart of our national birthstory." The second widespread assumption is that the Constitution is a conventional species of law—defined by its legal content and underlying legal purpose, susceptible to orthodox legal reasoning, interpretation, and adjudication, and thus the province of legal professionals to decode.[10]

At its inception, however, the Constitution was neither of these things in any clear or definitive sense. It would take more than the act of writing a constitution down to treat it as a distinctively linguistic artifact. In 1787, the Constitution was more often imagined as a system that needed to be brought to equilibrium than as words on parchment that meted out judgments. The written constitution was not a discrete, self-sufficient thing; embedded within a wider, dynamic, indivisible field of action, it was a script awaiting enactment. At the same time, the Constitution's status in relation to law was shrouded in uncertainty. Of course, in the most general sense, the Constitution was legal in character—a set of fundamental prescriptions distinguishing the lawful from the unlawful. But whether, beyond this capacious and imprecise sense, it resembled conventional law in more substantive ways was wholly unclear. Many Revolutionary-era Americans, for instance, were adamant that it was a "people's" constitution and expressly not a lawyer's. Even those who characterized it as a species of law meanwhile typically found the Constitution so novel and unprecedented that, to them, it bore no strict relationship to known legal canons. But since so many today take it as an article of faith that the Constitution simply must have been essentially textual and conventionally legal from the beginning, it is difficult to grasp how these attributes ever acquired such intuitive force, not to mention that the development of these two characteristics hardly exhausts all that went into defining the Constitution's core identity. Only by reconstructing Founding-era Americans' own distinct ways of perceiving the Constitution—their constitutional imaginations—does it become possible to see just how much of the American constitutional revolution of the 1770s and 1780s spilled over into the 1790s.[11]

IMAGINE that America's first constitutional disputants were playing a game. The Constitution was their ball and the object was to score, so everybody furiously tried to get their hands on it and tally as many points as possible. Most have assumed that, while these disputants may have fiercely disagreed over what made a score valid, they nonetheless had a good understanding not only of the rules of the game but also of what kind of ball they were playing with and what kind of court they were playing on. Given the deep uncertainty that engulfed the early Constitution, however, disputants had only a faint, contested grasp of how this game functioned. It was only by *playing* that a more definitive sense of the rules, the ball, and the court gradually emerged.

The logical extension of this analogy suggests that the key engine fueling constitutional imagination was debate, particularly political debate. While much about the Constitution was uncertain, its status as the final arbiter in all political dispute was clear. Ratification had assured at least this much: invested with the unmatched authority of the sovereign people, the Constitution was "the supreme law of the land." As James Wilson proposed in his famed "Lectures on Law," first delivered in the early 1790s at the College of Philadelphia, when "the supreme power of the United States has given one rule" and "the subordinate power in the United States has given a contradictory rule" the outcome was plain: "the former is the law of the land: as a necessary consequence the latter is void, and has no operation." The Constitution, in other words, always had the last word. Because political disputants recognized that the ultimate legitimacy of a position hinged on whether it could be justified in terms of the Constitution, there was, in all manner of disputes, cause to press the Constitution into greater and greater service, to constitutionalize politics ever more deeply. In the years immediately following ratification, a great many debates—often those in which the initial controversy was itself much narrower—rapidly mutated into contests over what the Constitution did or did not license. The decade of the 1790s saw, among other things, a great contest over rival practices of constitutional justification, a concerted effort—waged from all directions—to show how and why the Constitution permitted particular kinds of readings and usages and not others.[12]

Yet, precisely because of the Constitution's latent uncertainties, the consequences proved unpredictable. The Constitution was the ultimate source of justification, yet exactly how it justified anything was often unclear. Proving that a particular position was constitutional was vital, yet exactly what defined "constitutional" was an open question. The furious activity of drawing meaning from and appealing to the authority of the Constitution turned debates toward the ontological questions that had thus far gone unanswered. In arguing that the Constitution legitimized a particular argument or interpretation, disputants necessarily had to imagine that the Constitution itself was a certain way. The philosopher Robert Brandom has described human beings' core rational activity as playing the game of "giving and asking for reasons," and shown how this practice can so readily transform shared authoritative standards. This insight can help us understand constitutionalism in the 1790s. For Americans coping with an uncertain Constitution, the decade following ratification was a contest over *which* game of giving and asking for constitutional reasons they ought to be playing. Different games imagined the Constitution differently, meaning much more was on the line than merely one interpretation or another. The Constitution itself was at stake. If a certain game won out, then a certain conception of the Constitution would as well. This reality explains why post-ratification debates did so much to create the Constitution and why it has proved so difficult to bring into focus the transformation they wrought. Even though users of the Constitution after 1788 were not engaged in rewriting the document, by breathing life into certain norms and practices of constitutional justification they nonetheless gave an uncertain governing instrument shape and invested it with distinct kinds of authority.[13]

THROUGH the practice of justifying claims, then, early political disputants not only generated but also, over time, normalized certain ways of imagining the Constitution. How a wide swath of the American political community imagined the Constitution when it was written in 1787, or when the federal government first gathered under its auspices in 1789, was quite different from how that community imagined it a decade later. Many had initially assumed that the Constitution was an incomplete document, not least because they refused to think of it strictly, or even primarily, as a text. As a dynamic system that seamlessly blended text and surrounding practice, the Constitution was very much a work in progress. It was deeply indeterminate, by necessity and design, and accordingly the task of subsequent political generations would be to afford it ever-increasing coherence. But under the weight of debate, as certain kinds of justificatory practices cohered around the Constitution, many of these assumptions were remade. Along the way, a different way of imagining the Constitution took shape, one that conceived of it as complete and viewed its meaning as fixed. This process began when Americans started to imagine the Constitution as a textual artifact, one whose content was defined by the language in which it was written. Given the vagaries and indeterminacies of human language, though, fixing the Constitution's language, and with that its meaning, became an archival exercise, one that required excavating the archive of its creation and appealing to those who had constructed the document to resolve its inherent instability. As a decidedly textual way of thinking about the Constitution became entwined with an avowedly archival one, disputants who bitterly opposed each other converged on this particular game of giving and asking for constitutional reasons. By changing the core task of constitutionalism from invention to excavation, they reimagined the Constitution as an artifact circumscribed in time and space, in the process converging on a new object of constitutional imagination: the fixed Constitution.

This was neither the sole way of imagining the Constitution that survived the 1790s nor the only one that has informed American constitutionalism since. As Americans have argued over the Constitution and appealed to it to justify claims, they have exerted further pressure on its contents and character. But among constitutional imaginaries, the fixed Constitution has proved to be among the most dominant and enduring—not least because those who have seemingly rejected fixed constitutionalism nonetheless have often inhabited a paradigm created by it. In recent times, belief that the Constitution's meaning is historically or linguistically fixed has undergirded the theory of constitutional originalism (in its many guises). But, more importantly, the fixed constitutional imagination is typically what unites originalists and so many of their critics—especially living constitutionalists, who insist that the Constitution evolves with the times—by configuring the ground upon which so much constitutional combat is waged and so many disagreements turn. This imagination, in other words, is what has made this long-standing constitutional disagreement (in all its variations) intelligible and meaningful—not by mandating a particular theory of interpretation but by opening up the conceptual space in which certain (often opposing) theories could flourish.[14]

For one, the emergence of the fixed constitutional imagination in the 1790s transformed how many conceptualized the Constitution as an object. Daniel Hulsebosch has stressed the dynamism of early American constitutionalism by asking us to see the Constitution "in action" rather than in a "glass case." Certainly, in a vital sense, the early Constitution must be seen in action: both as embedded in a dynamic set of argumentative practices and as itself a dynamic object that was imagined as far more than an inert text. That said, a crucial outcome of this early dynamism was that it became possible to see the Constitution as anything but dynamic, as nothing *but* a static text. Once seen this way, it became hard to appreciate that the Constitution might ever have seemed otherwise. Constitutional disputants ever since, no matter their charged disagreements over that object's meaning, have often made reference to the same discrete, stationary object, precisely because it has so often seemed the only intuitive way of imagining the Constitution. The fixed constitutional imagination allowed Americans to think of the Constitution as something consigned to a glass case.[15]

An even more important consequence of the advent of the fixed constitutional imagination was that it remade the concept of constitutional fixity itself. After the 1790s, the older constitutional imagination Americans had long known, the one that had previously created and sustained the British constitution, would increasingly seem strange and out of place. Defenders of the British constitution—colonial Americans chief among them—had, without difficulty, assumed that their constitution was simultaneously fixed and yet perpetually changing. But American constitutional dispute helped pull these characteristics apart, in the process destroying the older constitutional imagination that had made this combination intelligible. The assumption thereafter that fixity and perpetual change were incompatible antagonists—no matter which of the two was privileged—signaled a new way of seeing a constitution, one founded on a peculiar conception of fixity. In 1787, many Americans would still have found it entirely logical that their Constitution was both stable and changing; by at least 1796, a new kind of constitutional imagination had upended this logic. As the Constitution was, all at once, refracted through language, tethered to acts of historical excavation, and imagined as an act of creation with defined authorship, an older understanding of constitutional fixity gave way to an explosively novel kind. Constitutional debates after 1787 helped transform American constitutional imagination, then, not by shifting attention wholly onto one single image of the Constitution, but by inaugurating a particular way of understanding it that structured the possible choices and their logical relations to one another. This explains why, even though the fixed constitutional imagination was not anticipated at the Constitution's birth, it has become seemingly essential to how the Constitution is conceived. Even as Americans have vacillated between the value of constitutional fixity and change, they have largely done so within a paradigm that was opened up by the rise of the fixed constitutional imagination in the 1790s—one that not only treats fixity and change as incompatible, but assumes that this incompatibility is natural, given, and inherent to constitutionalism itself.[16]

THIS BOOK is, thus, about a particular constitutional subject and brand of constitutional debate. It is about what kind of a thing the Constitution became in people's minds and how its character as an adjudicative and interpretive object was explicated and contested. It is not immediately centered on related constitutional topics of obvious importance, such as liberty, rights, institutional architecture, republican social order, or sovereignty. No doubt all of these were entangled with how people conceptualized the Constitution. For many years following ratification, Americans debated what kind of rights the Constitution protected. They struggled to demarcate clear boundaries between the three branches of the federal government. They wrestled with the peculiar ambiguities of federalism, and especially whether the new federal charter created a genuinely national polity, a compact among equal states, or something in between. They also argued over how the new United States and its Constitution fit into a wider cluster of sovereign nations. These points of constitutional controversy come into focus here only when, during these early years, they implicate deeper questions about the Constitution's core makeup as an object of interpretation and what it meant to be subject to its authority. We know far more about these constitutive elements of constitutionalism than we do about how the Constitution itself was imagined and reimagined during these formative years.[17]

Much the same can be said about the Constitution's relationship to political and social power. What the Constitution's architects and advocates were hoping to accomplish, or how their efforts overlay a broader struggle for power in the young republic—including the manifold ways in which the Constitution was used to protect the institution of slavery—mark significant stories that have been ably told. This book is about a different kind of power imprinted on the Constitution—the power it was given to legitimate some claims and discredit others. The two kinds of contests were intertwined, for the struggle over argumentative legitimacy would not have unfolded as it did without this broader struggle for political and social power that infused it with such meaning. But that makes it all the more urgent to grasp how high-stakes political and social contests gave way to particular battles over using and imagining the Constitution, with the latter holding real, and often explosive, implications for the former.[18]

Despite setting aside such matters, the story of post-1788 constitutional creation and change featured here is nonetheless wide-ranging, involving thousands of participants and innumerable episodes. Constitutional debate took place at all levels of society, in all regions of the country, and in all conceivable venues—newspapers, pamphlets, sermons, public speeches, coffeehouses, taverns, private correspondence, and legislative halls. It is also a story not easily confined to the decade after ratification. Although that period played a uniquely formative role in defining the Constitution's shape and content, the Constitution has continued to be debated and reimagined from its first appearance in 1787 right up to the present day. But the only way to bring the kind of dynamics that have hitherto been obscured into focus is to take a more concentrated look—to reconstruct important debates in sufficient detail that the practices of justification they occasioned and the consequences they subtly effected can be brought into sharp relief. Consequently, this book is almost exclusively centered around elite political debates, often held in formal settings, especially on the floors of the first Congresses.[19]

Privileging Congress makes sense because it was an ideal site from which to view the kind of constitutional debates that were most consequential in the earliest years of the republic. Contained within an institutional setting, structured by the formality of legislative proceedings, and organized around pressing questions of policy and law, these debates frequently concerned the Constitution and can be reconstructed in detail. As a laboratory of investigation, its value is without equal.[20]

But there is an even better reason for focusing on Congress: it was the principal site of constitutional development and transformation in these initial years. No group or entity more immediately confronted the open problems of constitutional uncertainty beginning in 1789, and perhaps no body had as much authority to shape the Constitution in such decisive ways. The First Congress was the next logical battleground over the Constitution after the ratification debates came to an end. Massachusetts statesman Samuel Osgood predicted that it would resemble a "second convention." James Madison seemed to grasp as much when he wrote during the ratification struggle that "all new laws, though penned with the greatest technical skill, and passed on the fullest and most mature deliberation, are considered as more or less obscure and equivocal, until their meaning be liquidated and ascertained by a series of particular discussions and adjudications." The first federal elections, held beginning in the fall of 1788, were in no small measure waged over what might come of the nation's supreme law when the First Congress gathered. Moreover, many of the principal disputants who had played such prominent roles during the previous years of constitutional reform—men like James Madison, Elbridge Gerry, Roger Sherman, Oliver Ellsworth, Abraham Baldwin, William Findley, Richard Henry Lee, and Aedanus Burke, to name just a few—populated the ranks of the first Congresses. On critical questions of far-reaching importance, many of which concerned the Constitution, Congress was the first mover, a fact Americans widely recognized. It preceded the executive or judiciary and, in fact, had to create executive departments and the federal court system from scratch during its first year in session. There was, in effect, no national government until Congress created one. The leading Revolutionary-era painter John Trumbull was not exaggerating when, in 1791, he remarked to John Adams on the First Congress, "by no Legislature, was ever so much done in so short a period for the establishment of Government, Order, public Credit & general tranquility." Prominent Massachusetts statesman James Warren thus captured a pervasive sentiment in the spring of 1789, when he wrote Elbridge Gerry, "All Eyes are looking up to Congress."[21]

Given the development of republican political thinking up to that point, especially in light of Americans' own experience with self-government as colonies and then independent states, it is not surprising that so many turned to Congress. Legislatures—and especially their lower houses—commanded distinctive authority in the Revolutionary American imagination. Inspired by the memory of colonial assemblies' efforts to thwart intrusions by the British crown, many believed that elected legislatures were the clearest embodiment of the people's interests and thus the safest repository of power. This conviction explains why so many state constitutions vested so much authority in them. By 1789, to be sure, some had turned against this sentiment, fearing that popularly elected legislatures were prone to tyranny. But this criticism otherwise reinforced the basic assumption. Legislatures were so threatening, and had wreaked such havoc in the states, precisely because they were uniquely powerful in republics predicated on popular will. Nobody articulated this point as vividly or incisively as Madison, who had long worried that the "legislative department is every where extending the sphere of its activity, and drawing all power into its impetuous vortex." Whatever one thought about the virtue of legislatures, they seemed to be the linchpin of constitutional design and the center of gravity in republican politics. Unsurprisingly, the Constitutional Convention's first, and arguably defining, task was to construct a new national legislature, and the proceedings' achievements largely hinged on conquering this assignment. When the First Congress gathered in the spring of 1789, then, many had reason to believe that it would shape political dynamics in a special way. In particular, many assumed that the House of Representatives—the new federal government's lower house, which, as Madison put it, would be made up of "the immediate representatives of the people"—would prove the defining body.[22]

Other settings besides Congress were no doubt also vital during these early years. Some scholars have explored the transformative actions of the executive branch during this period—exertions that cast doubt on the belief that the legislature was a singular force in republican politics. The judiciary, meanwhile, deserves fresh scrutiny—not because it has been neglected, but because examinations of its decisions have often presupposed a false affinity between constitutional worlds past and present. And then there are the countless sites beyond the formal halls of power. Even though there have been productive forays into this terrain, a full-blooded history of early popular constitutionalism—tracing in rich detail the Constitution's development in popular imagination and everyday life— cries out for attention. For now, even if a deep dive into how the Constitution was reimagined in the early Congresses will not reveal the full picture, it will illustrate its central features.[23]

THE POLITICAL and intellectual history of early republican debate is usually told in a different way. Through many bracing renditions, the age typically has been defined not by its constitutional debate but by its partisanship and its ideological fracturing. It is the period of Alexander Hamilton versus Thomas Jefferson, of commercial versus agrarian republicanism, of Federalists versus Republicans; when regional identities became noticeably partisan, slavery became a special political problem, and democracy took on more of a racial and gendered cast; when politics expanded and spilled out of its traditional settings, moving to the streets, to the partisan press, to the clubs—when the people "out of doors" announced their presence with hitherto unmatched potency, and "public opinion" took on new meaning and vitality. It was an anxious and chaotic time, when politicians were caught between the inherited imperatives of an aristocratic culture and the emerging norms of a democratic one; when they were forced to litigate the meaning of the American Revolution across numerous issues and contexts. Out of this explosive mixture emerged the nation's first political parties and the first stirrings of modern political sensibilities.[24]

In standard narrations of this age of aggressive partisanship, the Constitution often fades in and out of view, mainly as a proxy for the party wars. In the conventional telling, Hamilton and his Federalist allies favored broad construction of the Constitution, in order to advance their financial program and nationalist agenda, while Jefferson, Madison, and the Republicans seized on strict constitutional construction to combat them. An alternative approach has been to extract the Constitution from this messy context and chart its development independent of the richly textured world that early republican historians have rendered. But the Constitution should not be rescued from this crucial context; instead, it should be better understood within it. The 1790s was, indeed, a vigorously—and at times viciously—partisan decade. A great deal of political argument was motivated by regional, political, or socioeconomic interest. And political disputants were often forced to explain why their principles had conveniently changed to suit their partisan needs. All of this was especially true on the floors of Congress, where the decade's party wars played out most aggressively and clearly, where passions often reached a boiling point, where affairs of honor were the rule rather than the exception, and where economic and regional interests informed a vast array of decisions. Constitutional argument was no doubt laid over the messier realities made by these partisan imperatives and emotions.[25]

It is tempting, accordingly, to interpret individual arguments in light of the instrumental purposes that guided many of them—to care less about what politicians said than about what they were trying to accomplish.

Nothing about this inclination is mistaken, as long as it is kept in the right perspective. For too long a false dichotomy has bedeviled humanistic inquiry: that ideas and interests stand in fundamental opposition. In extreme cases, words and ideas have either been defended as principled commitments or dismissed as ephemeral superstructure. But here a distinction is helpful. Depending upon the questions one asks, it can be critical to take arguments seriously in their own right, or it can be entirely appropriate to wonder what motivations or purposes lay behind them. Those historians of early republican politics who have sought to understand what drove political debate and the formation of durable party coalitions have not been wrong to situate political argument in wider contexts and to ask what relationship different positions bore to economic stakes, regional pressures, or personal animosity. The same goes for the interplay between politics and the vectors of capital accumulation and economic and social power. This approach becomes unsuitable only when it is assumed that political argument is thus necessarily reducible to what motivated it, that its impact is purely a function of its instrumentality.[26]

If, however, the goal is not to explain political motivations but instead to understand the consequences of political argument—to understand how certain arguments reveal certain forms of constitutional imagination—then a different perspective is needed. While no doubt many political leaders were driven by socioeconomic interests, whether regional or personal, those motivations cannot explain exactly how disputants imagined the Constitution, or how some forms of imagination acquired power and resonance, or, most important, how some imaginings took on lives of their own—how the arguments underlying them were reproduced, appropriated, extended, and distorted in evolving contexts by multiple participants. In other words, arguments and the mental images they form are consequential, even if uttered by the least sincere, least scrupulous actors. Not only do authoritative norms explain and guide the provenance of arguments, but more critically, if one is interested in how authoritative norms originate and develop, only a careful study of discursive moves can suffice. With this goal in mind, it is often less critical to determine why arguments were articulated in the first place than to assess their long-term fate—whether they quickly disappeared or took on enduring force, if and how they grew and transformed over time, if and how they became premises for subsequent arguments. Exposing this dimension of political power means tracing the microdynamics of debate. To adopt a physical metaphor, it requires charting how certain arguments took on increased mass, force, and energy, came to dwarf competitors, and began attracting others into their orbit.[27]

Here, then, is where the Constitution fits into the aggressive partisanship of the early republic. Constitutional argument was more, not less, consequential when deployed in these political contexts. That disputants' motivations might have been anything but principled did not necessarily control or diminish the force of their constitutional appeals or the vitality of their constitutional imaginings. In fact, because politics—especially congressional politics—were infused with such passion and litigated with such zeal, political appeals to the Constitution only took on greater force. Partisanship only intensified the pace of debate, enabling the constitutional game of giving and asking for reasons to undergo abrupt and dramatic changes, while effectively obscuring the ways in which the Constitution was being remade. Because debates unfolded in such rapid succession and putatively turned on more evident political and economic issues, they did not lend themselves to the kind of self-conscious analysis necessary to uncover the transformative impact they had, in fact, wrought. Constitutional change was hard to keep up with before 1787, and much the same was true following 1789. Set against the backdrop of deep constitutional uncertainty, ferocious partisanship not only fueled but hastened the process of imagining and reimagining the Constitution.

THE NARRATIVE that follows is structured to bring a coherent portion of this sprawling story of early constitutional imagining and fixing into focus. Chapters 1 and 2 range widely across American constitutional discourse and debate between 1776 and 1788, to expose the important degree of constitutional uncertainty that ran through this period and endured beyond the ratification of the federal Constitution. These chapters explore the ways in which constitutional disputants began scratching the surface, however tentatively, of central issues pertaining to the Constitution's fundamental nature—especially its relationship to language—that would define the period that followed. With the uncertain Constitution in place, Chapters 3 through 7 examine in depth crucial congressional debates: disputes over the removal of executive officers in 1789, the addition of constitutional amendments later that year, Alexander Hamilton's proposal to charter a national bank in 1791, and the implementation of the controversial Jay Treaty in 1796. These were hardly the only congressional debates during this period that centered on the Constitution, but they are the ones that most immediately implicated the Constitution's character and did the most to transform how participants imagined it. The Epilogue explores how the brand of constitutional imagination that came into sharp relief during the debate over Jay's Treaty endured well beyond the eighteenth century.[28]

Many of these Founding-era moments are well studied. But my goal is not to elucidate the specific issues they raise. Rather, my objective is to identify within these debates the dynamic contests over the imaginative possibilities of the Constitution that they contained. At a time when it was unclear what the Constitution was, and the task of interpreting it was so novel, these debates helped transform how many Americans conceived of their fundamental governing instrument. Initial efforts to fix (resolve and construct) an uncertain Constitution unwittingly created a new way of imagining that Constitution as fixed (locked in place). This second constitutional creation was not inevitable, and its consequences were immense. They can still be felt to this day.

I

The Uncertainty of
Written Constitutionalism

Political prosperity resides, not in the words and letters of the *Constitu-tion;* but in the temper, the habits, and the practices of the people.
—Samuel Miller, A Sermon (1795)

Americans began creating their own constitutional order in 1776. With British authority effectively dismantled even before independence had been declared, the Continental Congress instructed the separate states "to adopt such government as shall . . . best conduce to the happiness and safety of their constituents." With a "blank sheet" to write upon, as Thomas Paine famously put it, Americans had the opportunity to design new frames of government from scratch. In manifold ways, many assumed they were paving the way for a novel constitutional order befitting their revolution. Indeed, so unshakably confident were they that they christened their creation—echoing Continental Congress secretary Charles Thomson's proposal for a national seal in 1782—a "novus ordo seclorum" (a new order of the ages).[1]

Often, due to these sorts of extravagant claims generated by the electrifying energies of revolution, it has been assumed that American Independence marked a decisive rupture in constitutional imagination, at the heart of which was a single innovation: the written constitution. Nearly two decades later, in 1795, Supreme Court justice William Paterson seemingly captured the significance of this development:

It is difficult to say what the constitution of England is; because, not being reduced to written certainty and precision, it lies entirely at the mercy of the parliament. . . . In England there is no written constitution, no fundamental law, nothing visible, nothing real, nothing certain. . . . In America the case is widely different: Every State in the Union has its constitution reduced to written exactitude and precision.

By reducing their constitutions to writing, Americans had fundamentally transformed the character of these instruments, expressly differentiating them from the British constitution they had long known and worshipped. Where previously a constitution had been descriptive and customary— embodying merely a working account of how government operated in practice—it was now prescriptive and codified—drawing bright lines demarcating what government could and could not lawfully do. It was a clean break. As the accomplished Virginia jurist St. George Tucker would write in his comprehensive explication of American constitutionalism in 1803, "the American revolution seems to have given birth to this new political phenomenon: in every state a written constitution was framed." And one that carried clear consequences. The act of writing constitutions down, of systematizing them via language, of erecting clear textual boundaries separating constitutional text from the conduct of rulers, had supposedly given constitutions a tangible, enforceable presence. The transformation in turn invented a new breed of fundamental law, one captured by John Marshall when he famously wrote in the Supreme Court's opinion in *Marbury v. Madison,* "all those who have framed written Constitutions contemplate them as forming the fundamental and paramount law of the nation." Many have long projected these kinds of remarks backward, assuming that, even though they were articulated a generation after independence, they speak to an understanding of the distinct character of American constitutionalism that developed in American minds shortly after 1776—that the consciousness they capture rapidly and inexorably emerged from recognizing, as one Philadelphian (believed to be Thomas Paine) put it, that "all constitutions should be contained in some written Charter." In turn, many have long believed that when Americans drafted their new federal Constitution in 1787, they had a clear understanding of what kind of thing they had devised. It was a *written* constitution—accordingly its contents and characteristics clearly derived from this fact alone.[2]

But while writing constitutions down fueled several transformations, doing so did not immediately or necessarily oblige Revolutionary-era Americans to imagine their constitutions as Paterson, Tucker, or Marshall later would. Nothing about the sheer act of reducing constitutions to paper either signaled a clear break from prior constitutional assumptions or automatically clarified anything about those new constitutions' basic attributes. Thus, when the federal Constitution first appeared, the simple fact that it was written offered only preliminary guidance.

To appreciate how early American constitutional imagination developed prior to 1787 requires understanding certain interrelated and complex developments. Americans did not initially believe that they had remade the concept of a constitution simply by reducing their frames of government to writing. Based on their experience living under the British constitution, especially drawing on it to justify their assorted claims to colonial liberty and governance (most notably during the imperial crisis that precipitated the American Revolution), they had long thought that a constitution's distinctive characteristic was that it offered a definitive standard of authority. What they knew about imagining and accessing fundamental law was embodied in practices that had been entrenched over decades of colonial experience. Moreover, written constitutions fit easily enough with ingrained constitutional habits. Other texts, going back to at least the Magna Carta, had been central to British constitutionalism, especially for American colonists who had invested their colonial charters and various charters of liberty with such significance. These written compacts, like other authoritative British constitutional texts, had blended seamlessly into a complex, dynamic whole defined as much by custom, history, and constitutional practice.

Meanwhile, it might be assumed that since the written and printed word acquired increased cultural authority as the Revolutionary period unfolded, this phenomenon encouraged a new emphasis on the importance of constitutional text that went hand in hand with the writing of American constitutions. But the written and printed word had enjoyed special power for some time, especially for pre-Revolutionary Americans. Since the Reformation, confessional life had increasingly revolved around written scripture; for well over a century, written contracts had become an entrenched part of western legal and economic life; and for decades people had grown accustomed to learning all manner of information through print. These separate developments had not automatically heightened the significance of constitutional text prior to the Revolution, so there is no reason to assume they automatically did so after 1776. If writing constitutions down did not unavoidably force Americans to acquire a new kind of constitutional imagination, neither did broader cultural trends sweeping the Atlantic world.[3]

While writing constitutions down did not alter their status as supreme arbiters, though, the experience of debating early state constitutions did lead many Americans to rethink exactly why constitutions were fundamental. Many began insisting that, in order to be authoritative, constitutions needed to be consciously chosen—authored and agreed to by real people in historical time. This new emphasis on conscious authorship focused constitutionalism, underscoring some of the implications of reducing constitutions to writing.[4]

In spite of these changes, Americans clung to many inherited assumptions; older nontextual ways of describing and appealing to constitutions powerfully lingered. To be sure, prior to 1787 constitutional discussion implicated the phenomenon of language as many began scratching the surface of what it meant to think about constitutions through a linguistic lens. But most striking was how fleeting, partial, and abortive this engagement often was. Writing constitutions down had wrought important changes. But most Americans still tended to imagine constitutions as dynamic interlocking systems of powers rather than inert objects defined by their textuality. In turn, they still tended to understand constitutional fixity as they long had. Constitutions, because of their fluid character, were simultaneously fixed yet changing.

This uncertainty that surrounded written constitutionalism reveals a deeper truth. American constitutional understanding, despite the searching inquiry and breakthroughs of the previous decade, was still in flux in 1787. Americans had begun reimagining their constitutional world—often in far-reaching ways—but they only partially comprehended what that process entailed. It remained unclear what exactly written constitutions were or how meaning could be credibly extracted from them. This uncertainty converged on the federal Constitution of 1787. Amid so much simultaneous rupture and continuity, it was unclear what kind of thing the new Constitution was when it first appeared—what defined its character, specified its content, or limned its boundaries. As far as the revolution in constitutional imagination had come, in many ways it had yet to begin.

Inherited Constitutional Assumptions

Although British constitutional authority over the thirteen mainland North American colonies evaporated in 1776, its legacy persisted. Virtually everything that Americans knew about constitutions they had learned while living under the British constitution. They had learned to talk about constitutions as authoritative standards. They had also learned how to think constitutionally—how to systematically relate their claims of rights, liberty, and the rule of law to those touchstones. As John Adams had written in 1771, "the Great Principles of the Constitution, are intimately known, they are sensibly felt by every Briton—it is scarcely extravagant to say, they are drawn in and imbibed with Nurses Milk and first air." Every aspect of American constitutional imagination was initially structured by the experience of conceptualizing and fighting over how to conceptualize the British constitution. Molded in this context, it was an imagination that bore the imprint of a distinct conceptual universe. Central to understanding it, therefore, is grasping that many of the distinctions or binaries that we may be inclined to see today simply did not exist within it.[5]

By the eighteenth century, the most basic fact about the British constitution was that it was fundamental and supreme. From the seventeenth century through American Independence, Britons and American colonists alike spoke confidently about the paramount status of their common constitution. Anything that violated its requirements was, by definition, null and void. Legitimizing a disputed power or right required successfully appealing to this ultimate, authoritative standard of justification.

It is not clear when an understanding of the British constitution as fundamental law first appeared, but it is evident that the seventeenth century played a special role in its entrenchment. The constitution emerged against the backdrop of a long-running disagreement between the king and Parliament—one that precipitated both the English Civil War of the 1640s and the Glorious Revolution of 1688. During this struggle, disputants began invoking, with a previously unmatched urgency, the concept of the constitution as fundamental law. Previously, the two concepts had been distinct. The idea of fundamental law had long been invoked, but often without much specificity. Different in theory—although rarely in usage—from "natural law," "divine law," or the "law of reason," fundamental law was an authoritative standard to which all earthly power was answerable. Its primary purpose had been to serve royal authority by theoretically checking that power. Monarchs were superior to all of their subjects, but because they were ultimately checked by fundamental law, their power was not arbitrary. Meanwhile, the word "constitution" had earlier emerged in common usage carrying at least two particular meanings. On the one hand, it referred to a recognized arrangement. The constitutions of nature, the elements, or the human body described how certain assemblages hung together and functioned. On the other hand, following Roman usage, the word referred to an enactment, typically of a legislative variety—be it a statute, decree, or some equivalent. Gradually, when used to describe government, the two usages began to blur. Samuel Johnson's definitive and widely referenced English dictionary (first published in 1755) thus defined "constitution" as "The act of constituting; enacting," and yet also as a "State of being" and an "Established form of government; system of laws and customs." A constitution of government could simultaneously refer to the established arrangement of political bodies and the legal enactment that had authorized that arrangement.[6]

Within the context of seventeenth-century English political dispute, this new understanding of a constitution blended with fundamental law. In the face of an expanding and threatening royal prerogative in the hands of the Stuart kings, several English commentators began drawing upon the idea of fundamental law (previously the tool of monarchs) to place limits on royal authority. The ensuing disputes freed the fundamental law of the land from the crown's exclusive grip and, in so doing, enabled the concept to merge with the inchoate understandings of a constitution. The latter now described not just an initial authorization of law but also a subsequent limitation on it, something that noted English Parliamentarian John Pym neatly captured in 1628 when he described "the ancient and fundamental law" as "issuing from the first frame and constitution of the kingdom." Out of this general formulation emerged the kingdom's constitution, a distinctly English source of fundamental law. Henry Parker, another staunch Parliamentarian, gave voice to this intellectual creation in 1640 when he insisted, "by the true fundamental constitutions of England, the beame hangs even between the King and the Subject." Thereafter, fundamental law and the constitution were often conjoined in powerful ways, especially among colonial Americans. As the Massachusetts lawyer and advocate for American rights James Otis would declare in 1764 during the early stages of the imperial crisis, *"acts against the fundamental principles of the British constitution are void."*[7]

But even if the British constitution was fundamental by the seventeenth century, it was no simple task to identify its contents, because the constitution was largely unwritten and thus enjoyed no physical locus. Above all, the constitution had become a mode of appealing to the past for authority, to the fundamental principles by which the nation had been governed since time immemorial. But as these principles were of ancient origin, evidence of their original enactment had long since vanished. Accordingly, the constitution was more the method for discovering or authoritatively invoking the ancient principles than it was the principles themselves, a distinction that underscored customary practice. "Inasmuch as the original of that pact or constitution of our government appears not," Matthew Hale, the leading seventeenth-century English jurist, explained, "we must . . . examine and measure it by those sound and authentical evidences of the laws and allowed customs and usages." Custom, in other words, determined constitutionality. If laws or institutions had received customary approval or broken with established practice, that was strong evidence of their standing. Moreover, new practices that were accepted over time became part of the constitution itself. Custom thus functioned as both evidence and authority, illuminating what was fundamental and sanctioning it in turn.[8]

Because the constitution was based in custom, it bore a distinct resemblance to the common law, which was rapidly becoming the dominant form of English law in the seventeenth and eighteenth centuries. What had begun as a set of rules and procedures organizing the monarch's central courts had slowly become a body of immutable principles from which those rules derived and a mode of reasoning for bringing them into tighter concert. By transcending procedures, the common law became a widely accepted cultural resource through which legal claims could be made and defended, ones that sanctified immemorial usage against the potential innovations of those in power. As with the constitution, the common law was trumpeted for its ancient origins. As famed eighteenth-century jurist William Blackstone wrote, "the goodness of a custom depends upon its having been used time out of mind; or, in the solemnity of our legal phrase, time whereof the memory of man runneth not to the contrary. This it is that gives it its weight and authority: and of this nature are the maxims and customs which compose the common law." Many suggested that the common law was its own kind of fundamental law and the strongest bulwark of liberty. But while key common law principles, such as the right to trial by jury, were considered part of the fundamental constitution, much of the common law was not. How the constitution and common law were related, then, was less substance than method, what Edward Coke, chief justice on the King's Bench, was getting at in explaining, "the common law itself is nothing but . . . [the] perfection of reason" or what came from "many successions of ages" in which the law "hath beene fined and refined . . . by long experience." It was this pervasive "common-law mind"—one that privileged custom, looked to history for precedent, and assumed that the application of reason would bring modern practices more closely in line with immutable principles—that helped furnish the constitution.[9]

The constitution's content was not only discoverable through custom, but also could be found in a widely recognized constitutional canon made up of foundational texts like Magna Carta, the Petition of Right of 1628, the Declaration of Rights of 1689, and, to a lesser extent, a series of notable statutes and learned treatises. Often these documents were authoritative because they were believed to be later reenactments of the constitution's original immutable principles. As Charles Herle observed in 1642, Magna Carta "was *Law* before 'twas *written.*" Such textual declarations, then, did not make principles so much as embody their meaning, making them an extension of custom, just further evidence of immemorial usage and the wisdom of the ages.[10]

Because the British constitution was primarily customary in character, it was as much a description of how law and government actually functioned as a prescription for how it ought to work. This was especially true when the constitution was identified in the political institutions that embodied it. The so-called mixed constitution balanced the three organic social estates of the realm—the crown, lords, and commons—by instantiating each in a coequal body of government—the monarchy, House of Lords, and House of Commons. Such a notion of mixed constitutionalism had existed for centuries, but the British incarnation was celebrated for curbing arbitrary authority and protecting liberty. Blackstone wrote in 1765 in his massively influential *Commentaries on the Laws of England,* "herein indeed consists the true excellence of the English government, that all the parts of it form a mutual check upon each other. . . . Like three distinct powers in mechanics, they jointly impel the machine of government in a direction . . . which constitutes the true line of liberty and happiness of the community."[11]

But while the constitution was often descriptive, it was nonetheless simultaneously prescriptive in character. It could be both located in government practices and yet distinguished from them. Writing in 1733, Henry St. John, Viscount Bolingbroke, captured this complex duality: "By constitution we mean, whenever we speak with propriety and exactness, that assemblage of laws, institutions and customs . . . that compose the general system." Yet, concurrently, the constitution was also "derived from certain fixed principles of reason . . . according to which the community hath agreed to be governed," making it both the assemblage of political and legal practices and yet something outside of them. Because the constitution was both a repository of resources for checking authority and a check on authority in its own right, it was no contradiction to equate the constitution with the constitution of government.[12]

Much as the British constitution was simultaneously descriptive and prescriptive, it was also at once immutable and changing. Because it was tacitly sanctioned by the collective wisdom of each generation, like the common law, the constitution improved over time. But, perhaps paradoxically, this change did not signal a break with the nation's Gothic roots. Matthew Hale vividly captured this dual character through metaphor: "the Argonauts Ship was the same when it returned home, as it was when it went out, tho' in that long Voyage it had successive Amendments, and scarce came back with any of its former Materials." Because the constitution could be deciphered only through the method of the common law, it could be both fixed and yet perpetually changing.[13]

Identifying the constitution's substance, however, revealed the somewhat contradictory basis of its fundamental authority. It was premised on consent, which, for centuries, had been a commonplace, if vague, foundation—all authority, even the king's, could be traced back to some kind of consent. Beginning during the civil war years, though, many radical Commonwealth Men emphasized a more concrete conception of popular will, out of which developed a more immediate conception of popular consent. To many doctrinaire Whigs whose ideology had emerged from the great controversies between crown and Parliament, this popular will blended with Parliament's authority. As long as Parliament controlled the crown's prerogative and legislated for the realm, English government was founded on consent. But this heightened anxiety produced a new worry: if the constitution rested on nothing more than custom and tacit consent, then it might not be a constitution at all. To alleviate this concern, some began stressing what had been "contrived by the people in its first constitution"—the original popular consent that had allegedly breathed life into the ancient constitution.[14]

At the same time, others contended that the British constitution's great virtue was that it had *never* been expressly chosen. The lawmaker Sir George Saville wrote, "no government ever was built at once or by the rules of architecture, but like an old house at 20 times up & down & irregular."

Accordingly, "principles have less to do than we suppose. The Critics['] rules were made after the poems. The rules of architecture after ye houses, Grammar after language and governments go *per hookum* & *crookum* & then we demonstrate it *per bookum*." Governments were not designed from prescriptions; to the contrary, prescriptions were later derived from the experience of government. In a similar vein, Edmund Burke claimed that one of the British constitution's chief advantages was that it lacked an author. "Our constitution is a . . . constitution whose sole authority is, that it has existed time out of mind. . . . [It] is a choice, not of one day, or one set of people, not a tumultuary and giddy choice; it is," he proclaimed, "a deliberate election of the ages and generations; it is a constitution made by what is ten times better than choice, it is made by the peculiar circumstances, occasions, tempers, dispositions, and moral, civil, and social habitudes of the people, which disclose themselves only in a long space of time." In privileging the implicit choice of numerous generations over the deliberative act of a single moment, Burke was not renouncing constitutional authorship or consent so much as clarifying both. He was favoring the constitutional equivalent of the common law's artificial reason, the kind of tacit consent that was slowly revealed through successive generations; in the process, he was explaining why it was safer to trust the disembodied will of numerous generations over the particular will of specific individuals.[15]

These two understandings—emphasizing and denigrating original consent—did not necessarily conflict. Instead they revealed something profound about the constitution's fundamentality. Just as many felt that the British constitution could be both descriptive and prescriptive as well as immutable and changing, so too did many emphasize that consent enjoyed both ancient and modern roots. None believed that custom and consent were contradictory; in fact, all considered custom the only true source of consent. To some, custom was the only surviving evidence of original consent; to others, custom itself embodied a superior brand of consent. In all cases, though, the actual preferences of a known group of people were less important than the logic of custom itself. Whether that custom captured an original consent or improved upon it, it was diffuse, meaning that the British constitution was, in a meaningful sense, not a product of choice. Even if it was made by popular enactment, it was not a product of will. It was a constitution without an author.

Enforcing the constitution followed a similar pattern—an uncertain patchwork of mechanisms cohered into a relatively stable system. Because

British Whigs placed their faith in Parliament, for many that body was a logical constitutional enforcer. Still others, especially common law lawyers, emphasized the importance of the common law courts and how their judges would uphold the law of the land. But perhaps the most cited resource, particularly after the civil war years of the 1640s, was the people-at-large, acting through any number of crucial mechanisms such as voting, petitioning, pamphleteering, serving on juries, or, if need be, taking action as a crowd. But just as it was not essential to limn the margins of constitutional content or to distinguish clearly between constitution-as-system and constitution-as-prescription, so too was it unnecessary to establish which entity, among several, enjoyed privileged authority to enforce the constitution.[16]

In short, the British constitution was an inchoate object. Primarily because much of it was unwritten and purely customary, it was diffuse and malleable, lacking clear boundaries and comprising dispersed materials. It had no concrete physical or temporal location. It was the collective, multi-generational wisdom of British political experience, captured in either formal texts or precedent. It blended easily with other sources of authority (such as natural law or divine law) that managed simultaneously to lie both beyond and within the constitution itself. It was as much a set of habits and practices as it was a concrete set of materials. And to the extent that it was the latter, it was more the activity of mobilizing and drawing meaning from such materials than the materials themselves. It was the product of consent, but not willful authorship. It was a tradition, or even a composite set of traditions, as much as it was an indisputable, tangible source of appeal. Because it was an object in motion, it promoted a constitutionalism that too was in motion.[17]

All that said, British subjects appealed to their constitution with frequency and conviction, betraying an evident confidence that others had a good sense of exactly what they were talking about. There may have been, as John Adams wrote in 1766, "much inquiry and dispute about the essentials and fundamentals of the constitution, and many definitions and descriptions have been attempted," but he was not, he declared, "at any loss about any man's meaning when he speaks of the British constitution, or of the essentials and fundamentals of it." While the constitution was amorphous, it still offered a commanding framework through which all political and legal argument was organized. Appeals to it were never empty; when made skillfully, they were forceful and authoritative. The constitution may have been unfocused, but its fundamental authority was readily apparent.[18]

American Constitutionalism Before Independence

In more ways than not, this constitutional tradition extended from Britain's metropole to its North American colonies. Importantly, the British constitution and the imperial constitution of the British Empire were not one and the same. Throughout the eighteenth century, as constitutional consensus increasingly defined life in the mother country, uncertainty engulfed the constitutional relationship governing Britain and its colonies. Within the fraught imperial context of colonial America, moreover, disputes typically implicated multiple, overlapping sources of law rather than the British constitution exclusively. Still, colonial Americans recognized and admired much the same British constitution that Britons long had. Their reverence for its "genius" knew virtually no match and, even in the decades preceding the Revolution, they celebrated it with remarkable vigor. "This glorious constitution," Stephen Hopkins, the governor of Rhode Island, proclaimed in 1764, was "the best that ever existed among men." They likewise acknowledged its primacy. While colonial laws might diverge from English laws based on local need and circumstance, they could never be "repugnant" (that is, directly contradictory) to English laws. Colonists had no doubt that they ultimately answered to the British constitution.[19]

Accordingly, especially after the Glorious Revolution, American colonists did not challenge the British constitution's fundamentality but instead tried to lay claim to its protections. They professed "an equitable claim to the full enjoyment of the fundamental rules of the British constitution" and proved successful in securing many customary British liberties. These gains typically came at the expense of metropolitan imperial designs, which bred conflict, but that meant each quarrel occasioned opportunity to invoke the British constitution, making constitutional talk ubiquitous. The most famous examples came after 1763, once the British ministry began intruding in American affairs with unprecedented urgency. But, by then, colonial Americans had already developed a sophisticated repertoire of constitutional arguments for comprehending and defending their liberties in the British Empire. When they declared independence in 1776, they were fully seasoned in the art of British constitutional reasoning. As Samuel Adams noted just years earlier, "You know there is a charm in the word 'constitutional.'"[20]

This robust constitutional know-how helps explain why colonial opposition to parliamentary taxation after 1763 was so immediate and finely tuned. As during the preceding decades, in combating controversial British policy from the Stamp Act through the Coercive Acts colonists revealed how deeply they had internalized the British constitution and its attendant habits of mind. They appealed to custom and precedent; they traced the prior history of the colonies and defended their colonial charters; they linked their cause to past Britons who had resisted arbitrary power; they invoked key constitutional texts; and they held up fundamental common law protections as rightfully their own. When, in 1774, the Continental Congress prefaced its defense of American rights by insisting that "the inhabitants of the English colonies in North-America, by the immutable laws of nature, the principles of the English constitution, and the several charters or compacts, have the following RIGHTS," they were demonstrating a well-honed British constitutional imagination.[21]

To be sure, as the pre-Revolutionary crisis deepened, it became increasingly clear that Britons and Americans were invoking at least two distinct conceptions of the constitution. Many in Britain, as captured most famously in Blackstone's *Commentaries,* were gravitating toward a newer constitution premised on parliamentary supremacy (in which Parliament was the final, indivisible source of all sovereignty in the empire, empowered to make and judge all law); while many in the colonies, meanwhile, harked back to an older constitution of customary restraint (in which immutable principles outside government checked all political power, whether wielded by crown or Parliament). As the American minister Johan Joachim Zubly declared, Britain had "not only a Parliament, which is the supreme legislature, but also a constitution," and Parliament received "its authority and power from the constitution, and not the constitution from the Parliament." While the British were beginning to recognize law as the command of the sovereign, Americans still assumed law was something distinct from human will. These divisions, however, nevertheless took shape within a shared constitutional imagination. Neither side abandoned either of the core elements of the British constitution—its principles or its practices. They simply emphasized different constitutive relationships between them. Moreover, throughout, they imagined constitutional fundamentality, character, and fixity in commensurate ways.[22]

For colonial Americans, as for metropolitan Britons, the British constitution was fundamental law, the highest known political and legal authority, an embodiment of "antient principles," discoverable in history and custom.

That is why Samuel Adams could write in 1769 that "at the [Glorious Revolution], the British constitution was again restor'd to its original principles . . . and stands as a bulwark to the natural rights of subjects." This conflation of natural and customary constitutional rights pointed to another conceptual similarity, as the British constitution melded with other sources of authority, including natural law. The Massachusetts House of Representatives resolved in the midst of the Stamp Act crisis, "there are certain essential rights of the British Constitution of government, which are founded in the law of God and nature, and are the common rights of mankind." Such sources of authority reinforced one another in a single constitutional perspective, enabling the British constitution to function as a particularly powerful source of appeal because rather than in spite of its capaciousness.[23]

American colonists likewise described the British constitution as simultaneously descriptive and prescriptive—a cluster of fundamental principles embedded in a systemic arrangement of institutions and powers. John Adams captured this tendency especially well. Much as a clockmaker might open a watch to understand its constitutive elements, Adams observed the workings of the British polity to understand how its component parts fit together, while insisting on the inadequacy of a purely descriptive account. He began:

> Some have defined [the constitution] to [be] the practice of parliament; others, the judgments and precedents of the King's courts; but either of these definitions would make it a constitution of wind and weather. . . . Some have call'd it custom, but this is as fluctuating and variable as the other. Some have call'd it the most perfect combination of human powers in society, which finite wisdom has yet contrived and reduced to practice. . . . This is rather a character of the constitution, and a just observation concerning it, than a regular definition of it; and leaves us still to dispute what it is.

Ultimately, he went on, "we can never judge of any constitution without considering the *end* of it." Thus, the British constitution was to be discovered not merely in its internal operations, but also through its animating purpose. "Liberty is its end, its use, its designation, drift and scope," he explained, "as much as . . . life and health [are] the designation of the human body." But that great end for which government was conceived was discoverable only through the institutional arrangements and protections in which it was embodied, especially "two branches of popular power, voting for members of the house of commons, and tryals by juries," which were "the heart and lungs, the main spring, and the center wheel," Adams wrote. "In these two powers consist wholly, the liberty and security of the people. . . . This is that constitution which has prevailed in Britain from an immense antiquity." The British constitution was, at once, a set of precepts outside a system and the system in which those precepts found their being.[24]

Building from this exact understanding, colonial Americans imagined constitutional fixity just as their counterparts in Britain did. As the explosive Massachusetts Circular Letter of 1768 stated, "in all free states the constitution is fixed." That "constitution ascertains and limits both sovereignty and allegiance." And since Parliament "derives its power and authority from the constitution, it cannot overleap the bounds of it, without destroying its own foundation." The British constitution was fixed and constant, yet because it was inherently customary and discoverable through usage and acquiescence, it was perpetually changing. Constitutional principle, as a 1766 essay published in Boston put it, was "sanctified by successive usage," which was "ratified by repeated authoritative acquiescence." The author explained, *English Liberty* was "founded on the original frame or constitution of our government," yet "time and a change of circumstances" extended it, as "usage and conveniency transformed" what was previously an "indulgence into a right." New allowances were thus basic modifications of fixed principles, but because such transformations were always understood as clarifications of those principles, rather than standing opposed, fixity and change worked in tandem.[25]

Because fixity was understood in these terms, few were interested in encoding constitutional liberty in the written word. As James Otis so vividly asserted in an influential Revolutionary pamphlet, "We want no foreign codes, nor canons here. The common law is our birthright. . . . [We] shall rest content with the laws, customs and usages . . . from age to age handed down." Such custom, predicated on and created by dynamic usage, was vastly superior to "Codes, pandects, novells, decretals of Popes" and similar written canons, which Otis thought were best characterized as "the flutter of a coxcomb; the pedantry of a quack, and the nonsense of a pettifogger." A most "strange gallimaufry" it all was. Thus, from within this distinctive brand of constitutional imagination, a great many colonial Americans believed constitutional principles were fixed, just not in language. For, as Otis quoted from Jonathan Swift's *A Tale of a Tub,* "Words are but wind."[26]

Meanwhile, disagreement over the constitution's meaning only strengthened the common conception of the constitution that Americans shared with their imperial antagonists. Colonists could reject British interpretations, particularly the understanding of parliamentary supremacy these authorized, while clinging to the ancient principles that the constitution embodied and the broader conceptual framework that it made. The Declaration of Independence, in fact, explicitly exhibited these habits—in "taking away our Charters, abolishing our most valuable Laws, and altering fundamentally the Forms of our Governments," it announced, King George III had "combined with others to subject us to a jurisdiction foreign to *our constitution.*"[27]

Consequently, after declaring independence and purging themselves of British impurities, Americans thought no grand reimagining was necessary. American political leaders remained as convinced as ever that they knew what fundamental authority was, how it regulated political and legal life, and how it could be accessed through argument. They considered themselves rightful heirs of the constitutionalism they had fiercely defended. What remained uncertain was how they might properly translate these inherited constitutional habits to suit American mores and needs.

The First Implications of Written Constitutions

Thus, in 1776, when Americans began constructing their own constitutional order—first, and most important, by drawing up constitutions in the newly independent states and then by drafting the Articles of Confederation uniting those states in common alliance—they had already deeply internalized a tenacious set of constitutional habits. Even as the Revolutionaries rejected monarchy and embraced republicanism, as they navigated the choppy waters of independence these habits remained central to their notions of constitutional authority. Americans still imagined constitutionalism as they long had, without many of the distinctions we tend to assume they must have drawn.[28]

Consequently, Americans set out to construct constitutions in the image of the one they had long known. The decision to draw up new governing principles sprang, in large measure, from pressing practical needs as British authority had collapsed and new institutions were needed to take the place of those that were now either defunct or incompatible with the spirit of republicanism. As petitioners in Pittsfield, Massachusetts, asserted in the spring of 1776, "the first step to be taken by a people in such a state for the Enjoyment or Restoration of Civil Government . . . is the formation of a fundamental Constitution." Needing to reestablish government, the Revolutionaries assumed that their new constitutions would be familiar standards of authority, fundamental just as the British constitution had been and embodying the principles that had long governed American lives. Many of these constitutions specified that neither existing nor new laws could be "repugnant to the rights and principles contained in this Charter," not out of a spirit of innovation, but with an eye toward mimicking British constitutionalism and the principle of repugnancy (that colonial legislation could not contradict the laws of Britain) that had been central to it. Illustrating the tenacity of basic constitutional assumptions, in two states—Connecticut and Rhode Island—Revolutionaries merely updated their existing charters (in the former through a statute and in the latter by replacing references in its governing documents to the king with the name of the state). While the final arbiter might have changed, the logic undergirding it had not. In the shadow of independence, much was fluid, but the basic conception of constitutional authority that had long structured American constitutional thinking remained undisturbed.[29]

The fact that these new constitutions were written texts did not mark a striking departure in their character or demand an immediate reworking of constitutional imagination. Many elements of the British constitution, especially the imperial constitution Americans knew best, had been textual, and prior to 1776 American colonists had routinely underscored the importance of their written charters and the political compacts that they formed. As James Iredell, eventual Supreme Court justice from North Carolina, had written in 1773, "I have always been taught . . . that the constitution of this country is founded on the provincial charter, which may well be considered as the original contract between the King and the inhabitants." These documents, however, were always embedded in a wider, more dynamic, more diffuse constitutional field. John Dickinson explained how in 1766 "charters were *declarations* but not *gifts* of liberties." Liberty was "not annexed to us by parchments and seals." These texts enjoyed power precisely because they rested on nontextual sources of authority. The concepts they embodied, not necessarily the language in which they were encoded, were what commanded authority. As the historian Mary Sarah

Bilder has put it, in "charters, words mattered, and yet, they also did not matter," for they derived from a cultural sensibility in which "words represented principles, but . . . the principles were not defined and limited entirely by the words." Their textuality was at once essential and insignificant. The same appeared to be true of the new state constitutions. The New Hampshire Constitution, for instance, proclaimed: "This form of Government shall be enrolled on parchment . . . and be a part of the laws of the land." Its textual component would be incorporated into the more diffuse body of fundamental law that comprised the "laws of the land." The new constitutions' written identity thus posed no necessary complications to what had long been assumed, and thus demanded no immediate reworking of established constitutional habits.[30]

Because writing constitutions did not automatically alter their fundamentality, doing so did not immediately inspire a new brand of constitutional imagination. As a result, many of the ways in which this act otherwise transformed constitutionalism were only slowly worked out. Its earliest stirrings can be traced to the early 1780s, as many Americans started to rethink how constitutions became fundamental and increasingly asserted that, in order to merit this status, constitutions had to be expressly chosen. They had to be both authored and agreed to by real people acting at some defined moment in time. Valorizing the importance of constitutional choice signaled a pronounced departure from certain features of the British constitution. Instead of celebrating custom, timelessness, tacit consent, and the absence of choice, many were beginning to privilege positive enactment, contingency, explicit consent, and concrete choice.

This development occurred alongside a broader celebration of the unique opportunity Americans had seized to willfully choose and construct their own governments. John Adams expressed a widely shared enthusiasm when he declared in *Thoughts on Government* (originally drafted as a private letter to the Virginian George Wythe), "You and I, my dear Friend, have been sent into life, at a time when the greatest lawgivers of antiquity would have wished to have lived. . . . When! Before the present epocha," he asked, "had three millions of people full power and a fair opportunity to form and establish the wisest and happiest government that human wisdom can contrive?" This fact instilled a special sense of pride in many. As one Pennsylvanian put it, "It has often been said that the Americans are the first people in the world that ever have been blessed with an opportunity of forming a government for themselves."[31]

As choice increasingly defined Americans' understanding of their Revolutionary experience, constitutional authorship took on heightened significance. Many Americans began emphasizing that only special constitutional conventions could legitimately produce constitutions. In 1776, most state constitutions were drawn up by the provincial conventions that acted as surrogate legislatures. But as more states began drafting constitutions, some began insisting that, as special conventions could alone instantiate the popular sovereignty upon which the Revolution was based, they alone could draft fundamental law. "CONVENTIONS," one Pennsylvanian insisted, "are the only proper bodies to *form* a Constitution, and Assemblies are the proper bodies to make Laws agreeable to *that* constitution." Nowhere was the importance of this emerging innovation more deeply appreciated than in Massachusetts (which was the last state to approve its constitution). Having canvassed the state's towns, the General Court eventually capitulated to the incipient will, that, as one town assembly put it, "a Convention for *this* and *this alone,* whose existence is known no longer than the Constitution is forming," was alone sufficient to draft the new document. Consequently, "a Convention for the sole purpose of framing a new Constitution" was eventually called. The practice so quickly came to be seen as indispensable that by the early 1780s, the dominant opinion among American political writers was that only conventions could legitimately draft constitutions. As Thomas Jefferson proclaimed in his *Notes on the State of Virginia,* only "special conventions" established "to form and fix . . . governments" could suffice.[32]

But it was not enough to draft a constitution in a certain way; it also needed a special form of popular approval. Initially, little thought was given to how state constitutions took effect—typically, sitting state legislatures merely decreed by fiat that constitutions were legitimate law. But many complained about this practice. In a June 1776 address protesting how constitutional construction was taking shape in their state, New York's mechanics proclaimed that "inhabitants at large should . . . judge whether it be consistent with their interest to accept or reject a constitution framed for that state of which they are members." Out of frustrations like these emerged the idea of constitutional ratification and the importance of ratifying conventions. By the mid-1780s, Jefferson captured a growing sentiment when he denounced the tacit consent upon which the Virginia Constitution allegedly rested. While it was true that Virginians had prudently acquiesced to the constitution drafted in May 1776, that did not mean this instrument enjoyed "an authority superior to the laws." The "proper remedy"—indeed the only remedy, he argued—was "a convention to fix the constitution." Jefferson drew inspiration from those in Massachusetts who had demanded a special convention to draft the state's constitution and insisted that it be ratified by popular referendum. Representatives of Berkshire County expressed this idea clearly: "To suppose the Representative Body capable of forming and imposing this Compact or Constitution without the Inspection and Approbation Rejection or Amendment of the people at large would involve in it the greatest Absurdity. This would make them greater than the people who send them, this supposes them their own Creators, formers of the foundation upon which they themselve[s] stand."[33]

As several scholars have shown, this sharp separation between constitutional conventions and legislatures gave new substantive meaning to the concept of popular sovereignty, as so many Americans began appreciating how an abstract creed could take operational form. Less appreciated, though, is how this emphasis on the mechanisms of constitutional choice similarly substantiated the concept of constitutional authorship. By privileging drafting and ratifying conventions, Americans more emphatically than at any time before connected the fundamentality of constitutions to identifiable authorship. Fundamental law was now embodied in the choices of specific people at concrete moments in time.[34]

With individual authorship taking on new importance, descriptions of constitutions changed in revealing ways. Corporeal metaphors began to give way to architectural ones. A constitution was not an organism akin to a human body but rather a frame or framework of government. Mechanical metaphors, meanwhile, remained common, but subtly changed. Constitutions were less often likened to self-regulating mechanisms like watches but increasingly imagined as machines that human beings set in motion and carefully monitored. In his 1787 pamphlet responding to John Adams's analysis of American constitutions, New Jersey inventor John Stevens "compare[d] a well-constituted government to a jack" (a machine that rotated meat while it roasted). To "counteract . . . the irregularities" and ensure "an equability of motion," a jack had to be carefully "regulated." It was not a machine that could run by itself. Whether emphasizing architectural or mechanical metaphor in order to underscore the importance of human construction, many described governments as artificial entities. Government was, as one Pennsylvania writer put it, an artifice, something to be built in the same way that "a carpenter . . . buil[t] a house, or a whitesmith . . . ma[d]e a smoke jack." It was, added James Bowdoin, later governor of Massachusetts, something that "requires the highest Skill in political Architecture." "Frames of government" or "machines" to be set "into motion" became more apt descriptions in part because it was assumed that, to be fundamental, constitutions needed to be built by human agents.[35]

In not only choosing their constitutions but making so much of the fact that they had done so, Americans changed the character of their inherited constitutional norms. A constitution could no longer be a product of custom or tacit consent, at least not exclusively; its legitimacy needed to be traceable to a specific moment in time when the people-at-large (however circumscribed in practice) expressly consented to its authority. Thus emerged a novel conception of what made constitutions fundamental. They preceded government, not merely in superiority but also in the time and manner of their creation. While little was new about constitutional fundamentality, then, in American hands the norm had taken new shape. And this novelty drew attention to another emerging implication of American constitutionalism: that constitutions, in being written, were more perceptible.[36]

Valorizing constitutional choice focused constitutionalism. As a result of having discrete and identifiable authors, American constitutions themselves became more discrete and identifiable, which made them more prescriptive, explicit, and distinct from politics. Their contents thinned, while the modes available to access them shrank. In a letter to Richard Dobbs Spaight in 1787, James Iredell explained that a constitution is not "a mere imaginary thing, about which ten thousand different opinions may be formed, but a written document to which all may have recourse."[37]

Just as constitutional instruments were now more distinguishable from ordinary government, so constitutionalism was now more clearly separated from politics. In complaining about the fact that Virginia's constitution was drafted by its legislature, Jefferson asserted, "but they have called it a constitution, which by force of the term means 'an act above the power of the ordinary legislature.'" His law teacher, George Wythe, made a similar point when assessing a legislature that had overstepped the state constitution. "To the usurping branch of the legislature," he declared, "you attempt worse than a vain thing," and "I, in . . . pointing to the constitution, will say, to them, here is the limit of your authority; and, hither, shall you go, but no further." In a related vein, "the constitution . . . should be the first and fundamental law of the State, and should prescribe the limits of all delegated power . . . paramount to all acts of the Legislature," argued Thomas Tudor Tucker of South Carolina.[38]

Constitutions, in turn, became more prescriptive, although the change was not total. At this early date, American constitutions were still readily imagined in descriptive ways; and the British constitutionalism out of which American attitudes developed had long been as much prescriptive as descriptive. But increasingly, the emphasis was changing. The shift was made plain in *The Essex Result*—the official response of the citizens of Essex County to the proposed Massachusetts Constitution of 1778—which stressed the importance of "fixed principles of government, and a stated regular recourse to them." As constitutions became more tangible and more obviously distinct from government, it became easier to explain how they prescribed political conduct. A constitution ought to "bind up the several branches of government by certain laws, which when they transgress their acts shall become nullities," Jefferson explained.[39]

Perhaps no piece of writing more evocatively advanced this point than the pamphlet *Four Letters on Interesting Subjects*, which was published in Philadelphia in 1776 and is believed to have been written by Thomas Paine. "Among the many publications which have appeared on the subject of political Constitutions," it began, "none . . . have properly defined what is meant by *a Constitution*, that word having been bandied about without any determinate sense being affixed thereto. A Constitution, and a form of government, are frequently confounded together, and spoken of as synonimous things"—its prescriptive and descriptive elements often blurred together. But they were distinct. And where "all countries have some form of government," in contrast, "few, or perhaps none, have truly a Constitution." This provocative remark was a dramatic by-product of contemplating some of the more radical implications of putting constitutions into writing. "If you ask an Englishman what he means when he speaks of the English Constitution," Paine dismissively explained, "he is unable to give you any answer. The truth is, the English have no fixed Constitution." Prior to 1787, very few had reached such extreme conclusions—here, as in much else, Paine was exceptional—but this insight was symptomatic of a developing tendency. A genuine constitution prescribed what the government could do; it did not merely describe what the government actually did do. Blending the two converted the government, according to Alexander Hamilton "into a government of *will* not of *laws*."[40]

Language and Its Discontents

These transformations were immense, but in certain ways limited. Americans still instinctively clung to older habits of mind. Conceptual relationships were rebalanced, but constitutions were still frequently described, as before, as structures of powers and systems of regulation. Ultimately, despite investing written constitutions with so much meaning in the decade after independence, American constitutional disputants still largely eschewed the topic of constitutional language. There were no doubt exceptions, instances when an inchoate written constitutional imagination came into view. Each occurrence made it easier, when attention turned to the federal Constitution, to identify language as a salient feature of constitutional analysis. But such moments mostly revealed the profound limitation and uncertainty of such engagement at this early stage.

Independent of constitutionalism, language itself had become an urgent problem in many corners of the eighteenth century as the prospect of linguistic instability haunted rhetoricians, grammarians, and philosophers alike. In terms of epistemology, there were grave concerns that language could not mirror reality or ideas in the mind; in terms of society and politics, there were pressing anxieties that language could not structure meaningful intersubjective exchange. Many shuddered to ponder the implications. If the defining medium of human expression was defective, all efforts at constructing stable foundations for knowledge or political order might be imperiled. Many linguistic reformers harbored hopes that language was in character universal, and thus capable of generating incontestable meanings; but others concluded that it was inherently historical and socially constructed, and thus incapable of generating fixed meanings.[41]

For decades, linguistic theorists had complained about the mutability and instability of language and had hoped to "fix" linguistic meaning once and for all, thus precluding users from distorting language while curtailing the confusion and uncertainty such manipulations typically engendered. The eighteenth century saw the publication of a slew of dictionaries and grammatical treatises devoted to this end. Few were more committed to this project than Jonathan Swift, the Irish-born writer and satirist. "What I have most at Heart," he claimed, near the start of the seventeenth century, "is, that some Method should be thought on for *ascertaining* and *fixing* our Language for ever, after such Alterations are made in it as shall be thought requisite. For I am of Opinion, it is better a Language should not be wholly perfect, than it should be perpetually changing." Meanwhile in 1755, the esteemed British lexicographer Samuel Johnson published *A Dictionary of the English Language*—one of the first rigorous attempts to systematize use of the English language—because he found "our speech copious without order, and energetic without rules." He set out to address the "abuse of words, which are often admitted to signify things so different, that, instead of assisting the understanding . . . produced error, dissension, and per-plexity." Through a comprehensive dictionary, he hoped that "the pronun-ciation of our language may be fixed, and its attainment facilitated; by which its purity may be preserved, its use ascertained, and its duration lengthened." Refining language meant fixing it, which meant standardizing the rules of its usage. Without clear rules, linguistic meaning would be governed by everyday practice, so over time, as that usage changed, so too would the meaning of words. It was incumbent upon the educated and learned to sta-bilize this flux by reining in the cavalier misuse of language.[42]

Not all linguistic reformers were sanguine about the prospects, though. Despite his hope that his dictionary would "fix our language, and put a stop to those alterations which time and chance have hitherto been suffered to make in it without opposition," Samuel Johnson had to admit that "I flat-tered myself for a while; but now begin to fear that I have indulged expecta-tion which neither reason nor experience can justify." Indeed, he conceded, there was not "a nation that has preserved their words and phrases from mutability"; there seemed no way to "embalm . . . language, and secure it from corruption and decay." As cultural development shaped it into new forms, language inexorably changed through usage. Contrary to their long-standing hopes, by the late eighteenth century linguistic reformers increas-ingly worried that language was historical, not universal, in character.[43]

There were also alarming epistemological concerns about language's capacity to adequately represent reality or ideas in the mind. Perhaps words, not ideas, posed the gravest threat to adequate knowledge and communica-tion. As Thomas Hobbes had asserted controversially in his objections to Descartes in the mid-seventeenth century, "All we can infer is whether or not we are combining the names of things in accordance with the arbitrary conventions which we have laid down in respect of their meaning." As a result, he added in *Leviathan,* "the significations of almost all words, are . . . ambiguous; and may be drawn in argument, to make many senses." Unte-thered from firm, natural referents, words could be perpetually bent into new and diverse shapes. Indeed, he observed, "there is scarce any word that is not made equivocal by divers contextures of speech, or by diversity of pronunciation and gesture."[44]

Because the same words could be used in infinite, and sometimes contradictory, ways, disagreement often turned specifically on the use of language. "Great and solemn disputes of learned men often terminate in controversies about words and names," Francis Bacon complained in 1620. Worse still, such failures were hard to identify, since language masked its own power to cloud. "Men register their thoughts wrong, by the inconstancy of the signification of their words," Hobbes observed, "by which they register for their conceptions, that which they never conceived; and so deceive themselves." Putting the point differently several decades later, the English churchman Robert South grumbled, "there is a certain *bewitchery* or fascination in words, which makes them operate with a force beyond what we can naturally give an account of."[45]

Many of these reflections remained partial and fractured, however, with the exception of John Locke's momentous 1690 *Essay Concerning Human Understanding,* which stitched together a comprehensive consideration of semantic instability. Locke turned tentative doubts about linguistic perspicuity into a full-blooded critique, while drawing out the more general implications of the alarming possibility that linguistic meaning was unstable. The simple fact that he devoted Book Three of the *Essay* to the philosophy of language marked an argument in itself. Locke recognized that it might "be thought by some to be much more than what so slight a subject required." But it was essential to realize "in the fallacies men put upon themselves, as well as others . . . how great a part is owing to words, and their uncertain or mistaken significations." Even if it seemed clear that ideas and experience theoretically came prior to language, it could not be assumed that either controlled language in practice; it was as possible, Locke believed, that language was the dominant agent in these relationships.[46]

Language acquired its unique authority in Locke's epistemological account primarily because of a specific kind of idea: the mixed mode. He argued that humans were born with a blank slate, which meant that all knowledge derived from experience. Empirical episodes generated simple ideas in the mind, from which people fashioned simple linguistic names to represent them. Out of those simple names, communities forged general names to stand in for common experiences. In this regard, language happily followed in line. But complex ideas were different. These were not passively received but actively compounded, indicating, Locke feared, that they could vary based on people's subjective experiences, perspectives, and judgments. Among the various complex ideas, none posed a greater threat to semantic stability than Locke's mixed modes. Unlike other complex ideas that had some natural basis, mixed modes (abstract ideas such as "murder," "gratitude," or "obligation" that were compounds of several other ideas) were "independent from any original patterns in nature" and were, instead, purely "an artifice of the understanding." Their meanings "arbitrary" and their composition sufficiently complex, mixed modes were "liable to great uncertainty and obscurity in their significations." Because nature could not regulate the meaning of these complex concepts, the only thing that might stabilize them were the social rules governing linguistic usage. But, while Locke sometimes spoke confidently of this possibility, he also cheerfully mocked it, pointing out that language use could not follow specified rules of propriety because it was impossible to identify where such rules had ever been promulgated. Whatever rules could be inferred from practice were not firm enough to limit humans' discretionary freedom—usually exercised unwittingly—to link words and ideas as their imaginations and habituation saw fit. To Locke, language afforded humans their greatest creative license and it was thus in words where obfuscation, subjective perception, and miscommunication proved most pronounced. Not easily regulated, words thus took on precisely the varied, diverse, indeterminate, and changing meanings that linguistic reformers found so alarming. Linguistic perspicuity was anything but assured. Although Locke held out hope for semantic stability, more striking is the extent to which he foregrounded the prospect of instability. "The very nature of words," he wrote, "makes it almost unavoidable for many of them to be doubtful and uncertain in their signification." Perhaps, he implied, linguistic meaning was perpetually indeterminate.[47]

While more immediately focused on semantics and philosophy, Locke, like the reformers who followed him, acutely appreciated how linguistic instability affected social authority, especially the domains of religion and law. "In the interpretation of laws, whether divine or human," he recognized, "there is no end." Given that language wriggled free from any "authority" that might plausibly "establish the precise signification of words," so too could humans exploit language to evade any social obligations encoded in language—alarming indeed.[48]

These far-ranging meditations on the perils of linguistic instability informed colonial American intellectual life. The works of Swift, Johnson, Locke, and others were well known, and, following 1740, a growing number of English grammars were published in North America. By the Revolution, some even called for reforms similar to those that had proliferated in England. Writing to Congress in 1780, for instance, John Adams proposed a "public Institution for refining, correcting, improving and ascertaining the English Language," one that would boast a complete language library and presiding officers supported at public expense. He had great hopes that Americans' experiment in self-government would promote linguistic reform in its own right, believing that "Republicks have produced the greatest purity, copiousness and perfection of Language." But as much as he believed this, he also recognized that language was always liable to corruption. So to ensure that Americans' linguistic usage remained pure, it was necessary "to have a public Standard for all persons in every part of the Continent to appeal to," something only a dedicated academy could establish and enforce. As he explained to William Tudor later that decade, "Our Fellow Citizens will never think alike nor act aright, untill they are habitually taught to Use the Same Words in the Same Sense." Since "Nations are governed by Words, as well as by Actions," for Adams, republican and linguistic reforms went hand in glove. Shortly thereafter, Noah Webster, Revolutionary America's leading lexicographer, articulated similar hopes. He began his 1783 *Grammatical Institute* denouncing Europe on the grounds that its "laws are perverted" and its "literature is declining," all because of the "folly, corruption and tyranny" that pervaded the continent. The United States, in contrast, enjoyed "the fairest opportunity of establishing a national language, and of giving it uniformity and perspicuity . . . that ever presented itself to mankind."[49]

As optimistic as these perorations often were, Revolutionary-era Americans, like the reformers who preceded them, nevertheless remained wary of the prospect of ever fixing linguistic meaning. Webster, despite his unbridled hopes, remarked but a few years after publishing his *Grammatical Institute* that any "attempt to fix a standard on the practice of any particular class of people is highly absurd . . . it is like fixing a light house on a floating island. It is an attempt to *fix* that which is in itself *variable*" for it will "shift with [users'] passions and whims." That the young nation's most incisive linguistic thinker so publicly vacillated between radically distinct views on linguistic meaning reveals the uncertainty that engulfed ideas about language at this time.[50]

Still others claimed that the problem of linguistic obscurity was a product, not of too little learned control, but of too much. No one made this argument more forcefully than Thomas Paine in his explosive pamphlet *Common Sense*. While Paine's primary goal was to impel Americans toward independence in the early months of 1776, he also sought to demolish the foundations upon which the ancien régime rested. That included the manipulation of language that he believed had helped propagate patently absurd beliefs. Descriptions of the British constitution were especially vulnerable to assault. "Some writers have explained the English constitution thus," Paine wrote: "the king, say they, is one, the people another; the peers are an house in behalf of the king; the commons in behalf of the people." But, he pointed out with evident frustration, "this hath all the distinctions of an house divided against itself; and though the expressions be pleasantly arranged, yet when examined they appear idle and ambiguous; and it will always happen, that the nicest construction that words are capable of, when applied to the description of something which either cannot exist, or is too incomprehensible to be within the compass of description, will be words of sound only, and though they may amuse the ear, they cannot inform the mind." The semantic corollary to Paine's common sense was bare, unadorned language. Much in the spirit of the Protestant plain style—which, in the wake of the Reformation, demanded that biblical interpretation stick closely to the word of scripture—Paine assumed this simple language could cure society of the pervasive ambiguity and indeterminacy that had not only corrupted writing and speech but also propped up a hierarchical social order. While his proposed solutions diverged dramatically from the elitism that animated Johnson or Webster, his diagnosis similarly implicated language and its capacity to obscure as an issue of intense political concern.[51]

Constitutionalism and Language

General commentaries on the problems of language were rare in Revolutionary America, and links between these problems and constitutionalism were rarer still. Nevertheless, as constitutional disputants began scratching the surface of the latent problem of constitutional language, they began to engage, however fleetingly, with the connections between constitutionalism and the problems that linguistic theorists had raised in the preceding centuries. Some commentators did not merely argue that constitutions needed to control political rulers (which was common) but also insisted that, in order to do so, these documents needed to be written in clear, unambiguous language. Even before independence was declared, for instance,

Thomas Jefferson had annotated Benjamin Franklin's proposed plan for articles of confederation and balked at the use of the phrase "general welfare" in the text. Asking what the phrase "their mutual and general welfare" means, he declared, "There should be no vague terms in an instrument of this kind." By contrast, its "objects should be precisely and determinately fixed." Similarly, a committee report (drafted by James Madison, James Varnum, and James Duane) that prefaced a proposed amendment to the Articles of Confederation in 1781 asserted that it was, "consonant to the spirit of a free Constitution that . . . all exercise of power should be explicitly and precisely warranted." Virginia's attorney general, Edmund Randolph, likewise insisted a year later while arguing a case that, in constitutions, "words must be free from ambiguity and decided, or cannot have supremacy." For a certain few, linguistic precision was especially urgent in declaring rights. The Reverend Samuel McClintock, in reflecting on New Hampshire's recently ratified constitution in 1784, marveled at the "precision [with which] the rights belonging to men in a state of society are defined in the *Declaration of Rights*."[52]

Others wondered, though—like Samuel Johnson and John Locke before them—if language would cooperate. Among the few who thought deeply on the matter was the Massachusetts jurist James Sullivan, who reflected on the crucial relationship between language, law, and constitutionalism in a 1786 newspaper essay. "It is necessary in every free government," he began, "to have the modes of doing justice at public tribunals, clear, precise and uniform, otherwise the judge and the officer would be the law makers and deciders, at the same time, and in their own manner." Maintaining the integrity of constitutional checks necessitated perspicuous constitutional language that could be "thoroughly understood by illiterate men." But "the imperfection of all language" dashed this hope. Indeed, "so vague are all the forms of expression ever yet hit upon," Sullivan lamented, "that the best we can do is affix, as well as we can, appropriate meanings to certain expressions, and carefully to use these in all parts of our systems of jurisprudence, so that we may render the laws as intelligible and technically certain as may be." For, he reckoned, "it is of infinitely more consequence to have the laws, as a rule of conduct, fully known, than it is to have them right." But perhaps even these modest desires would be thwarted. Sullivan recognized the general issues language posed. "Have we not the same difficulty in every other science as we have in law?" he asked. Perhaps "like other valuable attempts," such efforts "must, in this imperfect state, bear many marks of imperfection, and fall vastly short of the patriot[']s eager exertion."[53]

Other Americans made similar observations throughout the 1780s, chief among them James Madison, the Virginia politician who came of age during the Revolution and played an unparalleled role in the development of early American constitutionalism. Even though he never became a lawyer, Madison spent a portion of his post-collegiate career studying law, receiving training that sensitized him to problems of legal interpretation and language. His recently discovered law study notes reveal particular interest in the subject. He paid special attention to cases that exposed the problems of multiple meanings, the ambiguity of words, and the uncertainty of interpreting words across different legal instruments. In particular, such study awakened in him an abiding interest in and commitment to crafting pellucid legal language while also heightening his awareness of the inherent difficulty of the task.[54]

He brought this interest to his early career as a lawmaker, serving in both the Virginia House of Delegates and the Continental Congress. While most of his energies during these years was consumed by politics, at least some of his attention drifted to interpretive issues. These issues were similar to those that had animated his legal studies, but by the early 1780s Madison's focus was not statutory language, but something novel—constitutional language. In an exchange with his friend Edmund Randolph in 1784, the two statesmen discussed a recent interstate incident, in which a citizen of Virginia allegedly assaulted a public official in South Carolina, debating whether the accused should be extradited to the state in which the crime took place. Everything hinged on the meaning of "high misdemeanors," but whereas Randolph focused on how the two states' definitions of the offense diverged, Madison focused on how the Articles of Confederation defined the term. In looking to the Articles for guidance, though, he remarked that its relevant article "does not clear the ambiguity," a realization that led him to reflect, "The truth perhaps in this as in many other instances, is, that if the Compilers of the text had severally declared their meanings, these would have been as diverse as the comments which will be made upon it." Here he echoed James Sullivan's concession about the inherent ambiguity of language, but added a crucial twist, by tracing constitutional ambiguity to the multiplicity of its authorship. The document's assorted authors each imagined a different intent behind the chosen words. Had they appended the text with their understandings of its various meanings, the diversity of views would have overwhelmed the document. The ambiguous language hid a deeper truth about the inherently fractured character, not only of linguistic meaning, but of constitutional meaning in particular.[55]

During his time in Congress, Madison faced distinct, if related, questions about the scope of congressional authority under the Articles. Even if Congress, by the stipulation of Article II of the Articles of Confederation, enjoyed only the powers "expressly delegated," many assumed that it presided over issues of a general nature, reinforced by the sweeping descriptions of many of its powers. Madison and like-minded peers assumed that the Articles possessed "implied power[s]" to "carry into effect all the Articles." But when Robert Morris, superintendent of finance for the United States, unveiled a series of financial reforms in the early 1780s to help manage the war effort—one of which called for Congress to charter a bank—Madison probed the limits of implied power in new ways. Even though he acknowledged the "*importance* of the institution," he worried that "the Confederation gave no such power and that the exercise of it would not bear the test of a forensic disquisition"—that is, that important though this power was, it was not constitutional. Unable to locate a relevant power in the text of the Articles, and unwilling to assume, like most of his congressional peers, that it was simply "necessary that Congress should have power," Madison voted against the Bank of North America, an important early example of some Americans' willingness to imagine constitutions in terms of their text.[56]

Thus, traces of a written constitutional consciousness had only begun to take root in the 1770s and 1780s, as some began grasping that written constitutions placed a heightened burden on the interpretation of words. But these were exceptions. If broader meditations on linguistic instability pointed to the deeper implications of subjecting a republic to the rule of words, these issues remained largely unexamined. In the vast majority of instances, those who confronted the problem of constitutional language prior to 1787 deliberately avoided the matter, imagining constitutions as frameworks and systems more than as words.

Constitutional language would seem to have been especially significant in declaring rights. Seven of the new state constitutions were prefaced by declarations of rights, documents that contemporaneously elicited celebration and pride and that have since been cited as forerunners to the later federal Bill of Rights. Even though they seemingly entrenched constitutional rights via text, in more ways than not they were an extension of the decidedly nontextualist constitutional outlook that Alexander Hamilton had articulated in 1775: "The sacred rights of mankind are not to be rummaged for, among old parchments, or musty records. They are written, as with a sunbeam, in the *whole* volume of human nature." Declarations of rights were merely reminders, not sources, of this deeper inscription. This logic had governed British declarations—Magna Carta and the Declaration of Rights of 1689—and the dozens of similar texts that colonial Americans had drawn up to accompany their governing charters, such as the Massachusetts Body of Liberties (1641), New York's Charter of Liberties and Privileges (1683), and the Pennsylvania Charter of Liberties (1701). Animated by this logic, these new state declarations were an eclectic mix of enumerated rights and vague, sweeping suggestions, which read like instructive guidelines rather than definitive compilations or explicit legal commands. They read this way because they embodied a much different kind of constitutional imagination, one captured by leading Philadelphia politician and physician Benjamin Rush's contention that a "BILL OF RIGHTS should contain the great principles of *natural* and *civil* liberty" while a Constitution is simply "the executive part of the Bill of Rights." In other words, declarations of rights were designed less to constrain a constitutional grant of power than to outline the purposes that such a grant was meant to fulfill. In this regard, such declarations were not written to make fundamental rights or governing principles but only to codify what already existed and to gesture toward a larger repository of rights outside of government. Accordingly, they betrayed minimal concern for what might have been left out.[57]

Judicial and legal behavior immediately following independence also revealed an unwillingness to reduce constitutions to their text. Prior to 1787, American judges and lawyers tended to interpret constitutions according to their spirit, structure, and purpose. Rarely did they consider a constitution's language to be constitutive of its meaning or its defining feature. Often uninterested in seeing constitutions in this way, they seldom drew sharp distinctions between constitutional violations and transgressions against a more general sense of equity or "natural justice." Relatedly, they frequently lumped constitutions together with other kinds of fundamental authority—such as natural law, the law of nations, unalienable rights, Magna Carta, the Declaration of Independence, "common right or reason," or (perhaps most revealingly) the "Laws of the Land" that were independent of the written constitution. In this regard, judges and lawyers approached constitutions more or less as their legal forebears in the British tradition had. Obvious changes had carried them afield from that inheritance, but not enough to alter how they conceived of constitutions as objects of interpretation.[58]

Few cases better illustrate how much judges clung to older habits of mind than *Commonwealth v. Caton* (also known as the *Case of the Prisoners*), which came before the Virginia Court of Appeals in 1782. Three men had been condemned for treason. They had petitioned the legislature for a pardon, but while the House had approved their request the Senate had not. The Virginia Constitution empowered the House alone to grant pardons, but the Virginia Treason Act, passed after the constitution took effect, required both House and Senate approval. The defense thus argued that "the act of the assembly was contrary to the plain declaration of the constitution; and therefore void." Edmund Randolph, state attorney general, countered that the two texts were perfectly reconcilable. He rested his argument on "a difference of construction, which should prevail in interpreting the act of government, and an act of assembly," claiming that "in the former the liberality, necessary to catch its spirit, must be adopted," because "the constitution describes general outlines only" in order to "omit a part of that infinity of combination, of which the affairs of society are capable." By its character, then, a constitution was a general statement—one that demanded a different kind of interpretive protocol that could ensure that the "force of substantial sense" was not "subjected to the petty tyranny of grammatical rule." Chief Justice Edmund Pendleton concurred with Randolph's reasoning. The constitutional question "should be decided according to the spirit, and not by the words of the constitution," he asserted. "Either view of the subject satisfies the present enquiry," Pendleton concluded, "but I prefer the [state's argument], as most congenial to the spirit, and not inconsistent with the letter, of the constitution." Accordingly, he held that the legislature had not violated Virginia's constitution. Operating without distinctions that only later materialized, interpreting and enforcing a constitution meant grasping what had long been true of charter constitutionalism in the British Empire: that words were simultaneously important yet irrelevant since constitutions were at once fixed yet changing. Pendleton's stated impetus—that interpreters grasp, first and foremost, the spirit of the instrument—captured this logic, for the constitution's spirit was at once the embodiment of its words yet something that far transcended them.[59]

Then there was Americans' remarkably underexamined first national constitution. Before 1787, the majority of thinkers' attention was paid to the state constitutions, which meant that the substance and limits of the Articles of Confederation were deeply underdetermined. Even though, in hindsight, the Articles appear to have embodied a distinct conception of federalism, defined by a heavily circumscribed national government, its limitations did not seem so obvious to congressmen or constituents during the years of its operation. Due to Congress's ineffectiveness, most Americans simply ignored the body's work. Meanwhile, those who suffered within Congress tended to lament, not the textual limits that had been fixed on its power, so much as the states' refusal to honor their obligations. In their struggle to manage the war and postwar difficulties, congressmen devoted less attention to the meaning or limits of the Articles than they did to the practical necessities they faced. Hence, while Madison had articulated scruples about chartering the Bank of North America, most of the other delegates assumed that, either by implicit "constitutional power" or from "absolute necessity," Congress enjoyed the power to issue a corporate charter. The apparent distinction between these two kinds of justification was meaningful to few congressmen at the time. As hesitant as they were to sort out the exact relationship between the confederation and the states, they seemed even less interested in surveying the constitutional boundaries dividing them.[60]

While a handful of politicians grappled with the problem of constitutional language and most others ignored it, still another group outright denigrated the very idea that language, however lucid, could enforce constitutional barriers. Foremost among them was James Madison. In the second half of the 1780s, with the young republic facing a serious constitutional crisis, nobody expressed greater skepticism of the idea of grounding constitutions in text, even though, in a different context, he had found the problem of constitutional language so stimulating. Over the summer of 1785, he expressed profound doubts of its efficacy. In an extensive disquisition on state constitutional design written for Caleb Wallace, Madison noted that "if it were possible it would be well to define the extent of the Legislative power," but no matter the virtue of such an aim, "the nature of it seems in many respects to be indefinite," and thus impossible to delineate through language. The right way to control legislative power was to empower the right kinds of counterforces for "preserving [the] System." Less than two years later, on the eve of the federal Constitutional Convention, as America's most incisive constitutional thinker pondered the "vices of the American political system" and imagined what a reformed constitutional order might look like, Madison zealously expanded upon these earlier thoughts. In so doing, he resolutely imagined constitutional authority in dynamic terms and, in turn, even more strenuously rejected the effectiveness of constitutional language.[61]

Madison's disillusionment with the young confederation reflected his own personal experience. During his three and a half uninterrupted years in the Continental Congress from 1780 to 1783, he had witnessed firsthand the impotence of the system set up under the Articles of Confederation. The national government was ill equipped to tackle the financial challenges born of the war (including, especially, paying off its mounting debt), and because amending the Articles required the unanimous consent of the state legislatures, augmenting its powers proved almost impossible. A subsequent stint in the Virginia House of Delegates from 1784 to 1786, meanwhile, had exposed Madison to the perils of state lawmaking. State governments were not only unwilling to address the needs of union—a reality manifested most spectacularly in their refusal to make a good faith effort to raise the funds that Congress requisitioned—they were also enacting what Madison characterized as reckless and vicious legislation, specifically laws that provided a form of debtors' relief that caved in to majoritarian demands at the expense of creditors' property rights. Worse still, the impotent national government was powerless to do anything about this perceived injustice. Distressed by the deteriorating scene, he complained to Edmund Randolph that "our situation is becoming every day more & more critical. . . . The existing Confederacy is tottering to its foundation."[62]

Madison believed that these problems were foundational, exposing the issues inherent in republican government itself. Like other political leaders who shared his frustrations, he began sensing that dramatic, comprehensive reform was necessary to address "the mortal diseases of the existing constitution." The whole system needed to be reconstituted—not only the powers and makeup of the national government but also its relationship to the states and their citizens. The need became even more exigent in the aftermath of the disappointing Annapolis Convention of 1786—a meeting to address the problems of the confederacy that elicited delegates from only a handful of states—and a widespread agrarian uprising in western Massachusetts, which became known as Shays's Rebellion. The few delegates who gathered in Annapolis called for a general convention to meet the following May in Philadelphia. After Shays and his allies were put down only by force in early 1787, sending shockwaves across the confederacy, Congress approved the call for a general convention. Madison and his fellow reformers sensed their opening.[63]

To ensure that the convention's discussion would transcend the narrow focus of prior reform efforts, Madison prepared meticulously. With characteristic acuity and rigor, he drew on his learning and experience to diagnose the problems plaguing American constitutionalism while identifying a potential solution. His preparations took a variety of forms. He had already begun an analysis in his "Notes on Ancient and Modern Confederacies," which assessed the structures and weaknesses of all the prior confederacies he could document. Building from there, in the spring of 1787, in a memorandum entitled "Vices of the Political System of the United States," he identified what specifically ailed the American confederacy. The "Vices" hinted at a potential cure, but Madison spelled out his imagined solution in probing detail in private letters written to three Virginia confidants— Thomas Jefferson, Edmund Randolph, and George Washington. Within this penetrating, multipronged analysis lay a powerful statement about the character of constitutional power: that authority on paper was inherently insufficient.[64]

The problem, Madison asserted, was not simply that the Articles of Confederation gave the national government too few powers on paper, but that the "federal system" lacked "the great vital principles of a Political Cons[ti]tution." Madison's historical analysis of former confederacies had led him to conclude that such entities, by their very makeup, tended toward dissolution. The centrifugal force of their component parts perpetually strained the bonds of union. Herein lay the foundational problem of the American confederacy. On the one hand, the states were guilty of a catalogue of transgressions—against the national government (by failing to comply with congressional requisitions, by entering into rogue treaties, and by forming "unlicensed compacts"), against other states (by imposing restrictions on commerce and passing debtor relief measures that harmed creditors in other states), and against their own citizens (by passing multiple, mutable, and, above all, unjust laws, such as the aforementioned debtor relief). On the other hand, the national government lacked the practical capacity to do anything about these transgressions, to functionally hold the system together. The Confederation Congress could certainly have used additional powers, Madison conceded, but that was not the real problem. Madison himself had speculated as early as 1781 that Congress enjoyed "general and implied power" to execute and enforce all of the Articles.

The deeper issue, as he explained, was that a "sanction is essential to the idea of law, as coercion is to that of Government," yet the national government was "destitute of both." As "acts of Cong[ress] . . . depend[ed] for their execution on the will of the state legislatures," Congress's power was only "nominally authoritative" and, in fact, "recommendatory only." Congress's inability to exercise its power was less an issue of legal authority (it enjoyed the power) than a matter of practical legitimacy (the states simply did not allow it and Congress lacked the resources to coerce them). The core problem was that nominal authority—that is textual authority—was no authority at all. Something more was needed to form a "vital" "Political Cons[ti]tution."[65]

On this point, how Madison described and analyzed state transgressions is especially revealing. He began the "Vices" by complaining about how the separate states had violated different kinds of constituted authorities—the Articles, various treaties, and the Law of Nations. But, in fully understanding "the evils which viciate the political system" of the United States, he deemed it essential "to include those which are found within the States individually." Critically, the issue was not that the state governments were acting unconstitutionally (expressly violating something in the Articles or the state constitutions), but that their otherwise constitutional behavior was unjust and enervated the structure of the federal Constitution. Here Madison began developing his critique of republican majoritarianism and the problem of faction, built on the insight that, in a smaller republic (like the individual American states), nothing could protect minority rights from the tyranny of popular majorities. But, in so doing, he was also extending his indictment of textual authority. The national government required practical coercive power, not only to enforce its own authority and responsibilities but also, in order to preserve the constitutional system itself, to curb unjust state laws. In this regard, Madison framed transgression every bit as much in terms of a nebulous brand of republican justice as of formal constitutional authority. And Madison blurred these standards precisely because constitutional maintenance required it. "The great desideratum in Government," as he put it, "is such a modification of the Sovereignty as will . . . controul one part of the Society from invading the rights of another." Constitutionalism was not about vested power but about effective control. It was a matter of outfitting a political system that could hold itself together.[66]

Madison's decidedly structural conception of constitutionalism inspired his favored reforms. Curing the confederacy of its ills, he argued, required at least five fundamental changes. First, the national government's authority needed to rest on constitutional supremacy. Toward this end, "a ratification by the people themselves," independent of the states, would render a new constitution "clearly paramount" to the state governments and help ensure a "due supremacy of the national authority." Second, in tandem with the first, "a change in the principle of representation" was necessary; equal representation of the states (the existing arrangement under the Articles) had to be replaced by proportional representation, to be applied to both houses of a new national legislature. Third, since the existing Congress lacked the necessary powers, the national government "should be armed with positive and compleat authority in all cases which require uniformity." Fourth, a system of "national tribunals" was needed to enforce the supremacy of the national government over those of the states. It was the final proposal, though, that so strikingly revealed Madison's indictment of constitutional language. He insisted that the new government needed the requisite powers to reign in the states, most important of all a negative on state legislation *"in all cases whatsoever."* No power was more crucial since, as he explained to Randolph (and directly building on what he had written in the "Vices"), "without such a defensive power, every positive power that can be given on paper will be unavailing." No matter how "ample the federal powers may be made, or however Clearly their boundaries may be delineated, on paper," he told Jefferson, without a federal negative, "they will be easily and continually baffled." Constitutional language, no matter how strong or clear, was woefully inadequate. Reducing constitutionalism to the mode through which it was written reflected a misunderstanding of the tasks inherent to such a project. Policing constitutional transgression, and thus maintaining constitutional equilibrium, was a function of empowering the right counterforces with the right sorts of tools. Without empowering the right counterforces, constitutional text would prove feeble in the face of encroachments; with the right ones in place, finely calibrated text would prove irrelevant. Instead of ignoring constitutional language, as so many Americans had up to this point, Madison openly disparaged it.[67]

Written Constitutionalism at the Constitutional Convention

Through 1787, language played an altogether uneven role in shaping the American constitutional scene. The *writtenness* in written constitutionalism lay largely dormant when fifty-five delegates gathered in Philadelphia beginning in May 1787 to rethink the American constitutional system. While few worked as feverishly as Madison to diagnose the crisis facing the young confederacy, all delegates felt it in one way or another. The current system appeared to have reached a breaking point and many national leaders favored dramatic reform. Accordingly, when the delegates assembled, Madison and his fellow nationalists—especially George Washington, Alexander Hamilton, James Wilson, Gouverneur Morris, and Rufus King— expanded the scope of the project. Rather than merely revising the Articles—as some believed they had been instructed to do—they opted to construct a brand new constitutional order.

It marked a return to the mental world of the lawgiver that many had occupied a decade prior as delegates consciously focused on articulating constitutional rules and principles on a blank sheet. But even though the Convention's energies were focused on writing a new constitution, and even though the particular controversies implicated by expanding federal authority heightened awareness of the text's reach, following Madison's sentiments in the "Vices," delegates largely refused to imagine the project of writing a constitution through a textual prism. For most, constitutionalism still meant balancing powers and interests—building a functioning system of constituent political relationships—not policing linguistic barriers. The Philadelphia delegates were primarily focused on addressing the persistent challenges of the 1780s. For some, that meant reining in the abuses of the states. For others, that meant equipping the new government with augmented powers to raise revenue, dispose of western lands, satisfy foreign creditors, and project strength abroad. For everyone, however, that meant establishing a more energetic national government. That the Constitution might, first and foremost, function as a text defined by its textuality seemed far from most participants' minds. Illustrating the point, rather remarkably the delegates barely pondered how the document they were drafting might be interpreted by future users. Determining the literary structure of the Constitution, meanwhile, was a matter the framers put off to the very end of the debates, when they deferred the whole problem to the style and clever quill of Gouverneur Morris. As throughout the previous decade, there were no doubt moments when constitutional language came into focus as an immediate concern. But, throughout the summer of 1787, delegates only felt around the edges of written constitutionalism.[68]

Early on, reform-minded delegates ensured that the Convention would consider far-reaching change. Madison made a point of arriving in Philadelphia early, a week and a half before the Convention was scheduled to begin on May 14. During those days and several that followed, while delegates waited for a quorum to materialize, Madison worked with fellow reformers from the Virginia and Pennsylvania delegations to hammer out a plan for a new constitutional system. Formally presented in the Convention on May 29 by Virginia's governor and Madison's trusted associate, Edmund Randolph, the Virginia Plan scrapped the Articles and replaced them with a far more powerful national government. It embodied Madison's diagnosis of what ailed the union as well as many of his favored solutions. The plan reconstituted the national government, how it interacted with the existent states, and how it operated on the citizenry. Unlike the existing Confederation Congress, the proposed government would be complete in its own right, boasting independent executive and judicial branches to accompany the legislature, which now would be divided into two houses. Moreover, these various bodies would not simply represent the states; representation would be based on different schema such as population or wealth. Finally, this government would possess powers unknown under the Articles that would enable it to address long-standing national challenges and to curb the abuses of the states. Unlike the Articles, which, as Gouverneur Morris explained, were "a mere compact resting on the good faith of the parties," the proposed government would instead enjoy "a compleat and *compulsive* operation." The Virginia Plan successfully framed much of the Convention's subsequent discussion. While its more radical suggestions would be whittled down through various limiting compromises, it helped ensure that the Convention would constitute a new kind of national government.[69]

Initial objections to the Virginia Plan targeted the kind of powers it bestowed. But given that the plan proposed to strengthen the central government so dramatically, some delegates condemned not merely its underlying principles or projected workings but the open-ended text that conferred those powers. In particular, some objected to Resolution VI, which stipulated that "the National Legislature ought to be impowered to enjoy the Legislative Rights vested in Congress by the Confederation & moreover to legislate in all cases to which the separate States are incompetent, or in which the harmony of the United States may be interrupted." This clause granted the new federal government sweeping authority, especially in comparison to the Articles. Two South Carolinians—Charles Pinckney (who drafted and proposed his own rival plan and otherwise championed the nationalist cause) and John Rutledge (former governor and eventual Supreme Court justice)—"objected to the vagueness of the term *incompetent*," claiming "they could not well decide how to vote until they should see an exact enumeration of the powers comprehended by this definition." Roger Sherman, delegate from Connecticut and eventual federal congressman and senator, similarly complained that the government's powers were "too indifinitely expressed." Hoping to give the national government authority "within a defined province," Sherman later attempted replacing the seemingly broad mandate of the Virginia Plan with new language that—as Pinckney and Rutledge had demanded—enumerated powers.[70]

But Sherman's protests were routinely parried and his proposed enumeration soundly defeated. Even more revealing, though, were the arguments marshaled to counter his and others' objections. Some, like Edmund Randolph, were willing to acknowledge the credibility of the complaints. When Pierce Butler of South Carolina inquired into "the extent of [the] meaning" of the Virginia Plan's sweeping legislative grant, Randolph quickly "disclaimed any intention to give indefinite powers to the national Legislature." But few backtracked like this. Defenders instead condemned the very premise of the protest. Instead of claiming that the words in question had been misconstrued by its critics (as Randolph did), they disparaged the very idea that the new federal Constitution could be confined to the language of the proposal. James Wilson, for one, "observed that it would be impossible to enumerate the powers which the federal Legislature ought to have." Madison, meanwhile, claimed that while he came to the Convention with "a strong bias in favor of an en[u]meration and definition of the powers necessary to be exercised by the national Legislature," he "also brought doubts concerning its practicability." On that point, while "his wishes remained unaltered," nonetheless "his doubts had become stronger." Indeed, "at present he was convinced [enumeration] could not be done." Alexander Hamilton was even more adamant. Decrying the inadequacies of the Articles, he exclaimed, "How unwise and inadequate their powers! . . . this must ever be the case when you attempt to define powers." Congress's ills stemmed from the foolish exercise of delineating powers. Hence, Madison, like others, had severe doubts about the "practicability" of enumeration.[71]

The issue was not simply parceling power but distinguishing the national government's authority from that of the states. On this point, even Sherman agreed. "It would be difficult," he acknowledged, "to draw the line between the[se] powers." Hamilton seized on precisely this issue, insisting that, because "no boundary could be drawn between the National & State Legis-latures," the "former must therefore have indefinite authority." Madison concurred. "To draw the line between the two, is a difficult task," he noted. "I believe it cannot be done, and therefore I am inclined for a general government." His judgment derived from his studies of past confederacies and his personal experience witnessing the failures of Americans' own attempt at union under the Articles. In all those cases, the centrifugal pull of the component parts was far greater in principle than the centripetal force of union. Given this mechanical understanding of constitutional power, even if an "indefinite power should be given to the Gen'l Legislature" (something, importantly, the Virginia Plan did not propose to do), it did not "follow that the Gen'l Govt. wd. take from the States (any) branch of their power." It was thus pointless to parse text independent of a deeper understanding of how constitutional systems worked. Understanding their animating principles, Madison was arguing, revealed why concerns over seemingly open-ended text were utterly beside the point.[72]

Madison carried the day despite some limited protests, and the Virginia Plan's language was affirmed, first on May 31 by a near unanimous vote, and then again after Gunning Bedford of Delaware put forth a resolution tweaking the wording on July 17. More than anything else, the objections ended up illustrating how resistant most other delegates were to thinking of the Constitution like a text. Rufus King's protests revealed as much. The Massachusetts delegate was wary of "a dangerous encroachment on [the states'] jurisdictions," but "was aware" that his demand for a textual "security" for "the Rights of States in the National Constitution" would "be called a mere *paper security.*" King recognized, however, that many of his counterparts assumed that "fundamental articles of compact, are no sufficient defence against physical power"—what Madison had repeatedly insisted. As much as anything else, then, King's protest spoke to the persistent doubts surrounding enumeration.[73]

Given these prevailing habits of mind, it was not surprising that, across all kinds of disagreements, delegates construed the object they were constructing in avowedly nontextual ways. Some drew on scientific metaphor. John Dickinson, Delaware delegate who had been a celebrated voice of American resistance during the imperial crisis and leading author of the Articles of Confederation, "compared the proposed National System to the Solar System, in which the States were the planets, and ought to be left to move freely in their proper orbits." The "national council" would be "like the sun," and thus "illuminate the whole—the planets revolving round it in perfect order." Constituted as such, "the Planets" would be "repelled yet attracted," with the "whole moving regularly and harmoniously." Madison picked up on this theme to defend his favored congressional negative against state laws, calling it "the great pervading principle that must controul the centrifugal tendency of the States" without which they "will continually fly out of their proper orbits and destroy the order & harmony of the political system."[74]

While few other delegates invoked astronomical metaphors, most did reduce the task before them to constructing a "system." The term was by far the most common noun used to describe both the existent and proposed constitutions. The overarching goal was to either "preserve harmony," as Wilson put it, or, in Hamilton's words, "maintain . . . equilibrium." When introducing the Virginia Plan, Randolph claimed to "outline" a "system"; George Read of Delaware was opposed to "patching up the old federal System" as "it would be like putting new cloth on an old garment"; Madison talked about the need to purge "disturb[ances]" from "the system"; Pinckney defended Madison's negative "as the *corner-stone* of the present system"; Nathaniel Gorham of Massachusetts described a potential procedure for ratification as "giving effect to the System"; and, in his famous closing speech imploring the delegates to put aside their misgivings and consent to the Constitution, Benjamin Franklin was astonished "to find this system approaching so near to perfection."[75]

In addition to describing constitutions as systems, some delegates openly disparaged the idea of reducing constitutions to text. Madison made this point with clarity and force during the mature stages of the convention. "If a Constitutional discrimination of the departments on paper were a sufficient security to each [against] encroachments of the others," he contended, "all further provisions would indeed be superfluous." If paper discriminations carried any potency, they could solve most constitutional difficulties. "But experience," he continued, "had taught us a distrust of that security; and that it is necessary to introduce such a balance of powers and interests, as will guarantee the provisions on paper. Instead therefore of contenting ourselves with laying down the Theory in the Constitution that each department ought to be separate & distinct, it was proposed to add a defensive power to each which should maintain the Theory in practice." It was deeply misguided, in other words, to assume that a constitution could ever be reduced to its language, that its constituent powers could be established via "paper discriminations." Life under the Articles had confirmed as much. John Francis Mercer from Maryland shared these presuppositions. "It is a great mistake," he urged, "to suppose that the paper we are to propose will govern the U. States[.]" Instead, he contended, "it is The men whom it will bring into the Governt. and interest in maintaining it that is to govern them. The paper will only mark out the mode & the form—Men are the substance and must do the business." The Constitution was not, and could never be "the paper" the Convention was drafting. By necessity, it transcended such a limited frame. When the delegates conjured the Constitution in their minds, they looked far beyond the "paper" Mercer brought into view.[76]

Even if some delegates actively mocked "paper discriminations," crucial developments at the Convention encouraged a more searching consideration of constitutional language. The fate of Madison's cherished congressional negative against state laws helped mold the delegates' working constitutional imagination. Madison had stressed that the negative was the cornerstone of constitutional reform and, distrusting as he was of constitutional text, had believed that it should apply *in all cases whatsoever.*" By contrast, the Virginia Plan empowered Congress to negate only those laws "contravening in the opinion of the National Legislature the articles of Union." While affording the new legislature a remarkable degree of discretion to define the boundaries of transgression, this resolution stopped well short of Madison's hopes, sharpening the distinction between unconstitutional and unjust that he had consciously blurred. On June 8, with the help of Charles Pinckney, Madison attempted to expand the negative once again. Pinckney "urged that such a universality . . . was indispensably necessary to render it effectual," while Madison maintained that "an indefinite power to negative legislative acts of the States" was "absolutely necessary to a perfect system." Others picked up the banner. Dickinson, for instance, "deemed it impossible to draw a line between the cases proper & improper for the exercise of the negative," and Wilson agreed: only an indefinite negative could ensure "an effectual controul in the whole over its parts." Drawing out the larger point to which all of these defenses were gesturing—much the same one Madison had formulated in the "Vices"—Pinckney subsequently claimed that an undefined negative was the only way "to defend the national prerogatives" for it did not otherwise matter how "extensive they might be on paper." Without this power, properly fortified, all of the other prerogatives would prove meaningless. Extending the negative was thus a tacit indictment of paper constitutionalism.[77]

Most delegates were unconvinced, though, and Madison and Pinckney's motion was decisively defeated. Among the detractors, only Roger Sherman expressly questioned their underlying vision of the Constitution, assuring his fellow delegates that "the cases in which the negative ought to be exercised, might be defined." Others were as yet unwilling to explicitly defend the vitality of paper prerogatives, but by rejecting the extensive negative and the form of constitutional imagination it implied, the delegates nonetheless encouraged a new set of mental habits. No longer empowered with blanket discretion, the national legislature would approach state laws armed with nothing more than the Constitution itself. Thus, the only state laws that could be curbed—no matter how hasty, myopic, or unjust they were believed to be—were those that were incompatible with the Constitution. By abandoning the cornerstone of Madison's proposal and, thus, narrowing the mode of federal oversight, members of the Convention invited a different way of imagining constitutional enforcement: one in which state laws would be negated not because of the harm they might potentially cause, but instead because they violated the federal Constitution.[78]

Even more important, the reduced negative itself later went down to defeat. Whether extensive or limited, as an instrument of constitutional enforcement the negative bred a particular understanding of federal–state constitutional interaction. Under its auspices, state laws would be judged prior to becoming law. But the negative's place was taken, more or less by mid-July, by the "supremacy" clause and a series of restrictions on state authority. First proposed by Luther Martin, the attorney general of Maryland who became a bitter opponent of the Constitution, the supremacy clause became stronger as the Convention unfolded. By late August, it declared that the Constitution and its attendant treaties and laws "shall be the supreme Law of the Land," superior to all state constitutions and laws. Armed with this clause, federal officers (judges in particular) would, quite unlike the negative, adjudicate the constitutionality of state laws only after they took effect. This two-step transformation, from Madison's extensive negative to the defined negative to the supremacy clause and various attendant restrictions, placed greater emphasis on the authority of text. But it merely invited this shift; on its own it could not effect it. Nationalists who opposed the negative, such as Gouverneur Morris, were otherwise confident that "a law that ought to be negatived will be set aside in the Judiciary [department] and if that security should fail; may be repealed by a

WRITTEN CONSTITUTIONALISM

[national] law." Morris's use of "ought" was ambiguous, but he seemed to hint that the federal government would repeal the laws that it needed to. As hazy as the subject remained, though, the full defeat of the negative afforded constitutional text more vitality than it would have enjoyed in an avowedly Madisonian constitutional world.[79]

A dramatic change in the Convention's agenda did even more to heighten awareness of the Constitution's relationship to language. In late July, the Convention approved a motion to form a committee "to prepare & report a Constitution conformable" to the proceedings to date. While the Convention adjourned from July 27 to August 5, the five-person Committee of Detail—composed of John Rutledge, Edmund Randolph, James Wilson, Oliver Ellsworth, and Nathaniel Gorham—hammered out a working draft. Their starting point was the amended Virginia Plan, but they scoured all of the proposals, amendments, and votes thus far produced. While their ostensible duty was to bring coherence to what had already been agreed upon and they had no direct authority to resolve or clarify ongoing issues, the task of translating the Convention's proceedings into a working draft necessarily entailed creative discretion, conscious or not. The committee worked primarily in secret, making it hard to unravel how the final draft took shape. But it seems clear that Randolph was tasked with writing the first draft before Wilson took over and transformed Randolph's organizing premises into the final version. Along the way Rutledge played a significant collaborative role, amending the various drafts. The requirement of drafting, though, forced members of the committee to reckon with deeper questions about what kind of object the Constitution was and, especially, how it related to language.[80]

In the preface to his initial sketch, Randolph reflected on what issues deserved most attention "in the draught of a fundamental constitution," citing two things:

1. To insert essential principles only, lest the operations of government should be clogged by rendering those provisions permanent and unalterable, which ought to be accomodated [sic] to times and events. and

2. To use simple and precise language, and general propositions, according to the example of the (several) constitutions of the several states. (For the construction of a constitution . . . necessarrily [sic] differs from that of law).

Randolph had joined others at the Convention in favoring an examination of "essential principles" more than "language"—assuming that the former was the principal object of attention and the latter largely a distraction. The reason was captured in his first guiding principle. A constitution was categorically distinct from a law. As the Constitution was meant to rule over future generations, it needed to be constructed with only broad principles in mind, lest it prove inflexible and brittle. Echoing what he had previously argued as state attorney general in the *Case of the Prisoners*, this formulation betrayed a fluid conception of constitutionalism that sought to transcend the limitations of language. But Randolph's second principle cut in an entirely different direction. Rather than privileging or elevating principles above language, he linked the two. In implying that "simple and precise" words alone could embody essential principles, he tethered constitutional efficacy to determinate language. Randolph seemed to hover between two distinct brands of constitutional imagination.[81]

This tension carried over into his drafting, illustrated especially well in one of his major discretionary additions. Acting independently of any clear instructions, he replaced the Virginia Plan's sweeping grant of legislative authority with a list of enumerated powers. He had been the lone defender of the original Resolution VI who had otherwise conceded the thrust of critics' objections, insisting he had no intention of authorizing "indefinite powers." Just days earlier in the full Convention, he had objected to Gunning Bedford's slight modification to the legislative power clause, fearing it would imperil state autonomy. Unlike Madison, Hamilton, Wilson, and others who had dismissed such objections out of hand, Randolph seemed eager to stake out a middle ground. He seemed persuaded by his fellow committeeman Nathaniel Gorham's characterization of the Virginia Plan's legislative power clause on July 16: "The vagueness of the terms constitutes the propriety of them. We are now establishing general principles, to be extended hereafter into details which will be precise & explicit." That Rutledge subsequently moved to form a committee tasked with enumerating specific powers (a motion that had been defeated by a mere vote) likely convinced Randolph that many in the Convention expected such a list. But, having just decreed that a constitution should be composed of "essential principles only," he had a difficult time clarifying the scope of legislative power through precise language. His first draft illustrated his struggle as he awkwardly attempted to grant powers before limiting them through exceptions and restrictions. More generally, the whole section was littered with revisions—clauses were moved around and several deleted. In a seeming attempt to square the circle, Randolph settled on a final clause, which read: "all incidents without which the general principles cannot be satisfied shall be considered, as involved in the general principle." In addition to the enumerated powers, the national government could exercise any power incidental to carrying out the general principles upon which its authority was based. Perhaps, through this addition, the Constitution could be precise and general at the same time? Rutledge, however, was not satisfied. He promptly deleted the clause and rewrote it.[82]

Wilson, with Rutledge's close collaboration, thereafter assumed primary drafting responsibility. Wilson was perhaps America's most incisive legal thinker. What he lacked in tact and modesty he made up for in intellectual prowess. As William Pierce, a delegate from Georgia, wrote about him, "no man is more clear, copious, and comprehensive," or more capable of persuasion through the sheer "force of his reasoning." Above all, Wilson was a shrewd thinker and manipulator of language, which proved especially valuable to his cause on the Committee of Detail. Eager to vest the new national government with the sweeping authority he believed necessary, he attempted to fashion a working plan that could accomplish this aim without attracting too many objections. Thus, while he had openly questioned the premise of legislative enumeration, and had not expressed Randolph's wariness with a general grant of power, Wilson nonetheless followed his colleague's lead. While his initial draft for the committee had stated that the "Supreme legislative Power shall be vested in a Congress," "Supreme" was quickly deleted—perhaps at Rutledge's insistence—and his next draft enumerated powers in much the same way as the final Constitution would. Because he had previously opposed enumeration primarily because he questioned the basic efficacy of defining powers, he punctuated his version with a final power that echoed his colleagues' earlier drafts: the national legislature, he wrote, could "make all laws that shall be necessary and proper for carrying into execution" both "the foregoing powers, and all other powers vested by this Constitution" specifically "in the Government of the United States, or in any department or officer thereof." The "necessary and proper" clause, which would survive virtually intact through the end of the Convention, would prove among the most important in the new Constitution.[83]

While it bore a passing similarity to the language Randolph and Rutledge had initially produced, Wilson's creation subtly diverged from that of his fellow committee members. The wording "necessary and proper" was not, as so many have suggested, either novel and mysterious or a technical term of art that directly pointed either to a specific area of law or to jurisdictional constraints on the national government's power. Instead, it was an utterly ubiquitous phrase, used in countless contexts, that generally denoted the exercise of appropriate discretion. With this broader meaning in mind, as legal scholar John Mikhail has so carefully shown, Wilson did not merely ensure that Congress would have the power to execute its enumerated powers (the "foregoing powers" phrase—which incidentally was only added back in afterward, likely at Rutledge's suggestion), but also that Congress could carry out "all other Powers," a formulation suggesting that it was a standard "sweeping clause" (meant to combat the assumption that those powers enumerated were exhaustive). Moreover, Wilson vested what he styled "all other Powers" not in any specific government body, but more generally in the "Government of the United States." Such a construction pointed to powers beyond either those enumerated, those otherwise vested in other federal departments and officers, or merely instrumental powers needed to carry any of these powers into effect. In other words, by combining "all other Powers" with the "Government of the United States," Wilson was, in keeping with his long-standing assumptions, acknowledging the necessity of unenumerated powers. Whatever implications Wilson and others assumed or hoped the clause carried for national power and governance (no doubt a crucial matter), Wilson's construction of the "necessary and proper" clause also spoke to how he and others imagined the Constitution's character and its relationship to language. Wilson surely designed this clause in hopes of overcoming the challenge before him—that is, he no doubt aimed to appease critics of the Virginia Plan's legislative grant while capturing both the futility and potential harm of reducing power strictly to language. In so doing, he found a way to enumerate powers while also denying the deeper ontological assumption that the Constitution's identity was definitively textual.[84]

When the Convention reconvened, discussion turned to the concrete text crafted by the Committee of Detail and delegates began probing the place of language in their emerging scheme. Some, like Gouverneur Morris, were quick to remind colleagues of the proper priorities. It was "the thing, not the name" that mattered, he declared, for he "had long learned not to be the dupe of words." But as disagreements increasingly centered on precise wording and the scope of particular phrases, while talk of "fundamental articles" to be "fixed by the Constitution" became more common, language received a new kind of attention. No doubt the daily wordsmithing heightened awareness of the significance of constitutional text. At this point, Madison's latent interest in semantics and interpretation—his desire for "consistency, conciseness, perspicuity & technical propriety in the laws"—resurfaced and enabled him to define a new role for himself. Dejected by his failures to institutionalize signature aspects of the Virginia Plan, he coped with the resulting disappointment by gravitating toward a new preoccupation: editing and clarifying the document. He helped frame terminology—proposing strategic deletions or introducing subtle word changes—to help sidestep disagreements. His joint proposal to change Congress's power "to make war" into the authority "to declare war" marked a typical contribution. He suggested minimizing the Constitution's language to avoid encumbering it with unnecessary specifics and showcased a talent for capturing complex, multipronged ideas in simple language, while judiciously inserting words to "prevent doubts." By confronting so many of these compositional problems, he began glimpsing how ambiguities in language might play a leading role in the Constitution's operations.[85]

But even as attention on constitutional language no doubt intensified, delegates also continued to avoid its implications. The Committee of Detail's decision to enumerate powers, for instance, was met with almost complete silence (or, at least, nobody chose to record anything on the matter). Delegates pondered whether the committee had enumerated the right powers, and in some cases even parsed the meaning of certain key terms—such as when Luther Martin demanded that it "be made clear" how "duties" and "imposts" had the same meaning. But none of the prior disagreements over the issue, few as they had been, manifested themselves again. None of the nationalists who had been so wary of specifying congressional power raised a single objection. Perhaps, as many scholars have suggested, delegates (no matter how nationalist-minded) had always assumed that some kind of enumeration would have to take the place of the Virginia Plan's sweeping grant, that it was merely a placeholder until progress was made on larger issues. Perhaps, whatever misgivings remained, nationalist-minded delegates were comforted by Wilson's key addition—the "necessary and proper" clause. Perhaps, like Wilson, they assumed that this clause more or less saved the Constitution from the misguided impulse to define powers. But if that were true, then it is remarkable that there were no protests from earlier critics. Conspicuously absent from the enumeration was

THE SECOND CREATION

the language of Article II of the Articles of Confederation, which had declared that "Each state retains" all power not "expressly delegated to the
United States." This omission merited no comment as the Convention
debated the enumerated powers section, and it was similarly ignored when
the body took up the "necessary and proper" clause, a clause that strongly
underscored the conspicuous removal of the language of the Articles
and would later become explosively controversial for just this reason.
The Convention ultimately approved the "necessary and proper" clause, in
fact, with minimal discussion and no recorded disagreement. Maybe everybody was content. More likely, this stunning silence reveals the extent to
which delegates were relatively uninterested in the scope and tenor of the
enumerated powers section, not because they approved of its precise construction, but because they could not yet see why it merited careful scrutiny. Put differently, they did not yet instinctively imagine the Constitution in the sort of way that warranted a different reaction. Even though
the Convention's deliberations had encouraged new habits of mind, older
inclinations died hard.[86]

Not all controversy was avoided, though. Some delegates had grown
uneasy with the shape of the Constitution. As the proceedings neared completion, the three who refused to sign the final product—Edmund Randolph,
George Mason, and Elbridge Gerry—were forthright about their misgivings.
All of them pointed to the extent of national power. Mason's objections
were more conventional—he decried "the dangerous power and structure
of the Government," fearing it would culminate "in monarchy, or a tyrannical aristocracy." But Randolph and Gerry chose a different focus, harping
on the Constitution's language. To Randolph, the power was not only
dangerous but "indefinite." In particular, the "clause concerning necessary
and proper laws" was "general," and the "boundary between the General &
State Legislatures" was anything but "definite." Echoing this sentiment,
Gerry complained about the "general power of the Legislature" facilitated by the "necessary and proper" clause. While Mason did not himself
emphasize the clause in the waning days of the Convention, weeks earlier
in a draft of objections he had complained that "The sweeping Clause"—
what the "necessary and proper" clause would soon frequently be called—
"absorbs every thing almost by construction." These distinct objections
hinted that subsequent criticism might target structure, but might also focus
on text. Just which kind of Constitution would seize Americans' imagination when they had a chance to evaluate it, remained to be seen.[87]

The Uncertain Constitution

As delegates to the Federal Convention struggled to think through the relationship between language and constitutionalism, they revealed the deeper uncertainty surrounding the Constitution more generally. Whether it was an inert text that needed to be skillfully written or a dynamic system that needed to be fashioned in the right kind of way remained an unanswered question, illustrating just how much indeterminacy engulfed all facets of the effort. This kind of broader realization—about the more fundamental issues to which the fleeting debates over constitutional language had pointed—especially emerged during the Convention's debate over the proper mode for constitutional ratification.

Nationalist-minded reformers were eager to avoid the state legislatures at all costs, as these bodies were sure to be filled with representatives mindful of the power they stood to lose and thus hostile to the Convention's proposal. But bypassing established political authority carried consequences. In opposing Oliver Ellsworth's motion to send the Constitution to the state legislatures for ratification, Gouverneur Morris contended that the Connecticut delegate "erroneously supposes that we are proceeding on the basis of the Confederation." But "this Convention," he explained, "is unknown to the Confederation." Like the Constitution it was writing, the Convention stood outside the existing American legal framework. The logic gestured toward revolutionary principles, that appealing to the people could legitimize any constitutional act. As Madison claimed, "resorting to [the people], all difficulties were got over"—for only they "could alter constitutions as they pleased"; only they could resort to "first principles." The act of producing a new constitution, James Wilson confessed, demanded a return "to the original powers of Society." But beyond circumventing an existing legality, they were also claiming to be devising a superior one. Appealing to the people would place the Constitution on a stronger foundation than even those state governments that "were (not) derived from the clear & undisputed authority of the people." Such claims, however, unnerved Elbridge Gerry. By these arguments, reformers "prove an unconstitutionality in the present federal [system] & even in some of the State Govts." They suggested that Americans had, in fact, been living without constitutional government since they declared their independence.[88]

Madison drew out the deepest implication. Without meaning to be, Gerry was right. As Madison proclaimed, "the difference between a system founded on the Legislatures only, and one founded on the people," was the "true difference between a *league* or *treaty*, and a *Constitution*." Earlier in the Convention, Madison and many others had commonly referred to the Articles of Confederation as the "federal Constitution." Now, however, Madison was claiming that it had never really been a constitution at all but merely a treaty, a compact that had held a league of friendly, independent states together. In the "Vices" he had determined that the Articles were defective because, devoid of necessary powers, they lacked the "vital principles" of a political constitution. But this claim, which had centered on the makeup of the Articles and their lack of practical enforcement powers rather than their foundational essence, was fundamentally different than the claim he made at the Convention. His new argument underscored the importance of popular ratification in American constitutional thought—the logical fulfillment of remaking the foundations of a fundamental constitution. But it revealed something else as well. Not only would the new federal Constitution stand on superior footing, but it would possess a distinct character— it alone was a genuine constitution. As Gerry's retort illustrated, of course, this ontological classification was not readily accepted. Others believed that the Articles and the state compacts (including the majority that had not been popularly ratified) were also genuine constitutions. What, then, made the American Constitution a *constitution?* Did it share something fundamental with prior American constitutions or did it mark a decisive break? Madison's cataloguing had exposed resounding uncertainty.[89]

These open questions were reinforced by the Constitution's introductory words. In his Committee of Detail draft, Edmund Randolph had deemed a preamble "designating the ends of government and human polities . . . *is* unfit here." Such a flourish had been suitable in state constitutions but not the federal Constitution, which was dealing with people already "gathered into society." Rather than a "display of theory," the Constitution's opening words, he thought, should merely justify why the Convention had modified the Articles. But the Committee of Style, which drafted the final version of the Constitution expressly rejected Randolph's thinking. The finished Constitution began with a preamble (almost certainly written by Gouverneur Morris) altogether different than the kind Randolph assumed appropriate. Announcing the deed of "We the People" and the broad ends that people imagined their Constitution would serve, the preamble seemingly signaled the precise moment of "first formation" Randolph deemed inapposite. Beyond embodying the Constitution's basis in popular sovereignty, then, the preamble's presence raised precisely the questions Gerry had asked and Randolph and Madison had answered in such divergent ways. What kind of an object had a preamble like this?[90]

The same kind of question could have been posed, not merely with the preamble in mind, but the entire document. Drafting the final version of the Constitution fell to the Committee of Style, which assembled during the Convention's final days, and the committee primarily deferred the task to Gouverneur Morris, the dazzlingly talented Pennsylvania delegate who, next to Madison and Wilson, had contributed the most in Philadelphia. In charge of final drafting, Morris did more than add a preamble. He also fundamentally transformed the look and feel of the text. Similar to the state constitutions, the draft of the Constitution that had emerged in early August from the Committee of Detail had been arranged into twenty-three unwieldy articles (by comparison, many state constitutions had been divided into more than forty-five separate articles or sections). But Morris organized the eventual Constitution in a completely distinct fashion—arranging it into a tidy seven articles. As the Convention came to a close, it was unclear what meaning this novel composition held. But to initial observers it must have seemed striking. Perhaps in streamlining the document's text, Morris made it easier to see the Constitution as a linguistic artifact. In terms of its visual organization, however, the new Constitution sharply diverged from its obvious points of comparison, underscoring a more basic question: What kind of an object was this—a constitution that looked so different in kind from what had come before? Uncertainty surrounding the Constitution's relationship with language, in other words, spoke to broader uncertainties about the Constitution itself.[91]

WHEN THE Constitutional Convention adjourned, its delegates emerged with a brand new constitutional instrument in hand, one that dramatically expanded the power of the national government and altered its relationship with the states. Like the state constitutions and the Articles of Confederation that preceded it, the federal Constitution was a written text. But to what extent this lone fact revealed much about its content or makeup remained deeply unsettled.

Much had changed. The timeless, customary, unauthored British constitution had been replaced by a new brand of constitutionalism that stressed contingency, positive enactment, and conscious choice. But much had remained the same. As Benjamin Rush explained, the new Constitution "contains all the theoretical and practical advantages of the British constitution without any of its defects or corruptions." Many would have readily agreed. The dynamic, holistic brand of constitutionalism that had long structured American constitutional experience remained vital. Habitually, for most there was as yet no meaningful difference between constitution-as-text and constitution-as-system because it seemed impossible to talk about a constitution without focusing on the interworkings of the system that the text specified. Constitutional language was significant yet inconsequential because constitutions were fixed yet dynamic. That these inherited habits lingered so evidently among the delegates to the Constitutional Convention—the individuals seemingly in the best position to begin thinking in a new way—helps illustrate how widespread the phenomenon surely was. Even though Americans had written their constitutions down, they did not clearly exhibit a written constitutional imagination. They had not yet fully tethered authority to words.[92]

The new federal Constitution's murky relationship to language exposed uncertainty around what kind of an object it was, and thus how it could be used and understood. Delegates to the Convention had failed to sort out these issues, and nothing about the Constitution's writtenness immediately clarified them. In the fall of 1787, the new Constitution served as a microcosm of American constitutionalism more generally, embodied in Charles Inglis's prophetic question from a decade earlier: "For what is the constitution?—that word so often used—so little understood—so much perverted." Those who succeeded the delegates in Philadelphia would have to fathom what kind of a thing the Convention had created.[93]

2

Language and Power

But I have often wondered that a convention of such wise men should spend four months in making such an inexplicit thing. For . . . it appears too much like a fiddle with but few strings, but so fixed as that the ruling majority may play any tune they please upon it.

—William Manning, *The Key of Liberty* (1798)

Language finally exploded onto the American constitutional scene—if only in sporadic bursts—during the ratification debates, when a vast American political community vigorously contested whether to accept the federal Constitution that had emerged from the Constitutional Convention in September of 1787. Putting a constitution up for public debate was entirely novel, and the proposed instrument almost instantly consumed the nation's interest. As Madison reported to Jefferson not long after the document went public, it "engrosses almost the whole political attention of America." The divisive deliberations between just fifty-five delegates, however, foreshadowed the conversation that followed once the document was presented for public scrutiny. As a galvanized public sought to influence the special conventions that would meet in each state to decide whether to ratify or reject the proposed constitutional document in its entirety, spirited and often vitriolic debate ruled the next ten months (and beyond, in some states).[1]

Since the debate ultimately boiled down to this deceptively simple consideration—whether to accept or reject the new federal Constitution—disputants could be separated into two groups: the Federalists favored ratification, and the Anti-Federalists opposed it. But this division did not reflect organized parties or even people who shared a coordinated imagination, merely those who shared a common goal. So while the two sides' ultimate objectives were neatly focused, the same could not be said of the diverse arguments they mobilized or the vast conceptual terrain they canvassed. Federalists recognized from the beginning that they faced a daunting challenge, and they quickly inundated the American people with essays that conveyed the necessity of the proposed constitutional change. (They also utilized shrewd political tactics, some of which were heavy-handed and won them few converts.) Anti-Federalists likewise produced a raft of public writings, which warned about the dangers of ratification. In the midst of the process, Gouverneur Morris exaggerated only slightly when he remarked that the Constitution had been "the Subject of infinite Investigation Disputation and Declamation." In such an avowedly public debate, involving such a significant percentage of the population, and which produced such an astonishing volume of writing, this sprawling field of argument comprised many more ideological perspectives than the two crudely drawn camps—one for the Constitution, the other against—could hope to contain. Compounding matters, Federalists and Anti-Federalists punched and counterpunched so rapidly that it was hard for observers to see the debate whole.[2]

Amid the chaos, however, patterns emerged. At first, Federalists pitched the conversation broadly, claiming that the existing constitutional system's failure to address the political and economic problems of the 1780s marked a genuine emergency, necessitating drastic action. With an eye toward such large-scale problems and solutions, they drew invidious distinctions between the promising character of the proposed Constitution and the Articles of Confederation it was to replace. Anti-Federalists responded in kind, issuing one dramatic, frenzied warning after another, insisting that by radically expanding the might of a distant centralized power, the proposed Constitution threatened to vanquish the Revolutionary inheritance.[3]

But while Anti-Federalists issued their share of sweeping arguments, they also demanded greater specificity. They scrutinized the Constitution's details, insisting that Federalists defend its particular features and specific clauses—as well as quell fears about the dangers each provision supposedly posed. They complained about inadequate representation, unchecked taxing and military power, extravagant presidential prerogatives, an insulated Senate, and the absence of a bill of rights. They predicted, given these deficiencies, the abuses surely to flow from there: the growth of an unresponsive federal leviathan, the loss of state autonomy, and the destruction of customary legal liberties. In the process of highlighting these concerns, they also complained about the Constitution's language, asserting that its tyrannical character was as much a function of how it was written as what it said.[4]

The problem of constitutional language was merely one of many subjects of the ratification debates. But given the volume of polemics, it generated substantive attention. Moreover, the problem of constitutional language was discussed not merely in the abstract, but became entangled with other issues such as representation, legislative power, state autonomy, and judicial discretion. Beyond its importance to their own arguments, in stressing the problem of language Anti-Federalists forced Federalists to respond in kind, kindling a new sort of constitutional consciousness. At the same time, though, even as both sides began stressing the importance of constitutional language in different ways, uncertainty continued to engulf the Constitution. Debating its relationship to language did not clarify a common interpretive object—it simply exposed just how little agreement there was on its essential attributes. Beneath disagreements over particular constitutional clauses, in other words, lay a deeper form of flux. And even by the end of the ratification, it remained decidedly unclear what the Constitution, in fact, was.[5]

The Imperfect Constitution

Anti-Federalists began shining a light on the distinctively linguistic features of American constitutionalism in order to combat one of Federalists' most common justifications for the new Constitution: that it was a necessarily imperfect and incomplete document. Federalists claimed that this characteristic was actually one of its cardinal virtues. Easily changeable, the Constitution would grow with experience. Even though it would function as supreme, fundamental law, even though Federalists readily acknowledged that "we are forming a constitution for ages," simultaneously, and every bit as significantly, they argued that the Constitution embodied the beginning, rather than the end, of a long-developing conversation about self-government. It might have struck Anti-Federalists as devilishly ironic that Federalists, despite otherwise insisting that the confederation was on the brink of anarchy, also asked that an imperfect constitution be taken partly on faith. Indeed, many of those Anti-Federalists, clinging to once vital strands of Revolutionary ideology, were wary of the idea of constitutional growth, assuming that such change indicated decay and signaled irreparable corruption. But as dubious as this argument might have seemed to some, Federalists largely staked their case on it. It did not matter if the Constitution had certain deficiencies, they repeatedly asserted, because it was, by necessity and design, imperfect.[6]

Often Federalists stressed the imperfections of the Constitution in superficial ways. "I wish the Constitution which is offered had been made more perfect, but I sincerely believe it is the best that could be obtained at this time," George Washington asserted, a week after the Federal Convention adjourned. Henry Knox, meanwhile, conceded that the Constitution "might probably have been formed with greater consistency in the closet of a Philosophic—but a better could not be obtained by a free compromise." Federalists were fond of insisting that the Constitution's imperfections were a product of the inevitable compromises that came with balancing the diverse and clashing political and regional interests that had pervaded the Convention—the Constitution was "the reconcilement of jarring interests and opposing claims between the several states," as Oliver Ellsworth, the supremely talented Connecticut lawyer, put it.[7]

But as common as these reassurances were, Federalists justified the Constitution's inherent imperfections in deeper ways, ultimately resting that case on the imperfection of human beings themselves. Expectations for the new Constitution needed to begin with an acknowledgment of the fallibility of its authors. "The new constitution is not pretended to be a work of perfection—such is not to be expected from imperfect beings," declared Archibald Maclaine of North Carolina. "Men must be treated as Men and not as Machines," Gouverneur Morris likewise insisted. To be legitimate, a constitution had to embody a willful act of human beings. But this requirement came at a cost. For, as Benjamin Rush asked, "who ever saw any thing perfect come from the hands of man?" "'Tis not in the power of human wisdom to do more," argued Pelatiah Webster, "'tis the fate of human nature to *be imperfect and to err*."[8]

Because human beings were imperfect, their political creations, unlike works of divine or natural creation, were inherently flawed. Expecting "perfection in any institution devised by *man*," Edmund Pendleton conceded, "was as vain as the search for the philosopher's stone." That was because, as one Boston writer observed, "the Supreme Being ... alone is perfectly wise ... and it must be owned that the wisest human institutions are *imperfect*." For these reasons, it came as no surprise that the Constitution itself was imperfect. That an investigation of the instrument revealed oversights, errors, and confusions logically followed the character of its creators. James Innes noted in the Virginia ratifying convention, "in vain you will seek from India to the Pole, for a perfect Constitution. Though it may have certain defects, yet I doubt whether any system more perfect, can be obtained." Federalists did all they could to frame the debate on these terms.[9]

Most important, Federalists asserted, because the Constitution was imperfect, it was also necessarily unfinished. "I will not presume to say, that a more perfect system might not have been fabricated;—but," asked a New Yorker, "who expects perfection at once?" "At once" was the key caveat, implying that the Constitution presented to the American public was, by extension of its innate imperfection, radically incomplete. A Pennsylvania Federalist put a finer point on it. "Perfection, it has often been said, is not the lot of human nature, why then must this *Magna Charta* of American liberty be supposed to come at once into the world, like Minerva out of the head of Jupiter, in every respect finished and perfect?"[10]

If the Constitution was unfinished, however, it could be perfected over time. Experience would prove an ideal teacher. Few generations of political leaders trumpeted the incalculable value of experience quite like those who lived through the American Revolution. James Madison's logic would have been seen as axiomatic when he asked in *Federalist* 14, "But why is the experiment . . . to be rejected merely because it may comprise what is new? Is it not the glory of the people of America, that . . . they have not suffered a blind veneration for antiquity . . . to overrule the suggestions of their own good sense, the knowledge of their own situation, and the lessons of their own experience?" Federalists leaned heavily on experience's cultural purchase, seamlessly connecting it to their arguments about the Constitution's inherent imperfections. "The system yet requires much to make it perfect, and I hope experience will be our guide in taking from or adding to it," Edward Carrington avowed. Framing a perfect, timeless constitution was unfeasible. But the lessons drawn from subsequent experience could ensure its stability and endurance. As Tench Coxe explained, "there is no spirit of arrogance in the new federal constitution. It addresses you with becoming modesty, admitting that it may contain errors. Let us give it a trial." John Dickinson echoed this argument: "a little experience will cast more light upon the subject, than a multitude of debates."[11]

Yet allusions to experience and its corrective powers, pervasive as they were, often proved vague and mysterious. If one of the proposed Constitution's signature virtues was that it was unfinished and in need of improvement, how exactly would the knowledge born of experience translate into constitutional reform?

Federalists were often murky on the details—and had good political reason to keep their claims imprecise—but they repeatedly invoked two distinct mechanisms through which the Constitution would be perfected. The first was located in Article V—the provision for formally amending the Constitution. Amendments would prove necessary because no constitution could endure without changes. And, compared with the Articles of Confederation, which had proved almost impossible to amend since changing them required the unanimous approval of all the states, the new Constitution was much easier to change. "It has been asserted, that the new constitution, when ratified, would be fixed and permanent, and that no alterations or amendments . . . could afterwards be obtained," noted a Pennsylvania Federalist. But that objection was groundless. The Constitution, "in the clearest words," disproved this sentiment. While "perhaps [it] is certain that the New Constitution is not Perfect," Samuel McDowell conceded, "there is a doore left for Amendments." As one Federalist after another boasted, the capacity for change was integrated directly into the instrument. "The seeds of reformation are sown in the work itself," Archibald Maclaine argued, "there is express provision made for amendments, when its defects and imperfections shall be discovered in its operation." Seeds of reformation proved a powerful image. The Constitution was equipped for self-correction.[12]

Federalists also insisted that many, if not most, of the Constitution's deficiencies could be remedied by those political actors who would soon take office under its authority, especially in the first Congresses. Amendments and legislative discretion marked different modes of constitutional change. And, given that Americans had previously devised methods of constitutional construction and change that lay outside the normal channels of government, these procedures might have seemed contradictory. But to Federalists they worked in concert. As John Dickinson so revealingly put it, "by a gradual progress, as has been done in *England,* we may from time to time introduce every improvement in our constitution, that shall be suitable to our situation." Still seized by the logic of Britain's customary constitutionalism, and its concept of fixity, few seemed to worry about the differences between formal amendment and congressional discretion, instead hailing Congress's prospective role in the constitutional system every bit as much as the amendment provision.[13]

As no constitution could completely account for all potential contingencies, Congress would exercise necessary discretion to fill in remaining gaps. "In regard to a possible ill construction," James Iredell explained, "we must depend upon our future Legislature," because "it is impracticable to define every thing." Indeed, as he added in a later essay, "it was not possible for the Convention, nor is it for any human body, to foresee and provide for all contingent cases that may arise. Such cases must therefore be left," for "the general Legislature, as they shall happen to come into existence." Various "powers . . . are *defined* in the new constitution, as minutely as may be," Pelatiah Webster noted, but no matter how minutely they were framed, making use of them required setting them in motion, animating a duty necessarily "committed to the wisdom of Congress." "If some points are not amply clear now," Henry Knox insisted, "the first Legislature will enact such fundamental Laws, as will remove all doubts and apprehensions." As revealed by the latent ambiguity of Knox's striking usage of "fundamental Laws," it remained unclear where political discretion ended and amending began. But what was certain was that Federalists collectively imagined the Constitution as provisional and incomplete. Much of its practical content did not yet exist, and it was apparent that somebody (Congress) or something (amendments) would have to pick up where the Constitution left off.[14]

In manifold ways, Federalists went to great lengths to characterize the Constitution as nothing more than, as John Armstrong observed, a "first draught." This imagery betrayed a lingering attachment to the constitution-qua-system and embodied an avowed refusal to see the Constitution as a lifeless text. It was a work in progress, in need of activation and subsequent work—in essence an imperfect and unfinished object.[15]

The Abuse of Language

While Federalists emphasized the inevitability of constitutional imperfection, Anti-Federalists passionately decried it. They argued that an unfinished, inexact constitution would be an instrument of tyranny prone to endless interpretive manipulation. Accordingly, as Federalists celebrated the Constitution's provisional character, Anti-Federalists condemned its ambiguous and permissive language. In pitching the argument this way, Anti-Federalists tightly linked concerns about the abuse of power to the abuse of language. It was not simply that the imperfect, unfinished Constitution was a threat to liberty, but specifically that its language (and what could be done with it) was menacing. As a result, perfecting and finishing the Constitution meant affording it a linguistic precision that it previously lacked. Thus, in confronting the Federalist vision of an imperfect Constitution, Anti-Federalists focused their attention on the Constitution's words and, in the process, the phenomenon of language itself, demanding that all see the Constitution, however limitedly, as a text.

These Anti-Federalist complaints emerged from neither a prior interest in constitutional language nor, as is sometimes implied, a deep distrust of government itself and an attendant commitment to clearly enumerated constraints. If anything, Anti-Federalists were more sanguine about political power than Federalists were (at least of a certain kind that had dominated American politics up to that point). Anti-Federalists trusted the capacity of the state governments to reflect the will and interests of the people-at-large and, no matter Federalists' persistent complaints about them, Anti-Federalists remained confident that empowering local majorities was also the best way to protect the people's rights. "Government, to an American, is the science of his political safety," declared Cato (New York governor George Clinton) in a common refrain. And to Anti-Federalists like him, accurate representation was the surest safeguard. In government one could find the solution to government. Anti-Federalists' favored solution for combating threats to liberty had, thus, long been structural, not textual.[16]

Despite this long-standing preference, Anti-Federalists became preoccupied with language's capacity to regulate power. Their obsession was provoked by a specific fear about the federal Constitution itself—that such a distant, unrepresentative government would lack the structural safeguards otherwise essential to free government. As the "Federal Farmer" put it in his widely read letters, representative delegates "may do for a small republic," where those assembled in power might mirror "the interests, the views, feelings, and genuine sentiments of the people themselves," but such mechanisms could "never be admitted in an extensive country." If the proposed federal government could have been representative in the ways state governments were, Anti-Federalists' interest in constitutional language might not have materialized. Unable to rely on their trusted solutions, they instead pressed into service the one weapon—to that point largely ignored—

left to them: constitutional text. As Federalists relentlessly championed the Constitution as an unfinished project, that is, Anti-Federalists fell back on linguistic precision as the only mechanism that might wall off the dangers invited by vesting the Constitution with the kind of vast discretion that the Federalists' project necessarily required. While it may have been a last resort, this particular weapon proved effective because it seemed to grow so organically from the Federalists' own arguments. If Anti-Federalists pressed linguistic precision into service for highly contingent reasons, in any case their claims nevertheless proved enduring. They helped constitutional disputants learn how to begin thinking of the Constitution like a text.[17]

Anti-Federalists gravitated toward language as they launched a broader series of complaints. They were horrified by Federalists' blithe confidence in the Constitution's imperfections. Mercy Otis Warren fearfully remembered when Thomas Hutchinson, former royal governor of Massachusetts, had insisted in the years leading up to the Revolution that "no form of government of human construction can be perfect—that we had nothing to fear." History appeared to be repeating itself. The Constitution needed to be repaired (where it seemed manifestly deficient) and clarified (where vague or ambiguous) now, not later. "Is it a government for a moment, a day, or a year?" John De Witt (the pseudonym of a Massachusetts Anti-Federalist) asked rhetorically. "By no means—but for ages—Altered it may possibly be, but it is easier," he insisted, "to correct before it is adopted." Americans were constructing a constitutional system that was intended to endure in perpetuity. "When a building is to be erected which is intended to stand for ages," Brutus surmised, "the foundation should be firmly laid." For once it was set in stone, correcting it would prove nearly impossible. Anti-Federalists began tackling Federalists' conception of the unfinished Constitution by demanding that the Constitution be fixed now.[18]

According to Anti-Federalists, their opponents were wrong about the merits of constitutional malleability. As Nicholas Collin, a Philadelphia pastor who had emigrated from Sweden, claimed, "fixed principles and settled habits are necessary for the stability of Republics." A good constitution was not a work in progress but a stable and finished one. "In framing a government, we should consider a century to come as but a day, and leave the least possible for posterity to mend," declared one Philadelphian. "Hence we ought to aim at PERMANENCY in every part of a Constitution intended to endure." Capturing the point succinctly, another Philadelphian (perhaps

Benjamin Workman) declared, "a fragment of liberty cannot remain, if we once set it in motion in its imperfect state."[19]

That the Constitution could not achieve perfection, moreover, did not preclude the pursuit of excellence before it was adopted. An Old Whig writing in Philadelphia asked, "why then is a constitution which affects all the inhabitants of the United States, which is to be the foundation of all laws and the source of misery or happiness to one quarter of the globe; why is this to be so hastily adopted or rejected, that it cannot admit of a revision?" Indeed, he admitted, "these ideas of political felicity . . . may seem like the visions of an Utopian fancy. . . . But there is at least, this consolation in aiming at excellence, that, if we do not obtain our object, we can make considerable progress towards it." Before being persuaded by Federalists to lend the proposed document his support, Edmund Randolph (one of the three who refused to sign the Constitution at the Federal Convention and initially held out hope for a Second Convention) explained, "it is better to amend, while we have the Constitution in our power" because "a bad feature in government becomes more and more fixed every day."[20]

Anti-Federalists questioned the virtue of changeability, further, by turning one of Federalists' favored arguments on its head, insisting that constitutions needed to be completed at their inception precisely because human beings were imperfect. Brutus argued, "you are not however to expect, a perfect form of government, any more than to meet with perfection in man," but that meant attention "ought to be directed to the main pillars upon which a free government is to rest." Trusting congressional discretion, in other words, a cornerstone of the Federalist case, was foolish. Worse than that, perhaps, it was also lazy. William Symmes, a Massachusetts lawyer who became a delegate to the state's ratifying convention, certainly suggested as much: "A very wise Congress!" he intoned incredulously, "this Convention have really saved themselves a great deal of labour by this presumption." "It is one thing to authorise a well organized legislature to make laws, under the restraints of a well guarded constitution," Federal Farmer likewise proclaimed, "and another to assemble a few men, and to tell them to do what they please."[21]

But Anti-Federalists also thought Federalists were mistaken about the likelihood of changeability, insisting that constitutional change was far more difficult than Federalists claimed. As Richard Henry Lee explained, "it is neither prudent or easy to make frequent changes in government." Change was especially fraught since power, once relinquished, was exceedingly difficult to retrieve. "It is insisted," Brutus complained, "that this constitution must be received, be it ever so imperfect. If it has its defects . . . they can be best amended when they are experienced." Remember, though, he cautioned, "when the people once part with power, they can seldom or never resume it again but by force." Centinel asked rhetorically, "does history abound with examples of a voluntary relinquishment of power?"[22]

Even assuming the people's power could be regained, however, the possibility of future constitutional change was dim since the oft-celebrated amendment feature posed a nearly insurmountable obstacle. After walking through the modes prescribed by Article V, An Old Whig reflected, "this appears to me to be only a cunning way of saying that no alteration shall ever be made; so that whether it is a good constitution or a bad constitution, it will remain forever unamended." Summing things up in his characteristically plain-spoken style, Patrick Henry declared, "when I come to contemplate [Article V], I suppose that I am mad, or, that my countrymen are so: The way to amendment, is, in my conception, shut."[23]

These various criticisms led many Anti-Federalists to insist that the Constitution should be changed immediately, prior to ratification. An Old Whig, for instance, wondered why it was "impracticable, for us yet to correct such errors and imperfections . . . and whilst there is a possibility of procuring a better constitution, it is the duty of every good man to accomplish it." The Constitution was indeed imperfect and unfinished; that was why it required immediate attention.[24]

Out of this critique—drawn as it was in broad strokes—Anti-Federalists' focused complaints about constitutional language emerged. The Constitution was defective not simply because of the kinds of powers that it vested, but because of the mode through which it vested them. As William Petrikin, chief Anti-Federalist from western Pennsylvania, observed with typical acerbity, "every part of this constitution, either bears double meaning, or no meaning at all." Its vague and ambiguous language, language that would prove all too vulnerable to violent and constructive interpretation, would fail to control those in power. While the imperfections of the Constitution's language proved just one of many errors that Anti-Federalists highlighted, it was the flaw that emerged most logically from their attack on the Federalists' insistence that the Constitution was, by character and necessity, imperfect and unfinished.[25]

Anti-Federalists bombarded the public sphere with repeated complaints about the Constitution's "ambiguous," "indefinite," and "inexplicit" language. "Inexplicitness seems to pervade this whole political fabric," Cato complained. The Constitution seemed "designedly ambiguous," a Federal Republican suspiciously noted. At Virginia's ratifying convention, meanwhile, John Tyler observed that he found, "the Constitution is expressed in indefinite terms,—in terms" that were "liable to objections and different constructions." Accordingly, "the land-mark . . . between the powers that give, and the powers given," another Virginian objected, were neither "clearly drawn" nor, as a result, "clearly fixed." Inexplicit language was destined to undo the promise of the Revolution itself, which was captured in John Adams's oft-repeated injunction—drawn from the English political theorist James Harrington and deployed so conspicuously during the era of the American Revolution—that Americans must aspire to live in "an empire of laws and not of men." As Patrick Henry, long one of Virginia's most prominent voices, exclaimed with such concern, "it is not on that paper before you we have to rely, should it be received; it is on those that may be appointed under it. It will be an empire of men and not of laws."[26]

Whatever the chosen description, the moral—captured in several dramatic exhortations—was the same. Drawing upon oceanic metaphors that captured how the Constitution's ambiguous language signified to many an unknown and relentless force, Anti-Federalists launched themselves against the Constitution's text. As Cato warned, in "adopt[ing] a system so vague . . . you are about to precipitate yourselves into a sea of uncertainty." Mercy Otis Warren, in her lyrical style, likewise complained that certain powers "seem to be left as a boundless ocean, that has broken over the chart of the Supreme Lawgiver '*thus far shalt thou go and no further,*' and as they cannot be comprehended by the clearest capacity, or the most sagacious mind, it would be an Herculean labour to attempt to describe the dangers with which they are replete." Centinel seized on yet another metaphor: the bastard child passed off as legitimate heir. The Constitution, he argued, was the product of "the evil genius of darkness . . . came forth under the veil of mystery, its true features being carefully concealed, and every deceptive art has been and is practising to have this spurious brat received as the genuine offspring of heaven-born liberty." Whatever imaginary best captured the Constitution, it was an uncertain instrument, made so by its language. "If we adopt this constitution, it is impossible . . . to know what we give up, and what we retain," lamented John Williams. In sum, the Constitution was "a strange and unnecessary accumulation of words," as Brutus put it, "used to conceal from the public eye, what might have been expressed in . . . [a] concise manner."[27]

Dangerous Clauses

Of course, it was not simply the vague nature of the Constitution's language that was so alarming; it was the abuses of power that this characteristic would permit, if not encourage. Through the act of interpretation, through the clever manipulation of the document's words, those in authority would claim an astonishing array of powers. The Constitution would facilitate tyranny by many means, but few would operate quite as insidiously as its imprecise language. Warnings of tyrannical interpretation often took a general form. Centinel, for instance, complained that "the lust of power is so universal, that a speculative unascertained rule of construction" was sure to attend the Constitution's vague pronouncements. Those in power "may heap refinement upon refinement and subtilty upon subtilty, until they construe away every republican principle," John Williams warned similarly. Indeed, John De Witt added, those entrusted with authority, would by "tacit implication . . . bec[o]me possessed of the whole" of power.[28]

In this charged context, *implication* was a loaded word, one that neatly linked acts of interpreting language and consolidating power. "Implication," George Mason observed, "was capable of any extension, and," in the case of the Constitution, would "be extended to augment the Congressional powers." Setting the debate in a long, historical trajectory, Patrick Henry asserted that "implication in England has been a source of dissention. There has been a war of implication between the King and people. For 100 years did the mother country struggle under the uncertainty of implication. The people insisted [that] their rights were implied: The Monarch denied the doctrine. Their Bill of Rights in some degree terminated the dispute." British history, which had long been of such instructive importance for Americans, could be reduced to a war over implication. This struggle had been revived during Parliament's dispute with the American colonies, when, in 1766, after repealing the Stamp Act, Parliament issued the Declaratory Act, claiming authority to legislate for the colonies "in all cases whatsoever." As Henry continued, "by a bold implication, they said they had a right to bind us in all cases whatsoever. This constructive power we opposed, and successfully. Thirteen or fourteen years ago, the most important thing that could be thought of, was to exclude the possibility of construction and implication." And yet, in keeping with past patterns, those who had conquered the tyranny of implication had themselves, once in power, revived it.[29]

The Constitution that was most threatening was not the one in sight, but the one lurking in the shadows. That veiled Constitution was menacing precisely because it could be accessed so easily through the document's vague clauses. Its words failed to constrain the instrument, something Anti-Federalists repeatedly stressed. "Implication is dangerous, because it is un-bounded," explained Henry. If "no limits be prescribed, it admits of the utmost extension." This loose construction, in turn, would expose the young republic to despotism. As John De Witt noted ominously, "the in-trusion into society of that doctrine of tacit implication . . . has been the favorite theme of every tyrant from the origin of all governments to the present day."[30]

Broad criticisms such as these pervaded arguments over ratification. But they were outnumbered by a more focused kind of critique, one fixated not on the Constitution as a whole but on its most troubling clauses that prom-ised to extinguish American liberty. Of particular concern were the very first words of the Constitution:

We the People of the United States, in Order to form a more perfect Union, establish Justice, insure domestic Tranquility, provide for the common defence, promote the general Welfare, and secure the Bless-ings of Liberty to ourselves and our Posterity, do ordain and establish this Constitution for the United States of America.

Aside from the fact that the preamble began "We the People" rather than "We the States"—as many opponents of the Constitution certainly would have preferred—it also delineated grand, comprehensive ends that the Con-stitution putatively served. Even though much narrower articulations of specific federal powers followed, Anti-Federalists worried that the preamble's vague and open-ended language could be mobilized to expand the fed-eral warrant. Upon taking stock of its contents, George Clinton, governor of New York, concluded, "these include every object for which government was established amongst men," and, he reasoned, "in every dispute about the powers granted, it is fair to infer that the means are commensurate with the end." How much could be smuggled in under the license granted "to form a more Perfect Union" or "establish Justice" or even "secure the Bless-ings of Liberty"? The possibilities seemed limitless. "The great objects . . . are declared in this preamble in general and indefinite terms," Brutus complained. "The inference is natural that the legislature will have an authority to make all laws which they shall judge necessary for the common safety, and to promote the general welfare. This amounts to a power to make laws at discretion: No terms can be found more indefinite than these."[31]

Article I, which outlined the design and powers of Congress, caused similar consternation. Of particular concern was Section Eight, which enumerated the body's powers. Anti-Federalists did not make it far before worries mounted, for the section began with what they took to be a stunningly vague set of objects, that "Congress shall have Power to lay and collect Taxes, Duties, Imposts and Excises, to pay the Debts and provide for the common Defence and," most alarming of all, "general Welfare of the United States." "There is no Power," declared James Francis Mercer of Maryland, "which Congress may *think* necessary to exercise for the *general Welfare*, which they may not assume under this Constitution." Interpreting this article in the "most natural and grammatical" way, Brutus argued, "authorise[d] the Congress to do any thing which in their judgment will tend to provide for the general welfare." That "amounts," he reasoned, "to the same thing as general and unlimited powers of legislation in all cases." "Are these terms definite, and will they be understood in the same manner, and to apply to the same cases by every one?" he asked. "No one will pretend they will. It will then be matter of opinion, what tends to the general welfare; and the Congress will be the only judges in the matter." Not only would Congress then have discretion through linguistic definition, but according to Pennsylvania's dissenting minority—Anti-Federalists who angrily denounced the Constitution after Federalists rushed it through the state's ratifying convention—Congress could use that specific power to annihilate the state governments, "by construing every purpose for which the state legislatures now lay taxes, to be for the 'general welfare,'" and therefore within their power. In designing hands, the pliability of two words could lead to tyranny.[32]

The same opening clause also stated that Congress would have power to "lay and collect Taxes," a potentially blanket statement sure to unnerve those who had only recently clamored against the taxing authority of a distant, unrepresentative Parliament. Indeed, few parts of the Constitution received more criticism than the taxing power. As with the general welfare clause, complaints often centered on its indiscriminate text and the vast number of objects that could imaginably fall under it. "To detail the particulars comprehended in the general terms, taxes, duties, imposts and excises, would require a volume," argued Brutus. Based on this assessment, he added, "not only are these terms very comprehensive, and extend to a vast number of objects, but the power to lay and collect has great latitude." Centinel warned, "The words 'pursuant to the constitution' will be no restriction to the authority of congress; for the foregoing sections give them unlimited legislation" and through the "unbounded power of taxation" they would "have full dominion." Indeed, George Mason observed, "the present clause clearly discovers, that it is a National Government, and no longer a confederation. I mean that clause which gives the first hint of the General Government laying direct taxes," for it could not be interpreted in any other way. Such expansive language revealed that the new federal government would actually be a consolidated, national regime.[33]

Finally, Anti-Federalists took aim at the controversial "necessary and proper" clause, which punctuated Article I, Section Eight. More than any other portion of the Constitution, this clause, devised by James Wilson and criticized by the nonsigning delegates to the Constitutional Convention, seemed to carry the seeds of dangerous possibilities. For starters, "necessary and proper" was impossible to define, its meaning washing over any limiting constraints. As the Federal Farmer declared, "it is almost impossible to have a just conception of" what "may be deemed necessary and proper." John Williams found it "perhaps utterly impossible fully to define this power." Here he effectively quoted one of Brutus's earlier essays, which had concluded that the phrase was "truly incomprehensible. A case cannot be conceived of, which is not included in this power." The clause, Brutus elaborated, "may be given a construction to justify . . . passing almost any law." An Old Whig cried, meanwhile, it is "*undefined, unbounded, and immense power.*" Based on these troubling assessments of the clause's seemingly limitless reach, it was quickly labeled the "sweeping clause."[34]

Because the clause was impossible to define, it undercut the precise purpose of the section (and document more generally), which was to enumerate powers. "Under such a clause as this," asked An Old Whig, "can any thing be said to be reserved and kept back from Congress? Can it be said that the Congress have no power but what *is expressed?*" Here this Pennsylvania Anti-Federalist, like many others, hit on Wilson's crucial addition to the "necessary and proper" clause when he wrote it at the Convention—in which he had entrusted the national government to carry not only the "foregoing powers" of Article I, Section Eight into effect but also those required to carry out "all other Powers" as well. "What is the meaning of the latter part of the clause," An Old Whig asked uneasily—not the one that licensed laws necessary and proper to carry out the "foregoing powers" but the one "for carrying into execution ALL OTHER POWERS"? This additional "necessary and proper" clause unmistakably indicated, he felt, that "other powers may be assumed hereafter as contained by implication in this constitution." Focusing on the same troubling portion of the clause, The Republican Federalist in Massachusetts styled it the "*omnipotent* clause" for, he explained, he was as willing to believe "the man who says, that he can see in its *aphelion,* a comet which requires a century for its revolution," as he would trust the person "that says, he can see the extent to which an artful and arbitrary legislature, can by this clause *stretch* their powers."[35]

A Congress equipped with this bit of text, Anti-Federalists worried, would destroy the state governments. If the other clauses did not demolish whatever lines separated the two, this one surely would. "May not the powers of the Congress from the clause which enables them to pass all Laws necessary to carry this system into effect," former Virginia Continental Army officer George Lee Turberville asked James Madison, "be so operated upon as to annihilate the state Governments?" "It seams to me," William Russell, also a military veteran from Virginia, seemed to answer Turberville's question from afar, "if Congress, have a right to make all laws that may be necessary & proper, [then] no inferiour Legislature, can be more than a Mitaphysical nothing." This last phrase was an arresting way to describe the state governments—by insinuating that they were both ineffable and tangible. In arguments such as these, Anti-Federalists were gesturing toward language's similar dual character. Words were airy and insubstantial and yet, as was becoming clear, also markers of concrete power.[36]

Here lay the problem with implication, with language so pliable and ductile that it failed to constrain. "If you give to the United States" power to make "all laws necessary," argued James Monroe, then "there is no check in this Constitution." Instead, "there is a general power given" with "no limits pointed out." This meant that those in power would not be "restrained or controuled from making any law, however oppressive in its operation, which they may think necessary." Few were more aware of the relationship between supple words and interpretive techniques than Brutus. "The clause which vests the power to pass all laws which are proper and necessary . . . leaves the legislature at liberty, to do every thing, which in their judgment is best."

Indeed, "it implies that the constitution is not to receive an explanation strictly, according to its letter," but instead by its "spirit." The "necessary and proper" clause, in the final analysis, was threatening because it was language that nullified language; these were words that thrust the reader beyond explicit text into the indefinite realm of spirit.[37]

But such concerns—with language and its likely manipulation—were not reserved solely to Article I. With a vengeance, Anti-Federalists also focused their attacks on the second section of Article III, which specified the powers of the judiciary:

> The judicial Power shall extend to all Cases, in Law and Equity, arising under this Constitution, the Laws of the United States, and Treaties made, or which shall be made, under their Authority. . . . In all the other Cases before mentioned, the supreme Court shall have appellate Jurisdiction, both as to Law and Fact.

This portion of the text came under Anti-Federalist scrutiny in no small measure because many Americans viewed judges suspiciously at the time of the Constitution's drafting. Prior to independence, judges had been servants of the crown, and they still carried the burden of that legacy. The fact that so many future Anti-Federalists, suffering through the economic pains of the previous decade, had found themselves in debtors' court, moreover, only heightened their suspicion of judicial officers. Accordingly, Anti-Federalists—be they landed elites and middling professionals wary of centralized power or laborers and farmers who had acquired a distaste for judges—studied Article III with care. And what perhaps bothered them most was the ways in which Article III's language seemed so unlimited.[38]

The first objection they raised was Article III's wide latitude. As the judicial power extended "to all Cases of Law & Equity," observed Samuel Osgood, "the Extent of the Judicial Power is therefore, as indefinite & unlimited as Words can make it." Seemingly limitless, it was "of stupendous magnitude," remarked William Grayson. So much so, that it was "impossible for human nature to trace its extent. It is so vaguely and indefinitely expressed, that its latitude cannot be ascertained." About the article George Mason asked, "Will Gentlemen be pleased, candidly, fairly, and without sophistry, to shew us what remains? There is no limitation. It goes to every thing." This same fear led Melancton Smith of New York to conclude, "the judicial powers in this Constitution, are given in too general and indefinite terms; are so various and extensive, that they may easily be made by legal fiction to extend too far." This reasoning was striking—"indefinite terms" fueling "legal fiction"; unconstrained by language, judges could extend their powers as far as their imaginations.[39]

Article III's language was especially far-reaching in extending the judicial power to all cases, not just in law but also in equity. Equity connoted both a legal concept and an understanding of how it traditionally had been administered. Conceptually, equity conveyed broad principles of fairness, independent of the precise dictates of law, meaning powers to decide cases equitably carried vast discretion. Practically, in the Anglo-American legal world equity had primarily been administered by judges in equity courts. In seventeenth-century England, the administration of equity had been most tightly linked to the Court of Chancery, where the royally appointed Chancellor stood as substitute for the king's conscience and, on the basis of that authority, decided legal questions based on broad discretion. Opponents of the royal prerogative and champions of the common law (and the separate set of courts where it was administered) criticized Chancery for empowering judges to circumvent law through equity. Over time, though, equity was disaggregated from Chancery, and many opponents of Chancery defended equity as long as it was practiced by nonjudges, especially juries. Familiar with the institutional history of equity, Anti-Federalists were less concerned with the jurisprudence of equity itself than the fact that, under the Constitution, remote federal judges would control it. As a Democratic Federalist complained, "It is well known that the courts of chancery in England . . . introduce[d] a foreign mode of jurisprudence under the specious name of *Equity*." But, he added, "there is much more *equity* in a trial by jury." The real objection to equity, in other words, was institutional in character—that a federal judiciary would come to mirror the treacherous Chancery of yore. "It is a very dangerous thing to vest in the same judge power to decide on the law, and also general powers in equity," explained the Federal Farmer, "for if the law restrain him, he is only to step into his shoes of equity, and give what judgment his reason or opinion may dictate." This was especially true in the United States, since "we have no precedents in this country, as yet, to regulate the divisions as in equity in Great-Britain; equity, therefore . . . will be mere discretion." Via one slippery word, federal judges would be free from the burdens otherwise placed on them. As Brutus pointed out, "I might instance a number of clauses in the constitution, which, if explained in an *equitable* manner, would extend the powers of the government to every case." Similarly, Samuel Osgood predicted that if "any State should object to the exercise of Power . . . the legal Remedy is to try the Question before the supreme Judicial Court" as "they have Power, not confining themselves to the Letter of the general or State Constitutions, to consider & determine upon it, in Equity."[40]

Fearing that the federal judiciary would come to resemble the infamous Chancery, Anti-Federalists were especially concerned that the Supreme Court would have the power to determine matters of fact as well as law. Out of language granting it seemingly indefinite appellate power, Anti-Federalists conjured horrible visions—cases tried before local juries that would then be appealed to distant federal courts where judges would have power to evaluate not merely the application of legal principles but also the facts upon which those cases were based, a power that had long been reserved to those local juries. "If the jurisdiction of the jury be not final, as to fact," Federal Farmer warned, "it is of little or no importance." Building from this, Brutus worried, "if we understand the appellate jurisdiction in any other way, we shall be left utterly at a loss to give it a meaning." Under the common law, "in no case, when they are carried up, are the facts re-examined." But the words of Article III threatened to change that. As a Philadelphian put it, "the supreme continental court is to have, almost in every case, 'appellate jurisdiction both as to law and fact,' which signifies, if there is any meaning in words, the setting aside the trial by jury."[41]

Because judicial authority was conveyed through such far-reaching language, it would enjoy wide interpretive latitude. No Anti-Federalist author probed this dimension of the Constitution more thoroughly than Brutus. Through a series of remarkable analyses, he explained how the courts would extend their power through creative, constructive interpretations of the Constitution's words (first those applying to the judiciary and then, in time, the rest of the document). Using its malleable words, justices could find the power to unmoor the document from its textual foundation. As he explained, "the plan is so modelled, as to authorise the courts, not only to carry into execution the powers expressly given, but where these are wanting or ambiguously expressed, to supply what is wanting by their own decisions." Because Article III "vests the courts with authority to give the constitution a legal construction, or to explain it according to the rules laid down for construing a law," the Supreme Court would have "a certain degree of latitude of explanation." By "this mode of construction, the courts are to give such meaning to the constitution as comports best with the common, and generally received acceptation of the words in which it is expressed. . . . Where words are dubious, they will be explained by the context." But the matter would not stop there. Because the judiciary "are not only to decide questions arising upon the meaning of the constitution in law, but also in equity," it would be "empowered, to explain the constitution according to the reasoning spirit of it, without being confined to the words or letter." Because the judiciary was not properly constrained by the text, it could use that license to systematically destabilize the entire Constitution. Eventually, it would possess nothing save judge-made meaning.[42]

These dangers, moreover, were inescapable, since the Supreme Court, precisely because Article III was so imprecise, would become the final legal expositor in all the land. As a result, it would "have a right, independent of the legislature, to give a construction to the constitution and every part of it, and there is no power provided in this system to correct their construction or do it away," Brutus reasoned. "If, therefore, the legislature pass any laws, inconsistent with the sense the judges put upon the constitution, they will declare it void." Article III itself had made it thus. "Had the construction of the constitution been left with the legislature, they would have explained it at their peril," he reckoned, for "if they exceed their powers, or sought to find, in the spirit of the constitution, more than was expressed in the letter, the people from whom they derived their power could remove them." But no such recourse was available against the judiciary. Article III was strikingly indefinite, and that linguistic open-endedness was likely to produce a judicial Leviathan.[43]

The People's Text

The Constitution was thus vulnerable to misreadings, distortions, and sophistic interpretations of all sorts, leaving it susceptible, as Anti-Federalists derisively claimed, to lawyers' manipulation. Frustration with the legal profession was already endemic to American culture and would only intensify during and after ratification. Benjamin Austin's fiery essays—first published in the Massachusetts press on the eve of the ratification debates—were the most striking examples of this antipathy. Austin's critique was as extensive as it was searing, but it ultimately rested on a single idea: that through "chicanery and art," through the "wonderful mistery of *law craft*," the "sly art of *sophistry*," various "*false glosses* and *plausible cavils*," and "*metaphysical pleadings*," lawyers abused the people. Lawyers had fashioned a needlessly complex legal code by engulfing it in "hundreds of volumes" that rendered the whole "practice mysterious." Always "crying up the *intricacy of the law,*" the "'order' of lawyers . . . deceive the people" much "like Romish priests in matters of religion." Such obfuscation befitted monarchies, not republics. The Revolution should have ushered in "a system of laws of OUR OWN . . . made easy to be understood by every individual in the community." But lawyers had conspired against this republican goal since independence. Their "sophistry" was "the grand artillery" being used "to batter down every plain, rational principle of law" that kept America in a benighted state.[44]

Anti-Federalists intuitively tailored these sentiments to the context at hand. "The rights of the people," one Richmond writer put it, "should never stand in need of the comments or explanations of lawyers" who were "too apt . . . to entangle the plainest rights in their net of sophistry." And yet, Samuel Osgood complained, the Constitution writ large "is a Plan, that the common People can never understand—That if adopted—the Scribes & Pharisees only will be able to interpret, & give it a Meaning." The Constitution "thereby render[ed] Law," George Mason criticized, "as tedious intricate & expensive" as it too often had been. It was the kind of "incomprehensibleness" that suited "expounders of law."[45]

As these concerns reveal, the act of probing and highlighting the imprecision of the Constitution's language eventually led Anti-Federalists to assert that exact constitutions required clear language. If language in its own right needed to parcel and barricade power, if words as much as structural arrangements needed to police tyranny and corruption, then those words needed to be precisely written. In constitutions, the Reverend David Caldwell of North Carolina affirmed, "there is a great necessity for perspicuity." The "powers delegated to the government," the Federal Farmer observed, "must be precisely defined by the words that convey them." Nobody more incisively grasped the emerging connection between the importance of clear language and constitutional security than did the Massachusetts Anti-Federalist John De Witt. "Language is so easy of explanation, and so difficult is it by words to convey exact ideas," he wrote, "that the party to be governed cannot be too explicit. The line cannot be drawn with too much precision and accuracy." Precisely because linguistic precision was generally so elusive, constitutional language needed to be drafted with an obsessive focus on clarity.[46]

Arguments about the necessity of linguistic precision tended to imply what the Constitution ought to be rather than what it was. But that was not always the case. Harping on language served a variety of Anti-Federalist purposes, including underscoring what kind of a document they insisted the Constitution must be, irrespective of whether it was subsequently refined. To their minds, the Constitution was first and foremost a people's text, and thus emphatically not a legal text. No matter what might come of the Constitution's current language, it was imperative that it be read not as a legal statute or contract, but instead as a popular, nonlegal text. Given that the Constitution featured its share of cryptic language, the fear was that lawyers would cunningly impose technical meanings onto the Constitution's words. Clear language would not only help maintain the people's control over the Constitution, but also enforce the right kinds of interpretations of the Constitution's current words, interpretations that presupposed the document's accessibility. "A Constitution," contended Patrick Henry, "ought to be like a beacon, held up to the public eye so as to be understood by every man." Another Virginian, Denatus, employed a different metaphor: it "ought to be as evident to simple reason," he said, "as the letters of our alphabet." Most simply, as William Lenoir put it in the North Carolina ratifying convention, "a constitution ought to be understood by everyone."[47]

In contrast to lawyers' manipulations, Anti-Federalists insisted that the Constitution's words be given their ordinary signification. In a celebrated speech in the Massachusetts ratifying convention, Amos Singletary articulated this concern with unmatched imagery:

> These lawyers, and men of learning, and monied men that talk so finely and gloss over matters so smoothly, to make us poor illiterate people swallow down the pill, expect to get into Congress themselves; they expect to be the managers of this Constitution and get all the power and all the money into their own hands, and then they will swallow up all us little folks, like the great *Leviathan*, Mr. President, yes, just as the whale swallowed up *Jonah*.

This invocation of the biblical Jonah connected Anti-Federalist complaints about linguistic manipulation of the Constitution to the Protestant plain style that pervaded religious interpretation. Much as many Protestants had denounced church clerics' hermeneutical authority over scripture—as when the English political radical Henry Parker had claimed a century earlier that "the Pope's Arrogance" stemmed from his need "to interpret Scripture where it wants no interpreter"—so too did numerous Anti-Federalists preempt lawyers' claims to expert mediation over constitutional law by demanding that constitutional words be given their plain, unmediated meaning. "Are we to trust business of this sort to technical definitions?" asked George Mason skeptically. No, he demanded, what ought to be respected "is the plain meaning of the words."[48]

Increasing awareness of the Constitution as text, in other words, compelled Anti-Federalists to insist upon a particular way of imagining the Constitution's essence. If lawyers could claim that the document's meaning was, in character, legal, they could further distort it. "If Gentlemen pervert the most clear expressions, and the usual meaning of the language of the people, there is an end of all argument," announced Patrick Henry. But if the Constitution was read as ordinary people would, that could nullify much of this additional distortion. This is why Henry, upon being "told, of technical terms, and that we must put a liberal construction on it," replied, "we must judge by the common understanding of common men." The precise Constitution and the people's Constitution were one and the same.[49]

Thinking about what the Constitution was and what it ought to be gave new meaning to a constitutional feature that Anti-Federalists, like most Americans, had long revered: bills of rights. Anti-Federalists had begun emphasizing the value of constitutional language to combat otherwise flawed constitutional structure. If the structure itself could not be repaired and key powers returned to the state governments, then at least the Constitution could be given a precision it lacked, making it harder for national political leaders to exploit its authority. This strategy was extended when Anti-Federalists insisted that the proposed Constitution include a bill of rights. In certain ways, this demand fit comfortably in the long-standing logics of Anglo-American politics, which had placed so great a value on British forerunners (especially Magna Carta, the Petition of Right of 1628, and the English Bill of Rights of 1689), as well as Americans' own declarations of rights in several state constitutions. But against the backdrop of their emerging concerns over constitutional language, Anti-Federalists' attachment to bills of rights also signaled something new: an inchoate belief that constitutional text actually made constitutional substance. In this regard, their thinking about bills of rights owed at least as much to their complaints over the proposed Constitution's ambiguous and permissive language as to previous fondness for comparable instruments.

The demand for a federal bill of rights lay at the forefront of Anti-Federalist thinking from the beginning. George Mason helped ensure that it became an immediate component of Anti-Federalist resistance by including it so prominently in his widely read list of objections to the proposed Constitution. Because Mason enjoyed firsthand knowledge of the Constitution's drafting, his objections quickly became a template for Anti-Federalist criticism. Mason had been one of the few delegates to the Convention who had even pondered the need for a bill of rights. Having failed to convince others in attendance that the issue even merited consideration (it was unanimously rejected by the delegations), Mason made this one of the primary justifications for his refusal to sign. Capturing his friend's concerns, Richard Henry Lee insisted that "the new Constitution . . . be bottomed upon a declaration, or Bill of Rights, clearly and precisely stating the principles upon which this Social Compact is founded."[50]

But these complaints did not necessarily signal a new kind of constitutional orientation. They remained fully consistent with the kind of thinking that had informed state declarations of rights, which were important because they guided constitutional attitudes, not because they demarcated constitutional content. These prefatory declarations were not comprehensive enumerations; they were instead important statements of constitutional principle, proclamations that gestured toward the underlying purpose of what followed. Many Anti-Federalist complaints about the need for a bill of rights rested on these long-standing assumptions and called for a preamble to the federal Constitution that would function as a "sufficient guide." "This precious, this comfortable page," a Richmond Anti-Federalist explained, "will be the ensign, to which on any future contestation . . . the asserters of liberty may rally, and constitutionally defend it." He insisted, "let us then insert in the first page of this constitution as a preamble to it, a declaration of our rights, or an enumeration of our prerogatives, as a sovereign people; that they may never hereafter be unknown, forgotten or contradicted." As the Federal Farmer explained, "we do not by declarations change the nature of things, or create new truths, but . . . we give existence, or at least establish in the minds of the people truths and principles which they might never otherwise have thought of, or soon forgot."[51]

When Federalists responded to these early complaints, though, the Anti-Federalists' emphasis began to shift. No Federalist response was more consequential than James Wilson's speech in the Pennsylvania State House yard in October 1787. Wilson argued that a bill of rights was redundant, and even dangerous, in a system of enumerated powers. Unlike in the state constitutions, where "every thing which is not reserved is given," in the federal Constitution, "every thing which is not given, is reserved." Because, for instance, the federal government lacked authority to interfere with "the liberty of the press," there was no need to formally protect it. Federalists repeatedly invoked Wilson's core argument and built on it to justify the omission, including most notably Alexander Hamilton in *Federalist* 84 and James Madison in the Virginia ratifying convention. At the Constitutional Convention, Wilson, Hamilton, and Madison had all mocked the premise of enumerated powers. And seemingly they had only tolerated its eventual inclusion in the Constitution when they were satisfied that the construction of the document (especially Wilson's rendering of the "necessary and proper" clause) meant that enumeration made no substantive difference. Since enumerated powers posed no meaningful threat, when confronted by Anti-Federalist complaints about a lack of bill of rights, these Federalists were happy to emphasize this feature of the Constitution for strategic effect. But, in so doing, they helped generate a new kind of logic, one that altered how enumeration was understood and even led some Federalists to imagine the Constitution in a manner that was antithetical to how Wilson and his allies had understood it at the Convention. One Massachusetts Federalist even went so far as to argue that it was precisely because Britain "had no *written* constitution" that its people needed a bill of rights. But since American constitutions were "declared on paper," he argued, no such provisions were, in fact, necessary. Among Federalists, Wilson's argument thus inadvertently managed to underscore the importance of constitutional text.[52]

Most of all, though, Wilson's logic shaped how Anti-Federalists thought about the Constitution's language. In the face of Federalists' arguments defending the omission of a bill of rights and in concert with their growing fears of the insidious character of constitutional text, Anti-Federalists took the new Wilsonian logic to heart—except they inverted it. They agreed that the proposed federal Constitution was distinct (and indeed because it was written) but for altogether different reasons than Federalists emphasized. Where Federalists claimed omitted rights were irrelevant under a system of enumerated powers, Anti-Federalists claimed such omissions were alarming precisely because the Constitution's powers were enumerated. Only because Wilson's premise was sound did Anti-Federalists begin worrying about the status of rights not formally included in the proposed Constitution.

They realized they were no longer operating in the conceptual space opened up by the state constitutions, a space that placed little emphasis on textual omission. As long as custom, structure, and text formed a mutually reinforcing whole, such omissions were not immediately concerning. If text was embedded in a wider field of fundamental law, declarations did not need to be comprehensive. But as Anti-Federalists increasingly stressed the constitutive character of constitutional language, they cast doubt on the notion that custom, structure, and text still fused in traditional ways. In turn, following Wilson's premise to its logical conclusion, they implied that text was now the marker, rather than merely a reminder, of constitutional substance. And by emphasizing the boundary drawn by the Constitution's language—by insisting upon a starker contrast between what was within and without the text, what was immediately in the document's words as opposed to what could be found only in the document's more ethereal spirit—they placed greater emphasis on the text's omissions.

These developments explain why Patrick Henry could conclude, at the Virginia ratifying convention, that "the necessity of a Bill of Rights appear[s] to me to be greater in this Government, than ever it was in any Government before." In this evolving context, if "the people do not think it necessary to reserve [their rights]," then unlike under the state constitutions "they will be supposed to be given up." Thomas Wait, a printer from Maine, argued that because "there is a certain darkness, duplicity and studied ambiguity of expression runing thro' the whole Constitution," that made "a Bill of Rights peculiarly necessary." Meanwhile, George Mason "could see no clear distinction between rights relinquished by a positive grant, and lost by implication. Unless there were a Bill of Rights," he contended, "implication might swallow up all our rights." In seeing the Constitution through text, Anti-Federalists could not help but conclude that the instrument degraded whatever it did not explicitly include, that if something merited protection it needed to be codified in the source that otherwise delineated the Constitution's substance: language.[53]

Invocations of British constitutionalism best illustrated the change. "The most blind admirer of this Constitution must in his heart confess that it is as far inferior to the British constitution, of which it is an imperfect imitation as darkness is to light," proclaimed a Maryland Anti-Federalist. "In the British constitution," he went on, "the rights of men, the primary objects of the social Compact—are fixed on an immoveable foundation & clearly defined & ascertained by their Magna Charta, their Petition of Rights &

Bill of Rights." In comparison to these famous British documents, "in this new Constitution—a complicated System sets responsability at defiance & the Rights of Men neglected & undefined are left at the mercy of events." Here he recast Britain's most famous bills of rights in a new light—they possessed authority, not because they articulated fundamental liberties or had been reinforced by custom, but because they systemized rights in a specifically linguistic mode. As the Federal Farmer put it, "when the people of England . . . formed Magna Charta, they did not consider it sufficient, that they were indisputably entitled to certain natural and unalienable rights, not depending on silent titles"; rather, "they made an instrument in writing . . . to fix the contents of it in the minds of the people, as they successively come upon the stage." Less a continuation of prior constitutional logics, these calls for a bill of rights were an indication that a new kind of constitutional imagination was beginning to take shape.[54]

Through a cacophony of arguments—some sprawling, others focused; some devoted to specific clauses, others considering the document as a whole; some obsessed with the contents of the instrument, others with its omissions—Anti-Federalists began insisting that the Constitution was a text, an object whose contents were defined and whose boundaries were limned by its language. Their long-standing obsession with structural powers had not dissipated; most of their criticisms focused on the Constitution's structural failures—inadequate representation in the House of Representatives, the intermingling of executive and legislative power, dangerously long terms for officeholders, lack of mandatory rotation of office, and extravagant military and spending powers granted to the Congress and the president—and most of their demands centered on the amendments needed to repair them. But this preoccupation had been joined by a related, if distinct, fixation. Constitutions were not simply structures constructed of words; according to Anti-Federalists they were also just words, in the purest sense. As John De Witt revealingly put it, "the Compact itself is a recital upon paper." Constitutional limits were drawn by language, constitutional equilibrium was a function of linguistic choice and design, and a constitution's capacity to regulate power was a function of the interpretive modes that ought to be attached to it. These interlocking arguments helped Anti-Federalists arrive at this novel understanding: that comprehending the proposed Constitution meant grasping that it was constituted by language.[55]

The Indeterminacies of Language

Federalists would have been content to let their initial arguments for ratification stand. They preferred to sell the Constitution in sweeping terms and focus attention on the defects of the Article of Confederation and the state of emergency its shortcomings had seemingly occasioned. Moreover, in arguing that constitutional imperfection was not a failing of political science but an embodiment of its wisdom, they clearly sensed advantage in turning the document's potential weakness into a strength. But in the face of systematic and focused critiques, they could not help but respond in kind. Anti-Federalists had not merely broached but animated the problem of constitutional language, and Federalists soon took the bait.

Their responses took two different forms, though, showing how Anti-Federalist criticisms pushed Federalist argument in opposite directions. At times Federalists denied Anti-Federalists' premise about constitutional language; at other times they ceded that premise while, instead, rejecting their conclusion. Anti-Federalists warned that officeholders would lay claim to an astonishing expanse of power by manipulating the Constitution's language, all while being able to claim that they were respecting the document. The issue was not that those in power would ignore the Constitution, but that the Constitution itself would facilitate their tyranny. Anti-Federalists accordingly insisted that the Constitution needed more precise language and demanded the purging of its unnecessary and destructive indeterminacies and ambiguities. Perhaps those in power might still ignore these meanings, but they would do so at their own peril by acting in express violation of the Constitution's meaning. Accordingly, Anti-Federalists' premise was that language could police those in power if chosen aptly. Federalists overtly rejected this claim, doubling down on their commitment to an imperfect, unfinished Constitution and disparaging language in the process—whether it be its capacity to regulate power, close or complete the Constitution, or communicate determinate meaning. Properly understanding language meant appreciating that a viable Constitution could never be made or defined by this substance alone. Yet Federalists also, at times, accepted Anti-Federalists' premise about constitutional language before denouncing their conclusion by insisting that the Constitution was clear and Anti-Federalists had simply misread it. In so doing, though, Federalists exposed a deeper form of constitutional uncertainty. To show that the Constitution was clear and determinate, they began sketching the kinds of interpretive rules that ought to govern readings of the instrument. But they struggled to delineate what these rules were, precisely because they were still unsure what kind of an object the Constitution was. Thus, while the Federalist turn to interpretive rules underscored their willingness to legitimize constitutional language, the chaos surrounding these rules ended up illustrating that the Constitution remained a deeply indeterminate object.

Much of the time, then, Federalists mocked the idea that language might regulate politics. Finely drawn linguistic barriers—be they in constitutions generally or bills of rights specifically—were mere "parchment barriers." When it came to policing the powerful, they were utterly impotent, "not worth even the trouble of writing," as Roger Sherman (who had once defended enumeration at the Convention) emphatically declared. No Federalist made this point more incisively than Madison in *Federalist* 48:

> Will it be sufficient to mark with precision the boundaries of these departments in the Constitution of the government, and to trust to these parchment barriers against the encroaching spirit of power? . . . Experience assures us, that the efficacy of the provision has been greatly over-rated; and that some more adequate defence is indispensibly necessary for the more feeble, against the more powerful members of the government.

Just as some Anti-Federalists had refashioned understanding of state declarations of rights to insist upon linguistic barriers, Madison recast these declarations to denigrate such barriers. As he had already vigorously argued both prior to and during the Federal Convention, the experience of the previous decade had conclusively revealed their ineffectiveness. Noah Webster extended the point further, writing as "Giles Hickory" in his own *American Magazine.* "A *bill of rights,* a *perpetual constitution* on parchment guaranteeing that right, was a useless form of words," he asserted. "Liberty is never secured by such paper declarations . . . nor lost for want of them." This last point was critical. Not only were words powerless against the powerful, but they failed to explain why the powerful had authority. "Uncus," a Maryland author asserted that "the freedom of a nation does not so much depend on what a piece of parchment may contain,—as their virtue,—ideas of liberty—and *'the sense of the people at large.'* It was not *Magna Charta* written on parchment, which united the English Barons to oppose King John," he explained, "but, the united opposition of the Barons that *forced* from King John *Magna Charta*." The Articles of Confederation proved this point. As Edmund Randolph (having converted to the Federalist cause) pointed out, the Articles "had nominally powers, powers on paper, which it could not use." In essence, language could limit or instantiate power only if real power otherwise undergirded it.[56]

Accordingly, constitutions functioned and endured due to the structural equilibrium they achieved, not because of the textual impediments they erected. Even "if this Constitution was as perfect as the sacred volume is," the Reverend Samuel Stillman explained in the Massachusetts ratifying convention, "it would not secure the liberties of the people" because "nothing written on paper will do this." A bill of rights, Benjamin Rush claimed in much the same vein, was meaningless, for "there can be only *two* sureties for liberty in any government, viz. *representation* and *checks.* . . . Without them, a volume of rights would avail nothing." Echoing the point, Roger Sherman contended that "the Suffrage of the people" was "a much greater Security than" any "restraining clauses upon paper." This was another way of saying that "no bill of rights ever yet bound the supreme power longer than the *honey moon* of a new married couple, unless the *rulers were interested* in preserving the rights; and in that case they have always been ready enough to declare the rights, and to preserve them when they were declared." Safety, in short, lay in structure, not language. Belief in this precept led Madison to dismiss Patrick Henry's complaint at the Virginia ratifying convention that without a bill of rights the new Constitution left freedom of religion exposed. As Madison was only too quick to remind his antagonist, such textual protections had not precluded Virginians (Henry included) from pursuing a general assessment bill years earlier that violated freedom of conscience. Only a reconstitution of the federal system could check such majoritarian oppression. This belief also led Madison to repeatedly bemoan the defeat of his favored federal negative. Even if he claimed otherwise publicly, in a private letter to Jefferson written at the beginning of ratification debriefing his friend on the Constitutional Convention, Madison could not contain his disappointment and, in a fit of grief, renewed his defense of the provision's essential necessity. The discussion swelled far beyond its initial parenthetical character, no doubt because Madison remained firmly convinced, as he continued to be during ratification, that constitutional text presented few obstacles to those in power and thus few protections to those outside of it.[57]

When considering what would happen if those in power ignored or transgressed the limits of constitutional text, the superiority of constitutional structure became plain. James Iredell, for instance, argued that "if Congress, under pretence of exercising the power delegated to them, should, in fact . . . usurp" authority, "the people will be exactly in the same situation as if there had been an express provision against such power in particular, and yet they had presumed to exercise it. It would be," he concluded, "an act of tyranny, against which no parchment stipulations can guard." In such cases, Madison emphasized how indispensable popular political control was to any functioning constitutional system. The consequences of violating either the letter or the spirit of the Constitution, after all, would be the same: there would be cause "to mark the innovation, to sound the alarm to the people, and to exert their local influence in effecting a change of federal representatives." Beneath the structures highlighted by language lay an even stronger force: the people themselves. Without this foundation, textual forms were meaningless. Few were better attuned to this possibility than Noah Webster, whose deep interest in American language and identity went hand in hand with his more general fascination with national mores. It seemed obvious to Webster that "a paper declaration is a very feeble barrier against the force of national habits, and inclinations." If, he reasoned, "on paper a form is not accommodated to those habits, it will assume a new form," for there was no way something as flimsy as text could withstand something so potent as the disposition of a people.[58]

In fact, Federalists claimed it was actually dangerous to heed Anti-Federalists' demands and fetishize linguistic constitutional constraints. As Madison explained in *Federalist* 41, "it is in vain to oppose constitutional barriers to the impulse of self-preservation" because "it plants in the Constitution itself necessary usurpations of power, every precedent of which is a germ of unnecessary and multiplied repetitions." Hamilton had argued a similar point in *Federalist* 25. It was essential to avoid "fettering the government with restrictions, that cannot be observed; because," he argued, "every breach of the fundamental laws, though dictated by necessity, impairs that sacred reverence" for the "constitution of a country" and "forms a precedent for other breaches." Both authors were building on what Madison (with Hamilton's assistance) had earlier written in *Federalist* 20—where they had stressed, counterintuitively, that tyranny sprang more often from weak and defective constitutions than from properly empowered ones. Now, in *Federalist* 25 and *Federalist* 41, they were making that same argument about the phenomenon of constitutional text. Anti-Federalists did not appreciate that needlessly obsessing over clear and refined constitutional barriers, neatly drawn through expert word choice, inadvertently asphyxiated essential power which, in turn, fueled the precise usurpations they so anxiously feared. As Hamilton had put it, "how unequal parchment provisions are to a struggle with public necessity." Fetishizing constitutional language mobilized dangerous dynamics that a properly non-linguistic conception of constitutionalism mitigated.[59]

These arguments converged around the notion that a government could not be reduced to words. It was an entity in motion, a set of practices more than a bundle of stipulations. It was a "system" in which the "whole" and "the parts"—the "general authority" and the "subordinate authorities"—struggled to check each other's "encroachments." "I have found," declared Hamilton, "that Constitutions are more or less excellent, as they are more or less agreeable to the natural operation of things." Consequently, he explained, "I am therefore disposed not to dwell long on curious speculations, or pay much attention to modes and forms; but to adopt a system, whose principles have been sanctioned by experience; adapt it to the real state of our country; and depend on probable reasonings for its operation and result." There was so much within the realm of practical political life, Madison submitted—such as the "line of distinction" between the powers to regulate trade and draw revenue (which only two decades prior had helped ignite the American Revolution)—that, "on fair discussion," was in fact "absolutely undefinable." Gouverneur Morris made the point even more bluntly: "No Constitution is the same on Paper and in Life."[60]

Just as language could not police or imprint power, just as problematically, Federalists contended, it also could not produce a complete constitution. Language would not allow humans to articulate and enumerate a finished and closed system. Nor could its generalities adequately account for all possible contingencies. Federalists had stressed the impossibility of a finished constitution. Now they also insisted that this impossibility was, as much as anything else, a function of the linguistic medium through which constitutions were designed. The inherent character of language left constitutions inherently open-ended. Language perpetually undermined the act of fixing constitutions once and for all.

A constitution could not feature a complete and perfect enumeration of all relevant provisions, Federalists argued. As he explained the rationale that he thought guided the Constitutional Convention to George Washington, Madison noted that if that body "had in general terms declared the Common law to be in force, they would have broken in upon the legal Code of every State in the most material points; they wd. have done more, they would have brought over from G. B. a thousand heterogeneous & antirepublican doctrines." The only solution would have been to finely differentiate between what was operative, and thus included in the Constitution, and what was not, and thus excluded. But "if they had undertaken a discrimination, they must have formed a digest of laws, instead of a Constitution." At a later stage of ratification, Madison marshaled a similar defense of the "necessary and proper" clause. "Had the Convention attempted a positive enumeration of the powers necessary and proper for carrying their other powers into effect; the attempt would have involved a complete digest of laws on every subject to which the Constitution relates; accommodated not only to the existing state of things, but to all the possible changes which futurity may produce," a truly impossible task. A constitution could not be a "digest of laws"; such was not within the capacity of human language. "We must keep within the compass of human probability," Madison argued. "If a possibility be the cause of objection, we must object to every Government in America." A constitution delineated through words would always be unfinished.[61]

This linguistic conception of constitutional imperfection enabled Federalists to repurpose their arguments about the impossibility of mapping all future contingencies. "The contingencies of society are not reducible to calculations," explained Alexander Hamilton. "They cannot be fixed or bounded, even in imagination." Since future contingencies needed to be addressed as they emerged—rather than through linguistic provisions that had been earlier codified—the discretionary role of Congress acquired renewed importance. "Were it possible to delineate on paper, all those particular cases and circumstances in which legislation by the General Legislature would be necessary . . . I imagine no Gentleman would object to it," conceded Madison. "But this is not within the limits of human capacity." Particular and minute specification "might, and probably would be defective."[62]

The argument, then, was not simply that a constitution could not offer a complete enumeration, but also that it should not. Federalists could thus co-opt Anti-Federalists' obsession with permanence while still defending their own constitutional vision. As Hamilton put it, "Constitutions should consist only of general provisions: The reason is, that they must necessarily be permanent, and that they cannot calculate for the possible changes of things." Because a constitution could only be "general principles and maxims," it was not possible, Madison claimed, "to delineate on paper" all contingencies. Guided by this assumption, John Marshall asked Virginia's ratifying convention, "Why not leave it to Congress?" Congress would have to pick up where original authorship necessarily left off.[63]

But there was yet another crucial Anti-Federalist argument that Federalists appropriated as ratification wore on. If, as their opponents had claimed, the Constitution was to be a people's document, Federalists asserted, then instead of striving for a perfect and complete enumeration, the document needed to be deliberately succinct and limited in its ambitions. A constitution that truly belonged to the people, one that was accessible for all to read, would be an unfinished one. "Had [the Constitution] swelled into the magnitude of a volume," Oliver Ellsworth reasoned, "there would have been more room to entrap the unwary, and the people who are to be its judges, would have had neither patience nor opportunity to understand it." Indeed, he argued, had the Constitution "been expressed in the scientific language of law, or those terms of art which we often find in political compositions, to the honourable gentleman it might have appeared more definite and less ambiguous," but, most importantly, "to the great body of the people altogether obscure, and to accept it they must leap in the dark." He went on: "The people to whom . . . the great appeal is made, best understand those compositions which are concise and in their own language. Had the powers given to the legislature, been loaded with provisos, and such qualifications, as a lawyer who is so cunning as even to suspect himself, would probably have intermingled; there would have been much more danger of a deception in the case." Echoing his pre-Convention critique of "the vices of the political system," Madison observed that "it will be of little avail to the people that the laws are made by men of their own choice, if the laws be so voluminous that they cannot be read, or so incoherent that they cannot be understood." If Anti-Federalists genuinely believed that the Constitution needed to be wrested from the technical manipulations of lawyers, then they also needed to appreciate why it was so succinct a document. Had the Convention pursued an exhaustive enumeration, it would have created an utterly cryptic, entangled mess. Language could not execute a complete and finished constitution, and certainly not one that the people would embrace.[64]

Federalists also critiqued language directly, exposing its inherent imperfections. They insisted that the Constitution's makers had been inhibited by the essential nature of the written word. Language's purpose was to convey meaning, yet it was as likely to cloud its object as to cast it in sharp relief. As Ellsworth asserted, "the charge of being ambiguous and indefinite may be brought against every human composition, and necessarily arises from the imperfection of language." Considering "the several charges of ambiguity which gentlemen had laid to the Constitution," Theophilus Parsons, the future chief justice of Massachusetts, declared that "no compositions which men can pen, could be formed, but what would be liable to the same charge."[65]

No Federalist (or any other American for that matter) captured this point as penetratingly as Madison. The insight that language obscured as much as it revealed fueled his most incisive and monumental contribution to the entire ratification debate—*Federalist* 37. Here Madison explained the colossal difficulties faced by the Constitutional Convention in drafting not just the Constitution but any constitution. "Besides the obscurity arising from the complexity of objects, and the imperfection of the human faculties," he noted that "the medium through which the conceptions of men are conveyed to each other, adds a fresh embarrassment." Indeed, language itself caused the most peril:

> The use of words is to express ideas. Perspicuity therefore requires not only that the ideas should be distinctly formed, but that they should be expressed by words distinctly and exclusively appropriated to them. But no language is so copious as to supply words and phrases for every complex idea, or so correct as not to include many equivocally denoting different ideas. Hence it must happen, that however accurately objects may be discriminated in themselves, and however accurately the discrimination may be considered, the definition of them may be rendered inaccurate by the inaccuracy of the terms in which it is delivered. And this unavoidable inaccuracy must be greater or less, according to the complexity and novelty of the objects defined. When the Almighty himself condescends to address mankind in their own language, his meaning, luminous as it must be, is rendered dim and doubtful, by the cloudy medium through which it is communicated.

At no point during ratification did any participant offer a more sophisticated account of language, its inherent complexities, and the peculiar problems it posed for written constitutionalism. Effectively paraphrasing book III of John Locke's *Essay Concerning Human Understanding* in one remarkably concise passage, Madison articulated a two-phase epistemological process in which human beings first formed ideas and then tried to use words to accurately represent them. But since language was always partial and imperfect, never quite supple enough to capture the full depth of complex ideas, it tended to hold humans apart from the objects they were trying to understand as well as from their fellow interlocutors. Conveying determinate meaning through language was perpetually problematic. Given these imperfections, it was hardly surprising that the Constitution featured its share of linguistic ambiguities and indeterminacies. Given the "three sources of vague and incorrect definitions; indistinctness of the object, imperfection of the organ of conception, inadequateness of the vehicle of ideas," that Madison had highlighted, and recognizing that "any one of these must produce a certain degree of obscurity," it was clear that "the Convention . . . experienced the full effect of them all." Given the inherent character of language, any constitution would bear the imprint of its deep imperfections.[66]

All of these arguments revealed just how underdetermined the Constitution's meaning was. Only the experience of subsequently using the document could supply what it by necessity lacked. Accordingly, the remainder of *Federalist* 37 was devoted to this critical point. Madison's incisive examination of language followed a broader discussion of epistemological uncertainty and the frailty of human understanding. "When we pass from the works of nature, in which all the delineations are perfectly accurate, and appear to be otherwise only from the imperfection of the eye which surveys them," he explained, "we must perceive the necessity of moderating still farther our expectations and hopes from the efforts of human sagacity." As difficult as it was to accurately categorize the natural world, where observers could be confident of its ontological clarity and perfection (if not the epistemic skill of those seeking to understand it), it was immensely harder to attach stable definitions to human creations. Indeed, "no skill in the science of Government has yet been able to discriminate and define, with sufficient certainty, its three great provinces, the Legislative, Executive and Judiciary" or, relatedly, "the several objects and limits of different codes of laws and different tribunals of justice." Indeed, "questions daily occur . . . which prove the obscurity which reigns in these subjects, and which puzzle the greatest adepts in political science." This led Madison to his most crucial point: "All new laws, though penned with the greatest technical skill, and passed on the fullest and most mature deliberation, are considered as more or less obscure and equivocal, until their meaning be liquidated and ascertained by a series of particular discussions and adjudications." By unavoidable necessity, the Constitution's meaning was radically underdetermined. Only experience, mediated by the practice of discussion and adjudication, could settle it.[67]

Discussion was perhaps the pivotal word. The ratification debates, a searching discussion if ever there had been one, had revealed the indeterminacy and obscurity of the constitutional text—characteristics that the drafters had not intended to impart and likely had failed to notice. There was hope, however, in the practices that had revealed these imperfections; the debates that began during ratification would be resumed in the first Congress (and elsewhere). These discussions would help clarify an otherwise indeterminate text. For Madison, at least, Anti-Federalists were right about the Constitution's ambiguity but wrong about the possibility of eliminating this flaw as well as the young republic's capacity to cope with it. In other words, their observations about language were sound, if not the moral they took from them.[68]

The Clarity of Language

Federalists were moving in two directions at once, however. Their arguments about the failings and imperfections of language denied Anti-Federalists' premise that constitutional language needed to erect effective barriers. But they made a rival set of arguments that accepted this ground while instead rejecting the conclusion that Anti-Federalists subsequently reached—that the Constitution failed to erect such barriers by lacking determinate linguistic meaning. Precisely because the Constitution enjoyed sufficiently clear meaning, declared Madison, "all those alarms which have been sounded, of a meditated or consequential annihilation of the State Governments, must, on the most favorable interpretation, be ascribed to the chimerical fears of the authors of them."[69]

Federalists conceded Anti-Federalists' premise when they insisted that the Constitution was suitably explicit. "All the foundations . . . of the federal government, are . . . established, in the most clear, strong, positive, unequivocal expressions, of which our language is capable," trumpeted John Dickinson. "*Magna charta,* or any other law, never contained clauses more decisive and emphatic." Oliver Ellsworth declared, "It is an excellency of this Constitution that it is expressed with brevity, and in the plain common language of mankind." A western Massachusetts writer likewise asserted that the Constitution "with precision defines and limits" power, "thus firmly and stably fixeth the boundaries . . . beyond which they cannot pass."[70]

But Federalists sometimes turned the argument around on Anti-Federalists, accusing them of distorting the Constitution's plain meaning. Madison complained, "it gives me pain to hear Gentlemen continually distorting the natural construction of language; for, it is sufficient if any human production can stand a fair discussion." Language had both a natural construction and yet also obscured complex ideas (not an irreconcilable position, but one sufficiently tenuous that it revealed the complicated issues Federalists had brought forth). Alexander Hamilton, meanwhile, denounced those who "have laboured to invelope [the Constitution] in a cloud calculated to obscure the plainest and simplest truths." Zachariah Johnson, a delegate to the Virginia ratifying convention, made much the same point. "When we advert to the plain and obvious meaning of the words, without twisting and torturing their natural signification," most Anti-Federalist protests were groundless. Driving the point home, he added, "had we adverted to the true meaning, and not gone further, we . . . would have come to a decision long ago."[71]

Thus, even though Federalists pointed to the numerous ways in which the Constitution was provisional and unfinished, by defending its clarity and boasting about its "clear and precise expressions" they also emphasized its determinacy. This paradoxical tendency was most evident, not when they generically insisted upon the Constitution's lucidity, but when they explained, in concrete terms, how Anti-Federalists were guilty of misreading the Constitution and thus overstating the likelihood that its ambiguity would be its downfall. Rather than allowing Anti-Federalists' countless interpretations of particular clauses to stand unchecked, Federalists energetically combated each. In the process, they suggested that the Constitution's own words, properly understood, could resolve apparent ambiguities, a strategy that expressed a certain amount of faith in the capacity of constitutional language.[72]

In this vein, Federalists argued that Anti-Federalists had simply misread the "general welfare" clause. "Had no other enumeration or definition of the powers of the Congress been found in the Constitution," Madison acknowledged the criticism might have had merit. Even if this had been the case, "it would have been difficult to find a reason for so a[w]kward a form of describing an authority to legislate in all possible cases." As problematic as that would have been, the Constitution, of course, did not end with that clause but proceeded to offer an enumeration of Congress's powers. The inclusion of the particular, he felt, clearly transformed the meaning of the general. "For what purpose could the enumeration of particular powers be inserted, if," Madison continued, they "were meant to be included in the preceding general power? Nothing is more natural or common," he pronounced, "than first to use a general phrase, and then to explain and qualify it by a recital of particulars." If that was not enough, Madison noted that the "general welfare" clause had been largely copied from the Articles of Confederation, where it had produced no complaints. Edmund Randolph agreed with his friend's claims. In their readings Anti-Federalists were guilty of "treason against common language," a loaded condemnation indeed.[73]

Their opponents had likewise misconstrued the "necessary and proper" clause, Federalists alleged. And since Anti-Federalists had singled out this piece of text as the one most "replete with great dangers," Federalists were especially eager to defend its propriety. "Few parts of the Constitution have been assailed with more intemperance than this," charged Madison, "yet on a fair investigation of it, no part can appear more compleatly invulnerable." Indeed, "without the *substance* of this power, the whole Constitution would be a dead letter." He reasoned that the Convention might have done any one of four things: copied the language from the Articles prohibiting "the exercise of any power not *expressly* delegated"; enumerated every potential power "comprehended under the general terms 'necessary and proper'"; compiled a negative enumeration of powers not to be exercised; or remained silent, "leaving these necessary and proper powers, to construction and inference." The first would have crippled the government while the second and third were impractical. Properly understanding the implications of the fourth strategy, though, illustrated the clause's real value. Had the Convention tried nothing at all, the national government would have had all of the powers conveyed by the "necessary and proper" clause "by unavoidable implication" anyway because "no axiom is more clearly established in law, or in reason," Madison declared, "than that wherever the end is required, the means are authorised; wherever a general power to do a thing is given, every particular power necessary for doing it, is included." Hamilton best summed up this point: "The declaration itself, though it may be chargeable with tautology and redundancy, is at least perfectly harmless." In other words, the "necessary and proper" clause was superfluous, merely denoting powers that the government, by definition, already had. But, as several Federalists would argue, it made sense nonetheless to specify these powers clearly in order to remove any "pretext," as Madison put it, for "drawing into question essential powers of the union." In this regard, Federalists were not merely reiterating the assumptions that had guided James Wilson when he drafted the clause the summer before—that it was language that acknowledged the imperfections of language. Here, Federalists seemed to be taking the "necessary and proper" clause more seriously as a clause with its own textual value.[74]

In much the same spirit, Federalists asserted that Anti-Federalists had flagrantly misread the judicial powers clauses. Among Anti-Federalists' major objections had been the ease with which federal judges would exploit the seemingly indefinite power of judicial appeal. According to Alexander Hamilton—who, among Federalists, wrote most trenchantly on the judiciary's expected role—Article III needed to be understood within the context of the complex diversity of American judicial practice. Different states had different appeals practices, and modes of adjudication varied depending on whether the case in question implicated the common law. Given this complicated patchwork, "to avoid all inconveniencies, it will be safest to declare generally, that the supreme court shall possess appellate jurisdiction, both as to law and *fact,* and that this jurisdiction shall be subject to such *exceptions* and regulations as the national legislature may prescribe." A proper contextualist reading of the Constitution, he continued, made clear that "the supposed *abolition* of the trial by jury, by the operation of this provision, is fallacious and untrue." Anti-Federalists had also argued that the federal courts would enjoy wide interpretive latitude both under and over the Constitution. Here, according to Hamilton, it seemed as though Anti-Federalists, not hypothetical federal judges, were guilty of unconstrained interpretation. For "there is not a syllable in the plan under consideration," he declared, "which *directly* empowers the national courts to construe the laws according to the spirit of the constitution." The Constitution's opponents—Brutus especially—had simply allowed their imaginations to get the better of them. For this and related reasons, it was incorrect to read the Constitution as vesting the Supreme Court with final interpretive authority. It was a mistake, Hamilton explained, to "suppose a superiority of the judicial to the legislative power." The right of courts to review laws, instead, "only supposes that the power of the people is superior to both; and that where the will of the legislature declared in its statutes, stands in opposition to that of the people declared in the constitution, the judges ought to be governed by the latter, rather than the former." Yet again, Anti-Federalists had not exposed crippling ambiguities; they were simply guilty of misreading.[75]

The Chaos of Interpretive Rules

In claiming that Anti-Federalists had cavalierly misconstrued the Constitution, Federalists were beginning to concede that language—read the right way—could potentially constrain power. But in suggesting that the Constitution's language was clear, Federalists otherwise inadvertently exposed how unclear the Constitution's status as an object of interpretation truly was. This uncertainty was made manifest when they pivoted from criticizing Anti-Federalists' misreadings to advancing, however hesitantly, prospective rules of constitutional interpretation. It proved unclear which interpretive rules ought to govern usage of the Constitution, precisely because it remained so uncertain what the Constitution, in fact, was. Because all existing interpretive rules were tethered to certain kinds of interpretive objects, any proposal about rules necessarily implied an understanding of the Constitution's status as such an object. While suggestions about interpretive modes were made in order to defend the Constitution's clarity, they only ended up exposing the fraught character of the Constitution's essential character.

Edmund Randolph most plainly illustrated this difficulty in the Virginia ratifying convention while rebutting the Anti-Federalists' reading of the "necessary and proper" clause. The clause "gives no supplementary power" to Congress, he explained, "but only enables them to make laws to execute the delegated powers, or in other words, that it only involves the powers incidental to those expressly delegated." "By incidental powers," Federalists meant "those which are necessary for the principal thing.—That the incident is inseparable from the principal, is a maxim in the construction of laws." But, Randolph argued, "a Constitution differs from a law.—For a law only embraces one thing." A constitution, on the other hand, "embraces a number of things, and is to have a more liberal construction." He elaborated, "I need not recur to the Constitutions of Europe for a precedent to direct my explication of this clause, because in Europe there is no Constitution wholly in writing. The European Constitutions sometimes consist in detached statutes or ordinances:—Sometimes they are on record, and sometimes they depend on immemorial tradition." In contrast, "the American Constitutions are singular" and because of that, "their construction ought to be liberal. . . . If incidental powers be those only which are necessary for the principal thing, the clause would be superfluous." Randolph was defending a "liberal" reading of the "necessary and proper" clause based on the unique and unprecedented character of the American Constitution. The new Constitution was distinct from a law; and as a written text it was distinct from the constitutions that had preceded it. On the one hand, Randolph was showing a willingness to emphasize the Constitution's written character. On the other hand, however, he was doing so to insist upon its shear novelty as an object of interpretation. Many would agree with Randolph that the Constitution was unlike anything that had come before, and many, like Randolph, were confident that they knew how it should be interpreted in light of this novelty. Despite their confidence, these interlocutors rarely arrived at the same answer. Precisely because the Constitution bore no obvious relationship to existing objects of interpretation, few agreed on what kind of interpretive protocol it required.[76]

Invariably, the task of contemplating rules of constitutional interpretation provoked questions about the Constitution's fundamental status. What kind of an instrument was it? Was it a legal device? If so, what kind? Was it akin to a statute, a contract, a treaty, or perhaps something else entirely? (Treaties were interpreted more liberally than statutes, for instance, while the subjective intent of original parties was usually irrelevant when construing contracts.) Was it a kind of fiduciary trust, to be considered "a great power of attorney," as James Iredell put it in the North Carolina ratifying convention? Perhaps, far more plausibly, it was a corporate charter? Or was a constitution—or maybe just this constitution—a special category of legal object altogether? Maybe, though, Anti-Federalists were correct that the Constitution was not a legal instrument at all, but instead a "people's document"? Just about every possibility received consideration during the frenetic exchanges of 1787 and 1788. And to the extent there was a dominant opinion, it was simply that the Constitution was in character thoroughly distinct, a premise that only compounded the uncertainty. For even if the Constitution was a legal document, it seemed to be a decidedly unusual one given that its fundamental status rested (like some state constitutions before it) on the popular approval of a sovereign people. "This system is not a contract or compact," asserted James Wilson, "the system itself tells you what it is; it is an ordinance and establishment of the people."[77]

Little about the Constitution itself, then, clearly justified any particular interpretive protocol. So where might American interpreters turn to locate suitable interpretive rules? Of those already at Americans' disposal, perhaps none seemed more pertinent than the interpretive canons they inherited from the British common law tradition. For one, such canons seemed to offer substantial guidance—its tools for interpreting legal instruments had been finely honed over generations of practice. For another, such protocols had played a decisive role in molding specifically constitutional questions, including those that had shaped Americans' own thinking. Moreover still, British common law reasoning remained a crucial foundation of American legal training, not least because many American legal norms pre-dated independence. William Blackstone's *Commentaries on the Laws of England,* Edward Coke's *Institutes of the Lawes of England,* and Sir Matthew Hale's *History of the Common Law in England* had continued to be the most conspicuous common law texts in American libraries.[78]

No authority proved more influential than Blackstone, because nobody had done more to codify rules of common law interpretation, both by fixing the scope and meaning of important legal doctrines and by establishing protocols for interpreting legal instruments. Blackstone specified "the fairest and most rational method to interpret the will of the legislator," instructing interpreters on how and when to mobilize different exegetical techniques. Investigation began with an analysis of a statute's words, which were "to be understood in their usual and most known signification." Should matters remain dubious, then the interpreter was to turn, sequentially, to the linguistic context of the statute, its subject matter, the effects and consequences that followed from competing interpretations, and then, finally, the spirit or purpose that had animated it in the first place. Each procedure was tailored to address the potential limitations of the previous criterion, affording logic to their ordering and relationship. Here, in Blackstone's widely consulted writings, appeared a neatly refined recipe for interpretation.[79]

But uncertainty surrounded the eighteenth-century common law. For starters, its content was a matter of great debate in Britain itself. Blackstone's widely read work—which purportedly codified common law interpretation—was avowedly polemical, more a controversial set of suggestions for legislative action than the embodiment of well-established consensus. Writing in a context profoundly different from the seventeenth-century legal world that Coke and Hale had inhabited, at a point when the common law was in decline and the modern Parliament was exhibiting unprecedented control over lawmaking, Blackstone was trying to reinvigorate a fading authority. Given the realities of British political culture, he could find success only by synthesizing common law doctrine with Parliamentary supremacy, a merger that had not shaped earlier articulations. Consequently, Blackstone's systematic commentaries did as much to diversify as unify the content of the common law. Compounding the confusion, American common law differed from that found in Britain. A different environment had produced divergent legal norms. And since the common law was the accumulation of custom, the passage of time had only accentuated differences. As George Mason declared matter-of-factly, "the common law of England is not the common law of these States." Combined, these various points suggest that, by the late eighteenth century, the common law was contested ground covering far more than Blackstone's writings. It was certainly not reducible to a tidy, legible set of rules. Instead, it comprised disparate, at times contradictory, injunctions, rather than a unified whole. Madison was not alone in claiming that key aspects of it possessed "neither uniformity nor stability." Depending on where one looked across time or space, one might find different rules of common law construction and, with that, multivalent applications.[80]

This was to say nothing of the crucial background against which the common law was set. Each common law doctrine was inextricably tied to the jurisprudential perspective that had generated it, one that understood law as neither static nor permanent, but instead dynamic and evolving. As Edmund Randolph asserted, "the common law ought not to be immutably fixed." The content meant little, many Americans asserted, when it was divorced from this perspective. As each common law precept had been itself derived from the flow of history (by grasping the norms latent in usage), each was further susceptible to it. The common law's dual character inherently undermined the very idea that any one of its concepts was stable or fixed. The common law's rules were not only fractured but also unendingly embedded in a framework of perpetual change, further underscoring their pliability.[81]

Beyond all of this, several Americans argued that there was one deeper challenge still: the matter of common law rules' very applicability to American constitutionalism. Common law doctrines offered familiar precedent from which much could be stabilized and understood and, indeed, many judges and lawyers drew upon them instinctively. Crucial institutions like equity, admiralty, and jury trial along with several terms of art like "habeas corpus," "bill of attainder," and "ex post facto law" immediately informed American constitutionalism. But such doctrines also were inextricably tied to a tradition that sanctified Parliamentary supremacy and from which Americans had consciously—and bloodily—revolted. As Benjamin Austin asked disdainfully, "why should these States be governed by British laws? Can we suppose them applicable . . . ? Can the monarchical and aristocratical institutions of England, be consistent with the republican principles of our constitution? . . . We may as well adopt the laws of the Medes and Persians." Accordingly, this inheritance was deeply tenuous.[82]

This ambivalence about common law traditions could be glimpsed in the state constitutions, nowhere more clearly than New York's. While some of these documents stipulated that the common law remained in force, there was nothing self-evident about this declaration. As if recognizing the latent ambiguity, New York's Constitution, drafted in 1777, retained only those parts of the British common law that had been operable in the colony prior to April 19, 1775 (the day armed hostilities had broken out between Britain and its American colonies). In the midst of war such issues were easy to overlook, but by early 1787 in the state assembly Alexander Hamilton revealingly asked, "what is meant in the constitution, by this phrase 'the common law'?" It had two senses, he argued, "one more *extensive,*" which referenced most of the British constitutional inheritance, and "the other more *strict,*" which referenced a narrower set of legal procedures. While Hamilton thought the "more *extensive sense* may be fairly adopted," he nevertheless acknowledged the ambiguity. It was, he concluded, a "delicate and difficult question."[83]

So while many American commentators hoped or assumed that traditional common law reasoning would persist under the Constitution, the extent or character of the debt remained unclear. Thus, while James Iredell could aver that "the principles of the common law, as they now apply, must surely always hereafter apply," Thomas Jefferson, at virtually the same time, could "hold it essential . . . to forbid that any [recent] English decision . . . should ever be cited in a court," for there "is so much sly poison instilled into a great part of them." And then there were those, with the Revolution firmly in mind, who considered British legal norms irredeemably contaminated and rejected the inheritance entirely. William Findley put it most bluntly in the Pennsylvania ratifying convention, proclaiming, "England had always the common law," therefore "its Charter will not apply to us."[84]

This uncertainty over the content and applicability of common law rules of construction revealed, as much as anything, the broader issue at stake: that it was simply unclear at the time of ratification which rules of interpretation were appropriate for an object like the Constitution. Questions abounded. If conventional legal rules might play a valid role in constitutional interpretation—even if the Constitution itself was not a conventional legal instrument—it remained uncertain which ones and in which contexts. But it was also possible—given the Constitution's distinct character—that its interpretation marked a new frontier, meaning novel rules would be needed to construe it. In other words, even if Blackstone's rules had not been so controversial in their own right and even if there had not been questions about the applicability of English legal norms in the new United States, it would still have been logical to have rejected them anyway (as many did), on the grounds that rules for construing statutes were irrelevant to the interpretation of a constitution uniquely predicated on popular sovereignty. Everything, it seemed, was up for grabs. So when participants in the ratification debates—and Federalists in particular—suggested that the Constitution should be interpreted according to conventional rules of interpretation, it quickly became clear that nobody knew exactly what that meant. Instead of betraying confidence in recognizable conventions, such comments evinced a yearning desire to ground, however possible, a novel and deeply uncertain exercise.

Consequently, the interpretive rules that Federalists advanced amounted to a hodgepodge. The extent to which they justified interpretive conventions by appealing to such imprecise categories as "natural meaning," "rational meaning," or "common sense" revealed as much. Alexander Hamilton declared in *Federalist* 83 that "the rules of legal interpretation are rules of *common sense*." Yet, on another occasion, he suggested that interpreters ought to read a textual provision in light of its "natural operation." One could test, he argued at still a different point, whether it was "consistent with reason or common sense" or, alternatively, if it was "unnatural and unreasonable." Madison, meanwhile, deferred to what he called the "rules of construction dictated by plain reason," which, he later suggested, amounted to "degrees of probability" or "fair construction." In making these assertions, it was unclear whether these contributors were primarily trying to convince their interlocutors or first persuade themselves.[85]

At other times Federalists offered greater specificity. In *Federalist* 40, Madison asserted that there were "two rules of construction" that were dictated by rationality, "as well as founded on legal axioms." The first: "that every part of the expression ought, if possible, to be allowed some meaning, and be made to conspire to some common end." The other: "that where the several parts cannot be made to coincide, the less important should give way to the more important part; the means should be sacrificed to the end, rather than the end to the means." Text, simply put, needed to be read such that every word was afforded meaning. Meanwhile, in pursuit of a similar goal, Hamilton offered his own interpretive rule while responding to Brutus's critique about equitable interpretation. "I admit," he argued, "that the constitution ought to be the standard of construction for the laws, and that wherever there is an evident opposition, the laws ought to give place to the constitution." Importantly, though, "this doctrine is not deducible from any circumstance peculiar to the plan of the convention; but from the general theory of a limited constitution; and as far as it is true, is equally applicable to most, if not to all the state governments." Independent of what may have been intended by those who drafted the document, the "general theory of a limited constitution" was sufficient for deriving the rule.[86]

Many other Federalists underscored the same kind of partial consideration and confusion, but Hamilton's own divergent thoughts on the subject perhaps best capture the widespread uncertainty over interpretative rules. Hamilton was as good a commentator as any on the topic: he boasted an incisive legal mind, did not suffer from lack of confidence, had already thought deeply about how to interpret state constitutions, had served as a member of the Constitutional Convention, and, in writing so many installments of the *Federalist*—including all the essays on the judiciary—had been forced to think systematically about the document under consideration. Accordingly, he commented with some frequency on interpretive canons, often in an attempt to refute what he took to be evident misreadings by the Constitution's critics. In so doing he was seemingly of two minds. On the one hand, Hamilton often spoke confidently of the applicability of certain conventional legal rules, such as when he argued that "a specification of particulars is an exclusion of generals" and "the expression of one thing is the exclusion of another." In making these claims his goal was to disparage not that critics were using these rules, but their method of doing so. Relatedly, in an earlier essay he approvingly referred "to what lawyers call a NEGATIVE PREGNANT; that is a *negation* of one thing [is] an *affirmance* of another." And in a later contribution, in which he also favorably invoked Blackstone in order to justify restrictions on ex post facto laws, he followed Madison's assertion in *Federalist* 44 that every constitutional word had to be afforded meaning. Yet, despite these invocations, he also strenuously contended that certain legal maxims "would still be inapplicable to a constitution of government." Because, "in relation to such a subject, the natural and obvious sense of its provisions, apart from any technical rules, is the true criterion of construction." Even Hamilton was willing to maintain that a constitution was sufficiently different from other kinds of legal instruments that it merited a distinct interpretive protocol. Within the span of a few short months he was thus able both to affirm the propriety of legal rules and to cast profound doubt on their utility.[87]

When it came to interpretive rules, then, the only thing that was clear was that nothing was clear. These protocols were not fixed and readily understood, as so many have claimed, but instead highly volatile. Rules of interpretation were fractured, partial, and contradictory. Each of Federalists' and Anti-Federalists' diverse suggestions made some sense in its own right, but collectively they failed to cohere into a broader pattern for understanding the Constitution. Systematic theories would have to wait. Debates over interpretive rules thus revealed, more than anything else, just how much trouble early constitutional disputants had in establishing what kind of an object they were, in fact, talking about.[88]

The Written Constitution in Flux

The ratification debates—which reached an initial resolution in July of 1788 when New York became the eleventh state to approve the Constitution— traversed a vast and diverse rhetorical map. But language had proved an important topic. Federalists and Anti-Federalists had debated its relationship to constitutionalism in several different ways, in the process showing a greater willingness to think of the Constitution like a text than at any time before.

Ultimately, though, this sustained debate over language and the Constitution during ratification shows, above all, just how much remained in flux. A novel interest in constitutional language had not clarified the Constitution's status as a putatively written text; it had instead revealed a deeper uncertainty about its core identity and ontological makeup. Even if ratification disputants had begun scratching the surface of many novel and important issues, they had raised far more questions than they had answered. Several matters remained deeply unsettled by the end of 1788: the fundamental character of the Constitution (was it finished or unfinished?), its nature as an object (was it ultimately a text and, if so, what kind?), its meaning (clear and determinate or vague and indeterminate?), its relationship to subsequent political generations (were future leaders to flesh out and add to its meaning or simply to be constrained by its provisions?), and its interpretive imperatives (was it to be viewed in light of inherited sources or invented anew?). Vigorous debate over the importance and character of constitutional language had thrown all of these fundamental questions up into the air. It would take subsequent debates—not over accepting or rejecting the Constitution but, once it had become supreme law, over constructing a working polity under it—for American political leaders to begin answering them. In the process, they would finish creating their Constitution.

3

The Unfinished Constitution

I can easily conceive that you will at first meet with a great many perplexities in your progress of carrying the Constitution into effect.
—Samuel Johnston to James Madison, July 8, 1789

A "very interesting question has grown out of the silence of the
constitution," James Madison reported to Tench Coxe in June of 1789. It was
an issue, a Pennsylvania congressman explained, that "has employed us
every day" since it arose and that "has Engaged all the Abilitys of the house
[of Representatives]." This question had generated an unexpectedly tense
and time-consuming debate in the First Congress. Its drawn-out character
felt "tedious," featuring what Fisher Ames described as "unceasing speech-
ifying," but the significance of this "knotty business" seemed to grow with
each passing exchange. Representatives could not easily resolve or bypass
the debate they had stumbled into, even though they had every incentive
to move on to other urgent business.[1]

The First Federal Congress confronted a mountain of responsibilities and
challenges when its members first gathered in the spring of 1789. Many
would have agreed that "the object that presents itself to the Representatives of the U.S. [was] as ample in its dimensions and the most difficult to
accomplish that ever exercised the faculties of any body of men." Poor public
finances, mounting debt, and a struggling economy all demanded immediate attention. A country recently divided by the bitter ratification debate
still needed political healing. The nation's international credibility—and
its public credit—had to be established. And yet, "as to politics," one congressman reported, "almost everything is yet in an unfinished state." A few
months after Congress had settled down to begin its work, the lack of

progress was widely noticed. The French minister to the United States declared, "You would think after more than three months of existence this Congress, of which wonders are expected, would already have been able to let the American people taste the fruits of a revolution in government that is supposed to produce remedies for all the ills the people complained of." It was acknowledged that Congress's pressing tasks were "too numerous and intricate to be discussed in a moment," but, that said, the body "attend[s] too minutely to the detail of business." What minute question, stemming from the Constitution's silence, had bogged down Congress? And why did one member, capturing a pervasive sentiment, deem this seemingly minor matter "the most important question & the most solemn debate we have had," while another considered its resolution of profound importance, not merely "in the history of our own times, but in the history of mankind"?[2]

This "great constitutional question" grew directly out of the unfinished Constitution that had just been ratified: who could remove executive officers? It emerged unexpectedly as Congress began the vital task of constructing the federal government. Because the Constitution had provided only the outline for the executive branch, among the immediate tasks was the creation of the executive departments of government. Elias Boudinot of New Jersey first broached the subject in the mid-May, prompting debate about which kinds of departments were necessary. Among those deemed essential were departments of Foreign Affairs, Treasury, and War. Without anticipating that his proposal would ignite controversy, James Madison presented a motion to create the first of these three bodies:

> there shall be established an executive department, to be denominated the Department of Foreign Affairs; at the head of which there shall be an officer . . . who shall be appointed by the president, by and with the advise and consent of the senate; and to be removable by the president.

One particular feature of this submission caught the attention of William Loughton Smith of South Carolina. The clause vesting power of removal with the president needed to be struck out, Smith argued, because the Constitution was silent on the matter except where it provided for the impeachment of officials for "Treason, Bribery, or other high Crimes and

Misdemeanors." The Constitution specified no other method of removal. It stipulated how officers were to be appointed (by the president with the advice and consent of the Senate), but aside from impeachment, it said nothing about how they were to be removed.[3]

Many members believed that Smith's suggestion verged on the absurd, and few agreed that impeachment exhausted the options for removal. It was entirely uncertain, however, how and by whom officers were to be removed because it was also unclear how Congress could act in the face of constitutional silence. What might have been a quick procedural matter gave way to a prolonged debate. Some members thought that nobody could remove—the Constitution was silent, and that was that. Most thought that somebody could remove but disagreed about who had that authority. Those who sided with Madison believed that the president alone could do so, while others thought that the power belonged to the president and Senate in tandem. Complicating matters further, some believed that the Constitution did vest the power of removal, while others claimed that Congress had to bestow what the Constitution had failed to provide. After several weeks sorting through these overlapping positions, debate was finally brought to a close in the House of Representatives when Egbert Benson of New York suggested a pair of amendments that introduced sufficient ambiguity to earn the bill ample support. After passing the House, the legislation then went to the Senate, where Vice President John Adams cast the body's first tie-breaking vote. As a result, the president alone had now been vested with the power to remove executive officers, but only after Congress had spent two months of its precious time debating the matter.[4]

"Strange, that all this should arise from the executive magistrate's having the power of removal," Thomas Scott quipped deep into the proceedings. Beyond injecting a note of levity into the exhausting debate, his remark also raises a valid question. Given the daunting number of critical tasks facing the First Congress, how could its members have focused so intently on this single technical issue? Why did they believe, as Madison put it, "that it demands a careful investigation and full discussion"? Because congressmen sensed what has been easily missed: that they were grappling with more basic issues than a superficial account of the debate over removal would indicate. Ultimately, those in Congress were not debating just this issue, or even broader ones such as the scope of executive power or the separation of powers. Instead, they were debating the fundamental character of the Constitution itself.[5]

AS THE FIRST Congress gathered in New York in March 1789, the Constitution's character as an interpretive object, its definitive contents, its relationship to successive users, and what kind of meanings could be justifiably extracted from it all remained deeply underdetermined. As the Comte de Moustier, the French minister to the United States, tellingly remarked, "At present the consolidation of the United States exists only very imperfectly in language, since the Constitution cannot be regarded as fully established." Echoing the count's revealing remark, what remained especially unclear was the Constitution's relationship to the written word. Anti-Federalists had begun imagining it as a distinctively textual artifact, one whose substance and boundaries were drawn by language. Despite largely rejecting this mode of constitutional imagination, Federalists had unwittingly licensed it. But these debates had merely broached a massive subject, one whose full implications had yet to be probed. For the most part, the Constitution's basic ontology still needed to be mapped. As a result, as Madison noted with respect to early congressional disputation, "the exposition of the Constitution is frequently a copious source" of debate.[6]

Because the Constitution remained in flux, the removal debate quickly transcended its narrow object of focus. As congressmen soon learned, it proved impossible to argue about removing executive officers without continuing the conversation that had been opened up during ratification over the Constitution's essential character. From beginning to end, the debate focused on a deceptively simple question—should the words "to be removable by the president" be stricken from the Foreign Affairs Act?—but the debate was never really about this clause, for one could only answer that question after sorting out deeper issues. In particular, debate quickly revolved around two more fundamental questions, questions that in Elbridge Gerry's telling were at once related and distinct: "The first, whether the sovereignty of the union has delegated to the government the power of removal? And the second, to whom?" These two questions were intertwined throughout the debate, because arguing over who could remove was shaped by the consequences of first justifying why anybody at all could remove. Disputants were forced to ponder not which powers the president or Congress had (or ought to have), but in a more elemental sense how the

Constitution as a supreme source of authority conveyed orders. What did it mean to be subject to this particular Constitution's commands, especially when it appeared to be silent on the matter in question? Accordingly, nearly every argument about removal betrayed a deeper understanding about the Constitution's defining properties.[7]

While the debate's questions were entangled, they pulled disputants in competing directions. The first question—over whether anybody could remove executive officers—pitted all proponents of removal against William Loughton Smith and his few allies, who claimed that because the Constitution said nothing about ordinary removal, Congress had no choice but to accept that the power simply did not exist. Such an argument rendered the Constitution in starkly linguistic terms, suggesting that its contents ended at the text's edge and, based on that assumption, that the Constitution had a fixed meaning that Congress could not alter. Speakers on the other side acknowledged that the Constitution said nothing directly about removal, but they fiercely rejected the way in which Smith and company had imagined their governing instrument. Presupposing what Federalists had only recently insisted—that, because the Constitution was necessarily incomplete, Congress would play an outsized role in fleshing it out— defenders of removal claimed that, in the face of silence, it was the role of Congress to build upon the instrument. A dynamic system, the Constitution was far more than the words with which it was written, and it was incumbent upon successive users to keep that system in motion by exercising appropriate discretion and, where needed, adding meanings that did not previously exist. But this initial impasse between opponents and proponents of removal gave way to the second dispute, one among advocates of removal, over who could exercise that power: the president alone or the president and Senate combined. In debating these positions, those who had otherwise championed the unfinished, imperfect Constitution began hinting that the Constitution might be more complete than they had originally thought. Even though the Constitution appeared to be silent on the issue at hand, if subjected to the right kind of analysis, they argued, it could be made to speak.

Proponents of removal, in an attempt to adjudicate both questions at once, gestured in opposite directions. They claimed that the Constitution was incomplete yet also complete, simultaneously indeterminate yet also determinate. In both cases the Constitution was more than its language, but in the first instance they disparaged the Constitution-qua-text; in the second they took it more seriously. They were both extending the vision of the unfinished Constitution that Federalists had championed during ratification and advancing a novel form of constitutional imagination. It was neither wholly the unfinished, imperfect Constitution of the Federalists nor the distinctively textualist Constitution of the Anti-Federalists, but instead a strange hybrid of the two. But because the various arguments put forth circulated simultaneously—one participant marveled at "the vast field" of dispute, while another, "confounded with the diversity of arguments," complained, "I know not how to reply"—and because they were always reducible to the seemingly simple matter of whether to keep or remove a single statutory clause, it was hard for disputants to fully grasp these important contradictions. It is largely because the incongruities were obscured, however, that they tell an important story. For the removal debate at once managed to expose the vibrant possibilities of the imperfect Constitution, while revealing its potential complications and limitations. This tension, and the assumptions that underlay it, would prove among the debate's most crucial by-products as American political leaders continued to struggle to imagine their Constitution.[8]

A New World

Removal was among the initial topics to engulf the First Federal Congress. It was a testing ground for a new body that had to find its way. On March 4, 1789, bells rang throughout New York City and guns were fired into the harbor to commemorate the waning moments of the defunct Confederacy and the official opening of the new national government that would take its place. Not all was unsettled. As a national deliberative body, the inaugural federal Congress was in the broadest of strokes a carryover from the Confederation Congress that had preceded it. More generally, its shape and function would be guided by Americans' long experience in legislative politics—either directly in their colonial or state legislatures or indirectly through their keen interest in Parliament. Most members of the First Congress had gained experience in one of these prior bodies and could draw on the rules of parliamentary procedures, which they knew quite well. But even if this experience was a valuable guide, there were also striking discontinuities. Congress stood at the heart of a new constitutional order that had been constructed as a direct response to the failures of its predecessor. Armed with considerably more power, no longer beholden in the same ways to state legislatures, and confronting the daunting challenges that had inspired its formation, Congress could not simply follow established precedent. In many cases, after all, none existed. As Madison complained, "Scarcely a day passes without some striking evidence of the delays and perplexities springing merely from the want of precedents."[9]

In addition to these challenges, the First Congress also confronted unprecedented public scrutiny. The Continental Congress had operated mostly in deep obscurity—partly because its proceedings were closed to the public, but also because state politics overshadowed it. The same was not true of the new federal Congress in 1789. "The Public's expectation seems to be so highly wound up," observed Robert Morris, senator from Pennsylvania, upon arriving to take his seat. Many of his colleagues were hearing direct testimony confirming his suspicion. "The eyes of the people are upon you. We look up to you," a correspondent wrote to congressman George Thatcher. Meanwhile, another observer wrote to prospective House member Benjamin Goodhue, "the People this way are on *tiptoe* in their expectations, from Congress, we expect more than Angels can do From your Body." Public attention was fastened squarely on the assembling legislature.[10]

The people's fascination with the First Congress was rooted in the novelty of the House of Representatives. Unlike the Senate—whose members (as in most states under the Confederation Congress) were selected by the state legislatures—the House represented the people directly. More answerable to the people at large, House members opened their proceedings to the public from the beginning (Senate business, meanwhile, was conducted in secret until 1795). Even though some state legislatures had just recently begun allowing their debates to be published, this unchecked openness on the national stage was unprecedented and was greeted with great enthusiasm. Future jurist James Kent sat in the House galleries the first day they were opened, later recounting the rush of excitement he felt: "All ranks & degrees of men seemed to be actuated by one common impulse, to fill the galleries, as soon as the doors of the House of Representatives were opened for the first time," in order to take part in the "proud & glorious day" and to look "upon an organ of popular will, just beginning to breathe the Breath of Life."[11]

With the public's gaze fixed, seventy-nine congressmen (fifty-nine representatives and twenty senators) descended on New York City's Federal Hall. While the irascible Senator William Maclay sardonically called the renovated structure a "Great Baby House," most legislators were awed by the building's design and interior. Redesigned by Pierre Charles L'Enfant, the two-story building boasted impressive architectural features. Tuscan columns, a grand balcony, tall windows, and a large, ornate eagle adorned the exterior. Inside was a spacious hall that ascended to a glass cupola roof. The larger House chamber, with its viewing galleries, was located downstairs while the smaller Senate chamber was upstairs. In each hall, desks and chairs covered in blue damask were arranged in a semicircle facing the presiding officer's chair. The ceilings featured a sun surrounded by thirteen stars. Sufficiently captivated, Senator Oliver Ellsworth remarked that it "surpasses in elegance any building in this Country."[12]

As impressed as members were by the confines of their proceedings, they were less dazzled by their colleagues. Fisher Ames, a young upstart from Massachusetts, complained at one point of an absence of "demi-gods and Roman senators" and at another (alluding to the great British Parliamentary figures) that there were "no [Charles James] Foxes or [Edmund] Burkes." James Madison, that hard-working lawmaker, worried, "I see on the lists . . . a very scanty proportion who will share in the drudgery of business." But as much as anything else, this skepticism spoke to his uneasiness with the surrounding uncertainty. In truth, although the First Congress was composed of several younger, less seasoned members, it nonetheless boasted its share of political talents—not only Madison but Roger Sherman, Robert Morris, Richard Henry Lee, and Elbridge Gerry were among those who had played an outsized role in building the new American republic. Ames, meanwhile, was considered something of a prodigy whose talents would soon shine on the House floor.[13]

In these heavily scrutinized halls, congressmen fought to be heard. This was especially true in the House, which often chose to conduct its business assembled in a committee of the whole, which placed considerably fewer restrictions on debate. To some, this made the body raucous and unwieldy, fueling complaints of representatives' unhealthy love for speech making. Ames called it a "kind of Robin Hood society where everything is debated." He especially criticized the "unwieldy" practice of meeting in an entire body, which he likened to a "great, clumsy machine" being "applied to the slightest and most delicate operations—the hoof of an elephant to the strokes of [a] mezzotinto." Ames had an unusually sharp and sarcastic wit—he once began a letter to a favored correspondent from whom he had not heard in a while, "Are you dead, sick or married?"—but other congressmen reinforced his observations. Fellow Massachusetts House member Benjamin Goodhue complained of "needless and lengthy harangues" that were "actuated by the vain display of Oritorical abilities." Debates were indeed long, often exhausting entire days' proceedings. But with fewer subcommittee meetings, participants could concentrate on specific issues and better prepare themselves for discussions.[14]

While the tenor of the House was argumentative, it produced substantive and searching debate, conducted with an appropriate degree of seriousness. Despite his initial apprehensions about the new legislature's likely character, Madison was later struck by how well the "proceedings . . . are so far marked with great moderation and liberality." In part because discussions were so substantive, the freewheeling debates enjoyed an unusual capacity to force participants to confront fundamental issues. Congress became as much a debating salon, in which engaged disputants had the freedom and power to reshape the argumentative landscape, as a legislative hall. And that core characteristic proved important whenever debate implicated the Constitution. Here, the removal debate proved a paradigmatic and tone-setting example.[15]

Reckoning with Silence: New Constitutional Laborers

When the issue of removal first arose, few members thought it necessary to probe the Constitution in any depth. When William Loughton Smith initially objected to the proposed clause vesting removal power in the president—arguing that, "being once in office," an executive officer "must remain there until convicted upon impeachment"—most of his critics invoked common sense and raised practical concerns. Many felt that Elias Boudinot had it right when he concluded, "if . . . no officer whatever is to be removed in any other way than by impeachment, we shall be in a deplorable situation indeed." Whether it was the "dilatory and inefficient" process of impeachment, the obvious and extensive class of transgressions that fell short of high crimes and misdemeanors, the possibility that appointed officers might lose command of their faculties, or the all-too-common "total neglect of the duties" of office, "there were a thousand circumstances which would demand a removal from office" beyond impeachment, exclaimed Theodore Sedgwick. Even more than this, as Madison so urgently explained, if executive officers could "only be displaced . . . by impeachment," that "would give a stability to the executive department . . .

more incompatible with the genius of republican governments in general, and this constitution in particular, than any doctrine which has yet been proposed." It was simply unfathomable that executive officers would hold their offices not at pleasure but "by the firm tenure of good behavior." The executive department could not function if its officers, once appointed, could only be removed under exceptional circumstances. Theodorick Bland of Virginia clarified what all of these objections were getting at. "It seems to be agreed on all hands," he declared, "that there does exist a power of removal" as "the contrary doctrine would be a solecism of Government." Ames was even more succinct. With characteristic acidity, he deemed it simply "absurd to suppose that officers once appointed cannot be removed." No government could function without this power, so it made no sense to indulge Smith's fanciful objections.[16]

While many were persuaded by this logic, Smith had a powerful rebuttal. Even though he was not convinced impeachment was as unworkable as most suggested, he also found it utterly beside the point. For, ultimately, he asserted, "the argument does not turn upon the expediency of the measure. The great question is with respect to its constitutionality." And that matter hinged on an entirely different sort of analysis. Whether removal was essential to a functioning government or not, Smith replied, "if the power is not found in the constitution, we ought not to grant it." For "if [the Constitution] has not given [that power], we have no right to confer it." Arguments made in the name of "expediency . . . have tended rather to shew us what the constitution ought to be, than what it is." So, as "ridicule is said to be the test of truth," then "however ridiculously our arguments may be treated, I hope we shall preserve a due attention to" the only thing that counted: "the constitution." In agreement, Elbridge Gerry noted, "some gentlemen consider this as a question of policy," but they were wrong. At base, it was "a question of constitutionality."[17]

Smith's relentless prodding moved the Constitution to the very center of discussion. Hailing from a wealthy, established South Carolinian family that had strongly supported ratification, Smith nonetheless arrived in New York City suspicious of how his peers in the federal government might manipulate their authority. He did not share Anti-Federalists' general distrust of textual power, but he worried about how a cavalier attitude about the use of the Constitution and swollen executive power could threaten the institution of slavery and, thus, South Carolina's standing in the nation. The debate over executive removal tied concerns about constitutional manipulation and unchecked presidential prerogatives together. Whatever Smith's motivation, though, he forced his peers to reckon more immediately with their governing instrument. In the face of his insistence, it was not going to be sufficient merely to claim that the Constitution could not have meant to deny the federal government a power that happened to be convenient. A deeper reflection would be needed.[18]

But Smith was not simply pledging allegiance to the Constitution. Most, after all, happily agreed with him when he declared that nothing "can be otherwise performed than is directed by the constitution." Madison, for instance, stressed that he was "clearly of opinion with the gentleman from South-Carolina that we ought in this and every other case to adhere to the constitution, so far as it will serve to guide us." Indeed, he continued, "the powers of the government must remain as apportioned by the constitution." In a similar vein, Boudinot likewise assured his peers, "I shall certainly attend to the terms of the constitution." The Constitution's supremacy was not in dispute. Everyone claimed to take obedience to the Constitution for granted. The real issue that Smith raised was constitutional silence, which was a far more difficult problem.[19]

From his understanding of this matter, Smith vividly imagined the nature of the nation's governing instrument. "Examine the constitution," he insisted. "The powers of the several branches of government are there defined . . . you will find no such power as removing from office given to the president." He relentlessly and repeatedly pointed to the Constitution's tangible, textual presence while demanding answers. "I call upon gentlemen to shew me where it is said that the president shall remove from office." His confidence unwavering, he declared, "I know they cannot do it." If the power could not be found among the Constitution's words, he was arguing, then it did not exist. Benjamin Huntington of Connecticut fleshed out Smith's reasoning. Since "the constitution . . . must be the only rule to guide us on this occasion, as it is silent with respect to the removal, congress ought to say nothing about it; because it implies that we have a right to bestow it." Silence did not imply ambiguity, nor did it encourage congressional license. To the contrary, it represented a clear and transparent order not to act. "If this is wrong in the constitution," Smith explained, "it may be proper to amend it." But short of such a formal change, the Constitution was "as it now stands."[20]

Understanding silence in this way resuscitated the Anti-Federalists' image of the finished, linguistic Constitution by emphasizing the Constitution's words, the lines they drew, and the judgments they meted out. By exploiting constitutional silence and drawing an invidious distinction between text and its absence, Smith and his supporters betrayed a full-blooded written constitutional consciousness. Constitutional power was instantiated in constitutional text; without explicit language, there could be no attendant authority. This understanding of the Constitution signaled a clear relationship between the document and those who held power under it. Politicians were to obey the Constitution, not shape it, add it to, or embellish upon it. As Huntington said, it "must be the only rule to guide us." Ordinary politics was strictly confined to the space the Constitution's words created for it. The minute it spilled out from that defined space and politicians began following different rules than the ones prescribed, the Constitution ceased to exist.[21]

Those who protested recognized that the Constitution seemed to be silent on the question of executive removal. "It is admitted," John Laurance of New York conceded, "that the constitution is silent on this subject." Unlike the "power of appointing," Madison noted, "there was no express authority given" for removal. But these members made sense of the meaning and moral of constitutional silence in a radically divergent way than Smith and his allies, who had presupposed that the Constitution was complete and finished. So to push beyond mere expedience in order to defend their position, those who favored some kind of removal power revived Federalists' conception of the unfinished and imperfect Constitution from ratification. If the Constitution was necessarily incomplete, its silences looked much different.[22]

Champions of removal fleshed out their rival conception of the Constitution through a series of related arguments. They contended, for example, that the Constitution's omissions were to be expected. It was inherent to the project of constituting a government. As Abraham Baldwin of Georgia, who had been a member of the Constitutional Convention, explained, "some gentlemen seem to think there should be another clause in the constitution" stipulating removal. But this demand misconceived the Constitution. The list of potential contingencies that the instrument might have addressed was infinite. "There are other evils which might have been provided against, and other things which might have been regulated," Baldwin admitted. "But if the convention had undertaken to have done them, the constitution, instead of being contained in a sheet of paper, would have swelled to the size of a folio volume." No matter how extensive their efforts, the Convention was going to produce an unfinished Constitution, one that would serve only as the beginning, not the end, of an evolving conversation. As Egbert Benson insisted, "it is not in the compass of human wisdom to frame a system of government so minutely" that it would close all gaps and eliminate all silences. What the Convention did create was not only appropriately but intentionally brief, necessarily capturing its provisional status.[23]

Because silences were predictable, because they signaled the inherently unfinished character of constitutionalism, they called for additional creative constitutional work. The task of completing the Constitution had not fallen to the Convention that framed it; that body merely laid a foundation upon which subsequent constitutional laborers would build. Just as Federalists had insisted, the creative constitutional moment endured past 1788. As Madison observed, "we ought in this and every other case to adhere to the constitution, so far as it will serve as a guide to us." This comment recognized the instructions that were not only inherent in the Constitution's limitations—it could govern only a finite number of possible challenges—but also, more cleverly, its possibilities. The Constitution guided users in two ways: first, by directing them along known paths and, second, by steering them toward the uncertain terrain that needed to be surveyed. Heeding the Constitution, Madison was suggesting, meant acknowledging both. The Constitution, properly understood, guided users not merely to its firm directives, but also toward its unfinished work, encouraging them to tackle it in the process.[24]

Rendering the Constitution operable required this more capacious vision. John Vining dismissed the argument "that if the constitution does not vest the power of removal in the president, we have no right to give it." The "constitution authorizes a complete government," he argued—that was the only adequate way to understand its underlying purpose—"and leaves it to the legislature to organize it . . . on such principles as shall appear to be most conducive to the public good." The Constitution itself called for the work necessary to complete its design and function. Misunderstanding what the Constitution required, others foolishly sought to "narrow the operation of the constitution," placing it in a straightjacket, "render[ing] it impossible to be executed," complained Boudinot. With these precise objections in mind, Benson asked with a whiff of condescension, "can the gentleman be serious who tells us, that this is a case to be proposed as an amendment to the constitution?" Could Smith really believe "whenever a doubt arises in this house, (and it will be a doubt if an individual doubts,) with respect to the meaning of any part of the constitution, we must take that mode?" Did he "really suppose that we are never to take any part of the constitution by construction?" Such reasoning failed to grasp the Constitution's status or character and, in so doing, failed to appreciate "that a construction"—one which added to the Constitution's existent framework— "will, in some case[s], be necessary." Indeed, he concluded, "this is such a case." Baldwin, ordinarily a cautious speaker, captured the point most vividly. Speaking about the Senate in particular, but gesturing more broadly to the task at hand, he proclaimed, "we are fellow-laborers together, endeavouring to raise on the same foundation a noble structure, which will shelter us from the chilling blasts of anarchy, and the all-subduing storms of despotism." This striking imagery illustrated how proponents of removal imagined their efforts and their relationship to the new constitutional order. Those in power were not passive and obedient automatons hopelessly in thrall to the Constitution's commands. They were laborers erecting a "noble structure" on top of the foundation they had been given. Fetishizing constitutional silence was akin to marveling at an unfinished structure. The point was not to venerate such a skeleton, but to take up the unfinished work encouraged by its character.[25]

The character of silence thus turned on the character of the Constitution. If the latter was a dynamic system, as many were implying, then silences were to be filled rather than observed. And it was appropriate for Congress specifically to conduct this essential work. "The constitution has expressly pointed out several matters which we can do, and some which we cannot," Thomas Hartley, a former Continental Army colonel from Pennsylvania, explained, "but in other matters it is silent, and leaves them to the discretion of the legislature." Ames added that "the power of removal is incident to government, but not being distributed by the constitution, it will come before the legislature, and, like every other omitted case, must be supplied by law." Accordingly, it was "proper," as the pending measure proposed, "for the house to declare what is their sense of the constitution." Laurance echoed this precise logic. "If it is omitted, and the power is necessary and essential to the government, and to the great interests of the United States, who are to make the provision and supply the defect?" he asked rhetorically. "Certainly the legislature is the proper body." Summing matters up, Madison declared succinctly, "where the constitution is silent it becomes a subject of legislative discretion."[26]

Proponents of removal, then, had inverted Smith's conception of constitutional doubt. Whereas he demanded explicit clarity in order for Congress to act at all—claiming "if it were a matter of doubt, we ought by no means to interfere in adjusting or determining it"—his opponents argued the opposite. "Unless it is saddled upon us expressly by the letter of that work," legislators enjoyed the discretion to respond to such qualms in the manner they deemed best. Madison had emphasized the inevitability of constitutional doubt so strikingly in *Federalist* 37, maintaining that the Constitution would be "more or less obscure and equivocal" until its "meaning be liquidated and ascertained by a series of particular discussions and adjudications." Congress, repository of the nation's representatives, was the obvious site for these "discussions." Others reaffirmed this point and applied it to the issue at hand. Since "it cannot be said with certainty that it is unconstitutional in us to declare . . . the power of removal," Laurance assumed Congress could vest the authority. "If it relates to a doubtful part of the constitution," Madison reasoned, "an exposition of the constitution may come with as much propriety from the legislature" as anywhere else. Meanwhile, Fisher Ames would not "undertake to say, that the arguments," in favor of removal, "are conclusive." But, he added, "I do not suppose it is necessary that they should be so; for I believe nearly as good conclusions may be drawn from the refutations of an argument as from any other proof." What was clear was that constitutional doubt commanded action, not deference.[27]

Some members were even more adamant, insisting that Congress's creative discretion was not only appropriate but in fact necessary. They were "obliged," as Benson put it, "to take the constitution by construction." "It is true, we may decide wrong, and therefore there may be danger," Ames confessed, but, "we are sworn as much to exercise constitutional authority, for the general good, as to refrain from assuming powers that are not given to us." Congress had not simply the right but also a duty to exert constitutional authority. Representatives' deeper imperative was to promote the public good. And even "if it is complex and difficult, it is certainly disingenuous in us to throw off the decision," Ames asserted. For the guiding "principle" upon which the Constitution was constructed was "to give sufficient power to do all possible good." By refusing to act, members of Congress would not be deferring to the Constitution's authority, but actively compromising it. "With respect to this and every other case omitted," Laurance insisted, "the people look up to the legislature." They look to "legislative wisdom."[28]

Was this not why the "necessary and proper" clause, which had caused such turmoil during the ratification debates, had been inserted into the Constitution—so the new government could put a complete system into motion? As Hartley saw things, that clause "gives power to congress to make all laws necessary and proper" precisely "to carry the government into effect." The Constitution itself was instructing Congress to exercise those powers "they think proper," Richard Bland Lee of Virginia explained, powers that could not be anticipated or adequately conveyed by imperfect language. Through this clause, Peter Silvester of New York echoed, the Constitution gave them "ground to act upon," in order to address its own deficiencies.[29]

Those entrusted with power had a responsibility to bring the Constitution to fruition. "Would a regulation" of the sort demanded by Smith and his allies "be effectual to carry into effect the great objects of the constitution?" asked Laurance. Clearly not. Opposition to "carrying of the constitution into effect," he exclaimed, "must be rejected as dangerous and incompatible with the general welfare" (knowingly invoking part of the Constitution's preamble). His frustration evident, he declared, "hence all those suppositions, that, because the constitution is silent, the Legislature must not supply the defect are to be treated as chimeras and illusory inferences." Elias Boudinot similarly disagreed "that Congress have no right to modify principles established by the constitution; for," he explained, "if this doctrine be true, we have no business here." Underscoring the necessity of this activity, Boudinot wondered aloud, "can the constitution be executed, if its principles are not modified by the Legislature?" The Constitution was not set in stone. It was fixed yet in flux. Congressmen were supposed to add to its contents, to further construct its structure and edifice, to give it shape and body where previously it had none. In this regard, congressmen were not merely laborers; they were constitutional authors of a meaningful kind. The spirit of 1788 lived on in them.[30]

This extensive, layered defense of Congress's creative constitutional power spilled over into a broader consideration of the Constitution's basic status as an adjudicative instrument. What kind of an object it was helped determine which officer or institution had authority to arbitrate its doubtful contents and expand its scope. Nobody spoke more self-consciously or incisively on this subject than Madison. His meditations came as a direct response to one of Smith's specific assertions that Congress ought to step away from the issue so it could be "left to the decision of the judiciary."

The "judges" alone "would determine whether the president exercised a constitutional authority or not" as "it is the duty of the legislature to make laws" and "judges . . . to expound them." Elbridge Gerry agreed. As "constitutional umpires," the nation's courts presented "the proper tribunal" for arbitrating such doubt. Since judges would merely hear cases rather than engage in positive lawmaking, Smith and Gerry reasoned, they would be far less capable of adjudicating constitutional doubts for their own aggrandizement. Madison fiercely disagreed because he imagined the Constitution in a fundamentally different way. Smith's and Gerry's implication was clear, that "the legislature itself has no right to expound the constitution," that Congress had no role to play in constitutional construction "until the judiciary is called upon to declare its meaning." For much the same reasons that Madison favored congressional discretion on the question of removal, he was adamant that judges were not the final expositors of the Constitution; they had no monopoly over its meaning. Both points hinged on what kind of object the Constitution was and, accordingly, what ought to happen when its imperatives or structure were in doubt.[31]

The Constitution, according to Madison, was distinct from an ordinary legal instrument. Smith and Gerry had rendered its character in quasi-legal terms, assuming that judges would expound its contents much as they would an ordinary law. To Madison's mind, however, this reading misunderstood its essential character. "In the ordinary course of government," he acknowledged, "the exposition of the laws and constitution devolves upon the judicial." Others were not wrong to recognize that ordinary adjudications would likely pervade the system. But, crucially, such recourse was appropriate only during ordinary business. Moments of fundamental constitutional reckoning required radically different procedures, and the debate over removal marked just such a moment, both because it inspired doubt about the Constitution's meaning as it pertained to a particular practice and, more critically, because it isolated a practice that touched the constitutional structure itself. The power of removal implicated more broadly the balance of power between the federal government's branches. Given how fundamental this particular constitutional silence proved to be, then, it was necessary to remember the Constitution's foundational character. As the ratification debates had so strikingly revealed, the Constitution was a distinct kind of object. It was juridical in character but bore few clear relationships to other species of law. Most basically, as Madison explained, "the constitution is the charter of the people."[32]

Because the Constitution was, in essence, a popular charter, none of the individual institutions it empowered were uniquely authorized to arbitrate its inevitable and fundamental ambiguities. The Constitution "specifies certain great powers as absolutely granted, and marks out the departments to exercise them." But, Madison asserted, "if the constitutional boundary of either be brought into question, I do not see that any one of these independent departments has more right than another to declare their sentiments on that point." There was "not one government on the face of the earth"—and certainly not one in the United States—where "provision is made for a particular authority to determine the limits of the constitutional division of power between the branches of the government." For this reason alone, "the meaning of the constitution may as well be ascertained by the legislative as the judicial authority." And if the inherent and likely irreducible difficulties inherent in charting constitutional boundaries proved sufficiently controversial, "there is no recourse left," Madison believed, "but the will of community." Only the people themselves, instantiated in some form, could arbitrate moments of such fundamental doubt.[33]

But Madison was also suggesting that, even though the Constitution was inherently incapable of foreclosing all doubt, such recourse was not actually necessary. A better understanding of the Constitution's character pointed to another solution. "In all systems"—and it was essential to appreciate that the Constitution was a system—"there are points which must be adjusted by the departments themselves, to which no one of them is competent." Given that the Constitution required constant adjustment, to accommodate the motions of its various parts and to ensure that they moved in harmony, it was essential that first movers within the system enjoy the responsibility to conduct this work, which was why it was "highly proper to make a legislative construction." Here, then, Madison deployed his understanding of the Constitution's novel character both to refute the claim that the judiciary was better equipped to adjudicate the matter and to positively empower the legislature. As a people's charter meant to set republican politics in motion, the Constitution was both a supreme arbiter and a dynamic system of political relationships. As an arbiter, it elevated no branch above the others. But as a system, it uniquely empowered Congress to confront silences, to exercise discretion, and to build upon the Constitution to meet emergent needs. The process of pinning down what kind of a thing the Constitution was only reinforced the broader vision of congressional politics sketched by proponents of the power of presidential removal.[34]

A Firmer Constitution

Not all in Congress welcomed this talk of creative constitutional construction, however. It alarmed those who imagined the Constitution in a very different way. Even if they did not share Smith's doctrinaire position on removal, they did share the broader spirit of his opposition. More than this, they grasped that the debate transcended the issue of removal. Alexander White of Virginia, for instance, claimed it was "the most important question that has yet come before the legislature of the union." Indeed, "I am sure it is the most important question I ever had a voice in discussing, or a vote in determining, except that of adopting the constitution itself in the convention of Virginia." For this reason, "I consider the day, on which the sense of the house is to be taken on this subject, as a memorable day in the annals of America." To White, everything reduced to "whether we may grant to others, or assume to ourselves, powers which the constitution has not given, either in express terms, or by necessary implication. This," he concluded, "I conceive to be the true question." White perfectly captured why so many were worried. If the Constitution did not itself bestow the power of removal, and if Congress exercised discretion in vesting it anyway, the body threatened to rip the Constitution asunder. James Jackson, a former lieutenant colonel in the Georgia militia and wealthy lawyer-planter who was wary of the various ways commercially oriented northerners might harm southern interests, thought if Congress vested the power of removal that would "blast all those delightful buds of happiness which the establishment of the new constitution flattered us would expand and ripen into fruition." Although Jackson quickly earned a reputation as Congress's most boisterous speaker because his speeches teemed with obscure references, colorful expressions, and ad hominem critiques of his peers, his extravagant charge captured something revealing. While those who disagreed were inclined to mock these pronouncements as "the vagaries of a disordered imagination," they too saw a debate not simply about removal but about broader conceptions of the Constitution.[35]

Through their concerns, opponents of congressional discretion imagined the Constitution not as a dynamic system but as a static object tethered in place. They insisted on leaving the Constitution as it was. Jackson affirmed that "every power recognized by the constitution must remain where it was placed by that instrument." It "was out of the power of the house to alter it." Those subject to the Constitution's commands did not have the authority to modify its contents or character. "It is our business," Jackson commanded, "to preserve the constitution inviolate." The "constitution is already formed," White agreed. According to a later commentator, White thought of the Constitution as "his polar star," to be defended "against all meditated encroachments." Embodying this attitude on the House floor, White demanded that lawmakers not move "beyond the limits of the constitution." Not to be adjusted and refined, the Constitution was to remain exactly as Congress found it. "We are not at liberty," John Page of Virginia argued, "to vary [the Constitution] by implication." Champions of the power of removal had contended that the Constitution was perpetually incomplete and in constant need of supplement. But those like Roger Sherman of Connecticut vigorously disagreed. Implying that the Constitution was a finished instrument capable of handling novel developments on its own, he argued that "the best way will be to leave the constitution to speak for itself whenever occasion demands." Proponents of the right of removal were substituting their voice for the Constitution's when they ought to listen more carefully to what the Constitution already said.[36]

Leaving the Constitution as it was meant respecting the language in which it was written. Claiming "powers which are not fully within the letter of the constitution" would, warned White, provoke "alarm and terror." That vesting the removal power specifically violated the document's language mattered because, in America's federal republic, "the powers granted to carry [the Constitution] into effect, are specifically enumerated." This enumeration explained what kind of government they had—one of defined, textual powers. Their objection, summed up by Vining's evocative complaint, was plain: "this is not the language of the constitution."[37]

In celebrating their anointed role as constitutional laborers, and even, as some were suggesting, constitutional authors, defenders of congressional discretion were blurring the line between implementing and making a constitution. Elbridge Gerry feared that, seized by a spirit of invention, congressmen failed to perceive the looming danger. He predicted that, upon breaking "through the constitutional limits of their authority," proponents of congressional discretion "will find it very difficult to draw a boundary." But the problem ran deeper still. Even more disturbingly, those in favor of removal had fundamentally misunderstood the relationship between politicians and their constitution. They simply did not see what they were doing. "There is a great difference between organizing and modifying a department" on the one hand, Jackson cautioned, "and modifying the principles of the constitution" on the other. There was "great danger in this," particularly as offenders failed to grasp the implications of their proposals. Whereas proponents of removal imagined that constitutional stewardship would require ingenuity in the face of silence and ambiguity, opponents assumed that such stewardship, rightfully understood, precluded such license. By indulging their own constitutional creativity, removal advocates "shew us what *ought to be,* rather than what *is,* in the constitution," claimed William Loughton Smith. During the Senate debate that followed the House's, William Samuel Johnson of Connecticut drew a similarly invidious distinction between implementing and fashioning the Constitution. "We sit not here to make a [Constitution] but to execute the one we have," he said. "I want no Powers. I will usurp none." In a similar vein, William Paterson, senator from New Jersey, insisted, "we are not to enquire, whether the [Constitution] is wisely framed or not." By contrast, "we have it," it already existed, "and it is our Rule to walk by."[38]

Gerry felt more than a little vindicated by these debates. In the waning days of the Constitutional Convention, he had cautioned that the Constitution's vague and ambiguous language would leave the nation at risk. Then, throughout ratification, a multitude of Anti-Federalists had echoed his warnings. Now, before his very eyes, these prognostications were turning into reality. Even his misgivings about the "necessary and proper" clause were proving well founded. "The system, it cannot be denied, is in many parts obscure," Gerry noted. "It has been a strong objection to the constitution, that it was remarkably obscure; nay, some have gone so far as to assert, that it was studiously obscure," as Anti-Federalists had warned, "that it might be applied to every purpose by congress." Precisely because the Constitution was so obscure, congressmen needed to stick closely to the document. For "if congress have a right to exercise the power of giving constructions to the constitution different from the original instrument," if they could violate its clear meaning, then the "people of America can never be safe." Had they known the federal legislature would assume the kinds of powers being discussed, "I will be bold to say, this system of government would never have been ratified." Moreover, "if the people were to find that congress meant to alter it in this way, they would revolt at the idea; it would be repugnant to the principles of the revolution, and to the feelings of every freeman in the United States." Gerry had vigorously contested Federalists' vision of the imperfect, open-ended Constitution at the

Convention, during ratification, and, much to his chagrin, was being forced to raise the same objections again in the First Congress.[39]

To those who shared his concerns, removal advocates were charting an ominous path that threatened to fundamentally transform the Constitution. For one, legislative discretion on this scale was tantamount to amending the instrument. As Gerry warned, "consider the ground on which [we] tread. If it is an omitted case, an attempt in the Legislature to supply the defect will be in fact an attempt to amend the constitution." Attempting to alter the Constitution independent of Article V's stipulations for formal amendments "may be"—and here Gerry took some enjoyment in calling to mind the only cause the Constitution specified for removal of executive officers—"a high crime or misdemeanor, or perhaps something worse." For "there is no power on earth" that can amend, "except the people." Worse than amending, as Smith put it, "if the legislature can supply defects, they may virtually repeal the constitution." Perhaps, by "expos[ing] ourselves to most dangerous innovations by future legislatures, [we] may finally overturn the constitution itself," thus "destroying its beauty, consuming its spirits, and subverting its frame." This threat led Gerry to stridently declare that "all construction of the meaning of the constitution is dangerous or unnatural, and therefore ought to be avoided." Abandoning the Constitution's firm language, moving into the uncertain and uncontrolled realm of construction was both a dangerous and unnatural transgression, one so severe that the simple epithet "unconstitutional" would not suffice.[40]

At stake, most fundamentally, was whether the Constitution meaningfully controlled those subject to it. As Jackson worried, "if we begin once to construe and define the principles of the constitution"—if Congress, that is, filled all the gaps and silences as it saw fit—then alarmingly, "there is no end to our power." Free of any constraints, "we may begin with the alpha and go to the omega, changing, reversing and subverting every principle contained in it." This "never can be the meaning of the Constitution," he cried, "our constituents . . . never sent us here for the purpose of altering the system of government." Gerry, meanwhile, contended that "if congress are to explain and declare what [the Constitution] shall be, they certainly will have it in their power to make it what they please." Like clay in their hands, the Constitution could be molded into any shape they desired. "Strange constructions have been given," lamented Samuel Livermore of New Hampshire, that "will make the whole constitution nothing, or any thing, just as we please."[41]

Proponents of removal were perfectly content to rehash many of their previous arguments and accuse Smith, Gerry, Jackson, and their allies of misapprehending the guiding spirit of constitutionalism. But, in addition to reviving familiar claims, some proponents of removal attempted to turn their opponents' arguments against them. "The main ground on which the question is made to rest," Baldwin observed, "is, that, if we adopt this clause, we violate the constitution." This infidelity had been heightened by dramatic "reminde[rs] of our oaths" and "warn[ings] not to violate the solemn obligation." But, at bottom, the complaints made by Smith, Gerry, Jackson, and their allies assumed their point in order to prove their case. As Peter Silvester observed, "all their arguments are founded upon construction and implication, and lead to the very object which they caution us to avoid." Consequently, because their constitutional claims rested every bit as much on interpretive inference, every bit as much on exercising some manner of creative license, Baldwin hoped "gentlemen will change their expression, and say, we shall violate *their construction* of the constitution, and not the constitution itself"—unless, that is, "the gentlemen pretend to support the doctrine of infallibility, as it respects their decisions." There was no firm, stable, fixed Constitution to observe, heed, and honor. Any attempt to understand its contents or purposes, let alone what one sworn to follow it was meant to do, was destined to yield some manner of uncertainty, to require the user to subtly, perhaps unwittingly, fill silences and close gaps. So, in their own way without meaning to, removal opponents had proved the point they were combating: executing the Constitution invariably required some measure of congressional discretion, whether any of them were willing to admit it. Much as Madison and removal proponents had long been insisting, it was foolish to try to reduce the Constitution to the language in which it was written.[42]

Silent Meanings

As removal's proponents attempted to justify congressional discretion, however, they also articulated a distinct set of arguments. These were fueled, at least in part, by the pointed condemnations of their opponents—who were not shy about accusing them of subverting the Constitution. But more generally they were motivated by their need to rationalize why the power of removal needed to be lodged not merely somewhere within the government but instead with a particular officeholder. In trying to explain why the president or the president in conjunction with the Senate specifically should exercise this prerogative, they started to argue something quite different, namely that the Constitution itself vested the power of removal, that it was not silent after all. Subjecting the Constitution to the right kind of analysis, they asserted, revealed otherwise hidden meanings. Most who simultaneously held these two kinds of positions remained convinced that they were compatible, but they represented two different ways of imagining the Constitution: the act of emphasizing congressional discretion built out from constitutional silence, while its counterpart, the act of underscoring silent constitutional meaning pushed beneath constitutional silence. In stressing the latter, then, defenders of removal subtly undermined the imperfect Constitution they otherwise celebrated.

Given that so many removal proponents had already asserted that constitutional silence implied congressional discretion, it was hardly surprising that when it came time to decide who specifically was empowered to remove they justified their respective choices based, not on what the Constitution mandated, but on what they thought was best. As Fisher Ames explained, "if this is . . . a question undecided by the constitution, and submitted on the footing of expediency, it will be well to consider where the power can be most usefully deposited for the security and benefit of the people." Since the Constitution gave lawmakers no firm direction, they were at liberty to determine, as Hartley put it, what "ought to be." Much of the debate over whether the president alone or the president in combination with the Senate should possess the power to remove executive officers took this form.[43]

Accordingly, those who believed that removal should rest solely with the executive repeatedly made arguments that appealed to lessons derived from republican political theory rather than from constitutional necessity. They underscored the importance of maintaining a firm separation of powers. Found in most state constitutions and most celebrated political writings (Montesquieu and Locke above all), this "sacred" doctrine called for, as Madison explained, "the three great departments of government [to] be kept separate and distinct." To honor it, congressmen ought "to prevent an amalgamation of the legislative and executive powers," argued Egbert Benson, by not blending these two powers any more than the Constitution already had. Their consolidation, Baldwin claimed, had been "found to produce tyranny." That was why, Ames noted, so many ancient commonwealths had perished. Such a mixture was sure to enervate the new government by "infusing poison" through "an impure and unchaste connection." Madison, accordingly, implored his peers not to "make the executive a two-headed monster."[44]

Building from their commitment to executive independence, the advocates of removal insisted that the president needed to be equipped with the requisite responsibility and energy. For a number of congressmen, including several leading framers of the Constitution, this was a virtual obsession. They reminded colleagues of the weakness of the old Confederation, of the failures of past republics, and of the impotence of their own state governments during the recent War for Independence—all historical examples of, as Vining put it, the dangers of "clipping [the executive's] wings." To avoid these pitfalls, the president had to be "sufficiently energetic" so that he could swiftly carry out the full range of executive duties entrusted to him, and "as responsible as possible," so he was in complete command of the executive department and accountable to the people at large. By giving the Senate an equal say in removal, Madison complained, "you destroy the great principle of responsibility . . . defeating the very purposes for which an unity in the executive was instituted."[45]

Proponents of combined presidential–senatorial removal powers, on the other hand, disagreed, but often in the same key. In terms of why the "the senate ought to be joined with the president in removal," they spun dark tales about abusive executives throughout history—including the royal governors under whom colonial Americans had chafed on the road to revolution—in an effort to remind their colleagues of the great dangers attendant to executive power. "Behold," James Jackson implored, "the baleful influence of the royal prerogative!" John Page, an anxious republican, agreed. "This clause of the bill contains," he noted, "the seeds" of just that destructive power. Advocates of presidential removal had things backward. "Every thing which has been said in favor of energy in the executive may go to the destruction of freedom, and establish despotism." Indeed, calling on his talent for poetry, Page announced that "the doctrine of energy . . . is the true doctrine of tyranny." Could others not "see plainly," he asked, "that conferring this power" would turn the president into "an independent monarch"?[46]

Popular as such arguments were, however, those who believed the power of removal resided jointly with the president and the Senate more often made a different claim—not simply that it was bad policy to vest the president with this power exclusively, but that it was unconstitutional. Putting expedience and the wisdom of political theory aside, "if the power was deposited in any particular department," Jackson noted, "it was out of the power of the house to alter it." The "truth is," Page averred, "the constitution does give that power, and wisely gives it, to the senate." Sometimes their confidence wavered, and they conceded the indeterminacy of the question. But amid the uncertainty, they sketched an alternative approach to dealing with the problem of constitutional silence, one that deviated from Americans' long-standing understanding of "unconstitutional" by defining the term more immediately in relationship to constitutional text. While it was clear that the Constitution nowhere expressly gave the president and Senate combined removal power, those in favor nonetheless thought "the words of the constitution forcibly impl[ied]" it.[47]

To justify this claim, proponents of presidential–senatorial removal drew attention to the method of appointing executive officers stipulated in Article II: that it was to be done by the president "with the advice and consent of the Senate." Because "the power of removal is incident to the power of appointment," Alexander White contended, and because "the constitution gives this power" to the president and Senate in tandem, "consequently a dismission from office must be brought about by the same modification as the appointment." Roger Sherman argued, "I consider it as an established principle," one to be found "in law as well as reason," that "the power which appoints can also remove." According to a firm rule found outside of the Constitution, but that could otherwise be claimed to be part of the Constitution, the powers to appoint and remove were necessarily conjoined.[48]

To justify why politicians were beholden to inexplicit rules that were at once within and beyond the Constitution, advocates of presidential-senatorial removal leveraged the concept of natural necessity. As Samuel Livermore asserted, the "power of removal is incidental, and the natural consequence of the power of appointing." Theodorick Bland thought that it was "consistent with the nature of things"—with the essential, unchangeable way things were—"that the power which appointed should remove." Michael Jenifer Stone of Maryland echoed this precise phrase and its attendant logic: "in general every officer who is appointed should be removed by the power that appoints him: It is so in the nature of things." Because the Constitution was not completely silent, because it "has laid down the rule" of appointment, it was possible to draw upon essential logical relationships that existed outside of the Constitution to draw the connection to removal. Had the Constitution given the president sole power to appoint, the principle remained the same. What was essential was the inherent link between the two powers—it was "justice," as "clear and demonstrable" as could be. Even Elbridge Gerry, who was wary of all manner of constitutional inference, was willing to bite. It was "more natural," he conceded, for the president and Senate to remove in tandem, "because it is in the nature of things, that the power which appoints removes also." What accounted for this essential order of things, disputants would not say. Whether born merely of custom or something deeper, it roughly translated to "the way things were," a standard at once authoritative yet hopelessly vague, which also exposed the conceptual quicksand into which America's first constitutional users felt themselves sinking. Eager to grab a foothold anywhere, they propped up firm, essential order, independent of human pleasure or will, to help ground Congress's work.[49]

In response, proponents of presidential removal could have doubled down on their commitment to congressional discretion and continued to accuse their opponents of substituting their own highly contingent understanding of the Constitution for the instrument itself. But instead, unwilling to let these arguments stand unchallenged, they began dealing with the problem of silence in a similar way: by claiming that the Constitution implicitly bestowed the power of removal on the president exclusively rather than the president and Senate jointly. Vining, for instance, claimed there was "a strong presumption" the Constitution gave removal power to the president while Laurance said that "it pointed strongly in favor of the president." Ames, who otherwise proclaimed the Constitution "undecided" on the question, nonetheless thought that "revert[ing] to the principles, spirit, and tendency" of the Constitution betrayed "the highest degree of probability" that the power was vested in the president. Boudinot was most self-conscious about this seeming about-face. "It is said by some gentlemen to be an omitted case," he declared as if he had not conspicuously claimed so much himself. But "I shall take up the other principle . . . that it is not an omitted case" because, as he explained so revealingly, it "is easier to be maintained."[50]

Perhaps appreciating, like Boudinot, that this tack offered a more attractive mode of justification, advocates of presidential removal appropriated their opponents' premise and elucidated why these second order rules of natural necessity in fact confirmed their own position. In turn, this move breathed fresh life into the argument for executive authority. Observing what critics of presidential removal had said about the essential relationship between appointing and removing, Abraham Baldwin noted, "they say that it follows as a natural, inseparable consequence. This sounds like logic. But if we consult the premises, perhaps the conclusions may not follow." Proponents of presidential removal mocked the conclusions but respected the mode of deduction. Instead of fetishizing the appointment procedure, the key was, as Hartley explained, to "consider every other according to its nature." While such reasoning might have been what Senator William Maclay had in mind when he referred to Hartley as "a Strange Peice of Pomposity," nonetheless it captured what became a popular point. Others had obsessed over the alleged natural relationship between removal and appointing, but the better question was: What was the nature of the power to remove, when viewed independently of any other associations? "The power of removal," George Clymer of Pennsylvania answered in his characteristically matter-of-fact and reserved style, "was an executive power." In the Senate, William Paterson of New Jersey described removal as "a right incidental to the executive, inseparably connected with it, that grows up naturally and unavoidably out of the Thing itself." Given this essential feature, the right constitutional rule to study was not the appointment clause but the opening sentence of Article II, which "declares"—as Madison pointed out—"that the executive power shall be vested in a president of the United States." Advocates of presidential removal began hammering this point. Because, as Peter Silvester put it, "the president is invested with all executive power," then, as Clymer reasoned, he necessarily "has the power of removal as incident to his department." In this regard, "the nature of things" thus "restrains and confines the legislative and executive authorities," Madison concluded. Given these dictates, prohibiting the president from exercising what was his natural right, Vining complained, "surely . . . will be the most unreasonable thing in nature." Proponents of presidential–senatorial removal were right to respect nature's constraints; they simply misunderstood its instructions.[51]

For those who thought that the president alone should have the power to remove, grasping the nature of executive power also revealed the right way to understand the much-discussed appointment power. Like removal, the power to appoint was, by its nature, executive. As Madison asked, "if the constitution had not qualified the power of . . . appointing," would the president not "have the right by virtue of his executive power"? Thus, "the association of the senate with the president" in appointing "is an exception to the general rule"—the extra-constitutional rule given by the natural order of things. And "exceptions to general rules," he claimed, "are ever to be taken strictly" and not "extend[ed] or strain[ed] . . . beyond the limits precisely fixed for it."[52]

Madison, who was among those most confident that Congress was empowered to exercise its discretion, struggled to square his commitments. All at once he argued that the president had removal power merely by "inference" from a "fair construction of the words," yet also called his favored interpretation the Constitution's "true meaning." He recognized that his arguments had changed—"since the subject was last before the house," he noted at one point, before explaining "I have . . . examined the constitution with attention, and I acknowledge that it does not perfectly correspond with the ideas I entertained of it from first glance." Indeed, at times he even wondered "whether we are not absolutely tied down to the construction declared in the bill." Confronted with constitutional silence, he imagined the Constitution as necessarily unfinished and in need of perpetual maintenance but also as far more complete and self-fulfilling. Recognizing these competing pulls, at one point he alternately contended that the controversial clause vesting removal was either merely "explanatory" of what the Constitution otherwise meant or an explicit recognition of "a power the legislature" had "to confer." He openly acknowledged it was not necessarily one or the other, and even if it was, it was worth pondering how it might be either. If nothing else, this was an honest recognition of the contradictory argumentative strands he and several others were attempting to braid together.[53]

Thus, whether they favored presidential–senatorial removal or presidential removal, both groups came to be seized by the language of natural necessity, and they continued to wield this idiom back and forth. Proponents of combined presidential–senatorial removal claimed that the Senate was an executive body in its own ways, that removal was not executive in nature, and that general rules, fancifully pulled from history and reason, were irrelevant to the matter at hand since the Constitution created its own distinct set of rules. Defenders of presidential removal, meanwhile, pushed deeper, drawing on more historical examples and spinning out more theories of executive power, all while disparaging the Senate's claims to executive power and preaching about the nature of things. Beneath apparent silences, both were suggesting, could be found silent meanings, decipherable by silent rules. Decrypting such rules and constructing meanings out of them required a measure of congressional creativity, but of a vastly different sort from that which infused the vision of congressmen as new constitutional authors, generating new meanings where none existed.[54]

There was one final way, however, in which those who supported removal, regardless of which camp they belonged to, supported their position that the Constitution itself somehow vested this power. As justifications in the debate went, this view proved far less pervasive and relatively unimportant. But it inaugurated a particular way of conceiving the Constitution and its contents that would soon prove of the utmost significance. Instead of deeming the Constitution silent or presuming that natural essences of one kind or another might fill that silence, this alternative approach appealed to the original intent of those who had framed the Constitution. In Madison's rendering, it followed the principle that "we ought always to consider the constitution with an eye to the principles upon which it was founded."[55]

Ironically, it was William Loughton Smith, otherwise so doctrinaire in asserting the silence of the Constitution on the question of removal, who helped push his colleagues in this direction. Even though he remained confident throughout the debate that "there will be no doubt but the constitution does not give the power," he did note, with an air of concession, that "it has been the opinion of sensible men that the power" belongs "conjointly to the president and senate." He had in mind a "publication of no inconsiderable eminence, in the class of political writings on the constitution"—the *Federalist*. Written during the ratification debates and composed of eighty-five separate essays, it had argued in such complexity and detail how the Constitution ought to be construed. The papers' intended audience had been the citizens of New York, and the essays were initially read in few other states except Virginia. But while they were not yet cloaked in national mystique, and were far from being deemed the authoritative constitutional commentary they would later become, as early as the spring of 1789 they enjoyed wide purchase. And while the identity of their authorship was unclear, rumors had begun circulating. Smith knew that at least Madison and Alexander Hamilton were among its authors (John Jay was the third), and he deliberately played with that knowledge. "The author, or authors (for I have understood it to be the production of two gentlemen of great information) of the work published under the signature of Publius," he said, signaling that he knew a great deal more than he was willing to publicly admit, "has these words" to say on the matter. He then proceeded to quote at length the portion of *Federalist* 77 explaining how executive officers would be removed: "the consent of the [Senate] would be necessary to displace as well as to appoint." Smith was not claiming that Publius had it right. Instead, with feigned innocence, he was attempting to undermine one of its two lead authors (Madison, who so staunchly favored presidential removal on the House floor) by appealing to the authority of the other (Hamilton, who had written this particular installment of the *Federalist*). Despite these clever maneuvers, Smith was caught off guard the next day when—as he recounted to a correspondent—he received a note from across the House floor from Egbert Benson explaining that Hamilton's opinion had shifted. The note revealed that, "upon more mature reflection," Hamilton had "*changed his opinion,*" and was now "convinced" that the president alone should have the "power of removal at pleasure." While this revelation complicated Smith's use of the *Federalist,* it only reinforced his broader point: that his opponents were treating the Constitution as an object of freedom rather than of constraint.[56]

Whatever his motivation for appealing to past writings, Smith opened a new line of thought by invoking the understandings of those responsible for drafting and defending the Constitution prior to ratification as a way to fill in the document's silences. This move encouraged congressmen to travel back to Philadelphia to ponder what the members of the Constitutional Convention had specifically intended. Thus, Smith argued, "if the convention who framed the constitution meant that [the president] should have the power of removal, the propriety of inserting it must have occurred to them." The framers had no doubt been mindful of the example of the state constitutions—everybody would agree, he assumed, that they "furnished the members of the late convention with the skeleton of this constitution." And having "turned over" most of these documents, Smith had not found that "any of them have granted this power to the governor." This was because, in many of the states, there had been "grave doubts" about its exercise. Given this context and given that the power of executive removal was omitted in the federal Constitution, the conclusion was plain: "I take it for granted," Smith declared, that "they never intended to give it to him." Proponents of both kinds of removal invoked the Federal Convention in related ways. "It is our duty," Richard Bland Lee insisted in defense of presidential removal, perhaps guided by his youthful inexperience, "to vest all executive power, belonging to the government, where the convention intended it should be placed." In support of presidential–senatorial removal, meanwhile, James Jackson asked, if executive officers were merely creatures of presidential will, then "where is the necessity of calling them heads of departments in the constitution? Surely," he reasoned, "the convention did not use a redundancy of words, and insert a clause without a meaning." Relatedly, John Page, an ally of Jackson, declared, "the framers of the government had confidence in the senate, or they would not have combined them with the executive" in so many different ways.[57]

Such appeals, though, were fairly bland and offhand—unlike Smith who had invoked the *Federalist,* others made no effort to substantiate claims through documentation. They did, however, appeal to original debates over the Constitution by drawing on their own personal experience. As a former delegate to the Constitutional Convention, Abraham Baldwin played this card aggressively, insisting that he was "well authorised to say" that "mingling the powers of the president and senate was strongly opposed in the convention which had the honor to submit . . . the present system for the government of the union." Indeed, he claimed, "some gentlemen opposed it to the last; and finally it was the principal ground on which they refused to give it their signature and assent." In fact, "one gentleman" in particular—a reference to Elbridge Gerry, now among his colleagues listening in the House—"called it a monstrous and unnatural connection." Echoing this observation, Madison (who also, of course, had been a delegate to the Federal Convention) suggested, "perhaps there was no argument urged with more success, or more plausibly grounded, against the constitution, under which we are now deliberating, than that founded on the mingling of the executive and legislative branches . . . in one body." Given this original understanding of the Constitution's designed purpose, Baldwin asked, "Ought not we . . . be careful not to extend this unchaste connection any farther?"[58]

Proponents of presidential–senatorial removal quickly rebutted these claims with their own references to what earlier bodies had said and done— even if they themselves had not participated. Jackson was especially unpersuaded, demanding that opponents "prove to me that it was not the intention of this constitution to blend the executive and legislative powers." Indeed, he pointed out, "the celebrated Mr. [James] Wilson agrees with me in this sentiment; for he declares that the senate was constituted a check upon the president. Let gentlemen turn over his speeches, delivered in the convention of Pennsylvania," he suggested, "and they will find he asserts it as incontrovertible fact." If the ratifying conventions that had approved the Constitution potentially offered privileged access to the document's hidden meanings, then that evidence certainly did not support the case for presidential removal.[59]

Alexander White broadened the scope. Forget the removal power, he said, the crucial point to be inferred from the debates of 1787–1788 was that Americans had settled on a "system . . . differing in form and spirit from all other governments in the world." It was "a government constituted for particular purposes," one that bestowed specific powers. "This," he claimed, "was the ground on which the friends of government supported the constitution." Had "this principle . . . not been successfully maintained by its advocates . . . the constitution would never have been ratified." It did not matter whether executive power had a true nature that furnished some general rule from which inferences might be drawn, for the only nature the Constitution possessed was the one it had been given based on the particular facets of its design and the contingent purposes it had been fashioned to address. Appreciating the original mood of the nation and the basis upon which the Constitution became supreme authority would compel subsequent users, not to investigate "the nature of executive power," but merely to "look to the constitution." Grasping that the Constitution was distinct in kind, by its original intended design, confirmed that "the body [choosing] agents has the power of dismissing them." The Constitution was not subject to a logic beyond its own. Its contents, White was suggesting, were predicated on the kind of object it was and the precise context in which it was peculiarly devised.[60]

As striking of as some of these claims were, they appeared sparingly and were quickly shunted aside by rival arguments. But as fleeting as they were, they nevertheless intersected in intriguing ways with the alternative forms of constitutional imagination taking shape. Like appealing to natural necessity, appealing to original intent dug beneath silences instead of building out from them. Unlike appeals to nature, though, appeals to the ideas espoused by the Constitution's framers linked constitutional meaning to human will. Whether executive power had a true nature or appointing and removing enjoyed an essential relationship was less important than what the Constitution's authors had willfully and contingently constructed. By privileging the choices of real humans, appealing to the original framers mirrored congressional discretion in general logic. But by appealing to past actors at the expense of contemporary ones, such appeals otherwise reinforced the kind of essentialist constitutional imagination betrayed by the turn to the nature of things.

An Uncertain Resolution, an Uncertain Constitution

Given not only the dizzying diversity of argumentation but, especially, the contradictory defenses made for retaining the controversial clause that vested the right of removal, it was not surprising that participants were confused. Most thought that the Constitution was unfinished, but in what ways and to what extent was unclear. Perhaps all it meant was that the Constitution implied more than its text communicated. Or maybe the idea that the Constitution was incomplete meant that it had failed to specify a complete government. Or perhaps, most radically of all, it meant that sitting congressmen were empowered to add content to the Constitution that would have full constitutional force. Lacking a clear sense of the Constitution's properties or mandates, removal debate disputants had a difficult time disaggregating the different ways in which the Constitution might be unfinished, captured nowhere more clearly than in the dual position adopted by some removal proponents—that on the question of removal the Constitution was simultaneously silent yet spoke.

Content to make inconvenient and unpopular observations, William Loughton Smith unsurprisingly played up his own confusion on several occasions in order to get traction. Noting the distinct ways House members were justifying presidential removal, he remarked, "I apprehend that their reasoning is not perfectly consistent." Indeed, it seemed that only "one of these two ideas are just." Either "the constitution has given the president the power of removal, and therefore it is nugatory to make the declaration here," or "it has not given the power to him." Which was it? Did the president already have the power to remove by virtue of the Constitution, or did Congress have to give it to him? If the former was true, what was the point of retaining the clause that had caused so much consternation? Smith sensed he already knew the answer. "The extreme desire which gentlemen have manifested to retain this clause," he commented, "makes me suspicious . . . that gentlemen do not think the power is vested in him by the constitution." As usual, Smith displayed a rare capacity to instigate in the most effective way. Why did the bill establishing the first executive cabinet require language claiming the president could remove the department's chief officer, if the Constitution already gave him that power?[61]

Smith had called out the contradictory position that removal advocates had staked out for themselves and the confusion that had only intensified as the matter—which, in the words of James Jackson, had been "worn threadbare"—finally reached its merciful resolution. Egbert Benson, whose primary contributions in Congress came behind the scenes, conjured the innovation that finally closed debate in the House. Cleverly, he proposed two amendments. The first left the controversial clause "to be removable by the president" in place for the time being but altered the clause immediately following it, which had specified that beneath the proposed secretary of foreign affairs would be a chief clerk, by adding that "when ever the said principal officer shall be removed from office by the president," custody of all the records and papers pertaining to the office would fall to the clerk. This change thus overtly implied that the president had the power of removal without explicitly declaring as much. Benson made it clear that, once this amendment received a vote, he would immediately move, in his second amendment, to strike out the controversial removal clause.[62]

If the debate's internal contradictions had not previously come into focus, this proposal cast them in sharp relief. Opponents of removal were, predictably, frustrated. Smith, who had inaugurated the whole debate, immediately denounced these duplicitous maneuverings, arguing that removal advocates recognized the original impropriety but were "not willing to relinquish openly their principles." While he remained as convinced as ever that "any declaration whatsoever" was "an infringement on the constitution," nonetheless "if it be done, I hold it more candid and manly to do it in direct terms than by an implication like the one proposed." If the advocates of presidential removal were to circumvent the Constitution, better they should defend their avowed commitment in the bright light of day. Others who opposed presidential removal appreciated that proponents of removal appeared to be relenting but thought they needed to proceed all the way, striking out not just the original offending clause but also the new one describing the clerk's responsibilities.[63]

But even those who supported removal were not of one mind. Some who favored presidential removal, most especially Madison, were satisfied not only because they had carried the day, but also because they were increasingly convinced that the Constitution already vested the president with the power. The resolution, Madison asserted, "fully contains the sense of this house upon the doctrine of the constitution," while also appeasing those suspicious of congressional discretion. He was pleased at how it expunged ambiguity. Many more proponents of presidential removal, though, were wary, precisely because they felt the decision compounded, rather than eliminated, uncertainty. Some, like Theodore Sedgwick, were content to approve Benson's first amendment, "because it could do no harm," but could not support the move to strike out the original clause, for others, he worried, might deem "the constitution totally silent," in which case the words would be needed "to make an express grant of the power of removal." Hartley admitted that he personally doubted whether a legislative grant was necessary, but as he was convinced, in any case, that the president did enjoy the power he thought it absolutely necessary to retain the clause, lest any ambiguity remain. Still others, echoing what some had earlier implied, thought it no longer mattered whether they personally believed that Congress or the Constitution vested the power. Boudinot pointed to how the debate had consumed the body's attention for some time, worrying that "to strike out after such mature deliberation" would obscure the genuine outcome and inspire needless confusion.[64]

Far more than Madison's acquiescence, this ambivalence, which cut across both sides of the debate, captured the lingering uncertainty that the removal debate provoked. Benson's two amendments were approved, but by decidedly different majorities. Those who favored presidential removal in any shape or form voted for the first amendment. But the second amendment, which struck out the clause that had caused all of the problems, was approved by a strange combination of those like Madison and Fisher Ames (who now believed it was redundant) and Gerry and Smith (who had resisted it from the beginning). It was opposed, meanwhile, by those like Boudinot, Laurance, and Sedgwick (who, like Madison, staunchly believed that the president ought to have the power to remove but disagreed that a mere implication was sufficient to convey it). So even though the Department of Foreign Affairs had been created, at the head of which would be a secretary, to be appointed by the president with the advice and consent of the Senate, and to be removed (if necessary) by the president alone, the question of exactly why the president had this power—the source of the surprising and prolonged debate—was as confused as ever.[65]

Considerable ink has been spilled ever since by judges and legal scholars attempting to decipher whether members of the First Congress truly thought they were vesting removal power in the president by virtue of the Constitution or instead by their own discretion. And virtually all attempts to parse this question, invested as they have been in sorting out the true powers and character of the American presidency, have searched in earnest for a decisive answer. But, independent of the specific matter of presidential power, the basic ambiguity that consumed the debate, the ambiguity that made it so hard for proponents of removal to achieve clarity on when the Constitution was commanding them and when they were left to their own devices, confirmed as well as anything could have just how deeply in flux the Constitution was well into the first session of the First Congress. Indeed, the debate can be read as one extended, relentless, and ultimately uncertain attempt to decrypt the Constitution's fundamental properties and character.[66]

Did the Constitution end at the text's edge or spread out far beyond it? Madison, who had previously held constitutional language in such suspicion, now seemed trapped, like so many proponents of removal, between competing forms of constitutional imagination. As the debate was nearing conclusion, references to the removal debate filled his correspondence. In a letter to Edmund Pendleton, he defended presidential removal on the grounds that "the axiom relating to the separation of the Legislative & Executive functions ought to be favored" since, "in truth the Legislative power is of such a nature that it scarcely can be restrained either by the Constitution or by itself." If, he concluded, "the federal Government should lose its proper equilibrium within itself, I am persuaded that the effect will proceed from the Encroachments of the Legislative department." Channeling the dynamic structuralism that had oriented his constitutionalism for years, Madison imagined the Constitution as a system that needed to be balanced, making sense of removal based on that particular vision. He had highlighted identical dynamics in an earlier letter to Edmund Randolph and in his June 17 speech on the House floor. In this regard, as he told North Carolina governor Samuel Johnston, presidential removal was "most consonant to the *frame* of the Constitution." But other testimony spoke differently, betraying a different mentality at work. Rather than referring to the Constitution as a "frame," when he wrote Tench Coxe and Jefferson he explained that removal by the president was instead "most consonant to the *text* of the Constitution." Rather than perfecting a frame or stabilizing a system of moving parts, House members had engaged in a different sort of activity, parsing language and probing textual limits in an effort to square interpretation with that great arbiter: constitutional words. On their own, these dual characterizations were hardly incompatible. But set against the exhausting debate over removal, and the countless argumentative threads it had pulled, they gestured toward a meaningful distinction. They embodied different mental pictures that Madison (and so many others) formed in their minds in an attempt to clarify the outline and shape of the object at the heart of their struggle.[67]

Related to these questions about the Constitution's relationship to language was another: were politicians to leave its silences as they were or attempt to fill them? If they took the latter course, did that license them to exercise their own authorial creativity, to create meanings that did not otherwise exist, or did it call upon them to listen more carefully to what the Constitution was faintly saying? Again Madison exposed the emerging contradiction. As he began to believe that the Constitution, not Congress, vested the power of removal, he also began to believe that the "decision that is at this time made will become the permanent exposition of the constitution." The Constitution needed fixing, but in addressing that need it might also be fixed, perpetually. The Virginian who had otherwise celebrated the creative constitutional moment was now hinting that it might be limited, not substantively but chronologically. The Constitution was to be fleshed out, but Madison was now wondering, how long would this period last? As he revealingly observed,

> At present, the disposition of every gentlemen is to seek the truth. . . .
> The imagination of no member here, or of the senate, or of the president himself, is heated or disturbed by faction: If ever a proper moment for decision should offer, it must be one like the present.

This was not yet a time of ordinary politics. Perhaps only in the extraordinary context in which national politicians currently found themselves, in which they were putting the Constitution to work so closely on the heels of its adoption, was such creative constitutionalism permissible. The expansive and continuous horizons opened up by the imperfect Constitution were perhaps narrowing.[68]

The strange manner in which the question of removal was resolved illustrates how little clarity the debate yielded on any of the questions it raised—about the Constitution's fundamental makeup, on the extent to which it was a complete and finished instrument, or on its relationship to subsequent users. While the uncertain Constitution marched on, however, the debate had fleshed out existent modes of constitutional imagination while also generating new ones. It marked the first concerted, communal effort following ratification to draw upon the Constitution to justify claims, inaugurating a powerful set of practices for using and conceiving of the document that lingered well beyond the debate's conclusion. Whatever came of the power to remove executive officers (important though that was), the debate's impact on constitutional imagination far transcended it. As congressmen would continue to make sense of the Constitution, what soon became clear was that all subsequent attempts to imagine it would bear the removal debate's indelible mark.

4

The Sacred Text

Virginia has a Bill of Rights, but it is no part of the Constitution. By not saying whether it is paramount to the Constitution or not, it has left us in confusion. Is the Bill of Rights consistent with the Constitution? Why then is it not inserted in the Constitution? . . . This will produce mischief.

—Edmund Randolph, Virginia Ratifying Convention, June 9, 1788

Deep into the House of Representatives' debate over amending the Constitution, Thomas Sinnickson of New Jersey expressed confusion. "What was the question before the committee," he inquired, "for really debate had become so desultory" that he wondered if "it was lost sight of altogether." There was more truth in this complaint than perhaps even Sinnickson realized, for it gestures toward a more fractured, and interesting, story of the first constitutional amendments than often earns notice—and one that played an outsized role in further transforming American constitutional imagination. His comment invites us to reconsider the single narrative that has long dominated popular and scholarly understandings alike—one that treats the making of the Constitution's first amendments as the creation of the Bill of Rights.[1]

While this conflation is not without justification, it masks more than it reveals. For one, it is unclear whether the first ten amendments that Congress proposed in September 1789, and which were finally ratified by the requisite states by 1791, were actually considered a bill of rights at the time of their inception. This suggestion might come as a shock, for the first amendments are readily afforded this now-iconic label without the faintest consideration that they might have been described otherwise. Although the description "bill of rights" was used occasionally from the beginning, decades passed before it was habitually and authoritatively employed. At first, most simply called them "the amendments." Several former Anti-Federalists who had clamored for a federal bill of rights were most impressed by what distinguished the first ten amendments from the declarations of rights to which they had grown accustomed. These amendments, for example, were placed at the end of the Constitution, rather than its beginning. In the very first complaint about the Convention's original omission, George Mason had asked that the Constitution be "prefaced with a Bill of Rights." More-over, these amendments were written in a tone and style very different from the bills of rights that accompanied the first state constitutions. Conse-quently, many Anti-Federalists were profoundly disillusioned with the end result and thus not inclined to confer so distinguished a label on such paltry additions.[2]

It was not simply that the amendments failed to live up to a certain stan-dard, however, but also that the project of amending the Constitution entailed far more than merely adding a bill of rights. This was especially true among Anti-Federalists, who, despite fearing that the existing Consti-tution threatened individual liberty, never thought that adding a bill of rights was their exclusive or even primary aim. True, it was a consistent, core demand that they had reiterated at every stage of the ratification de-bates and then during the first federal elections of 1788–1789. Yet throughout, they tended to believe that fundamental changes to the Constitution's structure—ones that altered the federal government's powers and returned many of them to the states—were more urgent. Indeed, of the nearly two hundred amendments proposed by state ratifying conventions, the clear majority targeted structural issues with the Constitution, dwarfing calls for explicit protections for traditional liberties. This preference did not betray an indifference to individual liberty, but rather showed an avowed commitment to protecting it. To most Anti-Federalists, adding a federal bill of rights would help, but the far more effective way of protecting rights was to tilt the balance of powers back to the states. As one Virginian ex-plained, "There would be no need of a bill of rights, were the states prop-erly confederated." Articulating the underlying reasoning, Richard Henry Lee remarked that merely "stating Rights" was "small," for "right without power to protect it," he proclaimed, "is of little avail."[3]

Modern sensibilities—programmed to assume a combative relationship between liberty and the state—struggle to grasp this logic. It would seem obvious that those obsessed with protecting liberty would primarily be drawn to restraints on power over grants of power. But for many disputants (and not simply the Constitution's critics), the protection of liberty was often a matter of granting the right kind of power in the right kind of way. A devotion to individual liberty did not necessarily privilege the kinds of rights provisions that we now deem so basic to that commitment. Anti-Federalists in the First Congress were hardly comforted by the initial proposal for amendments—even though it closely resembled what became the Bill of Rights—and instead agreed with Aedanus Burke of South Carolina that James Madison's proposed amendments were "little better than whip-syllabub, frothy and full of wind, formed only to please the palate." Decidedly insubstantial, they were "like a tub thrown out to a whale, to secure the freight of the ship and its peaceable voyage." Drawing upon Jonathan Swift's 1704 *Tale of a Tub*—in which sailors distracted a looming whale by throwing an empty tub from their ship to divert its attention—those clamoring for more substantive amendments complained that these mere cosmetic changes to the Constitution represented a similar ploy. They claimed that the amendments were aimed not at genuinely altering a flawed structure and protecting liberty, but only at distracting the guileless and unsuspecting with flimsy modifications while the powerful new state escaped intact. Seeing these early amendments through the prism of the Bill of Rights makes it difficult to understand incisive criticism of this sort, because it both conceals the structural changes that many participants believed most urgent and distorts the very different way in which many of them made sense of rights.[4]

This perspective also makes it especially challenging to understand the congressional debates of 1789. Part of the danger of reading the modern conception of the Bill of Rights back onto the first amendments has been the tendency to presuppose the amendments' discrete characters. A corollary of anachronistically dividing the Constitution up into positive grants of power (the original articles) and restraints on its exercise (the Bill of Rights) has been the popular approach of carving the original amendments up one by one in order to narrate individual origin stories for each. Given that constitutional case law has developed around amendments individually and that many of the early amendments have acquired singular, iconic identities in American culture, it is easy to see why this atomistic approach has been attractive—especially when modern disputes ostensibly hinge on the original meaning of a particular amendment. But the debates surrounding the early amendments' creation were not dominated by the kind of searching inquiries into the nature of particular rights favored today.

That was because the problem facing members of Congress was not a specific one—highlighting and enumerating the rights that mattered—but a
more general one—figuring out how best to protect rights that former
Federalists and Anti-Federalists alike claimed to cherish within the broader
context of altering the Constitution. Portraying the early amendments as
isolated rights provisions equipped with autonomous identities, rather
than nodes in this wider story, too often frays the fabric that originally
linked the amendments one to another and gave them their full meaning.[5]

These issues run together with the most significant problem that plagues
a persistent emphasis on the formation of the Bill of Rights: it obscures the
story of amending, and with that the debate over what form amendments
should take. Altering the Constitution was not merely about what was to
be added, but at least as much about how such alterations needed to be
made in the first place. In turn, such revisions were about what the method
of addition revealed about the very document being amended. Debates over
amending the Constitution shaped the conversation over the fundamental
status of the Constitution that had begun to emerge during the ratification debates and had picked up such intensity during the debate over removal of executive officers. It especially did so by emphasizing the precise
mode of amendment—disputants divided over whether to amend through
incorporation or supplement. Incorporating amendments called for inte-
grating changes into the existing text, while supplementing amendments
called for leaving the original text intact and instead adding new, stand-
alone text. This debate, which consumed considerable time and emotional
energy, ultimately turned on what kind of an object the Constitution was.
This episode is hardly unknown, but its full implications and significance
have never fully been grasped. Few debates during these pivotal early years
did more to shape the Constitution's properties and possibilities in American minds. Only by resuscitating a constitutional imagination that has
long since collapsed, and recovering the relevant stakes for both sides, does
it become possible to make sense of the debate over amending.[6]

The task of wrestling with the very nature of amendments accelerated
the mental transformation already unfolding around the Constitution's
fundamental status and, in particular, its relationship to historical time.
As the debate between incorporation and supplement played out, it
became easier to think of the Constitution as an artifact fixed in time,
which in turn made it much simpler to imagine the Constitution as a
discrete, inert text. More than ever, American constitutional disputants began

imagining the Constitution as an archival object. Few participants were more affected by this transformation than James Madison, the amendments' chief architect. That fall, after the amendments had been submitted to the states for consideration, he approached and talked about the Constitution in a dramatically new way, signaling that the Constitution had taken on a new kind of shape and definition in his mind due to the prior year's debates. His constitutional imagination had begun to change. And he was not alone.

The Road to Amendments: Madison and Constitutional Text

Members of the First Congress set out to amend the Constitution in the shadow of ratification. Anti-Federalists' resolute demand for constitutional amendments had reverberated from every corner of the nation. Federalists had been able to secure majorities in the most divided ratifying conventions only on the good faith promise that amendments would be considered. Moreover, after ratification proved such a protracted and divisive fight, appeasing those who had lost marked an important, if secondary, priority. Lists of recommended amendments, in some cases numbering into the dozens, appended several states' official ratifying documents, showing both how far-reaching constitutional skeptics hoped future changes would be and how seriously they took Federalist promises. Meanwhile, many disaffected opponents of the new Constitution held out hope for a second convention. That prospect had gained momentum when the New York convention circulated a letter calling for a new general convention and, later, when Anti-Federalists in Pennsylvania actually gathered at one in the fall of 1788. These disgruntled activists were quick to interpret any available evidence as a sign of pervasive disapproval of the Constitution, so the slightest turbulence might help swell their ranks. The refusal of North Carolina and Rhode Island to ratify the Constitution—a damaging fact that could not be ignored—offered a further rationale for amendment. To combat these genuine threats to the Constitution's endurance, its supporters had good political reason to keep their promise regarding amendments. In their own recent ratification arguments, moreover, Federalists had insisted that one of the Constitution's signature virtues was that it could be amended—not simply but much more easily than the Articles of Confederation. An inherently imperfect document, they had insisted, could be altered and perfected with time.[7]

But none of this made amendments inevitable, certainly not in 1789. By the time the First Congress convened, opposition to the Constitution had notably waned. Many former Anti-Federalists had resigned themselves to the instrument, choosing to focus their efforts instead on its impending implementation. Some staunch opponents held out hope for another convention—captured most notably in Virginia's and New York's formal applications for Congress to call one right as the national legislature convened—but by the spring of 1789 support had dwindled. Even Patrick Henry conceded, "Federal and anti seem now scarcely to exist." While Edward Carrington told Madison that "Antifederal districts have become perfectly calm." Meanwhile, George Washington's official ascent to the presidency helped to comfort the unconverted. As open opposition diminished, Federalists' confidence mounted. Having won a vast majority of congressional seats in the fall elections, most were content to interpret their electoral success as tacit acceptance of the Constitution as it stood and accordingly saw little need to appease the minority they had recently bested. As John Vining characterized matters, "Altho' hitherto we have done nothing to tranquilize that agitation which the adoption of the constitution threw some people into, yet, the storm has abated, and a calm succeeds." Plus, as newspaper editor John Fenno worried, amending the Constitution ran the risk of "unhing[ing] the public mind, giv[ing] an opening to the artful, unprincipled, & disaffected—who are waiting with burning impatience for an opportunity to embroil & embarrass public affairs."[8]

Had it not been for James Madison's resolute commitment, in fact, it is doubtful whether Congress would have taken up the task at all, let alone with the urgency it did. Much has rightly been made about Madison's motives for championing amendments so doggedly. Throughout ratification, after all, he had staunchly opposed them. To his mind, the Constitution that emerged from Philadelphia was already deeply flawed (stripped of the congressional negative over state laws and without proportional representation in both houses of Congress, the instrument was less likely to curb the state governments' oppressive tendencies); amendments were likely only to compound these existent issues, increasing the likelihood of the instrument's eventual failure. Moreover, particularly when it came to adding a federal bill of rights, Madison had been an outspoken critic of these "parchment barriers," locating constitutional safety in well-built and managed structures, not overly refined words. Even when his good friend Thomas Jefferson (repeatedly) cited the absence of a bill of rights as the Constitution's "principal defect," Madison mostly clung to his long-standing beliefs on the subject, informing his comrade that "experience proves the inefficacy of a bill of rights on those occasions when its controul is most needed." His pivot, then, calls out for explanation.[9]

Regardless of his motivation, the task of justifying amendments forced Madison to begin entertaining, at least partially, a defense of constitutional language. As he had been so resistant to thinking in these terms up to this point, it was a notable shift. But more important than the fact of his defense was its novelty within American constitutional argument. Unwilling to dispense with his long-standing assumptions about constitutional text, but eager to take Anti-Federalist concerns seriously, Madison was left to fuse hitherto incompatible strands of thought. From this challenge emerged a somewhat different way of thinking of the Constitution as a text. On its own it did not initiate a deeper reworking of constitutional assumptions. But once the full debate over amending the Constitution had run its course, it took on heightened importance and helped form a distinct brand of written constitutional consciousness.

Madison's transformation began with a political predicament. Thanks to Patrick Henry's opposition, Madison failed to secure a seat from Virginia in the federal Senate. He then found himself embroiled in a fierce political contest with James Monroe for a seat in the United States House of Representatives, in part because Henry used his clout to help draw an unfavorable electoral district for Madison. To obtain victory, Madison had to offer public assurances that the Constitution needed amendments, including a declaration of rights, and that he would support adding them. All the while, from Paris, Jefferson continued to remind Madison of the fundamental value of such additions—which only reinforced the impression that Virginians were committed to this change. This political context was not lost on observers. Robert Morris would later jest, "poor Madison got so Cursedly fright[e]ned in Virginia that I believe he has dreamed of amendments ever since."[10]

If getting into Congress had required appeasing the Constitution's skeptics, getting amendments onto Congress's agenda meant convincing a body composed primarily of the Constitution's champions that the project merited attention. On June 8, when Madison made good on his campaign pledge and formally presented a proposal for amendments to the House, resistance was firm. Several congressmen, like Benjamin Goodhue, were "opposed to the consideration of amendments altogether." For some, this was because the Constitution was perfectly sufficient as it was. For others—channeling that popular Federalist argument from ratification—the Constitution would always be flawed, so desperately modifying it served no intrinsic purpose. "I do not suppose the constitution to be perfect," Roger Sherman confessed, "nor," he added, "do I imagine if congress and all the legislatures on the continent were to revise it, that their united labours would make it perfect. I do not expect any perfection on this side the grave in the works of man." For still others, no matter the intense criticism the Constitution had endured, its ratification marked meaningful public acquiescence to its contents, certainly significant enough to supersede any lingering disapproval. Notwithstanding the depth of the initial opposition, the "people" had "ratified that instrument," and they did so "in order that the government may begin to operate. If this was not their wish, they might as well have rejected the constitution, as North-Carolina has done, until the amendments took place." And then, finally, there were those who were worried that amending was simply "dangerous or improper."[11]

Others were not opposed to amendments in principle but thought the issue should wait. Amendments were "necessary," many thought, "but this was not the proper time to bring them forward." Many worried about the practical implications that would follow a descent into such a potential quagmire. "Are we going to finish it in an hour? I believe not; it will take us more than a day, a week, a month—it will take a year to complete it!" James Jackson exclaimed. "The great wheels of the political machine should first be set in motion," Elbridge Gerry suggested. Despite his earlier Anti-Federalism, he now opposed a second constitutional convention. "The vessel ought to be got under way," he believed, "lest she lays by the wharf till she beat off her rudder, and runs herself a wreck on shore." So many tasks awaited Congress—few more important than establishing the federal impost that had long eluded the national government—and if they were not addressed speedily, prospective foreign allies "will smile at our infantine efforts to obtain consequence, and treat us with the contempt we have hitherto borne by reason of the imbecility of our government." It did not make much sense, John Laurance protested, to "incur an absolute evil in order to rid themselves of an imaginary one."[12]

Many preached patience because amending required experience—the precise ingredient missing from congressional knowledge. Any amendments proposed at this early stage on the "untried constitution" would be "founded merely on speculative theory." An eighteenth-century Anglo-American truism if ever there was one, speculation and theory were inherently inferior to experience. As the Constitution had just been set in motion, and as such was untried, "let [it] have a fair trial, " exhorted James Jackson, "let it be examined by experience, discover by that test what its errors are, and then talk of amending." It was one thing if "we actually find the constitution bad upon experience," but until then congressmen were "pursuing a mere ignis fatuus" (or false hope).[13]

Madison worried that his congressional colleagues misunderstood the Constitution's current strength. He had long been convinced that committed opponents would exhaust "every effort that might endanger or embarrass" the new governing document. Critics such as Patrick Henry were bent on "the destruction of the whole System." Accordingly, Madison remained deeply worried about the prospect of a second general convention. As he had written just months earlier—in the shadow of New York's "pestilent" circular letter calling for one—if convened, a new convention would throw "all things into Confusion . . . subverting the fabric just established, if not the Union itself." To defend the urgency of amendments, he tried to shake his fellow House members' complacency. If a "re-consideration of the whole structure of the government . . . was opened," he warned, then it would be unlikely "to stop at that point which would be safe to the government itself." The Constitution's skeptics expected amendments. "If we . . . refuse to let the subject come into view," he worried, "it may occasion suspicions," which might "inflame or prejudice the public mind." Now was the time to "extinguish opposition" once and for all. For both Madison (whose political standing in Virginia partly hinged on the outcome) and the young republic (which might not survive a revival of Anti-Federalism), there was much to be gained from exhibiting a spirit of "moderation" and much to be lost from not.[14]

But while such pressing concerns helped motivate Madison, they do not explain the full range of justifications he offered for amendments or the impact those had on the discursive dynamics in which the Constitution was taking shape. Importantly, he advanced novel reasons in defense of amendments. He had gestured toward several of these during his extended, remarkable correspondence with Jefferson on the new Constitution that had dominated the period since the Constitutional Convention adjourned (at which time Jefferson was in Paris serving as the United States' diplomat to France). Now needing to defend amendments in Congress in the spring of 1789, Madison pushed his novel thinking even further. Whatever compelled him to favor amendments, rhetorically he did not take the easy way out. He could have simply defended amendments on the ground of expedience, by asserting that critics could be conciliated without "endangering any part of the constitution," that—as his friend Samuel Johnston, governor of North Carolina, put it—amendments were merely "the addition of a little Flourish & Dressing without injuring the substantial part." At times, Madison effectively claimed as much to his congressional colleagues: "We can make the constitution better in the opinion of those who are opposed to it, without weakening its frame, or abridging its usefulness, in the judgment of those who are attached to it." But, revealingly, he refused to stop there. A crucial component of Madison's case was that, in addition to strengthening the Constitution's image in the public's eye, amendments would also change the Constitution itself for the better; they would have a meaningful impact on its functioning.[15]

But here Madison rejected Anti-Federalist reasoning—the obvious alternative. He refused to hew to the demands of so many constitutional critics to rework the Constitution's structure—either by redistributing its powers or rewriting its allegedly ambiguous language. He was willing only to tolerate amendments that left the Constitution's formative "principles" and the "substance of [its] powers" in place. Hence, his June 8 proposal featured only two kinds of alterations. The first (of which there were very few) were structural amendments that, to Madison's estimation, changed nothing. The second, which comprised the bulk of his proposal, were rights-based provisions. He justified this disparity on the grounds that "the great mass of people who opposed [the Constitution], disliked it because it did not contain effectual provision against encroachments on particular rights," meaning most demands for change "relate," as he put it, "to what may be called a bill of rights." Disingenuous as this claim might have been (Madison had earlier conceded to Jefferson that calls for key structural changes dominated opposition to the Constitution), he nonetheless was proposing a popular Anti-Federalist remedy. But even here he rejected Anti-Federalist logic. He still refused to concede that textually entrenched rights provisions could serve their ostensible purpose and, more broadly, that language could police political power. As he had previously asserted—in the "Vices," at the Constitutional Convention, and throughout ratification—and as he had put it so forcefully to Jefferson just months earlier, "restrictions however strongly marked on paper will never be regarded when opposed to the decided sense of the public." As "repeated violations of these parchment barriers have been committed by overbearing majorities in every State," their "inefficacy" was clear. While he softened his language when making the point on the House floor, he nonetheless maintained that it "may be thought all paper barriers against the power of the community, are too weak to be worthy of attention."[16]

Madison was left with the far trickier project. Contrary to what Federalists had argued, he claimed that amending the Constitution—particularly through the addition of text-based rights—would somehow enhance the instrument, but not in any of the ways that Anti-Federalists thought. Madison needed to fuse Federalist assumptions with Anti-Federalist concerns, and the only way to do so was to subtly reimagine the Constitution he had known to that point.

This exercise teemed with irony, since it entailed Madison combating, however gently, many of the arguments he had recently championed. After all, at the Virginia ratifying convention he had stated plainly that "a solemn declaration of our essential rights" would be "unnecessary and dangerous." Now, on the House floor, he recited popular objections that had been made against such declarations as though he had not himself previously raised any of these doubts. For one, many had claimed bills of rights were "unnecessary articles of a republican government" as "the constitution is a bill of powers, the great residuum being the rights of the people." For another, a federal bill of rights was unnecessary as long as the state declarations of rights were operative (something the federal Constitution did not alter). Meanwhile, enumerating rights also threatened the authority of rights that were omitted (what James Wilson had famously argued during ratification). And, last, of course, text-based rights provisions were nothing more than "paper barriers." Madison surely sensed that, in challenging each of these points, he was arguing with himself as much as anybody else.[17]

But he went about trying to square the circle. He contended that it was insufficient that the Constitution was merely a "bill of powers," for "even if government keeps within those limits, it has certain discretionary powers with respect to the means, which may admit of abuse to a certain extent," none more significant than the much-diagnosed "necessary and proper" clause. Unlike Anti-Federalists, though, who championed precision in constitutional language in order to limit or even eliminate discretionary power, Madison proceeded from the opposite premise. As he himself had elucidated in several installments of the *Federalist,* discretionary powers were essential. Given as much, it was a mistake to assume that the residuum of power lay outside of government. To sharpen the precise scope of legitimate discretionary power, it thus made sense to enumerate "those cases in which the government ought not to act" to guard those rights that many had clamored to protect. Much the same went for appeals to the state declarations of rights. Several states lacked these instruments altogether while many others were defective or improper. But, more to the point, relying on partial state instruments was "too uncertain [a] ground to leave this provision upon, if a provision is at all necessary to secure rights." Perhaps declarations were pointless—again Madison was toggling between competing points of view—but if they served any purpose, their provisions had to be adequately drawn. Although the danger of enumerating was no doubt "one of the most plausible arguments" he had heard, he was confident that his proposal offered the necessary protection. In a forerunner to the eventual Ninth Amendment, he recommended a rule of constitutional construction: that the enumeration of some rights ought not be construed to disparage the existence of others.[18]

Then there was Madison's own long-favored argument that bills of rights were nothing more than "parchment barriers." He refused to abandon the underlying logic that had hitherto animated him—"I am sensible they are not so strong" he readily conceded and "perhaps the best way of securing" rights "in practice is to provide such checks, as will prevent the encroachment of . . . one [political body] upon the other." Yet, even if that remained true, "it does not follow," he reasoned, that they could not "have, to a certain degree, a salutary effect against the abuse of power." His point here can be easily misunderstood. Elaborating on this "salutary effect," he explained, "If [rights provisions] are incorporated into the constitution, independent tribunals of justice will consider themselves in a peculiar manner the guardians of those rights." Based on this aside, many have concluded that Madison was pointing toward the modern constitutional assumption that only enumerated rights are judicially enforceable. But his field of vision was broader. Not only did he have several effects in mind, he also had a distinctive idea of effect in mind. Enumerating rights via text neither afforded them fundamental status they otherwise lacked nor offered them a stronger form of protection.[19]

What enumerations, instead, could do—among federal judges, state legislators, the people at large, and everybody in between—was to "impress some degree of respect for them, to establish the public opinion in their favor, and rouse the attention of the whole community." Here he harked back to something he had written Jefferson the previous fall as part of their extensive discussion of the new Constitution. At that time, Madison had begun entertaining novel justifications for enumerated rights. "Political truths declared in that solemn manner," Madison had explained, "acquire by degrees the character of fundamental maxims of free Government," especially "as they become incorporated with the national sentiment." Moreover, even though republics were threatened more often by popular majorities than by ruling minorities, "there may be occasions on which the evil may spring from the latter sources," and in these instances, "a bill of rights will be a good ground for an appeal to the sense of the community." Now before his House colleagues he was drawing out the implications of these novel reflections to suggest that even if instantiating rights in text was redundant and did little to safeguard them from traditional threats, doing so could nonetheless serve valuable cultural and pedagogical purposes. What rights provisions could do—through their written presence—was serve as public markers, signals that could activate and sharpen public awareness, especially over time. Constitutional language might still have merited the appellation "parchment barriers," but it could nonetheless beget productive habits of mind. Bills of rights could not change anything about the Constitution itself, but they could alter its relationship to those who lived under it. They could be at once, as the notes from which he delivered his June 8 speech put it, "useful—not essential."[20]

Such was how constitutional text could be insubstantial and yet substantial at the same time. By uniting the underlying logic of Federalists' disdain for parchment barriers with the spirit of Anti-Federalists' respect for them, Madison arrived at a position that did not easily map onto the prevailing conceptual scheme. He managed to reject most Anti-Federalist defenses of rights provisions while arriving at their fundamental suggestion. Conversely, he managed to defend the deeper logic of Federalist thinking while rejecting its typical conclusion. Whatever his motivation for doing so, in articulating this position Madison was betraying a new kind of textual consciousness.

But the deeper implications would have to wait. Even though Madison's June 8 resolution included a full proposal for amendments, House members at first paid little attention to it, instead spending the bulk of their time pondering whether amendments ought to be entertained at all. Despite

Madison's impassioned plea, the project was tabled for the time being—but, thanks to Madison, not permanently. When discussion of the topic resumed several weeks later, participants referred the matter to a grand committee composed of a member from each state. Madison was Virginia's representative and the committee reported its work in late July. If Madison's June 8 remarks had forced at least some congressmen to follow their Virginia colleague in reimagining, however slightly, the Constitution upon which they were deliberating, the debate prompted by the committee's report that broke out in mid-August would fuel a greater, and more lasting, form of reckoning.[21]

Incorporating versus Supplementing

In one of his letters to Madison the previous summer, Jefferson had described the Constitution as "a good canvas on which some strokes only want retouching." But how did the Constitution need to be retouched? Much of the reason Madison's initial proposal for amendments had fit so uneasily amid Federalist criticisms and Anti-Federalist demands was because of the form in which he believed amendments would be added. He had referred to bills of rights in his post-Convention exchanges with Jefferson (in large measure because Jefferson, channeling his Anti-Federalist instincts, deployed the same term). Madison had occasionally flirted with this terminology during the House debate too. But mostly he eschewed it, talking not about adding a bill of rights but instead about the need to further safeguard certain cherished American liberties that constitutional skeptics had repeatedly emphasized. Part of the reason he spoke so uneasily of adding a bill of rights was because he already considered the Constitution itself a bill of rights—echoing the argument Alexander Hamilton had made in *Federalist* 84. Not only had Madison long privileged constitutional structure over textual declarations in the struggle to protect rights, but, relatedly, he refused to accept that amendments designed to protect certain rights ought to take a distinct form from what was already found in the Constitution. When Anti-Federalists demanded a bill of rights, they often imagined an addition distinct in kind from what the Constitution already was—an abridgement of power that would balance an otherwise dangerous grant of authority. But here Madison sharply disagreed. His instincts were not to add something new, but to extend the Constitution as it was, to add more of what currently existed. The Constitution already was an elaborate mechanism designed to protect rights. Safeguarding additional rights meant merely enhancing and refining that mechanism, not attaching something categorically distinct.[22]

This inclination—and the constitutional vision it presupposed—explains how Madison proposed amending the Constitution: through incorporation. Amendments would be woven into the existing document, rather than added as supplements at the end. Up to that point, Madison could not fathom an alternative mode and took no pains to conceal his preference. His June 8 proposal clearly advanced his favored method of amendment, as did the language by which he described the project throughout the early debate—he used the verbs "incorporate" and "revise" numerous times. Given that participants in the House debate saw no need to protest or suggest an alternative, perhaps Madison's instincts were in line with the dominant opinion. Or, given that the House was focused on other matters—not on how or what to amend but on whether amendments ought to be added at all—it could have been that nobody much noticed. Whatever the case, a new kind of context would soon clarify what had previously been inchoate. When the congressional committee tasked with proposing amendments emerged in late July with Madison's handiwork in tow, the ensuing debate turned entirely on how, in the words of Jefferson, the Constitution would be "retouched." It would not take long to realize the significance of the distinction between amending through supplement and amending through incorporation.[23]

As the House became embroiled in this debate, disputants would be forced to reckon—arguably like never before—with the Constitution's fundamental status as an interpretive object. By this point, now deep into the summer of 1789, the removal debate had come to an end. Having watched some opponents of removal find traction accentuating the Constitution's linguistic character, many disputants had acquired a new appreciation of the importance of constitutional language. Even if many still doubted its capacity to regulate political conduct, following Madison they likely recognized its broader cultural purchase. When the committee reported its work on amendments, these prior experiences helped crystallize what the debate over amending was really about and what was at stake. Madison's own deeper instinct, the one that had long led him to disparage constitutional text and to conceive of the Constitution as a dynamic object, would once again emerge in force as he defended his favored method for amendment. But much as the removal debate had forced him and others, despite their inclination, to refract the Constitution through a textual prism, so too would the House debate over adding amendments.

Madison took the initiative fashioning the proposal for amendments, and his fellow committee members deferred to his leadership. For his June 8 resolution, he had already sifted through the scores of amendments proposed by the separate state ratifying conventions before settling on a sampling that met his liking. These same suggestions now largely comprised the new proposal Madison put together on behalf of the committee. To add the proposed amendments to the Constitution, Madison also followed the exact method he had already utilized in his prior proposal: he incorporated them directly into the text. In other words, he literally amended the existing Constitution. For instance, in Article I, Section 9 (which specified prohibitions on Congress's authority), he proposed adding between the second and third paragraphs a restriction on establishing religion. There would be no First Amendment, as it were, just new bits of constitutional text seamlessly interwoven into the most relevant part of the original document.[24]

Now that the House's attention was centered squarely on the substance of amendments, Madison's method of incorporating them finally was noticed—and it met sharp resistance. The entire first day of debate (on August 13) focused on this single proposal. Roger Sherman of Connecticut, a long-standing and staunch opponent of amendments, was the most outspoken enemy of incorporation. In contrast to Madison's preferred approach, Sherman insisted that amendments be added by supplement— as an appendix to the original text. These opposing approaches framed the debate: over whether to incorporate or supplement, over whether to follow Madison or Sherman. Sherman quickly entered a formal motion to change Madison's chosen mode of amending, and as one of the reporters transcribing the action from the House of Representatives' viewing gallery put it, "a long and animated debate ensued."[25]

For Sherman, the stakes could not have been greater. Far older than many of his congressional colleagues, by 1789 Sherman had been serving in local or national politics for decades. A seasoned debater, "his train of thinking" exhibited "something regular, deep and comprehensive," according to William Pierce. Few boasted "a clearer Head" or were more "artful in accomplishing any particular object." Yet others surely would have agreed that, at the same time, Sherman exhibited a "strange New England cant" and was "as cunning as the Devil." No matter the "oddity of his address," the Connecticut statesman was a formidable adversary. And he was convinced that debating the appropriate mode of amendment cut to the core of the Constitution's essence, implicating its status as an interpretive object and, by extension, its relationship to subsequent users. Even though less than two years had passed since the Federal Convention had adjourned and the Constitution that had been the labor of its efforts had first appeared, Sherman (and soon others) instinctively contemplated the connection between that earlier work and the constitutional tasks confronting Congress. For Sherman, probing the Constitution's intergenerational character underscored the fundamentals of its composition and revealed why incorporating amendments was so threatening. This reaction might seem strange— needlessly dramatic and beside the point. But to Sherman, viewing the Constitution from a distinctively eighteenth-century perspective, it was entirely logical. It fast became clear that many shared his concerns.[26]

Those opposed to incorporation argued that the existing Constitution and its potential amendments embodied incompatible materials. Mixing them marked a category error. Sherman warned, "We ought not to interweave our propositions into the [Constitution] itself, because it will be destructive of the whole fabric." Rather than weaving a tighter cloth, amending through incorporation would tear at its threads, fraying each and unraveling the whole. "We might as well endeavor to mix brass, iron and clay, as to incorporate such heterogeneous articles; the one contradictory to the other," he concluded. James Jackson concurred. Invoking biblical imagery, he maintained that the Constitution should "not be patched up from time to time, with various stuffs resembling Joseph's coat of many colors."[27]

Precisely because the original Constitution and subsequent amendments represented two distinct kinds of materials, the original Constitution needed to remain untouched. Jackson's biblical comparison underlay his equally urgent appeal: "The constitution of the union has been ratified and established by the people, let their act remain inviolable." Samuel Livermore was similarly adamant that "whatever amendments were made to the constitution . . . they ought to stand separate from the original instrument." Why run the risk of confusing past and present? In claiming that "it would be convenient to have [everything] in one instrument that people might see the whole at once," champions of incorporation had things exactly backward. "Was it intended," Michael Jenifer Stone queried, "to have the constitution republished, and the alterations inserted in their proper places?" How exactly would additions be tracked in the public mind? Confusion was avoided, rather than encouraged, by amending through supplement. To support this point, Jackson encouraged his peers to "look at the constitution of Great Britain" and ask, "is that all contained in one instrument?" Clearly not, which had not caused a bit of difficulty. There had been numerous additions, changes, and improvements to it since Magna Carta had been devised in 1215. Yet, Jackson asked rhetorically, had it "been altered since by the incorporation of amendments?" Britain's constitution could function as a uniform whole despite not "striking out and inserting other words in the great charter." And even though "the constitution is composed of many distinct acts," nonetheless "an Englishman would be ashamed to own that on this account he could not ascertain his own privileges or the authority of the government."[28]

The British mode of amendment had thus offered clarity, but that only hinted at one kind of convenience. More important than what supplemental amendment might provide was the confusion it would help mitigate. "If the amendments are incorporated in the body of the work," Stone worried, "it will appear, unless we refer to the archives of congress"—and he assumed few would—"that George Washington, and the other worthy characters who composed the convention, signed an instrument which they never had in contemplation." Here was the core concern: if the original Constitution did not remain "inviolable," it could easily be confused with updated versions that succeeded it. Whatever merit those subsequent additions might claim, they were simply not what the Constitution's original authors—whose intent was emblazoned in their signatures punctuating the instrument—had devised.[29]

Incorporation would do far greater damage than merely mislead subsequent constitutional users, though. More fundamentally, it would do violence to the original Constitution—why Stone so passionately claimed that it was tantamount "to repeal[ing] the whole constitution." As Roger Sherman warned, incorporation signaled an intent "to destroy the whole and establish a new constitution." Samuel Livermore cautioned similarly, "if we destroy the base, the superstructure falls of course." Incorporation cut right to the Constitution's foundation. It was not peaceful or unobtrusive; as Jackson insisted, it could not be done "without mutilating and defacing the original." How could incorporation signify such permanent destruction? John Laurance of New York had a striking answer to that question. He "could not conceive how gentlemen meant to ingraft the amendments into the constitution" for, he explained, "the original . . . [being] lodged in the archives of the late congress, it was impossible for this house to take and correct and interpolate that without"—and here his formulation is especially revealing—"making it speak a different language." Even if the Constitution's original words remained unchanged, additions slipped in here and there would produce changes that would reverberate throughout the whole, mutating the Constitution's meaning, force, and import. Subtly, the document would speak differently than before. Laurance was equating the Constitution's content with the specific language it spoke. To modulate its idiom meant to fundamentally change it. From this perspective, to incorporate was to rewrite the Constitution. It was to destroy something that had existed and create something new in its place. It was to transmute the original Constitution, which otherwise was to remain safely in the archives.[30]

Importantly, then, incorporation signaled not only destruction but creation. It meant writing a wholly new Constitution, something that, opponents repeatedly stressed, fell beyond the legitimate activities of a sitting Congress. "We may propose *amendments to the constitution,*" Sherman stressed, but "[we may not] propose to repeal the old, and substitute a new one" in its place. James Jackson drew out the full implications "of repealing the present constitution, and adopting an improved one." As he explained, "if we have this power, we may go on from year to year, making new ones; and in this way we shall render the basis of the superstructure the most fluctuating thing imaginable," meaning, most disturbingly, "the people will never know what the constitution is." Forget what the Constitution meant or what language it spoke, its basic ontological makeup would remain forever in flux. If Congress after Congress could weave new amendments into existing text, the changes would be so far-reaching and so perpetual that no citizen—no matter how conscientious—could ever speak with confidence about the content of the nation's fundamental law. Between Laurance's anxiety about making the Constitution speak a new language and Jackson's concern about the people's confusion over its substance, opponents of incorporation were fully reducing the Constitution to a textual artifact. In so fiercely criticizing the consequences of melding new language with old, they were limning the Constitution's boundaries, defining its essence, and conceptualizing its core attributes in strikingly linguistic terms.[31]

In imagining their governing instrument this way, enemies of incorporation began sanctifying the original Constitution. James Jackson thought it "ought to remain inviolate," a beacon for all clearly to see. More revealingly, George Clymer (formerly one of Pennsylvania's delegates to the Constitutional Convention) thought "that the amendments ought not to be incorporated," because he hoped the existing Constitution "would remain a monument," so that "the world would discover the perfection of the original." By drawing not only a distinction between the original Constitution and its subsequently constructed additions, but a particularly invidious one—one that underscored the unvarnished perfection of the original—opponents of incorporation were building on the essentialism so recently born of the removal debate to fix the Constitution in place, as a distinct, tangible object frozen in time, as an artifact confined to the archives. This was why Sherman—in the face of scattered complaints that the debate was insubstantial—insisted that his position turned on something far more consequential than a "mere matter of form."[32]

Preserving the Uniform Constitution

On this particular point, Madison and his fellow defenders of incorporation firmly agreed. "Form . . . is always of less importance than the substance," Madison asserted; "but on this occasion," he concurred, "I admit that form is of some consequence." Indeed, the impassioned defense of incorporation demonstrated it was of the utmost consequence. Madison apparently had not given the mode of altering the Constitution much thought during the time he had been pondering the possibility of amendments. To amend was to incorporate; alternatives were not so much less appealing as wholly out of place. But, in the face of Sherman and company's opposition, it was now obvious that incorporation, were it to take effect, required a vigorous defense. In this regard, the opposition did not change Madison's mind, but it did inspire a new breed of self-consciousness, transforming what thus far had been merely stipulated supposition into an explicit justification. He had no doubt that "upon reflection" his core assumption would remain unchanged—that incorporation "shall appear to be the most eligible" method for amendment. But, having been thrust into this new disputation, it was the reflection that would prove novel and consequential. Madison and his energetic allies quickly developed not only a robust set of reasons why incorporation was so vital to the nation's constitutional culture, but also a vision of constitutionalism itself that stood in fundamental opposition to the one that the champions of supplementation were fast throwing into relief.[33]

At one point, Sherman had insisted that "the constitution . . . ought to remain entire." Defenders of incorporation stressed a similar point. As

William Loughton Smith—fresh off his command performance during the removal debate—proclaimed, amendments ought to "form one complete system" with the original Constitution. What the two sides had in mind, however, differed profoundly. Sherman meant that, for the Constitution to remain whole, the original Constitution had to remain as it was. In contrast, champions of incorporation thought that the Constitution needed to form one complete, harmonious, interlocking system, justifying their favored mode of amendment on the grounds that it alone satisfied this goal. Madison reasoned, "there is a neatness and propriety in incorporating the amendments into the constitution itself; in that case the system will remain uniform and entire." The point was to create a single, indivisible Constitution, not a tiered system of competing constitutional hierarchies. If, and only if, amendments "are placed upon the footing here proposed, they will stand upon as good foundation as the original work," and only then might the constitutional system Madison had in mind—and that he had devoted so much time to establishing—function most effectively and intelligibly. John Vining agreed. "If the mode proposed by [Sherman] was adopted," then "the system would be distorted, and like a careless[ly] written letter, have more matter attached to it in a postscript than was contained in the original composition." What kind of an interpretive object assumed such a misshapen form? If others presumed that something as prosaic as daily letters of correspondence should not contain such compositional deformities, then surely neither should a document as august as a constitution. "The constitution being a great and important work," Vining concluded, it "ought all to be brought into one view, and made as intelligible as possible." Only a seamless integration of new amendments could bring all—that is, the entire Constitution—into a single "view."[34]

Meanwhile, the work of making the Constitution as "intelligible as possible," as Vining put it, had several layers. Rendering it a single whole was the only way to make it comprehensible, to make it knowable. One constitution could be processed, could be known, whereas multiple constitutions fueled chaos—epistemological and ontological. If amendments "are supplementary," Madison warned, "its meaning can only be ascertained by a comparison of the two instruments"—the original Constitution and the added text. This "will be a very considerable embarrassment," for "it will be difficult to ascertain to what parts of the instrument the amendments particularly refer" and "will create unfavorable comparisons." To Elbridge Gerry, the problem was considerably more acute. If amendments were supplemented, it was unavoidable that "we shall have five or six constitutions, perhaps differing in material points from each other, but all equally valid." The resulting arrangement would be so fraught with complexity and confusion that it would "require a man of science to determine what is or is not the constitution." The Constitution would recede from sight, shrouded in perpetual mystery, which, given that "the several states are bound up not to make laws contradictory thereto, and all officers sworn to support it," meant that serious, perhaps intractable, problems would arise from constitutional actors not "knowing precisely what it is." William Loughton Smith echoed this critique. Unless incorporation was adopted, "the instrument is to have five or six suits of improvements," and "such a mode seems more calculated to embarrass the people than any thing else." There was no "juster cause of complaint than the difficulties of knowing the law, arising from legislative obscurities that might easily be avoided," and yet the proposal on the table ensured just that. The Constitution would melt into irresolvable intricacies, making its mere identification—a foundational task in constitutional reasoning if there was one—impossible. Why "run into such jargon in amending and altering the constitution," Vining asked, when members of Congress might instead "adopt a plainness and simplicity of style on this and every other occasion, which should be easily understood"?[35]

This confusion helps explain why a minority of participants drew parallels between the Constitution and ordinary laws. If, customarily, American laws had been amended in a certain fashion, with an interest in promoting holistic unity, then why should the Constitution not be so handled? John Page, for one, thought it best "to look at the constitution as a bill on its passage through the house, and to consider and amend its defects article by article." Smith, meanwhile, drew inspiration from his native South Carolina's example, which "in revising the old code" had chosen not to "mak[e] acts in addition to acts, which is always attended with perplexity." Instead, legislators "incorporated them, and brought them forward as a complete system, repealing the old." While such analogies did not predominate, they nonetheless illustrated the deeper impulse.[36]

The ontological and epistemological chaos against which champions of incorporation warned naturally bled into the interpretive realm as well. There was no way it could not, for what the Constitution was—what defined its contents, structure, and boundaries—and how easily that could be seen, identified, and rendered, formed the necessary preconditions of constitutional interpretation. The disorder that had already engulfed interpretive rules in the American republic—manifested so evidently throughout the ratification debates—directly sprung from the pervasive uncertainty that otherwise surrounded the Constitution's status as an object of interpretation. Debating the mode of amending that object reignited some of these uncertainties, leading proponents of incorporation to insist that constitutional interpretation would not be feasible unless the Constitution was amended in the right kind of way. As these disputants had already made clear, seeing the Constitution was the first step toward any meaningful understanding of its contents. Others now pushed this thinking further, beyond mere recognition and toward concrete exegesis. Madison drew a fundamental connection between a holistic Constitution and interpretive protocols: "when the amendments are interwoven into those parts to which they naturally belong . . . we shall then be able to determine its meaning without references or comparison." Deciphering constitutional meaning presupposed that the Constitution itself had been "naturally" constructed, that its parts had been woven together in accord with its essence. Such was why "systematic men frequently take up the whole law, and with its amendments and alterations reduce it into one act." Elbridge Gerry agreed. "If we" amend via supplement, he presumed, "the title of our first amendment will be, a supplement to the constitution of the United States; the next a supplement to the supplement, and so on, until we have supplements annexed five times in five years, wrapping up the constitution in a maze of perplexity." As problematic as this surely would be, nowhere would its damage be more painfully felt than in the realm of interpretation. For "as great and adept" as so many of America's constitutional thinkers were "at finding out the truth," nonetheless, should Sherman get his way, it would take the sort of prodigious skill and massive time investment most lacked "to ascertain the true meaning of the constitution."[37]

Beyond matters of conceptual and interpretive efficiency, champions of incorporation also stressed that the Constitution itself mandated this procedure. "The constitution has undoubtedly provided, that the amendments shall be incorporated," Gerry confidently maintained, "if I understand the import of the words, 'and shall be valid to all intents and purposes, as part of the constitution.' If it had said that the present form should be preserved, then it would be proper to propose the alterations by way of a supplement." But Article V made no such statement. The Constitution, interpreted properly through its own words, mandated incorporation. More generally, but no less forcefully, William Loughton Smith added that incorporation alone "was compatible with the constitution."[38]

Incorporation's advocates thought that the Constitution mandated their favored mode of amendment because it alone ensured that amendments (once ratified) would enjoy the same authority as the original articles written in Philadelphia. Incorporation was a response to the assurance, which Gerry had pulled from Article V, that amendments would be fully "part of the Constitution." Supporters of supplemental amendments, in sanctifying the original document, were diminishing the relative authority of amendments. For advocates of incorporation, the logic of this position was inescapable: amendments would not "have the same authority as the original instrument." As Gerry pointed out, though, "the congress of the United States are expressly authorised by the sovereign and uncontrollable voice of the people"—the same sovereign authority that undergirded the Constitution— "to propose amendments whenever two-thirds of both houses shall think fit." The only way to honor the popular sovereignty upon which the constitutional project rested, then, was to interweave amendments and the original into a seamless whole, such that every piece enjoyed the same status and authority as every other. This was why the signatures that punctuated the original Constitution were, contrary to what opponents of incorporation insisted, irrelevant. They would have given no "validity to the constitution if it was not ratified by the several states," so there was no need to worry about preserving the original signers' contributions as authors. Their wishes were inconsequential compared with the sovereign people's, whom Smith was convinced (from surveying the ratifying documents) were "of opinion that the phraseology of the constitution ought to be altered." The original drafters' wishes were also utterly unimportant compared with the more urgent task: maintaining a legitimate Constitution.[39]

If incorporation maintained the Constitution's uniformity, though, it did not prevent the Constitution from changing. Opponents of incorporation were, thus, not wrong that it would make the Constitution "speak a different language." Smith did not hide what he assumed "was intended to be done by the committee," that "the present . . . constitution was to be done away, and a new one substituted in its stead." Crucially, though, this was true despite the mode adopted. As Gerry put it, "if the amendments are incorporated it will be a virtual repeal of the constitution," but, he added, "I say the effect will be the same in a supplementary way." To amend was to create anew. Altering one part reverberated throughout the entire instrument. Opponents of incorporation were thus right, at least up to a point; they were only wrong about the likelihood of this transformation and, more importantly, its implications for amendments. Since amendments necessarily altered the whole Constitution, the key difference lay between change that was clear and credible and change that was imperceptible and dangerous. Holistic reweaving rendered the Constitution most clearly, while awkward supplementing encouraged the false belief that the original text remained unchanged. Since change was inevitable, it made little sense to adopt the mode that fueled confusion and bred illegitimacy. Should amendments be added via supplement, subsequent interpreters were liable to miss the transformations that amending had wrought and, in so doing, would fail to see the real Constitution. Only incorporation brought the genuine Constitution into relief.[40]

There was a more important issue yet, though, which cut to the heart of the debate and brought the deepest implications of supplementary amending to the surface. Nobody articulated it better than Gerry. He had worried that if amendments were added incorrectly, the Constitution might multiply; as he had complained, "we shall have five or six constitutions . . . requir[ing] a man of science to determine what is or is not the constitution." But he harbored a deeper anxiety about this potential splintering, one focused not on the additional constitutions that would spring forth but on the consequences this fracturing would have for the original Constitution. "If," he suggested, "it is the opinion of gentlemen that the original is to be kept sacred, amendments will be of no use, and had better be omitted." Opponents of incorporation misunderstood the character of amendments—assuming that only interwoven changes would affect the whole instrument—but they did so because of their deeper desire, one that the debate had clarified. They were bent on treating the original Constitution as a "sacred" text. That, above all, explained their favored method of amendment.[41]

Despite fundamentally disagreeing on the choice before them, the two sides had fully converged on a shared understanding of the relevant stakes. They were debating the fundamental character of the Constitution itself. In so doing, they were advancing competing visions for how the Constitution should be imagined—ones that implied very different understandings of the instrument's ontological character, its essential content, and its relationship to those subject to its jurisdiction. What was the Constitution? On this front, both sides were clear that "form" was anything but irrelevant.

Indeed, form was profoundly determinative. It is unclear how readily participants appreciated the implications of their arguments, let alone intended them. But whatever drove the competing positions, each outlook made it possible to imagine the Constitution in distinct fashion.

Incorporating or supplementing amendments helped determine whether the Constitution would be understood as an organic, evolving whole (the implication of Madison and his allies' position) or as layers of geological sediment marked in time (the implication of Sherman and his allies' stance). In effect, Madison proposed wrenching the Constitution out of fixed time by effacing the time stamp from each discrete addition. In effect, Sherman proposed just the opposite—fixing the original Constitution in time and starkly distinguishing it from any additions that followed. By emphasizing the Constitution's intergenerational character, Madison's method minimized its archival character. It promoted the kind of holistic constitutional dynamism that had long animated his thinking, that had otherwise led him to disparage the urge to see the constitution as text for so long. Again, Sherman's method gestured in the antithetical direction, enabling readers to see the original Constitution as a "sacred" text, as an untouchable historical artifact lodged in the archives. It created the possibility of, even if it by no means ensured, the kind of constitutional fixity so many had resisted or mocked since the United States' birth. It helped create the idea of the archival Constitution.

For this reason, Sherman's success in this debate numbers among the most important milestones in the entire sweep of American constitutional history. For reasons that still remain opaque, the House eventually adopted his position. Earlier, Sherman had warned that unless those pushing for amendments were willing to capitulate on the mode of alteration, the whole project might fall apart. While this threat failed at first, perhaps with time it ultimately persuaded the more impressionable members of the House. Madison later privately hinted that this rationale had made the difference, lamenting that his side had been forced "to give up the form by which the [amendments] when ratified would have fallen into the body of the Constitution" because it had become "an unavoidable sacrifice to *a few* who knew their concurrence to be necessary." Whatever the reasons, the consequences were immense. As Madison noted in that same letter, "it is already apparent . . . that some ambiguities will be produced by this change, as the question will often arise and sometimes be not easily solved, how far the original text is or is not necessarily superseded, by the supplemental act."

What Madison was getting at was that he and his allies had not merely lost the vote, but, with that, a broader struggle over how to imagine the Constitution itself. The "ambiguities" that Madison now assumed were inevitable would be a direct product of the constitutional multiplicity he had so fervently fought. No longer left to reckon with a single uniform whole, constitutional interpreters would now have to reconcile competing texts; they would likely be forced to relate one time-bound geological slice to another.[42]

Text over Structure

The *how* would soon be reinforced by the *what*. The resolution of the debate over incorporation versus supplementation was consequential in its own right. But its importance was enhanced as a result of the debate that followed—over which amendments would be added. In limiting the scope of amendments by keeping structural changes at bay during this portion of the debate, Madison ensured that the chosen amendments would almost exclusively be read as rights provisions. Ironically, though, because Madison and his allies had already lost the struggle over how the Constitution would be amended, this outcome helped initiate a structural transformation of its own—not the one Madison was combating, but a transformation nevertheless. Supplementing amendments (of any kind) made it easier to see the Constitution as a text, but supplementing specifically rights-based provisions made it especially easy. Madison and his allies, to be sure, did not intend to reinforce such changes, but—in molding the look and feel of the Constitution—their efforts had that effect.[43]

The irony was thick because Madison's entire commitment to amending the Constitution was predicated on ensuring that its "structure and stamina . . . are as little touched as possible." This had been the ground on which his otherwise divergent reasons for favoring amendments had converged. Politically, he exaggerated the importance of rights-based amendments—insisting in his June 8 speech that "the great mass of people" favored these additions rather than changes to the Constitution's "structure"—to accomplish his primary goal of avoiding fundamental alterations to the Constitution. Meanwhile, his more principled belief that a bill of rights could serve important pedagogical purposes already presupposed such an addition's main value: that it would not otherwise change the Constitution's basic design or function. Crucially, Madison consistently assumed that these new rights provisions would be incorporated into the existing Constitution—they would amount to redundancies here and there and were not likely to cause any harm. Once, though, it became clear these new provisions would be supplemented as an appendix—that they would stand alone as a discrete addition—they threatened to rework the very substance of the Constitution. Any supplementary amendments would have helped recast the original Constitution as a time-frozen, textual artifact. But rights provisions, in particular, amplified this feature by reinforcing the perspective that the first seven articles and the amendments that followed were distinct in kind.[44]

Whether such a possibility consciously worried Madison as the House's attention turned to the amendments themselves is unclear. Likely his primary aims remained political as he focused on assuaging moderate Anti-Federalist opinion. But fresh off his spirited debate with Sherman and the other advocates of supplementation—which had plainly revealed that Madison was acutely concerned about dividing the Constitution into discrete parts—it would not have been a stretch for him to have pondered this prospect. Whatever his state of mind, surely his primary focus turned toward guiding what remained of the committee's report through the House. Even if the first part of the proposal had been rejected, perhaps he could still shepherd his desired amendments through.

Securing this part of the agenda meant thwarting former Anti-Federalists. Few of the twenty proposed amendments in the report addressed their main structural concerns. Most instead focused on protecting rights—many of which have become celebrated constitutional safeguards, such as guarantees for rights to speech, press, worship, petition, and assembly, criminal justice protections, and restrictions against illegal searches and seizures. Some of these initially had been proposed as structural changes, as limitations on the federal government's power, but, presumably to soften their bite, Madison had turned them into rights guarantees. Meanwhile, most of the few structural amendments that were included—one altered the ratio between representatives and constituents, another entrenched the principle of separation of powers, and still another reserved the remainder of power to the states and the people—were chosen under the assumption they would leave the existent Constitution intact. Only two amendments seemed to promise real structural change. A new preamble (shortened from Madison's earlier proposal) would seemingly enhance the federal government's power—by expanding the Constitution's foundation and with that the national government's right to act. And a set of restrictions on state governments' power to interfere with certain rights, such as conscience, speech, and press, limited those governments' traditional authority.[45]

Not included at all in the proposal, then, were a variety of key structural amendments that would have substantially changed the Constitution, measures that constitutional skeptics had demanded throughout ratification and that filled the state ratifying documents from which Madison had culled his recommendations. These included amendments that expanded the size of the House of Representatives, limited the federal government's military and taxing powers (by effectively restoring the requisitions system that had existed under the Articles), restricted the government's authority over elections, restructured the Senate and presidency, and enabled constituents to issue formal instructions to their representatives. In proposing either to curb federal power or revive state power, these amendments all cut in the opposite direction of Madison's lone proposed structural changes. When these conspicuous omissions generated opposition, Madison feigned incredulity. Reiterating an earlier claim, he insisted that the report encapsulated the demands "most strenuously required by the opponents to the constitution." But those who previously had opposed the Constitution would not tolerate this sleight of hand. Aedanus Burke appealed "to any man of sense and candor, whether the amendments contained in the report were any thing like the amendments" people had clamored for. Far from capturing previous complaints, "all the important amendments were omitted in the report," the former Anti-Federalist protested, while those included were "not those solid and substantial amendments which the people expect."[46]

Former Anti-Federalists found Madison's deceit disquieting. Elbridge Gerry complained that Madison and his allies had done all they could to prevent "an open and full examination" of amendments lest it "lay bare the muscles and sinews of the constitution." Burke, who was outspoken and quick-tempered, warned that failing to discuss amendments satisfactorily "would occasion a great deal of mischief." While fellow South Carolinian Thomas Tudor Tucker cautioned similarly that unless amendments received appropriate consideration, many Americans "would feel some degree of chagrin at having misplaced their confidence in the general government" and, consequently, might "endeavor to obtain a federal convention" which could well revive that "party spirit" and those "animosities" that so many feared. The "consequences," he worried, "may be alarming."[47]

Distrust and resentment coursed through the House as a result of these challenges. Tempers flared, and members even challenged each other to duels. Madison came to describe the task as "the nauseous project." Amid the anger, Gerry put forward a motion demanding that the House consider all of the amendments the state conventions had proposed. Anti-Federalists were eager that they receive a fair hearing. But, in a great triumph for Madison's agenda, Gerry's motion was easily defeated. Some structural amendments did get a vote—such as those limiting Congress's authority to tax and permitting instructions to representatives—but they too were rejected with relative ease. Meanwhile, Tucker attempted to revise one of Madison's few structural amendments—that powers not enumerated were retained—by inserting "expressly" before "delegated" (as several states had explicitly requested). But this modification, too, was quickly defeated. After several tense days marked by sharp disagreement, the House approved the committee's report and sent it on to the Senate.[48]

Madison's gambit had worked—by privileging rights provisions he had staved off changes to the Constitution's core structure. Lingering frustrations were proof enough. Samuel Livermore, who supported Gerry's motion, worried that "unless something more effectual was done to improve the constitution," his "constituents would be dissatisfied." Disdainfully, he doubted they would value the proposed amendments "more than a pinch of snuff." Tucker, having failed to secure his desired changes and never one to hide his disdain, dismissed the House's work as "calculated merely to amuse, or rather to deceive." Meanwhile, Senator Richard Henry Lee, although willing to acknowledge that "some valuable Rights are indeed *declared,*" nonetheless complained that "the powers that remain are very sufficient to render them nugatory at pleasure." A similarly blunt assessment led Senator William Grayson to conclude that the submitted amendments "are so mutilated & gutted that in fact they are good for nothing" and, in lulling the American people into a false sense of assurance that their concerns had been addressed, would "do more harm than benefit." Madison had cause to rejoice.[49]

More broadly, he had accomplished many of his principal goals. He had successfully shepherded the amendments through the House, and even though the Senate proceeded to make numerous changes, many of his choices—not to mention the broader impulse that had organized them—survived intact and were submitted to the states for ratification. He was hopeful, if not outright confident, that the second convention movement had been stifled and with that the lingering traces of Anti-Federalism extinguished. On the matter of what was added, then, he could feel a fair manner of accomplishment. But the substance of these additions was as much how they would be added, and on that front Madison had decisively lost.[50]

The irony, then, was that, in working to avoid one kind of substantive reworking of the Constitution, Madison had only obtained another. It was not the transformation he was consciously combating—the amendments did not manifestly change the federal government's powers or its relationship to the states and citizens; but, in remaking the Constitution's basic structure as an interpretive object, it was a transformation nonetheless. It was not simply that amendments would be supplemental. While this fact alone would have encouraged interpreters to draw a meaningful distinction between the original seven articles and later additions, supplementing rights guarantees in particular invited observers to draw an invidious distinction between the two. This proved especially true after the Senate's revisions. Although the House committee report had proposed hardly any changes to the Constitution's structure, it had included a few notable alterations. But the Senate eliminated all of them—both amendments Madison had always assumed were meaningless (like the separation of powers guarantee) and the one he had most valued (protections of certain rights against state government infringement). Because of these final changes, not only was the Constitution divided into discrete parts—each physically set off from the other—but it was now easy to imagine each part as distinct in kind. Had structural amendments comprised the bulk of the additions, the Constitution's two parts, while separated, at least would have resembled each other. Both would have betrayed the kind of holistic structuralism that Madison and so many others had long favored, in which constitutional text and structure—along with the power and liberty they were simultaneously balancing—would have fused into a dynamic whole. But because the new amendments primarily were rights guarantees, the Constitution's separate parts seemed distinct in character—articles of power on the one hand and protections against that power on the other. While the division was hardly tidy, it made it easier to see one part as structure and the other as text.[51]

In a sense, Madison had hoped for just this division. He consciously selected amendments that by and large were rights guarantees to ensure that they would be primarily textual in character so that the existing constitutional structure would survive intact. He even included two amendments (what became the Ninth and Tenth Amendments) to deliberately weaken the textual additions even further. By prohibiting interpreters from considering the Constitution's new enumeration of protected liberties an exhaustive compilation of retained rights, the eventual Ninth Amendment indicted the very project of textualizing rights by implying that any attempt to do so was invariably incomplete. Madison was thus formally incorporating a concern that he had long identified. The previous October, in his most incisive letter on textuality and rights, he had warned Jefferson that "there is great reason to fear that a positive declaration of some of the most essential rights could not be obtained in the requisite latitude"—in other words, that enumerating rights actually limited their scope. Madison worried that his friend was obsessing over the wrong problem—how failing to constitutionally enumerate rights threatened them—when in fact the more dangerous problem was that textualizing rights risked weakening their authority by narrowing those that were enumerated and disparaging those left out. Meanwhile, in what became the Tenth Amendment, Madison had deliberately omitted "expressly" before "delegated" in the key stipulation that "powers not delegated by the Constitution" remained with the states—a conspicuous omission as the exact phrase, "expressly delegated," had been a prominent feature of the Articles of Confederation's own remainder of power provision. When Thomas Tudor Tucker moved to insert "expressly," Madison laid out his rationale for the omission: "it was impossible," he explained, "to confine a government to the exercise of express powers," for "there must necessarily be admitted powers by implication"; otherwise, "the constitution descended to recount every minutiae." Much as the soon-to-be Ninth Amendment indicted efforts to textualize rights, this other proposed amendment indicted efforts to textualize power. So collectively Madison minimized the effect of his proposed amendments by, first, privileging textual over structural changes, and, second, doing all he could to ensure that this new text would not unduly privilege constitutional language by including both a rule of interpretation and a declaration of the remainder of power that expressly discouraged subsequent interpreters from adopting such a narrow, textual perspective on the Constitution.[52]

But because, contrary to Madison's wishes, his textual additions were supplemented to the structure rather than incorporated within it, the division had the opposite effect. The original structure did not dwarf the meaningless text; instead the whole Constitution now seemed more like a text. This occurred for precisely the reason Madison had come to believe that rights guarantees had any value at all: that their form (as clear public markers) could be their substance. An appendix primarily composed of rights provisions not only invited viewers to see these additions as just such markers but also made it easier to see the whole Constitution in just this vein—to draw from the new amendments a model for how to render and read the entire instrument. Madison had gotten more than he bargained for. He had conceded that rights provisions had real pedagogical value, to justify redundancies woven throughout the Constitution, not to suggest that the whole Constitution ought to be seen and understood this way. Yet, by supplementing rights provisions, observers were encouraged to see the entire Constitution more as a set of textual guarantees than as an elaborate, interlocking, holistic system. In this way, the debate over *what* was added was ultimately part and parcel of the debate over *how* it would be added.

Coming to Terms with the "Sacred" Text

Moving forward, constitutional thinkers would literally see the Constitution differently. It is only because Sherman's side prevailed in the debate over incorporation—and, to a lesser extent, because Madison ensured that primarily rights-based guarantees would be added—that it became possible for much later generations to intuitively call the Constitution's first ten amendments a bill of rights. Had they not been supplemented as an appendix, visually set off from the original seven articles, it is inconceivable that they would have acquired this identity. They almost certainly would not have acquired a collective coherence, nor would they have been distinguished, in substance or form, from the rest of the document. Had they been interwoven into the existing text, as Madison had so fervently hoped, they and the original document would have more easily fused into a single form. Perhaps Madison's own, now foreign, conception of the Constitution as simultaneously a grant of power and a bill of rights—at once one and the same—might have endured. Perhaps Americans would have come to think about rights and their constitutional status in wholly different, nontextual ways. In the realm of constitutional imagination, there is no doubt much would have been different.

But, significant though these long-term consequences surely were, others were more immediately felt in the aftermath of the congressional debate, and nowhere more clearly—or revealingly—than in Madison's own constitutional imagination. As he came to terms with the transformative debates of the previous year, he began seeing the Constitution that had been at the heart of those struggles anew.

Throughout the fall of 1789, Madison had much to process. While he could take comfort in achieving his broader goal, he had suffered a decisive defeat. As summer turned to fall and he took stock of the magnitude of his loss, he began imagining the Constitution in a wholly new manner. He had no choice but to agree with something John Laurance had claimed in opposition to incorporation, that the "original [Constitution] . . . was lodged in the archives of the late congress." To think that Congress could subsequently reshape it was, he added, to "suppose several things which never were contemplated." Constitutional disputants now lived in the world that Laurance had mapped. The Constitution had assumed a more immediate temporal and physical character. Envisioned in this form, it more easily became a discrete, time-frozen object in people's minds, one that was permanently locked, both metaphorically and literally, in the historical archive. If any of Madison's arguments in favor of incorporation had been credible, then his own engagement with the Constitution had to alter in kind. He now saw—both figuratively and literally—the Constitution differently. As it became an archival object in his mind, one that was more clearly circumscribed in space and time, its linguistic boundaries sharpened. And, more than at any point previously, he envisaged the importance of the Constitution's language and history anew.[53]

Madison's newly transformed constitutional imagination manifested itself in a host of ways, none more revealing than a forgotten project that he took up anew. It now seems clear that, at this exact moment, Madison returned to his unfinished and relatively long-neglected notes from the Constitutional Convention. He had originally taken those notes—which remain the foundational historical source for understanding the Convention—principally to help him track the proceedings' debates as a participant. Such notes had less immediate purpose once the Convention adjourned, and, thanks to a combination of bad health and mounting committee work, they were incomplete in any case: even though the Convention ran until September 17, his note taking had largely petered out in late August. For two years he gave his unfinished notes little thought. But by the fall of 1789, his outlook had dramatically changed. Now that the Constitution was no longer a single whole but instead a series of discrete texts, each locked in time, he realized that ascertaining constitutional meaning would, at least partly, be a function of establishing the narrative and archive of its creation. With the Constitution taking on a new look that was haltingly coming into view, Madison's notes suddenly served a novel purpose, one not easily glimpsed just a few months prior. As the Constitution transformed as an object in the mind, so too did the notes. And as the notes then transformed in order to reckon with the changing Constitution, so too did the Constitution itself further change in his imagination.[54]

In the fall of 1789, Madison first completed the notes. To do so, he obtained the official records of the Convention—which had been kept by the Convention's secretary, William Jackson, and held in George Washington's custody during the intervening years—and made a personal copy. From these limited records—which consisted primarily of official motions, procedures, and vote tallies—and the rough notes that he still had in his possession, Madison tried to piece together the closing weeks of the Convention. Before long, though, the act of completing morphed into the act of revising. In particular, he chose to integrate the procedural details of the official records, not only in the later entries but throughout the entire corpus of his notes. This, along with additional changes that standardized tone and terminology, afforded the notes a consistency and coherence that they had previously lacked. In doing so, Madison unwittingly transformed his notes from a selective legislative diary written from the perspective of a situated participant to a transcription of legislative debates taken by a detached and meticulous record keeper. Madison's decision to incorporate material from the official records throughout his notes, however, was in some ways less important than the kind of material he chose to integrate. Specifically, he chose to incorporate every record of textual alterations made during the Convention, which meant, as Mary Sarah Bilder has observed, that "instead of reflecting Madison's earlier casual and sporadic interest in textual changes, the Notes silently absorbed the secretary's record of the official textual alterations." Put another way, through these revisions the notes now appeared as though, from the beginning, Madison had been animated by a sustained interest in the linguistic character of the Constitution. In making these changes, he was revealing more about the fall of 1789 than the summer of 1787; he was demonstrating how much his emerging constitutional imagination—the one that had been shaped so significantly by his congressional experience—diverged from the one that had guided him at Philadelphia. These were not conscious deceptions driven by a desire to manipulate the recent past; they were subtle changes brought forth by a new way of seeing the Constitution.[55]

As Madison was reworking his notes, purging them of inconsistencies and clarifying their terminology, he made one particular change that powerfully illustrates the shift. Throughout the summer of 1787, and fully in keeping with his understanding of constitutionalism up to that point, he had used the terms "government" and "constitution" interchangeably. But in revising his notes he found this conflation inapt. He changed the very first sentence, in which he had described the Articles of Confederation as the "federal Constitution," to the "federal system of government." More revealing still, at another point he changed a usage of "Constitution" to "government" because it did not refer to *the* Constitution. Prior to 1789, Madison had downplayed any firm distinction between constitution and government, not because he denied the fundamental character of constitutions but, instead, because he did not instinctively conceptualize constitutional governance as anything but an interlocking system that wove together text and practice into a single, indivisible whole. Now, however, he more clearly saw the Constitution—not necessarily as a system, but as a discrete artifact in historical time. This new field of vision, born most immediately of the debate over incorporating amendments, remade the Constitution as an interpretive object in his mind.[56]

At the same time that Madison was revising his notes, he received a remarkable letter from Jefferson that compelled him to articulate what had slowly been taking shape in his mind. Still in Paris, and now caught up in the throes of France's own revolutionary fervor, Jefferson reflected on the nature of constitutionalism and its relationship to human freedom. Deeply shaped by the ideological currents swirling around him, Jefferson proclaimed that "the earth belongs in usufruct to the living," and that "the dead have neither powers nor rights over it." For Jefferson, this insight impinged upon many separate domains of political, social, and economic life, especially landownership, a topic he had long mulled. But it had especially clear implications for constitutionalism, cutting to the core of its very foundation. If the earth belonged to the living, as he insisted, then "no society can make a perpetual constitution." Indeed, he argued, each constitution expired with the end of each generation (which, based on others' demographic calculations, he determined to last nineteen years). This principle of generational sovereignty superseded any formal acts of popular sovereignty, no matter how fundamental they might have been. Constitutions could be neither fixed nor permanent. When a new generation arrived on the scene, a new constitution needed to come with it.[57]

Madison did not receive this letter until the following January (when Jefferson returned to the United States), but the immediacy and incisiveness of his response reveals how much it consumed his attention. He respected none of his interlocutors as much as Jefferson, so given his deep concerns with his friend's radical zeal he took special care to lay out his disagreements. While Jefferson's belief that constitutions should be revised with each new generation might have been "applicable in Theory," Madison nonetheless insisted that "in practice" it succumbed to "powerful objections." Such "periodical revision" might upset the delicate constitutional balance so vital to republican liberty, and without which liberty (of any sort) remained endlessly elusive. On this score, Madison was channeling commitments that he had long nurtured to play the pragmatic foil to Jefferson's bouts of utopian excess. He had already developed many of these ideas in *Federalist* 49 and 50, explicitly framed as a reaction to Jefferson's earlier views on constitutional revision found in his *Notes on the State of Virginia*. The exchange spoke to a long-standing dynamic—the friction born of two thinkers' competing ideological proclivities and the respect with which they negotiated their disagreements. But it also revealed a new dynamic reflecting the distinct moment in which it took place. In his response, Madison was as troubled by what Jefferson's demand for periodic revisions might mean for "the fundamental Constitution of Government" as he had been when he wrote *Federalist* 49. But, as the revisions to his Convention notes reveal, that phrase, "the fundamental Constitution of Government," had taken on new meaning. So when he pivoted to his first skeptical question—about whether a constitution "so often revised" would "become too mutable to retain those prejudices in its favor which antiquity inspires, and which are perhaps a salutary aid to the most rational Government in the most enlightened age?"—it was refracted through the lens of the sacred, written constitutional text, and these older ideas took on a new resonance. The veneration and sanctity that constitutions required, and which the passage of time could alone ensure, took on new purchase. The fear that a constitution too frequently changed, too often amended, would never gain sacred stature in the public's mind, now meant something more specific. During the debate over amendments, Madison had worried about drawing a sharp distinction between the original Constitution and the alterations that followed. The Constitution needed to form a tightly woven fabric whose seams were undetectable. But now Madison was talking more like his opponents, those who had prevailed in the debate over incorporation and in whose constitutional world he had been forced to take up residence. In the face of Jefferson's striking suggestions, Madison found cause to single out the virtues of the "sacred" text.[58]

Not long thereafter, embroiled in a developing climate of political partisanship, Madison wrote an essay published in the *National Gazette* entitled "Charters." "America has set the example," he proudly proclaimed in it, "of charters of power granted by liberty." Fixating on the written presence of American power, he declared that such charters were "instruments, every *word* of which decides a question between power and liberty," that they were "metes and bounds of government" that "transcend[ed] all other land-marks." He wished "devoutly" that the people might be attached "to their governments as delineated in the *great charters.*" And he hoped, "with a holy zeal," that "these political scriptures" might be scrupulously guarded. The language of sanctity now saturated Madison's meditations on the Constitution as written word. "Parchment barriers" had become "political scriptures."[59]

The outcome of the debate over *how* to amend the Constitution brought momentous consequences—of which Madison's own personal transformation was but one especially striking example. The development of his own constitutional imagination was beginning to reverberate widely across the community of disputants that had been struggling with the Constitution throughout the first year in Congress, if not since it had first appeared. The change was not total or complete. For Madison, Sherman, Gerry, and others, a vision of the Constitution as an imperfect, dynamic system endured. But the next time Congress became embroiled in a debate over the Constitution's meaning, it would do so beneath the shadow cast by its sacred, archival character.

5

The Rules of the Constitution

> If therefore some interpretation of the constitution must be indulged, by
> what rules is it to be governed?
>
> —Fisher Ames, House of Representatives, February 3, 1791

At the very end of the First Congress's third and final session, in early
February 1791, members of the House of Representatives once again found
themselves embroiled in constitutional debate. In the midst of the heated
discussion, Fisher Ames posed the questions that seemed to be in dispute:
"May Congress exercise any powers which are not expressly given in the
constitution; but may be deduced by a reasonable construction of that instrument? And secondly, will such a construction warrant the establishment of the Bank?" As part of his far-reaching financial program, Secretary of the Treasury Alexander Hamilton had asked Congress to charter a
national bank. While the bill establishing such an institution had passed
the Senate with relative ease, disagreement had exploded in the House. The
bank's opponents in that chamber, in a last-ditch effort to prevent its passage, had transformed the matter into a constitutional issue. Setting aside
questions about the relative merits of such an institution, these critics instead asserted that chartering a bank was beyond the scope of Congress's
constitutional authority. Nowhere in the Constitution, they pointed out,
was there a clause empowering Congress to issue charters of incorporation.
The Constitution was once again front and center.[1]

While debate focused on the bank, it turned on how disputants imagined
the relationship between power and language. Picking up where previous
disputes had left off, the bank debate, as Ames succinctly explained, centered on how the Constitution conveyed power and what relationship that

had to the document's text and those tasked with interpreting it. Ames, who strongly supported chartering the bank, recognized why critics were demanding that Congress needed to stick to its expressly delegated powers. "The doctrine that powers may be implied which are not expressly vested in Congress," he noted, "has long been a bugbear to a great many worthy persons." Such people "apprehend that Congress by putting constructions upon the Constitution, will govern by its own arbitrary discretion; and therefore, that it ought to be bound to exercise the powers *expressly* given, and those only." James Madison, the leader of the opposition to the bank in the House, was one of the "worthy persons" Ames had in mind. Just a day earlier, the Virginian had warned that "the doctrine of implication is always a tender one. The danger of it has been felt in other governments. The delicacy was felt in the adoption of our own; the danger may also be felt," he cautioned above all, "if we do not keep close to our chartered authorities." Ames and Madison were both harking back to Anti-Federalists' urgently stated fears that American political leaders might circumvent the constitutional limits to their authority by way of implication—by creatively interpreting language to acquire more power. The solution was, as Ames discerned, to exercise only those "powers *expressly* given" or, as Madison put it, to "keep close to our chartered authorities"—that is, to stick closely to the Constitution's words.[2]

But while Ames recognized this argument, he sharply disagreed with it. Prodigiously gifted, he earned the moniker "the American Demosthenes" for his unmatched oratorical skill in Congress. This flair was on full display during the bank debate, as the youthful Massachusetts lawyer, whose supreme self-regard and acerbic wit cured him of all deference, led the countercharge against Madison's resistance. Like other bank supporters, Ames felt that Congress's authority was not limited to its express powers because it could not be. Although he "did not contend for an arbitrary and unlimited discretion in the government to do every thing," he believed, "we can scarcely proceed without [implied power]." Thankfully, then, at the end of Article I, Section 8, of the Constitution, there was a clause "which empowers Congress to exercise all powers necessary and proper to carry the enumerated powers into execution." Ames "did not pretend" that this clause "gives any new powers," but he did think it clearly "established the doctrine of implied powers" in the Constitution itself. The "necessary and proper" clause—which had been so explosively controversial during the ratification debates—became the dominant means for justifying how Congress enjoyed the power to charter a national bank. Those opposed to the bank responded in turn by claiming that bank supporters had profoundly misread this enigmatic clause.[3]

But this debate over implied powers and the "necessary and proper" clause soon gave way to a broader dispute over not merely what the Constitution said but what the Constitution was. At bottom, it was a debate over what the Constitution demanded. Debating the "necessary and proper" clause forced disputants to ponder what the Constitution necessitated in a weightier sense. Did it necessitate that users stick closely to its words (as bank opponents demanded) or that they exercise their own discretion (as bank supporters insisted)? These rival answers betrayed a deeper disagreement over the Constitution's character, whether it was fully reducible to language and, relatedly, whether it was a complete and finished instrument. Unlike prior debates that had foregrounded the idea that the Constitution was necessarily incomplete, the bank debate compelled disputants to consider, above all, whether the Constitution was complete in a specific sense, namely, whether it offered a complete set of rules. The Constitution provided one set of rules—prescribing what officeholders could do—but did it also provide an additional set of rules explaining how to apply the first set? In other words, did the Constitution come with built-in rules for interpreting such difficult articles like the "necessary and proper" clause? Or, alternatively, was some other authority or institution, operating independently of the instrument, necessary to fill this void and thus bring the incomplete Constitution to life? In many ways, the bank debate became an investigation into this feature of the Constitution's character. Probing it generated fresh problems. And in fashioning solutions to cope with these issues, disputants began imagining the Constitution in explosive new ways.

In particular, in coming to terms with the incomplete Constitution, participants in the bank debate began bringing together different strands of constitutionalism that had thus far remained scattered. It was not evident how the kind of textual imagination pioneered by Anti-Federalists and enhanced during the removal debate—which refracted the Constitution through its words—related to the other kind of textual imagination that had taken shape during the amendments debate—which conceived of the Constitution as a distinctively archival object. The bank debate boasted both dimensions. It was a fight over the Constitution's specific words, a process that further heightened the significance of constitutional language. But the bank debate also became a fight over the history of the Constitution's creation, over what its framers and ratifiers had intended it to mean. Why the bank debate was especially significant, though, was its fusion of these two distinct approaches—a convergence that transformed claims about linguistic meaning into claims about historical meaning. As a way of combating the incomplete Constitution, the opponents of the bank linked the textual Constitution with the sacred, archival Constitution. In so doing, they imagined a new way of fixing the Constitution in all its guises.

The Constitution in a Charged Political Age

The Constitution returned to the center of congressional debate against the backdrop of intense ideological fracturing among the United States' leadership class. While congressmen had continued to debate the document, 1790 witnessed no equivalent to the transformative disputes of 1789. But now in early 1791, just months after the national government had moved to Philadelphia, and because controversial issues were dividing the congressional ranks, the Constitution once again became a dominant subject of political debate.[4]

The ascendance of Alexander Hamilton was the catalyst. Hamilton was an exceptional talent. The New Yorker who had been born into obscurity in the Caribbean was a remarkably quick study, acquiring a commanding knowledge of political science, political economy, and law in short order. During his service in the Continental Army as a staff officer, through his remarkable capacity to organize and analyze information, he had made himself indispensable to Commanding General George Washington. After the war, like his longtime ally James Madison, Hamilton had been deeply influenced by his experience holding public office. During his stint in the Confederation Congress in 1782–1783 especially, he had been horrified by the impotence of the national government and the refusal of the state governments to address the needs of the nation. He had been especially appalled that Congress lacked the crucial financial powers needed to address the massive Revolutionary War debt and stabilize the nation's credit. Obsessed with the importance of public credit, and increasingly convinced that it was the key to any nation's health, throughout the 1780s he became an outspoken leader of the nationalist movement and a fervent advocate for constitutional reform. As a delegate to the Constitutional Convention, he had heartily supported all efforts to strengthen the national government and had defended the resulting document as vigorously as anyone, writing fifty-one of the eighty-five installments of the *Federalist* (by comparison, Madison wrote only twenty-nine). Having already impressed Washington during the war, the first president appointed Hamilton to run the newly created Treasury Department. In September 1789, the Senate confirmed his nomination.[5]

As treasury secretary, Hamilton immediately got to work constructing an ambitious program that aimed to completely overhaul and revitalize the nation's finances and, in the process, remake the American political economy. The Constitution had created the potential for a stronger national government; now Hamilton set his sights on exploiting that new reserve of power to transform the country from, as he saw it, a fledgling, poor, and weak nation into a strong, wealthy, and powerful one. He presented the first wave of reforms in his initial "Report on Public Credit," delivered to the House of Representatives in January 1790. It called for the national government, first, to fund the unpaid national debt and, second, to assume the unpaid state debts in order to consolidate a single public debt. The next piece of his program was unveiled in his "Second Report on Public Credit," sent to the House in December 1790. It recommended chartering a national bank.[6]

These were anything but modest proposals, not least because they were designed to do far more than straighten out national finances; they were also engineered to modify American society itself. Funding, assumption, and the national bank were aimed at consolidating a wealthy creditor class, furnishing a steady national debt, and further transforming the nascent United States from an agrarian into a commercial society. If the United States were to thrive, Hamilton felt its unparalleled natural resources would have to be harnessed, which meant increasing the supply of available investment capital. He believed that a merchant class, properly supported by the government, would produce the kind of surplus wealth that would enable the nation to live beyond the edge of subsistence. And he believed that a properly funded national debt could provide precisely the source of capital merchants needed to effect this transformation. Stabilizing a creditor class that could furnish an available source of capital became paramount. Funding the debt ensured that those who held the old government securities—which thanks to speculation following the war were primarily wealthy merchants in the Northeast—would be confident in repayment, thus turning the debt into a large pool of valuable capital. Assuming the debt consolidated it, tightening the reciprocal link between the national government and the creditor class. A national bank was a further mechanism by which the full strength of the nation's debt could be capitalized, enabling security holders to place wealth in a centralized location available to the entire mercantile community. It would also introduce a stable national currency that merchants could exploit to expand commercial investment. Hamilton and his numerous supporters thus not only envisioned commerce and republicanism as fundamentally intertwined, but also trusted that the kind of commercial development promised by these reforms would help secure the promise of the Revolution.[7]

By embodying such a far-reaching social vision, Hamilton's proposals for the nation's political economy elicited vociferous political opposition. To southerners—especially James Madison (who had long been Hamilton's political ally) and Thomas Jefferson (the secretary of state, recently returned from France, who would become Hamilton's most virulent critic)—the proposed financial program portended a very different America than the one the treasury secretary envisioned. As engines of commercial consolidation, Hamilton's proposals would explode the virtuous base upon which Madison, Jefferson, and others imagined that American republicanism was built—agriculture and the independent yeomen farmers who engaged in it. These changes would encourage frenetic speculation, especially in bank securities—"a mere scramble for so much public plunder" fueled by a "spirit of gambling," as Madison and Jefferson would come to describe it—which would simultaneously sap republican virtue while concentrating power and influence in northeastern commercial markets. By recreating the corrupt traces of Britain in America, Hamilton's program, far from ensuring the promise of the Revolution, fundamentally imperiled it. Finally, at the heart of the southern, agricultural republic Madison and Jefferson sought to defend was the institution of slavery—an institution they professed to be compatible with an independent yeomanry. Hamilton's policies, they feared, would threaten slavery's vitality and, in turn, Virginia's core source of economic and political strength.[8]

The recommendations in the first "Report on Public Credit" were controversial, but nothing divided the political class quite like the proposed national bank. The bank's symbolism sharpened commercial and agrarian interests, underscored the character and distribution of wealth, and helped launch the incipient formation of national political parties. It clarified the inchoate opposition and ideological worldview that the earlier proposals had helped generate. If the bank was chartered, different social groups and geographic regions promised to gain (and significantly so) from such a dramatic restructuring of the nation's capital markets. Southerners and westerners were not foolish to worry that such an institution, to be established in Philadelphia, might favor eastern mercantile interests and entrench their economic and political power. As the primary holders of the nation's consolidated national debt, easterners were likely to purchase the bank's stock. James Jackson, a southerner, began the House debate complaining that "the proposed bank" would "giv[e] undue advantages to the city of Philadelphia" and that "the commercial interest and not the agricultural would receive all the advantage derived from it." It would prop up "an aristocracy which would be possessed of the extraordinary privilege of creating fortunes" through bank stock. Moreover, southerners and westerners had cause to worry that the recently brokered deal locating the nation's new capital on the Potomac River might fall apart if Philadelphia claimed the nation's central financial institution.[9]

Believing that the bank would corrupt America but badly outnumbered politically, those House members who were opposed to its chartering decided to leverage the one tool they hoped might even the odds: the Constitution. By February 1791, the proposed bank had faced little resistance. Even though some senators had opposed it, the bill incorporating it had passed the Senate with relative ease. The irascible William Maclay of Pennsylvania was among the opponents, but with characteristic wit he conveyed in his diary the futility of that opposition: "This day the Bank bill reported, It is totally in vain to oppose." It then appeared poised to pass the House just as easily. Despite three separate readings, no amendments were proposed and no opposition sounded. But then, on February 1, when debate began on whether to approve the measure, some members raised a challenge. The next day, Madison took the floor and after a learned analysis of banks' general utility, he reduced the debate to a single consideration: "Is the power of establishing an *incorporated bank* among the powers vested by the Constitution in the Legislature of the United States?" This speech conformed to the essential paradigms of his best political writing; it was detailed, extensively researched, and organized by careful distinctions, and it laid out three potential grounds on which Congress could claim the authority to charter a bank: "1. The power to lay and collect taxes to pay the debts, and provide for the common defence and general welfare: Or, 2. The power to borrow money on the credit of the United States: Or," most important of all, "3. The power to pass all laws necessary and proper to carry into execution those powers." But upon "Reviewing the constitution," it was "not possible," Madison claimed, "to discover in" any of these clauses "the power to incorporate a Bank."[10]

In claiming that none of these clauses licensed the power to charter a bank, Madison was not only disagreeing with Fisher Ames's broader belief that the Constitution relied upon implied powers or his narrower one that these powers were most clearly authorized by the "necessary and proper" clause; Madison was also, it might have seemed, disagreeing with his earlier self. After all, at the Constitutional Convention he had defended the Virginia Plan's sweeping grant of power on the assumption that enumerating powers was inherently fraught. Then, during ratification, he had defended the "necessary and proper" clause (also known as the sweeping clause) on the basis that complete enumeration was impossible. And finally, during the congressional debate over amendments, he had defended what became the Tenth Amendment on the grounds that no government could ever be reduced to express powers. Time and again, as part of his general suspicion of textualized power, he had refused to reduce the Constitution to its words. He had then defended this form of constitutional imagination when he advocated Congress's right to vest the power of executive removal in the president alone. Unlike Anti-Federalists who had demanded that the Constitution, and the sweeping clause in particular, be shorn of its pervasive indeterminacies, Madison had insisted that Congress required discretionary power since the Constitution's language, on its own, could neither adequately empower nor constrain authority.[11]

Madison's defense of Congress's necessary discretionary authority in these earlier disputes reflected Hamilton's own understanding of the Constitution. In *Federalist* 33, the New Yorker had explained the logic behind the "necessary and proper" clause. It was "only declaratory of a truth, which would have resulted by necessary and unavoidable implication from the very act of constituting a Federal Government, and vesting it with certain specified powers." It was expressly to ensure that the government could execute those specified powers "that the sweeping clause . . . authorises the national legislature to pass all *necessary and proper* laws." If the clause merely made explicit what was already implicit, why was it included? While Hamilton called it a "tautology," he also sketched out a deeper rationale. It was added, he argued, "to guard against all cavilling refinements in those who might hereafter feel a disposition to curtail and evade the legitimate authorities of the Union." Here he alluded to an important point he had made in *Federalist* 25: "Wise politicians will be cautious about fettering the government with restrictions, that cannot be observed," he contended, for "how unequal parchment provisions are to a struggle with public necessity." In other words, the "necessary and proper" clause was not merely an explicit acknowledgment of incidental powers, but more broadly, and more importantly, a recognition that all governments would eventually require powers to serve the public interest that, at an earlier date, would have proved impossible to anticipate. This was exactly why, when Hamilton asked, "who is to judge of the *necessity* and *propriety* of the laws to be passed for executing the powers of the Union?," he insisted that "the national government . . . must judge in the first instance of the proper exercise of its powers." Experience under the fledgling confederation had convinced Hamilton, like most Federalists, that the Constitution authorized Congress to set up a complete government. "If the Federal Government should overpass the just bounds of its authority," he explained, then "the people" can "take such measures to redress the injury done to the constitution." But the importance of these political checks, instead of constitutional checks, presupposed the necessity of implied powers and discretionary authority.[12]

Hamilton carried this thinking forward into the Treasury Department and, through his intimidating presence, helped ensure that it was standard thinking in the First Congress. Consistent with the creative constitutional discretion exhibited and defended during the removal debate, during the disputes over funding and assumption many congressmen defended a power to legislate in the general interest. Accordingly, the debates largely turned on political and policy grounds. Both Michael Jenifer Stone of Maryland and James Jackson of Georgia argued that assumption was unconstitutional. But their claims were mere whispers drowned out by the louder chorus. And, revealingly, even though Madison opposed assumption and even though at one point he expressed doubt that the Constitutional Convention had intended that Congress could assume state debts, he did not explicitly deny that Congress indeed had the power to do so. Meanwhile, both his established hope that Congress would repay Virginia for the portion of the debt the state had already paid, as well as his willingness to negotiate with Hamilton over assumption when they compromised on the location of the national capital implied that Madison thought Congress indeed had the power to assume state debts. This attitude was so prevalent that even Elbridge Gerry—who had consistently denounced implied powers and congressional discretion during the Federal Convention, ratification as an Anti-Federalist, and the removal debate—not only supported assumption but in fact argued that the "necessary and proper" clause, which he had previously vilified, authorized the power. In other words, by late 1790, Hamilton's conception of the Constitution more or less reigned supreme. Madison's decision to challenge it thus marked a fresh departure in constitutional dispute.[13]

Madison's constitutional challenge was so novel, in fact, that not only had no one up to that point thought to oppose the bank on these grounds, but it seems Madison himself only arrived at this position well after Hamilton first called for Congress to charter a national bank. Until early February 1791 when Madison made his fateful speech, the proposed bank had faced virtually no constitutional resistance, even though it had been proposed nearly two months earlier. When the bank was finally taken up by the Senate, none of the senators who sympathized with Jefferson's and Madison's republican opposition to Hamiltonian finance (several of whom had previously harbored Anti-Federalist sympathies) openly questioned the federal government's constitutional right to charter a bank. Hamilton's own report had betrayed this dominant assumption. In fourteen thousand words of analysis, justifications, and responses to hypothetical challenges, the treasury secretary offered not a word on Congress's constitutional authority to charter the bank—it did not even occur to him that he might have to counter such a concern. For weeks, nobody seemed to disagree. Fisher Ames was seemingly not exaggerating when he met Madison's initial objections with incredulity: at a time when so much was disputed, "not a whisper has been heard against [Congress's] authority to establish a bank."[14]

Perhaps Madison feared that challenging the bank on constitutional grounds would contradict his earlier positions, because when he finally opposed the bank on this basis his colleagues in the House were quick to charge him with inconsistency. Theodore Sedgwick, an ardent bank supporter, recalled "the time" before Madison resisted implied powers, "when the energy of [Madison's] reasoning, impressed . . . a conviction, that the power of removal from offices . . . was by construction and implication, vested, by the constitution, in the president." But Madison's change of heart was hardly the only one singled out. William Loughton Smith and Elbridge Gerry, the two most outspoken critics of presidential removal, had become fierce supporters of the bank. As with Madison, the irony was not lost on their peers. Michael Jenifer Stone hoped (with a wink) that "Mr. Smith . . . and some other gentlemen who had opposed [executive removal] would review the arguments they had used upon that occasion," before rethinking their support of the bank. Meanwhile, in so fully gravitating toward Hamilton's vision, Gerry had effectively abandoned the Anti-Federalism that had previously guided him. Madison took Gerry, based on his commentary on the bank, to now be arguing that "Congress may do what they please," which was odd since, recurring to 1787, Gerry had believed that "the powers of the constitution were then dark, inexplicable and dangerous." But now, "perhaps as the result of experience," Madison mocked, "they are clear and luminous!" Such charges of unscrupulous inconsistency pervaded the dispute over the bank.[15]

In studying the debate, it has been logical to see these shifts in constitutional principle as symptomatic of the charged, and increasingly partisan, political culture in which the constitutional debate over the bank developed. By extension, it has been easy to fixate on what motivated members of Congress to interpret the Constitution as they did and, in so doing, to stress the undeniable importance of regional and personal interest. As one congressman shrewdly observed, channeling a prevailing sentiment, "the opinions respecting the constitution seem to be divided by a geographical line"—a blunt way of acknowledging the divisions and interests born of rival modes of production and forms of labor that the bank promised to advance or threaten. That, for example, Madison hailed from a region that so strongly opposed Hamilton's financial program or that the Gerry family's highly profitable mercantile firm stood to benefit from a national bank escaped no one at the time or since. While it is important to recognize that the bank provoked legitimate constitutional issues that, especially in the case of Madison, received thoughtful intellectual engagement, it is also clear that no congressman could fully escape the political dynamics in which their positions took shape.[16]

That said, in terms of how the Constitution was imagined as an object of interpretation and the kind of conceptual freight it came to carry, motivations for mobilizing constitutional argument in the House of Representatives were less important than the ways disputants used the document to justify claims and the images of the Constitution those justifications brought into focus. The motivations—driven by such weighty stakes—helped invest the justifications with particular force. But no matter how important such external factors were, they could not help disputants determine what game of giving and asking for constitutional reasons they ought to be playing. These political and economic factors could not show congressmen how to imagine the Constitution. To grasp how the bank debate further transformed American constitutional imagination, then, requires seeing it as not only a fight over republicanism or slavery or economic power or even simply the Constitution's meaning. Instead, it should be seen as a fight over what practices ought to regulate use of the Constitution and, by proxy, as a fight over what kind of a thing the Constitution needed to be. On this score, constitutional arguments—deeply embedded as they were in the vectors of early national capital and power—carried their own far-reaching implications.[17]

What the Constitution Necessitated

Madison's exceptionally long speech of February 2 that launched the bank debate in the House did not simply center on the Constitution—it centered on the concept of necessity, and specifically on what the Constitution necessitated. In many ways this was because Madison, like virtually all disputants who would follow him, parsed the uncertain meaning of the "necessary and proper" clause and, with that, what it meant to claim that Congress could exercise all powers deemed "necessary" and "proper." As one disputant put it, "the question rested in a great measure on the meaning of the words *necessary* and *proper*." The phrase itself was ubiquitous at the time. But as the ratification debates had already revealed, when wording that was otherwise common and used in several different contexts was thrust into the tentative world of early American constitutionalism, its ubiquity could actually become the source of its deep uncertainty. James Wilson might have had one meaning in mind when he drafted the clause in the Constitutional Convention, but precisely because the phrase was so quotidian its constitutional meaning easily became fraught. In the bank debate that uncertainty was magnified. And in turn, the connections between the clause and the broader concept of constitutional necessity became especially urgent. Thus, while bank supporters thought the "necessary and proper" clause sanctioned implied powers, whereas bank opponents believed it forbade them, these rival positions were just the starting place. In probing the clause's meaning, debate quickly expanded outward and implicated a broader notion of constitutional necessity, one centered not on the meaning of any specific clause but on what the Constitution, in the broadest sense, necessitated. This obligation conjoined two related questions: First, what did the Constitution authorize, and second, what did the Constitution

require of members of Congress who swore an oath to protect it? As Elbridge Gerry remarked at one point, "gentlemen on different sides of the
question do not disagree with respect to the meaning of the terms *taxes, duties, imposts, excises, &c.* or of *borrowing money.*" Instead, they disagreed on
the meaning "of the word *necessary.*" And they diverged because at bottom it
was "a question," as Fisher Ames put it, "of duty." To a large extent, the bank
debate hinged on this issue. All disputants claimed to pay fealty to what the
Constitution necessitated, but the two sides understood this obligation
quite differently. In sketching out their rival conceptions of necessity, they
imagined the Constitution in dramatically divergent ways.[18]

In order to defend the necessity of implied constitutional powers, bank
supporters laid out why the Constitution was, by necessity, an incomplete
instrument. Much like Federalists had repeatedly argued during ratification,
Elias Boudinot of New Jersey stressed the Constitution's inherent imperfections. "As it was very apparent that so long as the human powers were
limited," he claimed, "some inconvenience and difficulties would attend the
most perfect system that could be devised." Accordingly, constitutional users
"would be careful not to be misled by looking for perfection when nothing
higher than human prudence and foresight ought to be expected." Because
perfection was ever elusive in the realm of constitutional design, clearly and
completely enumerating powers was unfeasible. "The ingenuity of man,"
Ames noted, "was unequal to providing, especially before hand, for all the
contingencies that would happen." It was simply impossible "to declare, in
detail, every thing that government may do."[19]

Due to this impossibility, implied powers were necessary. Looking over
the Constitution, Theodore Sedgwick—a talented lawyer from western
Massachusetts whose devotion to Hamilton's policies knew no equal—
observed, "Congress has power to lay and collect taxes, but every thing
subordinate to that end," such as "the means, the instruments," for carrying
it into effect, were implied. The same was true of the government's authority to borrow money. This was because "the subordinate means are so
numerous, and capable of such infinite variation, as to render an enumeration impracticable." These powers must, Sedgwick argued, "therefore be left
to *construction, and necessary implication.*" Boudinot reinforced the point:
"whenever a general power was given," declared the former president of the
Continental Congress, "every necessary means to carry it into execution
were necessarily included." This, to his mind, was "the common sense
of mankind," without the benefit of which "it would require a multitude

of volumes to contain the original powers of an encreasing government that must necessarily be changing its relative situation every year or two."[20]

Correctly interpreted, bank supporters argued, the "necessary and proper" clause itself stressed this understanding of the Constitution. That Article I, Section 8, of the document, which outlined Congress's legislative powers, was punctuated by the so-called sweeping clause seemed to clearly indicate that the Constitution itself acknowledged the necessity of additional powers beyond those enumerated. As noted, Ames thought that "it established the doctrine of implied powers." Sedgwick, meanwhile, in trying "to determine with precision, what was the meaning of the words *necessary and proper,*" what seemed clear, he thought, was that "they do not restrict the power of the legislature, to enacting such laws only as are indispensible." For "such a construction would be infinitely too narrow and limited," defeating the very purpose for having such a clause in the first place, which was to allow the government "to employ" all the "means, *necessary and proper, to* effectuate the ends which are expressed." Elbridge Gerry complained that bank opponents "give the whole clause . . . no meaning whatever," by denying that it pointed to broader powers. "Where the words bear no signification," where the inclusion of the "necessary and proper" clause was interpreted as nothing more than an empty redundancy, he insisted, "we must deviate a little" and give the words in question "a more liberal construction." The clause was built-in acknowledgment of the Constitution's incomplete character.[21]

Because the Constitution was necessarily incomplete, it could not be strictly reduced to the language in which it was written—it could not, as it were, be understood as a written text. Sedgwick believed that "probably no instrument, for the delegation of power, could be drawn with such precision and accuracy, as to leave nothing to *necessary implication.*" Given as much, it was misguided to think that the Constitution was wholly encased within its words. Seemingly operating under this flawed assumption, bank opponents complained that the authority to charter a bank was not expressly enumerated among Congress's powers. "If by *expressly,* express words are meant, it is agreed," Boudinot conceded, "that there are no express words." But, building from the idea that the Constitution was radically incomplete, he thought that "this is the case with most of the powers exercised by Congress," and "if the doctrine of necessary implication is rejected," he did "not see what the supreme legislature of the union could do in that character." Also emphasizing the word "expressly," Gerry insisted that the real question was, "what powers are *delegated?*" It was therefore foolish to think that such powers "only are delegated as are *expressed.*" If this was the case, if constitutional power was fully reducible to language, then, Gerry added, "our whole code of laws is unconstitutional." Summing matters up, John Vining dismissed "objections deduced from the letter of the constitution" because such "definitions" were "so contracted, that they went to explain away every power of Congress." Confining the Constitution to its express words was a recipe for its destruction since "the constitution was a dead letter if implied powers were not to be exercised." Because the Constitution was necessarily incomplete—because, as Boudinot had put it, the government set up by the Constitution "must necessarily be changing" with each passing year— the Constitution could not be imagined as a "dead letter." By necessity, it was to be imagined as a dynamic system.[22]

Once the Constitution was freed from these linguistic shackles, it became possible to understand the value of its words. The key was not that the authority to charter the bank had been omitted from Congress' enumerated powers but instead, as Vining explained, that "no express inhibition of the exercise of the power . . . could be found in the constitution." The Constitution's words were a starting place for interpretation, an entry point into a necessarily unfinished system. It mattered far less that the power to incorporate a bank was omitted than the fact that it was not expressly denied. Since there was nothing in the Constitution clearly forbidding the power, John Laurance, representative of New York and close friend of Alexander Hamilton, reasoned, "we ought not to deduce a prohibition by construction." This logic made good sense to Fisher Ames. As "it would be endless, useless, and dangerous" to specify everything a government could do, it seemed obvious to him that "exceptions of what it may not do, are shorter and safer." Much as the "necessary and proper" clause necessitated implied powers, so too did the soon-to-be-ratified Tenth Amendment necessitate this understanding of the constitutional text. That amendment stated that "the powers not delegated to the United States by the Constitution" were reserved to the states and the people. During the House debate over amendments, Thomas Tudor Tucker had tried to insert "expressly" before "delegated," but his proposal had been soundly defeated. In defending his reading of the Constitution, Laurance explicitly invoked this amendment—and especially the fact it merely said "delegated"—as evidence of the legitimacy of "constructive interpretation." The purpose of the Constitution's words was to expressly deny, not delimit, power. Meaning, except in cases of clear prohibitions, the Constitution delegated far more authority than a confining reading of its words implied. The soon-to-be Tenth Amendment, in concert with the necessary and proper clause, revealed as much. Appreciating that the Constitution was something distinct from a mere text, something its own words in fact made plain, fundamentally altered how interpreters were to make sense of the document's silences.[23]

Convinced that the Constitution's fundamental character necessitated implied powers, bank supporters went about explaining how these unstated powers could be discovered. They readily acknowledged that "the construction of the Constitution . . . must be," as Ames put it, "guided and limited." The government could not do everything. Bank supporters thus tried to discern implied powers based on the logic of necessity, based on what the Constitution itself, rightly understood, necessitated. Gerry was assured that, by certain "rules of construction," the "constitution, authorize[d]" the proposed bank. Similarly, Ames argued that "the power to incorporate a Bank" was "a necessary incident to, the entire powers to regulate trade and revenue, and to provide for the public credit and defence." Meanwhile, if interpreters looked to "the context of the constitution," Laurance believed, they would find that "a full uncontroulable power to regulate the fiscal concerns of this union is a primary consideration in this government." Thus, he went on, "it clearly follows, that it must possess the power to make every possible arrangement conducive to that great object." So while it was a "construction" to claim that the Constitution sanctioned the authority to charter a bank, given this kind of logical connection between what the Constitution required and what then followed, Laurance judged it "an easy and natural construction." Boudinot drew out the logic of this thinking. While the power to charter a bank "was not contained in express words," nonetheless, he argued, "it was necessarily deduced by the strongest and most decisive implication." This was because, as he contended, the bank "*was a necessary means to attain a necessary end.*"[24]

Tracing the logic of necessity, in other words, meant linking ends and means. Congress had the authority to charter a bank because it was the means for carrying out essential ends. Often, bank supporters insisted, those ends were specific and located in the Constitution itself, nowhere quite as dramatically as in the preamble. These opening words of the document best captured, according to Laurance, "the principles of the government and the ends of the constitution." They offered a sweeping overview of the Constitution's guiding purpose and the national government's charge. Agreeing with this assessment, Gerry insisted that the Constitution was "the great law of the people." And their sovereign authority was nowhere more clearly instantiated than in the document's opening words: "We, the people." What followed these momentous words, and which Gerry read aloud, identified "the great objects for which the constitution was established" and "in administering it," he instructed, "we should always keep them in view." Especially important were the great ends of providing for "the common defence and promoting "the general welfare," as both were not only in the preamble but also restated among Congress's expressed powers in the first clause of Article I, Section 8. "The means" for obtaining these objects were so important, Gerry stressed, "we ought not to omit a year, month, or even a day." Bringing the bank into this picture, Ames announced that "the preamble of the constitution" showed "that a Bank is not repugnant to the spirit and essential objects of that instrument."[25]

Sometimes the ends were implied, though, based less on what the preamble or other parts of the document directly emphasized and more on what was required of the kind of government the Constitution was meant to set up. Unlike the individual state governments, the new national government was alone responsible for addressing broad problems that confronted the nation as a whole. There were certain powers, Vining argued, that "appertain[ed] to a nation" and were automatically delegated to the general government presiding over that nation. While not explicitly laying out this requirement, the preamble itself clearly pointed in this direction, Ames inferred, especially by empowering the federal government to look after the "general welfare," for it "vested Congress with the authority over all objects of national concern or of a general nature." Indeed, the "necessary and proper" clause itself—by identifying a set of powers that were vested not in Congress or any specific department but generally "in the Government of the United States"—invited this broader reading of the preamble. But even if the Constitution had failed to make this clear, any national government, by definition, possessed general powers that none of the states were competent to exercise. James Wilson had forcefully made this point in 1785 in his penetrating essay *Considerations on the Bank of North America*. Now, in 1791, bank supporters were doing the same. "The power to establish a national bank must reside in Congress," William Loughton Smith contended, "for no individual state can exercise any such power." In this regard, several bank advocates claimed that the national government established by the Constitution (like the proposed bank) was itself akin to a corporation, insofar as "it has tacitly annexed to its being," Ames explained, "various powers which the individuals who framed it did not separately possess," but that were "essential to its effecting the purposes for which it was framed."[26]

The prior example of the Bank of North America, which had been chartered by the Continental Congress in 1781 and had been the subject of Wilson's 1785 defense, further illustrated the legitimacy of general powers, bank supporters argued. Since nobody denied that "the present government is vested with powers" at least "equal to those of the late confederation," Laurance noted, it was revealing that "the old government possessed certain very limited powers over the United States, and yet they had incorporated a bank." In spite of the limitations of the Articles, the bank had been valid because the separate states were inherently incapable of managing certain national responsibilities. But, as importantly, the bank's legitimacy had been confirmed by the public's acceptance of it. Clearly the previous Congress had not exceeded its constitutional mandate, bank supporters reckoned, for it had never been "criminated for so doing." Despite lacking any "*expressly* delegated" power, Congress had faced no opposition from the states. In fact, Ames and Gerry averred, the "public sense" fully "supported the measures." The public had already tacitly recognized that establishing a national bank legitimately fell under the inherent ends of national government. Consequently, the new Congress (that otherwise had more power than the previous Congress) was fully justified in pursuing this course.[27]

More often, however, the essential ends that bank supporters emphasized, and for which they claimed chartering the bank was necessary, were even farther removed from the Constitution's contents. Appeals to the nature of national governance, and what it necessitated, had already begun carrying them in this direction, and from there they only drifted farther afield. Several defenders of the bank stressed the more general ends for which the Constitution was originally adopted. Reminding House members of the "defects and incompetency" of the "late confederation," Laurance "inferred" that "the constitution under which we now act was formed" supposing that the national government would have the powers it had so miserably lacked under the Articles of Confederation. Assuming otherwise, he insisted, "involves the grossest absurdity." Gerry added, "The causes which produced the constitution were an imperfect union, want of public and private justice, internal commotions, a defenceless community, neglect of the public welfare and danger to our liberties." If, Gerry reasoned, "these weighty causes produced the constitution," and ensured it received the powers for dealing with them, then it was also safe to assume that these causes "authorize[d] Congress to make all laws necessary and proper" for addressing these problems that had originally inspired the Constitution.[28]

Even more remote from the Constitution, bank supporters also deduced that the Constitution guaranteed a complete government. If some power was necessary and essential to that end, it was thus fairly sanctioned. "If we have not the power to establish" a bank, Ames figured, then the government could not easily address sudden emergencies—such as the capacity to quickly raise money to pay for sudden wars. If this was the case, he concluded, "our social compact is incomplete." Vining, who despite being one of Congress's more measured members had a penchant for ostentatious metaphor, made much the same point in particularly poetic fashion. To those who refused to assume that the nation's governing document provided all necessary authority, he compared "the constitution to a horse finely proportioned in every respect to the eye, and elegantly capari[s]oned, but deficient in one, and the most essential requisite, that of ability to carry the owner to his journey's end." Vining said he would rather "mount the old confederation, and drag on in the old way, than be amused with the appearance of a government so essentially defective." By force of simile, the new government had to possess all necessary power.[29]

Bank supporters also defended the necessity of chartering the bank on the basis of the vaguest of all ends: public utility. Congress's presumed right to incorporate the bank, Sedgwick claimed, was consistent with "common sense" since it was based on the assumption that "laws should be established on such principles and such an agency" as to "effect the ends expressed in the constitution, with the greatest possible degree of public utility." Ames meanwhile defended a particular "rule of interpretation," in part because it "promotes the good of society." If these sorts of ends were necessary, then it was anything but obvious which kinds of ends were unnecessary.[30]

Bank supporters' refusal to differentiate between specific and general ends spoke to a deeper form of constitutional uncertainty with which they were struggling. While they were fond of claiming that implied powers were easily discoverable in the Constitution, strikingly, just as often they conceded that these powers were indeterminate, that they were not in fact so easily derived from a sound reading of the instrument. At these moments, bank supporters stressed how all interpretations of implied powers were invariably subjective. Even if these readings were not "arbitrary," nonetheless Ames conceded, they could never be "absolutely certain." This realization did not invalidate these interpretations, but it did characterize them in a new light. It emphasized that they were as much born of human judgment as derived from the Constitution's putative contents.[31]

This acknowledgment of interpretative uncertainty began with the concept of necessity itself. Among bank supporters, nobody probed the subject quite like Elbridge Gerry. As a contemporary observed, Gerry possessed "a great degree of confidence and goes extensively into all subjects that he speaks on," no matter how clumsily or unconventionally. Speaking on this topic proved no exception. With so many different disputants defining "necessary," he laid a firmer foundation from which to understand its meaning. To do so, he quoted one of the most famous interpretive rules found in William Blackstone's *Commentaries on the Laws of England:* "'the fairest and most rational method to interpret the will of the legislator, is by exploring his intentions at the time when the law was made, by *signs* the most natural and probable,'" and among "these signs" were the words themselves. With respect to these, Gerry noted, "the Judge observes that 'they are generally understood in their usual and most ordinary signification, not so much regarding the grammar as their *general* and *popular* use.'" Herein lay the object of investigation, to illuminate the meaning of "necessary" by looking outside the Constitution to popular usage of the term in question. And, upon investigation, Gerry was convinced that "the word does not admit of a definite meaning" because it "varies according to the *subject* and *circumstances*." Lacking an essential meaning, "necessary" changed based on its context. Gerry invoked several examples—the physical necessity of surrendering a garrison when surrounded, the legal necessity of paying a creditor, the artificial necessity of providing a lawyer more than legal fees—before parsing each. If the soldiers did not surrender, they would be deprived of sustenance and perish. If the debtor failed to pay the creditor, he would be jailed but not want for sustenance. If a client did not provide his lawyer more than legal fees, he would have violated the dictates of custom, but would walk away free to tell the story. "To determine the time, quantum, mode, and every regulation *necessary* and proper" was endlessly complex. There was no necessity, in other words, to the meaning of necessary. It was not a product of the sweeping clause, or even the Constitution; it was instead a function of linguistic usage and thus evolved with convention.[32]

If "necessary" could not be pinned down, how could constitutional users tell the difference between a necessary implied power and an unnecessary one? Perhaps such a task was mired in uncertainty, a possibility most powerfully examined by Theodore Sedgwick, whose congressional speeches were as cogent as they were penetrating. Noting the resistance to implied powers, he remarked that whichever way bank supporters moved they were met by claims that "*the constitution is in danger.*" The only way, it seemed, to make use of the Constitution involved "attempting, what perhaps would be found impracticable," which was "to fix by general rules, the nice point within which Congress would be authorized to assume powers by construction and implication, and beyond which they may be justly considered as usurpers." In other words, even though implied powers were essential to a correct understanding of the Constitution, it was impracticable, arguably impossible, to fix by general rules the exact distinction between those implied powers that could be legitimately exercised and those that could not. From the beginning, bank supporters acknowledged that this was the crucial dividing line. As William Loughton Smith conceded, nobody was arguing that "whatever the legislature thought expedient was therefore constitutional." But now Sedgwick was admitting something more revealing—that even though there was a difference between authorized and unauthorized implied powers, and even if it was critical to ascertain that distinction, nonetheless it was impossible through prior rules to differentiate legitimate from illegitimate authority. The Constitution could not, on its own, establish the distinction.[33]

Given this residual uncertainty, all that could distinguish a credible exercise of power from an unlicensed one was human judgment. Nothing else would suffice. While Fisher Ames had "no desire to extend . . . beyond the limits prescribed them," still "in cases where there was doubt as to its meaning and intention," he "thought it his duty to consult his conscience and judgment to solve them." And "even if doubts" would still "remain on two different interpretations"—as would often be the case involving disputed implied powers—Ames would "embrace" the reading "least involved in doubt." Similarly, "in cases where the question was, whether a law was necessary and proper to carry a given power into effect," Smith mused, "the members of the legislature had no other guide but their own judgments." Ultimately, in sorting out whether a potential implied power was legitimate or not, "each member," Gerry avowed, "must determine for himself." This was what Sedgwick meant when he noted that "the whole business of legislation, was a practical construction of the powers of the legislature." It was a practice, an activity that invariably relied upon human judgment. Most revealing of all, Gerry defended bank supporters by arguing that "the liberty we have taken in interpreting the Constitution, we conceive to be *necessary.*" At bottom, the Constitution necessitated interpretive liberty—the need to exercise the kind of judgment that alone could clarify outstanding indeterminacies.[34]

All of this brought bank supporters to their decisive point: that the Constitution was, by necessity, incomplete precisely because it could not exhaustively delineate the rules for its own application. The Constitution was a set of supreme rules for all subsequent political practice. In theory, these rules arbitrated what was permissible. But if the Constitution was a cluster of rules, did it come with an accompanying set of instructions for applying them? Some bank supporters sounded doubt by stressing the problem of infinite regress. A rule could seem clear and unambiguous. But the application of that rule to a concrete situation, perhaps novel and unanticipated, could be done well or poorly. Thus, presumably another rule was needed to explain how to apply the first rule. But the original rule would need a second rule explaining how to apply it, and a third rule would be needed to explain how to apply the second—and so on and so forth. Discretionary application was inevitable, and the Constitution, despite containing the overarching principles through which law could be made, could never itself fully explain how to apply those principles. Judgment was inevitable precisely because the Constitution lacked, by necessity, an accompanying prior set of rules completely explaining application. As Fisher Ames so powerfully explained, "The Constitution contains the principles which are to govern in making laws; but every law requires an application of the rule to the case in question." Thus, crucially, "We may err in applying it," and because of that, "we are to exercise our judgments, and on every occasion to decide according to an honest conviction of its true meaning."[35]

Because the Constitution was an incomplete rule giver, interpretation was never a passive act. Gerry made this point most emphatically. "The interpretation of the constitution, like the prerogative of a sovereign, may be abused," he acknowledged, "but from hence the disuse of either cannot be inferred." Since the task of interpreting the Constitution could not be wholly prescribed by prior rules, it was equivalent in its own right to a power of government. It involved active judgment and exertion of authority. It was inevitable; its "disuse" was impossible. The key, thus, was recognizing that, because constitutional interpretation could never swing free of politics, constitutional checks meshed seamlessly with political judgments. "In the exercise of prerogative the minister is responsible for his advice to his sovereign," Gerry added, "and the members of either House are responsible to their constituents for their conduct in construing the constitution." Since interpreting the Constitution always required judgment, the final check on constitutional interpretation lay in the people themselves. As Hamilton had insisted in *Federalist* 25, the people, not the Constitution, were the only genuine check on the Constitution's meaning. The Constitution, in no meaningful sense, could serve as a complete, final check on its own usage.[36]

Echoing what Federalists had anticipated during ratification and so many defenders of removal had subsequently trumpeted, this invariable need for contemporary judgment emphasized and justified the pivotal role that Congress had to play in the constitutional scheme. If judgment was required, no entity was better positioned or more legitimately authorized to exercise it. "It is for the house to judge," Ames declared adamantly, "whether the construction which denies the power of Congress" to incorporate a bank "is more definite and safe." Laurance reminded his fellow House members, "the constitution was in their hands," which meant "they were the interpreters of it." Constitutional uncertainty was left, Sedgwick contended, "to the honest and sober discretion of the legislature." Because such discretionary authority was unavoidable, exercising it was not a choice but a necessity.[37]

Moreover, congressional discretion was not merely theoretical. To bank supporters it had already become a staple of federal governance under the Constitution ever since the First Congress had initially assembled. Both William Loughton Smith and Boudinot each cited several instances when "Congress exercised power by implication." Ames was even more emphatic. "If Congress may not make laws comformably to the powers plainly implied, tho not expressed in the frame of government," he argued, "it is rather late in the day to adopt it as a principle of conduct." Because "a great part of our two year's labor" would be "lost," he claimed, since "we have scarcely made a law in which we have not exercised our discretion." The bank bill did not stand alone in this respect; on trial was the entirety of the First Congress's work.[38]

Bank supporters thus conveyed, with a tacit philosophical power, the reasons why implied powers were defensible, which had less to do with the power to construct a bank or even the imperatives of the "necessary and proper" clause than with the Constitution's essential character. What kind of rule giver would the Constitution be? Never, the argument went, a fully complete one. From "the nature of things this must ever be the case," Sedgwick insisted, "for otherwise, the constitution must contain" not only all necessary laws, "but also a code so extensive, as to adapt itself to all future possible contingencies." To fully function, not only did the Constitution need a complete set of laws (one set of rules) but also a sufficiently extensive code (a separate set of rules that dictated how the first set would be applied). Such a feat was simply beyond the powers of human construction. By failing to appreciate the inherent dynamism of the Constitution, bank opponents threatened to turn the instrument into a "dead letter," into a meager, useless text.[39]

The Necessity of the Written Constitution

If bank supporters contended that the Constitution could never be reduced to a set of rules, decipherable independent of the judgment of constitutional users, it became the task of bank opponents to show why supporters were wrong, to show that the Constitution necessitated something else. "The latitude of interpretation required by the bill," Madison argued, "is condemned by the rule furnished by the constitution itself." The Constitution itself furnished a rule; it was just a matter of finding and applying it, of showing how the Constitution was something distinct from the radically incomplete instrument bank supporters had claimed it to be. Even though they were significantly outnumbered, bank opponents that joined Madison—including most notably James Jackson, Michael Jenifer Stone, and William Branch Giles—spent much of their energy trying to accomplish just this: to demonstrate that the Constitution was a self-contained instrument and that Congress's primary job was not to exercise creative discretion, but to decipher the tasks necessarily prescribed for it by that instrument. This meant that where bank defenders had imagined the Constitution an incomplete, dynamic system, bank opponents instead imagined it distinctively as a complete and static text.[40]

In so doing, bank critics revived Anti-Federalists' anguished pleas from the ratification debates that the Constitution's vague provisions, particularly the "necessary and proper" clause, had to be tied down in some way, fixed to some set of determinate interpretive rules. But despite this similarity, opponents of the bank faced an altogether distinct task than the Anti-Federalists had. The latter had demanded that the Constitution's most troubling clauses be purged of its pervasive ambiguities precisely because they suspected future congressmen would credibly make use of them just as bank supporters had—as permission to exercise vast political discretion. Bank opponents thus somehow had to explain how the Constitution as constructed reined in the tendencies Anti-Federalists had otherwise assumed inevitable.

Critics of the bank began by denouncing their opponents' understanding of "necessary." In surveying the bill, Madison attended to the "diffuse and ductile terms which had been found requisite to cover the stretch of power contained in the bill." He then "compared them with the terms *necessary* and *proper*," asking if bank supporters' definitions were "a fair and safe commentary on the other." Giles, a young, outspoken Virginian who had joined the House only two months prior to take the place of the deceased Theodorick Bland, was not shy about voicing his opposition to the bank. Edward Carrington had told Madison that Giles possessed "real genius" and would prove a worthy ally. The young Virginian did his best to earn that praise. He claimed that bank supporters, "finding the usual import of the terms used in the Constitution to be rather unfavorable . . . [have] favored us with a new exposition of the word *(necessary)*" one that "as applicable to a mean to produce an end, should be construed so as to produce the greatest possible quantum of public utility." Giles, in contrast, suggested, "the true exposition of a necessary mean to produce a given end, was that mean, without which the end could not be produced." Contrary to what bank advocates insisted, the word "necessary" did not suggest implied license or "unlimited discretion"; it denoted only what was essentially connected, and thus absolutely necessary, to a given end. The clause's "meaning must, according to the natural and obvious force of the terms and context," Madison claimed, "be limited to means *necessary* to the *end,* and *incident* to the *nature* of the specified powers." Stone, one of the House's most frequent and effective speakers, fully grasped the import of Madison's observation. "Gentlemen tell us that if we tie up the constitution too tight, it will break; if we hamper it we cannot stir; if we do not admit the doctrine, we cannot legislate at all." The problem, Stone thought, lay in the accompanying inference, that "with a kind of triumph," bank supporters "say that implication is recognised by the constitution itself" in the "necessary and proper" clause. But this clause was hardly the condemnation of constitutional language that bank supporters claimed. Instead, he went on, it "was intended to defeat those loose and proud principles of legislation which had been contended for. It was meant to reduce legislation to some rule." The clause hardly constituted a tacit recognition of the impossibility of interpretive rules. Properly understood, it was precisely such a rule.[41]

In parsing the sweeping clause, bank opponents maintained that there were inherent limits to congressional interpretive discretion. "Whatever meaning this clause may have," Madison asserted, "none can be admitted, that would give an unlimited discretion to Congress." The fact that incidental powers, some of which surely had to exist in the Constitution, were difficult to define, was not sufficient reason to defer so willingly to congressional judgment. For, as Stone put it, "the sober discretion of the legislature . . . was the very thing intended to be curbed and restrained by our constitution." Indeed, "never did any country more compleatly unite in any sentiment," he added, "than America in this—'That Congress ought not to exercise, by implication, powers not granted by the constitution.'" Giles challenged how quickly bank defenders gave up on the possibility that the Constitution might, on its own, furnish a usable set of interpretive rules. "I presume the great object of the constitution was to distribute all governmental rights between the several State governments and the government of the United States," he argued; "the expediency therefore of the exercise of all constitutional rights . . . is properly contemplated and decided by the constitution, and not by the governments amongst which the distribution is made." Surely the Constitution could speak for itself; surely it could command those who were subject to its authority.[42]

For the bank's detractors, part and parcel of constraining their opponents' conception of the Constitution was undermining the ends–means distinction that was central to it. The means needed to flow from a firmer set of rules than bank supporters allowed. Madison had warned about the doctrine of implication, what Stone poetically likened to a "serpent" poised "to sting and poison the constitution." There had to be limits, Madison thought, to how freely legislators could move from stated ends to seemingly implied means. As he imagined hypothetically, if the federal government could borrow money and if that end implied the means of accumulating capital, then what would stop anybody, based on that first inference, from assuming that the power to accumulate capital was now itself a legitimate end, one that then legitimated other means, including the authority to charter a bank? "If implications, thus remote and thus multiplied, can be linked together," Madison warned, "a chain may be formed that will reach every object of legislation."[43]

Especially unnerving was how bank supporters had exploited the Constitution's preamble, claiming that it was a comprehensive statement of ends. Madison was shocked that these opening words had "produced a new mine of power." After reading it aloud, Stone cried, "Here is your constitution! Here is your bill of rights! Do these gentlemen require any thing more respecting the powers of Congress, than a description of the ends of government? . . . I would ask if there is any power under heaven which could not be exercised within the extensive limits of this preamble?" Giles charged similarly that, were bank supporters right, "the detail of the constitution would have been wholly unnecessary farther than to designate the several branches of the government, which were to be intrusted with this unlimited, discretionary choice of *means* to produce these specified ends." By bank supporters' logic, Jackson complained, the two words, "'general welfare,'" could alone "justify the assumption of every power." Simply put, the extensive text of the Constitution alone cut against bank supporters' conception of the document. Had the diffuse, holistic context they had trumpeted been sufficient, the specific provisions of Article I never would have proved necessary. Surely the document's other specifications could supply interpretive guidance. The ends specified in the preamble, Giles observed, merely gestured toward "the subsequent regulations of which the constitution is composed." Any patient observer of the Constitution would recognize that interpretive regularities were hardly the product of subsequent construction, but were fixed within the document itself.[44]

To bank opponents, the recently proposed amendments to the Constitution (which in early 1791 were on the verge of being ratified by the requisite number of states) further condemned bank supporters' misreading of the "necessary and proper" clause and the belief in implied powers they had claimed it licensed. Madison, who of course was most responsible for the existence of these amendment, specifically cited what would become the Ninth and Tenth Amendments. He argued that the former—which laid out that the enumeration of certain rights in the Constitution should not be read to deny others—afforded "a rule of construction" that excluded "the latitude of interpretation" that bank supporters "contended for." Meanwhile, the soon-to-be Tenth Amendment worked in tandem with the preceding amendment by "excluding every source of power not within the constitution itself." Madison's understanding of these two amendments had changed dramatically since he first introduced them in the House—and several bank defenders were happy to push back against his new logic by invoking his prior commitments. When Madison had originally defended what would become the Tenth Amendment, and particularly its omission of "expressly" before "delegated," he had maintained, in insisting that no government could be confined to express power, that implied powers were unavoidable. By 1791, though, his constitutional imagination had much changed. Previously a critic of enumeration, Madison now deemed the "essential characteristic" of the government established by the Constitution to be that it was one "of limited and enumerated powers."[45]

Other bank opponents built on Madison's new logic to articulate what kind of thing the Constitution was. They used the eventual Tenth Amendment to help pull together their many strands of argument—regarding the meaning of "necessary," the difference between means that were essential to an end and those that were merely incidental to it, and the point of enumerating powers—to imagine the Constitution in a radically distinct way from their opponents. As Giles asserted, in their various arguments bank supporters "seem to have forgotten the peculiar nature of this government," a nature which "Congress themselves have made an express declaration in favor of" in the Tenth Amendment. The "*sine qua non*" of the new federal government set up by the Constitution was, "it being composed of mere chartered authorities," that "all authority not contained within that charter" was retained outside of that government. The eventual Tenth Amendment was textual reminder of the Constitution's textual identity. This was its essence—the necessary starting place for understanding what it necessarily entailed and exactly why Madison declared that the bank bill "was condemned by its tendency to destroy the main characteristic of the constitution."[46]

The Constitution's writtenness also negated another of bank supporters' favored arguments: that the chartering of the Bank of North America under the previous Congress had established the necessity of implied, general powers. The previous bank, James Jackson noted, had been chartered "in time of war" when "publick exigencies pleaded" for it, but neither dire circumstances nor popular support could change the fact that it represented "an infraction of the constitution" from which the Continental Congress had derived its authority. It was "an illegitimate, a bastard production," he contended, affording no legal precedent. As "the child of necessity," Madison added, it never could have been justified by the Articles. It was, revealingly, an "infraction of parchment rights." Madison had objected to the original chartering back in 1781 (something he was quick to remind his congressional peers of), but most of his colleagues a decade ago had paid little attention to questions of textual constitutional authority. Madison was now projecting a strong conception of written constitutionalism back onto this notable episode, a choice that betrayed how bank opponents were coming to conceptualize their Constitution in terms of the language in which it was codified.[47]

Thinking in terms of this avowedly written constitutional imagination, bank critics issued their strongest condemnation of all: that, most ominously, bank supporters' arguments threatened to eliminate the Constitution itself. By "levelling all the barriers which limit the powers of the general government," as Madison put it, proponents of the bank bill were gravitating far from the legitimate locus of their power: the Constitution's language. If powers were "not there"—not in the words themselves—"the exercise of it involves the guilt of usurpation." Stone argued, "if gentlemen are allowed to range in their sober discretion for the means, it is plain they have no limits. By the cabalistical word incident, your constitution is turned upside down; and instead of being *a grant of particular powers,* guarded by an *implied negative* to all others, it is made to *imply all powers.*" Worse still, instead of "the people fairly g[iving] up their liberty," through "subtle constructions," they would be "unexpectedly tricked out of their constitution." If proponents of the bank bill did not tread carefully, their opponents charged, the Constitution might exist in name alone. Having usurped all relevant power, the nation would be governed by the will of an unchecked majority.[48]

The Constitution's written character was pressed into service to upend the image of constitutional stewardship bank champions had so studiously constructed. If incorporating the bank was merely "left to legislation," at the discretion of Congress, "all written compacts were nugatory," Stone declared. In a similar vein, Jackson complained, "if the sweeping clause . . . extends to vesting Congress with such powers . . . we shall soon be in possession of all possible powers, and the charter, under which we s[i]t, will be nothing but a name." Stone tendered the most urgent and animated plea:

Nay, if the principles now advocated are right, it is the duty of the legislature of the union to make all laws—not only those that are necessary and proper to carry the powers of the government into effect, but all laws which are convenient, expedient, and beneficial to the United States. Then where is your constitution! . . . Is it written? No. Is it among the Archives? No. Where is it? It is found in the sober discretion of the legislature—it is registered in the brains of the majority.

Bank opponents were imagining the Constitution fundamentally as a text. As its very existence was bound up in its language and the barriers it erected, the only way to preserve its identity was to police the boundaries that its words set. No alternative could preserve its tangible existence. Since the instrument's capacity to protect liberty was derived from its felt existence, this marked no small insight. Should bank supporters get their way, the Constitution would exist only in the mind, bending to the will of the majority of legislators, based on whatever they deemed necessary. For Stone, two conceptions of the Constitution thus hung in the balance: one real and identifiable, the other fabricated and imagined. Only bank opponents, he suggested, appreciated "the sacredness of the written compact."[49]

Despite these frustrations, bank opponents had a difficult time specifying how to secure the internal constitutional regulations they demanded. They were emphatic about the existence of these regulations and could extensively explain why abandoning the search for them violated the Constitution's defining character. But it appeared as though the bank's defenders had a point. Eventually, no matter how clear its meanings, the Constitution would need additional rules to bring it life. Even if it was distinctively a written text, something beyond the text would be required to resolve the ambiguities inherent in its language. As Fisher Ames put it, it was easy to illuminate the "danger[s] of implied power." But, despite such protestations, despite denouncing bank supporters' readings of the "necessary and proper" clause and, more broadly, the Constitution itself, bank opponents had offered no credible substitute in their place. "While the opposers of the Bank exclaim against the exercise of this power by Congress, do they," Ames asked skeptically, "mark out the limits of the power which they will leave to us, with more certainty than is done by the advocates of the Bank?" To the contrary, "their rules of interpretation . . . will be found as obscure . . . as that which they condemn." Rather than identifying plausible rules, Ames concluded, "they only set up one construction against another"—what amounted to endless criticism devoid of positive suggestion, subjective inference dressed up as objective constitutional essence. Try as they otherwise might, bank opponents tacitly conceded this ground. "It is not pretended," Madison granted, "that every insertion or omission in the constitution is the effect of systematic attention. This is not the character of any human work, particularly the work of a body of men." Madison could not fully abandon his earlier arguments—he still accepted that the Constitution was, in a certain sense, incomplete. Meanwhile, when Giles proclaimed, "observations arising from the constitution itself were of two kinds: The right of exercising this authority is either expressed in the constitution, or deducible from it by necessary implication," he was exposing the difficulty that Ames had highlighted. A certain form of deduction was required—not to criticize others' uses of the Constitution, but to delineate appropriate uses of the sweeping clause from invalid ones. If judgment were indeed required, then what rule of interpretation would put judgment on the right path?[50]

Diving into the Past

Madison had anticipated and answered this challenge by appealing to the history of the Constitution's creation, arguing that the bank bill "was condemned by the apparent intention of the parties which ratified the constitution." In his original, lengthy February 2 speech that had launched the whole debate, historical appeals were pivotal to his stipulated "rule of interpretation"—one that acknowledged the need for constitutional interpretive judgment while undercutting Congress's right to exercise it. When constitutional meanings were unclear, "the meaning of the parties to the instrument, if to be collected by reasonable evidence, is a proper guide." In moments of doubt like those bank supporters had claimed were inevitable, the meaning of the Constitution could be determined by appealing to the original intent of its framers. No matter how strongly one could infer rules of interpretation from the Constitution's evident contents, there would always be uncertainties, moments when judgment was required. To bank supporters, Madison was willing to concede at least this much. But the judgment need not belong to Congress; it could be the original parties to the instrument. Exasperated, Stone had asked, "where is your Constitution? . . . Is it among the archives?" Madison, in an intriguing move, was suggesting that it was. Through "reasonable evidence" available from "contemporary and concurrent expositions," congressmen could find the discretion required without exercising any of their own. Rules of application were indeed needed, but there was another way to locate them without entrusting sitting politicians with the sovereign prerogative (to invoke Gerry's powerful expression) of constructive interpretation. Those rules of application were the original intent of those who had authored and approved of the Constitution. Appealing to the archive of the Constitution's creation—no matter how self-interested, partial, or inaccurate that excavation might turn out to be—became a solution to the conviction that, in a profound sense, the Constitution was incomplete. After fighting the archival Constitution so strenuously during the amendments debate, Madison now proactively appealed to it.[51]

With this move, constitutional exegesis converged with historical excavation. Eager to fix a set of interpretive rules to the Constitution—and desperate to gain traction in this bruising political fight—Madison and other members of Congress began appealing to the archive of the Constitution's creation. The removal debate had featured similar invocations, such as William Loughton Smith's appeal to *Federalist* 77, but only as fleeting curiosities. Now they were afforded a logic and significance they had previously lacked. Even if such appeals were driven as much by partisan need as by principled commitment, and even if, in Madison's case, they carried more than a little bit of self-aggrandizement, nonetheless, in the realm of constitutional imagination, they carried important implications.[52]

Madison subtly gestured toward original intent before more systematically making his case. The basis of his opposition to the bank bill he claimed to have "entertained . . . from the date of the Constitution," since he "well recollected that a power to grant charters of incorporation had been proposed in the General Convention and rejected." Drawing upon alleged firsthand experience, he suggested that, no matter what shifts had taken place in the intervening years, the Constitutional Convention had been opposed to the federal government's power to charter corporations. Turning attention to the ratifying conventions, he argued that "the explanations" in them "all turned on the same fundamental principle, and on the principle that the terms necessary and proper gave no additional powers to those enumerated." Upon reading speeches from the debates of the Pennsylvania, Virginia, and North Carolina conventions (likely those made by James Wilson, Thomas McKean, George Nicholas, James Iredell, and himself), he concluded that these selections revealed "the grounds on which the Constitution had been vindicated by its principal advocates, against a dangerous latitude of its powers, charged on it by its opponents."

Bank antagonists had maintained that the "necessary and proper" clause could not be interpreted as a doctrine of implied powers, but they struggled to demonstrate how the Constitution's own contents proved the point. However, "the grounds" upon which the document "had been vindicated by its principal advocates," offered more conclusive evidence, or so bank opponents claimed. The judgment exercised in the Federal Convention and the ratifying conventions (because of the purpose that brought delegates to those sites and the immediacy they enjoyed to the moment of constitutional creation) was superior to that exercised in Congress and could supply a more legitimate brand of constitutional meaning.[53]

Because the ratifying conventions especially expressed a pure form of popular sovereignty—acting as unique deliberative assemblies convened at a special time for a special purpose—their surviving testimony trumped subsequent arguments. "With all this evidence of the sense in which the Constitution was understood and adopted, will it not be said," Madison concluded, "if the bill should pass, that its adoption was brought about by one set of arguments, and that it is now administered under the influence of another set; and this reproach will have the keener sting," he reckoned, "because it is applicable to so many individuals concerned in both the adoption and administration." Congress ought to consider the arguments made in the ratifying conventions against those made during the bank debate, judging the legitimacy of the latter based upon how successfully it represented the spirit of the former. The problems generated by the indeterminate Constitution were thus answered by the archival Constitution.[54]

Had Madison's extended foray into the archive of the Constitution's creation stopped there, or had bank supporters ignored or rejected his argument, Madison's approach might never have taken on the justificatory weight that it eventually enjoyed. Fisher Ames was dismissive, claiming that such "rules of interpretation by contemporaneous testimony" were "obscure." In his private correspondence he disparaged Madison's appeals to the historical record as "full of casuistry and sophistry" and "very little to the purpose." He even claimed that many congressmen "laughed at the objection" when Madison first offered it. But beyond indulging his biting sense of humor, Ames also sounded a telling note of uncertainty. Acknowledging that Madison "spoke with his usual ability," he conceded, "what impression he made I cannot say." Other bank supporters were far less inclined to dismiss Madison's reasoning out of hand. Many were surely exasperated by his ploy, feeling that Madison had deliberately manipulated earlier debates to save his unpopular position on the bank. Partly out of frustration and partly because they thought they could retain their advantage, many bank supporters instead began challenging Madison on his own terms. But by quibbling with his sources rather than challenging the premise of his investigation, they reinforced the legitimacy of historical excavation. To aggressively favor a specific historical moment (albeit one in recent living memory), as Madison had, called attention to the use of historical materials. Madison claimed, offhandedly, that he "did not undertake to vouch for the accuracy or authenticity of the publications" from which he quoted. But he thought "the complexion of the whole . . . fully justified the use . . . made of them." Madison opened the door to historical excavation, but others freely chose to walk through it, an act that proved decisive in its development as a credible argumentative practice.[55]

Bank supporters unwittingly strengthened Madison's position, meeting him squarely on the terrain he had staked out by denouncing his characterization of the Federal Convention. John Vining thought that "the opinion of the gentleman, in this instance, was, if not singular, different from that of his contemporaries." Since "a similar objection had not been sta[t]ed by those gentlemen of the Senate, who had been members of the convention," Madison's recollections alone were not "sufficient authority . . . for Congress at the *present* time to construe the constitution." The issue, though, lay not with Madison's appeal to history but with his specific representation of it. Elbridge Gerry vigorously critiqued Madison's recollection of the Federal Convention. Hinting that Madison was mischaracterizing what had happened, he asked, "are we to depend on the memory of the gentleman for an history of their debates and from thence to collect their sense?" That "would be improper, because"—not so subtly alluding to the fact that he too had been a delegate to the Convention—"the memories of different gentlemen would probably vary." And "if not," Gerry added, "the opinions of the individual members who debated are not to be considered as the opinions of the convention." But even if it was appropriate to do what Madison had done, it was important to understand that "the sense of the Convention is in favor of the bill." Madison was simply wrong that the Convention had considered a power to charter a bank. The "measure which the gentleman has referred to," Gerry explained, was "merely to enable Congress to erect *commercial* corporations." Indeed, "no motion was made in that convention, and therefore none could be rejected for establishing a national bank."[56]

Gerry was ultimately less interested in the Federal Convention than he was in the state ratifying conventions, however. What made Madison's claims especially problematic was not that the testimony was irrelevant, but that it had been deciphered from such poor sources. "The debates of the state conventions, as published by the short hand writers," Gerry remarked skeptically, "were generally partial and mutilated." Gerry was hardly a neutral commentator. His personal experience at the Massachusetts convention had been peculiar. Anti-Federalists had invited him to attend as a nondelegate to answer questions about the Constitutional Convention. A few days into the proceedings, though, after hearing his name in the debate Gerry intervened in the discussion, igniting animated disagreement over the propriety of his interruption. Afterward he was confronted by an angry Federalist delegate. Gerry never returned, nor was he invited again. Anti-Federalists subsequently complained about the accuracy of the published accounts of the convention debates, objections Gerry (perhaps still irked by how he had been treated while in attendance) was now happy to share in the House of Representatives. Meanwhile, Madison had "quoted the opinions, as recorded in the debates of [Pennsylvania] & North-Carolina, of two of our learned judges. But," Gerry objected, "the speech of one member is not to be considered as expressing the sense of a convention; and if, it was, we have no record which can be depended on, of such speeches." The speeches that Madison had quoted were drawn from a fragmentary record. But, again, the issue lay in sources, not in the legitimacy of appealing to them. Bank supporters, even if they had no intention to do so, were beginning to sanction historical appeals. Even if they merely conceded Madison's premise in hopes of exploding his case, they helped reinforce the interpretive foundation the Virginian had begun to erect.[57]

The most significant manner in which bank defenders legitimized historical excavation was in their use of the *Federalist* papers. These made an early appearance in the debate when James Jackson read sections from *Federalist* 44, which he believed to have been written by "the author of the present plan before the house" (that is, Hamilton) and which he believed showed that Hamilton had previously thought that chartering a bank was "contrary to the constitution." Jackson charged the treasury secretary with a change of sentiment, assuming that he had departed from his prior commitments for the same partisan reasons so many congressmen had defected from their earlier beliefs. What better way to nullify Hamilton than to appeal to his own opinions in defense of the Constitution's ratification?[58]

Nobody challenged Jackson's arguments more forcefully than Elias Boudinot. Had Jackson not quoted the *Federalist* "to shew a different contemporaneous exposition of the Constitution," he might have concluded his speech without further comment. But since Hamilton "is not here to speak for himself," Boudinot noted in his characteristically jocular style, the treasury secretary "ought to have the next best chance, by having what he then wrote, candidly attended to." Boudinot then quoted *Federalist* 44 at length:

> Had the convention attempted a positive enumeration of the powers necessary and proper for carrying their other powers into effect; the attempt would have involved a complete digest of laws on every subject . . . not only to the existing state of things, but to all the possible changes which futurity may produce; for in every new application of a general power, the *particular power*, which are the means of attaining the general power, must always necessarily vary with that object, and be often properly varied whilst the object remains the same.

Through his reading, Boudinot hit every major point. The "necessary and proper" clause was built-in proof that the Constitution could not possibly specify every detail of its application. The general powers laid out by the Constitution always afforded whatever means were necessary to its security. And, as the surrounding context shaping that relationship would constantly shift, some subsequent source of judgment would have to deduce what kinds of means were necessary for those ends. For all these reasons, given the tenor of both Hamilton's proposal and the debate over the bank, "how these sentiments can be said to be a different contemporaneous exposition," Boudinot could not decipher.[59]

There was, however, a fascinating irony at work here. Both Jackson and Boudinot erroneously assumed that Hamilton was the author of the paper in dispute. But he was not; Madison was. Amazingly, without the slightest recognition, Boudinot was laying out in Madison's own words, with recourse to Madison's own conception of historical appeal, reasons why Madison's recent interpretation of the "necessary and proper" clause was wrong. Nobody appreciated this irony, except, of course, Madison, who was forced to listen to his own contradictory testimony. He was unique in his capacity for self-reflection, and this blessing likely became a curse as he watched his peer, who was none the wiser, use his own words against him.[60]

This irony, and the ignorance that accompanied it, was emblematic of what in part made this debate so important. Madison was not trying to venerate historical excavation for its own sake. He was simply trying to undermine the bank bill. Boudinot, meanwhile, was merely trying to square Hamilton's commitments. But nobody—not even the original authors—wholly owns arguments or justifications. Once unleashed, they take on lives of their own. Neither Madison, nor Boudinot, nor any other member of Congress, was necessarily trying to reimagine the Constitution. And yet, they were collectively, if unintentionally, contributing to that end. By giving the *Federalist* papers a new purchase, and in so doing affording "contemporaneous testimony" an enduring legitimacy, they were suggesting that constitutionalism turned on historical excavation. They were helping solidify the idea of the archival Constitution and with that a particular conception of fixed constitutional meaning.

To Veto or Not to Veto?

After over a week of debate, the House decisively voted in favor of the bill. What had long been assumed was now formally secured, but a great deal had unfolded in between. Madison and his supporters likely doubted that they could ever prevail on the floor, but their arguments had an important impact nevertheless, helping change how people could talk about the Constitution, a lasting consequence that exceeded the narrow parameters of the bank debate. But, more immediately, they also shaped how President George Washington viewed the bill he was now expected to sign. Washington had never seriously considered the veto to that point in his presidency. As with everything else he gauged while in office, precedent was his obsession. He was not inclined to use the veto unless matters truly demanded it. That Madison—as strong an authority on the Constitution as perhaps existed and long his trusted advisor and friend—so spiritedly opposed the bank's constitutionality seemed to give the veto credence. In the weeks that followed the bill's passage, the two Virginians held several meetings in which Washington allowed Madison to speak freely on the topic.[61]

Washington's respect for the congressman was so great that he commissioned three official opinions on the topic. The first two were delivered by his fellow Virginians, Attorney General Edmund Randolph and Secretary of State Thomas Jefferson. The third, requested only after the others were in hand, came from Hamilton, who was afforded the benefit of surveying the other two. All extended the congressional debate and vividly illustrated how the bank debate was altering constitutional imagination.[62]

Both Randolph and Jefferson opposed the bank, but neither of their opinions was especially long. Some of their arguments simply echoed what opponents had articulated in Congress: the preamble did not render the rest of the Constitution's contents superfluous; the "necessary and proper" clause merely authorized what was necessary to carry out the enumerated powers and not the general ends of union and government; by what would become the Tenth Amendment the state governments claimed the remainder of power; and the rights to borrow money, tax, and protect the common defense did not imply the power to charter a bank. But other arguments they made extended those that preceded them, offering novel shape to otherwise familiar terrain.[63]

At the heart of Randolph's opinion was an argument about the kind of thing that the Constitution was and, based on that, what sort of interpretive rules necessarily followed. What ultimately nullified bank supporters' interpretations was the fact that the Constitution was a written text. If "the power of creating Corporations" was merely "implied in the nature of the Federal government," he argued, that "would beget a doctrine so indefinite, as to grasp every power." To Randolph this possibility was alarming; but what mattered was what made it illegitimate. "Governments, having no written Constitution," he explained, "may perhaps claim a latitude of power, not always easy to be determined." In contrast, "those, which have written Constitutions"—like the United States federal government—"are circumscribed by a just interpretation of the words contained in them." Reading so much into the sheer writtenness of the federal Constitution revealed the extent to which Randolph imagined it as a distinctively textual instrument.[64]

But it was especially striking for Randolph to adopt this position because he had previously argued exactly the opposite. In the famous *Case of the Prisoners* that came before the Virginia Court of Appeals, Randolph (in his position as state attorney general) had claimed that the language of the state constitution was largely irrelevant to the case because of the kind of object it was—it was not a law but a constitution. Surely remembering this argument (which he had consciously drawn on when helping to draft the Constitution as a member of the Committee of Detail), Randolph attempted to reconcile his past and present opinions. In his bank opinion, he reiterated his earlier argument: "There is a real difference between the rule of interpretation, applied to a law & a Constitution. The one comprises a summary of matter, for the detail of which numberless Laws will be necessary; the other is the very detail. The one is therefore to be construed with a discreet liberality; the other with a closer adherence to the literal meaning." Just as he had argued in the Virginia Court of Appeals, because constitutions were general statements of principle, inherently incapable of anticipating all future contingencies, they required (and indeed permitted) liberal interpretations of their contents.[65]

In his opinion for Washington, however, Randolph introduced a novel consideration. "When we compare the modes of construing a state, and the federal, constitution," he explained, "we are admonished to be stricter with regard to the latter, because there is a greater danger of Error in defining partial than general powers." The federal Constitution was defined not simply by its writtenness, but by the fact that it was written in a particular idiom (to vest partial powers). From this idiom could be derived "the rule" of interpretation: that as each of the Constitution's textually specified powers "includes those details which properly constitute the whole of the subject, to which the power relates, the details themselves must be fixed by reasoning." Because of the kind of object the federal Constitution was, interpreters were compelled to treat its distinctly linguistic contents as "fixed." Never mind that Randolph had argued the precise opposite in the Virginia ratifying convention, in trying to justify the "necessary and proper" clause no less. There he had applied his understanding of constitutional interpretation from the *Case of the Prisoners* directly to the new federal Constitution. Quite unlike before, then, Randolph exhibited a staunch willingness to see the Constitution as a text.[66]

Randolph's striking faith in linguistic perspicuity carried him away from Madison. He dismissed historical excavation—why should "an almost unknown history . . . govern the Construction?"—arguing, in contrast, "ought not the Constitution to be decided on by the import of its own expressions?" Yet here, in claiming that the Constitution (by virtue of being written) was not only complete but armed with its own interpretive rules, he fell back on the same vague pronouncements that had proliferated during ratification. The Constitution's words could be fixed, he claimed, by appealing "to common sense and common language." Why this rule gave the "necessary and proper" clause one particular meaning and not another, though— especially in light of the vociferous disagreement just evidenced in the House—remained unclear. In this regard, Randolph's new, quasi-Anti-

Federalist confidence in the Constitution as text left him with the same difficulties that had inspired others, like Madison, to appeal to the Constitution's history in the first place.[67]

Jefferson's opinion harped on related themes but, in character, was noticeably different. Unlike other protagonists in this constitutional struggle, Jefferson had missed the drafting and ratification of the Constitution. He had returned from France—where he had been United States minister since 1784—only in late 1789. During his first year as secretary of state, his constitutional thinking reflected his absence. Even as so many disputants awkwardly struggled between rival forms of constitutional imagination, Jefferson was clearly locked in a past moment. When issuing an opinion on the constitutionality of the Residence Bill that moved the federal capital to the Potomac River, he largely sidestepped the Constitution, defending the bill on the grounds of Congress's "natural right of governing itself" and only drawing upon the Constitution in reference to how this natural right (some version of which he mentioned a dozen times) had not been abridged by that new charter. When, the following year, he turned his attention to the bank, this brand of constitutional reasoning lingered. Before even discussing the Constitution, Jefferson began his opinion by contending that the bank bill violated a variety of different features of common law derived from the law of mortmain, alienage, and descents, to forfeiture and escheat, distribution, and monopoly—strange sources of authority with which to lead. "Can it be thought," he asked, "that the Constitution intended . . . to break down the[se] most antient and fundamental laws?" as if these fundamental laws, and not the Constitution, controlled the case of the bank. Only after laying this unusual groundwork did he turn to the familiar constitutional arguments that bank opponents in the House and Randolph had explored, equating transgression of the "boundaries . . . specially drawn around the powers of Congress" with taking "possession of a boundless feild of power, no longer susceptible of any definition." If what was "convenient" could be substituted for "necessary," he argued, "such a latitude of construction . . . would swallow up all the delegated powers," destroying the very essence of the Constitution in the process. Like so many Americans, Jefferson could disparage and fetishize, ignore and emphasize constitutional language in the same breath.[68]

But the point where Jefferson most evidently diverged from Randolph was not over the relevance of the Constitution's language (despite his idiosyncratic perspective, he ultimately agreed that the Constitution's words built a clear barrier against chartering the bank) but over the history of its creation. Whereas Randolph had dismissed the value of such excavations, to a striking degree Jefferson rested his case on them. He could appeal to the Constitutional Convention because he had access to Madison's notes of its proceedings—the very notes that Madison had returned to with such interest in the wake of the amendments debate. With the help of Madison's record, Jefferson wrote at a critical juncture in his opinion,

> It is known that the very power now proposed *as a means,* was rejected *as an end,* by the Convention which formed the constitution. A proposition was made to them to authorize Congress to open canals, and an amendatory one to empower them to incorporate. But the whole was rejected, and one of the reasons of rejection urged in debate was that then they would have a power to erect a bank, which would render the great cities, where there were prejudices and jealousies on that subject adverse to the reception of the constitution.

Citing an episode in the Convention in which the delegates had rejected Madison's proposal to vest Congress with the power to incorporate canals, Jefferson thought such evidence proved that the framers of the Constitution had considered and consciously rejected general incorporation powers. But he went a step further, arguing that in rejecting this proposal some delegates had claimed that their reason for doing so was to avoid vesting in the federal government a power to incorporate not canals but a bank. This was nothing if not a highly tendentious reading of Madison's notes. But that was not the point. It spoke to how Jefferson—like his good friend upon whose notes he based his claims—had been seized by a particular way of imagining the Constitution and what justified its interpretation.[69]

Neither Randolph's nor Jefferson's opinions, however, matched Hamilton's in breadth or complexity. The treasury secretary had the benefit of reading the other arguments and the luxury of offering the final word. Washington, who probably hoped to sign the bill in to law (wary as he was to veto), was soliciting an authoritative opinion that could trump those already issued. Hamilton presented a bevy of arguments, many of which, like those issued in his rivals' opinions, echoed claims made in the House. Following bank supporters' lead, he stressed a vision of the Constitution that far transcended its mere words. He suggested that an "aggregate view of the constitution" implied a broad sweep of powers that could never be specified. While some had complained throughout the debate that the "moment the literal meaning is departed from, there is a chance of error and abuse," Hamilton insisted that "an adherence to the letter of [the Constitution's] powers would at once arrest the motions of the government." Thus, all had to agree that "the exercise of constructive powers is indispensible." Thankfully, then, the Constitution recognized the necessity of implied powers. Like he had long thought and like bank supporters in the House had repeatedly argued, "there are *implied,* as well as *express* powers," and, Hamilton explained, "the former are as effectually delegated as the latter." The government could exercise all *delegated* powers, but, contrary to what bank opponents—including, especially, Randolph—had insisted, these powers included both those that were *expressed* as well as others that were *implied.* By grasping the difference between delegated and expressed power, it became possible to see how the Constitution itself licensed unwritten authority.[70]

A proper understanding of the Constitution's character elucidated the meaning of the "necessary and proper" clause. Echoing bank defenders in the House, Hamilton linked ends and means. "Every power" delegated to the national government, he maintained, carried with it "a right to employ all the *means* requisite, and fairly *applicable* to the attainment of the *ends* of such power." This implied power to exercise all means necessary to carry out specified ends was "*inherent* in the very definition of *Government.*" But the "necessary and proper" clause embodied far more than this baseline principle, since (as Hamilton had established) the powers delegated to the federal government far exceeded those expressly enumerated. Most of these unenumerated delegated powers, or "*resulting* powers," were "objects of National . . . administration"—powers that fell to the federal government by virtue of the fact that it presided over national matters. And especially those means required to address "national exigencies" were "of such infinite variety, extent and complexity" that there needed to be a "great latitude of discretion" in their application. This unavoidable reality was exactly what the "necessary and proper" clause acknowledged. Whereas bank opponents— none more so than Jefferson—foolishly assumed that "necessary" meant only what was absolutely indispensable, Hamilton was sure that the "whole turn of the clause" tacitly recognized that "the powers contained in a constitution of government," especially those which concerned "general administration," "ought to be construed liberally, in advancement of the public good." The "necessary and proper" clause, by appreciating the "indispensible authority of the United States," was built-in acknowledgment of the dynamic character of the Constitution.[71]

These observations brought Hamilton to another crucial and familiar point, and one upon which much of his opinion otherwise turned: that constitutional rules could not fully apply themselves. The necessarily incomplete character of the Constitution necessitated discretionary judgment. "The truth is," he wrote, "that difficulties on this point are inherent in the nature of the federal constitution." By dividing legislative power between distinct levels of government (national and state), the Constitution created cases that fell clearly within the authority of the national government, those that clearly fell outside of it, and a ubiquitous "third class, which will leave room for controversy & difference of opinion." In these unavoidable cases, "a reasonable latitude of judgment must be allowed." The Constitution itself could not clearly and completely divide what was constitutional from what was not. Users would have to sort out the full scope of the Constitution's unanticipated implications.[72]

But in addition to recapitulating and fleshing out arguments painting the Constitution as a necessarily incomplete object, Hamilton also followed Madison's and Jefferson's path of historical excavation, a decision that cut against the general thrust of the rest of his opinion. A brilliant legal mind, Hamilton surely meant to decimate Madison and Jefferson on their own chosen ground. But while his forays on this point were few and tactical, at one point his engagement was indeed striking. Hamilton found it remarkable that "the State Conventions who have proposed amendments" related to this point have requested that "'Congress shall not grant monopolies, nor *erect any company* with exclusive advantages of commerce,'" thus simultaneously insinuating "that the power to erect trading companies or corporations, was inherent in Congress." What was not criticized in the state ratifying conventions, Hamilton concluded, must then have been assumed. Exclusive corporate monopolies merited restriction only if corporations were otherwise permitted. That the ratifying conventions conceded this point gave the Constitution a meaning it otherwise might have lacked. Madison had first suggested that the ratifying conventions could adjudicate interpretation. Hamilton was now following suit. He was willing to play the same game of giving and asking for reasons. In so doing, no matter his intention, he was willing to see the Constitution in the same light.[73]

Randolph imagined the Constitution as a text, one defined by its language and whose meanings were relatively clear. Jefferson both embraced and rejected Randolph's conception, but ultimately redeemed it by imagining the Constitution as an archival object whose contents were illuminated by an understanding of the history of its construction. Hamilton adamantly refused to see the Constitution as the kind of linguistic artifact betrayed by Randolph. But in his efforts to refute his opponents he tacitly legitimized Jefferson's chosen mode, which showed that, in effect if not intent, he was closer to Jefferson—not on principles but on the more basic image of the Constitution that he held in his mind—than he would have been prepared to admit.

DIFFERENT conceptions of the Constitution had emerged since 1787. Even though they had come in conflict in the interim, they had managed to coexist, more or less peacefully. But during the bank debate they began clashing violently. Probing the Constitution's language, particularly the "necessary and proper" clause, and, relatedly, whether the document came with its own rules of interpretation, helped clarify the differences between rival modes of constitutional imagination that had developed to that point. Familiar scripts, first sketched by Federalists and Anti-Federalists in 1787–1788, were repurposed and redeployed. While many continued to insist that the Constitution was necessarily ambiguous, incomplete, or its application uncertain, others insisted that the Constitution—as a rule-proffering text—could specify a complete set of prescriptions for application that gave the Constitution the kind of determinate meaning it was said to lack. But as sharp as this divide was, it proved difficult to explain how some kind of discretionary human judgment was not inevitable to close off the Constitution's indeterminacies. Echoing Madison's searching reflections from *Federalist* 37, like language itself no human artifact could be completely shorn of its ambiguities and imperfections. This realization inspired another, more powerful, if more subtle division. While some privileged the contemporary discretion of sitting congressmen (choosing to imagine the Constitution as an unfinished structure that needed to be built out), others dealt with its uncertainties and gaps, not by building out but by digging below and excavating its historical record (choosing to imagine the Constitution as a time-locked archival text). This excavation elevated the historical judgments of the Constitution's creators above those currently sitting in Congress. This became a powerful way of acknowledging the Constitution's inability to apply itself while also undermining the kind of contemporary discretion deemed so necessary. It became a way of fixing the Constitution—both repairing its blemishes and stabilizing its otherwise fluctuating contents.

Washington signed the bill into law, which chartered the national bank for the next twenty years and brought the congressional debate over its constitutionality to a close. The bill had passed with overwhelming support, and a great number of the justifications that accompanied its passage had imagined the Constitution as imperfect and incomplete. It certainly mattered that the bank defenders' favored arguments—which expressed, in rather sophisticated detail, why the Constitution was perpetually unfinished—had carried the day. But it mattered, too, that historical appeals had acquired fresh vitality, and on both sides of the dispute. The tensions between contemporary discretion and historical excavation had manifested themselves, and they would continue to do so well after this dispute had faded. The broader debate over the Constitution's fundamental character—over how to conceive of it and make use of it—would continue apace.[74]

Something important did change after the bank debate, however, something that Madison alluded to during his closing remarks on the House floor. Brimming with frustration that his carefully drawn arguments had persuaded none in the majority, the Virginian contended that "the enlightened opinion and affection of the people [were] the only solid basis for the support of this government." Therefore, "if the appeal to the public opinion is suggested with sincerity, we ought to let our constituents have an opportunity to form an opinion on the subject."[75]

Nearly a year later, in an exchange with Virginia governor Henry Lee, Madison reiterated this point and signaled not only where constitutional debate had been, but also where it was going. Writing to Lee, Madison derided Hamilton's latest economic proposal announced in the "Report on Manufactures," which called for the federal government to subsidize American manufacturing. In that report, unveiled toward the end of 1791, Hamilton had defended Congress's authority to issue these subsidies based on the legislature's constitutional right to "provide" for the "general welfare." The phrase was deliberately vast, the secretary explained, in order to anticipate powers "susceptible neither of specification nor of definition." Believing that this constitutional defense restated precisely the problematic logic upon which the bank had been defended earlier that year, a frustrated Madison told Lee that "if not only the *means*, but the *objects* are unlimited"—what, to Madison, Hamilton's reading of "general welfare" clearly implied—then "the parchment had better be thrown into the fire at once." In imagining the Constitution so vividly as a text, Madison was identifying the problem. But, in his next letter to Lee, he also gestured toward a new solution, one that echoed his passing reference to public opinion from the waning moments of the bank debate. Hamilton and his supporters were defying the "true & universal construction" of the Constitution, but what remained to be seen, Madison thought, was "whether the people of this country will submit to a constitution" they had "not established." Accordingly, it was essential that the people at large "should have as fair an opportunity as possible of judging for themselves."[76]

Thereafter, constitutional politics would no longer be confined to the halls of government. Madison, Jefferson, and their friends in the press would make sure that constitutional questions were brought before the public like never before. In the process, the meaning and practice of public opinion would take on vast new significances in America. In the world made of those transformations, the pressures that had already shaped the Constitution would only intensify.

6

The "People's" Constitution

The constitution supposes . . . that the voice of the people ought to govern, and if that voice was competent to decide upon a form of government, it must be equally, if not more capable to judge of those regulations made under it. In assigning to the President and Senate the power of making treaties, can it be supposed, that it contemplated a treaty which would be ratified by them in opposition to the almost unanimous voice of America!

—Hancock, "For the Aurora," *Aurora General Advertiser,* August 21, 1795

Edward Livingston claimed merely to want information. In a resolution proposed in the House of Representatives in early March 1796, the New York congressman requested access to sensitive government papers in possession of the president. But this plea, supposedly issued only for the House's edification, made others suspicious. To "determine on its propriety," Livingston would need to state "the reason which urged the motion," asserted Uriah Tracy of Connecticut. This was a "delicate subject," he went on. The House had a right "to pass the resolution, but they could not do it without good cause." So why did the House need the papers? Albert Gallatin, who was sympathetic to Livingston's motion, tried to clarify. "The President tells the House that he has made a Treaty," and has laid it before the House to be carried into execution. Regardless of how the House might proceed—potentially having "an agency and a discretion in carrying it into effect," or possibly just needing "to express our opinion"—"the information called for will be useful, by showing the reasons which induced the adoption of the Treaty." To "render this information public," Gallatin explained, "must then answer to a valuable purpose." The House consequently demanded to know more about the circumstances that had produced the treaty in front of them.[1]

The treaty in question was the Treaty of Amity, Commerce, and Navigation, Between His Britannic Majesty and the United States of America—better known as the Jay Treaty, after its American negotiator, Chief Justice John Jay. It had been concluded in London on November 19, 1794, ratified by the Senate in Philadelphia on June 24, 1795, and approved and signed by President Washington on August 18, 1795. It took effect on February 29, 1796, when the two nations formally exchanged their separate ratifications. But days later, Livingston, new to Congress but hailing from a powerful political family, deeply confident in his own abilities, and believing that "the late British Treaty must give rise in the House to some very important and Constitutional questions," moved: "That the President of the United States be requested to lay before the House a copy of the instructions to the Minister of the United States, who negotiated the Treaty with the King of Great Britain, communicated by his Message of the first of March, together with the correspondence and other documents relative to the said Treaty."[2]

Daniel Buck, representative from Vermont, was skeptical of Livingston's proposal and attempted to decode its latent intent. Buck opposed the resolution, not because the papers could serve no value, but because a right to examine the papers assumed a right to judge the treaty. "If we are to take upon ourselves the right of judging whether it was expedient to make the Treaty or not . . . if we are to assume the power of judging upon them merits as well as the constitutionality of it," he declared, "then we . . . possess the right to call for those papers." Requesting privileged information that shed light upon the negotiations was inappropriate unless the House possessed a right to judge the constitutionality of the treaty. And any prima facie reading of the Constitution would disclose that the House had no role in treaty making. All that Article II stipulated was that the "[President] shall have Power, by and with the Advice and Consent of the Senate, to make Treaties, provided two thirds of the Senators present concur." That said, Livingston had prefaced his resolution by insinuating—with what exact meaning was not yet clear—that the late treaty gave rise to important constitutional questions that the House could not ignore. Through a series of rhetorical questions, Buck began putting the pieces together. "From whence do we derive this right and power? . . . Do we possess the right merely because we are the Representatives of the people?" More to the point, "Are we to derive this right from popular opposition to the Treaty, and from thence say, that it is the will of the nation that we should exercise this right of inquiry?" The president, acting with the advice and consent of the Senate, had entered the Jay Treaty into law. But, subsequently, the treaty had been met with intense, at times violent, popular opposition throughout the country. Members of the House, Buck was saying, were ignoring their constitutional role and trying to force their way, rather slyly, into treaty making, purely because the Jay Treaty had inspired such a passionate reaction. They had ignored their true master—the Constitution—in order to serve the spurious whims of the people.[3]

The Jay Treaty was as controversial as any development that roiled the early United States, encouraging those in power to take notice. But those who supported Livingston's resolution believed they had a constitutional right to the papers. They were not merely arrogating power in response to public pressure; they believed that the Constitution permitted the House a role in treaty making and that those who claimed otherwise misunderstood its full meaning. By advancing this constitutional claim, they initiated a protracted and penetrating debate that, according to Theodore Sedgwick of Massachusetts, turned on "the most important question which had ever been debated in this House."[4]

The far-reaching debate—which consumed the House for every single day from early March through the end of April 1796—was, yet again, a struggle over the Constitution's essential character and what it meant to be subject to its authority. Narrow initial questions—Why did the House need the papers? Why did it matter that the public was outraged? Why did the House have any role whatsoever in debating a ratified treaty?—gave way to more extensive ones: What was the House's relationship to treaties? What was the relationship between public opinion, the Constitution, and the political will of the nation? If certain constitutional interpretations were at odds with the evident will of the public, to which master should representatives pledge allegiance? Ultimately, all of these questions begged a simpler, yet omnipresent consideration: Was the bundle of meanings that comprised the Constitution's contents a fixed and settled matter? Was the Constitution, in other words, a finished product?

The debate over the Jay Treaty must be treated at length. Not only was it markedly complex, implicating and shaping American constitutional imagination in numerous important ways. But, more significantly, it marked the climax of our particular story—the moment when a distinctive mode of imagining the Constitution (which, since 1789, had slowly been taking shape) came starkly into view.

Understanding how this episode revealed this transformation requires first grasping how the debate over the Jay Treaty implicated the indeterminate Constitution. By insisting that the House of Representatives had a role in treaty making not obviously licensed by the Constitution, proponents of Livingston's resolution conjured the image of the imperfect, unfinished, dynamic instrument that the ratification debates had first introduced. In the face of protests that took the Constitution at face value—and assumed that treaty making was vested exclusively in the president and Senate and that the House was excluded from the process—proponents of the resolution had to explain why the Constitution's meaning was more than initially met the eye. That meant exposing the contradictions that emerged from a prima facie reading of the document and substantiating why the House of Representatives, due to its special relationship with "the people," was uniquely positioned to adjudicate the contradictions. By exercising creative constitutional discretion, the "nation's representatives" in the House could alone uphold the "people's" Constitution.

These latest efforts to imagine the Constitution unfolded against the evolving American political landscape. A good deal had changed since the First Congress permanently adjourned in the early months of 1791. The intervening years had given way to an altogether more raucous, more public, and more partisan arena than Americans had ever known. The fight over the Jay Treaty, and the effect this battle had on the way Americans came to think about the Constitution's defining properties, would reflect and sharpen the broader developments that were remaking the United States.

Partisan Fires Ablaze

Treaties are rarely the stuff of controversy. But embedded in an explosive context, the Jay Treaty made a profound impression on the public consciousness and became a charged symbol of the partisan and ideological rancor consuming American politics. For one, the treaty was forged with Great Britain, thus evoking the powerful, lingering traces of Revolutionary sentiment that informed dealings with this country. As Theodore Sedgwick reminded the House, "if this Treaty had been formed with any other Power, with the precise stipulations it now contained" it was questionable "whether there ever would have existed this doubt of constitutionality."[5]

In the wake of the Revolution, relations with the former mother country were inherently charged. By the time the federal Constitution was ratified, resistance to Great Britain had defined many American lives. Memories of the invasive imperial policies that had precipitated revolution and the brutal violence of the war that followed were still fresh. And British conduct since the Treaty of Paris had done little to temper Americans' animosity. Many Americans seethed about Britain's refusal to honor certain requirements of the peace, transgressions that made a mockery of the international legitimacy of the new United States. This smoldering resentment connected with a deeper frustration. To many, independence from Britain—the heart of the Revolutionary project—had scarcely been achieved by the 1790s. Political separation was insufficient; cultural and economic independence needed to follow. In pursuit of this goal, several members of the early national government, led by James Madison, sought to undermine America's reliance on British trade by passing navigation and tonnage laws that discriminated against British ships.[6]

Of course, not everybody shared these concerns. Alexander Hamilton had been especially enthusiastic about promoting favorable economic relations with Britain, and much of his financial program relied upon the steady flow of commerce. Furthermore, Hamilton and his supporters were comfortable modeling the emerging federal government on the underlying principles of the British nation-state—a large national debt and national bank, a standing army, and expansive executive patronage. The simple fact that Hamilton, as treasury secretary, was exerting so much influence over the administration fueled the fires of Anglophobia and with that anti-monarchism. As Jefferson complained, "the zealous apostles of English despotism" had "increased the number of its disciples." Those who shared his frustrations accused the Washington administration of attempting to transform the young nation into a monarchy.[7]

Britain's symbolic importance in America only intensified following the outbreak of the French Revolution. To sworn enemies of the English, the new French republic was the perfect counterpoint to which to stake their hopes and visionary claims. Popularity for the French cause swept across the United States as citizens donned tricolor cockades, sang revolutionary songs, and toasted to their sister revolution across the Atlantic. While approval waned with the outbreak of the Terror and the execution of the king and queen of France, a large swath of the American population remained intensely devoted to the French. The experience had confirmed how deep and visceral many Americans' hatred for Britain remained.[8]

The mounting fear that Hamilton and his associates were bent on transforming the young republic into a fiscal-military state akin to Britain motivated Madison and Jefferson to increase their opposition to both his program and his political influence. This fateful decision had far-reaching consequences. Where political debate had been merely vitriolic and personal before 1791, it became formally partisan from late 1792 onward, spilling over to the wider and more public domain of print. Shortly after the bank bill became law, Jefferson and Madison invited Philip Freneau to Philadelphia in the hope that he would establish a newspaper to challenge John Fenno's strongly pro-administration *Gazette of the United States.* Freneau obliged. The *National Gazette,* which became the mouthpiece of the administration's critics, began its run shortly thereafter.[9]

As partisanship consumed the press, formal party affiliations crystallized. As early as the congressional races of 1792, House Clerk John Beckley, a spirited critic of the administration who would become one of the United States' first seasoned political operatives, declared that in most states it was plain that the contests were a "struggle between the Treasury department and the republican Interest." The labels "Federalist" and "Republican" (while not resembling modern parties) began to coalesce around leading national figures and political divisions—Federalists supported the Washington administration while Republicans opposed it—along with the worldviews and interests they represented and the metaphors for social order and morality tales their allies in the partisan press propagated. Catharine Maria Sedgwick, the talented daughter of Theodore, later recounted "the general diffusion of the political prejudices of those times," noting dryly that "no age nor sex was exempt from them." Explaining how she had "been bred, according to the strictest sect of my political religion, a federalist," she captured the emotional intensity of party connection during the 1790s. Republicans fashioned themselves the "friends of the people" and treated their enemies as secret monarchists, while Federalists portrayed themselves as defenders of traditional social order and good government and their opponents as dangerous "democrats" bent on "setting mobs above law" and reducing the polity to chaos. Both alone claimed to embody the public interest and insisted that the other was intent on destroying the Constitution and the young republic. Even though politicians denied the existence of parties (as the political mores of the era demanded), with each passing year partisanship only became more familiar, more acceptable, and more intense.[10]

The Constitution was soon served up to this public, partisan arena. After the French Revolutionaries executed their king in early 1793, they declared war on Britain. While few Americans believed that the United States should intervene militarily in the European war, a great many thought the nation should remain loyal to France. For Washington and his administration, this was no abstract issue, since it was an open question whether the United States' 1778 treaties with France, which had been forged during the War for Independence required America to support the new republic across the Atlantic. While Washington was willing to meet with the French republic's minister, Edmund Charles Genet (soon to be christened "Citizen Genet"), he was adamant that the United States ought to stay out of the conflict. On at least this much Hamilton and Jefferson could agree and the president issued a proclamation of neutrality in April. But the two secretaries fiercely disagreed over the spirit of the resolution. Hamilton believed that the United States owed France virtually nothing and the proclamation established full impartiality; in contrast, Jefferson assumed that the proclamation merely deferred to Congress, which alone could declare war. With the aim of earning support for his understanding of the proclamation, Hamilton wrote seven extensive newspaper essays over the course of that summer under the pseudonym "Pacificus." In making his arguments he transformed the issue of neutrality into a wider constitutional matter centered on foreign affairs and executive power. A few months later, angry that Hamilton's views had yet to be challenged, Jefferson wrote Madison, imploring him to respond. "Nobody answers him, and his doctrine will therefore be taken for confessed," Jefferson complained. "For god's sake . . . take up your pen, select the most striking heresies, and cut him to peices in the face of the public." Reluctantly, Madison agreed, and under the pseudonym "Helvidius" penned five essays of his own.[11]

The "Pacificus"–"Helvidius" debate foreshadowed, and laid some of the groundwork for, important features of the Jay Treaty debate that would follow. While it was a wide-ranging discussion that touched on numerous issues, it illustrated how partisan antipathy over foreign affairs could incite rival accounts of constitutional authority over treaty making. Hamilton and Madison agreed on the constitutionality of Washington's proclamation; they instead disagreed on the relative constitutional powers of the president and Congress. According to Hamilton, Washington alone could declare neutrality because issues of foreign affairs were inherently executive in nature and the Constitution vested all executive authority in the president, save a handful of express exceptions. Hamilton acknowledged that one of these qualifications was the Senate's role in making treaties, like Congress's right to declare war, but because it was an exception it was "to be construed strictly—and ought to be extended no further than is essential to [its] execution." He limited legislative authority even further by insisting that while Congress could exercise its own powers, "the Executive in the exercise of its constitutional powers, may establish an antecedent state of things" which "ought to weigh" on congressional decisions. Madison vigorously disagreed with Hamilton's attempt to enlarge executive power at the expense of the legislature. Consulting "the nature and operation" of the power to make treaties, Madison believed it was clear that treaty making "can never fall within a proper definition of executive power" since a treaty was to have "the force of a *law*" and the "natural province" of "the legislature is to make laws." In defending the rights of Congress in treaty making, Madison was merely drawing attention to the Senate's express role in the process. But the thrust of his point was more radical, which became more evident when he defended Congress's exclusive right to declare war. As he revealingly put it, on this front "the legislature is made the organ of the national will" and served as a necessary check on "executive aggrandizement." Madison was objecting generally to constitutional intrusions against the legislature, stressing that body's unique right to make laws and represent the nation. Recognizing that some might conclude that he had retreated from the position he had taken earlier on executive removal, he stressed that the powers of making treaties and war were distinct in kind and, consequently, uniquely linked with the legislature. When it came to treaty making in this partisan climate, it remained to be seen exactly how far legislative control in fact extended. When Jay's Treaty reared its head, there would be cause to find out.[12]

If the French Revolution had exposed deep-seated antipathy toward Britain, the Jay Treaty would as well. At a time when all connections between the United States and Britain were controversial, tensions between the two nations ran high. As a response to escalating warfare with France, in the fall of 1793 Britain effectively blockaded the entire French West Indies, claiming the right to seize any cargo, whether belligerent or neutral, arriving or departing from French ports. News of this order reached the United States in December 1793, accompanied by distressing reports that the British navy had seized American ships in the Caribbean and British officials had attempted to drum up anti–United States hostility among Native Americans along the American–Canadian border. This latter aggression especially irked Americans because the British military, in direct violation of the Treaty of Paris, had still refused to vacate a variety of northwestern military posts. War seemed imminent.[13]

When it became clear that the British were eager to avoid hostilities, however, Americans seized the opportunity to dispatch a special envoy to Britain to address all outstanding grievances. Washington chose to send Chief Justice John Jay to serve in this role. For the most part, Jay proved successful. The British agreed to compensate American merchants whose ships had been seized, to vacate the northwestern forts by June 1796, and to allow American ships access to the West Indies. Both sides agreed to mixed arbitral commissions that would determine the formal boundary between the United States and Canada and to allow each other to trade across the border with Native Americans. The United States not only agreed to give Britain favored nation status, which meant that Madison would have to do without his discriminatory commercial legislation, but also agreed to repay British creditors what was owed them from before the Revolutionary War (if they could not otherwise obtain recompense through the ordinary course of judicial proceedings). The agreement laid the groundwork for future peace, a project to which Jay, who was arguably America's most experienced diplomat, was dearly committed. In late 1794, both parties consented to the agreement and Jay sailed home. Instead of receiving a hero's welcome, though, Jay soon found himself brandished a traitor.[14]

When news of the treaty reached American shores, "so general a burst of dissatisfaction never before appeared against any transaction," Jefferson claimed. "The whole body of the people . . . have taken a greater interest in this . . . than they were ever known to do in any other." William Manning, a Massachusetts tavern keeper, would write of the treaty, "When the monster first came into view, it was reprobated from one end of the continent to the other." Even in a political world so riven with contest, the Jay Treaty had few equals. Opposition mounted immediately, even before the treaty was made public. Washington was adamant about maintaining its secrecy, but that failed to allay the outrage. Some anger stemmed from disconcerting reports that Jay had conceded too much. Some was directed at the clandestine nature of the whole affair. But, most of all, anger stemmed from Americans' deep-seated loathing for Britain and its monarchism. "The British brib'd that scoundrel Jay, / To pass his country's rights away," one poem began. Meanwhile, "there is not a nation upon earth so truly and justly abhorred by *the People* of the United States as

Great Britain," raged a zealous Republican writing under the name "Franklin." Friendship with Britain was so vile to so many because it also meant betrayal of France. Franklin went on, "Can any *honorable* reason be given, why the United States have *courted* a treaty with great Britain and have *neglected* the overtures from France? . . . France is the only ally of the United States . . . she is combatting for the liberties of mankind," and deserved "the support of every Republican upon earth." Hatred of Britain gave the partisan press all necessary pretext to eviscerate the treaty.[15]

Overcoming his own reservations about the treaty, Washington finally laid it before the Senate in June 1795. After a heated and exhausting discussion, senators voted along party lines, approving the treaty by the slimmest possible margin. Throughout the Senate debate, public outcry over the secrecy of the treaty, which had been intense since Jay's return, became particularly acute. "The Constitution of the United States gives to the President and Senate the power of making Treaties; but it communicates no power to hatch those things *in darkness,*" cried an author in Benjamin Franklin Bache's virulently anti-administration *Aurora General Advertiser.* As the treaty moved to the president's desk, Washington heeded Hamilton's counsel and authorized publication for July 1. But a leaked copy originating with Virginia senator Stevens Thomson Mason made its way to Bache, and the public finally learned of the treaty's contents on the pages of the *Aurora* days before the Washington administration's planned publication date. Publication was going to cause a firestorm regardless, but the circumstances of the treaty's eventual dissemination only intensified opposition.[16]

Protest flared up across the nation. Public meetings criticized the treaty daily, newspaper essays denounced it as unconstitutional, Jay was burned in effigy, the British flag was dragged through the streets, Philadelphia rioters took out their frustrations on the residences of the British minister and several Federalist senators in Philadelphia, and in New York an angry protester pelted Hamilton with a stone while he was making a speech. Alongside these denunciations, Washington was inundated with petitions, pamphlets, remonstrances, and resolutions demanding that he not sign the treaty. For several anxious weeks, the president evaluated his options carefully. The treaty had obvious merit and would ensure a lasting peace; but the popular will was plainly against it. In mid-August, he finally decided to ratify.[17]

The business of the treaty appeared to have been completed. But the unparalleled opposition it engendered ensured that matters were far from over. The following spring, the House of Representatives would formally receive the treaty with the implied task of executing it. What did it mean for a treaty to be at once constitutionally ratified and yet reviled by the public? In the context of crystallizing party divisions, what had it meant to announce, as Madison had, that "the people themselves" were "the best keepers of the people's liberties"? What did it mean now that, as Jefferson put it, "the whole mass" of the people "have condemned [the treaty] in the most unequivocal manner"? These questions, and all of the constitutional implications they carried, weighed heavily on the minds of the nation's federal representatives.[18]

Central to the new kind of politics that had shaped opposition to the Jay Treaty was a novel understanding of publicity. "How does the *secrecy* of the Senate, in relation to the Treaty, comport with THE SOVEREIGNTY of the people?" one Republican writer asked. The Constitution would be beholden to the public in a new kind of way. True, the American constitutional experience had already featured unprecedented public scrutiny. The ratification debates had been notably democratic, and proceedings in the House of Representatives, of course, had been open to spectators. But neither of these developments fully anticipated the kind of vital and empowered public that had emerged by the mid-1790s. Fueled in part by the democratic energies unleashed by the Revolution and mobilized by Republican politicians and partisans—who repeatedly celebrated "the people" while denouncing the elitism, archaic gentility, and outmoded calls for deference made by their Federalist opponents—the people at large, outside the formal halls of government, were taking a more active role in political life. Through parades, festivals, public assemblies, organized protests, and politicized clubs, the public aggressively asserted itself in politics. The clubs were an especially striking site of popular political participation. In part inspired by the French Revolutionary Jacobin clubs, the Democratic-Republican societies (as they have since been called) were local voluntary organizations that served as a conduit for democratic political association and expression. They were organized on the premise that "the people" needed to vigilantly watch those in power, judging and commenting on leaders and their chosen policies. More broadly, members of the clubs believed that the promise of the American Revolution was tethered to the active political engagement of the people at large. The spread of partisan newspapers, meanwhile, accelerated the public's new role in politics, both by bringing constituents closer to the political process and by expanding their participation in the sphere of political debate. As politics spilled out into the streets and saturated daily life, political leaders had to take fresh account of the powerful public to which they answered. Now as much controlled by, as in control of, "the people" they had helped empower, Republicans, in particular, had to reckon with the democratic fires they had stoked.[19]

Attempts to come to terms with widespread political participation gave rise to new understandings of public opinion. Although it had long been assumed that government was answerable to the people at large, it was only in the 1790s that Americans began speaking of this concept with any precision. Few were as innovative as James Madison, who had probed the subject in one of his *National Gazette* essays (one of eighteen installments he had anonymously written for that venue in order to articulate the principles of the Republican opposition). Drawing heavily upon French political writings, he proclaimed, "Public opinion sets bounds to every government, and is the real sovereign in every free one." As much as this formulation legitimized popular opposition to the Washington administration, Madison also limited its potency by drawing a distinction between public opinion and popular will. Public opinion was a distilled, rational version of its vulgar counterpart. In this regard it bore a resemblance to the favored Federalist distinction—that "the dispassionate will of the people" needed to be separated from "the reign of popular frenzy, anarchy, and confusion." But Madison's version nonetheless gestured in a radically different direction. Federalists were insisting that duly elected leaders embodied the will of the people whereas extrapolitical organizations (none more glaringly than the Democratic-Republican societies) represented merely a portion of the public. Accordingly, between elections the people at large were meant to remain quiet and inactive. Madison, in contrast, was identifying a perpetual force existing outside of government and beyond the ordinary political process to which "the stability of all governments and security of all rights may be traced." Public opinion was what ultimately kept power on its "regular path."[20]

Public opinion, expressed through popular political protest, directly informed the ongoing debate over the Jay Treaty. The treaty had been denounced in countless public venues while the president had been bombarded with numerous petitions. Once the treaty was ratified and signed, public protest took the form of extensive pamphleteering. Several Republicans took up their pens to denounce the treaty in serialized essays. Even Federalists felt obliged to engage in this forum. Over the course of eighteen months, Hamilton—a literary army of one—alone produced thirty-eight separate essays defending the treaty and its constitutionality. He was joined by a host of other Federalists, including several congressmen, who wrote their own essays and pamphlets supporting the treaty. But these Federalist efforts could not contain the public's anger, which continued to be stoked by each new incendiary condemnation of the treaty in the Republican press. Even Washington himself, long spared partisan censure, became an object of intense public criticism.[21]

Soon, all of this public outrage, construed by so many as evidence of the treaty's illegitimacy, converged on the House of Representatives, "the people's" branch of government—which happened to be controlled by a Republican majority. As an essay in the *Aurora* noted suggestively, "the Independent representation of the people in Congress assembled, that constituted authority of our country, to whose sovereign voice, even the President and Senate must yield, have yet to pronounce on this much talked of treaty." Accordingly, many expected that the House—with its superior "sovereign voice"—would take a stand. Jefferson wrote to Edward Rutledge, "I trust the popular branch of our legislature will disapprove of it, and thus rid us of this infamous act, which is really nothing more than a treaty of alliance between England & the Anglomen of this country against the legislature and people of the United States." By late 1795, petitions began pouring into the House. Betraying the new understanding of popular politics, Republicans claimed that the Constitution's meaning might be reconsidered in light of the sheer volume of pleas. "If these popular proceedings were to be considered as an expression of public opinion," and "the petitions on the table of the House were more numerous than . . . on any question whatever," then, William Branch Giles of Virginia explained, "from these . . . it will be found that the people had recognized the power of the House to interfere" in this matter. As the staunch Republican writer William Manning later put it, "all our hopes lay in the federal House of Representatives." Federalists, too, recognized that the House had become the battlefield. "[It] will draw all eyes upon its proceedings," predicted Fisher Ames. But "what are we to hope from a body so deeply infected with the spirit of folly and jacobinism," he asked. "A crisis will soon come."[22]

The House of Representatives that confronted Jay's Treaty in the spring of 1796 faced different pressures than their predecessors. Since the bank debate had ended, Vermont and Kentucky had joined the union, and Tennessee was soon to be admitted as well. As a result of the first federal census of 1790 and the admission of new states, moreover, House membership had nearly doubled. Representatives from frontier settlements, which had expanded the nation north and westward, now brushed elbows with southern planters, mid-Atlantic merchants, and northern lawyers. Some new members, above all John Swanwick from Philadelphia, had been ushered into Congress on a populist, democratic wave in what Madison described as "a stunning change for the aristocracy." Albert Gallatin, a Swiss-French émigré, and William Findley, a Scotch-Irish immigrant, represented the boisterous, virulently anti-aristocratic reaches of western Pennsylvania—the region that had just nearly risen up in armed rebellion against the federal government in protest of Hamilton's excise tax on whiskey distilleries in 1794. Findley in particular, who had once been an arch-Anti-Federalist, was on the vanguard of the new democratic forces remaking American politics. Representing the other end of the political spectrum was William Cooper of upstate New York. A wealthy judge and landlord who had consolidated power on the early republican frontier, he practiced gentility as best he could, fashioning himself as the social better of the new political and social upstarts who had harnessed the Republican persuasion. But Cooper, himself a parvenu of humble origins who had begun his climb only a bit sooner, embodied the same brand of political culture that had elevated the likes of Swanwick and Findley. Whether through his willingness to wrestle locals in the mud, his excessive partisanship, or his clumsily constructed congressional speeches, Cooper revealed his rough-hewn character. Madison had complained about the inexperience of the First Congress, but now its membership was more untried than ever. Republicans had recently swept into power, and many members of their coalition had embraced the new brand of popular politics that had seized hold of so much of the republic. It created a volatile atmosphere. Describing the tenor of the House in early 1796, the characteristically forthright Ames reported, "faction is preparing its mines, and getting all ready for an explosion." Within this roiling, partisan cauldron, the transformation in constitutional imagination that was already well under way would only accelerate.[23]

Constitutional Rights

On March 1, 1796, Washington finally delivered the treaty to the House. Before the treaty could take full effect, the House would have to appropriate the necessary funds. The next day, Edward Livingston presented his fateful resolution. On its face, his motion might have seemed innocuous enough. All he sought was more information about the treaty's construction to assist the House's efforts. "The object of the resolution [is] only to obtain that knowledge necessary for an enlightened decision," claimed John Swanwick.[24]

But a more radical sentiment lurked beneath the surface, one that divided Republicans themselves. Madison and the other de facto Republican leaders in the House were proceeding cautiously, anxious of confronting Washington directly. But Livingston was among a younger cadre of House Republicans who had grown impatient. The first-term New York congressman was especially brash. An ostentatious speaker and dresser, he had ridden the support of New York City's Democratic-Republican society into office. No longer willing to wait on Madison and eager to satisfy the popular anger against the treaty, Livingston seized the initiative and, without permission, introduced his resolution. Taken aback and irritated, Madison tried to soften the motion, but he proved unsuccessful. Livingston's proposal would dominate the next month of debate in the House, largely because it effectively translated the essential democratic attitude that had driven Republican opposition to the treaty since the previous summer into a defense of the House's constitutional rights. As affirmed by Albert Gallatin, the future secretary of the treasury who made the Republican case as skillfully and vigorously as anyone in the debate, "it was supposed that the President and the Senate were the best judges" of the treaty, "because they possessed the best information." Accordingly, "to render this information public, must then answer to a valuable purpose." The president and Senate were the best judges of treaties, not because the Constitution afforded them this right, but because they had better intelligence than anybody else. If afforded the same information, the House would judge every bit as well. Drawing out the most important point, Gallatin avowed, "the House were the grand inquest of the nation," turning, in the context of the Jay Treaty, what had been a commonplace into a provocative statement.[25]

Federalists, suspicious of such insinuations, found Livingston's request pernicious. As William Loughton Smith, ever the willing challenger, knowingly asked, "Was the language, then, that this House might interfere and defeat the Treaty?" To Federalists, the request for papers betrayed a particular understanding of the Constitution—complete with a certain conception of what kind of discretionary rights were implied in its contents, who among the government's officers were justifiably positioned to exercise those, and how, in light of that discretion, uncertainties could be settled. Putting the components together, Livingston's motion suggested that the House of Representatives possessed a carte blanche interpretive authority. The resolution "was designed," William Vans Murray of Maryland announced, "as the ground-work of a very dangerous doctrine, that the House had a right to adjudge, to adopt, or to reject treaties generally." This request, therefore, was not merely about the treaty. Had that been the case, its proponents would have specified why they needed the information—what selective constitutional function (impeachment, appropriations, something else) would be carried out more successfully with the papers in hand. Republicans had instead embarked upon a fishing expedition. To Federalists, consequently, the request was not about properly carrying into effect specific constitutional functions. What Republicans seemed to be asserting, however opaquely, was broad authority for "the people's" representatives to pass judgment on certain features of the Constitution. This was "a Constitutional question . . . of the highest magnitude," Nathaniel Smith of Connecticut explained, "no less than whether the House of Representatives have a right to judge over the heads of the President and Senate on the subject of Treaties."[26]

Republicans insisted they had no malign intentions. Gallatin found it amazing that "a call for papers" was treated as an appeal "to disorganize the Government, and to erect the House into a National Convention." But neither did they shy away from the challenge. Some defended the House's right to request the papers. "If the papers called for contain information concerning the state of the Union," William Findley reasoned, "there can be no doubt but we have a right to call for them." To such claims, Republicans added another: that the House had a role in treaty making. "In the present case," Virginian John Nicholas asserted, "the House had a voice." Giles went further: "the House had a right, and, if it was a right, it must also be their duty," not simply to weigh in on the controversy, but, in fact, "to oppose [the Treaty's] execution by all the Constitutional means in their power."[27]

The Constitution specified that treaties were to be made by the president with the advice and consent of the Senate. How the House figured into this equation was hardly obvious, and explaining how it might would suggest something deeper about the Constitution's core characteristics. Thus, in affirming the House's role in treaty making, Republicans engulfed the body in a discussion that far transcended the immediate questions raised by Jay's Treaty. The resolution under debate "had unexpectedly involved in its discussion a question of a serious and interesting nature," observed Nathaniel Freeman, a truly "delicate Constitutional question." Madison himself reflected that "the direct proposition before the House, had been so absorbed by the incidental question which had grown out of it, concerning the Constitutional authority of Congress in the case of Treaties," that, no matter what anybody thought, they had no choice but to broaden their horizons and probe the Constitution itself. As he reported matter-of-factly to Jefferson, "the point in debate is the Constitutional right of [Congress] in relation to Treaties."[28]

The Sanctity of the Constitution

It took several rounds of intense exchanges on the House floor, however, before it became clear to members that, as Joshua Coit put it, "they stood now on the pure ground of an abstract Constitutional question." From there, attention quickly turned to what sort of object congressmen took the Constitution to be. Since its ratification, it had become commonplace to emphasize the Constitution's supremacy. In a common refrain, John Williams of New York stressed, "[our] powers were limited" as "the Constitution" alone "was [our] guide." But, as evidenced so vividly during both the removal and bank debates, this picture of supremacy was easily reconcilable with another image that accommodated the creative discretion of Congress: the Constitution could be simultaneously supreme and unfinished. The Jay Treaty debate featured something new, though, as several disputants (primarily Federalists) underscored not just the Constitution's supremacy but its sanctity. The 1789 debate over amendments had brought into focus the notion of the "sacred" text—although it was issued at first as a term of abuse. What was now distinct about invocations of the Constitution's vaunted status was the authority with which these appeals were deployed. It was an image that was acquiring a hitherto unprecedented power.[29]

Talk of constitutional sacredness became ubiquitous. "To support the Constitution it was necessary to preserve public faith. To promote the public happiness it was essential to hold sacred . . . [all] public engagements," Theodore Sedgwick, still a commanding presence in the House, explained. More precisely highlighting the Constitution, William Cooper suggested, "surely the good sense of the United States will frown into atoms the man who shall attempt to violate the sacred volume." Meanwhile, in the same vein, Ezekiel Gilbert of New York contended, "The rules and regulations prescribed by the nation through this organ"—that is, the Constitution—"are of . . . transcendant authority." The Constitution earned these paeans, which flew with marked frequency, not only because it was a supreme source of power, but also because its nature categorically distinguished it from other kinds of objects. All citizens, but especially those in office, had to "duly respect the sacred obligations they were under to support the Constitution."[30]

The document was no ordinary text; it was a timeless artifact. As William Vans Murray, one of the Federalists' most capable voices in the House, evocatively put it, "were despotism to cover the face of human society like a sweeping deluge, if preserved in some sacred sanctuary, [the Constitution] would, when made known again, be the rallying point from which genius, and patriotism, and justice, might restore to man his rights and happiness, however obscured by time and accident." Impervious to the accidents of time, the Constitution, no matter how poorly understood, would remain agelessly preserved. For this reason, it was to be venerated. "Our Constitution . . . is the law and the testimony, [the] sacred volume," James Holland of North Carolina declared. "The sacredness depends upon the attention to the principles that procured its adoption," he went on; "when that is contravened a violence is made upon the rights of the people." The Constitution demanded not only reverence but frequent acts of devotion, both of which would reinforce its sacred status. The only way to adhere to the Constitution was, as with religious belief, to pay ritualistic homage to its principles. Constitutional faithlessness equated to violence precisely because the Constitution was the "sacred volume." Building on this theme, Richard Brent of Virginia added, "Though a departure from the Constitution at one time may bestow some fugitive advantages," nonetheless, "such deviations would go finally to its destruction. If a single departure from the Constitution be once permitted, the Government will be subject to constant violation."[31]

This talk led many to equate infidelity to the Constitution with genuine revolution. "To overturn this Constitution is not merely to oppose it by violence," said Murray in reference to the Republican claim that the House could decline to execute the treaty until it had the executive papers in hand. "To refuse to act, to withhold an active discharge of the duties it enjoins upon the different branches," he went on, "would as effectually prostrate it as open violence could do." Believing that people had a revolutionary right to ignore laws, William Cooper worried that "it was in that confused state of things that Congress might repeal Treaties by not filling that middle ground they are placed in by refusing to grant appropriations; but both must be considered as in rebellion against the Constitution of the United States." Meanwhile, "as little taste as" Joshua Coit "had for revolutions," he "would not . . . be induced to join gentlemen, either by fraud or force, to overturn the Constitution."[32]

By depicting the Constitution in such sacrosanct terms, Federalists drew a particularly strong distinction between the tasks of creating a constitution and of expounding its meaning. "We were not making a Constitution, but construing one already made," Jeremiah Smith of New Hampshire pointed out. "Were we in Convention, and forming a Constitution, it might have weight; but in a cool discussion of a Constitution already formed and adopted," Uriah Tracy concluded, "it could not be proper." The task was "to inquire not what ought to be, but," summed up Connecticut's James Hillhouse, to determine "what *was* the Constitution of the United States?" Roger Griswold helped answer this question. "It was sufficient to say, that the people had, by their Constitution, in express words, deposited the Treaty power with the President and Senate," he explained. "As the House did not sit to make a Constitution, but to execute one, it was of no consequence whether the deposite was judicious, or otherwise." The Constitution was its express words. Its literal linguistic content comprised the substance of its creation. Ignoring those words—and the clear picture they painted—was tantamount to creating a new Constitution.[33]

This conception of the Constitution's essential character pointed toward a more exacting understanding of how it ought to restrain those seeking to make sense of it. Sedgwick assumed "that we were to resort to the Constitution, to know the extent and limits of our power, and if we found not there a clear evidence of its existence, we ought to abandon the exercise." Some congressmen, even more strongly than they had in earlier debates, drew a putative difference between the Constitution itself and what one could say about it. With this sharp distinction in mind, Federalists were especially distrustful of arguments that seemed to distort the Constitution into something it was not. "This practice of doing away the Constitution by construction," warned Hillhouse, "if once admitted, would lead to the most dangerous consequences." "All men must now see," Cooper proclaimed, "who are willing to be bound down by the letter of the Constitution, and who are desirous to break through all shackles." Through creative readings, Republicans were avoiding and evading the Constitution's own textual constraints and, in so doing, destroying the very document they were trusted to protect.[34]

Stressing the sacredness of the Constitution thus emphasized its fundamental linguistic character. As Federalists drew progressively more invidious distinctions between the Constitution and the blasphemous readings pronounced by Republicans, they increasingly rendered it a text. This led Federalists to stress the Constitution's face-value meaning. Appearances were not deceiving; the Constitution meant what it said. Any honest reading of the text would condemn the pending resolution as an act of usurpation. According to Sedgwick, the issue, when reduced to its essence, was "no less than whether this House should, by construction and implication, extend its controlling influence to subjects which were expressly, and . . . exclusively, delegated by the people to another department of the Government." "Construction and implication"—a loaded phrase to be sure—stood in stark contrast to what the Constitution quite evidently was. Along similar lines, Chauncey Goodrich, a recently elected lawyer from Connecticut, explained, "if we substitute constructive reasoning in place of the express letter of the Constitution, the form of our Government . . . would undergo perpetual changes." Constructive reasoning, another evocative phrase, unmoored the Constitution from its stable foundation, transforming it into something new with each passing construction. As Murray asserted, "we act under a Government and Constitution so extremely definite and precise," that any constructive liberty, taken "upon any important part of the Constitution, will forever be a hazardous experiment." An examination of the Constitution's words, on the other hand, conducted with "a sacred regard to their plain import," left little room for the "inventive faculties." Congressmen, as William Loughton Smith put it—as if channeling his earlier, spirited contributions to the removal debate—"were to understand the Treaty from the face of it," and nothing else.[35]

Indeed, for Federalists, only "by examining the law itself"—be that the Constitution or Jay's Treaty—would its meaning be clear. Samuel Lyman explained, "in forming an opinion relative to the constitutionality or unconstitutionality of a Treaty," all that was needed was "the Treaty and the Constitution, and then, by comparing the two instruments together, and upon that comparison alone," inquirers could "form their judgment." As Daniel Buck added, "The instrument is then before us; let us compare it with the Constitution" to see "if there is one article, sentence, word, or syllable in the Treaty, which clashes with, or is contradictory to, the Constitution." Robert Goodloe Harper of South Carolina elaborated on this comparison at length. Once such an ardent Republican that he had joined, and even led, one of Charleston's leading Democratic-Republican clubs, Harper had grown so disillusioned with the French Revolution that after joining Congress in 1795 he zealously converted to the Federalist cause. Undeterred by the pointed criticism he received for his betrayal, on the House floor he passionately married the Federalist position on the Jay Treaty to the inherent worth of written records themselves:

> As to its constitutionality, it must be decided by the instrument itself; it must be compared with the Constitution, and judged by the result. If Constitutional, on the face of it, none of the previous negotiations by which it was brought about, none of the instructions under which it was framed, could make it otherwise. So, on the other hand, if unconstitutional in itself, the defect cannot be cured by the instructions or previous correspondence. So, as to doubtful passages, it was a constant and invariable maxim that every deed, every law, every written instrument of any sort, was to be judged of and explained by itself, and not by recurrence to other matter. . . . Should this rule be departed from . . . all the advantages of written records would be lost, and we should wander into the wide fields of uncertainty and opinion.

Judging the constitutionality of the treaty required a simple comparison—putting the text of the Constitution to one side and the text of the treaty to the other. No additional documents, evidence, inferences, or constructions were necessary. The entire benefit of having "written records," Harper was insisting, was the clarity they provided. Congressmen were at risk of dispensing with that pellucidity, for seemingly no reason, and, as a result, wandering onto the "wide fields of uncertainty and opinion." In this realm of frightening indeterminacy, nothing could ground opinion; any reading of the Constitution would be as justified as any other.[36]

This comparison between the treaty and the nation's fundamental law worked so effectively because of the Constitution's clarity. "That instrument is so admirably constructed," rhapsodized Hillhouse, "that there is not a single superfluous word to be found throughout the whole." "The people have declared that the President and Senate shall make Treaties, without a single exception," Isaac Smith argued, "and, lest there should be any mistake or cavilling about it, they have put it in written words . . . too plain to be doubted, too positive to be contradicted." Joshua Coit, meanwhile, confessed that in looking to "the Constitution itself," the "light was there so clear that nothing more" was needed. The document's written contents were explicit and transparent, betraying no ambiguity. They called out for no further interpretation. As Fisher Ames (who, much to his frustration, missed most of the debate due to illness) wrote, will "the casuists quibble away the very words, and adulterate the genuine spirit, of the Constitution? . . . Sophistry may change the form of the question . . . yet the fact will speak for itself." Because it was written, and written with such care, there could be no doubt about the Constitution's meaning.[37]

In manifold ways, Federalists underscored clarity—clarity of the Constitution, clarity of the treaty, clarity of public instruments of any kind. In a lengthy and substantive speech, Murray referred to the Constitution as an "explicit and luminous body" made up of "strong and plain language" with "powers . . . so very definitely measured" that they ought be considered only from a "plain, unlettered, and self-consistent construction." Meanwhile, "The word Treaty," Jeremiah Smith insisted, was "as certain and definite in its meaning as any word in the language." Why the confusion, therefore, over what was otherwise so clear? Why were some ignoring "the common and most obvious meaning of words"? Given the document's evident lucidity, William Cooper asked, "why this new mode of explaining the Constitution?" To that point, "it had been understood from the school-boy to the Senator according to its true meaning. Why, to gratify party rage, shall [Republicans] attempt a new explanation of this criterion of their happiness?" The Constitution's "true meaning" had not escaped even the most inexperienced of its readers.[38]

Their Republican opponents, however, seemed to insist upon a fiction that, if conceded, would erode the Constitution's foundation. As John Williams explained with alarm, "if we ourselves do not understand the Constitution, it is not likely that our constituents at large should understand it." How could they know, he asked, "if we do not understand the Constitution after it has been in operation for nearly eight years?" What did it mean, in other words, to be subject to a Constitution if its orders and regulations were largely unknowable? The Constitution, he seemed to suggest, rested on epistemological foundations as much as political ones. Williams was exaggerating—Livingston and his fellow Republicans were not insisting on this brand of epistemic nihilism—but Federalists certainly convinced themselves otherwise. Williams's reference to the near decade of experience under the Constitution advanced a related argument. Republicans needed only look back at their own constitutional arguments over the preceding eight years—arguments that betrayed confidence in the document's contents—to find the most potent responses to their current position.[39]

If comparing the Constitution and the treaty provided a sufficient test, adequate in itself, Federalists reasoned, then any recourse to external documentation—above all Washington's instructions to Jay—would be superfluous and distracting. As Harper had pointed out in his extensive speech, if the treaty on its own was constitutional, nothing could make it unconstitutional. And, vice versa, those instructions could not redeem an otherwise unconstitutional instrument. "If it is not a Treaty in the view of the Constitution, nothing that we can do can make it Constitutional," Murray explained. "Either the paper upon the table is a Treaty, and as such is obligatory upon us as being part only of the nation, because it binds the nation; or it cannot be a Treaty." There was no middle ground, because it "cannot be a neutral inchoate act." Surrounding documents could underscore the "signification" of a written text, but they could not remake the text itself. Federalists hammered this point. While the papers could serve certain purposes, William Loughton Smith argued, "it was obvious, the question of constitutionality should be determined from the face of the instrument." The "knowledge of the preparatory steps which led to its adoption, could throw no light upon it" whatsoever.[40]

Ultimately, all of the Federalists' arguments that emphasized face-value meaning and interpretation leveraged the Constitution's writtenness—its embodiment in language—by identifying it as the object's defining characteristic. Harper had complained that Republicans threatened to destroy the value inherent in written records. Other Federalists elaborated on this point, grumbling that Republicans were trying to nullify the singular advantage Americans enjoyed in their constitutional system. "Much has been said about the British constitution," Cooper offered, but "their charter was nothing more than long usage, or practice reduced to precedent; and from that uncertain source their present unpleasant situation may have arisen." Britain's unwritten customary constitution had only created problems. What happily distinguished the American situation, though, was that "they had the book and page." Added Samuel Lyman, the "Constitution of this country is written," and within it "the powers of several Departments of Government are clearly and accurately defined." No mystery remained. Since it could appeal to the clear, unambiguous temple of language the United States could not descend into corruption as Britain had—as long, that is, as Republicans, who were doing everything they could to unravel the nation's constitutional fabric, did not get their way.[41]

Digging beneath the Constitution's Surface

Opposition to Livingston's resolution had brought to the surface a particular vision of the Constitution. What was sacred was unshakeable, and what was unshakeable spoke for itself. But as powerful and relentless as this opposition was, Livingston's request for executive papers enjoyed a greater measure of support. Pressured by their constituents' intense Anglophobia, Republicans clung to their constitutional position: the House of Representatives ought to have a role in treaty making. Explaining why, though, compelled Republicans to challenge the Federalists' rival vision of the Constitution by destabilizing its basic tenets and offering a compelling alternative. The goal was to force the House into the realm of treaties. But, in justifying this position, they clarified a broader understanding of the Constitution. At the heart of this rendering was a single theme to which they relentlessly returned, one that cut to the very foundation of Federalists' objection: understanding the Constitution required digging beneath its surface.

How clear was the Constitution's treaty provision—Republicans asked? Federalists were insistent on its clarity—the president with the advice and consent of the Senate made treaties, which then became part of the supreme law of the land, while the House plainly had no role in the process. Republicans vehemently disagreed. As Abraham Baldwin contended, "those few words in the Constitution on this subject, were not those apt, precise, definite expressions, which irresistibly brought upon them the meaning" many supposed. Pursuing this line, Baldwin "begged" his colleagues "to review the few words in the Constitution on which they rested so much, and to ask whether they appeared to be such labored expressions as they supposed—so apt and definite as to mean exactly what they contend for, and nothing else." It was spurious, he concluded, to suggest that the treaty clause was such a model of perspicuity. Quite the contrary, a simple reading of it invited as many questions as answers.[42]

The Constitution, on its face, was insufficient to arbitrate the pertinent question. "It was to be regretted," Madison observed, "that on a question of such magnitude as the present, there should be any apparent inconsistency, or inexplicitness in the Constitution, that could leave room for different constructions." While perhaps unfortunate, however, there was nothing shameful about acknowledging this deficiency. As Baldwin noted, "it was not to disparage the instrument, to say that it had not definitely, and with precision, absolutely settled everything on which it had spoke." The only shame came in dishonestly claiming otherwise. Albert Gallatin found Federalists' assertion that "their doctrine rested on the letter of the Constitution, whilst that of those who contended for the powers of the House was grounded only on construction and implication," utterly baseless. The Constitution was nothing if not complex. It was more than met the eye and, accordingly, required patient, careful study. Invidious distinctions drawn between strict and constructed interpretations, between clear and unclear passages, were typically just attempts to obscure clever readings. As Madison put it, reviving some of his earlier commentary on linguistic indeterminacy, "No construction might be perfectly free from difficulties."[43]

Given this evident uncertainty, Republicans argued, the Constitution's treaty-making power required more probing than Federalists were willing to concede. The issue was not—as Federalists obsessively framed it—*that* the Constitution constrained those in power, but *how* exactly it constrained them. As Jonathan Havens of New York explained, even if "the will of the people had been expressed in [the Constitution], and that therefore we ought to submit" to it, "such an assertion did not remove the difficulty," because it still remained "to be determined what the people had said when they expressed their will in the Constitution," and, from there, whether "they did not intend that a Treaty containing Legislative regulations should receive the assent of the House of Representatives before it was carried into effect." Making much the same point, Madison claimed that the "true question . . . before the Committee, was, not whether the will of the people expressed in the Constitution was to be obeyed, but *how* that will was to be understood," that is, "what construction would best reconcile the several parts of the instrument with each other, and be most consistent with its general spirit and object."[44]

The treaty-making clause needed to be situated in the context of the whole Constitution. In a celebrated speech, Gallatin adeptly explained why. "That general power of making Treaties, *undefined* as it is by the clause which grants it," he noted, "may either be expressly *limited* by some other positive clauses of the Constitution, or it may be *checked* by some powers vested in other branches of the Government." Because treaty making was sufficiently "undefined," one had to look elsewhere in the Constitution and ponder whether other constitutional provisions contradicted the treaty-making clause. Republicans were confident in where this led. A face-value reading of the treaty clause, they claimed time and again, was "limited by other parts of the Constitution."[45]

The Constitution, Republicans asserted, was plainly contradictory. "The question may arise," Gallatin observed, "whether a Treaty made by the President and Senate containing regulations touching objects delegated to Congress, can be considered binding without Congress passing laws to carry it into effect." This question could not be ignored. "A difference of opinion may exist as to the proper construction" of the Constitution, but it was incumbent upon interpreters "to reconcile those apparently contradictory provisions." More pointedly, if the treaty-making power and the specific powers vested in the House of Representatives were fully admitted, "we are reduced to a dilemma," William Findley declared, for then "the Constitution is necessarily admitted to have instituted two interfering Legislative authorities, acting in direct competition with each other on the same subjects, and both making supreme laws of the land." As William Lyman of Massachusetts stressed, "two persons could not be possessed fully and completely of the same thing and at the same time," and yet, from a cursory glance, that was what the Constitution seemed to ensure.[46]

This glaring contradiction between Federalists' reading of the Constitution and the powers of the House of Representatives demanded serious consideration because, if admitted, Federalists' understanding of the treaty-making power was admitted, it would cripple the core constitutional rights and obligations of the House. One right empowered Congress to exercise complete authority over all legislative matters; another gave the House exclusive authority over all appropriations (which the Jay Treaty required to take effect); still another—linked to the matter of appropriations—granted the House sole oversight over all commerce (the treaty, of course, was among other things a commercial agreement). Republican argument was saturated with references to these rights.[47]

The House, according to Republicans, had a fundamental, non-eliminable, right to make laws. As Havens characterized it, "the Constitutional question . . . when stated in as concise terms as possible" came down to this: "Is there not . . . an apparent interference between the Treaty-making power, vested by the Constitution in the President and Senate, and the Legislative power vested in Congress?" Article I of the Constitution vested an enumerated set of legislative powers in Congress. It did so just as clearly as the treaty clause seemed to delegate power to the president and Senate. And yet the Jay Treaty also required the House to pass certain laws to bring that agreement into effect. If the treaty mandated that the House pass those laws, did the House really enjoy constitutional control over legislation? Where there was "a concurrence of powers, where they interfere in their exercise," explained Findley, "one of the powers must yield absolute and implicit obedience to the other. . . . The submitting power must, in the event, be annihilated by the paramount power, or become a mere formal and inefficient agent." The Jay Treaty pitted fundamental constitutional obligations against one another. The House's basic power as a legislative agent would be annihilated if, even once, it was subjected to the unilateral will of the president and Senate. As Madison argued, "if the Treaty power alone could perform any one act for which the authority of Congress is required by the Constitution, it may perform every act."[48]

More specific than the right to legislate were the particular legislative powers that fell under congressional authority more generally, and often the House's authority in particular. The Jay Treaty was, in essence, a commercial agreement. It regulated commerce between the United States and Great Britain, by forbidding either nation from imposing higher duties on the other than they levied on other nations (thus eliminating the possibility of discriminating against British trade, a move Madison had long favored). Should the House, vested with the right to regulate all interstate and foreign commerce, not have some say in such an agreement, Republicans asked? Robert Rutherford assumed that none would claim that "this branch of the great National Council have not complete control over the commerce, naturalization, &c., of the United States." John Page of Virginia added "that as that Treaty would be a commercial regulation, and as Congress is expressly empowered by the Constitution to regulate commerce," Congress must "sanction the ratification of such Treaty." James Holland was particularly adamant about the role of the House in these transactions: "This is a Treaty of Commerce, and therefore has involved Legislative objects." Consequently, it "requires Legislative sanction; a contrary construction would be a violation of the Constitution."[49]

Republicans did not see why, in the face of this contradiction, the House should capitulate. If anything, it was the treaty-making power that needed to be checked. At the very least, the two contradictory powers deserved equal respect. "If still it is insisted that Treaties are the supreme law of the land, the Constitution and laws are also," Gallatin maintained, meaning that the real question was "which shall have the preference? Shall a Treaty repeal a law or a law a Treaty?" Madison echoed this sentiment. If disputants were honest and willing to recognize the constitutional contradiction exposed by Jay's Treaty, then they would realize that "where the act of one department of Government interferes with a power expressly vested in another," then "the latter power must be exercised according to its nature." And if it was legislative power, "it must be exercised with that deliberation and discretion which is essential to the nature of Legislative power." If the House could give up any of its powers, Findley argued, "it may on the same principle, dispense with or transfer every power with which it is vested." That defeated the purpose of constituting legislative power. Relatedly, if the House could relinquish its authority, that would render the Constitution cripplingly dysfunctional. As Republican House member William Branch Giles put it so vividly in a letter to Jefferson, Federalists' interpretation of "the treaty makeing power completely Checkmates the whole constitution."[50]

At stake was whether the House would enjoy its powers as a constitutional equal. Federalists' reading promised to reduce the body to dependency in relationship to the other bodies of government. As Swanwick cautioned, in a description that evoked the most pointed of racialized horrors, "the House [would] become mere automatons, mere Mandarine members, like those who nod on a chimney-piece, as directed by a power foreign to themselves." Similarly, Madison worried that the House "would be the mere instrument of the will of another department, and would have no will of its own." In insisting upon "this doctrine," Gallatin warned, Federalists "should deny the free agency of the House." Stripped of its agency, treated "like machines," the House would be stripped of its constitutional being. In a culture in which the meaning of political liberty often stressed the importance of being subject to one's own will—what made popular representation in the House so vital to so many—these were alarming concerns.[51]

Republicans further explained that Federalists' common retort to these fears—that the House exercised discretion by carrying the treaty into effect—misunderstood the nature of its willful agency. "If the subject were less serious," Livingston joked without much humor, "one would be tempted to smile at the efforts that are made to reconcile the Constitutional predestination contended for, with the free agency of discretion." It was as tricky to understand "as the most entangled theological controversy," and, he continued, "like most disputants in that science, they concluded with anathemas against all who could not comprehend, or would not believe them." To so distort the true meaning of free agency and equate it with predestination gave Federalist logic the appearance of the most abstruse religious doctrine. The House had no discretion at all if it was "only to execute the injunction of the Constitution." As Gallatin so urgently explained, an "essential principle of our Constitution . . . which was the basis of our Revolution, and of all our Governments," was that "the sacred principle that the people could not be bound without the consent of their immediate Representatives." And yet, "Deprived of their discretion, of the freedom of their will," these representatives "must implicitly obey and execute laws made by another set of agents of the people."[52]

More troubling still, consigning the House to a dependent fate compromised one of the Constitution's essential ends. "It is the height of folly to contend that the American people ever intended to give any authority an unlimited operation. If the Constitution be examined," and probed right to its core, Giles contended, "it will be found grounded on a jealousy against all rulers." The Constitution was constructed to limit the exercise of power; if anything about it was clear, it was that. This characteristic was fundamental to its mission. In light of this principle, Gallatin wondered why friends of Livingston's resolution were being branded revolutionaries, "stigmatized as rebellious disorganizers, as traitors against the Constitution?" To his mind, they were not claiming a dangerous, active power, just "the right of checking the exercise of a general power" when it clashed with "the special powers expressly vested in Congress by the Constitution." It was those opposed to the resolution, those unwilling to dig deeper and consider the treaty-making power more fully, who were actually undermining the document.[53]

At every turn, Republicans insisted that a face-value reading of the Constitution failed not only to uphold the purpose for which the instrument was constructed but also to do justice to the multiple—at times conflicting—imperatives embedded within its contents. "It is not contended," Giles suggestively offered, "that there are words in the Constitution expressly" authorizing the House to control treaties; but that did not mean the House lacked the power. As William Lyman explained, "in the interpretation and construction of laws or Constitutions, the following rules had always been deemed sound": to, among other things, always "regard the true spirit and meaning, and not merely the letter. It was a maxim very ancient, and at the same time very common . . . that he who adhered only to the letter stuck in the bark, and never arrived at the pith." Republicans were gesturing toward an altogether different conception of the Constitution, one that probed beneath its surface, and which was less wedded to its words and more sensitive to its spirit. At stake, then, was not just the House's role in treaty making. More broadly this was a contest over the kind of object that the Constitution was and what sorts of interpretive norms ought to structure its usage.[54]

Republicans' core claim was that the Constitution had to be seen whole. No single component could be divorced from the rest. Only by appreciating how its interlocking pieces fit together could one comprehend what it was saying. As John Page laid out, "No rule of construction is more universally known and established in explaining any Constitution, law, contract, or Treaty than this: that the whole must be taken together," meaning that "whatever seeming contradiction may appear in different parts, those parts must be construed so, if possible, as to be consistent with each other, and with the whole; and by no means so as to contradict the general tenor and design of the whole instrument." This was the requirement in construing "all writings," William Lyman claimed, "to receive such interpretation and construction as to render them consistent with themselves." The goal of constitutional exegesis, especially, was "to preserve the symmetry of the fabric, and keep the balance," Richard Brent explained. William Branch Giles applied this line of reasoning to the Jay Treaty: "if there was no other clause" than the one Federalists were obsessing over, then they might have had a point. But "when they quote this clause, [they] stop, as if there were no other words in it," from there assuming "that the people had, in fact, delegated an unchecked power." In "referring to particular portions, and not attending to the whole," Gallatin argued, "absurdities must arise." And, as Madison pointed out, "the first task in constitutional interpretation was to remove all absurdities." Since it "could never [be] suppose[d] so great and pernicious an absurdity was contemplated by the Constitution" as the one that Federalists were endorsing, it was clear that they were reading the Constitution incorrectly.[55]

The Meanings of Supremacy

What, then, was the best way to see the Constitution "whole"? Attending to the instrument's latent contradictions naturally provoked this question. Early on, Madison took stock of the debate in his incisive style, characteristically distinguishing the five constructions implicated by the debate. He laid them out one by one:

I. The Treaty power, and the Congressional power, might be regarded as moving in such separate orbits, and operating on such separate objects, as to be incapable of interfering with, or touching each other. II. As concurrent powers relating to the same objects; and operating like the power of Congress, and the power of the State Legislatures, in relation to taxes on the same articles. III. As each of them supreme over the other, as it may be the last exercised; like the different assemblies of the people, under the Roman Government, in the form of centuries, and in the form of tribes. IV. The Treaty power may be viewed, according to the doctrine maintained by the opponents of the proposition before the Committee, as both unlimited in its objects, and completely paramount in its authority. V. The Congressional power may be viewed as co-operative with the Treaty-power, on the Legislative subjects submitted to Congress by the Constitution . . . [as] exemplified in the British Government.

The first, second, and third constructions were all naive, premised on the assumption that the treaty power and congressional power, if left to their own devices, would not interfere with one another. The Jay Treaty had exposed that absurdity. Option four captured Federalists' favored argument, but it had already collapsed under scrutiny. Option five, meanwhile, sufficiently reduced House discretion as to render it impotent. So none of these choices sufficed.[56]

The debate had exposed contradictions in the Constitution's provisions, ones that Republicans were quick to exploit to carve out a role for the House in treaty making. But they still had to explain why the House itself (rather than another entity) was capable of reconciling the incongruities. In tilting the conversation in this direction, they focused first on the supremacy clause and next on the relationship between the House and "the people." Federalists tried to undermine each of these Republican claims. But by engaging their opponents on this ground, Federalists suggested that the Constitution was less clear than their appeals to face-value meaning had otherwise insisted. By playing this particular game of giving and asking for reasons, they acknowledged that constructive reasoning of some kind was necessary to resolve the Constitution's inconsistencies. By forcing Federalists to take House treaty discretion seriously, in other words, Republicans got both sides to dig beneath the Constitution's surface.

House members delved into the many meanings of supremacy in the American constitutional scheme—the supremacy of treaties compared with laws, the supremacy of "the people" compared with the textual meaning of the Constitution, the supremacy of the Constitution compared with everything else. This discussion was complex, moving in numerous directions at once. Most evidently, it was about resolving the constitutional contradictions exposed by Jay's Treaty. More broadly, it was about the many valences of constitutional supremacy. And broadest of all, it was about the Constitution's functional character—whether it truly constituted a complete and closed system, a rule-proffering mechanism in need of no external inputs.

Federalists first made the debate about supremacy, since they were convinced that emphasizing this constitutional theme bolstered their cause. "It was said, yesterday," Madison cynically observed on March 10, "that a Treaty was paramount to all other acts of Government." His disbelief aside, he was not wrong to think that it was becoming a standard refrain. Like most Federalists, William Vans Murray considered "a Treaty, constitutionally made, to be the supreme law of the land." He and other Federalists were pointing to Article VI of the Constitution, which read: "This Constitution, and the Laws of the United States which shall be made in Pursuance thereof; and all Treaties made, or which shall be made, under the Authority of the United States, shall be the supreme Law of the Land." The vaunted "supremacy clause"—previously a source of compromise at the Federal Convention and of intense controversy during the ratification debates—fast became a staple of the House debate over Jay's Treaty.[57]

Federalists happily underscored what the supremacy clause seemed to be saying—that treaties, once properly ratified, were supreme law. "If we were to rest the subject here, it would seem to follow irresistibly, and to be incapable almost of higher proof," Theodore Sedgwick reasoned, "that whenever a compact . . . was of such a nature as to be properly denominated a Treaty, all its stipulations would thereby, and from that moment, become 'supreme laws.'" The supremacy clause, in this regard, reconciled the apparent contradiction between treaty making and lawmaking by giving priority to the former. As Theophilus Bradbury of Massachusetts put it, "the Constitution declares, that Treaties, all Treaties, without exception or limitation, made under the authority of the United States . . . shall be the law of the land." Given this declaration, the Republicans' understanding, which "teaches and asserts, that they shall not be the law of the land, although so made, until sanctioned by an act of the Legislature," was especially strange. How could treaties be supreme and yet at once susceptible to legislative sanction? "If the sanction of the House is to be given by a law, this absurdity seems to be involved in it," Jeremiah Smith pointed out with exasperation, "that a law is necessary to give" it the validity that the Constitution declares it to already have.[58]

But Republicans argued that their opponents had completely misunderstood the supremacy clause. In fact, far from privileging treaty making above lawmaking, the clause merely underscored the importance of House discretion. "It had been argued," Baldwin observed, that "the Treaty-making power must be paramount. The truth is," though, "the Treaty-making power must be what the Constitution has made of it." And "the most natural meaning," he claimed, was far different than the one Federalists had defended.[59]

Specifically, Republicans asserted that the supremacy clause did not cover the relationship between national treaties and federal laws, but instead only the relative authority of federal and state law. As Gallatin contended, "the clause does not compare a Treaty with the law of the United States. . . . It only compares all the acts of the Federal Government with the acts of the individual States," declaring that the former shall be paramount to the latter. "The clause by no means expresses," he continued, "that Treaties are equal or superior to the laws of the Union, or that they shall be supreme law when clashing with any of them." Once properly deciphered, Swanwick argued, "it is obvious that the supremacy of the law is over the Constitution and laws of the separate States." As a result, the supremacy clause "does not affect the powers of this House." Madison argued even more forcefully that "the term *supreme,* as applied to Treaties, evidently meant a supremacy over the State Constitutions and laws, and not over the Constitution and Laws of the United States."[60]

Moreover, while treaties were included in the supremacy clause, so were laws; neither was superior to the other, they enjoyed the same constitutional authority. Federalists, Republicans complained, had struggled to explain precisely what they meant when they claimed that treaties were supreme law of the land. As Jonathan Havens argued, Federalists "consider[ed] Treaty law of so transcendant a nature as almost to form a part of the Constitution itself." But "they appeared," at the same time, "to place it in a grade or sphere a little below the Constitution, but far above any Congressional law."

These conclusions failed to make sense of the fact "that the Constitution has declared the Congressional law shall be the supreme law of the land as well as Treaty law." According to Republicans, Federalists had elevated treaties beyond the realm of law, equal to the Constitution itself. These peculiar distortions seemingly had no purpose except to limit the power of the House and, in any case, they were not grounded in the Constitution, since, as Madison contended, "treaties and laws, whatever the nature of them may be, must, in their operation, be often the same." Being "on the same footing in the Constitution," they "must share the same fate."[61]

Since the supremacy clause simply underscored the equal standing of treaties and laws, it did nothing to reconcile the contradiction at hand between the relative authority of lawmaking compared to treaty making. "It was as absurd to say that a Treaty could repeal a law," Gallatin argued, "as to say that a law could repeal a Constitution." "The argument was as strong the other way," claimed Madison. "Congress are as much the organs of the people, in making laws, as the President and Senate can be in making Treaties." Put in the most sweeping of terms, Gallatin argued, the "Constitution is paramount to both laws and Treaties." Thus, "when gentlemen ground their arguments on the position that Treaties are superior or equal to the laws of the Union, they take for granted the very thing which is to be proved." The supremacy clause simply could not arbitrate the conflict.[62]

Invocations of the supremacy clause, Republicans contended, instead merely emphasized the House's legitimate role in treaty making. It certainly could not be the case that "the House must remain silent spectators in the business of a Treaty," as Giles put it. For the supremacy clause to make sense (much like the rest of the Constitution of which it was a part), politicians would have to integrate lawmaking with treaty making. When treaties "contain stipulations bearing a relation to the specific power vested in the Legislature," Richard Brent argued, "the House had a right to take cognizance of it, and such Treaty could not become supreme law until sanctioned by the Legislature." Rather than futilely elevating one power above another, Havens contended, it was instead "necessary to adopt such a principle of construction as will give both these powers full operation and effect." The only way to make sense of the supremacy clause, in other words, was to permit the House a role in treaty making.[63]

Yet, for Republicans, there was a deeper reason still why the House had to be involved in treaty making—one that most fully captured their conception of the "people's" Constitution. Republicans expressed skepticism that the Constitution was a complete system of rules. William Lyman articulated the point most clearly. "The right or power of making Treaties was," he argued, one of those examples that "were so many and various, that it was impossible to prescribe certain rules antecedent to the case." Just like the debate over chartering a national bank had brought this issue to the surface, so too had the debate over Jay's Treaty. Precisely because the Constitution could not resolve its own contradictions, it required additional judgment. In moments of constitutional doubt, Lyman professed, constitutional rules "could only be [elucidated] by the whole people, or by their Legislature." Republicans asserted that the House, in particular, was uniquely suited to exercise this judgment because of its special role in the constitutional scheme. The rules necessary to apply the Constitution to emergent situations involved recognizing the connection between the "whole people" and "their Legislature." The House was supreme among equals because it was the one institution closest to "the people."[64]

Republicans' belief that the House played a special constitutional role stemmed from a peculiar understanding of both the newfound importance of publicity in the young republic and the unique relationship connecting the House to "the people" who made up that forceful public. The Jay Treaty had indeed prompted a national crisis. Opposition to it had consumed the nation since Jay first returned from Britain. But fierce antagonism, expressed through any number of extra-political means, was not merely the cause of Republicans' opposition in the House. More strikingly, it was also claimed as legitimate grounds for their intervention. In general, Republicans stressed the importance of publicity. "The doctrine of publicity," suggested Baldwin, "had been daily gaining ground in public transactions. . . . The passion for mystery was exploded . . . the greater the publicity of measures the greater the success." John Williams added, "in a Republican Government there ought to be no secrets." Rutherford declared even more emphatically that "the majesty of this great people justly entitles them to all possible publicity." Against the background of these broader defenses, John Heath of Virginia justified Livingston's resolution on two grounds: "first, that the request or call for those papers . . . is a Constitutional right of this House to exercise now, and at all times, founded upon a principle of publicity essentially necessary in this, our Republic," and, building from there, "secondly . . . since the Treaty lately negotiated with Great Britain has created so much uneasiness and solicitude in the public mind, we therefore ought to pursue every method in our power to allay their sensibility." This statement, stunning in is implications, captured a pervasive sentiment. "The petitions in favor of the Treaty, and those which were presented against it," Livingston claimed, "both acknowledged the right of the House to interfere." Republicans were suggesting that the Constitution took on novel shape based on the needs of the people at large.[65]

"The people" boasted a significance they had not previously enjoyed, and in the Republican view, the House of Representatives comprised, in a special sense, "the people's" representatives. While much about American constitutionalism had been transformed since 1776, the debate over the Jay Treaty revealed that at least one crucial idea retained power—the notion that there was a special affinity between the people at large and their lower houses of assembly. As Nathaniel Freeman Jr. argued, "The consent of the people" was essential, "and by their Constitution the Legislature are the organ to express the public will." Gallatin was one of several members to call the House "the Representatives of the People." Samuel Smith of Maryland echoed him. "We . . . are the immediate delegates of the people," he proclaimed, and thus members needed "to retain those privileges given to the House by the Constitution," to hand "to their successors inviolate." Some had said that the president and Senate were equally the representatives of the people. But the "Constitution has appointed that Representatives shall be chosen by the people in proportion to their population," so, Aaron Kitchell asked, "were the Senate so chosen? No. The people have no vote at all in choosing them. Are they amenable to the people for their conduct? No." Given these facts, "in no shape can they be called the Representatives of the people." Only the House "represented . . . the people at large." Only the House could enforce the "people's" Constitution.[66]

Federalists challenged this alleged special relationship, drawing a distinction between the Constitution and the popular will. The Constitution, they argued, was the only true embodiment of the people. Accordingly, each branch of government was merely a custodian of that trust, simultaneously as close and as far away from the people as all the others. The president and Senate could control treaty making in its entirety without compromising the popular sovereignty on which the Constitution rested. If members of the House were the people's only representatives, Sedgwick asked, "who then . . . were the Senators? Were they unfeeling tyrants, whose interests were separated from and opposed to those of the people?" Like all other representatives, they sprang from "the confidence of the people, and the free choice of their electors." Roger Griswold added that "the laws were the laws of the people, and not the laws of the House of Representatives. And shall not the people who made the laws by one set of agents, repeal them, if they please, by another?" Isaac Smith hammered home the point: "Here rests the fallacy. The people knew, whether they knew or not, that they chose the President, and they firmly believe, as well they may, that he is their guardian. The people knew, also, that they chose the Senators, and they likewise think they are their guardians." Explaining how the House alone represented the people, he wryly insisted, "will require a modesty superior to that of New England to explain."[67]

In fact, reverence for the people's sovereignty encouraged a swift rejection of Livingston's resolution. "The Constitution is the will of the people," declared Robert Goodloe Harper, "in whom the sovereign power resides, and we . . . obey it." Indeed, it was "his love of the Constitution, his love of the people, his respect for their rights, and his belief in their sovereignty, which induced" him to oppose the resolution. Spelling out this logic, Ezekiel Gilbert humorously asked, "should one branch complain because it had not been placed in the station of another? Should the foot complain because it had not been made the hand, or the hand murmur because it has not been made the head?" Treaties, then, were as much the will of the people as were laws. In summation, "the people had fixed barriers to the different branches of the Constitution," explained John Williams, "which could not be overleaped without endangering the whole fabric."[68]

That Williams referenced the Constitution's "whole fabric" was revealing. For, despite what they were otherwise trying to accomplish, in arguing over the supremacy clause and the document as a whole, Federalists had been dragged into the Republicans' game. Such engagement represented a tacit acknowledgment that the Constitution might indeed contain some of the contradictions that Republicans had complained about. In looking to other parts of the Constitution, like the supremacy clause, and thus beyond the prima facie meaning of the treaty-making clause, Federalists were invoking their own, gentler brand of constitutional holism. Chauncey Goodrich conceded, "that to expound the Constitution fairly we must compare its parts together." Similarly, James Hillhouse "felt an irresistible impression," which was "to give the Constitution such a candid and fair construction as to admit every part to have its full operation." William Vans Murray, meanwhile, argued "that no construction of the Constitution which defeated and rendered either null or unnatural in its enjoyment any grants of power in the

Constitution, could possibly be the true one." The treaty's "relation," he concluded, "is to the whole."[69]

While they never conceded Republicans' primary assertion that the House needed to sanction commercial treaties, over the course of the debate, Federalists acknowledged that the Constitution was less clear than they had initially suggested. In denying Republicans' conclusion, Federalists had licensed their premise. This dialectical process and the practices it produced gestured toward a kind of constitutional indeterminacy.

The Contradictory Constitution

"The natural construction of the Treaty-making power, was this," Gallatin concluded at one point, "as far as a Treaty negotiated by the Executive embraced Legislative objects, so far it required the sanction of the Legislature." This "natural construction" of the treaty clause, which afforded the House a discretionary role, was premised on an implicit recognition of the Constitution's contradictions. Madison agreed: "On comparing the several passages in the Constitution," he reflected, "it appeared, that if taken literally, and without limit, they must necessarily clash with each other." The upshot of all this argumentation was that the House's sanction was tied to a particular conception of the Constitution, one that was based on the notion that its meaning was buried somewhere beneath its textual surface.[70]

At first, Republicans' assault on face-value meaning implied a strong vision of constitutional incompleteness. The only way to harmonize the Constitution's discordant parts was through political discretion, which could best be exercised by the House of Representatives because of its unique capacity to speak for the sovereign people who had so zealously announced their presence beyond the corridors of government. Federalists had challenged this conception of the "people's" Constitution at every turn by emphasizing the sanctity of the Constitution's face-value meaning. But even if they never explicitly relinquished this commitment, they did engage with Republicans on their own terms, conceding not only that the Constitution was more than met the eye but that additional judgment was needed to piece together the instrument's contradictory elements. They never endorsed Republicans' brand of constitutional imagination, but they did license some of its possibilities.

As much as the contradictory Constitution pushed congressmen toward constitutional imperfection, however, ultimately the Jay Treaty debate led to a much different place. During this episode the conception of the Constitution as uncertain and incomplete was ultimately crowded out, replaced in emphasis and immediate appeal by another. From the debate's beginning until its end, Republicans endorsed the House's authority to ratify commercial treaties and Federalists denounced that commitment. But as the manner in which both sides justified their positions subtly shifted, a rival form of constitutional imagination came to dominate the scene.

7

The Apotheosis
of the Fixed Constitution

The infant periods of most nations are buried in silence or veiled in
fable. . . . The origin & outset of the American Republic contain lessons
of which posterity ought not to be deprived: and happily there never
was a case in which every interesting incident could be so accurately
preserved.

—James Madison to William Eustis, July 6, 1819

The debate over Jay Treaty barreled on. As it did, it increasingly came
to revolve around a different kind of argument—one that was not focused
on the Constitution's words or structure, but rather on the history surrounding its creation. The wider public had vehemently opposed the
treaty, and the debate in the House of Representatives had begun with
Republicans stressing (and celebrating) the Constitution's inherent contradictions. Federalists' face-value reading of the Constitution would not
suffice, a point Federalists obliquely conceded, even as they continued to
oppose Republicans' broader purpose. Both sides dug beneath the surface, desperate to resolve the Constitution's complexities. But rather
than concluding—as so many had before—that the Constitution was perpetually incomplete, they gravitated toward a much different image of its
fundamental character. In the process, they invented a much different way of
coping with the long-standing ambiguities of constitutional fixity, one that
radically reconceived its relationship to time and the historical archive.[1]

Appeals to the history of the Constitution's construction had slowly acquired purchase after the document's ratification. During the debate over
removal of executive officers, they infrequently but conspicuously fortified

important arguments. Then, during the debate over chartering a national bank, the relevance and power of these invocations grew. In a last-ditch effort to challenge the bank's constitutionality, Madison and others had drawn on historical evidence of original intent as a way of handling the problem of interpretive regress without licensing congressional discretion, a move that, however unsuccessful in thwarting the creation of the bank, nonetheless encouraged some opponents to make similar appeals. These appeals, combined with the fateful decision to add amendments by supplementation rather than incorporation, had brought the archival Constitution—which imagined the document as a distinctively time-locked object—into focus. But even if the archival Constitution had come into view, it still lurked primarily in the shadows throughout the first half of the 1790s. During the Jay Treaty debate, though, historical excavation moved from the periphery to the center, remaking constitutional imagination in the process.

The transition in the Jay Treaty dispute from one conception of the Constitution to another was complex. Appeals to the constitutional discretion of the House of Representatives were not wholly replaced by appeals to the history of the Constitution's construction—let alone in one simple move or at one decisive point. Both kinds of arguments (and all of the related arguments that accompanied each) were laid over each other from the debate's beginning to close. Seeing the debate whole, though, reveals an important shift in emphasis—how the initial possibilities opened up by the debate ended up producing a distinct set of consequences. By episode's end, historical excavation into the Constitution's origins enjoyed a new vitality and relevance.

The ease with which the debate's participants licensed historical excavation was stunning. Both Republicans and Federalists assumed its relevance with virtually no debate. Two groups that had split over virtually every detail of the Jay Treaty—the House's right to call for supporting papers, the House's discretionary role in treaty making, the meaning of the Constitution's face value—had at last found something on which they could agree: the premise of historical appeals was readily accepted by congressmen for the first time. Both sides increasingly concurred that the original intent and understanding of those who drafted and ratified the Constitution could arbitrate the questions at issue. They had converged on a particular game of giving and asking for constitutional reasons. The convergence was not total, and it did not automatically necessitate a particular brand of constitutional consciousness. But through this convergence the debate's participants invented and helped to entrench a particular way of looking at the Constitution. Independent of the treaty's fate, the aggressive and sustained appeals they made to the archive of the Constitution's creation crystallized a form of constitutional imagination that, over the prior decade, had slowly been germinating: the idea of the fixed Constitution.[2]

In contrast to the indeterminate, unfinished Constitution—whose contents were in flux—the contents of the fixed Constitution were locked in time. Several distinct conceptual pieces needed to coalesce for this particular understanding of the Constitution to take shape. First, it required conceiving of the Constitution as a linguistic artifact, one whose contents and boundaries were drawn by words. But indeterminacies, instabilities, and contradictions remained, as the Jay Treaty debate—like the removal and bank debates before it—had so manifestly revealed. Disputants during the bank debate had managed to devise an inchoate way of overcoming this difficulty—by tethering the textual Constitution that Anti-Federalists had first conceived during ratification to the archival Constitution that the debate over amendments had helped bring into focus. Second, then, fixing the Constitution meant tethering its words to the archive of its creation.

Yet, even when taken on their own, these ingredients might not have produced a time-locked notion of fixity. Still another step was required to complete the creation. The Constitution's textual and archival character had to be linked to a separate idea that Founding-era Americans had otherwise emphasized: the concept of contingent, willful constitutional authorship. The American Revolutionary generation came of age immersed in the logic of the British constitution. Like the Argonauts' ship—which Matthew Hale so revealing explained "was the same when it returned home, as it was when it went out, tho' in that long Voyage it had successive Amendments, and scarce came back with any of its former Materials"—the British constitution was understood to be at once fixed and perpetually changing. This dual character proved unproblematic. So appeals to the constitutional past were perfectly consistent with the notion that the Constitution grew more perfect over time. By remaking the concept of constitutional authorship, however, by replacing Edmund Burke's wisdom of the ages with an image of concrete creators at specific moments in time, Revolutionary Americans began altering the imagined relationship between the constitutional past and present. And leveraging this novel understanding of constitutional authorship after 1788 helped archival excavation take on a distinct form. Rather than searching for original underlying purposes or principles, this new conception of time-locked authorship pushed excavators toward the time-locked understandings of original authors. In so doing, historical excavation was increasingly imagined as a means of sharply distinguishing between past and present Constitutions, rather than a means of uniting the two. Unlike before, constitutional fixity could be markedly disaggregated from constitutional growth. So even though appealing to the past for guidance and authority had been a dominant feature of Anglo-American constitutional culture for centuries, in this new context this familiar activity carried novel implications. By braiding together these different strands—the textual Constitution, the archival Constitution, and the contingently authored Constitution—the process of fixing the Constitution became a distinctly historical exercise, one that required excavating the archive of its creation, with the implicit effect of circumscribing the Constitution in time.[3]

Importantly, then, nothing about the original Constitution that had emerged from the Constitutional Convention necessitated this peculiar development. The distinct form of constitutional imagination that made the fixed Constitution intelligible was not a discovery but an invention. It required, first, the independent and contingent emergence of numerous constitutional fragments between 1787 and 1796. It required, second, the creative combination of those different elements into a single, unique fusion. The Jay Treaty debate marked the culmination of that imaginative process—of the invention of the fixed Constitution.

Looking to the Past

Skeptical as they were of the Constitution's face value meaning, Republicans early on in the struggle over Jay's Treaty could not help but be drawn to the parallel implications of Edward Livingston's request of President Washington. They had insisted that they could not adequately understand the Jay Treaty without access to the papers that accompanied John Jay's diplomatic mission. In other words, original surrounding documentation was necessary to bring to life an otherwise inert and veiled instrument. "It is not enough for me to know that this Treaty did happen," James Holland proclaimed, "I wish to know the causes that produced it, which will best be known by adverting to the papers contemplated in the resolution." The papers ought to be seen "not only as useful, but as necessary to know the true meaning and intention of certain articles in the Treaty," insisted John

Page. Abraham Baldwin summed the matter up more generally: "the only question, then, was, whether to take up the subject unexplained as it was, merely from the instrument and petitions, or to request any information that might be thought useful to the discussion," and lead congressmen "to a proper result." Rather than "merely" studying the treaty itself, disputants might understand the deeper meaning of its contents by knowing something about its creation. Republicans hammered this point relentlessly.[4]

If Jay's papers could shed light on the meaning of the treaty, why would the Constitution's "original papers" not shed similar light on the meaning of the nation's founding document? As Republicans gestured from the particular to the general, they hinted at this connection. "It is admitted, as a sound rule of construction," Richard Brent asserted at one juncture, "that to discover the true meaning of any instrument, it is fair to have recourse to the existing circumstances that produced it." William Lyman stressed how valuable it was "to resort to the context or other parts of a law or writing for a true interpretation," because doing so offered "a window" that "let in light upon the subject." At the same time, Federalists were conceding the merits of this logic. "By referring to the contemporaneous expositions of that instrument, when the subject was viewed only in relation to the abstract power, and not to a particular Treaty," William Loughton Smith permitted, "we should come at the truth." Meanwhile, Theodore Sedgwick believed that "a contemporaneous exposition of any instrument, and especially by those who were agents in its fabrication . . . was, in fact, among the best guides to finding its true meaning." Nearly all of these characterizations of the value of obtaining "contemporaneous expositions" were built upon such revealing descriptions—locating "true" meanings or interpretations; casting "light" on what was otherwise opaque.[5]

Both sides in the dispute, for reasons that had everything to do with the subject of the debate itself, agreed that historical excavation should prove the ultimate arbiter of their constitutional fight. To Federalists, if some kind of constitutional construction was required, then something external to the document might be needed to clarify its indeterminate contents. Given that they had spent the debate otherwise stressing the sanctity of the Constitution, it was much better to make that agent the original intent of the document's framers, they reasoned, than to rely on the current members of the House. Appealing to the voices of the past would provide the interpretive latitude needed to resolve apparent contradictions in the Constitution while still maintaining both their preferred version of the treaty power and the conception of the sacred Constitution they had so fervently defended. Republicans, who were most invested in asserting the House's role in treaty making, were attracted to anything that weakened the legitimacy of a prima facie reading of the treaty-making clause. But Republicans' own, much stronger appeal to holism—and its implication that the Constitution's true meaning might lay hidden—encouraged precisely the kind of digging central to historical excavation. It was thus tempting, by their own studiously fashioned logic, to probe the recent past and to move the field of conflict away from the Constitution's literal words and onto the events of 1787 and 1788.

Thus, at different points in the debate, two House members whose views placed them on opposite ends of the political spectrum could nevertheless agree on the interpretive legitimacy of appealing to the Constitution's history. Edward Livingston, the staunch Republican from New York whose explosive request for executive papers had helped launch the House debate over the treaty, remarked halfway through the debate, "In looking for the true construction of [the Constitution], we should consider the state of things at the time it was proposed and adopted." Even though Theodore Sedgwick was an archetypical Federalist from Massachusetts, who had vigorously defended Congress's authority to charter a national bank and every other core Federalist position that had followed, just a week earlier he had issued a statement that fundamentally aligned with Livingston's. "The real inquiry was," Sedgwick claimed, "what opinion was entertained on this subject by those who ratified the Constitution. If," he submitted, "that opinion could be discovered, with honest minds it must be conclusive on the present debate." Fully compatible in every way, these two statements betrayed the underlying beliefs of those who appealed to the Constitution's history—the belief in the existence of a single "true" meaning, the belief that historical excavation could yield that meaning, and belief in the epistemological capacity to see that method through to completion. To locate the Constitution's genuine meaning, inquirers ought to return to the moment when the document was "proposed and adopted." They could decipher the opinion on "this subject" (the relationship between commercial treaties and the House of Representatives) by reference to those "who ratified the Constitution" and, assuming this opinion could be known (the epistemological question), "it must be conclusive." As a method, it at once claimed that the Constitution's "true meaning" was fixed (because it was locked in place at inception) and offered a method for actually fixing that meaning (by privileging it above potential rivals). Livingston and Sedgwick, like most of their Republican and Federalist peers, were miles apart on the question of the treaty, but they agreed on how, ultimately, the question ought to be adjudicated. In that regard, they converged on a common idea of the Constitution, one set in a common logical space of reasons, made by a common set of justificatory practices.[6]

Both Republicans and Federalists quickly assumed the authoritative character of historical testimony. They debated, then, two problems, each of which shaped the possibilities of these sorts of appeals. The first pertained to evidence—among the plethora of surviving sources, which were most revealing and why? More specifically, of the three distinct phases of original constitutional construction (the framing, the public debate during ratification, and the ratifying conventions themselves), examination of which revealed the document's true meaning? The second, and more dominant, focus of the debate centered on application—did the original understanding of the Constitution justify or deny the House of Representatives a role in treaty making?

Thinking Archivally

Americans generally agreed they were a fortunate people. Unlike the members of most other political societies, they knew and remembered the origins of their polity. This was because of a defining, and novel, feature of American constitutions. Their legitimacy as sources of supreme authority derived from their origins. These constitutions had been purposefully created by known people at distinct moments in time. The federal Constitution—drafted in Philadelphia in the summer of 1787 and ratified over the following year in special state conventions—perfectly embodied these principles; there was absolutely no mystery about where it came from or how it became authoritative.

Accordingly, constitutional disputants spoke fondly about knowing their Constitution. "In the construction of other Constitutions," declared William Vans Murray, "some formed by mere charters of privileges, others rising from practice, we find the historian and the commentator obliged, in the support of theory, to resort to records unintelligible." But "in construing our Constitution, in ascertaining the metes and bounds of its various grants of power, nothing at the present day is left for expediency or sophistry." Much of this was no doubt due to the proximity of the creation. "We have all seen the Constitution from its cradle," Murray went on, "we know it from its infancy and have the most perfect knowledge of it, and more light than ever a body of men in any country have ever had of ascertaining any other Constitution." Even if proximity was encouraging, confidence also stemmed from the documentation available. That circumstance, perhaps above all other factors, made the origins of the United States highly unusual. Speaking of historical sources, Sedgwick noted, "it would be too tedious . . . to consult all the materials which might be within our reach on this subject." Although the Constitutional Convention was conducted in secret, ratification had been remarkably open. Not only were many of the convention debates reproduced in local newspapers or printed separately as pamphlets or books, but the public record from the entire ratification struggle was replete with contemporaneous commentary on the Constitution. Members of Congress could get their hands on any number of original disquisitions or debates, often with relative ease. Americans enjoyed this rare luxury and openly boasted about it.[7]

Although sources were readily available, however, the documentary record was problematic. Despite the relative abundance of materials, in 1796 House members had access only to a fraction of what has since become available. The archive of the Federal Convention was partial and limited. While "the Journals of that Convention which formed [the Constitution] still exist[ed]," Murray noted they were "not public." Since the Convention had adjourned, they had been in George Washington's private custody. That meant disputants had to rely more than they might have liked on the subjective memories of individual delegates to the Federal Convention. Few members of that body had kept contemporaneous notes, and those that did exist (like Madison's) were not yet public.[8]

Turning, as Sedgwick put it, from those "who formed" to "those who received and approved" the Constitution did not solve the problem. The records of the ratification debates were far more extensive than those of the Constitutional Convention, but they were plagued by similar issues. Several accounts of the separate state ratifying conventions had been published and were available, but they were hardly comprehensive. Although some state convention debates had been published contemporaneously in local newspapers, only material from the Pennsylvania, Massachusetts, Virginia, New York, and (first) North Carolina conventions had been printed in book form by 1796. Much of this material was partial, too. For instance, Thomas Lloyd's *Debates of the Convention* featured nothing beyond major speeches made by Federalists James Wilson and Thomas McKean, while New York's published account was considerably less detailed for the second half of the convention. Then there were questions of accuracy. Some in Massachusetts complained that Federalist convention members had helped the printer, Benjamin Russell, edit speeches for publication. The final published version of the proceedings of Massachusetts's ratifying convention, moreover, featured convention speeches that had never appeared in the local newspapers while the proceedings were ongoing. Virginia's debates, meanwhile, were published in three volumes based on the shorthand notes of David Robertson, a prominent local lawyer. Several participants complained that Robertson was biased in favor of the Federalists, however, and thus unlikely to have authentically replicated Anti-Federalist speeches. They also assumed that he allowed Federalists to modify their speeches prior to publication. Robertson himself acknowledged the shortcomings of his efforts, noting forthrightly in the final volume of the published account that he had been forced to sit some distance from the speakers in the gallery of the Richmond state house and could not always hear the speeches over the noise of delegates entering and exiting the chamber.[9]

Participants in the Jay Treaty debate recognized these limitations. "In referring to the debates of the State Conventions as published," Madison "wished not to be understood as putting entire confidence in the accuracy of them." This was true "even [of] those of Virginia"—the convention in which he had participated. Even though—acknowledging the complaints about Robertson—they "had been probably taken down by the most skillful hand, (whose merit [Madison] wished by no means to disparage)," nonetheless, even these records "contained internal evidence in abundance of chasms and misconceptions of what was said." In general, the "agitations of the public mind on that occasion, with the hurry and compromise" that was true of all of the proceedings, "would at once explain and apologize for the several apparent inconsistencies which might be discovered." During the bank debate, congressmen had already questioned the veracity of these sources in similar ways. Madison himself had refused "to vouch for the accuracy or authenticity of the publications," assuming "it probable that the sentiments delivered might in many instances have been mistaken, or imperfectly noted." Elbridge Gerry, meanwhile, had been even more strident: "The debates of the state conventions, as published by the short hand writers," he asserted, "were generally partial and mutilated." So it was not shocking that, during the Jay Treaty debate, Edward Livingston conceded that the ratifying conventions "were called in haste, they were heated by party," and many of them had concluded "without having fully debated the different articles" of the Constitution. Given the available records, Uriah Tracy "acknowledged, that, from such debates, the real state of men's minds or opinions may not always be collected with accuracy." It was hard, in short, to avoid "the several apparent inconsistencies which might be discovered" in the sources.[10]

Issues with the original sources spoke to a broader epistemological uncertainty. "If," Murray observed, "at this day, so full of light shining upon every part of [the Constitution]," there were nonetheless "doubts [concerning] some of its plainest passages, what is the prospect of that posterity which is to be deprived of those lights"? Would the Constitution's true meaning not be lost forever to the mists of time? But to those like Murray, this was exactly why it was imperative to return to the moment of inception now, at this time when, with the surrounding events fresh in participants' minds, so much about it could be known. "One hundred years hence, should a great question arise upon the construction [of the Constitution], what would not be the value of that man's intelligence, who, allowed to possess integrity and a profound and unimpaired mind, should appear in the awful moments of doubt, and, being known to have been in the illustrious body that framed the instrument, should clear up difficulties by his contemporaneous knowledge? Such a man would have twice proved a blessing to his country." Resorting to the original construction of the Constitution would help to clarify not only the instrument's meaning but also the method by which that meaning was obtained. It would enable future generations, further removed from the document's origins, to revive and perpetuate the Constitution's genuine meaning. Thus, despite what misgivings he might have harbored, Sedgwick nonetheless "dared to appeal to the recollection of every gentleman who was in a situation to know the facts." And William Loughton Smith, no matter what he otherwise knew or said, insisted (like so many others during the debate) that "the discussions which took place at the time of [the Constitution's] adoption by the Convention of the several States," were capable of "prov[ing] beyond a doubt" the key issues under investigation.[11]

Beyond source difficulties—some were unavailable, while others were untrustworthy, incomplete, or contradictory—there was a deeper question still: Which of the different sources should be considered preeminent? If the available evidence was abundant and pristine, where should one look, first and foremost, to the Federal Convention that framed the Constitution, the ratifying conventions that agreed to it, the public debate that preceded and surrounded the state conventions, or the "amendments proposed by the several Conventions"? Along with the other ratification materials that had thus far been published, House members could draw on Augustine Davis's compilation of state ratification forms and proposed amendments, published in 1788 as a pamphlet, *The Ratifications of the New Federal Constitution, Together with the Amendments, Proposed by the Several States.* At one point during the Jay Treaty debate, Madison claimed that these amendments—which he had carefully sifted through seven years earlier to compile his proposal for constitutional amendments—"were better authority" than most available sources as they could "throw light on [the] opinions and intentions on the subject in question." No matter how carefully they handled these historical materials, Jay Treaty disputants would have to demonstrate not only that historical sources could speak clearly but also that the kind of sources they appealed to were more credible than others. While most House members tried to avoid these questions, choosing instead to inundate their interlocutors with a sheer abundance of historical evidence, eventually they came to the fore.[12]

Imagining the Founding: The Federalists

Federalists went to work building their case. "In order to show that the Treaty power was solely delegated to the PRESIDENT and Senate by the Constitution," William Loughton Smith thought he "should not confine himself to a mere recital of the words." Instead, he would "appeal to the general sense of the whole nation at the time the Constitution was formed, before any Treaty was made under it, which could, by exciting passion and discontent, warp the mind from a just and natural construction of the Constitution." In order to make his case, in short, Smith would look beyond the Constitution's words and beyond the political prejudices of the current moment to understand how the treaty-making clause was understood when first devised. "On all subjects of this sort," Sedgwick added, "the real inquiry was and ought to be, what was the intention of the parties to this instrument?"[13]

Was it the Constitutional Convention's own sense of the document they crafted that was, in fact, most critical? Arguably no group more directly authored the Constitution than the fifty-five individuals who comprised this body (or perhaps the thirty-nine who signed it). If the treaty-making power was intended to be limited, if it was meant to distinguish commercial treaties from other kinds of agreements, and if it was to rely on the sanction of the House, then how, James Hillhouse asked, "can we account for the total silence of the Constitution on this subject, and that there should not be a single sentence in the whole instrument that even looks that way?" As Joshua Coit added, "the meaning of the Constitution was well understood, in the Convention which formed it, to vest the Treaty-making power completely in the PRESIDENT and Senate." Consequently, "it would require strong arguments" to convince him "that the Constitution placed any such power in that House, contrary to the unanimous understanding of the members of the Convention who formed it."[14]

Federalists also drew meaning from the fact that the Constitution's framers had not qualified the treaty-making clause. "If any limitation was intended," Hillhouse reasoned, "the Convention certainly knew that it was necessary it should be inserted." The original drafters would not have left Americans in such a sorry state, forced to struggle with such an ambiguous instrument. "Did not the framers of the Constitution know the nature of these two authorities, their respective and relative offices?" asked Chauncey Goodrich of Connecticut. "Or, is it more rational," he added, "to suppose that they instituted these two authorities, and left them to range at random until they could find their true destiny" from future considerations? "Is it not fully evident that the framers of the Constitution and the people have considered this subject," he went on, "and declared their will in respect to a check? And shall we, in contradiction to that declaration, from remote and uncertain construction, multiply checks?" As Ezekiel Gilbert argued, this made a mockery of "the enlightened framers of the Constitution."[15]

Describing the framers as "enlightened" underscored an important part of appealing to their intent. Portraying the unique wisdom of the drafters reinforced the sanctity of the original Constitution. "When we examine the Constitution," Hillhouse declared, "and see with what accuracy and care it is drawn up, how wonderfully every part of it is guarded, that there is not a single word but appears to have been carefully examined," and when "we call to mind the members of that Convention, and find them to have been the ablest and most accurate men of our country," upon doing that, "we cannot presume that we should have been left to the sad alternative, for the purpose of explaining so important an article of our Constitution, which might have been so easily made definite." The Constitution's clarity corresponded to the beauty of its construction, to the qualities that made it sacrosanct. This character was an extension of the wisdom of its framers. Because the original Constitution was sacred, because it was inconceivable that its authors would have committed such an oversight, the Republicans' interpretation of the treaty clause fell apart.[16]

Federalists believed that the history surrounding the construction of the Senate raised particularly important questions about the original understanding of the treaty power. The Senate was composed, against the wishes of many in the Convention, to safeguard small states' interests by giving each state equal representation in that body. Given that context, Federalists argued that it was impossible to conclude that the treaty-making power could have been susceptible to a further check from the House. If that was the expected application, delegates of the small states would have been outraged. "The Convention had many difficulties to surmount in this article," explained John Williams, "to do away the discordant interests of the different States, and to give the small States satisfaction." Accordingly, "in the Treaty-making power each State hath an equal voice. To extend it further, for another check, without the consent of the smaller States," would eradicate "that power which the small States had retained." Republicans' arguments about the treaty power made little sense from the perspective of this original dynamic.[17]

These sorts of arguments were primarily the product of logical deduction. By referencing the stylistic choices in the Constitution or the surrounding context that surely shaped the drafters' decisions, Federalists claimed they could identify the authors' intentions. A similar sort of deduction, based instead on original constitutional critics, informed another Federalist point. If the instrument had not vested the treaty-making power solely with the president and Senate, Federalists asked, why would critics have claimed that it had? Anti-Federalists had singled out this precise feature as a cardinal reason to reject the Constitution. Moreover, in the face of this criticism, why then would Federalists (many of whom were now members of Congress and claiming otherwise) have affirmed that Anti-Federalists were correct about how the power worked? As William Loughton Smith explained, he would "confidently appeal to the opinions of those who, when the Constitution was promulgated, were alarmed at the Treaty power," because it was alone vested in the President and Senate. In addition to these critics, he would appeal "to its advocates, who vindicated it by proving that the power was safely deposited with these branches of the Government." If, in other words, Federalists and Anti-Federalists had seemingly agreed on the contours of the treaty-making power—no matter their belief in its relative merits—how could Republicans subsequently claim that their otherwise heterodox reading was well founded? To Federalists in 1796, evidence of the original debate over the Constitution exposed the feebleness of the Republicans' interpretation. During ratification, Federalists had enjoyed every political incentive to accept the Republicans' current understanding. But they had done no such thing. Instead, as Sedgwick pointed out, "they admitted the power, proved the necessity of it, and contended that it would be safe in practice." Federalists assumed this risk during ratification, all because "they certainly knew what they had so recently intended."[18]

But as much as Federalists relied on deduction, they rested their argument, as much as anything else, on an empirical reading of the historical record. It was not all inferences about what must have been meant. As Robert Goodloe Harper explained, "nobody could doubt that the American people might, when they were framing their Constitution, have bestowed this power on any other branch of the Government." The crucial "question was had they restricted it? Not what they could do, but what they did." Many Federalists combed the ratification debates and state ratifying convention records to build an empirical case, to prove not what the original constitutional authors likely did, but instead what they in fact had done.[19]

Like disputants had during the bank debate, Federalists drew on the *Federalist* papers to support their position on the treaty power. As he had in prior debates, William Loughton Smith quoted from them directly. Uriah Tracy noted that the papers had been used to support the doctrine that the House of Representatives was involved in treaty making. But, by his reading, "it was an unfounded assertion." Indeed, he "was much mistaken if all would not acknowledge that the opinions of the *Federalist* were," in fact the opposite, to "not . . . associate the House of Representatives with the PRESIDENT in the making of Treaties." Federalists were confident that Publius was on their side.[20]

But Federalists were even more confident relying on the state ratifying conventions to prove that the Constitution had vested the president and Senate alone with the power to make treaties. John Williams charged Republicans with relying "on too contemporaneous a construction," one too determined by the present, in claiming "that the House were better able to judge of the meaning of the Constitution than the Conventions which were held to consider upon its adoption." Here he explicitly conceded Republicans' premise (that the treaty-making power, and thus the Constitution, required supplemental judgment) while undercutting their conclusion (by elevating the judgment of the ratifying conventions above the sitting House). Many Federalists concurred. John Reed argued, "the almost unanimous understanding of the members of the different Conventions in the States" favored Federalists' interpretation. Much as the Constitution's meaning was complete only when inquirers consulted its original authors, treaties were complete when the president and Senate agreed to them.[21]

Federalists especially appealed to the recommended amendments that had accompanied ratification in many states, the same proposals that Madison had sorted through in 1788–1789 while preparing formal amendments for the First Congress. "The Convention of Virginia," argued William Loughton Smith, "had proposed an amendment, which of itself overturned all [Republican] reasonings." He and other Federalists quoted from Virginia's proposal, which required the concurrence of two-thirds of all senators (rather than merely those "present," as the Constitution specified) to ratify commercial treaties. Since, Smith reasoned, this amendment reflected Anti-Federalists' original understanding of what the treaty-making power lacked (indicating nothing, in turn, about the House having a role in the process), it was impossible to conclude that Virginians had "conceived that the check which is now contended for existed in the Constitution." They simply "could not have been guilty of such an absurdity." The proposed amendment was hardly trivial. "Here is the voice, not of a few individuals, but of the people of Virginia," Hillhouse declared, "expressed, not on a sudden or trivial occasion, but when they were called for the express purpose of deliberating and deciding on an instrument the most important ever offered to the consideration of a nation." All possible dangers connected to an unlimited treaty power had been considered during ratification, and yet, Smith noted, "Virginia required no further check than the one . . . recited." The Virginia Convention, Federalists argued, had proposed its amendments assuming the House could not check treaty making. The argument now being pedaled by Republicans was, thus, "like rowing a boat one way and looking another."[22]

Other recommended amendments told a similar story, particularly those from Pennsylvania. In that state, Anti-Federalists had proposed alterations to the Constitution that the Federalist-dominated convention had brusquely rejected. Angered, the embittered convention minority made sure to include a slew of proposed amendments in the scathing denunciation of the Constitution they published shortly after the convention adjourned. Federalists in the House of Representatives made great use of the minority's dissent, claiming it underscored the same critical point as Virginia's amendments. William Loughton Smith quoted one proposed amendment in particular: that no treaty would become law until "'assented to by the House of Representatives in Congress.'" He argued that "this amendment was the most satisfactory evidence that the proposers of it did then believe that, without that amendment," instruments such as the Jay Treaty "would be valid and binding, although not assented to by this House." This evidence exposed Republicans' invented "check" on the treaty power for what it was: an "*ex post facto* construction."[23]

Among Federalists, Theodore Sedgwick and Benjamin Bourne dug deepest into the state ratifying conventions. Each of them turned entire days of the House debate into exhaustive exhibitions of historical documentation. Sedgwick, ever the skilled litigator, engaged in a time-consuming analysis of the Virginia convention. He felt it "admitted as the best authority" since "the subject there was examined by eminent talents, and by minute and scrupulous investigation." In particular, he quoted speeches from leading Anti-Federalists such as George Mason, James Monroe, and Patrick Henry and leading Federalists including Madison, George Nicholas, Francis Corbin, and Governor Edmund Randolph, who, by that point in the ratification process, had become an advocate for the Constitution. Bourne, meanwhile, a Rhode Island lawyer who had attended his own state's ratifying convention, probed the first North Carolina convention records in tedious depth, reading "extracts from the debates of that Assembly" that were "applicable to the present question." In doing so, he reported that he had "clearly discover[ed] that all agreed that the Treaty-making power was exclusively vested in the President and Senate." He quoted from William Davie (a former Revolutionary War officer and eventual governor of North Carolina), Samuel Spencer, James Porter, and Archibald Maclaine. Through their archival investigations, Sedgwick and Bourne hammered home three points: that both Federalists and Anti-Federalists had believed that the House was wholly removed from treaty making; that treaties were to be understood as supreme law of the land; and that the treaty power, as constituted, was unchecked. These were arguments that Federalists in the House had made numerous times before, but now they were explicitly justified by historical evidence. While the conclusion remained constant, the source of argumentative authority had decisively shifted.[24]

On the House floor, Federalists tried to demonstrate that, from the beginning of the ratification debates, Anti-Federalists had complained that the House was not involved in treaty making. Sedgwick read from one of Patrick Henry's speeches: "'That if two-thirds of a quorum would be empowered to make a Treaty, they might relinquish . . . our most valuable commercial advantages. In short, should anything be left it would be because the President and Senators were pleased to admit it.'" Bourne made the same point by quoting Samuel Spencer, "'If the whole Legislative body— if the House of Representatives—do not interfere in making Treaties, I think they ought to at least have the sanction of the whole Senate.'" The Constitution's original supporters, meanwhile, had never denied the exclusion of the House from treaty making. Sedgwick quoted another speech from the Virginia ratifying convention, this one from the Federalist Francis Corbin: "'If there be any sound part in the Constitution, it is this clause. The Representatives are excluded from interposing in making Treaties, because large popular assemblies are very improper to transact such business. . . . It is therefore given to the President and Senate . . . conjointly. In this it differs from every Government we know.'" The last line struck Sedgwick as especially crucial. Given that the American Constitution evidently deviated from other known governments with respect to treaty making, it was all the clearer, as Corbin had suggested during the Virginia debates, that the choice was intentional. To Sedgwick and Bourne, the original constitutional dispute inescapably presupposed Federalists' understanding of the treaty power.[25]

The Federalists of 1796 likewise pointed out that the Federalists of 1787 and 1788 had been adamant that, if anything, treaties were the supreme law of the land. Clearly relishing the irony, Sedgwick noted that Madison had declared as much in the Virginia convention. The Massachusetts representative read from the Virginian's speech: "'Are not Treaties the law of the land in England? I will refer you to a book which is in every man's hand, "Blackstone's Commentaries"; it will inform you, that Treaties made by the King are to be the supreme law of the land; if they are to have *any* efficacy, they must be the law of the land. They are so in every country.'" To make the identical point, Bourne quoted Archibald Maclaine of North Carolina. Meanwhile, shifting attention to the New

York convention, of which he had been a member, John Williams read from the documentary record to establish that Treaties were "considered to be paramount to any law."[26]

Both the Constitution's original critics and its supporters, Federalists in the House contended, had argued that the treaty power was unchecked. Beginning with those opposed to the Constitution, Sedgwick quoted Edmund Randolph—the only member of the Washington administration who had protested the Jay Treaty—"'It is said, there is no limitation of Treaties.'" George Mason had also said in the Virginia convention, "'It is true it is one of the greatest acts of sovereignty, and therefore ought to be most strongly guarded. The cession of such power, without such checks and guards, cannot be justified; yet, I acknowledge such a power must rest somewhere: It is so in all Governments.'" Sedgwick found this commentary deeply revealing. "Strange," he said with more than a note of irony, "that this gentleman did not discover, or was not told, that Treaties before they should become laws, must receive Legislative sanction." The original Federalists also had contended that the treaty-making power was unchecked. Sedgwick quoted Madison before concluding, "[he] had stated the checks which the Constitution had in fact provided," never imagining "that the consent of this House was among them." Somehow, in the intervening years, Madison had come to change his mind (not about what constituted sound treaty making, but about what the Constitution inherently meant). Through such a brazen presentation, Sedgwick was coming close to impugning Madison's honor, but given how self-serving most Federalists had long viewed Madison's use of the Founding, no doubt Sedgwick felt justified.[27]

Other Federalists likewise noted Madison's seeming turn of mind. With evident sarcasm, Murray confessed surprise that neither Madison nor Abraham Baldwin (two of the four House members in 1796 who had been delegates to the Constitutional Convention) had "favored the Committee with the view which either they or others had taken of this important point in the Convention." The implication was clear. Madison and Baldwin were loath to share their remembrances of what had happened in Philadelphia because they knew such evidence would contradict their current political agenda. That Madison's original commentary in the Virginia ratifying convention diverged so sharply from his current commitments hinted as much. Theophilus Bradbury was even more direct, declaring matter-of-factly of Madison, "the gentleman had altered his opinion." To Federalists, though, whether Madison was being disingenuous was less important than what his original testimony, when corroborated by the testimony of so many others, revealed: a clear glimpse of the Constitution's genuine meaning, the meaning Federalists in the House had attached to the treaty clause.[28]

Wherever Federalists looked in the documentary record, they felt vindicated. Taking stock of Virginia's archive, Sedgwick confidently declared, "it was manifest, beyond all doubt . . . that the Convention of that State supposed, that the Constitution . . . delegated to the President and Senate, and to the exclusion of the House, the whole power of making and ratifying Treaties." Although his evidence came from this one ratifying convention, he assured listeners, "it was not Virginia alone," for he was "persuaded every other State had given precisely the same construction." Why he felt this way, he did not say. But he surely felt justified when, the following week, Bourne presented a bevy of North Carolina sources seemingly confirming many of the same points. Sedgwick, like other House Federalists, was convinced that, from this original testimony, honest inquirers could "derive all reasonable satisfaction that we had discovered the truth."[29]

Imagining the Founding: The Republicans

Republicans fiercely disagreed. They thought that the balance of historical evidence affirmed their position, and they looked upon their rivals' arguments with confusion and bemusement. "In opposition to the resolution, it is asserted, that this doctrine is new," William Findley expressed in dismay. "To me, the opposite opinion is novel and surprising." To Republicans, a careful examination of the same sources yielded a conclusion much different than the one their opponents had drawn.[30]

In appealing to history, Republicans, like Federalists, could be vague and speculative, relying on personal knowledge, experience, and memory or just general inferences drawn from the text of the Constitution or the perceived expectations that must have accompanied its construction. But on the whole, and especially when they were parrying Federalists' claims, Republicans were more substantive, analyzing many of the same sources—the resolutions of the Pennsylvania minority, the recommended amendments that had been proposed by the states, and the debates in the Massachusetts, North Carolina, Virginia, and Pennsylvania ratifying conventions—to illustrate, as William Lyman decisively concluded, that their "interpretation was given to the Constitution in most of the State Conventions at the time of its adoption."[31]

In particular, Republicans found Federalists' interpretations of the Pennsylvania and Virginia conventions deeply misleading. "The minority of the ratifying Convention of Pennsylvania," announced Findley, "has been adduced to prove, that [Republicans' position] was not believed to be the meaning of the Constitution at the time." Findley spoke with confidence, and a sense of irony, since he had been a leading member of the Pennsylvania minority. The Federalists' conclusion was based on one of the minority's specific amendments—that the House ought to be given the right to authorize or reject all treaties that might alter federal or state laws. Findley was willing to concede, first of all, that "this clause would go far to prove the right of Congress to exercise a formal negative over Treaties of every description," and that this was what the Pennsylvania convention minority "plead for" in their amendment. He was likewise willing to admit that "I did not then believe it was secured in the Constitution, nor do I contend for it now." But—and here he was adamant—neither concession denied that Republicans' current conception of treaty making was otherwise part of the Constitution; both simply showed that Pennsylvania Anti-Federalists had been especially wary of the treaty-making power—whether the House was involved or not.[32]

To Findley, this distortion yet again illustrated the imprecision of the kind of face-value readings Federalists were insisting upon. Federalists had misread the minority's resolution much as they had the Constitution. "Only the arguments in favor of the Constitution made in [the Pennsylvania convention] were preserved," he reflected, "but, being a member of it, and in the minority, I have a good recollection of the sentiments expressed in it." Knowledge of what happened in the convention itself made a significant difference. Just as the Constitution could not be understood without the supporting context from which it issued, just as Jay's Treaty could not be understood without the supporting papers that accompanied its construction, so too could the Pennsylvania minority's resolutions not be understood without knowledge of the convention from which they emerged. In recalling his personal experience in the ratifying convention, Findley remembered something that James Wilson, the leading Pennsylvania Federalist, had said. Wilson had "maintained that an effective, though indirect check on the Treaty-making power, would naturally grow out of the exercise of the Legislative authority." Pennsylvania Federalists and Anti-Federalists alike presumed that legislative authority would evolve to check the treaty power. The latter merely "objected to the effects which Treaties might have on the State Governments; and that, in some cases, the Constitution itself might be infringed by it." In other words, the minority's proposed amendment rested on issues of federalism, not treaty making. Surely they had hoped to secure greater authority for the House of Representatives, but even if this proposed amendment failed (and it had), it did not follow that the House lacked a controlling power. In fact, an understanding of the deeper context out of which the Pennsylvania amendments emanated confirmed that Pennsylvanians had assumed—at that time and ever since—that the House enjoyed a role in treaty making.[33]

According to Republicans, similar reasoning undercut Federalists' reading of the Virginia amendments. "The amendment in question goes to providing, that no Commercial Treaty shall be concluded without the consent of two-thirds of the [Senate]; but surely," argued Richard Brent, this did not "prove that they conceived the House had no voice in those Treaties, directly or indirectly." Virginian Anti-Federalists had indeed proposed an amendment that reflected their deeper dissatisfaction with the treaty-making power, "but how would it apply in the sense [Federalists] wished?" asked William Branch Giles. The objection simply had been that "the check in the Senate, provided in the Treaty-making power," was insufficient, so they had proposed a more stringent check, as "they conceived the Treaty-making power to be a subject of extreme delicacy, and . . . wished additional checks consequently added." All the amendment revealed was contemporary dissatisfaction with the Constitution's treaty-making provision, not that treaty making itself lacked fundamental checks.[34]

Albert Gallatin, in a lengthy speech, simultaneously strengthened and undermined the use of all of these proposed amendments to establish an authoritative source of information about what the ratifiers had intended. The amendments had not been "brought forward as a test of . . . the true construction of the Constitution" because, he explained, "those amendments were adopted in order to conciliate the opinions of a majority, and they were proposed as much with a design to explain doubtful articles as with a view to obtain alterations." The amendments did not reflect constitutional omissions—they were simply crafted to ensure safer interpretations. Furthermore, "not one of the amendments which had been read," or which he had seen, "applied to the question now under discussion." Instead, "they all tended to give a different construction to the Constitution from that . . . now contended for," and, in that regard, could "have been proposed by Conventions, or by individuals, who understood the Constitution in the same sense" as Republicans did, but who favored "some further alterations, some further security, some further check, than even the construction now contended for, by the advocates of the motion." The amendments could easily have been proposed by individuals already under the impression that the president's and Senate's capacity to make treaties was, in certain ways, limited. And there was no reason to think that they were not.[35]

The closer Republicans looked, the more they discredited the interpretive value of amendments they had once drafted and defended. "The sentiments of those who objected to the adoption of the Constitution," and who had authored the amendments in question, "could not have much weight as a rule of construction," Gallatin claimed. Instead, he concluded, "the only contemporaneous opinions which could have any weight . . . were those of the gentlemen who had advocated the adoption of the Constitution." Findley, as zealous an Anti-Federalist as there had been, was even more pointed. Nobody could "expect the sentiments of a minority," he exclaimed, "acting under peculiar circumstances of irritation, and consisting of but about one fifth of the members, to be quoted as a good authority for the true sense of the Constitution on this occasion." Things had indeed turned upside down. That Findley was now complaining that Federalists were taking his once impassioned claims about the Constitution too seriously confirmed as much.[36]

Instead, to make their claims, Republicans, like their Federalist opponents, relied most heavily on the state conventions themselves. Putting aside amendments, minority protests, or general inferences, they argued, the direct evidence culled from those chambers strongly substantiated their interpretation of the Constitution. Even though Federalists were repeatedly bolstering their claims with evidence drawn from these conventions, the genuine spirit of these debates from 1787 and 1788, Republicans felt, pointed toward a much different conclusion. As Samuel Smith put it, Republicans' "doctrine was not novel, but as old as the Constitution" itself, captured by the fact that it was "generally admitted in the Conventions."[37]

Just like Federalists, Republicans were eager to make appeals based on the proceedings of the Virginia ratifying convention. Richard Brent, himself a Virginian, was surprised that Theodore Sedgwick had declared that Republicans' doctrine was "novel," when, "by recurring to the very debates he produced," the Republicans' understanding of the treaty clause "was unequivocally laid down." Gallatin reiterated the point: "the debates of Virginia had first been partially quoted," but "when the whole was read and examined," he argued, it "clearly appeared" that "the general sense of the advocates of the Constitution there" aligned with the Republican position. Federalists were guilty not only of selective reading but also of ignoring the ambiguity of their sources. To prove this point, Brent quoted at length from the Virginia convention records. Among his choices was a speech of then-Federalist Francis Corbin, in which Corbin had marked out the differences between commercial and noncommercial treaties (in Britain as well as the American confederation), to illustrate that commercial treaties demanded legislative approval. Under the then-proposed Constitution Corbin had asked what was necessary to ratify "'a commercial Treaty?'" Answering his own question he had remarked, "'the consent of the House of Representatives,'" because of the "'correspondent alterations that must be made in the laws.'" To Brent, the Jay Treaty bore a striking similarity to Corbin's hypothetical treaty, thus suggesting that Virginia's original voices supported Republicans' current conception of the Constitution.[38]

Republicans cast doubt in similar ways on their opponents' reading of the North Carolina debates. Not only had references to this convention relied on Anti-Federalists, a skeptical Brent pointed out, but there had been no acknowledgment that the original convention, in fact, had rejected the Constitution. The second North Carolina convention—the one that had actually approved the document—supported Republicans' reading of the treaty clause. James Holland, a House member who had been a delegate to that second convention, confirmed as much. Among those who had favored the Constitution, he stressed, it had been clear "that commercial regulations had been previously and expressly given to Congress." By this understanding, commercial treaties required the assent of the House. Gallatin drew on the same convention, quoting James Iredell, North Carolina's leading constitutional advocate who, since 1790, had served as a Supreme Court justice. In a 1788 speech, Gallatin noted, Iredell had addressed the alleged dangers of the treaty-making power and had reassured skeptics that because the House would have authority over money bills, its members would be able to exert some control over treaties. "'The authority over money will do every thing,'" Iredell had said. "'Our Representatives may, at any time, compel the Senate to agree to a reasonable measure by withholding supplies till the measure is consented to.'" Did this not suggest, Gallatin asked, that the House would enjoy a check on treaties?[39]

With every bit the same fervor, Republicans scrutinized the Massachusetts ratifying convention. Even though he had primarily focused on

North Carolina to defend Federalists' position, earlier in the debate Bourne had made an offhand remark about the Massachusetts convention, claiming that "no one" in that meeting had "suggested that the House of Representatives had any control over, much less a participation in, [the treaty] power." But William Lyman fiercely disagreed. In analyzing the surviving materials, he presented two revealing quotations. One came from Federalist Rufus King: "'The Treaty-making power would be found as much restrained in this country as in any country in the world'"; the other from John Choate: "'As the regulation of commerce was under the control of Congress, it could not be regulated by Treaty without their consent and concurrence.'" Once again, in the face of Federalists' cavalier misrepresentations, Republicans attempted to show that history had redeemed their side of the story.[40]

Whether they appealed to the imagined logic that had guided the Constitutional Convention, the amendments proposed by the states, or the state ratifying conventions, Republicans were all moving in the same direction. In a single question, Gallatin drew out and vigorously defended the more basic point upon which all Republican arguments converged. After hearing "such pointed contemporaneous expositions of the true meaning and spirit of the Constitution," he piercingly asked, "would it still be asserted, that the opinions now expressed [by Republicans] were a new-fangled doctrine; unheard of, and unthought of, till the British Treaty became a subject of discussion; inconsistent with former opinions . . . and the general sense of mankind?" In short, the "true meaning and spirit" of the Constitution—once again the favored phrase of historical excavations—had adjudicated the question in Republicans' favor. Given how strained Republican argument had become, it is unclear if Gallatin, or any of the rest, genuinely believed their stated conclusions. No matter what they thought, however, their public commitments were bringing a new conception of the Constitution into relief. Digging into the past had shown that Republicans, in their rush to ensure contemporary House discretion, were willing to legitimize a rival image of the nation's fundamental instrument, one in which the Constitution was anything but incomplete, but instead already possessed an operative meaning, discoverable in the fixed past.[41]

Washington's Archive

Finally, after weeks of exhaustive debate, Jonathan Dayton, the speaker of the House, called for a vote. On Thursday, March 24, the House approved

Livingston's original resolution by a wide margin, 62 to 37, and the next day it was formally presented to President Washington. For the better part of the next week Washington weighed his options. The entire treaty episode had taken a toll on him, and he had been especially wounded by the severity of the personal critiques that Republican newspaper writers had leveled at him. No doubt worn down and frustrated, he finally replied to the House on March 30.[42]

Washington's response revealed how deeply rooted historical-constitutional thinking had become. A few days earlier he had finally deposited the official records of the Constitutional Convention in the State Department, making them part of the public record. He passed them on to his secretary of state, Timothy Pickering, who meticulously recorded the receipt of each and every page. Washington did so for much the same reason that Madison had eventually completed and revised his notes of the Convention and Jefferson had subsequently made a copy of them. In a constitutional world in which it was ever easier to see and talk about the Constitution as an archival artifact, and to appeal to the history of its creation to adjudicate contemporary disputes, it was slowly becoming clear that those who controlled the constitutional archive could control interpretation of the Constitution's language, and perhaps with that fundamental authority over the Constitution itself. History had become the stuff of power.[43]

Washington, in particular, had a unique opportunity to contribute to the American constitutional archive. A last-minute motion by the delegates to the Constitutional Convention had made Washington responsible for keeping the meeting's official records. Since he had served as president of the Convention, he seemed the logical choice to take custody of them. For years he seemed to give records little thought. But in the explosive context of the Jay Treaty dispute, they had taken on new, urgent meaning. In the last of the thirty-eight "Defence" essays he wrote supporting the policy and constitutionality of the treaty some three months earlier, Alexander Hamilton had complained about the apparent inscrutability of the proceedings of the Constitutional Convention. "As to the sense of the Convention, the secrecy with which their deliberations were conducted does not permit any formal proof of the opinions and views which prevailed in digesting the power of Treaty [making]," he observed. While he was confident that Federalists' interpretation of the treaty clause was nonetheless supported by all available historical sources, when it came to the Convention he had to concede the lack of "direct proof." Much still remained unknown about the circumstances of the

Constitution's construction, and especially about the Convention that framed it. But over the subsequent course of the Jay Treaty debate, it became clear that the official record Washington had yet to furnish might offer the "direct proof" Hamilton coveted. Depositing the records in the State Department was a power play in a new world of constitutional power.[44]

Having deposited the records, Washington then issued his response. Primarily drafted by Pickering—with some input from Attorney General Charles Lee—it demonstrated a detailed grasp of the House debate. "I trust," it read, "that no part of my conduct has ever indicated a disposition to withhold any information which the Constitution has enjoined upon the President, as a duty, to give, or which could be required of him by either House of Congress as a right." Through the response, Washington underscored the importance of secrecy in foreign negotiations, a consideration that helped explain why the treaty-making power had been vested solely in the president and Senate. "It does not occur," he went on, "that the inspection of the papers asked for can be relative to any purpose under the cognizance of the House of Representatives, except that of an impeachment; which the resolution has not expressed."[45]

Washington could have stopped there, but he did not. Instead, he challenged the premise upon which Livingston's resolution calling for the release of the Jay Treaty papers had been built, disputing its underlying constitutional logic. As he explained, "the course which the debate has taken on the resolution of the House leads to some observations on the mode of making Treaties under the Constitution of the United States." This brought him to the history of the Constitution's creation. "Having been a member of the General Convention, and knowing the principles on which the Constitution was formed," he began authoritatively,

> I have ever entertained but one opinion on this subject, and from the first establishment of the Government to this moment, my conduct has exemplified that opinion, that the power of making Treaties is exclusively vested in the President, by and with the advice and consent of the Senate, provided two-thirds of the Senators present concur; and that every Treaty so made, and promulgated, thenceforward becomes the law of the land.

Washington then turned, like both Federalists and Republicans in the House before him, to the state ratifying conventions to further reinforce his claims. "There is also reason to believe," he wrote, "that this construction agrees with the opinions entertained by the State Conventions, when they were deliberating on the Constitution, especially by those who objected to it"—here he invoked the proposed amendments as so many had before him. He continued, "it is a fact, declared by the General Convention, and universally understood, that the Constitution of the United States was the result of a spirit of amity and mutual concession. And it is well known, that under this influence, the smaller States were admitted to an equal representation in the Senate, with the larger States"—drawing upon the already-established context of the Senate's creation—"and that this branch of the Government was invested with great powers; for, on the equal participation of those powers, the sovereignty and political safety of the smaller States were deemed essentially to depend."[46]

This unusually strong and pointed argument (for Washington anyway) concluded with one final point that directly drew on the constitutional archive he had just personally created. "If other proofs than these, and the plain letter of the Constitution itself, be necessary to ascertain the point under consideration, they may be found in the Journals of the General Convention, which I have deposited in the office of the Department of State. In those Journals it will appear, that a proposition was made [on August 23, 1787], 'that no Treaty should be binding on the United States which was not ratified by a law,' and that the proposition was explicitly rejected." Taking advantage of the archive he had just constructed, Washington argued that the House's vision of treaty making had been expressly considered by the Constitution's authors before being rejected. As they had rejected it, so too must he reject the House's request. If anybody objected, they were free to consult the record. In making this argument, Washington had redeemed the textual Constitution—the "plain letter of the Constitution"—by tethering it to the archival Constitution.[47]

Madison's Last Stand

The House stood chastened, Washington having rejected its formal request. But Republicans were not done. Thomas Blount, a North Carolina Republican, "observed, that the President[']s Message stands upon the Journals of the House"; therefore, "the House should state upon their Journals the reasons which influenced them to make the request." Giles agreed with his colleague. "This call had given rise to a great Constitutional question; the

President had stated the reasons of his opinion; if the House were not convinced by them (and he owned that, for one, he was not) then it would be proper that they should present to the public their reasons for differing with him." Blount added, "that the President refers, in his Message, to the debate in the House, and insinuates that the House contend for a right not given them by the Constitution. This," he noted, "was the first instance of any importance of a difference between the House of Representatives and the Executive respecting a Constitutional point; it was then proper," he surmised, "to make such a disposal of the Message as to enable the House to state their reasons in support of their opinion." Consequently, Republicans called for the president's message to be referred to the Committee of the Whole so that the House might deliberate upon its response. No matter the resolution of the broader debate, Republicans were anxious that their constitutional reasons would become a matter of public record.[48]

Federalists were strident in their opposition. George Thatcher of Massachusetts assured members that all speeches would be printed in pamphlet form and anybody looking for explanations or justifications for different positions could find them there. In agreement, Samuel Sitgreaves of Pennsylvania argued, "the House have made a demand on the President; the President refused it; this must naturally put an end to the correspondence on this subject. The difference of sentiment between the two branches is not sufficient reason for converting the Journals of the House into a volume of debates." Sedgwick, again translating his disdain into biting sarcasm, asked, "Were the Committee of the Whole to turn authors and write a dissertation on part of the Constitution? The people did not send their Representatives here for any such purpose," he complained. "If the reasons of the House were to be drafted . . . they would reach the end of their political career before the discussion . . . would be brought to a close." His mockery then turned even more barbed. "If the gentlemen would write books, [I am] confident every body would buy them."[49]

Yet deliberately or not, Washington himself seemed to invite the Republicans' request for a referral of his response to the committee. As Gallatin reasoned, the president had not simply rejected the request, he had also articulated his reasons for doing so. Indeed, "he had adverted to the debates had in the House. He may be mistaken as to the motives he ascribed to the House. In this delicate situation," the Pennsylvanian felt, "it is certainly right to notice the Message, and to explain the real motives of the House, in support of the motion." Findley, meanwhile, spoke more generally about why the House should record its reasons for challenging the constitution-ality of the Jay Treaty. Drawing on his experience in the Pennsylvania state legislature, he recalled that he "had often known the sentiments of men long dead, brought forward there. It was not for themselves, but for pos-terity, that their reasons for calling for the papers in question should be en-tered upon the Journals." Perhaps it was only natural that in a debate that had sanctified the archival record of past debates, House members de-manded memorialization. The House concluded business that day by in-deed referring the president's message to the Committee of the Whole.[50]

When the House again considered the question the following week, Nathaniel Smith, a young Federalist lawyer from Connecticut, pleaded with his peers to move on to a consideration of the treaty itself. Under the terms of the Jay Treaty, the British were set to vacate the western forts on June 1 and, assuming it would take a month for word of the House's con-sent to be received, that left less than a month to deliberate on the treaty's actual details. As a Federalist, Smith presumed the House to have no business in treaties beyond formal execution, and he reiterated that opinion. But, regardless of whether the House had the right, members clearly possessed the raw power to break the treaty. The British no doubt had been made aware of the House's deliberations, he argued, and would likely not carry out any of the treaty's stipulations until the House had approved the necessary appropriations for the treaty to take effect—even if the House lacked formal constitutional authority to do otherwise.[51]

But House Republicans refused to give up their interest in the deeper constitutional question. Led by Madison, on April 2 they fatefully gathered to hold their first formal party caucus. They collectively decided to continue the struggle against the treaty, agreeing to two specific resolutions, both of which intended to clarify the House's constitutional rights. On April 6, heeding the instructions of the caucus, Thomas Blount introduced the Re-publicans' resolutions. The first conceded that the House did not have immediate agency in forming treaties (that was left to the president and Senate), but added "that when a Treaty stipulates regulations on any of the subjects submitted by the Constitution to the power of Congress, it must depend, for its execution, as to such stipulations, on a law or laws to be passed by Congress." It went on, "it is the Constitutional right and duty of the House of Representatives, in all such cases, to deliberate on the expedi-ency or inexpediency of carrying such Treaty into effect, and to determine and act thereon, as, in their judgment, may be most conducive to the public good." The second resolution stated that in requesting information, "which may relate to any Constitutional functions of the House," the House did not need to specify its reasons—a claim that directly contradicted Washington's message.[52]

At this point—Washington having rejected Livingston's request and House Republicans resolved to make their constitutional beliefs clear—Madison readied a response. He was convinced, as he told Jefferson, that "resolutions declaring the Const[itutiona]l. powers of the House as to treaties" were imperative, not least because of Washington's "reprehensible measure" denying the House the executive papers. But he knew that the ground of debate had shifted. As Madison told Jefferson, "if you do not at once perceive the drift of the appeal to the Genl. Convention & its journal," then one need only consult "one of Camillus' last numbers, & read the latter part of Murray's speech." Not only had Washington shone a bright light on the proceedings of the Constitutional Convention, but so too had Alexander Hamilton and William Vans Murray. Even worse, as if sensing what the president had subsequently documented, Hamilton and Murray had done so specifically to call out Madison, by reminding the public that Madison possessed rare firsthand knowledge of what had happened at the Federal Convention that could illuminate the original understanding of the treaty power. Writing as "Camillus" in his last "Defence" essay backing the Jay Treaty way back in January, Hamilton had claimed that Federalists' understanding of the treaty provision "was understood *by all* to be the intent" of the Constitutional Convention. He "appeal[ed] for this with confidence to every member of the Convention—particularly to those in the two houses of Congress"—one of whom was "Mr. Madison." "I feel a confidence," Hamilton concluded, "that neither of them will deny the assertion I have made. To suppose them capable of such a denial were to suppose them utterly regardless of truth." Meanwhile, just weeks prior Murray had been even more flagrant on the House floor. With a performer's instinct and zeal, he focused attention squarely on Madison:

> The gentleman from Virginia had borne an exalted rank among those who framed the very instrument. To his genius and patriotism . . . were we indebted for the Constitution. Would it not be expected that he who had helped to speak through the Constitution would be well prepared to expound it by contemporaneous opinions? Would it not be desirable that, if there are doubts, if we wander in the dark, the

gentleman should afford us light, as he had it in abundance? If the Convention spoke mysterious phrases, and the gentleman helped to utter them, will not the gentleman aid the expounding of the mystery? If the gentleman was the Pythia in the temple, ought he not to explain the ambiguous language of the oracle? To no man's exposition would he listen with more deference. If any cause could justify the intrusion of curiosity upon a deposite of secrets in a very sanctuary itself, it would be this doubt, and he should almost feel at liberty to open the Journals of the Convention, to see at least what they meant who spoke a language to others ambiguous, but to himself plain, incontrovertibly plain.

Through heavy-handed praise and with false credulity and deference, Murray set Madison up as the nation's high oracle, daring him to use the Convention's proceedings in order to show how the body's original intent deviated from Federalist orthodoxy. As if he had knowledge of what Washington would shortly document, Murray gestured directly to the Convention journals, convinced, it seems, that their contents would embarrass the Virginian who "had helped speak through the Constitution."[53]

Madison was clearly mindful of these challenges, but it was really Washington's decision to deposit the Convention records that had given such appeals to the Constitutional Convention, and the direct challenge they embodied, a new kind of authority. In complaining about Washington's tactic in a note to Jefferson, Madison revealed as much. "According to my memory & that of others, the Journal of the Convention was by a vote deposited with the P. to be kept sacred untill called for by some competent authority. How can this be reconciled with the use he has made of it?" Imagining the Constitution in terms of the hallowed archive in which it was embedded, Madison chastised Washington for effectively exploiting the journal for partisan gain. (Perhaps Madison only too easily recognized the effectiveness of this maneuver.) But proprieties aside, Washington's ploy had captured disputants' attention. Likely speaking for most Federalists, Fisher Ames privately reported, "Mr. Madison is deeply implicated by the appeal of the President to the proceedings of the General Convention, and most persons think him irrecoverably disgraced, as a man void of sincerity and fairness." Madison surely heard the whispers and noted the innuendo. Whether wounded, angered, or emboldened, he remained convinced that Washington's use of the Convention records was flawed. He told Jefferson "you will perceive that the quotation is nothing to the purpose," as he believed the August 23 discussion from the Convention that Washington had quoted focused on a fundamentally different set of issues than those raised by the House debate. But without his own notes handy (which, unlike the official record, actually captured the debate surrounding the failed amendment to the treaty power) and otherwise wary of how his personal record might be exploited if made public, he instead opted for a different strategy. He challenged Washington—and, by extension, Hamilton and Murray—not by litigating the record of the Convention, but by deflecting attention away from it entirely.[54]

Madison's response to these challenges came in an extensive speech on the House floor on April 6. Up to that point, he had been biding his time, contributing less frequently to the debate than had been customary in part because he continued to have mixed feelings about Livingston's ploy. But Madison now made up for his earlier reticence. "If there were any question which could make a serious appeal to the dispassionate judgment," he began, "it must be one which respected the meaning of the Constitution." He went on, "if any Constitutional question could make the appeal with peculiar solemnity, it must be in a case like the present, where two of the constituted authorities interpreted differently the extent of their respective powers." What happened in moments like these, when two agents tasked with carrying the Constitution into effect differed over its interpretation? The Constitution did not specify how to handle such meta-disputes, but Madison thought "there were three most precious resources against the evil tendency of them": the responsibility that every department felt to the public will, "ordinary elective channels," and the sovereign people's capacity to amend the document. Such solutions mirrored the initial thrust of the Jay Treaty debate—that the Constitution's contradictions empowered "the people," whose will was best manifested in the House of Representatives, to exercise creative constitutional discretion. But these arguments were quickly overwhelmed by Madison's appeal to the history of the Constitution's creation, which became the centerpiece of his remarks. In this regard, his speech was a microcosm of the treaty debate as a whole. As he had told Jefferson just days before, he was most preoccupied by Washington's appeal to the "proceedings in the General Convention, as a clue to the meaning of the Constitution."[55]

Attuned to thinking archivally and driven by necessity, this particular historical appeal became Madison's obsession. To establish the House's right to judge certain treaties, and thus ensure that the Republican cause prevailed, meant refuting the foundation of Washington's argument. And doing that meant disaggregating the original meaning of the Constitution from the Convention that had framed it. Madison could have pursued his initial narrative, explaining how the House enjoyed a discretionary right to vest the Constitution with meaning that could not be fixed and settled before such judgment was exercised. But he did not. In keeping with those who had preceded him in the debate, he followed Washington into the archive. He conceded that the method employed by the president, as well as by so many other House members, was entirely appropriate for fixing constitutional meaning. The issue merely centered on which archive and which kind of historical meaning.

Madison underscored the interpretive problems surrounding the Constitutional Convention. "When the members of the floor, who were members of the General Convention"—of whom he was one—"were called on in a former debate for the sense of that body on the Constitutional question, it was a matter of some surprise, which was much increased by the peculiar stress laid on the information expected." Part of the issue was memory. "This was the ninth year since the Convention executed their trust," he explained, and he had "not a single note in this place to assist his memory." But here Madison was being clever. Beneath this supposed lamentation about the imperfection of human memory lay a deeper problem. Announcing that he did not have one note "in this place" drew conspicuous attention to his personal Convention notes, whose existence was well known by this point, and the fact that they were not with him in Philadelphia. But Madison's point was not that his notes might function as a panacea (or a rival documentary record that would overturn Washington's use of the Convention journals). Instead, he was insinuating that, even if he did have access to his notes, the problem of asking Convention members to provide "information, not merely of their own ideas of that period, but of the intention of the whole body" remained. This debate in particular had cast doubt on the recovery of such a single intention. Thus far, he pointed out, "a sense had been put on the Constitution by some who were members of the Convention, different from that which must have been entertained by others, who had concurred in ratifying the Treaty." Here, in an especially ironic move in a speech otherwise loaded with them, Madison then hailed Elbridge Gerry's previous denunciation of the act of appealing to the Convention. Gerry had issued this warning during the bank debate specifically to chasten Madison for having done so. This fact did not stop Madison from quoting Gerry's earlier remarks in full. Obvious inconsistencies and partisan maneuvering aside, the Virginian had arrived at a clear point. To avoid the intractable indeterminacy that arose from trying to draw a single intention from the Federal Convention, interpreters needed to look elsewhere.[56]

Madison then directly tackled Washington's use of evidence to suggest that the proceedings of the ratifying conventions, rather than the Federal Convention, should be given pride of place in any effort to interpret the "true meaning" of the Constitution. While Madison considered the Convention journal that Washington had made use of "to be much more precise than any evidence drawn from the debates in the Convention, or resting on the memory of individuals," he still rejected the notion that it made sense to admit "the record of the Convention to be the oracle that ought to decide the true meaning of the Constitution." One needed to look elsewhere. In perhaps the most important conceptual statement issued during the entire debate, Madison then declared:

> But, after all, whatever veneration might be entertained for the body of men who formed our Constitution, the sense of that body could never be regarded as the oracular guide in expounding the Constitution. As the instrument came from them it was nothing more than the draft of a plan, nothing but a dead letter, until life and validity were breathed into it by the voice of the people, speaking through, the several State Conventions. If we were to look, therefore, for the meaning of the instrument beyond the face of the instrument, we must look for it, not in the General Convention, which proposed, but in the State Conventions, which accepted and ratified the Constitution.

Whatever evidence could be gleaned from the records of the Constitutional Convention, Madison was arguing, was ultimately meaningless. The Constitution that emerged from there was merely a proposal, an idea, a "dead letter." The ratifying conventions, acting in the name of the people's sovereign authority, breathed "life and validity" into it. If, then, inquirers were to look for the true meaning of the instrument, then the ratifying conventions were the only place to look.[57]

Consequently, the remainder of Madison's speech drew on the ratifying conventions instead of the Federal Convention. Not to "fatigue the Committee with a repetition of the passages then read to them," he opted not to quote from the debates—though his notes show he was poised to draw on speeches given by James Iredell and James Wilson at the North Carolina and Pennsylvania conventions, respectively, which both implied that there were checks on the treaty power. Instead, he insinuated that what had already been introduced on the floor was conclusive. Alternatively, he quoted from the various amendments proposed by the state conventions, claiming they were "better authority" than the ratifying debates themselves if one was attempting to uncover the intent of the ratifying conventions. Here he almost certainly relied on Augustine Davis's compilation of proposed amendments from ratification. They "would be found," he confidently promised, "to favor the sense of the Constitution which had prevailed in the House." In rapid succession, he read from the Virginia convention's proposed declaration of rights, the identical words laid down by North Carolina's convention, and further amendments that had been put forth by those two states along with ones proposed by New York and New Hampshire, all of which, he felt, presupposed an assumption that congressional consent was necessary for the exercise of important federal powers. On the basis of this presentation, he asked "whether it ought to be supposed that the several Conventions," who had showed such concern for commercial powers, often demanding that two-thirds or three-fourths of both branches of the legislature approve the exercise of this kind of authority, "could have understood that, by the Treaty clauses in the Constitution, they had given to the President and Senate, without any control whatever from the House of Representatives, an absolute and unlimited power over all those great objects?" That conclusion, he asserted, seemed unlikely. Surveying the testimony that emanated from those chambers, it was impossible to miss the deep presumption that the House of Representatives controlled the power of ratification of commercial treaties.[58]

No doubt compelled by political exigencies at many turns, Madison's thinking had evolved considerably. His appeals to constitutional history revealed a striking revision of his past commitments. In vaulting the powers of the House ahead of the president and Senate, he now minimized his earlier suspicion of popular legislative assemblies, a suspicion that had dominated his sober diagnosis of the "vices of the political system" in the 1780s, had led him to lobby so aggressively for a federal negative over state laws, and had underlay his fear, after the Constitutional Convention adjourned, that the House of Representatives would slowly swallow up the powers of the other federal branches. By 1796, Madison was in fact defending the alleged rights and powers of the federal House of Representatives, a body that should have been susceptible to the exact shortcoming a Madisonian theory of republicanism attempted to overcome. Clearly much had changed.[59]

A New Imagination

But this story transcends Madison and republicanism. More broadly, it reveals how Americans' conception of the Constitution, as an interpretive object, was changing. This transformation had remade not only Madison's ideological convictions but also how he imagined the Constitution's content and the means available for deciphering it. The inadequacies of the Constitution's face-value meaning had exposed contradictions, confusions, and ambiguities, all of which compelled enthusiastic Republicans and resistant Federalists to dig beneath the surface of the instrument. At first, House Republicans had used this opportunity to stress creative constitutional discretion, explaining why, in the new world of political publicity, the House of Representatives was uniquely empowered to manage, clarify, and adjudicate constitutional contradictions. But, along with Federalists, Republicans soon disappeared into history, probing the archive of the Constitution's creation in an attempt to locate testimony that might resolve those contradictions, gradually replacing contemporary discretion with fixed historical meaning. The "people's" Constitution thus gave way to the framers' Constitution. Madison had tried to justify why they were one and the same, why the records of the ratifying conventions captured the supreme popular sovereignty upon which the nation's fundamental law was based. But he was supplanting one image of the Constitution with another. In the process, he, like so many congressional disputants, had afforded deep meaning to the authorship that underlay the Constitution. Because constitutions were only legitimate, as Americans had long believed, because they had been drafted and ratified by known people in known time, Madison and his peers had turned to the Constitution's original authors in order to join present and past. Tethering constitutional meaning to original constitutional authorship signaled a shift, a new way of imagining what the Constitution was and how its contents should be debated and understood.

The Jay Treaty debate had helped solidify a new way of thinking about the Constitution, but ironically, for all this wrangling, it had failed to settle much about the treaty itself. By the middle of April, most practical aspects of the agreement had yet to be resolved. As much time as members of the House had spent debating every possible angle of Livingston's resolution and Washington's rejection of that request, they still had to struggle with the finer points of the treaty and determine, ultimately, if they were going to authorize the requisite appropriations. This consideration would consume the rest of the House's time that April. Public opinion began to shift on the treaty, fueled by an economic surge and Federalists' own spirited campaign to drum up public support for it by warning of economic collapse and war with Britain if the treaty was not implemented. Having apparently overcome their distaste for popular politics, Federalists ensured that a stream of petitions in support of the treaty flooded the House. As debate began on appropriations, many Republicans wavered and some openly defected. Gallatin, in a last-ditch effort, systematically criticized every aspect of the treaty. Shaken by the developments, Madison receded quietly into the background. At the end of the month, Fisher Ames—the Federalists' most eloquent orator who had been ill throughout the spring—mustered the energy to deliver the most celebrated speech of his congressional career, a speech that effectively ended debate. "We hear it said," he began, "that this is a struggle for liberty, a manly resistance against the design to nullify this assembly, and to make it a cypher in the Government . . . to force the Treaty down our throats." But "our Constitution has expressly regulated the matter differently," its "true doctrine" pointing in a different direction. It was only because Republicans had succumbed to irrational passions that they appeared willing "to tear up the settled foundations of our departments." Juxtaposing Federalists' rational commitment to the Constitution with Republicans' emotional assault on it, Ames successfully sapped the strength of his opposition. The Republicans' majority was now clearly in doubt. The next day when the question was called, the Committee of the Whole was evenly divided, 49–49. Frederick Muhlenberg, a Pennsylvania Republican who had served as the first speaker of the House and faced pressure from the Philadelphia merchant community (led by the merchant whose daughter Muhlenberg's son was hoping to wed), broke the committee deadlock by voting to allow it a full floor vote. Then on the following day, April 30, despite final protests, the appropriation for the Jay Treaty passed the full House by a vote of 51–48, and at long last the treaty was the supreme law of the land.[60]

In the end, crucial though this was, in terms of the Constitution it mattered far less. Regardless of how the House decided to resolve the important question of whether and how to implement the treaty, the debate surrounding it had already taken a deeper toll. The treaty's fate might have remained open for consideration. Yet new forms of constitutional imagination had already taken shape.

One understanding in particular had emerged in force. Disputants in the Jay Treaty debate had converged on a particular way of justifying constitutional claims, by excavating the history of the Constitution's origins to uncover its true, buried meaning. From this new perspective, the Constitution was no longer imagined as necessarily incomplete and unfinished. Instead, it was born complete; and when there were doubts about its meaning or commands—doubts that its own language could not resolve—the right kind of digging, into the right piece of its archive, revealed what the vagaries of human language and the passage of time had otherwise obscured.

While Federalists and Republicans perhaps came to believe that they were appealing to the history of the Constitution's creation, discovering its one, true fixed meaning, however, they were actually, in the process, both creating the Constitution and fixing it themselves. By underwriting the practices of justification that invested such moves with authority, and tightly tethering them to a conception of the Constitution, they were constructing this brand of constitutionalism as much as they were relying on it. In sanctifying 1787 and 1788, Jay Treaty disputants had created something new in 1796. "Fixing" signaled both a condition and an activity. Congressmen increasingly imagined the Constitution as fixed by conceiving it as a finished text whose ambiguities were resolved at the time of its birth. But they did so by themselves actually fixing it—by pulling together various constitutional strands that had earlier taken shape and fusing them into a distinct arrangement. Independent of the practices and image of the Constitution that gave the constitutional archive authority, it did not much matter what that archive contained. The fixed Constitution was, thus, not discovered but invented, as a certain form of constitutional imagination acquired coherence and power. The Jay Treaty debate marked its apotheosis and, with that, the culmination of a pivotal, and often obscured, portion of the story of American constitutional creation.

Epilogue

The Endurance of Fixity

The language of our Constitution is already undergoing interpretations unknown to its founders.

—James Madison to Henry Lee, June 25, 1824

Noah Webster, the early American lexicographer who devoted his life to liberating American English from its British roots, completed his masterwork, *An American Dictionary*, in 1828. Webster hoped his creation would replace Samuel Johnson's *A Dictionary of English Language* in American usage. First published in 1755, Johnson's handiwork had gone through several editions and was widely considered the definitive resource of its kind. United by a common language, but separated by nearly three-quarters of a very tumultuous century, their dictionaries betray how constitutional imagination had changed. To "constitute," Webster declared, in its first sense, denoted "To set; to fix." "Fix," in turn, he insisted, meant, among other things, "To set or establish immovably" or "To withhold from motion." In contrast, Johnson had defined "constitute" as merely "1. To give formal existence . . . to produce . . . 2. To erect; to establish." The entry said nothing about "fixing."[1]

The fixed Constitution was not the only way of imagining America's governing instrument to emerge from the 1790s. Like Webster's dictionary, it was not without its rivals. But it has proved surprisingly enduring. By the end of the eighteenth century, it had become a fully formed player on the American constitutional stage. Since then, it has played a starring role during some moments, and receded into the background at others. But it has never left the stage. All constitutional performers, moreover, have inhabited a theater that has been itself shaped by it. The fixed Constitution, as concept, has, thus, endured in this twin sense—its presence has proved permanent in an arena that distinctively bears its mark.

The idea of the fixed Constitution has had such an enduring legacy not because all (or even most) constitutional users have subscribed to it, but instead because it remade the concept of constitutional fixity itself. By creating a constitutionalism that is frozen in time, it forever disaggregated constitutional fixity from constitutional change. Prior to the 1790s, fixity and change had been entwined in Anglo-American constitutional imagination—with each view informing the other at every turn. Now, in the aftermath of a decade of debate over how to understand the United States Constitution, they were understood as mutually exclusive antagonists. As a result, the fixed Constitution and its competitors are often defined on the same terms. While some Americans believe the Constitution is fixed in place and others think it is constantly changing, both reach these conclusions based on a common understanding of fixity, one that did not exist before American political leaders fought one another about the limits and possibilities of their governing document during the twilight of the eighteenth century.

This shared understanding both grew out of and has subsequently been enforced by a common conception of the Constitution itself. No matter how bitterly Americans have disagreed since the 1790s about how they ought to interpret the Constitution or the right way to discover its meaning, more often than not they have imagined the Constitution in much the same ways—as a written, discrete, inert, historically conceived object composed of words, contained on parchment, and enforced by judges. Regardless of whether they claim that this object's meaning is unchanging, or insist that its meaning evolves over time; no matter that some privilege the text itself, while others emphasize the layers of precedent and doctrine built upon it—nonetheless it is a common object born of a common understanding of fixity organizing a common field of vision and argumentation. Beneath disagreement about the Constitution's meaning, in other words, often lies a shared conception of the Constitution's constitution. But the emergence of that common object was not inevitable; it was not a necessary result of any inherent feature of the Constitution itself, its initial construction, or the assumptions that informed that process. Instead, it was the unexpected by-product of a unique brand of constitutional imagination, and the distinctive conception of constitutional fixity it betrayed, which political debates following 1788 contingently brought into existence.

EVIDENCE of the tenacious pull of the fixed Constitution is how deeply it transformed James Madison's own understanding of the constitutional order that he had done so much to create. No single figure played as significant a role in either the creation of the American Constitution or the fixed constitutional imagination that came to accompany it. It is perhaps not surprising that as early as 1829 he was christened the "father of the Constitution." He had offered the most penetrating diagnosis of what ailed the nation's constitutional system in the 1780s. He had drawn upon that analysis to frame the agenda at the 1787 Constitutional Convention and to propel the proceedings toward the kind of far-reaching reform he had deemed essential. During ratification, he had produced some of the most incisive commentaries of the proposed Constitution and he had repelled the vigorous criticisms of vaunted Anti-Federalists on the floor of the Virginia ratifying convention. Once he succeeded in installing the Constitution as the nation's governing document, he had then been the most active member of the House of Representatives during the 1790s, helping to bring the inert Constitution to life through—as he had put it in the *Federalist Papers*—"a series of particular discussions and adjudications." In the process, he helped create and sanction the justificatory practices that created the idea of the fixed Constitution.[2]

Madison's political career extended far beyond 1796, but much about his constitutional imagination remained the same. After retiring from Congress shortly after the Jay Treaty episode had run its course, he was soon dragged back into public life to help his longtime political ally Thomas Jefferson and fellow Republicans combat the gravest Federalist threat yet—legislation known as the Alien and Sedition Acts, which muzzled criticism of most federal representatives, made citizenship harder to attain, and expanded the powers of the presidency. From 1798 to 1800, Madison and Jefferson laid the groundwork for the next presidential contest by protesting these laws. They secretly authored resolutions, passed by the Republican-controlled state legislatures in Virginia and Kentucky, proclaiming the Alien and Sedition Acts unconstitutional. Following Jefferson's ascent to the presidency in 1801, Madison served under him as secretary of state for eight years.

Then for two terms immediately thereafter he served as president himself. Throughout these eventful years he continued to grapple with the Constitution and its interpretation. Some of his constitutional assumptions acquired new shape and definition; but many of his core attitudes remained strikingly consistent.[3]

After he had receded from the public stage and retired to Montpelier, he continued to reflect on many of the same questions that had long animated him. New problems emerged, most frequently those that stemmed from either intensifying partisanship or sectional tensions that threatened to tear the union apart. As trusted correspondents and confidants solicited his opinions on the Missouri Crisis and the problem of slavery in the early 1820s or the nullification crisis and the problem of final constitutional authority that exploded later that decade, Madison revealed what had come of his constitutional imagination. What stands out in his remarkable correspondence from these years is how powerfully the concept of the fixed Constitution still consumed him. If anything, as Madison had ample time to reflect, particularly on the democratic energies that were rapidly remaking the United States, this mode of imagination had only solidified. While Madison was merely a single individual in a far-flung nation, and while such allusions to constitutional fixity speak to only some of the mental habits that engrossed his ever-active mind, they nonetheless vividly demonstrate the persistence of what the 1790s had so consequentially unleashed.[4]

In these later years, Madison was still preoccupied by the intersection of language and constitutionalism. Many of the same concerns that had animated *Federalist* 37 lingered. As he remarked in 1824, "defining the terms used in argument" was "the only effectual precaution against fruitless & endless discussion." Indeed, he went on, "this logical precept is peculiarly essential in debating Constitutional questions, to which for want of more appropriate words, such are often applied as lead to error & confusion." The problem was partly language but also partly constitutionalism—at least as Americans had experienced it. "Known words express known ideas." But what happened, Madison wondered, when there were "new ideas, such as are presented by our Novel & Unique political System?" They "must be expressed either by new words, or by old words with new definitions. Without attention to this circumstance, volumes may be written which can only be answered by a call for definitions, and which answer themselves as soon as the call is complied with." Radical innovation—of the sort unleashed when Americans remade their constitutional world—left language, inherently impoverished, lagging behind. Without a language capable of representing the complex ideas generated by the Constitution, constitutional dispute could not help but yield its fair share of indeterminacy—which is why he still conceded in 1833, much as he always had, that "no government of human device and human administration can be perfect."[5]

While Madison's fascination with language and constitutionalism continued into the 1820s and 1830s, however, he increasingly drew different lessons about the relationship between them than he had decades earlier when he helped write the *Federalist*. "Whilst few things are more difficult, few are more desirable," he claimed in 1826, "than a standard work, explaining, and as far as possible fixing the meaning of words & phrases." Given that "all languages . . . are liable to changes from causes, some of them inseparable from the nature of man, & the progress of society," accordingly "a perfect remedy for the evil must therefore be unattainable. But," and here he began to show how much had changed, "as far as it may be attainable, the attempt is laudable, and next to compleat success is that of recording with admitted fidelity the State of a language at the epoch of the Record."[6]

The mutability of language, he now asserted, was especially problematic for constitutions. "In the exposition of laws, & even of Constitutions, how many important errors, may be produced by mere innovations in the use of words & phrases," he asked. "If the meaning of the text be sought in the changeable meaning of the words composing it," then "the shape and attributes of the Government must partake of the changes to which the words and phrases of all living languages are constantly subject." Language, he had come to believe, not only obscured ideas but—every bit as problematically—changed through usage. "What a metamorphosis would be produced in the code of law," he remarked, "if all its ancient phraseology were to be taken in its modern sense." Indeed, "the change which the meaning of words inadvertently undergoes" has already led to "misconstructions of the Constitutional text." All of this meant that "the language of our Constitution" had been forced to bear "interpretations unknown to its founders."[7]

Madison worried that through linguistic change the Constitution would slowly disappear. Constitutions were predicated on stability and were built to regulate the political, social, and economic order. But, as Madison insisted, if all available "authoritative interpretations" and all the potential study and explication "cannot settle" the Constitution's "meaning and the intention of its authors, we can never have a stable and known Constitution." Unless the "meaning of a Constitution" was "fixed and known," it would be as mutable and changeable as the language in which it was written, "producing that instability which is incompatible with good government." Under "written constitutions," unless there was concerted effort to settle their meaning, then the "effect of time in changing the meaning of words and phrases" would eliminate the Constitution altogether.[8]

According to Madison in these later years, there was only one available remedy to this unsettling problem. Constitutional words needed to be "controuled by a recurrence to the original and authentic meaning attached to them." As words were constantly liable to break away from the meanings once paired with them, it became the job of constitutional stewards to re-join constitutional words to their original meanings—to fix constitutional language. As only original meanings were "authentic" meanings, fixing meant excavating. It meant perpetually returning, through rigorous acts of historical exhumation, "to the sense in which the Constitution was accepted and ratified by the nation," because "in that sense alone it is the legitimate Constitution." Only a fixed constitution understood in this specific sense, in other words, was a genuine constitution.[9]

Gripped by the idea of the fixed Constitution, Madison studiously prepared his notes from the Constitutional Convention of 1787 for posthumous publication. He had seen far too many "departures from the true & fair construction of the Instrument . . . by rules, or rather the abandonment of all rules, of expounding it, which were capable of transforming it into something very different from its legitimate character." Since he believed "it was the duty of all to support [the Constitution] in its true meaning as understood *by the Nation* at the time of its ratification," he considered it his special responsibility to help lay the archival foundation from which such judgments could be derived. He remembered how a paucity of historical knowledge had hindered his own constitutional investigations in the 1780s and thus claimed in his later years to have long hoped to contribute to "the fund of materials for the History of a Constitution on which would be Staked the happiness of a people." By the 1820s especially, his correspondence focused on the events of 1787 and 1788 as he demonstrated a growing interest in communicating his version of the Founding to younger confidants while encouraging their own research into the subject.[10]

Publication of a competing narrative of the Constitutional Convention—*The Secret Proceedings and Debates of the Convention,* based largely on Robert Yates's convention notes—made Madison all the more anxious to ensure that his notes would become part of the public record. Doctored portions of Yates's account had first been published after his death in 1808, but they appeared in their entirety with the 1821 publication of the *Secret Proceedings*. The latter portrayed the Convention as a secret cabal bent on destroying the state governments. But whether Yates's original notes were faithfully reproduced in the published pamphlet was of less concern to Madison than, as he complained in one letter after another, what an "inaccurate" and "grossly erroneous" narrative they formed. While he took personal umbrage at the accusation that he had been among the nationalist plotters, he was particularly concerned about the integrity of the historical record. Yates had left the Convention along with his fellow New York delegate, John Lansing, in protest on July 10 (more than two months before it adjourned) and thereafter had become an arch Anti-Federalist. Not only was Yates, Madison noted, "present during the early discussions only," but, worse yet, "prejudices guided his pen." In contrast, Madison "possess[ed] materials for a pretty ample view of what passed" at that time. Even if his notes had been revised—a reality he struggled to come to terms with—he believed they better captured the spirit of the Founding than anything Yates could have authored. So while Madison had difficulty settling on the exact timing and manner of the publication of his notes, he was clear that it had never been his "intention that they should for ever remain under the veil of secrecy." In many instances he still privileged the authoritative character of the ratifying conventions, but—especially in light of the publication of Yates's account—he appreciated that his own notes at the Federal Convention could meaningfully contribute to the broader record of the Constitution's origins. As he explained to one correspondent, the "key to the sense of the Constitution, where alone the true one can be found" was to be discovered "in the proceedings of the Convention, the co[n]temporary expositions, and above all in the ratifying Conventions of the States." Consequently, after Madison's death in 1836, his widow, Dolley, ensured "that the report [of the Convention] as made by me should be published" and delivered the notes to the federal government. They were published shortly thereafter, in 1840.[11]

If understanding the "true sense" of the Constitution meant restoring its original character by properly exhuming its lost meaning and fixing it in place, as Madison had come to believe, then an adequate archive of its creation was essential. Because the Constitution was embodied in language and because language was so fickle, historical excavation offered the only available mode to prevent it from "transforming . . . into something very different from its legitimate character." In Madison's eyes, the Constitution was thus intimately, and essentially, linked to its own history.

The Madison of the "Vices," the Constitutional Convention, the ratification debates, and the removal debate had drawn a much different moral from his reflections on the indeterminacy of language. That Madison had denigrated "parchment barriers" and the related idea that constitutions could be reduced to words, while embracing the active political construction of constitutional meaning. That Madison had assumed the Constitution was incomplete, partial, and in critical ways indeterminate and believed that ongoing discussions and experiences would help make new meanings that would flesh out the unfinished edifice that he had helped construct. That Madison had thought constitutions were systems of practices, not discrete objects. Now, late in life, shaped as he was by the logic of fixed constitutionalism, he drew a radically different set of conclusions, so much so that the Madison of earlier years might well have been shocked by them. As he had long thought, thanks to the unfortunate character of language, the Constitution could never be purely determinate. Some of its contents would always be shrouded in uncertainty. But this subsequent Madison was no longer content with this reality; he was now deeply unnerved by it. He no longer assumed that the deficiencies of language could serve constitutionalism; he now believed that they threatened it. Rather than taking comfort in the new meanings generated through ongoing debates and adjudications, he instead sought to escape these processes, by freezing language in its place, by checking its relentless dynamism, and by tethering the original meaning of the Constitution to its words. Madison was insisting on recovering, fixing, and respecting the Constitution as it originally was. But, ironically, in so doing he was disparaging the Constitution he himself had originally imagined.[12]

THERE WERE several ways to imagine the Constitution—its possibilities, its characteristics, its meanings. But it was the idea of a fixed Constitution, a Constitution with an inherent meaning that had to be deciphered through acts of excavation, that dominated public consciousness after the 1790s and consumed the most engaged and incisive Founding-era constitutional thinker until his death. Even Madison's good friend Jefferson, who so often played Madison's constitutional foil, had been seduced by its charms. Jefferson's obsession with generational sovereignty and constitutional change lingered, captured most powerfully in the evocative commentary he wrote to Samuel Kercheval in 1816 regarding Virginia's constitution:

> Some men look at Constitutions with sanctimonious reverence, & deem them, like the ark of the convenant, too sacred to be touched. [T]hey ascribe to the men of the preceding age a wisdom more than human, and suppose what they did to be beyond amendment. I knew that age well: I belonged to it and labored with it. [I]t deserved well of its country. [I]t was very like the present but without the experience of the present: and 40 years of experience in government is worth a century of book-reading: and this they would say themselves, were they to rise from the dead.

Yet, at the same time, Jefferson betrayed a much different kind of constitutional imagination. While pondering whether it was constitutional to execute the Louisiana Purchase with France in 1803, he worried about assuming the power to do so "by a construction" of, of all things, the treaty clause. "Our peculiar security is in the possession of a written constitution," he remarked; "let us not make it a blank paper by construction." Even if there were great costs associated with looking upon "constitutions with sanctimonious reverence" and ascribing to figures in the past "a wisdom more than human," nonetheless, stabilizing a written constitution entailed, he wrote near the end of his life in 1823, "carry[ing] ourselves back to the time when the constitution was adopted." Rather than "trying what meaning may be squeezed out of the text, or invented against it," interpreters should look backward, probing the Constitution's origins, in order to "conform to the probable one in which it was passed." Jefferson, too, was inclined to fuse the Constitution's language with the archive of its creation in order to fix it in place.[13]

But as quickly and powerfully as the idea of the fixed Constitution emerged after the Constitution's construction, nothing about the Constitution itself necessitated its development. It was the product of a complex set of forces—including, above all, convictions that constitutions were deliberately authored, that they were fundamentally made and defined by language, that they were largely complete systems of adjudication, and that filling in their gaps and indeterminacies meant excavating meanings that had been locked into them at the moment of their inception. Each of these characteristics was contingent, each was developed along a slightly different trajectory, each was mobilized, then normalized, in peculiar ways in the context of political combat, and each was necessary for the fixed constitutional imagination to fully take shape. Neither their individual developments nor the way they slowly cohered were necessitated by the Constitution itself. They instead developed out of an explosive set of debates, begun during ratification and continued in the halls of Congress, that put enormous argumentative pressure on the Constitution and, in the process, strengthened certain modes of using the Constitution to justify claims. As these practices became entrenched, certain habits of mind followed—ones that betrayed a textual, then an archival constitutional consciousness—until what had once been largely unthinkable became commonplace.

The irony of the endless search for the original Constitution is that such an inquiry will never reveal a fixed document. These efforts can only ever expose—should its inquirers be willing to see it—the story of how a contingent set of practices made it possible thereafter to imagine the Constitution in that way, a narrative about how the activities of fixing ended up producing a fascination with fixity. Once it is appreciated that an entirely optional set of norms made this conception of the Constitution—and that, in turn, any conception of the Constitution is made by a similarly optional set of norms—it will then cease to make much sense to search for any essential set of constitutional practices that could have been hardwired into the Constitution. Appreciating how the idea of a fixed Constitution was invented, in other words, should encourage us to imagine anew, in our own way, what the Constitution ought to be.

NOTES

ACKNOWLEDGMENTS

INDEX

Notes

Abbreviations

AC   *Annals of Congress* or *The Debates and Proceedings in the Congress of the United States; with an Appendix, containing Important State Papers and Public Documents, and all the Laws of a Public Nature; with a Copious Index, Compiled from Authentic Materials by Joseph Gales, Senior* (Washington, DC: Gales and Seaton, 1834), 42 volumes.

Creating   *Creating the Bill of Rights: The Documentary Record from the First Federal Congress,* ed. Helen E. Veit, Kenneth R. Bowling, and Charlene Bangs Bickford (Baltimore: Johns Hopkins University Press, 1991).

Debates   *The Debates in the Several State Conventions of the Adoption of the Federal Constitution,* ed. Jonathan Elliot (Washington, DC: United States Congress, 1827–1830), 5 volumes.

DHFFC   *The Documentary History of the First Federal Congress of the United States of America, 4 March 1789–3 March 1791,* ed. Linda Grant De Pauw, Charlene Bangs Bickford, Kenneth R. Bowling, and Helen E. Veit (Baltimore: Johns Hopkins University Press, 1976–), 22 volumes.

DHFFE   *The Documentary History of the First Federal Elections,* ed. Merrill Jensen, Robert A. Becker, and Gordon DenBoer (Madison: University of Wisconsin Press, 1976–1989), 4 volumes.

DHRC   *The Documentary History of the Ratification of the Constitution,* ed. John Kaminski, Gaspare J. Saladino, Richard Leffler, Charles H. Schoenleber, and Margaret A. Hogan (Madison: State Historical Society of Wisconsin, 1976–), 29 volumes.

JCC   *Journals of the Continental Congress, 1774–1789,* ed. Worthington C. Ford, Gaillard Hunt, John C. Fitzpatrick, and Roscoe R. Hill (Washington, DC: Government Printing Office, 1904–1937), 34 volumes.

JER   *Journal of the Early Republic*

Letters	*Letters and Other Writings of James Madison* (Philadelphia: J. B. Lippincott, 1865), 4 volumes.
PAH	*The Papers of Alexander Hamilton,* ed. Harold C. Syrett and Jacob E. Cooke (New York: Columbia University Press, 1961–1987), 27 volumes.
PJA	*The Papers of John Adams,* ed. Robert J. Taylor (Cambridge, MA: Harvard University Press, 1977–), 18 volumes.
PJA Legal	*The Legal Papers of John Adams,* ed. L. Kinvin Wroth and Hiller B. Zobel (Cambridge, MA: Harvard University Press, 1965), 3 volumes.
PJM	*The Papers of James Madison, Congressional Series,* ed. William T. Hutchinson, William M. E. Rachal, and Robert Allen Rutland (Chicago: University of Chicago Press, 1962–1977; Charlottesville: University of Virginia Press, 1977–1991), 17 volumes.
PJM RS	*The Papers of James Madison, Retirement Series,* ed. David B. Mattern, J. C. A. Stagg, Mary Parke Johnson, and Katherine E. Harbury (Charlottesville: University of Virginia Press, 2009–), 3 volumes.
PTJ	*The Papers of Thomas Jefferson,* ed. Julian P. Boyd, Charles T. Cullen, John Catanzariti, Barbara Oberg, and James P. McClure (Princeton, NJ: Princeton University Press, 1950–), 43 volumes.
PTJ RS	*The Papers of Thomas Jefferson, Retirement Series,* ed. James P. McClure and J. Jefferson Looney (Princeton, NJ: Princeton University Press, 2004–), 14 volumes.
Records	*The Records of the Federal Convention,* ed. Max Farrand (New Haven, CT: Yale University Press, 1911–1937), 4 volumes.
Supplement	*Supplement to Max Farrand's Records of the Federal Convention,* ed. James H. Hutson (New Haven, CT: Yale University Press, 1987).
WFA	*Works of Fisher Ames,* ed. W. B. Allen (Indianapolis: Liberty Fund, 1983), 2 volumes.
WJM	*The Writings of James Madison,* ed. Gaillard Hunt (New York: G. P. Putnam's Sons, 1900–1910), 9 volumes.
WMQ	*William and Mary Quarterly.*

Introduction

Epigraph: Comte de Moustier to Comte de Montmorin, June 9, 1789, *DHFFC,* 16:735.

1. James Jackson, June 8, 1789, *DHFFC,* 11:812; John Vining, Feb. 8, 1791, *DHFFC,* 14:472.

2. On the original Constitution's authoritative aura, see Jack N. Rakove, *Original Meanings: Politics and Ideas in the Making of the Constitution* (New York: Knopf, 1996), ch. 1. On reverence for the Constitution throughout American history, above all see Michael Kammen, *A Machine That Would Go of Itself,* 2nd ed. (1986; New Brunswick, NJ: Transaction, 2006); Sanford Levinson, *Constitutional Faith* (Princeton, NJ: Princeton University Press, 1988), ch. 1. On similarities drawn between constitutional

veneration and religious scripture and faith, see Thomas C. Grey, "The Constitution as Scripture," *Stanford Law Review* 37 (Nov. 1984), 1–25; Anne Norton, "Transubstantiation: The Dialectic of Constitutional Authority," *University of Chicago Law Review* 55 (Spring 1988), 458–472; Jaroslav Pelikan, *Interpreting the Bible and the Constitution* (New Haven, CT: Yale University Press, 2004); Jamal Greene, "On the Origins of Originalism," *Texas Law Review* 88 (Nov. 2009), 1–89; Jack M. Balkin, *Constitutional Redemption: Political Faith in an Unjust World* (Cambridge, MA: Harvard University Press, 2011); Peter J. Smith and Robert W. Tuttle, "Biblical Literalism and Constitutional Originalism," *Notre Dame Law Review* 86 (Mar. 2011), 693–763; Jill Lepore, "We the Parchment," in *The Story of America* (Princeton, NJ: Princeton University Press, 2012), 72–90. On battling over the Founders, see David Sehat, *The Jefferson Rule: How the Founding Fathers Became Infallible and Our Politics Inflexible* (New York: Simon and Schuster, 2015); Andrew M. Schocket, *Fighting over the Founders: How We Remember the American Revolution* (New York: New York University Press, 2015); Jill Lepore, *The Whites of Their Eyes: The Tea Party's Revolution and the Battle over American History* (Princeton, NJ: Princeton University Press, 2011); R. B. Bernstein, *The Founding Fathers Reconsidered* (New York: Oxford University Press, 2009), 115–143; Michael G. Kammen, *A Season of Youth: The American Revolution and the Historical Imagination* (New York: Knopf, 1978); "Symposium on *Hamilton, An American Musical,*" *JER* 37 (Summer 2017), 251–303. For important examples of how the Constitution has been trussed to its origins, see Charles A. Beard, *An Economic Interpretation of the Constitution of the United States* (New York: Macmillan, 1913); Ronald Dworkin, *Freedom's Law: The Moral Reading of the American Constitution* (Cambridge, MA: Harvard University Press, 1996); David Waldstreicher, *Slavery's Constitution: From Revolution to Ratification* (New York: Hill and Wang, 2009); George Van Cleve, *A Slaveholder's Union: Slavery, Politics, and the Constitution in the Early American Republic* (Chicago: University of Chicago Press, 2010), chs. 3–4; Randy E. Barnett, *Restoring the Lost Constitution: The Presumption of Liberty,* rev. ed. (2004; Princeton, NJ: Princeton University Press, 2014); Clement Fatovic, *America's Founding and the Struggle over Economic Inequality* (Lawrence: University Press of Kansas, 2015); Gary Gerstle, *Liberty and Coercion: The Paradox of American Government from the Founding to the Present* (Princeton, NJ: Princeton University Press, 2015); Ganesh Sitaraman, *The Crisis of the Middle-Class Constitution: Why Economic Inequality Threatens Our Republic* (New York: Knopf, 2017).

3. Thomas Paine, *Common Sense* (1776), ed. Isaac Kramnick (New York: Penguin Press, 1982), 98 (speaking generally of law). On the Constitution's relationship to American identity, see especially John Fabian Witt, *Patriots and Cosmopolitans: Hidden Histories of American Law* (Cambridge, MA: Harvard University Press, 2007), 3–5. On the sanctity of the Declaration of Independence, see Pauline Maier, *American Scripture: Making the Declaration of Independence* (New York: Knopf, 1997), ix–xxi, 175–215.

4. The literature on originalism is massive. For its development, as well as a guide to the work of originalists, see Jonathan Gienapp, "Constitutional Originalism and

History," *Process: A Blog for American History,* Mar. 20, 2017, available at http://www
.processhistory.org/originalism-history/. For introductions from leading originalists, see
Lawrence W. Solum, "What Is Originalism? The Evolution of Contemporary Originalist Theory," in *The Challenge of Originalism: Theories of Constitutional Interpretation,*
ed. Grant Huscroft and Bradley W. Miller (New York: Cambridge University Press,
2011), 12–41; Keith E. Whittington, "Originalism: A Critical Introduction," *Fordham
Law Review* 82 (Nov. 2013), 378–387.

5. The foundational works on the making of the U.S. Constitution include Bernard Bailyn, *The Ideological Origins of the American Revolution,* enl. ed. (1967; Cam-
bridge, MA: Harvard University Press, 1992); Gordon S. Wood, *The Creation of the
American Republic, 1776–1787,* 2nd ed. (1969; Chapel Hill: University of North Carolina
Press, 1998); Rakove, *Original Meanings;* Michael J. Klarman, *The Framers' Coup: The
Making of the United States Constitution* (New York: Oxford University Press, 2016). Also
see Clinton Rossiter, *1787: The Grand Convention* (New York: Macmillan, 1966); Merrill
Jensen, *The Making of the American Constitution,* 2nd ed. (1964; Huntington: R. E.
Krieger, 1979); Forrest McDonald, *Novus Ordo Seclorum: The Intellectual Origins of the
Constitution* (Lawrence: University Press of Kansas, 1985); Richard B. Bernstein and
Kym S. Rice, *Are We to Be a Nation? The Making of the Constitution* (Cambridge, MA:
Harvard University Press, 1987); Woody Holton, *Unruly Americans and the Origins of the
Constitution* (New York: Hill and Wang, 2007); David O. Stewart, *The Summer of 1787:
The Men Who Invented the Constitution* (New York: Simon and Schuster, 2007); Richard
Beeman, *Plain, Honest Men: The Making of the American Constitution* (New York:
Random House, 2009); David Brian Robertson, *The Original Compromise: What the
Constitution's Framers Were Really Thinking* (New York: Oxford University Press, 2013).

6. Complaints that the Constitution is broken and in need of fundamental re-
pairs have become common. For a start see, for example, Sanford Levinson, *Our
Undemocratic Constitution: Where the Constitutions Goes Wrong (And How We the
People Can Correct It)* (New York: Oxford University Press, 2006); Daniel Lazare, *The
Frozen Republic: How the Constitution Is Paralyzing Democracy* (New York: Harcourt,
Brace, 1996); Robert A. Dahl, *How Democratic Is the American Constitution?* 2nd ed.
(2002; New Haven, CT: Yale University Press, 2003); William G. Howell and
Terry M. Moe, *Relic: How Our Constitution Undermines Effective Government—and
Why We Need a More Powerful Presidency* (New York: Basic Books, 2016).

7. James Madison to Thomas Jefferson, June 30, 1789, *PJM,* 12:268. Several
scholars have persuasively emphasized that the Constitution's meaning was contested
from the moment it appeared; see especially Rakove, *Original Meanings;* Saul Cornell,
The Other Founders: Anti-Federalism and the Dissenting Tradition in America, 1788–1828
(Chapel Hill: University of North Carolina Press, 1999); H. Jefferson Powell, "The Political Grammar of Early Constitutional Law," *North Carolina Law Review* 71 (Apr. 1993),
949–1009. Meanwhile, appreciating that the Constitution has always been rife with ambiguities, constitutional originalists have begun emphasizing the concept of construction—

when the Constitution's meaning is irredeemably ambiguous, vague, or indetermi-nate, it falls to contemporary political and judicial actors to construct meaning, to fill the document's gaps and resolve its ambiguities. But they foreground the indetermi-nacy of constitutional *meaning* (uncertainty about bits and pieces of text) without considering what this book primarily scrutinizes: the indeterminacy of constitutional *ontology* (uncertainty about the Constitution's basic properties). Thus, the account of constitutional indeterminacy offered here is profoundly and categorically different from this alternative. For some leading examples of construction originalism, see Keith E. Whittington, "Constructing a New American Constitution," *Constitutional Commentary* 27 (Fall 2010), 119–138; Jack M. Balkin, *Living Originalism* (Cambridge, MA: Harvard University Press, 2011), 3–6, ch. 12, 297–305; Lawrence B. Solum, "Orig-inalism and Constitutional Construction," *Fordham Law Review* 82 (Nov. 2013), 453–537. For more citations and discussion, see Jonathan Gienapp, "Making Constitutional Meaning: The Removal Debate and the Birth of Constitutional Essentialism," *JER* 44 (Fall 2015), 375–418, esp. nn13–14.

8. Others have emphasized the Constitution's uncertainty post-1788 in various ways, and this book is indebted to them. See, above all, Jack N. Rakove, "Thinking like a Constitution," *JER* 24 (Spring 2004), 1–26; Mary Sarah Bilder, *Madison's Hand: Re-vising the Constitutional Convention* (Cambridge, MA: Harvard University Press, 2015); Caleb Nelson, "Originalism and Interpretive Conventions," *University of Chicago Law Review* 70 (Spring 2003), 519–598; David M. Golove and Daniel J. Hulsebosch, "A Civi-lized Nation: The Early American Constitution, the Law of Nations, and the Pursuit of International Recognition," *N.Y.U. Law Review* 85 (Oct. 2010), 932–1066; Terence Ball and J. G. A. Pocock, eds., *Conceptual Change and the Constitution* (Lawrence: University Press of Kansas, 1988). The most important work on American constitutional develop-ment between 1776 and 1787 remains Wood, *Creation of the American Republic.* While more focused, also valuable is Eric Nelson, *The Royalist Revolution: Monarchy and the American Founding* (Cambridge, MA: Harvard University Press, 2014).

9. On the Constitution's rapid sanctification, see Linda Grant DePauw, "The Anticlimax of Antifederalism: The Abortive Second Convention Movement, 1788–1789," *Prologue* 2 (1970), 98–114; Lance Banning, "Republican Ideology and the Triumph of the Constitution," *WMQ* 31 (Apr. 1974), 167–188; Michael Lienesch, *New Order of the Ages: Time, the Constitution, and the Making of Modern American Political Thought* (Princeton, NJ: Princeton University Press, 1988); David J. Siemers, *Ratifying the Re-public: Antifederalists and Federalists in Constitutional Time* (Stanford, CA: Stanford University Press, 2002), chs. 2–3. For takes at odds with this prevailing view, see Kammen, *A Machine That Would Go of Itself,* 46–57; James Roger Sharp, *American Politics in the Early Republic: The New Nation in Crisis* (New Haven, CT: Yale University Press, 1993), 5–8, 13–14. On the Anti-Federalists' transition from combating the Constitution to struggling over its interpretation, see Cornell, *Other Founders,* 136–171; DePauw, "Anticlimax of Antifederalism"; John H. Aldrich and Ruth W. Grant, "The

Anti-Federalists, the First Congress, and the First Parties," *Journal of Politics* 55 (May 1993), 295–326; R. B. Bernstein, "A New Matrix for National Politics: The First Federal Elections, 1788–1790," in *Inventing Congress: Origins and Establishment of the First Federal Congress,* ed. Kenneth R. Bowling and Donald R. Kennon (Athens: University of Ohio Press, 1999), 109–137. For work that examines the Constitution post-1788, see Banning, "Republican Ideology and the Triumph of the Constitution"; Thornton Anderson, *Creating the Constitution: The Convention of 1787 and the First Congress* (University Park: Pennsylvania State University Press, 1993); David P. Currie, *The Constitution in Congress: The Federalist Period, 1789–1801* (Chicago: University of Chicago Press, 1997); Joseph M. Lynch, *Negotiating the Constitution: The Earliest Debates over Original Intent* (Ithaca, NY: Cornell University Press, 1999); H. Jefferson Powell, *A Community Built on Words: The Constitution in History and Politics* (Chicago: University of Chicago Press, 2002).

10. Akhil Reed Amar, *America's Unwritten Constitution: The Precedents and Principles We Live By* (New York: Basic Books, 2012), xii. On how the existence of a written constitution is taken for granted, see Rakove, "Thinking like a Constitution," 5. For examples of works that view the Constitution as a written text, see Keith E. Whittington, *Constitutional Interpretation: Textual Meaning, Original Intent, and Judicial Review* (Lawrence: University Press of Kansas, 1999), esp. chs. 3–4; Barnett, *Restoring the Lost Constitution,* 102–111; Gary L. McDowell, *The Language of Law and the Foundations of American Constitutionalism* (New York: Cambridge University Press, 2010), esp. 4, 48–54, 222–226, 322–327; Antonin Scalia and Bryan A. Garner, *Reading Law: The Interpretation of Legal Texts* (St. Paul, MN: West, 2012), 15–28, 78–92. For examples of works that view the Constitution as a legal text, see John O. McGinnis and Michael B. Rappaport, *Originalism and the Good Constitution* (Cambridge, MA: Harvard University Press, 2013), ch. 7; and Gary Lawson and Guy Seidman, *"A Great Power of Attorney": Understanding the Fiduciary Constitution* (Lawrence: University Press of Kansas, 2017), esp. ch. 1.

11. On the Constitution as a "people's" instrument at its inception, see Saul Cornell, "The People's Constitution vs. the Lawyer's Constitution," *Yale Journal of Law and the Humanities* 23 (Summer 2011), 295–337. On how the Constitution was originally seen as distinct from conventional law, see Sylvia Snowiss, Judicial Review and the Law of the Constitution (New Haven, CT: Yale University Press, 1990), esp. ch. 1; Gordon S. Wood, "The Origins of Judicial Review Revisited, or How the Marshall Court Made More out of Less," Washington and Lee Law Review 56 (Summer 1999), 794–799.

12. United States Constitution, Article VI; James Wilson, "Lectures on Law," in *The Collected Works of James Wilson,* ed. Kermit L. Hall and Mark David Hall, 2 vols. (Indianapolis: Liberty Fund, 2007), 1:742. Others have stressed that American constitutionalism is principally a language or culture of debate; see Powell, "Political Grammar of Early Constitutional Law"; Levinson, *Constitutional Faith;* Balkin, *Constitutional Redemption.*

13. Robert B. Brandom, *Perspectives on Pragmatism: Classical, Recent, Contemporary* (Cambridge, MA: Harvard University Press, 2011), 148. The use of these ideas is based on a sustained engagement with Anglo-American pragmatist philosophy. For more discussion of this topic, see Jonathan Gienapp, "The Transformation of the American Constitution: Politics and Justification in Revolutionary America" (Ph.D. diss., Johns Hopkins University, 2013), introduction; and, for a more focused take, see Jonathan Gienapp, "Historicism and Holism: Failures of Originalist Translation," *Fordham Law Review* 84 (Dec. 2015), 935–956. Put another way, in 1789 the Constitution could be profitably thought of as, in the famous language of H. L. A. Hart, a set of primary rules in need of secondary rules of recognition. According to Hart, these secondary rules were needed to give the primary rules practical meaning and substance by not only identifying the primary rules but also affording them criteria of validity. If, in these early years, the Constitution existed, these secondary rules did not. The Constitution only fully existed, then, when a set of secondary rules took shape and were unified with the primary rules already laid down. See H. L. A. Hart, *The Concept of Law,* 3rd ed. (1961; New York: Oxford University Press, 2012), esp. ch. 5, 100–110. Relatedly, Founding-era Americans lacked a clear or instinctive understanding of constitutional status and content. Richard Primus has effectively illustrated the multivalent complexity of constitutional status today; see Richard Primus, "Unbundling Constitutionality," *The University of Chicago Law Review* 80 (Summer 2013), 1079–1153. It pays to consider that, immediately following ratification, the uncertainty of constitutional status ran many times deeper still.

14. On pressure exerted on the Constitution throughout American history generally, see Bruce Ackerman, *We the People,* 3 vols. (Cambridge, MA: Harvard University Press, 1991–2014), vols. 2–3; Kammen, *A Machine That Would Go of Itself,* parts II–IV. On how constitutional creativity spilled over into the first half of the nineteenth century, see Alison L. LaCroix, "The Interbellum Constitution: Federalism and the Long Founding Moment," *Stanford Law Review* 67 (Feb. 2015), 397–445. On originalism's guiding assumptions, see Gienapp, "Constitutional Originalism and History." On the varieties of originalism and what unites them, see Solum, "What Is Originalism?" For examples illustrating the centrality of unchanging fixity to originalism, see Whittington, *Constitutional Interpretation,* 53–59; Scalia and Garner, *Reading Law,* 78–92, 403–405; Lawrence B. Solum, "The Fixation Thesis: The Role of Historical Fact in Original Meaning," *Notre Dame Law Review* 91 (Nov. 2015), 1–78. For good examples of the ubiquitous perceived antagonism between fixity and change, see Morton J. Horwitz, "The Constitution of Change: Legal Fundamentality without Fundamentalism," *Harvard Law Review* 107 (Nov. 1993), 30–117; Herman Belz, *A Living Constitution or Fundamental Law? American Constitutionalism in Historical Perspective* (Lanham, MD: Rowman & Littlefield, 1998); Barnett, *Restoring the Lost Constitution,* esp. introduction; McDowell, *Language of Law,* esp. 9–11; David A. Strauss, *The Living Constitution* (New York: Oxford University Press, 2010); John W. Compton,

The Evangelical Origins of the Living Constitution (Cambridge, MA: Harvard University Press, 2014), esp. introduction and conclusion; James E. Fleming, *Fidelity to Our Imperfect Constitution: For Moral Readings and against Originalisms* (New York: Oxford University Press, 2015). The point being made here is different from, for instance, Jack Balkin's claim that originalism and living constitutionalism are "two sides of the same coin," as that otherwise presupposes the constitutional logic that has disaggregated them; *Living Originalism*, 20.

15. Daniel J. Hulsebosch, "The Constitution in the Glass Case and Constitutions in Action," *Law and History Review* 16 (Summer 1998), 397–401. On how disagreements in constitutional law often converge on this common image of the Constitution, see David A. Strauss, "Does the Constitution Mean What It Says?" *Harvard Law Review* 129 (Nov. 2015), 4.

16. Given the contingencies of Anglo-American constitutional culture, Americans wrestled with constitutional fixity in a distinct manner from those who faced related challenges during the French Revolution. Whereas the latter struggled with a widening gap between revolution and constitution, Americans struggled with the relationship between fixity and constitutionalism itself. On efforts to fix a constitution during the early years of the French Revolution, see the stimulating analysis in Keith Michael Baker, *Inventing the French Revolution: Essays on French Political Culture in the Eighteenth Century* (New York: Cambridge University Press, 1990), ch. 11. On how such efforts were abandoned in favor of a wider project of permanent revolution, see Dan Edelstein, "From Constitutional to Permanent Revolution: 1649 and 1794," in *Scripting Revolution: A Historical Approach to the Comparative Study of Revolutions,* ed. Keith Michael Baker and Dan Edelstein (Stanford, CA: Stanford University Press, 2015), 118–130. For a suggestive take on how Americans avoided the problems of their French counterparts, see Jack N. Rakove, "Constitutionalism: The Happiest Revolutionary Script," in *Scripting Revolution*, 103–117.

17. The literature is enormous, but on these better-known kinds of constitutional ideas, see Wood, *Creation of the American Republic;* Rakove, *Original Meanings;* Nelson, *Royalist Revolution;* McDonald, *Novus Ordo Seclorum.* On federalism in particular, see Peter S. Onuf, *The Origins of the Federal Republic: Jurisdictional Controversies in the United States, 1775–1787* (Philadelphia: University of Pennsylvania Press, 1983); Jack P. Greene, *Peripheries and Center: Constitutional Development in the Extended Polities of the British Empire and the United States, 1607–1788* (Athens: University of Georgia Press, 1986), chs. 8–9; Peter Onuf and Nicholas Onuf, *Federal Union, Modern World: The Law of Nations in an Age of Revolutions, 1776–1814* (Madison: University of Wisconsin Press, 1993); David C. Hendrickson, *Peace Pact: The Lost World of the American Founding* (Lawrence: University Press of Kansas, 2003); Douglas Bradburn, *The Citizenship Revolution: Politics and the Creation of the American Union, 1774–1804* (Charlottesville: University of Virginia Press, 2009); Alison L. LaCroix, *The Ideological Origins of American Federalism* (Cambridge, MA: Harvard University Press, 2010); Eliga H. Gould, *Among the Powers of*

the Earth: The American Revolution and the Making of a New World Empire (Cambridge, MA: Harvard University Press, 2012), 130–134; Max M. Edling, "'A Mongrel Kind of Government': The U.S. Constitution, the Federal Union, and the Origins of the American State," in *State and Citizen: British America and the Early United States,* ed. Peter Thompson and Peter S. Onuf (Charlottesville: University of Virginia Press, 2013), 150–177. For a good overview of this literature, see Alan Gibson, *Interpreting the Founding: Guide to the Enduring Debates over the Origins and Foundations of the American Republic,* rev. ed. (2006; Lawrence: University of Kansas Press, 2009), 96–109. On the Constitution in an international context, an area that has enjoyed a recent effervescence of interest, see Golove and Hulsebosch, "A Civilized Nation"; Tom Cutterham, "The International Dimensions of the Federal Constitution," *Journal of American Studies* 48 (May 2014), 501–515; Daniel J. Hulsebosch, "Constitution-Making in the Shadow of Empire," *American Journal of Legal History* 56 (Mar. 2016), 84–91.

18. On the kind of national political power that the Constitution's leading advocates hoped to bring into being, see Max D. Edling, *A Revolution in Favor of Government: Origins of the U.S. Constitution and the Making of the American State* (New York: Oxford University Press, 2003). For the best renditions of the struggle for social power that defined so much of the 1780s and in which the Constitution played such an important role, see Holton, *Unruly Americans and the Origins of the Constitution;* Tom Cutterham, *Gentleman Revolutionaries: Power and Justice in the New American Republic* (Princeton, NJ: Princeton University Press, 2017). On the Constitution's particular entanglement with the institution of slavery, see Waldstreicher, *Slavery's Constitution;* Van Cleve, *Slaveholder's Union.*

19. For stimulating accounts of how such a process has worked, see Ackerman, *We the People*; Balkin, *Living Originalism,* chs. 2, 13, 14. The latter has captured constitutional change under the helpful concept of "constitutional historicism"; see Balkin, *Constitutional Redemption,* 12–16, 177–186. On how the debate surrounding the Thirteenth Amendment forced Americans to fundamentally reconceptualize the Constitution, see Michael Vorenberg, *Final Freedom: The Civil War, the Abolition of Slavery, and the Thirteenth Amendment* (New York: Cambridge University Press, 2001), esp. 5–7.

20. For more on the first Congresses, see the introduction in *DHFFC,* 1:vii–xiii; and more generally, Charlene Bangs Bickford and Kenneth R. Bowling, *Birth of the Nation: The First Federal Congress, 1789–1791* (Madison: Madison House, 1989); Kenneth R. Bowling, *Politics in the First Congress, 1789–1791* (New York: Garland, 1990); Fergus M. Bordewich, *The First Congress: How James Madison, George Washington, and a Group of Extraordinary Men Invented the Government* (New York: Simon and Schuster, 2016). Also see these informative volumes that cover a variety of different aspects of the first Congresses: Bowling and Kennon, *Inventing Congress;* Kenneth R. Bowling and Donald R. Kennon, eds., *Neither Separate nor Equal: Congress in the 1790s* (Athens: Ohio University Press, 2000); Kenneth R. Bowling and Donald R. Kennon, eds., *The House and Senate in the 1790s: Petitioning, Lobbying, and*

Institutional Development (Athens: Ohio University Press, 2002). Recounting early congressional debates requires drawing upon surviving congressional sources. The Senate's proceedings were closed (until 1795), so all that survives are some participants' notes. Because the House of Representatives made its proceedings open to the public, though, newspaper scribes could record the debates from the public galleries and later from the front of the chamber. Technological limitations made full transcription impossible, and the volume and rapidity of politicians' speech could vary dramatically. Some complained about the accuracy of transcriptions, but they tended to inspire confidence. See *DHFFC*, 9:xi–xviii, 10:xvi–xxiii; Eric Slauter, *The State as a Work of Art: The Cultural Origins of the Constitution* (Chicago: University of Chicago Press, 2009), 148–166.

21. Samuel Osgood to Elbridge Gerry, Feb. 19, 1789, *DHFFE*, 1:657; Publius [Madison], "The Federalist 37," New York *Daily Advertiser*, Jan. 11, 1788, *DHRC*, 15:346; John Trumbull to John Adams, Mar. 20, 1791, *Founders Online*, National Archives, available at http://founders.archives.gov/documents/Adams/99-02-02-1228; James Warren to Gerry, Apr. 19, 1789, *DHFFC*, 15:287. On the importance of the first Congress, see *DHFFC*, 1:vii–viii; Bickford and Bowling, *Birth of a Nation*; Currie, *Constitution in Congress*, ix–x. On the first federal elections, see introduction to *DHFFE*, 1:vii–xi; Bernstein, "New Matrix for National Politics." On the composition of the first Congress, see Jack N. Rakove, "The Structure of Politics at the Accession of George Washington," in *Beyond Confederation: Origins of the Constitution and American National Identity*, ed. Richard Beeman, Stephen Botein, and Edward C. Carter II (Chapel Hill: University of North Carolina Press, 1987), 275–294. Twenty members of the first Congress (nine in the House, eleven in the Senate) had been delegates to the Constitutional Convention; while forty-two members of the first Congress (twenty-eight in the House, fourteen in the Senate) had been delegates to the state ratifying conventions.

22. Publius [Madison], "The Federalist 48," *New York Packet*, Feb. 1, 1788, *DHRC*, 16:4; Publius [Madison], "The Federalist 63," *New York Independent Journal*, Mar. 1, 1788, *DHRC*, 16:297. On Revolutionary-era Americans' deep attachment to their legislatures, see Wood, *Creation of the American Republic*, 162–173, 226–237. On loss of faith in the states' legislative bodies during the 1780s, see Wood, *Creation of the American Republic*, chs. 8–11; Rakove, *Original Meanings*, chs. 2–3; Nelson, *Royalist Revolution*, ch. 4. On the centrality of Congress in American constitutional design, see Keith E. Whittington, "The Place of Congress in the Constitutional Order," *Harvard Journal of Law & Public Policy* 40 (2017), 573–574.

23. On how the early executive remade certain features of the original Constitution, see Golove and Hulsebosch, "A Civilized Nation," 1015–1061. Outsized attention has been paid to Founding-era judges, usually with an interest in deciphering the origins of judicial review. For overviews, see Mary Sarah Bilder, "Idea or Practice: A Brief Historiography of Judicial Review," *Journal of Policy History* 20 (2008), 6–26; Philip Hamburger, *Law and Judicial Duty* (Cambridge, MA: Harvard University Press, 2008), introduction. On the decontextualized character of most histories of this subject, see

Jack N. Rakove, "The Origins of Judicial Review: A Plea for New Contexts," *Stanford Law Review* 49 (May 1997), 1031–1064. Debate has also raged over how narrowly the period's judges interpreted statutes; see especially the opposing perspectives in John F. Manning, "Textualism and the Equity of the Statute," *Columbia Law Review* 101 (Jan. 2001), 1–127; William N. Eskridge Jr., "All About Words: Early Understandings of the 'Judicial Power' in Statutory Interpretation, 1776–1806," *Columbia Law Review* 101 (June 2001), 990–1106. Much of what is known about the early judiciary is established in the monumental *The Documentary History of the Supreme Court of the United States, 1789–1800*, ed. Maeva Marcus, 8 vols. (New York: Columbia University Press, 1985–2007). It reveals how much remains to be studied. For the important starting points to studying popular constitutionalism, see Larry D. Kramer, *The People Themselves: Popular Constitutionalism and Judicial Review* (New York: Oxford University Press, 2004); Cornell, *Other Founders*. Nothing like Kammen, *A Machine That Would Go of Itself*—the bulk of whose attention falls after the Civil War—has been attempted for the decades immediately following ratification. Hopefully marking a sign of changes to come, see the new work on popular antebellum constitutionalism, Aaron Hall, "Claiming the Founding: Slavery and Constitutional History in Antebellum America" (Ph.D. diss., University of California, Berkeley, in progress); and on how cultural understandings of the Constitution changed during its first half-century, see Simon Joseph Gilhooley, "The Textuality of the Constitution and the Origins of Original Intent" (Ph.D. diss., Cornell University, 2014).

24. The most thorough overview of elite politics is Stanley Elkins and Eric McKitrick, *The Age of Federalism, the Early American Republic, 1788–1800* (New York: Oxford University Press, 1993). On elite political norms and their turbulent character, see Joanne B. Freeman, *Affairs of Honor: National Politics in the Early Republic* (New Haven, CT: Yale University Press, 2001). For a start on politics "out of doors," see Jeffrey L. Pasley, Andrew W. Robertson, and David Waldstreicher, eds., *Beyond the Founders: New Approaches to the Political History of the Early Republic* (Chapel Hill: University of North Carolina Press, 2004). On newspaper politics and politicking, see Jeffrey L. Pasley, *"The Tyranny of Printers": Newspapers Politics in the Early American Republic* (Charlottesville: University of Virginia Press, 2001); Jeffrey L. Pasley, *The First Presidential Contest: 1796 and the Founding of American Democracy* (Lawrence: University Press of Kansas, 2013). For regional and national consciousness, see David Waldstreicher, *In the Midst of Perpetual Fetes: The Making of American Nationalism, 1776–1820* (Chapel Hill: University of North Carolina Press, 1997). On democracy's troubled relationship with race and gender during this period, see Nicholas Guyatt, *Bind Us Apart: How Enlightened Americans Invented Racial Segregation* (New York: Basic Books, 2016); Caroll Smith-Rosenberg, *This Violent Empire: The Birth of an American National Identity* (Chapel Hill: University of North Carolina Press, 2010); Rosemarie Zagarri, *Revolutionary Backlash: Women and Politics in the Early Republic* (Philadelphia: University of Pennsylvania Press, 2007).

25. The best portrayal of the raucous, personal, honor-obsessed world of elite early national politics is Freeman, *Affairs of Honor*. Also see Marshall Smelser, "The Federalist Period as an Age of Passion," *American Quarterly* 10 (Winter 1958), 391–419; John R. Howe, "Republican Thought and the Political Violence of the 1790s," *American Quarterly* 19 (Summer 1967), 147–165. For an explicit version of the view that constitutional argument was a function of political need, see Lynch, *Negotiating the Constitution*, 6, 146, 161.

26. On this problematic dichotomy, see Jonathan Gienapp, "Using Beard to Overcome Beardianism: Charles Beard's Forgotten Historicism and the Ideas-Interest Dichotomy," *Constitutional Commentary* 29 (Summer 2014), 367–381.

27. This approach is indebted in important ways, above all, to the following: Quentin Skinner, *Meaning and Context: Quentin Skinner and His Critics,* ed. James Tully (Princeton, NJ: Princeton University Press, 1988), esp. 29–67, 231–288; Baker, *Inventing the French Revolution,* esp. ch. 1; J. G. A. Pocock, *Virtue, Commerce, and History: Essays on Political Thought and History Chiefly in the Eighteenth Century* (New York: Cambridge University Press, 1985), esp. introduction; Daniel T. Rodgers, *Age of Fracture* (Cambridge, MA: Harvard University Press, 2011).

28. For a thorough overview of all the constitutional debates that consumed Congress between ratification and the end of the eighteenth century, see Currie, *Constitution in Congress.*

1. The Uncertainty of Written Constitutionalism

Epigraph: Samuel Miller, *A Sermon, delivered in the New Presbyterian Church, New-York, July Fourth, 1795* (New York: Thomas Greenleaf, 1795), 23.

1. May 10, 1776, *JCC,* 4:342, 340–341; The Forester [Thomas Paine], "Letter III," *Pa. Packet,* Apr. 22, 1776, 4. Also see Congress's recommendations to New Hampshire and South Carolina to form new governments on November 3, 1775, and its de facto declaration of independence on May 15, 1776, *JCC,* 3:319, 4:357–358.

2. *Vanhorne's Lessee v. Dorrance,* 2 U.S. (2 Dall.) 308 *C.C.D.Pa.* (1795); St. George Tucker, *View of the Constitution of the United States with Selected Writings* (1803) (Indianapolis: Liberty Fund, 1999), 104; *Marbury v. Madison,* 5 U.S. (1 Cranch) 177; [Thomas Paine perhaps], *Four letters on interesting subjects* (Philadelphia: Styner and Cist, 1776), 15. Also see St. George Tucker's opinion in *Kamper v. Hawkins,* 3 Va. (1 Va. Cas.) 20 (1793). The literature emphasizing the transformative turn to written constitutions before 1787 is seemingly endless. Much of it carefully and sophisticatedly charts a messy process by which the implications of writing constitutions down were worked out, one that developed out of searching debate over the new state constitutions and traced a complex and circuitous trajectory. That said, it is nonetheless widely presumed that, no matter how quickly it took shape, this process was completed by the time the

federal Constitution was drafted. See Charles McIlwain, *Constitutionalism: Ancient and Modern* (Ithaca, NY: Cornell University Press, 1940), 10–14; Bernard Bailyn, *The Ideological Origins of the American Revolution,* enl. ed. (1967; Cambridge, MA: Harvard University Press, 1992), 175–193; Gordon S. Wood, *The Creation of the American Republic, 1776–1787,* 2nd ed. (1969; Chapel Hill: University of North Carolina Press, 1998), 259–343, 593–615; Donald S. Lutz, *Popular Consent and Popular Control: Whig Political Theory in the Early State Constitutions* (Baton Rouge: Louisiana State University Press, 1980); Michael Warner, *The Letters of the Republic: Publication and the Public Sphere in Eighteenth-Century America* (Cambridge, MA: Harvard University Press, 1990), ch. 4; Sylvia Snowiss, *Judicial Review and the Law of the Constitution* (New Haven, CT: Yale University Press, 1990), chs. 1–2; Philip A. Hamburger, "Natural Rights, Natural Law, and American Constitutions," *Yale Law Journal* 102 (1993), 907–960; H. Jefferson Powell, "The Political Grammar of Early Constitutional Law," *North Carolina Law Review* 71 (Apr. 1993), 952–955; Vivien Hart and Sannon C. Stimson, eds., *Writing a National Identity: Political, Economic, and Cultural Perspectives on the Written Constitution* (New York: Manchester University Press, 1993), 9–20, 41–58; David E. Kyvig, *Explicit and Authentic Acts: Amending the U.S. Constitution, 1776–1995* (Lawrence: University Press of Kansas, 1995), ch. 1; Marc W. Kruman, *Between Authority and Liberty: State Constitution Making in Revolutionary America* (Chapel Hill: University of North Carolina Press, 1997); John Howe, *Language and Political Meaning in Revolutionary America* (Amherst: University of Massachusetts Press, 2004), 38–39, 54–62; Jack N. Rakove, *Revolutionaries: A New History of the Invention of America* (Boston: Houghton Mifflin, 2010), ch. 4. None have placed more emphasis on the writtenness of American constitutionalism than constitutional lawyers, most of all originalists, and, when appealing to the historical development of American constitutionalism, they often portray a particularly straightforward and immediate break with inherited constitutional norms. The selections that follow offer just a taste of the literature, and virtually every one of these authors has advanced this argument in multiple settings: see Philip Bobbitt, *Constitutional Fate: Theory of the Constitution* (New York: Oxford University Press, 1982), 9–10; Richard S. Kay, "Constitutionalism," in *Constitutionalism: Philosophical Foundations,* ed. Larry Alexander (New York: Cambridge University Press, 1998), 27–39; Herman Belz, *A Living Constitution or Fundamental Law? American Constitutionalism in Historical Perspective* (Lanham, MD: Rowman & Littlefield, 1998), introduction, ch. 1; Keith E. Whittington, *Constitutional Interpretation: Textual Meaning, Original Intent, and Judicial Review* (Lawrence: University Press of Kansas, 1999), esp. 47–61, 89–90, 104–105, 110, 176–177, 215; Randy E. Barnett, *Restoring the Lost Constitution: The Presumption of Liberty,* rev. ed. (2004; Princeton, NJ: Princeton University Press, 2014), 102–111; Akhil Reed Amar, "The Document and the Doctrine," *Harvard Law Review* 114 (Nov. 2000), 26–134; Saikrishna B. Prakash and John C. Yoo, "The Origins of Judicial Review," *University of Chicago Law Review* 70 (Summer 2003),

914–921; Michael Stokes Paulsen, "Does the Constitution Prescribe Rules for Its Own Interpretation?" *Northwestern University Law Review* 103 (Spring 2009), 857–921; Gary L. McDowell, *The Language of Law and the Foundations of American Constitutionalism* (New York: Cambridge University Press, 2010), esp. 4, 48–54, 222–226, 322–327; Jack M. Balkin, *Living Originalism* (Cambridge, MA: Harvard University Press, 2011), 35–41; Antonin Scalia and Bryan A. Garner, *Reading Law: The Interpretation of Legal Texts* (St. Paul, MN: West, 2012), 15–28, 78–92. Meanwhile, some have downplayed such a rupture between British and American constitutionalism; see Larry D. Kramer, *The People Themselves: Popular Constitutionalism and Judicial Review* (New York: Oxford University Press, 2004); Daniel J. Hulsebosch, *Constituting Empire: New York and the Transformation of Constitutionalism in the Atlantic World, 1664–1830* (Chapel Hill: University of North Carolina Press, 2005); Kate Elizabeth Brown, *Alexander Hamilton and the Development of American Law* (Lawrence: University Press of Kansas, 2017), esp. 9–12, ch. 6; James R. Stoner Jr., *Common Law and Liberal Theory: Coke, Hobbes, and the Origins of American Constitutionalism* (Lawrence: University Press of Kansas, 1992); Robert Lowry Clinton, *God and Man in the Law: The Foundations of Anglo-American Constitutionalism* (Lawrence: University Press of Kansas, 1997), 58–61, 71–72, ch. 8. While still others have stressed the unwritten components of eighteenth-century American constitutionalism; see Edward S. Corwin, "The 'Higher Law' Background of American Constitutional Law," *Harvard Law Review* 42 (Dec.–Jan. 1928–1929), 149–185, 365–409; Thomas C. Grey, "Origins of the Unwritten Constitution: Fundamental Law in American Revolutionary Thought," *Stanford Law Review* 30 (May 1978), 843–894; Suzanna Sherry, "The Founders' Unwritten Constitution," *University of Chicago Law Review* 54 (Fall 1987), 1127–1177.

3. On the Protestant emphasis on the "word alone" (sola scriptura), especially its vitality in colonial and Revolutionary America, see Mark A. Noll, *In the Beginning Was the Word: The Bible in American Public Life, 1492–1783* (New York: Oxford University Press, 2016), 45–47, 98–114, 191–197, 201–205, 289–292; David D. Hall, *Worlds of Wonder, Days of Judgment: Popular Religious Belief in Early New England* (Cambridge, MA: Harvard University Press, 1990), ch. 1. On the increasing centrality of written instruments in early modern British legal and economic culture, see Craig Muldrew, *The Economy of Obligation: The Culture of Credit and Social Relations in Early Modern England* (New York: St. Martin's Press, 1998); and in colonial America, for example, see Bruce H. Mann, *Republic of Debtors: Bankruptcy in the Age of American Independence* (Cambridge, MA: Harvard University Press, 2002), 9–18. For those who have argued that print was acquiring new authority during the last third of the eighteenth century, see Warner, *Letters of the Republic;* Cathy N. Davidson, *Revolution and the Word: The Rise of the Novel in America,* rev. ed. (1986; New York: Oxford University Press, 2004); including by uniting law and literature, see Robert A. Ferguson, *Law and Letters in American Culture* (Cambridge, MA: Harvard University Press, 1984), esp. part I. But these developments grew out of a culture that already centered on the importance of print; see David D. Hall, *Cultures of Print: Essays in the History of the Book* (Amherst: University of Massachu-

setts Press, 1996); Richard D. Brown, *Knowledge Is Power: The Diffusion of Information in Early America, 1700–1865* (New York: Oxford University Press, 1989).

4. For more, see Wood, *Creation of the American Republic,* esp. chs. 9–11; Jack N. Rakove, "Thinking like a Constitution," *JER* 24 (Spring 2004), 1–26.

5. Adams's Diary Notes on the Right of Juries, Feb. 12, 1771, *PJA Legal,* 1:230. On constitutional engagement prior to 1763, see Craig Yirush, *Settlers, Liberty, and Empire: The Roots of Anglo-American Political Thought, 1675–1775* (New York: Cambridge University Press, 2011); Richard L. Bushman, *King and People in Provincial Massachusetts* (Chapel Hill: University of North Carolina Press, 1985), chs. 1–4. On constitutional appeals during the imperial crisis, see John Phillip Reid, *Constitutional History of the American Revolution,* 4 vols. (Madison: University of Wisconsin Press, 1986–1993); Jack P. Greene, *The Constitutional Origins of the American Revolution* (New York: Cambridge University Press, 2011), chs. 2–4.

6. Samuel Johnson, *A Dictionary of the English Language,* 2 vols. (London: W. Strahan, 1755); J. G. A. Pocock, *The Ancient Constitution and the Feudal Law: A Study of English Historical Thought in the Seventeenth Century,* reissued ed. (1957; New York: Cambridge, 1987); J. W. Gough, *Fundamental Law in English Constitutional History* (New York: Oxford University Press, 1955), chs. 2–4; Hulsebosch, *Constituting Empire,* 33; Grey, "Origins of the Unwritten Constitution," 850–854. On the meaning of "constitution" in seventeenth- and eighteen-century Anglo-America, see Gerald Stourz, "*Constitution:* Changing Meaning of the Term from the Early Seventeenth to the Late Eighteenth Century," in *Conceptual Change and the Constitution,* ed. Terence Ball and J. G. A. Pocock (Lawrence: University Press of Kansas, 1988), 35–54; Philip Hamburger, *Law and Judicial Duty* (Cambridge, MA: Harvard University Press, 2008), 87–88; McIlwain, *Constitutionalism,* ch. 2; and, across Western Europe more generally, Keith Michael Baker, *Inventing the French Revolution: Essays on French Political Culture in the Eighteenth Century* (New York: Cambridge University Press, 1990), 254–258. Only after the Act of Union of 1707, which united England and Scotland into the Kingdom of Great Britain, did the term "British constitution" become common.

7. John Pym, "Speech at Manwaring's Impeachment," June 4, 1628, in *The Stuart Constitution, 1603–1688: Documents and Commentary,* ed. John Phillips Kenyon (Cambridge: Cambridge University Press, 1986), 15; Henry Parker, *The Case of Shipmoney Briefly Discoursed* (London: 1640), 7; James Otis, *The Rights of the British Colonies Asserted and Proved* (Boston: Edes and Gill, 1764), 72 (Otis articulated a nearly identical formulation three years earlier during the "writs of assistance" controversy); Hamburger, *Law and Judicial Duty,* 81–90; Hulsebosch, *Constituting Empire,* 32–36; John Phillip Reid, *The Ancient Constitution and the Origins of Anglo-American Liberty* (DeKalb: Northern Illinois University Press, 2005), 8–12, 23–27.

8. Sir Matthew Hale, *The Prerogatives of the King,* ed. D. E. C. Yale (London: Selden Society, 1976), 10; Pocock, *Ancient Constitution,* 46–55; John Phillip Reid, *Constitutional History of the American Revolution: Abridged Edition* (Madison: University of

Wisconsin Press, 1995), 3–8, 19–25; Kramer, *People Themselves,* 9–18; Reid, *Ancient Constitution,* chs. 3–5.

9. Sir William Blackstone, *Commentaries on the Laws of England* (1765–1769), 4 books, 2 vols. (Philadelphia: J. B. Lippincott, 1893), 1:66; Sir Edward Coke, *The First Part of the Institutes of the Laws of England; or, a Commentary upon Littleton* (1628), ed. Francis Hargrave and Charles Butler, 2 vols. (London: James and Luke G. Hansard and Sons, 1832), 1:sect. 138; Pocock, *Ancient Constitution,* chs. 2–3; Gough, *Fundamental Law in English Constitution History,* ch. 3; Hulsebosch, *Constituting Empire,* 28–32. It might seem that common lawyers were of at least two minds on the character of the common law in privileging both immemorial custom and accumulated reason; see J. W. Tubbs, *The Common Law Mind: Medieval and Early Modern Conceptions* (Baltimore: Johns Hopkins University Press, 2000), chs. 6–7, 9. But on how these approaches happily fit together, see David Lieberman, *The Province of Legislation Determined: Legal Theory in Eighteenth-Century Britain* (New York: Cambridge University Press, 1989), 36–49, 85–87.

10. Charles Herle, *A Fuller Answer to a Treatise Written by Doctor Ferne* (London: John Bartlet, 1642), 6; Hulsebosch, *Constituting Empire,* 34–35; Hamburger, *Law and Judicial Duty,* 90–91; R. H. Helmholz, "The Myth of Magna Carta Revisited," *North Carolina Law Review* 94 (June 2016), 1492–1493.

11. Blackstone, *Commentaries on the Laws of England,* 1:154–155; J. G. A. Pocock, *The Machiavellian Moment: Florentine Political Thought and the Atlantic Republican Tradition* (Princeton, NJ: Princeton University Press, 1975), 77–80, 361–400; Wood, *Creation of the American Republic,* 10–17; Jonathan Scott, *Commonwealth Principles: Republican Writing of the English Revolution* (New York: Cambridge University Press, 2004), ch. 6; David Lieberman, "The Mixed Constitution and the Common Law," in *The Cambridge History of Eighteenth-Century Political Thought,* ed. Mark Goldie and Robert Wokler (New York: Cambridge University Press, 2006), 317–346.

12. Henry St. John, 1st Viscount Bolingbroke, "Letter X," in *The Works of Lord Bolingbroke,* 4 vols. (Philadelphia: Carey and Hart, 1841), 2:88.

13. Sir Matthew Hale, *The History of the Common Law of England* (1713), ed. Charles M. Gray (Chicago: University of Chicago Press, 1971), 40. For more, see Pocock, *Ancient Constitution,* 36–41; Gough, *Fundamental Law in English Constitutional History,* ch. 1; Reid, *Constitutional History: Abridged Edition,* 7; Kramer, *People Themselves,* 14–18.

14. Herle, *A Fuller Answer,* 6. On consent and the rule of law, see Greene, *Constitutional Origins,* 7; John Phillip Reid, *Rule of Law: The Jurisprudence of Liberty in the Seventeenth and Eighteenth Centuries* (DeKalb: Northern Illinois University Press, 2004), 18–19. On popular will, see Eric Nelson, *The Royalist Revolution: Monarchy and the American Founding* (Cambridge, MA: Harvard University Press, 2014), chs. 1–2; Hulsebosch, *Constituting Empire,* 35–37; Scott, *Commonwealth Principles,* ch. 16; and, in connection with the Levelers' distinctive radicalism, see Dan Edelstein, "From Constitutional to Permanent Revolution: 1649 and 1794," in *Scripting Revolution: A Historical Approach to the Comparative Study of Revolutions,* ed. Keith Michael Baker

and Dan Edelstein (Stanford, CA: Stanford University Press, 2015), 120–125. On original consent, see Hamburger, *Law and Judicial Duty,* 90–95.

15. Sir George Saville to [Jonathan Acklom], 1766, in *The Athenaeum Journal of Literature, Science, the Fine Arts, Music, and the Drama, July to December, 1903* (London: Athenaeum, 1903), 317; Edmund Burke, "Speech on a Motion for a Committee to Inquire into the State of the Representation of the Commons in Parliament" (1782), in *The Writings and Speeches of Edmund Burke,* 12 vols. (Boston: Little, Brown, 1901), 7:94–95; Pocock, *Ancient Constitution,* 34–36; Tubbs, *Common Law Mind,* 162–167; J. G. A. Pocock, "Burke and the Ancient Constitution: A Problem in the History of Ideas," in *Politics, Language, and Time: Essays on Political Thought and History* (New York: Atheneum, 1971), 202–232.

16. On Parliament's authority, see Reid, *Constitutional History: Abridged Edition,* 22–24. On judges enforcing the law of the land, see Hamburger, *Law and Judicial Duty,* chs. 4–7; Kramer, *People Themselves,* 18–29. On crowd action, see E. P. Thompson, "The Moral Economy of the English Crowd in the Eighteenth Century," *Past and Present* 50 (Feb. 1971), 76–136; and, on crowd action in colonial America, see Pauline Maier, *From Resistance to Revolution: Colonial Radicals and the Development of American Opposition to Britain, 1765–1776,* 2nd ed. (1972; New York: Norton, 1991), esp. ch. 1.

17. Relatedly, see Daniel J. Hulsebosch, "The Constitution in the Glass Case and Constitutions in Action," *Law and History Review* 16 (Summer 1998), 397–401.

18. John Adams, Earl of Clarendon, to William Pym III, Jan. 27, 1766, *PJA,* 1:165. On Adams's three "Clarendon" essays, see Richard Alan Ryerson, *John Adams's Republic: The One, the Few, and the Many* (Baltimore: Johns Hopkins University Press, 2016), 53–59.

19. James Wilson, *Considerations on the Nature and Extent of the Legislative Authority of the British Parliament* (Philadelphia: William and Thomas Bradford, 1774), 19; [Stephen Hopkins], *The Rights of Colonies Examined* (Providence: William Goddard, 1765), 4; Mary Sarah Bilder, *The Transatlantic Constitution: Colonial Legal Culture and the Empire* (Cambridge, MA: Harvard University Press, 2004), on repugnancy and divergence, esp. 1–6, 40–46; Hulsebosch, *Constituting Empire;* Mary Sarah Bilder, "Expounding the Law," *George Washington Law Review* 78 (Sept. 2010), 1137–1140.

20. Massachusetts Circular Letter to the Colonial Legislatures, Feb. 11, 1768, in *Speeches of the Governors of Massachusetts from 1765 to 1775* (Boston: Russell and Gardner, 1818), 134; Samuel Adams to Joseph Warren, Sept. 1774, *The Writings of Samuel Adams,* ed. Harry Alonzo Cushing, 4 vols. (New York: G. P. Putnam's Sons, 1904–1908), 3:157. On the importance of the Glorious Revolution in the colonies, see David S. Lovejoy, *The Glorious Revolution in America* (New York: Harper and Row, 1972); Bushman, *King and People,* chs. 1–3; Owen Stanwood, *The Empire Reformed: English America in the Age of the Glorious Revolution* (Philadelphia: University of Pennsylvania Press, 2011). On the development of robust constitutional arguments in the North American colonies prior to 1763, see Greene, *Constitutional Origins,* 16–18, ch. 1; Yirush, *Settlers,*

Liberty, and Empire, chs. 1–6; Jack P. Greene, *The Quest for Power: The Lower Houses of Assembly in the Southern Royal Colonies, 1689–1763* (Chapel Hill: University of North Carolina Press, 1963). On the ubiquity of constitutional argument throughout the eighteenth-century British Empire, see David Armitage, *The Ideological Origins of the British Empire* (New York: Cambridge University Press, 2001).

21. Oct. 14, 1774, *JCC*, 1:67. The character of colonists' appeal was complex and changing; see Reid, *Constitutional History*; Greene, *Constitutional Origins*, chs. 2–4; Grey, "Origins of the Unwritten Constitution," 865–891.

22. [John Joachim Zubly], *An Humble Enquiry into the Nature of the Dependency of the American Colonies upon the Parliament of Great-Britain, and the right of Parliament to lay taxes on the said colonies* (Charleston: 1769), 5. On these divergent constitutions, see Reid, *Constitutional History: Abridged Edition*, 20–25; Bailyn, *Ideological Origins*, 178–181; Hamburger, *Law and Judicial Duty*, ch. 8; Nelson, *Royalist Revolution*, chs. 1–2. On the idea of a multiplicity of constitutions in the empire, see Greene, *Constitutional Origins*, xiv, 50–54, 64–66; Hulsebosch, *Constituting Empire*, ch. 3.

23. Thomas Jefferson, *A Summary View of the Rights of British America* (Williamsburg, VA: Clementinarind, 1774), 18; [Samuel Adams], *Boston Gazette*, Feb. 27, 1769, 3; Resolutions of the House of Representatives of Massachusetts, Oct. 29, 1765, in Edmund S. Morgan, *Prologue to Revolution: Sources and Documents of the Stamp Act Crisis, 1764–1766* (Chapel Hill: University of North Carolina Press, 1966), 56. On Revolutionary Americans' use of British history, see Trevor Colbourn, *The Lamp of Experience: Whig History and the Intellectual Origins of the American Revolution* (Chapel Hill: University of North Carolina Press, 1965); Bailyn, *Ideological Origins*, 30–54, 66–86; Nelson, *Royalist Revolution*, ch. 1. Confusion has often shrouded the relationship between customary constitutionalism and natural rights, as most have privileged one source of authority at the expense of the other rather than grasping how they intersected and reinforced one another. For excellent treatments that properly historicize natural rights in the Founding era, see Jud Campbell, "Republicanism and Natural Rights at the Founding," *Constitutional Commentary* 32 (Winter 2017), 85–112; Jud Campbell, "Natural Rights and the First Amendment," *Yale Law Journal* 127 (Nov. 2017), 246–321; Dan Edelstein, *On the Spirit of Rights* (University of Chicago Press, forthcoming 2018), ch. 6. For good representations of the orthodox positions: emphasizing natural rights, see Thomas L. Pangle, *The Spirit of Modern Republicanism: The Moral Vision of the American Founders and the Philosophy of Locke* (Chicago: University of Chicago Press, 1988); Michael Zuckert, *The Natural Rights Republic: Studies in the Foundation of the American Political Tradition* (South Bend, IN: University of Notre Dame Press, 1996); Thomas G. West, *The Political Theory of the American Founding: Natural Rights, Public Policy, and the Moral Conditions of Freedom* (New York: Cambridge University Press, 2017), esp. part I; emphasizing customary constitutional rights, see Edmund S. Morgan and Helen M. Morgan, *The Stamp Act Crisis: Prologue to Revolution* (Chapel Hill: University of North Carolina Press, 1953); John Phillip Reid, *Constitutional History of the American Revolu-*

tion: The Authority of Rights (Madison: University of Wisconsin Press, 1986); and attempting to strike a balance, while assuming an opposition, see James T. Kloppenberg, "The Virtues of Liberalism: Christianity, Republicanism, and Ethics in Early American Political Discourse," *Journal of American History* 74 (June 1987), 9–33. For a good overview, see Eric Slauter, "Rights," in *The Oxford Handbook of the American Revolution,* ed. Edward Gray and Jane Kamensky (New York: Oxford University Press: 2013), 447–464.

24. Adams, Earl of Clarendon, to William Pym III, Jan. 27, 1766, *PJA,* 1:165, 167, 169. For more, see Bailyn, *Ideological Origins,* 67–77.

25. Massachusetts Circular Letter, 134; Aequus, "From the Craftsman," *Massachusetts Gazette,* or *Boston News-Letter,* Mar. 6, 1766, in *American Political Writing during the Founding Era, 1760–1805,* ed. Donald S. Lutz and Charles S. Hyneman, 2 vols. (Indianapolis: Liberty Fund, 1983), 1:63–64. On the centrality of usage and custom, and the corresponding imperative of avoiding pernicious precedents, in American constitutional thinking during the imperial crisis, see Reid, *Constitutional History: Abridged Edition,* 5–8, 27–31, 82–84.

26. [James Otis], *A Vindication of the British Colonies . . .* (Boston: Edes and Gill, 1765), 32. On how written legal codes marked out only the minimum, not the limits, of rights in colonial American thinking, see Bailyn, *Ideological Origins,* 78–79.

27. Declaration of Independence, July 4, 1776, emphasis mine.

28. Wood, *Creation of the American Republic,* 10–45; Reid, *Constitutional History: Abridged Edition,* 3–25; John M. Murrin, "A Roof without Walls: The Dilemma of American National Identity," in *Beyond Confederation: Origins of the Constitution and American National Identity,* ed. Richard Beeman, Stephen Botein, and Edward C. Carter II (Chapel Hill: University of North Carolina Press, 1987), 334–340. On how easily American Revolutionaries took to reestablishing constitutional authority, see Jack N. Rakove, "Constitutionalism: The Happiest Revolutionary Script," in *Scripting Revolution: A Historical Approach to the Comparative Study of Revolutions,* ed. Keith Michael Baker and Dan Edelstein (Stanford, CA: Stanford University Press, 2015), 103–117.

29. Pittsfield Petitions, May 29, 1776, in *The Popular Sources of Political Authority: Documents on the Massachusetts Constitution of 1780,* ed. Oscar Handlin and Mary Handlin (Cambridge, MA: Harvard University Press, 1960), 90; New Jersey Constitution of 1776, Article XXII; Bilder, *Transatlantic Constitution,* 186–187; Willi Paul Adams, *The First American Constitutions: Republican Ideology and the Making of the State Constitutions in the Revolutionary Era,* expanded ed. (1980; New York: Rowman and Littlefield, 2001), 64–65; Kramer, *People Themselves,* 39–41. Other state constitutions that included explicit repugnancy clauses were: Delaware Constitution of 1776, Article XXV; Georgia Constitution of 1777, Article VII, and Article XLII; New York Constitution of 1777, Article XXXV; Massachusetts Constitution of 1780, Part II, Ch. I, Sect. I, Article IV, and Part II, Ch. VI, Article VI; New Hampshire Constitution of 1784, Part II, "Confirmation of Laws."

30. James Iredell, "Essay on the Court Law Controversy," Sept. 10, 1773, in *The Papers of James Iredell,* ed. Don Higginbotham, Donna Kelly, and Lang Baradell, 3

vols. (Raleigh: North Carolina Division of Archives and History, 1976–), 1:164; [John Dickinson], *An Address to the Committee of Correspondence in Barbados* (Philadelphia: William Bradford, 1766), 4; Mary Sarah Bilder, "Charter Constitutionalism: The Myth of Edward Coke and the Virginia Charter," *North Carolina Law Review* 94 (June 2016), 1590; New Hampshire Constitution of 1784, Part II, "Provision for a Future Revision of the Constitution." On charters generally, see Bailyn, *Ideological Origins,* 189–193; Reid, *Constitutional History: Authority of Rights,* ch. 19; John Phillip Reid, *Constitutional History of the American Revolution: The Authority to Tax* (Madison: University of Wisconsin Press, 1987), 57–60, ch. 9; John Phillip Reid, *Constitutional History of the American Revolution: The Authority to Legislate* (Madison: University of Wisconsin Press, 1991), ch. 13; Bushman, *King and People,* 11–14, 102–103, 111–114; Yirush, *Settlers, Liberty, and Empire,* 72–73, 153–154, 187–189; Nelson, *Royalist Revolution,* 34–36, 46–54, 99–104. In a fascinating study of British author Daniel Defoe's political and literary writings, Bernadette Meyler has revealed how Defoe valorized written constitutionalism (particularly in the context of colonial charters) as early as the first decades of the eighteenth century. However, Defoe appears to have been highly unusual in this regard, revealing, as much as anything, the rarity of this kind of thinking. See Bernadette Meyler, "Daniel Defoe and the Written Constitution," *Cornell Law Review* 94 (Nov. 2008), 73–132.

31. John Adams, *Thoughts on Government: Applicable to the Present State of the American Colonies. In a Letter from a Gentleman to his Friend* (Philadelphia: John Dunlap, 1776), 27; E., "Remarks on the Constitution of Pennsylvania," in *Pa. Packet,* Sept. 24, 1776, 2; Gordon S. Wood, "America's Enlightenment," in *America and Enlightenment Constitutionalism,* ed. Gary L. McDowell and Johnathan O' Neill (New York: Palgrave Macmillan, 2006), 159–175.

32. "The Alarm: Or, an Address to the People of Pennsylvania on the Late Resolve of Congress" (Philadelphia: 1776), 3; "To the Representatives of the Town of Boston," *Independent Chronicle* (Boston), June 4, 1778, 3; "Call for a Convention, June 1779," in Handlin and Handlin, *Popular Sources of Political Authority,* 402; Thomas Jefferson, *Notes on the State of Virginia* (1785), ed. Frank Shuffelton (New York: Penguin Press, 1999), 131; Wood, *Creation of the American Republic,* ch. 7.

33. "Address of the Mechanics of New York City, June 14, 1776," in *Principles and Acts of the Revolution in America . . . ,* ed. Hezekiah Niles (Baltimore: William Ogden Niles, 1822), 442; Jefferson, *Notes on the State of Virginia,* 130, 136; "Statement of the Berkshire County Representatives," in Handlin and Handlin, *Popular Sources of Political Authority,* 377. On ratification, see Wood, *Creation of the American Republic,* 328–343, 372–389; Jack N. Rakove, *Original Meanings: Politics and Ideas in the Making of the Constitution* (New York: Knopf, 1996), 96–102. On how state constitutions were adopted, see Adams, *First American Constitutions,* 63–98.

34. On popular sovereignty, above all see Wood, *Creation of the American Republic,* 306–389; also see Edmund S. Morgan, *Inventing the People: The Rise of Popular Sover-*

eignty in England and America (New York: Norton, 1988), chs. 7–11; Christian Fritz, *American Sovereigns: The People and America's Constitutional Tradition before the Civil War* (New York: Cambridge University Press, 2008), chs. 2–4.

35. [John Stevens], *Observations on Government Including Some Animadversions on Mr. Adams's Defence of the Constitutions . . . by a Farmer, of New-Jersey* (New York: W. Ross, 1787), 31, 32; "Legislative," in *Pa. Evening Post* (Philadelphia), Mar. 16, 1776, 135; "Address of the Convention, Mar. 1780" in Handlin and Handlin, *Popular Sources of Political Authority,* 436; Eric Slauter, *The State as a Work of Art: The Cultural Origins of the Constitution* (Chicago: University of Chicago Press, 2009); Rakove, *Revolutionaries,* 159–161; John Fabian Witt, *Patriots and Cosmopolitans: Hidden Histories of American Law* (Cambridge, MA: Harvard University Press, 2007), 61–67.

36. For a similar version of the same point, see McIlwain, *Constitutionalism,* 14.

37. James Iredell to Richard Dobbs Spaight, Aug. 26, 1787, *Papers of James Iredell,* 3:308–309.

38. Jefferson, *Notes on the State of Virginia,* 129, and generally 129–130, and generally 129–130; George Wythe, *Commonwealth v. Caton* (1782), in *Reports of Cases Argued and Decided in the Court of Appeals of Virginia,* ed. Daniel Call (Richmond: Robert I. Smith, 1833), 4:8; Philodemus [Thomas Tudor Tucker], *Conciliatory Hints . . .* (Charleston: Printed for A. Timothy, 1784), 30. For more, see Wood, *Creation of the American Republic,* 273–305; Snowiss, *Judicial Review and the Law of the Constitution,* 23–33.

39. [Theophilus Parsons], *The Essex Result* (Newburyport: John Mycall, 1778), 33; Jefferson, *Notes on the State of Virginia,* 136.

40. [Paine perhaps], *Four letters on interesting subjects,* 18; Alexander Hamilton, *A Second Letter from Phocion,* Apr. 1784, *PAH,* 3:551. On Paine's authorship, see A. Owen Aldridge, *Thomas Paine's American Ideology* (Newark, DE: University of Delaware Press, 1984), 219–220.

41. Howe, *Language and Political Meaning,* ch. 1; Caleb Nelson, "Originalism and Interpretive Conventions," *University of Chicago Law Review* 70 (Spring 2003), 530–534; Murray Cohen, *Sensible Words: Linguistic Practice in England, 1640–1785* (Baltimore: Johns Hopkins University Press, 1977). The problem of linguistic instability extended well beyond the English-speaking world. On its central importance in France, and its crucial connection to the French Revolution, see Sophia Rosenfeld, *A Revolution in Language: The Problem of Signs in Late Eighteenth-Century France* (Stanford, CA: Stanford University Press, 2001); and on how a shared preoccupation with the problem of language united scientific and political dispute, see Jessica Riskin, "Rival Idioms for a Revolutionized Science and a Republican Citizenry," *Isis* 89 (June 1998), 203–232.

42. Jonathan Swift, *A Proposal for Correcting, Improving, and Ascertaining the English Tongue* (London: Printed for Benj. Tooke, 1712), 31; Samuel Johnson, Feb. 22, 1752, in *The Rambler* (London: Jones and Company, 1825), 341; Samuel Johnson, *The Plan of a Dictionary of the English Language,* 2nd ed. (London: W. Strahan, 1755–1756), 1:2; Samuel Johnson, *The Plan of a Dictionary of the English Language* (London: 1747),

32; Howe, *Language and Political Meaning*, 18–19. This English project and the conflict it implied paralleled, in striking ways, disputes among eighteenth-century French scientists—while some thought scientific language should be "cultural," growing spontaneously through accretions, others believed it should be "social," engineered through deliberate prescription; see Riskin, "Rival Idioms," 207–213. The desire to stipulate rules for linguistic usage was thus widely felt.

43. Samuel Johnson, *A Dictionary of the English Language*, 4th ed. (London: 1777), 1:preface.

44. Thomas Hobbes, in *The Philosophical Writings of Descartes*, trans. John Cottingham, Robert Stoothoff, and Dugald Murdoch, 3 vols. (New York: Cambridge University Press, 1985), 2:178; Thomas Hobbes, *Leviathan* (1651), ed. C. B. Macpherson (New York: Penguin Press, 1968), 326; Thomas Hobbes, *The Elements of Law Natural and Politic* (1640), trans. and ed. J. C. A. Gaskin (New York: Oxford University Press, 1994), 37. On these philosophical concerns, see Hannah Dawson, *Locke, Language, and Early Modern Philosophy* (New York: Cambridge University Press, 2007), chs. 5–6; on most European philosophers' faith in language despite philosophical concerns, see ch. 4. On Hobbes's conception of language and meaning, see Philip Pettit, *Made with Words: Hobbes on Language, Mind, and Politics* (Princeton, NJ: Princeton University Press, 2008), 40–41, 129–132; Stewart Duncan, "Hobbes on Language: Propositions, Truth, and Absurdity," in *The Oxford Handbook of Hobbes*, ed. A. P. Martinich and Kinch Hoekstra (New York: Oxford University Press, 2016), 60–75.

45. Francis Bacon, *Novum Organum* (1620), ed. Joseph Devey (New York: P. F. Collier, 1902), 31; Hobbes, *Leviathan*, 102; Robert South, "Of the Fatal Imposture and Force of Words," in *Twelve Sermons Preached upon Several Occasions*, 2 vols. (London: J. H., 1692–1694), 2:456.

46. John Locke, *An Essay Concerning Human Understanding* (1690), ed. Roger Woolhouse (New York: Penguin Press, 1997), book III, ch. 5, sect. 16, ch. 9, sect. 21:391, 435. On the depth of Locke's critique of semantic stability, see Dawson, *Locke, Language*, chs. 7–9. For this critique's implications for social and political authority, see Dawson, *Locke, Language*, ch. 10; and (for a valuably different version) Hannah Dawson, "Locke on Language in (Civil) Society," *History of Political Thought* 26 (Autumn 2005), 397–425.

47. Locke, *An Essay Concerning Human Understanding*, book III, ch. 5, sect. 5, 9, ch. 9, sect. 1, 9:385, 388, 426, 424. This analysis draws heavily on Dawson, *Locke, Language*, ch. 8, esp. 222–224, 233–238. On Locke's hopes of stabilizing words through the clarity of ideas, see Dawson, *Locke, Language*, ch. 9. For an account that misses Locke's deeper struggle with semantic instability, see McDowell, *Language of Law*, 123–132.

48. Locke, *An Essay Concerning Human Understanding*, book III, ch. 9, sect. 9, 8:428, 427. See Dawson, *Locke, Language*, ch. 10.

49. John Adams to the President of Congress, Sept. 5, 1780, *PJA*, 10:128, 127; John Adams to William Tudor, June 28, 1789, *DHFFC*, 16:870; Noah Webster, *A Grammatical Institute of the English Language*, 3 parts (Hartford: Hudson and Goodwin, 1783–

1785), 1:14; Noah Webster, *Dissertations on the English Language* (Boston: Isaiah Thomas, 1789), 36; Howe, *Language and Political Meaning*, 27–37; Christopher Looby, *Voicing America: Language, Literary Form, and the Origins of the United States* (Chicago: University of Chicago Press, 1996), 28–40. On Webster's project, see Jill Lepore, *A Is for American: Letters and Other Characters in the Newly United States* (New York: Knopf, 2002), ch. 1; and Tom Cutterham, *Gentleman Revolutionaries: Power and Justice in the New American Republic* (Princeton, NJ: Princeton University Press, 2017), 49–53, 61–64. On the ubiquity of Lockean epistemology in eighteenth-century America, particularly as it related to education, see Jay Fliegelman, *Prodigals and Pilgrims: The American Revolution against Patriarchal Authority, 1750–1800* (New York: Cambridge University Press, 1982), 12–29, 38–40, 58–60, 111. Contemporaneously, French Revolutionaries were obsessed with engineering language to mold republican citizens and a polity devoid of deliberate distortions and misunderstandings; see Riskin, "Rival Idioms," 223–231.

50. Webster, *Dissertations on the English Language,* 25. On the contradictions in Webster's linguistic vision, see Michael Kramer, *Imagining Language in America: From the Revolution to the Civil War* (Princeton, NJ: Princeton University Press, 1991), ch. 1.

51. Thomas Paine, *Common Sense* (1776), ed. Isaac Kramnick (New York: Penguin Press, 1982), 70. For more on Paine's revolutionary arguments, especially their relationship to the socio-epistemic tradition against which he was reacting, see Sophia Rosenfeld, *Common Sense: A Political History* (Cambridge, MA: Harvard University Press, 2011). For more on the "plain style" and its relationship to the Protestant hermeneutics of "sola scriptura," see H. Jefferson Powell, "The Original Understanding of Original Intent," *Harvard Law Review* 98 (Mar. 1985), 889–894; Saul Cornell, *The Other Founders: Anti-Federalism and the Dissenting Tradition in America, 1788–1828* (Chapel Hill: University of North Carolina Press, 1999), 58–59. On sola scriptura generally, especially its vitality in colonial and Revolutionary America generally, see Noll, *In the Beginning Was the Word*, 45–47, 98–114, 191–197, 201–205, 289–292; Hall, *Worlds of Wonder, Days of Judgment*, ch. 1. On the counterintuitive influence Paine had on Webster, see Kramer, *Imagining Language in America*, 44–49.

52. Thomas Jefferson, "Annotated Copy of Franklin's Proposed Articles of Confederation," *PTJ*, 1:181; Mar. 12, 1781, *JCC*, 20:470; Edmund Randolph, Notes of Virginia laws, Ms. Notes of Argument in *Commonwealth v. Lamb &c.,* Library of Congress, James Madison Papers, 91:104, 3, available at https://www.loc.gov/item/mjm021836/; Samuel McClintock, *A Sermon Preached before the Honorable Council* (Portsmouth, NH: Robert Cerrish, 1784), 23.

53. Zenas [James Sullivan], *Independent Chronicle* (Boston), Apr. 27, 1786, 1. Also see Hamburger, *Law and Judicial Duty,* 275–303.

54. Mary Sarah Bilder, "James Madison, Law Student and Demi-Lawyer," *Law and History Review* 28 (May 2010), 437–443.

55. James Madison to Edmund Randolph, Mar. 10, 1784, *PJM,* 8:3–4; also see editors' supporting notes.

0

56. Articles of Confederation and Perpetual Union, Article II; Mar. 12, 1781, *JCC*, 20:469; Madison to Edmund Pendleton, Jan. 8, 1782, *PJM*, 4:22–23; Pendleton to Madison, Jan. 28, 1782, *PJM*, 4:49. On the bank, see May 26, 1781, *JCC*, 20:546–548. On Morris's financial reforms, see Jack N. Rakove, *The Beginnings of National Politics: An Interpretive History of the Continental Congress* (New York: Knopf, 1979), 298–307; E. James Ferguson, *The Power of the Purse: A History of American Public Finance, 1776–1790* (Chapel Hill: University of North Carolina Press, 1961), 117–155.

57. Alexander Hamilton, *The Farmer Refuted: or, A more impartial and comprehensive view of the dispute between Great-Britain and the colonies* (New York: James Rivington, 1775), 38; Benjamin Rush, *Observations upon the Present State of the Government of Pennsylvania* (Philadelphia: Steiner and Cist, 1777), 3; Bailyn, *Ideological Origins*, 193–198; Wood, *Creation of the American Republic*, 271–273; Rakove, *Original Meanings*, 306–308; Lutz, *Popular Consent and Popular Control*, 61–66; Donald S. Lutz, *The Origins of American Constitutionalism* (Baton Rouge: Louisiana State University Press, 1988), 111–112; Richard Primus, *The American Language of Rights* (New York: Cambridge University Press, 1999), 93–94; David Thomas Konig, "Why the Second Amendment Has a Preamble," *UCLA Law Review* 56 (June 2009), 1317–1324. On Magna Carta in eighteenth-century British imagination, see Helmholtz, "Myth of Magna Carta Revisited." The states boasting such declarations were (in order of passage) Virginia, Delaware, Pennsylvania, Maryland, North Carolina, Massachusetts, and New Hampshire. For more, see Kruman, *Between Authority and Liberty*, 37–49.

58. James Iredell to Richard Dobbs Spaight, Aug. 26, 1787, *Papers of Iredell*, 3:308; James Varnum, *The Case, Trevett against Weeden* (Providence: John Carter, 1787), 30; Wayne D. Moore, "Written and Unwritten Constitutional Law in the Founding Period: The Early New Jersey Cases," *Constitutional Commentary* 7 (Summer 1990), 352, and generally 352–358; William Michael Treanor, "Judicial Review Before *Marbury*," *Stanford Law Review* 58 (Nov. 2005), 473–497; Brown, *Hamilton and the Development of American Law*, ch. 6, 212–213; Sherry, "Founders' Unwritten Constitution," 1134–1146; Kramer, *People Themselves*, 41–43. Revolutionary-era judges did not always draw a clear distinction between legislation and adjudication either, often seeking to discover law by appealing to reason and equity as common law jurists long had. On the persistence of this ambiguity in American legal thinking after 1776, see Wood, *Creation of the American Republic*, 293–305.

59. *Commonwealth v. Caton* (1782), in Call, *Reports of Cases*, 4:7; Randolph, Notes of Virginia laws, Ms. Notes of Argument in *Commonwealth v. Lamb &c.*, 3; Edmund Pendleton, *Commonwealth v. Caton* (1782), in Call, *Reports of Cases*, 4:19–20; William Michael Treanor, "The *Case of the Prisoners* and the Origins of Judicial Review," *University of Pennsylvania Law Review* 143 (Dec. 1994), 491–570.

60. Virginia Delegates to Governor Benjamin Harrison, Jan. 8, 1782, *PJM*, 4:19; Rakove, *Beginnings of National Politics*, ch. 8; David C. Hendrickson, *Peace Pact: The Lost World of the American Founding* (Lawrence: University Press of Kansas, 2003),

ch. 20. For a more explicit, later defense of Congress's right to charter the bank, see James Wilson, *Considerations on the Bank of North America* (Philadelphia: Hall and Sellers, 1785).

61. Madison to Caleb Wallace, Aug. 23, 1785, *PJM*, 8:351. While Madison disparaged the possibility of legislative enumeration in this letter, he did say that it was practicable to enumerate exceptions. At this time, though, much of his constitutional thinking was in flux, and as the 1780s unfolded this provisional faith in enumerating exceptions would wane.

62. Madison to Randolph, Feb. 25, 1787, *PJM*, 9:299. For the fullest discussion of Madison's political experience in the 1780s, see Ralph Ketcham, *James Madison: A Biography* (1971; Charlottesville: University of Virginia Press, 1990), chs. 7–9. On the problems faced by Congress under the Articles, see Rakove, *Beginnings of National Politics,* chs. 12, 14; Michael J. Klarman, *The Framers' Coup: The Making of the United States Constitution* (New York: Oxford University Press, 2016), ch. 1; Max D. Edling, *A Revolution in Favor of Government: Origins of the U.S. Constitution and the Making of the American State* (New York: Oxford University Press, 2003), chs. 5 and 10; Calvin H. Johnson, *Righteous Anger against the Wicked States: The Meaning of the Founders' Constitution* (New York: Cambridge University Press, 2005), ch. 1; George William Van Cleve, *We Have Not a Government: The Articles of Confederation and the Road to the Constitution* (Chicago: University of Chicago Press, 2017), chs. 1–6. On the specific issues of finance and taxation, see Roger H. Brown, *Redeeming the Republic: Federalists, Taxation, and the Origins of the Constitution* (Baltimore: Johns Hopkins University Press, 1993), chs. 1–2; Ferguson, *Power of the Purse,* ch. 11. On Congress's difficulties projecting its authority, see Benjamin H. Irvin, *Clothed in the Robes of Sovereignty: The Continental Congress and the People out of Doors* (New York: Oxford University Press, 2011). On the general economic and social problems of the 1780s and the responses these elicited, see Woody Holton, *Unruly Americans and the Origins of the Constitution* (New York: Hill and Wang, 2007), parts I–III; Klarman, *Framers' Coup,* ch. 2; Van Cleve, *We Have Not a Government,* chs. 1–3, 7; Brown, *Redeeming the Republic,* chs. 4–11.

63. Madison to Jefferson, Mar. 19, 1787, *PJM*, 9:318. On how Madison's political experience in the 1780s impacted his constitutional thinking, above all see Rakove, *Original Meanings,* ch. 3; Lance Banning, *The Sacred Fire of Liberty: James Madison and the Founding of the Federal Republic* (Ithaca, NY: Cornell University Press, 1995), ch. 2, 115–121. For the broader sense of reform and justice this new thinking inspired, see Wood, *Creation of the American Republic,* chs. 10–11; Cutterham, *Gentlemen Revolutionaries,* esp. chs. 3–4, 142–151, conclusion. For a suggestive account that privileges Madison's commitment to representative government, see James T. Kloppenberg, *Towards Democracy: The Struggle for Self-Rule in European and American Thought* (New York: Oxford University Press, 2016), 373–380, 385–394. There is disagreement on how much Shays's Rebellion fueled the turn toward dramatic constitutional reform: on its importance, see Klarman, *Framers' Coup,* 88–101; Holton, *Unruly Americans,* 218–220; on its

limited importance, see Van Cleve, *We Have Not a Government,* 229–242; Johnson, *Righteous Anger,* 213–222.

64. Madison, "Notes on Ancient and Modern Confederacies," c. Apr.–June 1786, *PJM,* 9:4–22; Madison, "Vices of the Political System of the United States," Apr. 1787, *PJM,* 9:348–357; Madison to Jefferson, Mar. 19, 1787, *PJM,* 9:317–322; Madison to Randolph, Apr. 8, 1787, *PJM,* 9:368–371; Madison to George Washington, Apr. 16, 1787, *PJM,* 9:382–387.

65. Madison, "Notes on Ancient and Modern Confederacies," *PJM,* 9:6–7, 11, 16–18; Madison, "Vices of the Political System of the United States," *PJM,* 9:348, 351, 352; "Proposed Amendment of the Articles of Confederation," [Mar. 12, 1781], *PJM,* 3:17. On this critical point, that Madison thought the national government already possessed many of the powers it needed, also see Rakove, *Beginnings of National Politics,* 289–296; Banning, *Sacred Fire of Liberty,* 161–162; Klarman, *Framers' Coup,* 43–48.

66. Madison, "Vices of the Political System of the United States," *PJM,* 9:353, 354, 357.

67. Madison to Jefferson, Mar. 19, 1787, *PJM,* 9:318; Madison to Randolph, Apr. 8, 1787, *PJM,* 9:369, 370; Madison to Washington, Apr. 16, 1787, *PJM,* 9:383, 384. On the holistic dynamism of Madison's constitutionalism, see Jonathan Gienapp, "How to Maintain a Constitution: The Virginia and Kentucky Resolutions and James Madison's Struggle with the Problem of Constitutional Maintenance," in *Nullification and Secession in Modern Constitutional Thought,* ed. Sanford Levinson (Lawrence: University Press of Kansas, 2016), 53–90. For complimentary accounts, see Jack N. Rakove, "The Madisonian Moment," *University of Chicago Law Review* 55 (Spring 1988), 473–505; George Thomas, *The Madisonian Constitution* (Baltimore: Johns Hopkins University Press, 2008), ch. 1.

68. On hopes of vesting vital fiscal-military powers in the new Constitution, see Edling, *Revolution in Favor of Government;* Brown, *Redeeming the Republic,* chs. 1–2, 12–13; David M. Golove and Daniel J. Hulsebosch, "A Civilized Nation: The Early American Constitution, the Law of Nations, and the Pursuit of International Recognition," *N.Y.U. Law Review* 85 (Oct. 2010), parts I–II, esp. 989–1015. On delegates' lack of interest in future interpretation, see Powell, "Original Understanding of Original Intent," 903–904; Charles A. Lofgren, "The Original Understanding of Original Intent?" *Constitutional Commentary* 5 (Winter 1988), 81–82.

69. Gouverneur Morris, May 30, 1787, *Records,* 1:34. On the Virginia Plan, see Klarman, *Framers' Coup,* 133–144; Richard Beeman, *Plain, Honest Men: The Making of the American Constitution* (New York: Random House, 2009), 86–92, 99–104.

70. Virginia Plan, May 29, 1787, *Records,* 1:21; Charles Pinckney and John Rutledge, May 31, 1787, *Records,* 1:53; Roger Sherman, May 31 and July 17, 1787, *Records,* 1:59 (William Pierce's Notes), 133, 2:25. It has often been assumed that Resolution VI was written or significantly influenced by Madison, but there is compelling reason to think that James Wilson (or another Pennsylvanian) was responsible for its creation; see

John Mikhail, "The Necessary and Proper Clauses," *Georgetown Law Journal* 102 (Apr. 2014), 1071–1086.

71. Pierce Butler, May 31, 1787, *Records*, 1:53; Randolph, May 31, 1787, *Records*, 1:53, 2:26; James Wilson, May 31, 1787, *Records*, 1:60 (Pierce's Notes); Madison, May 31, 1787, *Records*, 1:53, 60 (Robert Yates's Notes); Hamilton, June 18, 1787, *Records*, 1:298.

72. Sherman, July 17, 1787, *Records*, 2:25; Hamilton, June 19, 1787, *Records*, 1:323; Madison, June 21, 1787, *Records*, 1:364 (Yates's Notes), 357. For Madison's historical argument about the tendencies of confederacies, see June 21, 1787, *Records*, 1:356. For a related point, stressing the lack of sustained debate at the Convention over the appropriate objects of the union, see Max M. Edling, "'A Mongrel Kind of Government': The U.S. Constitution, the Federal Union, and the Origins of the American State," in *State and Citizen: British America and the Early United States,* ed. Peter Thompson and Peter S. Onuf (Charlottesville: University of Virginia Press, 2013), 161–162.

73. King, June 30, 1787, *Records*, 1:492–493. For the votes, see May 31, 1787, *Records*, 1:53–54; July 17, 1787, *Records*, 2:27.

74. John Dickinson, June 7, 1787, *Records*, 1:153, 157 (Yates's Notes), 159 (Rufus King's Notes); Madison, June 8, 1787, *Records*, 1:165. On scientific metaphor in Founding-era American political thinking, see Michael Foley, *Laws, Men, and Machines: Modern American Government and the Appeal of Newtonian Mechanics* (New York: Routledge, 1990); I. Bernard Cohen, *Science and the Founding Fathers: Science in the Political Thought of Jefferson, Franklin, Adams, and Madison* (New York: Norton, 1995), 243–244, 257–262.

75. Wilson, June 4, 1787, *Records*, 1:100; Hamilton, June 22, 1787, *Records*, 1:376; Randolph, May 30, 1787, *Records*, 1:34; George Read, June 6, 1787, *Records*, 1:136–137; Madison, July 17, 1787, *Records*, 2:27; C. Pinckney, June 8, 1787, *Records*, 1:169 (Yates's Notes); Nathaniel Gorham, July 23, 1787, *Records*, 2:90; Benjamin Franklin, Sept. 17, 1787, *Records*, 2:642. One must be careful as Madison often translated speeches into his own favored political vocabulary; see Mary Sarah Bilder, *Madison's Hand: Revising the Constitutional Convention* (Cambridge, MA: Harvard University Press, 2015), 38, 192–198. But since enough of these references to "system" are found in other delegates' notes, this observation about its prevalence is justified.

76. Madison, July 21, 1787, *Records*, 2:77; John Francis Mercer, Aug. 14, 1787, *Records*, 2:289.

77. Virginia Plan, May 29, 1787, *Records*, 1:21; C. Pinckney, June 8, 1787, *Records*, 1:164; Madison, June 8, 1787, *Records*, 1:164, 165; Dickinson, June 8, 1787, *Records*, 1:167; Wilson, June 8, 1787, *Records*, 1:167.

78. June 8, 1787, *Records*, 1:168; Sherman, June 8, 1787, *Records*, 1:166. Also see Hugh Williamson, June 8, 1787, *Records*, 1:165; Elbridge Gerry, June 8, 1787, *Records*, 1:165; Gunning Bedford, June 8, 1787, *Records*, 1:167–168.

79. United States Constitution, Article VI; July 17, 1787, *Records*, 2:27–29; G. Morris, July 17, 1787, *Records*, 2:28. For the various strengthenings of the supremacy clause, see

Draft of Committee of Detail, *Records*, 2:183; Rutledge, Aug. 23, 1787, *Records*, 2:389. On the shift from the negative to the supremacy clause, see Jack N. Rakove, "The Origins of Judicial Review: A Plea for New Contexts," *Stanford Law Review* 49 (May 1997), 1041–1050; Alison L. LaCroix, *The Ideological Origins of American Federalism* (Cambridge, MA: Harvard University Press, 2010), 158–174; Klarman, *Framers' Coup*, 154–159.

80. July 23, 24, and 26, 1787, *Records*, 2:95–96, 97, 117–118; Beeman, *Plain, Honest Men*, 246–247, 263–276; Clinton Rossiter, *1787: The Grand Convention* (New York: Macmillan, 1966), 200–202. For an especially detailed discussion of the Committee of Detail and the difficulties and controversies surrounding interpretation of the surviving evidence, particularly questions of authorship, see William Ewald, "The Committee of Detail," *Constitutional Commentary* 28 (Fall 2012), 197–285.

81. Committee of Detail [Edmund Randolph's Draft], *Records*, 2:137.

82. Nathaniel Gorham, July 16, 1787, *Records*, 2:17; Rutledge, July 16, 1787, *Records*, 2:17; Committee of Detail [Randolph's Draft], *Records*, 2:144. On Randolph's authorship of this first draft, see Ewald, "Committee of Detail," 242–244. The Committee of Detail had Pinckney's plan (which has never been located) in their possession. Since it appears that his plan enumerated powers, quite possibly the Committee of Detail drew on it for guidance; see Committee of Detail [Outline of the Pinckney Plan], *Records*, 2:136. For more, see J. Franklin Jameson, "Portions of Charles Pinckney's Plan for a Constitution, 1787," *American Historical Review* 8 (Apr. 1903), 509–511; Andrew C. McLaughlin, "Sketch of Pinckney's Plan for a Constitution, 1787," *American Historical Review* 9 (July 1904), 735–741; and, on Pinckney's plan generally, see Beeman, *Plain, Honest Men*, 93–98.

83. "William Pierce: Character Sketches of Delegates to the Federal Convention," *Records*, 3:92; Committee of Detail [Randolph's Draft], *Records*, 2:144; Committee of Detail, Wilson's First Draft, *Records*, 2:152; Committee of Detail, Wilson's Second Draft, *Records*, 2:168; Committee of Detail, Final Draft, *Records*, 2:182. For evidence that Wilson principally authored this draft, see Ewald, "Committee of Detail," 216, 246, 259. On Wilson's personality and intellect, see Witt, *Patriots and Cosmopolitans*, ch. 1, esp. 71–75; Mark David Hall, *The Political and Legal Philosophy of James Wilson, 1742–1798* (Columbia, MO: University of Missouri Press, 1997), esp. 20–30; Charles Page Smith, *James Wilson: Founding Father, 1742–1798* (Chapel Hill: University of North Carolina Press, 1956), 319–323, 391–394.

84. This analysis is indebted to the detailed research and persuasive arguments found in Mikhail, "Necessary and Proper Clauses," esp. 1086–1106 (on the construction of the clause, rightfully understood as three distinct clauses, and Wilson's role as primary author); 1107–1121 (on the meaning of "necessary and proper" at the time); 1058–1071, 1121–1128 (on the meaning of "all other Powers" at the time); and 1047–1050, 1055–1056, 1100–1101, 1121–1124 (on Wilson's and other nationalists' potential motives, in terms of expanding the powers of the national government, for devising the clause). For those who have argued that the necessary and proper clause was irredeemably

enigmatic, see Mark A. Graber, "Unnecessary and Unintelligible," *Constitutional Commentary* 12 (Summer 1995), 167–170; Lynch, *Negotiating the Constitution,* 4; or completely novel, see Ewald, "Committee of Detail," 272. For those who have contended that the clause was a legal term of art, claiming that it was either a familiar offshoot of agency or of corporate law, see Gary Lawson, Geoffrey Miller, Robert G. Natelson, and Guy I. Seidman, *The Origins of the Necessary and Proper Clause* (New York: Cambridge University Press, 2010). And then for those who have stressed that the clause, especially the addition of "proper," denoted jurisdictional constraints, see Gary Lawson and Patricia B. Granger, "The 'Proper' Scope of Federal Power: A Jurisdictional Interpretation of the Sweeping Clause," *Duke Law Journal* 43 (Nov. 1993), 285–326; Barnett, *Restoring the Lost Constitution,* ch. 7. Those who have presumed that the clause was a legal term of art or a safeguard of federalism have typically assumed, by extension, that it merely licensed powers otherwise enumerated. But this has problematically required only stressing the "foregoing powers" provision while ignoring the "all other Powers" portion of the clause, thus privileging Randolph's and Rutledge's authorship at the expense of Wilson's; see Mikhail, "Necessary and Proper Clauses," 1049–1050, 1068–1069. Thus, the phrase "necessary and proper" was neither wholly mysterious nor a legal term of art and, consequently, the necessary and proper clause that emerged from the Committee of Detail, and survived until the end of the Convention, was intended to authorize the exercise of unenumerated, nonincidental powers. In so doing, it emphasized the Constitution's unwritten character.

85. G. Morris, Aug. 7, 1787, *Records,* 2:202; Madison, July 21, Aug. 10, and Aug. 17, 1787, *Records,* 2:74, 249–250, 318. This analysis is based on Bilder, *Madison's Hand,* ch. 6, esp. 127–137. Also see Beeman, *Plain, Honest Men,* ch. 15, 306–307.

86. Luther Martin, Aug. 16, 1787, *Records,* 2:305; Articles of Confederation and Perpetual Union, Article II, Aug. 20, 1787, *Records,* 2:344–345. Intriguingly, Pierce Butler (delegate from South Carolina) prepared, but never introduced, alternative language to replace the "necessary and proper" clause that would have eliminated the "all other Powers" vested in the "Government of the United States" clause; see *Supplement,* 231. That the provision was neither introduced nor received additional attention, though, otherwise underscores the key point. For those who have assumed that most delegates expected an enumeration of powers, see Rakove, *Original Meanings,* 177–180; Beeman, *Plain, Honest Men,* 288; Klarman, *Framers' Coup,* 147. For an especially strong argument that Madison always anticipated this change, see Banning, *Sacred Fire of Liberty,* 161–162. Madison hinted at a likely substitution in early July; see Madison, July 7, 1787, *Records,* 1:551. Then, late in life, he portrayed the expectations of the Convention in exactly this way; see Madison to John Tyler (unsent), 1833, *WJM,* 9:505, 507–508; Madison to Andrew Stevenson, Mar. 25, 1826, *Letters,* 3:520–521; Madison to Thomas S. Grimke, Jan. 6, 1834, *WJM,* 9:531–532. There is truth to this, but the issue must be properly framed. If Madison thought about enumeration differently in 1787, it was not necessarily because he was an avowed nationalist, but more that he was gripped by a constitu-

tional imagination that placed less emphasis on constitutional language. For a different take altogether, arguing that the Committee of Detail sharply diverged from the Convention's expectations, see John C. Hueston, "Altering the Course of the Constitutional Convention: The Role of the Committee of Detail in Establishing the Balance of State and Federal Powers," *Yale Law Journal* 100 (Dec. 1990), 765–783. Given the controversy the "necessary and proper" clause soon inspired, it is unlikely that it was simply a familiar offshoot of agency law, as claimed in Gary Lawson and Guy Seidman, *"A Great Power of Attorney": Understanding the Fiduciary Constitution* (Lawrence: University Press of Kansas, 2017), 85–86. For the suggestive argument that the combination of enumerated powers plus the "necessary and proper" clause represented an implicit compromise between northern and southern states (with Madison stuck in the middle) that resolved conflict by deferring disagreement, see Lynch, *Negotiating the Constitution*, 19–26.

87. George Mason, Sept. 15, 1787, *Records*, 2:632; Randolph, Sept. 10 and 15, 1787, *Records*, 2:563, 564, 631; Gerry, Sept. 15, 1787, *Records*, 2:633; "Objections to the Constitution, attributed to George Mason," Aug. 30, 1787, *Supplement*, 249; also see 251.

88. G. Morris, July 23, 1787, *Records*, 2:92; Madison, Aug. 31, 1787, *Records*, 2:476; Wilson, Aug. 30, 1787, *Records*, 2:469; Mason, July 23, 1787, *Records*, 2:89; Gerry, July 23, 1787, *Records*, 2:89.

89. Madison, July 23, 1787, *Records*, 2:93; Madison, "Vices of the Political System of the United States," *PJM*, 9:351. On how Federalists were not just circumventing existing law but creating a new kind of constitutional legality, see Rakove, *Original Meanings*, 102–108, 128–130. On how delegates were engaged in illegality, see Bruce Ackerman, *We the People: Foundations* (Cambridge, MA: Harvard University Press, 1993), 41–42; Richard S. Kay, "The Illegality of the Constitution," *Constitutional Commentary* 4 (Winter 1987), 57–80. For a rebuttal, see Akhil Reed Amar, *America's Constitution: A Biography* (New York: Random House, 2005), 21–33.

90. Committee of Detail [Randolph's Draft], *Records*, 2:137; Committee of Style Report, *Records*, 2:590; Beeman, *Plain, Honest Men*, 347–348.

91. Committee of Detail, Final Draft, *Records*, 2:177–189; Committee of Style Report, *Records*, 2:590–603; Beeman, *Plain, Honest Men*, 345–346. The Committee of Style, which met from September 8 to 11 and presented its draft on September 12, had five members: William Samuel Johnson (chair), Gouverneur Morris, James Madison, Rufus King, and Alexander Hamilton. Evidence for Morris's role as primary drafter comes from years later. Morris himself wrote that the Constitution "was written by the fingers, which write this letter"; see Morris to Timothy Pickering, Dec. 22, 1814, *Records*, 3:420. Madison claimed, "The *finish* given to the style and arrangement of the Constitution fairly belongs to the pen of Mr. Morris"; see Madison to Jared Sparks, Apr. 8, 1831, *WJM*, 9:448. For contemporary commentary on Morris's talents for argument and reasoning, see "William Pierce: Character Sketches of Delegates to the Federal Convention," *Records*, 3:92.

92. Benjamin Rush to John Coakley Lettsom, Philadelphia, Sept. 28, 1787, *DHRC,* 13:263.

93. [Charles Inglis], *The True Interest of America Impartially Stated* (Philadelphia: James Humphreys, 1776), 18.

2. Language and Power

Epigraph: William Manning, *The Key of Liberty: The Life and Democratic Writings of William Manning, "A Laborer," 1747–1814,* ed. Michael Merrill and Sean Wilentz (Cambridge, MA: Harvard University Press, 1993), 148.

1. James Madison to Thomas Jefferson, Dec. 9, 1787, *PJM,* 10:311. On ratification as a whole, see Pauline Maier, *Ratification: The People Debate the Constitution, 1787–1788* (New York: Simon and Schuster, 2010); Michael J. Klarman, *The Framers' Coup: The Making of the United States Constitution* (New York: Oxford University Press, 2016), chs. 5–6. For useful state-by-state treatments, see Patrick T. Conley and John P. Kaminski, eds., *The Constitution and the States: The Role of the Original Thirteen in the Framing and Adoption of the Federal Constitution* (Madison: Madison House, 1988); Michael Allen Gillespie and Michael Lienesch, eds., *Ratifying the Constitution* (Lawrence: University Press of Kansas, 1989).

2. Gouverneur Morris to James LaCaze, Williamsburg, Virginia, Feb. 21, 1788, *DHRC,* 16:171. For overviews of the Federalist and Anti-Federalist debate, see Bernard Bailyn, "The Ideological Fulfillment of the American Revolution," in *Faces of Revolution: Personalities and Themes in the Struggle for Independence* (New York: Knopf, 1990), 225–278; Jack N. Rakove, *Original Meanings: Politics and Ideas in the Making of the Constitution* (New York: Knopf, 1996), ch. 6; Klarman, *Framers' Coup,* ch. 5; Jürgen Heideking, *The Constitution before the Judgment Seat: The Prehistory and Ratification of the Constitution, 1787–1791,* ed. John P. Kaminski and Richard Leffler (Charlottesville: University of Virginia Press, 2012), ch. 3. Other more focused portrayals are also valuable: on debates over centralized financial powers, see Max D. Edling, *A Revolution in Favor of Government: Origins of the U.S. Constitution and the Making of the American State* (New York: Oxford University Press, 2003); on the two sides' rival conceptions of social authority, see Gordon S. Wood, *The Creation of the American Republic, 1776–1787,* 2nd ed. (1969; Chapel Hill: University of North Carolina Press, 1998), 483–564; Gordon S. Wood, "Interests and Disinterestedness in the Making of the Constitution," in *Beyond Confederation: Origins of the Constitution and American National Identity,* ed. Richard Beeman, Stephen Botein, and Edward C. Carter II (Chapel Hill: University of North Carolina Press, 1987), 93–109; on how ratification cultivated a certain democratic sensibility, see James T. Kloppenberg, *Towards Democracy: The Struggle for Self-Rule in European and American Thought* (New York: Oxford University Press, 2016), ch. 9; on Anti-Federalist ideology and its diversity, see Saul Cornell, *The Other Founders:*

Anti-Federalism and the Dissenting Tradition in America, 1788–1828 (Chapel Hill: University of North Carolina Press, 1999), esp. chs. 1–4.

3. See generally Edling, *Revolution in Favor of Government;* Roger H. Brown, *Redeeming the Republic: Federalists, Taxation, and the Origins of the Constitution* (Baltimore: Johns Hopkins University Press, 1993), esp. chs. 10–16.

4. Cornell, *Other Founders,* chs. 1–3, esp. 26–34; Bailyn, "Ideological Fulfillment," 232–246; Herbert Storing, *What the Anti-Federalists Were For* (Chicago: University of Chicago Press, 1981); Jackson Turner Main, *The Anti-Federalists: Critics of the Constitution, 1781–1788* (Chapel Hill: University of North Carolina Press, 1961); Cecelia Kenyon, "Men of Little Faith: The Anti-Federalists on the Nature of Representative Government," *WMQ* 12 (Jan. 1955), 3–43.

5. For a much different take on language and the ratification debates, see John Howe, *Language and Political Meaning in Revolutionary America* (Amherst: University of Massachusetts Press, 2004), ch. 7.

6. Robert R. Livingston, New York Ratifying Convention, June 27, 1788, *DHRC,* 22:1942. For a radically different take, see Michael Lienisch, *New Order of the Ages: Time, the Constitution, and the Making of Modern American Political Thought* (Princeton, NJ: Princeton University Press, 1988). On corruption in republican thought, see Bernard Bailyn, *The Ideological Origins of the American Revolution,* enl. ed. (1967; Cambridge, MA: Harvard University Press, 1992); Wood, *Creation of the American Republic;* J. G. A. Pocock, *The Machiavellian Moment: Florentine Political Thought and the Atlantic Republican Tradition* (Princeton, NJ: Princeton University Press, 1975); and on the republican tradition generally, see Daniel T. Rodgers, "Republicanism: The Career of a Concept," *Journal of American History* 92 (June 1992), 3–38. On republican decay and the Constitution, see Lance Banning, "Republican Ideology and the Triumph of the Constitution," *WMQ* 31 (Apr. 1974), 167–188.

7. George Washington to Former Virginia Governors, Mount Vernon, Sept. 24, 1787, *DHRC,* 13:224; Henry Knox to Jean-Baptiste Gouvion, New York, Feb. 19, 1788, *DHRC,* 16:142; The Landholder X [Oliver Ellsworth], *Connecticut Courant,* Mar. 3, 1788, *DHRC,* 16:306. Also see Madison to Jefferson, Oct. 24, 1787, *PJM,* 10:208.

8. Publicola [Archibald Maclaine], "An Address to the Freemen of North Carolina," *State Gazette of North Carolina,* Mar. 20, 1788, *DHRC,* 16:438; Morris to Washington, Philadelphia, Oct. 30, 1787, *DHRC,* 13:514; Benjamin Rush to David Ramsay, *Charleston Columbian Herald,* Apr. 14, 1788, *DHRC,* 17:97; A Citizen of Philadelphia [Pelatiah Webster], *The Weaknesses of Brutus Exposed,* Nov. 8, 1787, *DHRC,* 14:68.

9. Edmund Pendleton, Virginia Ratifying Convention, June 12, 1788, *DHRC,* 10:1201; Poplicola, *Boston Gazette,* Dec. 24, 1787, *DHRC,* 15:73; James Innes, Virginia Ratifying Convention, June 25, 1788, *DHRC,* 10:1524. Also see "Strictures on the Proposed Constitution," *Philadelphia Freeman's Journal,* Sept. 26, 1787, *DHRC,* 13:244; John Sullivan, "Speech to the New Hampshire General Court," *New Hampshire Mer-*

cury, Jan. 30, 1787, *DHRC,* 14:409; Zachariah Johnson, Virginia Ratifying Convention, June 25, 1788, *DHRC,* 10:1534.

10. Caesar II, New York *Daily Advertiser,* Oct. 17, 1787, *DHRC,* 13:396–397; *Philadelphia Freeman's Journal,* Oct. 10, 1787, *DHRC,* 13:361. It has been suggested that Alexander Hamilton was "Caesar," but that is disputed; see *DHRC,* 13:287.

11. Publius [James Madison], "The Federalist 14," Nov. 30, 1787, *New York Packet, DHRC,* 14:317; Edward Carrington to William Short, New York, July 26, 1788, *DHRC,* 18:293; [Tench Coxe], "On the Federal Government," Oct. 21, 1787, *DHRC,* 13:437; Fabius VIII [John Dickinson], *Pennsylvania Mercury,* Apr. 29, 1788, *DHRC,* 17:250. Also see Wilson, Pennsylvania Ratifying Convention, Dec. 11, 1787, *DHRC,* 2:557; A Countryman V [Roger Sherman], *New Haven Gazette,* Dec. 20, 1787, *DHRC,* 15:55; John Marshall and James Innes, Virginia Ratifying Convention, June 10 and 25, 1788, *DHRC,* 9:1125, 10:1524. On the pervasiveness of "experience" in Revolutionary American culture, see Daniel J. Boorstin, *The Genius of American Politics* (Chicago: University of Chicago Press, 1953), 8–35; Trevor Colbourn, *The Lamp of Experience: Whig History and the Intellectual Origins of the American Revolution* (Chapel Hill: University of North Carolina Press, 1965); Douglas G. Adair, "Experience Must Be Our Only Guide: History, Democratic Theory, and the American Constitution," in *Fame and the Founding Fathers,* ed. Trevor Colbourn (New York: Norton, 1974), 107–123; Jack P. Greene, "'An Instructive Monitor': Experience and the Fabrication of the Federal Constitution," in *Imperatives, Behaviors, and Identities: Essays in Early American Cultural History* (Charlottesville: University of Virginia Press, 1992), 317–326. For a different and valuable take, not disputing the concept's pervasiveness, but its non-speculative impulse, see Daniel T. Rodgers, *Contested Truths: Keywords in American Politics Since Independence* (Cambridge, MA: Harvard University Press, 1987), 17–44.

12. A Friend of Society and Liberty [Coxe], *Pennsylvania Gazette,* July 23, 1788, *DHRC,* 18:283; Samuel McDowell to William Fleming, Mercer County, Dec. 20, 1787, *DHRC,* 15:54; Publicola [Maclaine], "An Address to the Freemen of North Carolina," *State Gazette of North Carolina,* Mar. 20, 1788, *DHRC,* 16:438. Also see Wilson, "Speech at a Public Meeting in Philadelphia," Oct. 6, 1787, *DHRC,* 13:343; A Citizen of New Haven [Roger Sherman], *Connecticut Courant,* Jan. 7, 1788, *DHRC,* 3:527; Henry Lee III, Virginia Ratifying Convention, June 9, 1788, *DHRC,* 9:1081; William Pierce, "Oration," Savannah, Georgia, July 4, 1788, *DHRC,* 18:252. For a related take, see David E. Kyvig, *Explicit and Authentic Acts: Amending the U.S. Constitution, 1776–1995* (Lawrence: University Press of Kansas, 1995), ch. 4. For more on how Federalists portrayed Article V this way, see Klarman, *Framers' Coup,* 544–545; Richard B. Bernstein with Jerome Angel, *Amending America: If We Love the Constitution So Much, Why Do We Keep Trying to Change It?* (New York: Times Books, 1993), 22–29.

13. Fabius VIII [Dickinson], *Pennsylvania Mercury,* Apr. 29, 1788, *DHRC,* 17:250.

14. Marcus II [James Iredell], *Norfolk and Portsmouth Journal,* Feb. 27, 1788, *DHRC,* 16:242–243; Marcus IV [Iredell], *Norfolk and Portsmouth Journal,* Mar. 12,

1788, *DHRC*, 16:379; A Citizen of Philadelphia [Webster], "The Weaknesses of Brutus Exposed," Nov. 8, 1787, *DHRC*, 14:66; From Henry Knox, New York, Sept., 1787, *DHRC*, 13:279. Also see Wilson, "Speech at a Public Meeting in Philadelphia," Oct. 6, 1787, *DHRC*, 13:340; Publius [Madison], "The Federalist 34," *New York Packet*, Jan. 4, 1788, *DHRC*, 15:260; Aristides [Alexander Contee Hanson], *Remarks on the Proposed Plan*, Jan. 31, 1788, *DHRC*, 15:535; Henry Pendleton, South Carolina Ratifying Convention, May 14, 1788, *DHRC*, 27:346–347; Alexander Hamilton, New York Ratifying Convention, June 20, 1788, *DHRC*, 22:1729; Richard Harison, New York Ratifying Convention, June 23, 1788, *DHRC*, 22:1804.

15. John Armstrong Sr. to George Washington, Carlisle, Pennsylvania, Feb. 20, 1788, *DHRC*, 16:150.

16. Cato I [perhaps George Clinton], *New York Journal*, Sept. 27, 1787, *DHRC*, 13:255; Cornell, *Other Founders*, 32–33.

17. Federal Farmer [perhaps Melancton Smith or Elbridge Gerry], *An Additional Number of Letters to the Republican*, May 2, 1788, Letter VIII, *DHRC*, 17:288.

18. A Columbian Patriot [Mercy Otis Warren], *Observations on the Constitution*, Boston, Feb. 1788, *DHRC*, 16:283–284; John De Witt I, Boston *American Herald*, Oct. 22, 1787, *DHRC*, 4:111; Brutus II [perhaps M. Smith], *New York Journal*, Nov. 1, 1787, *DHRC*, 13:524–525.

19. Foreign Spectator [Nicholas Collin], *Philadelphia Independent Gazetteer*, Oct. 2, 1787, *DHRC*, 13:290; "Strictures on the Proposed Constitution," *Philadelphia Freeman's Journal*, Sept. 26, 1787, *DHRC*, 13:244; Philadelphiensis XI [perhaps Benjamin Workman], *Philadelphia Independent Gazetteer*, Mar. 8, 1788, *DHRC*, 16:365. For a similar portrayal of Anti-Federalism embedded within a much different take on the debate over constitutional permanence, see Philip Hamburger, "The Constitution's Accommodation of Social Change," *Michigan Law Review* 88 (Nov. 1989), 239–327.

20. An Old Whig IV, *Philadelphia Independent Gazetteer*, Oct. 27, 1787, *DHRC*, 13:498, 500; Edmund Randolph, "Letter to the Speaker of the Virginia House of Delegates," *DHRC*, 15:133.

21. Brutus III [perhaps M. Smith], *New York Journal*, Nov. 15, 1787, *DHRC*, 14:119; William Symmes Jr. to Peter Osgood Jr., Andover, Massachusetts, Nov. 15, 1787, *DHRC*, 14:115; Federal Farmer [perhaps M. Smith or Gerry], *An Additional Number of Letters to the Republican*, May 2, 1788, Letter IX, *DHRC*, 17:288. Also see An Old Whig VIII, *Philadelphia Independent Gazetteer*, Feb. 6, 1788, *DHRC*, 16:54.

22. Richard Henry Lee to Governor Edmund Randolph, *Petersburg Virginia Gazette*, Dec. 6, 1787, *DHRC*, 14:367; Brutus I [perhaps M. Smith], *New York Journal*, Oct. 18, 1787, *DHRC*, 13:413; Centinel II [Samuel Bryan], *Philadelphia Freeman's Journal*, Oct. 24, 1787, *DHRC*, 13:467.

23. An Old Whig I, *Philadelphia Independent Gazetteer*, Oct. 12, 1787, *DHRC*, 13:377; Patrick Henry, Virginia Ratifying Convention, June 5, 1788, *DHRC*, 9:955.

24. An Old Whig IV, *Philadelphia Independent Gazetteer,* Oct. 27, 1787, *DHRC,* 13:498.

25. Aristocrotis [William Petrikin], *The Government of Nature Delineated; or An Exact Picture of the New Federal Constitution* (Carlisle: Kline and Reynolds, 1788), 24.

26. Cato V [perhaps Clinton], *New York Journal,* Nov. 22, 1787, *DHRC,* 14:182–183; A Federal Republican, *A Review of the Constitution,* Philadelphia, Nov. 28, 1787, *DHRC,* 14:262; John Tyler Sr., Virginia Ratifying Convention, June 25, 1788, *DHRC,* 10:1525; Denatus, *Virginia Independent Chronicle,* June 11, 1788, *DHRC,* 10:1602; John Adams, *Thoughts on Government: Applicable to the Present State of the American Colonies. In a Letter from a Gentleman to his Friend* (Philadelphia: John Dunlap, 1776), 8; Patrick Henry, Virginia Ratifying Convention, June 23, 1788, *DHRC,* 10:1465. Also see William Symmes Jr. to Peter Osgood Jr., Andover, Massachusetts, Nov. 15, 1787, *DHRC,* 14:116; William Findley, Pennsylvania Ratifying Convention, Nov. 30 and Dec. 7, 1787, *DHRC,* 2:439, 523; "The People: Unconstitutionalism," *Middlesex Gazette,* Dec. 10, 1787, *DHRC,* 3:494; John Smilie, Pennsylvania Ratifying Convention, Dec. 12, 1787, *DHRC,* 2:592. For the original reference to an "empire of laws, and not of men," see James Harrington, *The Commonwealth of Oceana* (1656), ed. J. G. A. Pocock (New York: Cambridge University Press, 1992), 8.

27. Cato V [perhaps Clinton], *New York Journal,* Nov. 22, 1787, *DHRC,* 14:183; A Columbian Patriot [Warren], *Observations on the Constitution,* Boston, Feb. 1788, *DHRC,* 16:279; Centinel IV [Bryan], *Philadelphia Independent Gazetteer,* Nov. 30, 1787, *DHRC,* 14:321; John Williams, New York Ratifying Convention, June 27, 1788, *DHRC,* 22:1936; Brutus III [perhaps M. Smith], *New York Journal,* Nov. 15, 1787, *DHRC,* 14:120.

28. Centinel II [Bryan], *Philadelphia Freeman's Journal,* Oct. 24, 1787, *DHRC,* 13:460; John Williams, New York Ratifying Convention, June 27, 1788, *DHRC,* 22:1936; John De Witt II, Boston *American Herald,* Oct. 29, 1787, *DHRC,* 4:159.

29. George Mason, Virginia Ratifying Convention, June 16, 1788, *DHRC,* 10:1317; Patrick Henry, Virginia Ratifying Convention, June 7, 1788, *DHRC,* 9:1046.

30. Patrick Henry, Virginia Ratifying Convention, June 7, 1788, *DHRC,* 9:1046; John De Witt II, Boston *American Herald,* Oct. 29, 1787, *DHRC,* 4:159.

31. United States Constitution, Preamble; George Clinton, New York Ratifying Convention, July 11, 1788, *DHRC,* 22:2146; Brutus V [perhaps M. Smith], *New York Journal,* Dec. 13, 1787, *DHRC,* 14:423. Also see "The Dissent of the Minority of the Pennsylvania Convention," *Pennsylvania Packet,* Dec. 18, 1787, *DHRC,* 15:25.

32. United States Constitution, Article I, Section 8; [James Francis Mercer], Address to the Members of the New York and Virginia Conventions, Post-April 30, 1788, *DHRC,* 17:259; Brutus XII [perhaps M. Smith], *New York Journal,* Feb. 7, 1788, *DHRC,* 16:75; Brutus VI [perhaps M. Smith], *New York Journal,* Dec. 27, 1787, *DHRC,* 15:114–115; "The Dissent of the Minority of the Pennsylvania Convention," *Pennsylvania Packet,* Dec. 18, 1787, *DHRC,* 15:22. Also see William Symmes Jr., Massachusetts Ratifying Convention, Jan. 22, 1788, *DHRC,* 6:1311.

33. United States Constitution, Article I, Section 8; Brutus V [perhaps M. Smith], *New York Journal,* Dec. 13, 1787, *DHRC,* 14:424–425; Centinel V [Bryan], *Philadelphia Independent Gazetteer,* Dec. 4, 1787, *DHRC,* 14:345; Mason, Virginia Ratifying Convention, June 4, 1788, *DHRC,* 9:936. Also see A Farmer, *Philadelphia Freeman's Journal,* Apr. 16, 23, 1788, *DHRC,* 17:142. On the perceived sweep of the taxing power, see Robin L. Einhorn, *American Taxation, American Slavery* (Chicago: University of Chicago Press, 2006), 173–174.

34. United States Constitution, Article I, Section 8; Federal Farmer [perhaps M. Smith or Gerry], *Letters to the Republican,* 1787, Letter IV, *DHRC,* 14:44; John Williams, New York Ratifying Convention, June 26, 1788, *DHRC,* 22:1918; Brutus V [perhaps M. Smith], *New York Journal,* Dec. 13, 1787, *DHRC,* 14:425; Brutus I [perhaps M. Smith], *New York Journal,* Oct. 18, 1787, *DHRC,* 13:416; An Old Whig II, *Philadelphia Independent Gazetteer,* Oct. 17, 1787, *DHRC,* 13:402. Also see Mason, "Objections to the Constitution of Government formed by the Convention," *DHRC,* 13:350; Cincinnatus II [Arthur Lee], "To James Wilson, Esquire," *New York Journal,* Nov. 8, 1787, *DHRC,* 14:14; William Russell to William Fleming, Aspenville, Virginia, Jan. 25, 1788, *DHRC,* 15:468; Address of the Anti-Federalist Minority of the Maryland Convention, May 1, 1788, *DHRC,* 12:663; Henry, Virginia Ratifying Convention, June 16, 1788, *DHRC,* 10:1324; Melancton Smith and George Clinton, New York Ratifying Convention, June 27 and July 11, 1788, *DHRC,* 22:1923, 2146.

35. An Old Whig II, *Philadelphia Independent Gazetteer,* Oct. 17, 1787, *DHRC,* 13:402–403; The Republican Federalist VI, *Massachusetts Centinel,* Feb. 2, 1788, *DHRC,* 5:846. Also see Brutus V [perhaps M. Smith], *New York Journal,* Oct. 18, 1787, *DHRC,* 13:416; A Countryman V [De Witt Clinton], *New York Journal,* Jan. 17, 1788, 20:623; Sydney [Abraham Yates Jr.], *New York Journal,* June 13, 14, 1788, *DHRC,* 20:1159. On this point, see John Mikhail, "The Necessary and Proper Clauses," *Georgetown Law Journal* 102 (Apr. 2014), 1059–1060, 1129–1130.

36. George Lee Turberville to Madison, Richmond, Virginia, Dec. 11, 1787, *DHRC,* 14:407; Russell to Fleming, Aspenville, Virginia, Jan. 25, 1788, *DHRC,* 15:468. Also see Brutus V [perhaps M. Smith], *New York Journal,* Oct. 18, 1787, *DHRC,* 13:416; A Federal Republican, *A Review of the Constitution,* Nov. 28, 1787, *DHRC,* 14:269; Robert Whitehill, Pennsylvania Ratifying Convention, Nov. 30, 1787, *DHRC,* 2:426; Agrippa XII [James Winthrop], *Massachusetts Gazette,* Jan. 15, 1788, *DHRC,* 5:722–723; A Farmer, Philadelphia *Freeman's Journal,* Apr. 16, 23, 1788, *DHRC,* 17:142.

37. James Monroe, Virginia Ratifying Convention, June 10, 1788, *DHRC,* 9:1112; Brutus XI [perhaps M. Smith], *New York Journal,* Jan. 31, 1788, *DHRC,* 15:515. Also see An Old Whig II, *Philadelphia Independent Gazetteer,* Oct. 17, 1787, *DHRC,* 13:402–403; John Williams, New York Ratifying Convention, June 26, 1788, *DHRC,* 22:1917–1918.

38. United States Constitution, Article III, Section 2. On judges in Revolutionary American culture, see Saul Cornell, "The People's Constitution vs. the Lawyer's Constitution," *Yale Journal of Law and the Humanities* 23 (Summer 2011), 295–337; Gordon S.

Wood, *Empire of Liberty: A History of the Early Republic, 1789–1815* (New York: Oxford University Press, 2009), ch. 11; and Jack N. Rakove, "The Origins of Judicial Review: A Plea for New Contexts," *Stanford Law Review* 49 (May 1997), 1060–1064. On fears of debtors' court and the resentment it bred, see Woody Holton, *Unruly Americans and the Origins of the Constitution* (New York: Hill and Wang, 2007), 43–45, 100–107; Terry Bouton, *Taming Democracy: "The People," the Founders, and the Troubled Ending of the American Revolution* (New York: Oxford University Press, 2007), ch. 4; Cornell, "The People's Constitution vs. the Lawyer's Constitution," 306–307; Bruce H. Mann, *Republic of Debtors: Bankruptcy in the Age of American Independence* (Cambridge, MA: Harvard University Press, 2002).

39. Samuel Osgood to Samuel Adams, New York, Jan. 5, 1788, *DHRC*, 15:264–265; William Grayson, Virginia Ratifying Convention, June 21, 1788, *DHRC*, 10:1447; Mason, Virginia Ratifying Convention, June 19, 1788, *DHRC*, 10:1401; Melancton Smith, New York Ratifying Convention, July 17, 1788, *DHRC*, 23:2214–2215.

40. A Democratic Federalist, *Pennsylvania Herald*, Oct. 17, 1787, *DHRC*, 13:389; Federal Farmer [perhaps M. Smith or Gerry], *Letters to the Republican,* 1787, Letter III, *DHRC,* 14:41; Brutus XII [perhaps M. Smith], *New York Journal,* Feb. 14, 1788, *DHRC,* 16:120; Osgood to S. Adams, New York, Jan. 5, 1788, *DHRC,* 15:265; Bernadette A. Meyler, "Substitute Chancellors: The Role of the Jury in the Contest between Common Law and Equity," *Cornell Law Faculty Publications,* Paper 39, 2006; Daniel J. Hulsebosch, *Constituting Empire: New York and the Transformation of Constitutionalism in the Atlantic World, 1664–1830* (Chapel Hill: University of North Carolina Press, 2005), 242–243. Also see William Grayson, Virginia Ratifying Convention, June 21, 1788, *DHRC,* 10:1446.

41. Federal Farmer [perhaps M. Smith or Gerry], *An Additional Number of Letters to the Republican,* May 2, 1788, Letter XV, *DHRC,* 17:341; Brutus XIV [perhaps M. Smith], *New York Journal,* Feb. 28, 1788, *DHRC,* 16:258; Philadelphia *Freeman's Journal,* Nov. 21, 1787, *DHRC,* 14:165; Meyler, "Substitute Chancellors," 31–38; Hulsebosch, *Constituting Empire,* 243–244. Also see A Democratic Federalist, *Pennsylvania Herald,* Oct. 17, 1787, *DHRC,* 13:388; Luther Martin's Speech before the Maryland House of Delegates, Nov. 29, 1787, *DHRC,* 14:290; Candidus I [Benjamin Austin], *Independent Chronicle,* Dec. 6, 1787, *DHRC,* 4:397; John Smilie, Pennsylvania Ratifying Convention, Dec. 7, 1787, *DHRC,* 2:521; William Findley, Pennsylvania Ratifying Convention, Dec. 7, 1787, *DHRC,* 2:523; "The People: Unconstitutionalism," *Middlesex Gazette,* Dec. 10. 1787, *DHRC,* 2:494–495; Luther Martin, "Genuine Information X," Baltimore *Maryland Gazette,* Feb. 1, 1788, *DHRC,* 16:8–10; Aristocrotis [Petrikin], *Government of Nature Delineated,* 20; Address of the Anti-Federalist Minority of the Maryland Convention, May 1, 1788, *DHRC,* 12:664; Melancton Smith, July 17, 1788, *DHRC,* 23:2214–2215. On the celebrated role of juries in eighteenth-century American legal consciousness, particularly as finders of legal fact, see William E. Nelson, *Americanization of the Common Law: The Impact of Legal Change on Massachusetts Society, 1760–1830* (Cambridge, MA: Harvard University Press, 1975), 20–30.

42. Brutus XI [perhaps M. Smith], *New York Journal,* Jan. 31, 1788, *DHRC,* 15:512, 513–514. Also see Brutus XV [perhaps M. Smith], *New York Journal,* Mar. 20, 1788, *DHRC,* 16:433; Federal Farmer [perhaps M. Smith or Gerry], *An Additional Number of Letters to the Republican,* May 2, 1788, Letter XV, *DHRC,* 17:333–342.

43. Brutus XV [perhaps M. Smith], *New York Journal,* Mar. 20, 1788, *DHRC,* 16:433, 431, 435. Also see George Mason, "Objections to the Constitution of Government Formed by the Convention," *DHRC,* 13:349; Federal Farmer [perhaps M. Smith or Gerry], *Letters to the Republican,* 1787, Letter III, *DHCR,* 14:40.

44. Honestus [Benjamin Austin], *Observations on the Pernicious Practice of the Law* (Boston: Adams and Nourse, 1786), 4, 12, 13, 38, 20. On Austin's thinking, see Aaron T. Knapp, "Law's Revolution: Benjamin Austin and the Spirit of '86," *Yale Journal of Law and the Humanities* 25 (Summer 2013), 276–281, 295–324. On anti-lawyer sentiment, see Cornell, "The People's Constitution vs. the Lawyer's Constitution"; Richard E. Ellis, *The Jeffersonian Crisis: Courts and Politics in the Young Republic* (New York: Oxford University Press, 1971), 111–116, 253–256; Nathan O. Hatch, *The Democratization of American Christianity* (New Haven, CT: Yale University Press, 1989), 26–28; Christopher Grasso, *A Speaking Aristocracy: Transforming Public Discourse in Eighteenth-Century Connecticut* (Chapel Hill: University of North Carolina Press, 1999), 431–449; John Fabian Witt, *Patriots and Cosmopolitans: Hidden Histories of American Law* (Cambridge, MA: Harvard University Press, 2007), 25–26, 40–44.

45. A True Friend, Richmond, Dec. 6, 1787, *DHRC,* 14:377; Osgood to S. Adams, New York, Jan. 5, 1788, *DHRC,* 15:264; Mason, "Objections to the Constitution of Government Formed by the Convention," *DHRC,* 13:349; A Bostonian, *American Herald,* Feb. 4, 1788, *DHRC,* 5:851. Also see Timoleon, "Extraordinary," *New York Journal,* Nov. 1, 1787, *DHRC,* 13:536; Centinel XV [Bryan], *Philadelphia Independent Gazetteer,* Feb. 22, 1788, *DHRC,* 16:189–190; Agrippa XII [Winthrop], *Massachusetts Gazette,* Jan. 15, 1788, *DHRC,* 5: 726; Aristocrotis [Petrikin], *Government of Nature Delineated,* 18–20.

46. David Caldwell, July 29, 1788, *Debates,* 4:187; Federal Farmer [perhaps M. Smith or Gerry], *An Additional Number of Letters to the Republican,* May 2, 1788, Letter XVI, *DHRC,* 17:345; John De Witt II, Boston *American Herald,* Oct. 29, 1787, *DHRC,* 4:158. Also see Timoleon, "Extraordinary," *New York Journal,* Nov. 1, 1787, *DHRC,* 13:535; Grayson to William Short, Nov. 10, 1787, *DHRC,* 14:82; A True Friend, Richmond, Virginia, Dec. 6, 1787, *DHRC,* 14:377; Melancton Smith, New York Ratifying Convention, June 27, 1788, *DHRC,* 22:1921–1922. This obsession with linguistic precision was especially strong among plebeian Anti-Federalists; see Saul Cornell, "Constitutional Meaning and Semantic Instability: Federalists and Anti-Federalists on the Nature of Constitutional Language," *American Journal of Legal History* 56 (Mar. 2016), 22, 25–27.

47. Henry, Virginia Ratifying Convention, June 23, 1788, *DHRC,* 10:1466; Denatus, *Virginia Independent Chronicle,* June 11, 1788, *DHRC,* 10:1600; William Lenoir, North Carolina Ratifying Convention, July 30, 1788, *Debates,* IV, 201.

48. Amos Singletary, Massachusetts Ratifying Convention, Jan. 25, 1788, *DHRC,* 6:1346–1347; Henry Parker, *Observations upon some of His Majesties late answers and expresses* (London, 1642), 36; Mason, Virginia Ratifying Convention, June 17, 1788, *DHRC,* 10:1361. This discussion is indebted to Cornell, "The People's Constitution vs. the Lawyer's Constitution"; Caleb Nelson, "Originalism and Interpretive Conventions," *University of Chicago Law Review* 70 (Spring 2003), 570–571, 578–581. On the plain style, see Cornell, *Other Founders,* 58–59; and on Protestant hermeneutics in Founding-era constitutional interpretation generally, see H. Jefferson Powell, "The Original Understanding of Original Intent," *Harvard Law Review* 98 (Mar. 1985), 889–894. On the long-standing evangelical opposition to lawyers, which likened the dangerous presumptions of legal rationality to those of religious rationality, see Richard E. Ellis, *Jeffersonian Crisis,* 253–256. On Protestant interpretive sensibilities in Revolutionary America generally, see Mark A. Noll, *In the Beginning Was the Word: The Bible in American Public Life, 1492–1783* (New York: Oxford University Press, 2016), 191–197, 201–205, 289–292.

49. Henry, Virginia Ratifying Convention, June 20, 1788, *DHRC,* 10:1423, 1420.

50. Mason, "Objections to the Constitution of Government Formed by the Convention," *DHRC,* 13:348–351; Richard Henry Lee's Amendments, Confederation Congress, Sept. 27, 1787, *DHRC,* 13:239. On Anti-Federalists' obsession with the omission of a bill of rights, see Cornell, *Other Founders,* 26–34; Maier, *Ratification,* 46–49; Klarman, *Framers' Coup,* 548–555; John P. Kaminski, "The Making of the Bill of Rights, 1787–1792," in *Contexts of the Bill of Rights,* ed. Stephen L. Schechter and Richard B. Bernstein (Albany: New York State Commission on the Bicentennial of the United States Constitution, 1990), 18–64.

51. A Citizen of the State of Maryland, "Remarks Relative to a Bill of Rights," *DHRC,* 17:92; A True Friend, Richmond, Virginia, Dec. 6, 1787, *DHRC,* 14:376; Federal Farmer [perhaps M. Smith or Gerry], *An Additional Number of Letters to the Republican,* May 2, 1788, Letter XVI, *DHRC,* 17:343.

52. Wilson, "Speech at a Public Meeting in Philadelphia," Oct. 6, 1787, *DHRC,* 13:339; One of the Middling-Interest, *Massachusetts Centinel,* Nov. 28, 1787, *DHRC,* 4:329; Publius [Hamilton], "The Federalist 84," New York, May 28, 1788, *DHRC,* 18:127–135; James Madison, Virginia Ratifying Convention, June 24, 1788, *DHRC,* 10:1507. For other examples of how Federalists justified the omission, see Benjamin Rush, Pennsylvania Ratifying Convention, Nov. 30, 1787, *DHRC,* 2:434; A Landholder V [Oliver Ellsworth], *Connecticut Courant,* Dec. 10, 1787, *DHRC,* 3:490; Charles Cotesworth Pinckney, South Carolina Ratifying Convention, Jan. 18, 1788, *DHRC,* 27:157–158; Joseph Bradley Varnum, Massachusetts Ratifying Convention, Jan. 23, 1788, *DHRC,* 6:1315; James Iredell, North Carolina Ratifying Convention, July 28, 1788, *Debates,* 4:148. On Wilson's speech, see Maier, *Ratification,* 77–82.

53. Henry, Virginia Ratifying Convention, June 16, 1788, *DHRC,* 10:1328, 1329; Thomas B. Wait to George Thatcher, Portland, Maine, Jan. 8, 1788, *DHRC,* 15:285;

Mason, Virginia Ratifying Convention, June 16, 1788, *DHRC*, 10:1328. Also see Brutus II [perhaps M. Smith], *New York Journal*, Nov. 1, 1787, *DHRC*, 13:529. For a related take, see Jack N. Rakove, "Thinking like a Constitution," *JER* 24 (Spring 2004), 17.

54. [James Francis Mercer], Address to the Members of the New York and Virginia Conventions, Post-April 30, 1788, *DHRC*, 17:260; Federal Farmer [perhaps M. Smith or Gerry], *An Additional Number of Letters to the Republican*, May 2, 1788, Letter XVI, 17:344.

55. John De Witt II, Boston *American Herald*, Oct. 29, 1787, *DHRC*, 4:158. Also see Brutus V [perhaps M. Smith], *New York Journal*, Dec. 13, 1787, *DHRC*, 14:424; Fabius IX, *Pennsylvania Mercury*, May 1, 1788, *DHRC*, 17:263; Henry, Virginia Ratifying Convention, June 20, 1788, *DHRC*, 10:1421; Grayson, Virginia Ratifying Convention, June 21, 1788, *DHRC*, 10:1450.

56. A Countryman II [Roger Sherman], *New Haven Gazette*, Nov. 22, 1787, *DHRC*, 14:173; Publius [Madison], "The Federalist 48," *New York Packet*, Feb. 1, 1788, *DHRC*, 16:4; Giles Hickory III [Noah Webster], "Government," *American Magazine* (New York), Feb. 1788, 141; Uncus, *Maryland Journal*, Nov. 9, 1787, *DHRC*, 14:81; Randolph, Virginia Ratifying Convention, June 6, 1788, *DHRC*, 9:985. Also see Publius [Hamilton], "The Federalist 84," *DHRC*, 18:129–132; Randolph, Virginia Ratifying Convention, June 9, 1788, *DHRC*, 9:1084; George Nicholas, Virginia Ratifying Convention, June 16, 1788, *DHRC*, 10:1334.

57. Samuel Stillman, Massachusetts Ratifying Convention, Feb. 6, 1788, *DHRC*, 6:1460; Rush to Ramsay, *Charleston Columbian Herald*, Apr. 14, 1788, *DHRC*, 17:96; From Roger Sherman, New Haven, Dec. 8, 1787, *DHRC*, 14:386–387; A Countryman II [Sherman], *New Haven Gazette*, Nov. 22, 1787, *DHRC*, 14:173; Madison, Virginia Ratifying Convention, June 12, 1788, *DHRC*, 10:1223–1224; Madison to Jefferson, Oct. 24, 1787, *PJM*, 10:209–214.

58. Marcus IV [Iredell], *Norfolk and Portsmouth Journal*, Mar. 12, 1788, *DHRC*, 16:379–380; Publius [Madison], "The Federalist 44," *New York Packet*, Jan. 25, 1788, *DHRC*, 15:473; Giles Hickory III [Webster], "Government," *American Magazine* (New York), Feb. 1788, 140, 141. The salience of constitutional structure undergirded many Federalists' defense of federalism; see Publius [Hamilton], "The Federalist 26," *New York Independent Journal*, Dec. 22, 1787, *DHRC*, 15:65–69; Publius [Hamilton], "The Federalist 28," *New York Independent Journal*, Dec. 26, 1787, *DHRC*, 15:102–105; "The Federalist 46," *New York Packet*, Jan. 29, 1788, *DHRC*, 15:488–493. On this point, see Rakove, *Original Meanings*, 188–201.

59. Publius [Madison], "The Federalist 41," *New York Independent Journal*, Jan. 19, 1788, *DHRC*, 15:420; Publius [Hamilton], "The Federalist 25," *New York Packet*, Dec. 21, 1787, *DHRC*, 15:63; Publius [Madison], "The Federalist 20," *New York Packet*, Dec. 11, 1787, *DHRC*, 14:412. *Federalist* 20 is among the fifteen installments of the *Federalist* whose authorship is disputed. The current belief is that Madison probably wrote all of

them, although it is thought that Hamilton assisted him on this particular one; see *DHRC,* 13:486–490.

60. Madison to Jefferson, Oct. 24, 1787, *PJM,* 10:209–210, 211; Hamilton, New York Ratifying Convention, June 21, 1788, *DHRC,* 22:1767–1768; Morris to Washington, Philadelphia, Oct. 30, 1787, *DHRC,* 13:514.

61. Madison to Washington, Oct. 18, 1787, *PJM,* 10:197; Publius [Madison], "The Federalist 44," *DHRC,* 15:472; Madison, Virginia Ratifying Convention, June 14, 1788, *DHRC,* 10:1295.

62. Hamilton, New York Ratifying Convention, June 27, 1788, *DHRC,* 22:1956; Madison, Virginia Ratifying Convention, June 16 and 19, 1788, *DHRC,* 10:1323, 1396. Also see A Countryman III [Sherman], *New Haven Gazette,* Nov. 29, 1787, *DHRC,* 14:296.

63. Hamilton, New York Ratifying Convention, June 28, 1788, *DHRC,* 22:1984; Publius [Hamilton], "The Federalist 27," *New York Packet,* Dec. 25, 1787, *DHRC,* 15:95; Marshall, Virginia Ratifying Convention, June 20, 1788, *DHRC,* 10:1433. Also see generally Hamburger, "Constitution's Accommodation of Social Change."

64. A Landholder V [Ellsworth], *Connecticut Courant,* Dec. 3, 1787, *DHRC,* 14:335; Publius [Madison], "The Federalist 62," *New York Independent Journal,* Feb. 27, 1788, *DHRC,* 14:236.

65. A Landholder V [Ellsworth], *Connecticut Courant,* Dec. 3, 1787, *DHRC,* 14:335; Theophilus Parsons, Massachusetts Ratifying Convention, Jan. 25, 1788, *DHRC,* 6:1348. Also see Henry Knox to Benjamin Lincoln, New York, June 13, 1788, *DHRC,* 18:176–177.

66. Publius [Madison], "The Federalist 37," New York *Daily Advertiser,* Jan. 11, 1788, *DHRC,* 15:346–347. On Madison's use of Locke in *Federalist* 37, see Jack N. Rakove, "Joe the Ploughman Reads the Constitution, or, The Poverty of Public Meaning Originalism," *San Diego Law Review* 48 (May 2011), 593–595; and on how he used Locke to leverage linguistic ambiguity, see Michael Kramer, *Imagining Language in America: From the Revolution to the Civil War* (Princeton, NJ: Princeton University Press, 1991), ch. 4.

67. Publius [Madison], "The Federalist 37," *DHRC,* 15:345–346. Also see Publius [Hamilton], "The Federalist 82," New York, May 28, 1788, *DHRC,* 18:111.

68. Here Madison also broke with Locke's more pessimistic conclusions about language; see Hannah Dawson, *Locke, Language, and Early Modern Philosophy* (New York: Cambridge University Press, 2007), chs. 7–10. He also broke with the linguistic purity demanded by many French Revolutionaries; see Sophia Rosenfeld, *A Revolution in Language: The Problem of Signs in Late Eighteenth-Century France* (Stanford, CA: Stanford University Press, 2001), ch. 4. Some have doubted how much Madison privileged the concept of deliberation, citing, in part, how it disappeared from his later writings; see the careful analysis in Jeremy D. Bailey, *James Madison and Constitutional Imperfection* (New York: Cambridge University Press, 2015), ch. 3. But much about Madison's

constitutional imagination changed after 1788, and during ratification this concept was central to how he negotiated the possibilities and perils of constitutional indeterminacy.

69. Publius, "The Federalist 46," *DHRC*, 15:493.

70. Fabius II [Dickinson], *Pennsylvania Mercury*, Apr. 15, 1788, *DHRC*, 17:126; A Landholder V [Ellsworth], *Connecticut Courant*, Dec. 3, 1787, *DHRC*, 14:335; Anti-Cincinnatus, *Northampton Hampshire Gazette*, Dec. 19, 1787, *DHRC*, 15:37. Also see Rufus King and Nathaniel Gorham, Response to Elbridge Gerry's Objections, *DHRC*, 13:552; "A. B." to Gerry, *Massachusetts Centinel*, Nov. 14, 1787, *DHRC*, 4:229; A Citizen of New Haven [Roger Sherman], *Connecticut Courant*, Jan. 7, 1788, *DHRC*, 3:525; Caleb Strong, Massachusetts Ratifying Convention, Jan. 16, 1788, *DHRC*, 6:1216; Civis, *Maryland Journal*, Feb. 1, 1788, *DHRC*, 11:276; Henry Lee III, Virginia Ratifying Convention, June 9, 1788, *DHRC*, 9:1080; William Johnston, North Carolina Ratifying Convention, July 25, 1788, *Debates*, 4:64.

71. Madison, Virginia Ratifying Convention, June 6, 1788, *DHRC*, 9:989; Publius [Hamilton], "The Federalist 32–33," *New York Independent Journal*, Jan. 2, 1788, *DHRC*, 15:222; Z. Johnson, Virginia Ratifying Convention, June 25, 1788, *DHRC*, 10:1531. Also see "Social Compact," *New Haven Gazette*, Oct. 4, 1787, *DHRC*, 13:311–313; A Federal Centinel, *South Carolina Weekly Chronicle*, Oct. 9, 1787, *DHRC*, 13:356.

72. Publius [Madison], "The Federalist 41," *New York Independent Journal*, Jan. 19, 1788, 15:425. Also see Publius [Madison], "The Federalist 45," *New York Independent Journal*, Jan. 26, 1788, *DHRC*, 15:479.

73. Publius [Madison], "The Federalist 41," *New York Independent Journal*, Jan. 19, 1788, *DHRC*, 15:424, 425; Randolph, Virginia Ratifying Convention, June 17, 1788, *DHRC*, 10:1350.

74. Nicholas, Virginia Ratifying Convention, June 10, 1788, *DHRC*, 9:1135; Publius [Madison], "The Federalist 44," *DHRC*, 15:471, 472, 473; Publius [Hamilton], "The Federalist 32–33," *DHRC*, 15:221. Also see Wilson, Pennsylvania Ratifying Convention, Dec. 1 and 4, 1787, *DHRC*, 2:454–455, 482; Thomas McKean, Pennsylvania Ratifying Convention, Dec. 10, 1787, *DHRC*, 2:539; Aristides [Hanson], *Remarks on the Proposed Plan*, Jan. 31, 1788, *DHRC*, 15:531–532; A Native of Virginia, *Observations upon the Proposed Plan of Federal Government*, Apr. 2, 1788, *DHRC*, 9:675; Edmund Pendleton, Virginia Ratifying Convention, June 16, 1788, *DHRC*, 10:1325; Nicholas, Virginia Ratifying Convention, June 16, 1788, *DHRC*, 9:1135, 10:1327.

75. Publius, "The Federalist 81," New York, May 28, 1788, *DHRC*, 18:110; Publius [Hamilton], "The Federalist 81," *DHRC*, 18:103–104; Publius [Hamilton], "The Federalist 78," New York, May 28, 1788, *DHRC*, 18:90; Hulsebosch, *Constituting Empire*, 237–253. Also see Wilson, Pennsylvania Ratifying Convention, Dec. 7, 1787, *DHRC*, 2:517–518; Marshall, Virginia Ratifying Convention, June 20, 1788, *DHRC*, 10:1437.

76. Randolph, Virginia Ratifying Convention, June 17, 1788, *DHRC*, 10:1347–1348.

77. Iredell, North Carolina Ratifying Convention, July 28, 1788, *Debates,* 4:148; Wilson, Pennsylvania Ratifying Convention, Dec. 11, 1787, *DHRC,* 2:556, and more generally 555–556. On rules for reading various legal devices, see Nelson, "Originalism and Interpretive Conventions," 561–573. Numerous scholars have assumed that the Constitution is inherently a legal text, supporting this position with references to eighteenth-century attitudes; for example, see John O. McGinnis and Michael B. Rappaport, *Originalism and the Good Constitution* (Cambridge, MA: Harvard University Press, 2013), ch. 7; Powell, "Original Understanding of Original Intent," 894–924; Antonin Scalia and Bryan A. Garner, *Reading Law: The Interpretation of Legal Texts* (St. Paul, MN: West, 2012), 403–405; Gary L. McDowell, *The Language of Law and the Foundations of American Constitutionalism* (New York: Cambridge University Press, 2010), 248–251; Robert G. Natelson, "The Founders' Hermeneutic: The Real Understanding of Original Intent," *Ohio State Law Journal* 68 (2007), 1239–1305; John F. Manning, "Separation of Powers as Ordinary Interpretation," *Harvard Law Review* 124 (June 2011), 2025; Gary Lawson and Guy Seidman, *"A Great Power of Attorney": Understanding the Fiduciary Constitution* (Lawrence: University Press of Kansas, 2017). This last work has recently contended that the original Constitution was specifically thought of as a "power of attorney," but beyond Iredell's comment there were hardly any claims to this effect during ratification; nor, for that matter, did the Constitution resemble contemporary powers of attorney. On how several prominent members of the Founding generation analogized the Constitution to a corporate charter, see John Mikhail, "The Constitution and the Philosophy of Language: Entailment, Implicature, and Implied Powers," *University of Virginia Law Review* 101 (June 2015), 1082–1084, 1097–1103; David Ciepley, "Is the U.S. Government a Corporation? The Corporate Origins of Modern Constitutionalism," *American Political Science Review* 111 (May 2017), 418–435. Others have recognized some of the problems with the assumption that the Constitution was a conventional legal text. On how the Constitution marked a new kind of fundamental law since it relied on the sovereign people's ratification, see Charles A. Lofgren, "The Original Understanding of Original Intent?" *Constitutional Commentary* 5 (Winter 1988), 82–85; and, for a deeper elaboration, see Larry D. Kramer, *The People Themselves: Popular Constitutionalism and Judicial Review* (New York: Oxford University Press, 2004), chs. 3–5. Relatedly, on the original differences between fundamental and ordinary law in American constitutional thinking, see Sylvia Snowiss, *Judicial Review and the Law of the Constitution* (New Haven, CT: Yale University Press, 1990), esp. ch. 1. On how so many Founding-era Americans thought the Constitution was not a legal text, see Cornell, "The People's Constitution vs. The Lawyer's Constitution."

78. For the ubiquity of the common law in eighteenth-century American legal training and reasoning, see Bailyn, *Ideological Origins,* 30–31; Bernadette Meyler, "Towards a Common Law Originalism," *Stanford Law Review* 59 (Dec. 2006), 582–584; Mary Sarah Bilder, "James Madison, Law Student and Demi-Lawyer," *Law and*

History Review 28 (May 2010), 395–399, 404, 413–415; Julian S. Waterman, "Thomas Jefferson and Blackstone's *Commentaries,*" *Illinois Law Review* 27 (1933), 630–634.

79. Sir William Blackstone, *Commentaries on the Laws of England* (1765–1769), 4 books, 2 vols. (Philadelphia: J. B. Lippincott, 1893), 1:59, and generally 59–61. On the widespread use of Blackstone by Revolutionary Americans, see Horst Dippel, "Blackstone's *Commentaries* and the Origins of Modern Constitutionalism," in *Re-Interpreting Blackstone's* Commentaries, ed. Wilfrid Prest (Portland, OR: Hart Publishing, 2014), 199–214; Albert W. Alschuler, "Rediscovering Blackstone," *University of Pennsylvania Law Review* 145 (Nov. 1996), 4–9; David A. Lockmiller, *Sir William Blackstone* (Chapel Hill: University of North Carolina Press, 1938), ch. 10.

80. Mason, Virginia Ratifying Convention, June 19, 1788, *DHRC,* 10:1390–1391; Madison, Aug. 17, 1787, *Records,* 2:316. This analysis is heavily indebted to Meyler, "Towards a Common Law Originalism," 559–572. On the pivotal context in which Blackstone formulated his conception of the common law, see David Lieberman, *The Province of Legislation Determined: Legal Theory in Eighteenth-Century Britain* (New York: Cambridge University Press, 1989), 13–28, chs. 1–2. On how Founding-era Americans were often influenced by Blackstone's critics, see David Thomas Konig, "Why the Second Amendment Has a Preamble," *UCLA Law Review* 56 (June 2009), 1313–1317. On the divergences between colonial and British common law, see Mary Sarah Bilder, *The Transatlantic Constitution: Colonial Legal Culture and the Empire* (Cambridge, MA: Harvard University Press, 2004); Nelson, *Americanization of the Common Law,* 8–10, ch. 1; William E. Nelson, *The Common Law in Colonial America,* 3 vols. (New York: Oxford University Press, 2008–2016). The portrait of the common law offered here runs counter to the static one so many constitutional interpreters problematically fall back on; for example, see Antonin Scalia, "Common-Law Courts in a Civil-Law System: The Role of United States Federal Courts and the Law," in *A Matter of Interpretation: Federal Courts and the Law* (Princeton, NJ: Princeton University Press, 1997), 3–47.

81. Randolph, Virginia Ratifying Convention, June 17, 1788, *DHRC,* 10:1352; Meyler, "Towards a Common Law Originalism," 581–592. On the historical perspective embedded in the common law, see J. G. A. Pocock, *The Ancient Constitution and the Feudal Law: A Study of English Historical Thought in the Seventeenth Century,* reissued ed. (1957; New York: Cambridge, 1987), ch. 2; and on how this historical perspective generated an American common law mind, see Stephen A. Conrad, "The Constitutionalism of 'the Common-Law Mind,'" *Law and Social Inquiry* 13 (Summer 1988), 619–636; James R. Stoner, *Common-Law Liberty: Rethinking American Constitutionalism* (Lawrence: University of Kansas Press, 2003), ch. 1; David T. Konig, "James Madison and Common-Law Constitutionalism," *Law and History Review* 28 (May 2010), 507–514.

82. Honestus [Austin], *Observations on the Pernicious Practice of the Law,* 12; also see 37. On controversy over the common law's applicability beyond ratification, see

Meyler, "Towards a Common Law Originalism," 572–580; Morton J. Horwitz, *The Transformation of American Law, 1780–1860* (New York: Oxford University Press, 1978), 9–30. On the uneasy refraction of British common law culture through American legal developments, see Mary Sarah Bilder, Maeva Marcus, and R. Kent Newmyer, eds., *Blackstone in America: Selected Essays of Kathryn Preyer* (New York: Cambridge University Press, 2009); Nelson, *Americanization of the Common Law*. In contrast, some have uncritically assumed that it was expected that the Constitution would simply be read in accordance with the Anglo-American common law; see Robert Lowry Clinton, *God and Man in the Law: The Foundations of Anglo-American Constitutionalism* (Lawrence: University Press of Kansas, 1997), ch. 8, 111–113, 116–117; Natelson, "Founders' Hermeneutic," 1246–1249. In terms of one particular area of English law, it has been persuasively shown that the English Habeas Corpus Act of 1679 did indeed deeply influence American constitutionalism; see Amanda L. Tyler, *Habeas Corpus in Wartime: From the Tower of London to Guantanamo Bay* (New York: Oxford University Press, 2017), chs. 4–5.

83. New York Constitution, Article XXXV (1777); Hamilton, "New York Assembly. Remarks on an Act for Settling Intestate Estates, Proving Wills, and Granting Administrations," Feb. 14, 1787, *PAH*, 4:69. On Hamilton's distinctive understanding of the ambiguity of the common law's applicability, see Kate Elizabeth Brown, *Alexander Hamilton and the Development of American Law* (Lawrence: University Press of Kansas, 2017), 175–177, 181–182, 188–189, 192–198; and particularly in terms of the New York Constitution, see 175–176.

84. Marcus I [Iredell], *Norfolk and Portsmouth Journal*, Feb. 20, 1788, *DHRC*, 16:164; Jefferson to John Brown Cutting, Oct. 2, 1788, *PTJ*, 13:649; William Findley, Pennsylvania Ratifying Convention, Nov. 30, 1787, *DHRC*, 2:439. This uncertainty was precisely what inspired leading Virginia jurist St. George Tucker (based on frustrations he had teaching law at William and Mary) to heavily annotate, and thus republicanize, Blackstone's *Commentaries* in the 1790s before publishing the five-volume product in 1803. For more, see Cornell, *Other Founders*, 263–264; Alschuler, "Rediscovering Blackstone," 11–16.

85. Publius [Hamilton], "The Federalist 83," *DHRC*, 18:115–116; Publius [Hamilton], "The Federalist 32–33," *New York Independent Journal*, Jan. 2, 1788, *DHRC*, 15:219; Publius [Madison], "The Federalist 40," *New York Packet*, Jan. 18, 1788, *DHRC*, 15:404; James Madison, Virginia Ratifying Convention, June 16, 1788, *DHRC*, 10:1318–1319; Publius [Madison], "The Federalist 40," *DHRC*, 15:404.

86. Publius [Madison], "The Federalist 40," *DHRC*, 15:404; Publius [Hamilton], "The Federalist 81," New York, May 28, 1788, *DHRC*, 18:104. Also see Publius [Madison], "The Federalist 44," *DHRC*, 15:472–473; Publius, "The Federalist 82," *DHRC*, 18:112.

87. Publius [Hamilton], "The Federalist 81," *DHRC*, 18:115; Publius [Hamilton], "The Federalist 32–33," *DHRC*, 15:218; Publius [Hamilton], "The Federalist 84,"

DHRC, 18:129; Publius [Hamilton], "The Federalist 83," *DHRC,* 18:116. On Hamilton as lawyer—his prodigious legal mind, how legal practice and principles informed his constitutional and political thinking, and his searching consideration of the applicability of inherited British legal norms to the new American constitutional order—see the incisive analysis in Brown, *Alexander Hamilton and the Development of American Law.*

88. Thus, the long-standing obsession with discovering the Founders' original interpretive intent must be fundamentally rethought. For leading examples, see McGinnis and Rappaport, *Originalism and the Good Constitution,* ch. 7; Powell, "Original Understanding of Original Intent"; Raoul Berger, "'Original Intention' in Historical Perspective," *George Washington Law Review* 54 (Jan. and Mar. 1986), 296–337; Lofgren, "Original Understanding of Original Intent?"; Leonard W. Levy, *Original Intent and the Framers' Constitution* (New York: MacMillan, 1988); Clinton, *God and Man in the Law,* 111–113, 116–117; Natelson, "Founders' Hermeneutic"; McDowell, *Language of Law,* 50–51, and generally chs. 6–7. For a compelling critique of this tendency, see Saul Cornell, "Meaning and Understanding in the History of Constitutional Ideas," *Fordham Law Review* 82 (Nov. 2013), 733–740. For alternative takes more appreciative of the dynamism of early interpretive modes, see Jack N. Rakove, "The Original Intent of Original Understanding," *Constitutional Commentary* 13 (Fall 1996), 159–186; Nelson, "Originalism and Interpretive Conventions"; Kurt T. Lash, "Originalism All the Way Down?" *Constitutional Commentary* 30 (Winter 2015), 154–165.

3. The Unfinished Constitution

Epigraph: Samuel Johnston to James Madison, July 8, 1789, *PJM,* 12:285.

1. James Madison to Tench Coxe, June 24, 1789, *PJM,* 12:257; Thomas FitzSimons to Benjamin Rush, June 20, 1789, *DHFFC,* 16:819; Benjamin Goodhue to Samuel Phillips Jr., June 21, 1789, *DHFFC,* 16:826; Fisher Ames to George Richards Minot, June 23, 1789, *DHFFC,* 16:840; George Clymer to Rush, June 18, 1789, *DHFFC,* 16:804.

2. Epes Sargent to Goodhue, Mar. 23, 1789, *DHFFC,* 15:97; George Thatcher to Benjamin Brown, June 12, 1789, *DHFFC,* 16:763; Comte de Moustier to Comte de Montmorin, June 9, 1789, *DHFFC,* 16:730; William Loughton Smith to Edward Rutledge, June 21, 1789, *DHFFC,* 16:832; Richard Bland Lee, June 18, 1789, *DHFFC,* 11:962. On the situation's urgency and the lack of progress, also see Reverend James Madison to Madison, Mar. 1, 1789, *PJM,* 11:454; Abraham Baldwin to Joel Barlow, June 14, 1789, *DHFFC,* 16:774. On the question's importance, also see Madison, June 17, 1789, *DHFFC,* 11:921; Ames to Minot, June 23, 1789, *DHFFC,* 16:841; Lee to Leven Powell, June 27, 1789, *DHFFC,* 16:866. On the challenges faced by the First Congress, see *DHFFC,* vii–viii; Fergus M. Bordewich, *The First Congress: How James Madison, George Washington, and a Group of Extraordinary Men Invented the Government* (New York: Simon and Schuster, 2016), 3–9, 12–13.

3. Lee to Powell, June 27, 1789, *DHFFC*, 16:866; Madison, May 19, 1789, *DHFFC*, 10:725; United States Constitution, Article II, Section 4. For Boudinot's introduction and Smith's reaction, see May 19, 1789, *DHFFC*, 10:722–723, 726–727. For the power to appoint executive officers, with the advice and consent of the Senate, see United States Constitution, Article II, Section 2. For Madison's formal resolution, see *DHFFC*, 4:693–694.

4. Egbert Benson, June 22, 1789, *DHFFC*, 11:1028. For the debate's conclusion, see, *DHFFC*, 1:83–87.

5. Thomas Scott, June 18, 1789, *DHFFC*, 11:972; Madison, June 17, 1789, *DHFFC*, 11:921. Historians have offered some brief portrayals of the debate; see Jack N. Rakove, *Original Meanings: Politics and Ideas in the Making of the Constitution* (New York: Knopf, 1996), 347–350; Charlene Bangs Bickford and Kenneth R. Bowling, *Birth of the Nation: The First Federal Congress, 1789–1791* (Madison: Madison House, 1989), 37–43; Thornton Anderson, *Creating the Constitution: The Convention of 1787 and the First Congress* (University Park: Pennsylvania State University Press, 1993), 185–190. On specifically Madison's relationship to the debate, see Lance Banning, *The Sacred Fire of Liberty: James Madison and the Founding of the Federal Republic* (Ithaca, NY: Cornell University Press, 1995), 276–279; Mary Sarah Bilder, *Madison's Hand: Revising the Constitutional Convention* (Cambridge, MA: Harvard University Press, 2015), 172–174. That said, constitutional lawyers and political scientists have been the primary students of this debate—what is often called the "Decision of 1789"—and, by and large, their focus has been on what it revealed about the scope of presidential power and, relatedly, the separation of powers; see Charles C. Thach, *The Creation of the Presidency, 1775–1789* (Baltimore: Johns Hopkins University Press, 1922), ch. 6; Edward S. Corwin, *The President's Removal Power under the Constitution* (New York: National Municipal League, 1927), 10–23; James Hart, *The American Presidency in Action, 1789: A Study in Constitutional History* (New York: Macmillan, 1948), 155–214; Leonard D. White, *The Federalists: A Study in Administrative History* (New York: Macmillan 1948), 20–25; Louis Fisher, *Constitutional Conflicts between Congress and the President,* 6th ed. rev. (1978; Lawrence: University Press of Kansas, 2014), 57–62; Lawrence Lessig and Cass R. Sunstein, "The President and the Administration," *Columbia Law Review* 94 (Jan. 1994), 22–27; Steven G. Calabresi and Saikrishna B. Prakash, "The President's Power to Execute the Laws," *Yale Law Journal* 104 (Dec. 1994), 642–645; Gerhard Casper, *Separating Power: Essays on the Founding Period* (Cambridge, MA: Harvard University Press, 1997), 35–40; David P. Currie, *The Constitution in Congress: The Federalist Period, 1789–1801* (Chicago: University of Chicago Press, 1997), 36–41; Curtis A. Bradley and Martin S. Flaherty, "Executive Power Essentialism and Foreign Affairs," *Michigan Law Review* 102 (Feb. 2004), 656–664; Saikrishna Prakash, "New Light on the Decision of 1789," *Cornell Law Review* 91 (July 2006), 1021–1078; Saikrishna Prakash, "Removal and Tenure in Office," *Virginia Law Review* 92 (Dec. 2006), 1815–1830, 1837–1840; Steven G. Calabresi and Christopher S. Yoo, *The Unitary Executive: Presidential Power from Washington to Bush* (New Haven, CT: Yale University Press, 2008),

35–36; Akhil Reed Amar, *America's Unwritten Constitution: The Precedents and Principles We Live By* (New York: Basic Books, 2012), 319–324; J. David Alvis, Jeremy D. Bailey, and F. Flagg Taylor IV, *The Contested Removal Power, 1789–2010* (Lawrence: University Press of Kansas, 2013), ch. 1; Saikrishna Bangalore Prakash, *Imperial from the Beginning: The Constitution of the Original Executive* (New Haven, CT: Yale University Press, 2015), 195–197; Jeremy D. Bailey, *James Madison and Constitutional Imperfection* (New York: Cambridge University Press, 2015), 61–69. Some have pushed beyond issues of executive power and productively explored how the debate turned on questions of implied powers; see Joseph M. Lynch, *Negotiating the Constitution: The Earliest Debates over Original Intent* (Ithaca, NY: Cornell University Press, 1999), 54–65; or constitutional interpretation more generally, see Kent Greenfield, "Original Penumbras: Constitutional Interpretation in the First Year of Congress," *Connecticut Law Review* 26 (Fall 1993), 82–107.

6. Comte de Moustier to Comte de Montmorin, Apr. 7, 1789, *DHFFC,* 15:219; Madison to Samuel Johnston, June 21, 1789, *PJM,* 12:250.

7. Elbridge Gerry, June 17, 1789, *DHFFC,* 11:928. For overviews of the debate from participants, see Madison to Edmund Randolph, June 21, 1789, *PJM,* 12:251–253; Ames to Minot, June 23, 1789, *DHFFC,* 16:840–841. For thorough overviews from scholars, see Hart, *American Presidency in Action,* 155–184; Greenfield, "Original Penumbras," 82–107; Prakash, "New Light on the Decision of 1789," 1034–1042; Alvis, Bailey, and Taylor, *Contested Removal Power,* ch. 1. Given the focus here, these variations are less vital than the assumptions that underlay them.

8. Theodore Sedgwick, June 18, 1789, *DHFFC,* 11:959; John Vining, June 19, 1789, *DHFFC,* 11:1019.

9. Madison to Randolph, May 31, 1789, *PJM,* 12:190. Also see Jeremiah Hill to Thatcher, Mar. 4, 1789, *DHFFC,* 15:11. On legislative continuities, see Donald S. Lutz, "The Colonial and Early State Legislative Process," in *Inventing Congress: Origins and Establishment of the First Federal Congress,* ed. Kenneth R. Bowling and Donald R. Kennon (Athens: University of Ohio Press, 1999), 49–75; R. B. Bernstein, "Parliamentary Principles, American Realities: The Continental and Confederation Congresses, 1774–1789," in Bowling and Kennon, *Inventing Congress,* 76–105. On the Confederation Congress generally, see Jack N. Rakove, *The Beginnings of National Politics: An Interpretive History of the Continental Congress* (New York: Knopf, 1979). On the novelty of the new Congress, see *DHFFC,* 1:vii–viii; Charlene Bangs Bickford, "'Public Attention Is Very Much Fixed on the Proceedings of the New Congress': The First Federal Congress Organizes Itself," in Bowling and Kennon, *Inventing Congress,* 138–165. On its undecided character, see Joanne B. Freeman, *Affairs of Honor: National Politics in the Early Republic* (New Haven, CT: Yale University Press, 2001), 1–10.

10. Robert Morris to Gouverneur Morris, Mar. 4, 1789, *DHFFC,* 15:11; Ezra Ripley to Thatcher, Mar. 30, 1789, *DHFFC,* 15:161; William Pickman to Goodhue, Mar. 3, 1789, *DHFFC,* 15:9.

11. James Kent to Elizabeth Hamilton, Dec. 2, 1832, as quoted in *DHFFC*, 10:xvii. On the House's publicity and the Anglo-American background that laid the groundwork, see *DHFFC*, 10:xi–xxiii; Jack N. Rakove, "The Structure of Politics at the Accession of George Washington," in *Beyond Confederation: Origins of the Constitution and American National Identity*, ed. Richard Beeman, Stephen Botein, and Edward C. Carter II (Chapel Hill: University of North Carolina Press, 1987), 290–294; Eric Slauter, *The State as a Work of Art: The Cultural Origins of the Constitution* (Chicago: University of Chicago Press, 2009), 23–24, 124–127; Mary Sarah Bilder, "How Bad Were the Official Records of the Federal Convention?" *George Washington Law Review* 80 (Nov. 2012), 1636–1640. On the secrecy of eighteenth-century politics, see Gordon S. Wood, "The Founders and Public Opinion," in *Revolutionary Characters: What Made the Founders Different* (New York: Penguin Press, 2006), 244–274. On the documentary record of the Senate's earliest debates—which mostly consist of William Maclay's famous journal—see *DHFFC*, 9:xi–xviii.

12. William Maclay to Rush, *DHFFC*, 15:78; Oliver Ellsworth to Abigail Ellsworth, Mar. 8, 1789, *DHFFC*, 15:42. Also see *New York Daily Gazette*, Mar. 6, 1789, *DHFFC*, 15:33; Alexander White to Mary Wood, Mar. 8, 1789, *DHFFC*, 15:46; William Paterson to Euphemia Paterson, Mar. 24, 1789, *DHFFC*, 15:109; Ames to William Tudor, Apr. 1, 1789, *DHFFC*, 15:180; George Partridge to Samuel Holten, May 20, 1789, *DHFFC*, 15:600. On Federal Hall, see *DHFFC*, 15:26–35; Bordewich, *First Congress*, 25–26.

13. Ames to Minot, May 27, 1789, *DHFFC*, 15:636; Ames to Tudor, Apr. 25, 1789, *DHFFC*, 15:351; Madison to Randolph, Mar. 1, 1789, *PJM*, 11:453. For other disdainful views, see Baldwin to Barlow, Mar. 1, 1789, *DHFFC*, 15:1; Rush to John Adams, Mar. 19, 1789, *DHFFC*, 15:79–80; Comte de Moustier to Comte de Montmorin, Mar. 20, 1789, *DHFFC*, 15:84. For optimistic takes, see Sargent to Goodhue, May 11, 1789, *DHFFC*, 15:516; Tudor to Adams, May 18, 1789, *DHFFC*, 15:589. On the generally impressive makeup of the First Congress, see Rakove, "Structure of Politics at the Accession of George Washington," 276–277. For a more pessimistic assessment, see James Roger Sharp, *American Politics in the Early Republic: The New Nation in Crisis* (New Haven, CT: Yale University Press, 1993), 31–32. On Ames's talents, see Winfred Bernhard, *Fisher Ames: Federalist and Statesman, 1758–1808* (Chapel Hill: University of North Carolina Press, 1965), 25–30, 37–46, 58–70, 92–93.

14. Ames to Thomas Dwight, June 11, 1789, *DHFFC*, 16:748; Ames to Minot, July 8, 1789, *DHFFC*, 16:978; Ames to Dwight, Jan. 2, 1791, *DHFFC*, 21:295; Goodhue to Cotton Tufts, July 20, 1789, *DHFFC*, 16:1084. On the character of the proceedings, see Gordon S. Wood, *Empire of Liberty: A History of the Early Republic, 1789–1815* (New York: Oxford University Press, 2009), 60–61.

15. Madison to Thomas Jefferson, May 27, 1789, *PJM*, 12:186. Complimenting Congress's proceedings, also see Madison to Randolph, May 31, 1789, *PJM*, 12:189; Lee

to Powell, Apr. 13, 1789, *DHFFC*, 15:259; Lee to David Stuart, June 4, 1789, *DHFFC*, 16:698.

16. W. Smith, May 19, 1789, 10:727; Elias Boudinot, May 19, 1789, *DHFFC*, 10:730; Vining, June 16, 1789, *DHFFC*, 11:870; Sedgwick, June 16 and 22, 1789, *DHFFC*, 11:865, 1035; Madison, June 17 and 18, 1789, *DHFFC*, 11:922, 988; Theodorick Bland, May 19, 1789, *DHFFC*, 10:737; Ames, June 18, 1789, *DHFFC*, 11:978. Also see Vining, May 19, 1789, *DHFFC*, 10:728; Madison, May 19, 1789, *DHFFC*, 10:727, 734–735; Ames, June 16 and 18, 1789, *DHFFC*, 11:880, 980–981; Thomas Hartley, June 17, 1789, *DHFFC*, 11:905; Benson, June 17, 1789, *DHFFC*, 11:931. In the eighteenth century, when it came to "good behavior" tenure, it was not necessarily presupposed that impeachment was the implicit remedy for misbehavior; see Saikrishna Prakash and Steven D. Smith, "How to Remove a Federal Judge," *Yale Law Journal* 116 (Oct. 2006), 88–121; although in Revolutionary America some were beginning to link this tenure with this remedy, yet this reasoning usually applied to judges, not executive officers; see 109–110, 114–121. Perhaps for this reason, during the removal debate most disputants assumed a tight connection between good behavior and impeachment; see for instance Benson, May 19, 1789, *DHFFC*, 10:728; W. Smith, May 19, 1789, *DHFFC*, 10:732.

17. W. Smith, June 16, 17, and 18, 1789, *DHFFC*, 11:878, 934, 876, 985–986; Gerry, June 16, 1789, *DHFFC*, 11:878. Also see White, June 18, 1789, *DHFFC*, 11:954. For Smith's engagement with practical arguments, see *DHFFC*, 11:876–877.

18. On Smith's political background, see *DHFFC*, 14:845–852; on Smith more generally, see George C. Rogers Jr., *Evolution of a Federalist: William Loughton Smith of Charleston (1758–1812)* (Columbia: University of South Carolina Press, 1962).

19. W. Smith, June 16, 1789, *DHFFC*, 11:863; Madison, June 16, 1789, *DHFFC*, 11:866, 867; Boudinot, June 18, 1789, *DHFFC*, 11:965. Also see Ames, June 18, 1789, *DHFFC*, 11:979; Peter Silvester, June 19, 1789, *DHFFC*, 11:1010.

20. W. Smith, June 16, 1789, *DHFFC*, 11:861–862, 877; Benjamin Huntington, June 16, 1789, *DHFFC*, 11:864. Several years later, Smith admitted that he had been wrong about removal; see W. Smith to James McHenry, Oct. 1797, in Bernard C. Steiner, "Correspondence of William Smith, American Minister to Portugal," *Sewanee Review* 14 (Jan. 1906), 87.

21. Huntington, June 16, 1789, *DHFFC*, 11:864.

22. John Laurance, June 17, 1789, *DHFFC*, 11:908; Madison, June 18, 1789, *DHFFC*, 11:988. Also see Benson, May 19, 1789, *DHFFC*, 10:728; Madison, June 16, 1789, *DHFFC*, 11:869; Hartley, June 17, 1789, *DHFFC*, 11:905; Ames, June 18, 1789, *DHFFC*, 11:978.

23. Baldwin, June 19, 1789, *DHFFC*, 11:1006; Benson, June 17, 1789, *DHFFC*, 11:932.

24. Madison, June 16, 1789, *DHFFC*, 11:866.

25. Vining, June 19, 1789, *DHFFC*, 11:1021; Boudinot, May 19, 1789, *DHFFC*, 10:730–731; Benson, June 17, 1789, *DHFFC*, 11:932; Baldwin, June 19, 1789, *DHFFC*, 11:1007. On Baldwin's speaking temperament, see *DHFFC*, 14:553.

26. Hartley, June 17, 1789, *DHFFC*, 11:906; Ames, June 16, 1789, *DHFFC*, 11:882, 884; Laurance, June 17, 1789, *DHFFC*, 11:909; Madison, June 16, 1789, *DHFFC*, 11:867–868. Also see Silvester, May 19, 1789, *DHFFC*, 10:733; Madison, June 22, 1789, *DHFFC*, 11:1031.

27. W. Smith, June 17, 1789, *DHFFC*, 11:937; Madison, May 19, 1789, *DHFFC*, 10:735; Publius [Madison], "The Federalist 37," New York *Daily Advertiser,* Jan. 11, 1788, *DHRC*, 15:346; Laurance, June 17, 1789, *DHFFC*, 11:907; Madison, June 16, 1789, *DHFFC*, 11:866; Ames, June 18, 1789, *DHFFC*, 11:979. Also see Hartley, June 17, 1789, *DHFFC*, 11:906; Vining, June 17 and 19, 1789, *DHFFC*, 11:939, 1021; Baldwin, June 19, 1789, *DHFFC*, 11:1005; Silvester, June 19, 1789, *DHFFC*, 11:1008.

28. Benson, May 19, 1789, *DHFFC*, 10:728; Ames, June 16 and 18, 1789, *DHFFC*, 11:880, 979; Laurance, June 17, 1789, *DHFFC*, 11:910.

29. Hartley, June 17, 1789, *DHFFC*, 11:906; Lee, June 18, 1789, *DHFFC*, 11:963; Silvester, June 19, 1789, *DHFFC*, 11:1009. Also see Vining, June 17, 1789, *DHFFC*, 11:939.

30. Laurance, June 17, 1789, *DHFFC*, 11:909; Boudinot, June 18, 1789, *DHFFC*, 11:965.

31. W. Smith, June 16, 1789, *DHFFC*, 11:864, 876; Gerry, June 19, 1789, *DHFFC*, 11:1022; Madison, June 17 and 18, 1789, *DHFFC*, 11:926–927, 987. Also see White, June 16 and 18, 1789, *DHFFC*, 11:872, 873, 957; John Page, June 18, 1789, *DHFFC*, 11:991; Baldwin, June 19, 1789, *DHFFC*, 11:1007–1008.

32. Madison, June 17, 1789, *DHFFC*, 11:926.

33. Madison, June 17 and 18, 1789, *DHFFC*, 11:926–927, 987.

34. Madison, June 17 and 18, 1789, *DHFFC*, 11:926–927, 987.

35. White, June 18, 1789, *DHFFC*, 11:951; James Jackson, June 19, 1789, *DHFFC*, 11:999; Scott, June 18, 1789, *DHFFC*, 11:971. Also see Gerry, June 16, 1789, *DHFFC*, 11:879. For Jackson's angry response to Scott's mockery, see June 18, 1789, *DHFFC*, 11:974. On Jackson's political background, see *DHFFC*, 14:555–559; and on his temperament in Congress, see *DHFFC*, 14:557.

36. Jackson, May 19 and June 19, 1789, *DHFFC*, 10:729, 11:1003; White, June 16, 1789, *DHFFC*, 11:872; *DHFFC*, 14:929; Page, June 22, 1789, *DHFFC*, 11:1031; Roger Sherman, June 18, 1789, *DHFFC*, 11:978. Also see Michael Jenifer Stone, June 19, 1789, *DHFFC*, 11:1011; Gerry, June 19, 1789, *DHFFC*, 11:1021. On White's ideological commitments, see *DHFFC*, 14:928–931.

37. White, June 18, 1789, *DHFFC*, 11:957, 953; Vining, June 19, 1789, *DHFFC*, 11:1017. Also see Gerry, June 17 and 19, 1789, *DHFFC*, 11:927–928, 1021–1022; Page, June 18, 1789, *DHFFC*, 11:989.

38. Gerry, June 18, 1789, *DHFFC*, 11:976; Jackson, June 18, 1789, *DHFFC*, 11:969; W. Smith, June 17, 1789, *DHFFC*, 11:934, emphasis mine; William Samuel Johnson, July 14, 1789, "Notes of William Samuel Johnson," *DHFFC*, 9:466; William Paterson, July 16, 1789, "Notes of William Paterson," *DHFFC*, 9:488.

39. Gerry, June 17, 1789, *DHFFC*, 11:930. Also see White, June 18, 1789, *DHFFC*, 11:953–954; Stone, June 19, 1789, *DHFFC*, 11:1010–1011.

40. Gerry, June 17, 1789, *DHFFC*, 11:929, 931; W. Smith, June 17, 1789, *DHFFC*, 11:935; Jackson, June 19, 1789, *DHFFC*, 11:1001; Gerry, June 19, 1789, *DHFFC*, 11:1022. Also see Thomas Sumter, June 24, 1789, *DHFFC*, 11:1043.

41. Jackson, June 18, 1789, *DHFFC*, 11:969–970; Gerry, June 17, 1789, *DHFFC*, 11:930–931; Samuel Livermore, June 18, 1789, *DHFFC*, 11:983.

42. Baldwin, June 19, 1789, *DHFFC*, 11:1003, emphasis mine; Silvester, June 19, 1789, *DHFFC*, 11:1008. Also see Vining, June 17, 1789, *DHFFC*, 11:939. For Gerry's response to Baldwin, see June 19, 1789, *DHFFC*, 11:1021–1022.

43. Ames, June 16, 1789, *DHFFC*, 11:882; Hartley, June 17, 1789, *DHFFC*, 11:907. Also see Laurance, May 19, 1789, *DHFFC*, 10:733; Sedgwick, June 18, 1789, *DHFFC*, 11:961, 983.

44. Madison, June 17 and 22, 1789, *DHFFC*, 11:1032, 923, 925; Benson, June 17, 1789, *DHFFC*, 11:931; Baldwin, June 19, 1789, *DHFFC*, 11:1005; Ames, June 18, 1789, *DHFFC*, 11:981–982. Also see Vining, May 19 and June 17, 1789, *DHFFC*, 10:739, 11:938; Sedgwick, June 16, 1789, *DHFFC*, 11:865–866; Boudinot, June 16 and 18, 1789, *DHFFC*, 11:873, 874, 967–968; Hartley, June 17, 1789, *DHFFC*, 11:905; Lee, June 18, 1789, *DHFFC*, 11:963–964; Goodhue, June 18, 1789, *DHFFC*, 11:973.

45. Goodhue, June 18, 1789, *DHFFC*, 11:973; Vining, June 19, 1789, *DHFFC*, 11:1017 and 1017–1020; Ames, June 18, 1789, *DHFFC*, 11:982; Goodhue, May 19, 1789, *DHFFC*, 10:734; Madison, June 17, 1789, *DHFFC*, 11:925–926. Also see Madison, May 19, 1789, *DHFFC*, 10:727, 735; Vining, June 16, 1789, *DHFFC*, 11:870; Boudinot, June 16, 1789, *DHFFC*, 11:875; Ames, June 16 and 18, 1789, *DHFFC*, 11:880, 979; Clymer, June 17, 1789, *DHFFC*, 11:915; Lee, June 18, 1789, *DHFFC*, 11:964; Scott, June 18, 1789, *DHFFC*, 11:972. On Madison's particular investment in executive responsibility, see Bailey, *James Madison and Constitutional Imperfection*, 61–69. On how a commitment to energy and responsibility informed the creation of the American presidency at the Constitutional Convention, see Rakove, *Original Meanings*, ch. 9; Michael J. Klarman, *The Framers' Coup: The Making of the United States Constitution* (New York: Oxford University Press, 2016), 213–238. On how attachment to an energetic executive with powerful prerogative powers had long been a commitment of many American constitutional reformers, see Eric Nelson, *The Royalist Revolution: Monarchy and the American Founding* (Cambridge, MA: Harvard University Press, 2014), esp. chs. 3–5.

46. Silvester, May 19, 1789, *DHFFC*, 10:734; Jackson, June 17, 1789, *DHFFC*, 11:913, and generally 912–914; Page, June 17 and 18, 1789, *DHFFC*, 11:917, 990–991, 959, and generally 989–992. Also see Livermore, June 16, 1789, *DHFFC*, 11:884–885; White, June 18, 1789, *DHFFC*, 11:955; Jackson, June 18 and 19, 1789, *DHFFC*, 11:970, 1000–1002; Page, June 22, 1789, *DHFFC*, 11:1031. On fears of executive power in Revolutionary America, see Bernard Bailyn, *The Origins of American Politics* (New York: Knopf,

1968), esp. 71–91, 136–139; Ralph Ketcham, *Presidents Above Party: The First American Presidency, 1789–1829* (Chapel Hill: University of North Carolina Press, 1984), ch. 4. On how the state constitutions reflected this anxiety, see Gordon S. Wood, *The Creation of the American Republic, 1776–1787*, 2nd ed. (1969; Chapel Hill: University of North Carolina Press, 1998), 132–143. On Anti-Federalists' concerns about presidential power, see Nelson, *Royalist Revolution*, 203–226. On how monarchism and its discontents played a crucial role at the dawn of the new republic, see Gordon S. Wood, *Empire of Liberty: A History of the Early Republic, 1789–1815* (New York: Oxford University Press, 2009), ch. 2. On Page's ideology and penchant for poetry, see *DHFFC*, 14:920–922.

47. Jackson, May 19, 1789, *DHFFC*, 10:729; Page, June 18, 1789, *DHFFC*, 11:992; Jackson, June 19, 1789, *DHFFC*, 11:1001–1002. Also see Gerry, May 19, 1789, *DHFFC*, 10:736; White, June 18, 1789, *DHFFC*, 11:955. For a conscious acknowledgment of the issue's uncertainty from somebody who otherwise displayed confidence, see Page, June 22, 1789, *DHFFC*, 11:1030–1031.

48. White, June 16, 1789, *DHFFC*, 11:872; Sherman, June 17, 1789, *DHFFC*, 11:917. Also see Jackson, May 19, 1789, *DHFFC*, 11:729; Livermore, May 19 and June 18, 1789, *DHFFC*, 10:736–737, 11:984–985; White, June 16, 1789, *DHFFC*, 11:860.

49. Livermore, June 18, 1789, *DHFFC*, 11:984–985; Bland, May 19, 1789, *DHFFC*, 10:729; Stone, June 17, 1789, *DHFFC*, 11:918; Gerry, June 19, 1789, *DHFFC*, 11:1022. Also see Stone, June 19, 1789, *DHFFC*, 11:1014–1015; Maclay, July 14, 1789, "The Diary of William Maclay," *DHFFC*, 9:110; William Grayson, July 16, 1789, "Notes of William Paterson," *DHFFC*, 9:487. On how the Constitution would need to be amended if, indeed, it was so problematic that presidential and senatorial power was blended, see Jackson, June 17, 1789, *DHFFC*, 11:912.

50. Vining, May 19, 1789, *DHFFC*, 10:728; Laurance, June 17, 1789, *DHFFC*, 11:909; Ames, June 18, 1789, *DHFFC*, 11:978; Boudinot, June 18, 1789, *DHFFC*, 11:966. Also see Madison, May 19, 1789, *DHFFC*, 10:735.

51. Baldwin, June 19, 1789, *DHFFC*, 11:1004; Hartley, June 17, 1789, *DHFFC*, 11:905; "The Diary of William Maclay," May 9, 1790, *DHFFC*, 9:263; Clymer, May 19 and June 17, 1789, *DHFFC*, 10:738, 11:915; Madison, June 17 and 22, 1789, *DHFFC*, 11:922, 1032; William Paterson, July 16, 1789, "Notes of William Paterson," *DHFFC*, 9:489; Silvester, June 19, 1789, *DHFFC*, 11:1008; Vining, June 17, 1789, *DHFFC*, 11:938. Also see Sedgwick, June 16 and 18, 1789, *DHFFC*, 11:866, 960; Madison, June 16, 1789, *DHFFC*, 11:869; Ames, June 16, 1789, *DHFFC*, 11:880; Boudinot, June 18, 1789, *DHFFC*, 11:966–967; Ellsworth, July 15, 1789, "Notes of John Adams," *DHFFC*, 9:445; George Read, July 16, 1789, "Notes of John Adams," *DHFFC*, 9:448. On Clymer's speaking style, see *DHFFC*, 14:775–776.

52. Madison, June 16, 17, and 22, 1789, *DHFFC*, 11:866, 922, 1032. Many denied the Senate had legitimate appointment power, rather than mere advisory power; see Clymer, May 19, 1789, *DHFFC*, 10:738; Vining, June 16, 1789, *DHFFC*, 11:869–870;

Ames, June 16 and 18, 1789, *DHFFC*, 11:881, 979–980; Laurance, June 17, 1789, *DHFFC*, 11:908; Benson, June 17, 1789, *DHFFC*, 11:932–933; Silvester, June 19, 1789, *DHFFC*, 11:1008–1009.

53. Madison, May 19, June 16, 17, and 18, 1789, *DHFFC*, 11:727, 927, 986, 867, 868.

54. For some of these arguments, see White, May 19, 1789, *DHFFC*, 10:738–739; Gerry, June 16, 17, and 19, 1789, *DHFFC*, 11:878, 930, 1023–1024; Jackson, June 17, 1789, *DHFFC*, 11:912; Stone, June 17 and 19, 1789, *DHFFC*, 11:920, 1012; Sherman, June 18, 1789, *DHFFC*, 11:977; Page, June 18, 1789, *DHFFC*, 11:992.

55. Madison, June 22, 1789, *DHFFC*, 11:1032. For other accounts that have drawn attention to this feature of the debate, albeit with much different focuses in mind, see Rakove, *Original Meanings*, 347–351; Leonard W. Levy, *Original Intent and the Framers' Constitution* (New York: MacMillan, 1988), 5–6; Greenfield, "Original Penumbras," 97–102; Louis J. Sirico Jr., "Original Intent in the First Congress," *Missouri Law Review* 71 (Summer 2006), 695–696, 698–699, 704–705, 710–711, 716–717; Robert G. Natelson, "The Founders' Hermeneutic: The Real Understanding of Original Intent," *Ohio State Law Journal* 68 (2007), 1300–1303.

56. W. Smith, June 17 and 16, 1789, *DHFFC*, 11:937, 861; also see 935; Publius [Alexander Hamilton], "The Federalist 77," *New York Independent Journal*, Apr. 2, 1788, *DHRC*, 17:8; W. Smith to Rutledge, June 21, 1789, *DHFFC*, 16:832–833. Also see White, June 18, 1789, *DHFFC*, 11:970. On rumors about the *Federalist*'s authorship, see *DHRC*, 12:488–490. On the limited circulation of the *Federalist* during the ratification debates, see Pauline Maier, *Ratification: The People Debate the Constitution, 1787–1788* (New York: Simon and Schuster, 2010), 84–85; Trish Loughran, *The Republic in Print: Print Culture in the Age of U.S. Nation Building, 1770–1870* (New York: Columbia University Press 2007), 112–121; Elaine F. Crane, "Publius in the Provinces: Where Was *The Federalist* Printed outside New York City?" *WMQ* 21 (Oct. 1964), 589–592.

57. W. Smith, June 17 and 16, 1789, *DHFFC*, 11:937; 877; Lee, June 18, 1789, *DHFFC*, 11:964; Jackson, June 18, 1789, *DHFFC*, 11:969; Page, June 18, 1789, *DHFFC*, 11:957. Also see White, June 18, 1789, *DHFFC*, 11:956. Many referenced a more general intent too; see Boudinot, May 19, 1789, *DHFFC*, 10:731; Gerry, June 16, 1789, *DHFFC*, 11:879; Madison, June 16 and 17, 1789, *DHFFC*, 11:867, 921; Sherman, June 18, 1789, *DHFFC*, 11:977; Vining, June 19, 1789, *DHFFC*, 11:1017. William Loughton Smith was among the few during the debate who explicitly invoked the state constitutions. He was right that, generally speaking, few state governors explicitly enjoyed the power to remove executive officers. To an extent this was because these constitutions identified few executive officers to begin with, partly because most constitutions created councils of state to advise the state's executive. To an even greater extent, though, state governors lacked this power because, fueled by anti-monarchical sentiment, most state constitution makers stripped executives of most meaningful prerogative powers. Accordingly, where state officers—judicial officers, council members, and other civil

officers—did not serve under good behavior, they were controlled by the legislature. Only Maryland's constitution explicitly alluded to an executive power to remove "civil officers of government" who did not otherwise serve on good behavior, see Maryland Constitution of 1776, Article XLVIII. On how early state constitutions stripped state executives of traditional prerogative powers, see Wood, *Creation of the American Republic*, 132–143. On Richard Bland Lee's inexperience, see *DHFFC*, 14:902–903.

58. Baldwin, June 19, 1789, *DHFFC*, 11:1003–1004; Madison, May 19, 1789, *DHFFC*, 10:735–736. Also see Boudinot, June 18, 1789, *DHFFC*, 11:966.

59. Jackson, June 19, 1789, *DHFFC*, 11:1002–1003.

60. White, June 18, 1789, *DHFFC*, 11:952–953; Stone, June 19, 1789, *DHFFC*, 11:1014–1015. Also see W. Smith, June 18, 1789, *DHFFC*, 11:985.

61. W. Smith, June 16 and 18, 1789, *DHFFC*, 11:876, 861, 986, and generally 863–864. Also see Sherman, June 18 and 19, 1789, *DHFFC*, 11:977, 1024.

62. Jackson, June 18, 1789, *DHFFC*, 11:969. For the proposed amendments, see June 22, 1789, *DHFFC*, 11:1028. On Benson in Congress, see *DHFFC*, 14:711–712; and on his quiet parliamentary skill, see John D. Gordan III, "Egbert Benson: A Nationalist in Congress, 1789–1793," in *Neither Separate nor Equal: Congress in the 1790s*, ed. Kenneth R. Bowling and Donald R. Kennon (Athens: Ohio University Press, 2000), 68–90.

63. W. Smith, June 22, 1789, *DHFFC*, 11:1029; Page, June 22, 1789, *DHFFC*, 11:1030–1031; Gerry, June 22, 1789, *DHFFC*, 11:1033; Vining, June 22, 1789, *DHFFC*, 11:1035–1036. Also see Thomas Tudor Tucker, June 22, 1789, *DHFFC*, 11:1034–1035; Andrew Moore, June 22, 1789, *DHFFC*, 11:1033.

64. Madison, June 22, 1789, *DHFFC*, 11:1031–1032; Sedgwick, June 22, 1789, *DHFFC*, 11:1030; Hartley, June 22, 1789, *DHFFC*, 11:1035; Boudinot, June 22, 1789, *DHFFC*, 11:1034. Also see Ames, June 18, 1789, *DHFFC*, 11:883–884; Clymer, June 17, 1789, *DHFFC*, 11:915; Baldwin, June 19, 1789, *DHFFC*, 11:1007; Page, June 22, 1789, *DHFFC*, 11:1028; Laurance, June 22, 1789, *DHFFC*, 11:1034.

65. The first amendment passed 30–18 and the second 31–19. For the decidedly different majorities that passed each, see *DHFFC*, 3:92–93. The final vote on June 24 was 29–22; see *DHFFC*, 3:95. For the final bill, see *DHFFC*, 4:689–690.

66. Capturing the attention that has been lavished on the so-called "Decision of 1789," the late Supreme Court justice Antonin Scalia once wrote, "it might well take thirty years and 7,000 pages" to decipher the original meaning of presidential removal power; see "Originalism: The Lesser Evil," *University of Cincinnati Law Review* 57 (1989), 852. In the decades immediately following the decision, several contemporaries concluded that the president enjoyed the power by virtue of the Constitution alone; see [Alexander Hamilton], "Pacificus," No. 1, June 29, 1793, *PAH*, 15:33–43; John Marshall, *The Life of George Washington*, 5 vols. (Philadelphia: C. P. Wayne, 1804–1807), 5:196–200. Over a century later, Chief Justice of the Supreme Court William Howard Taft reached the same conclusion; see *Myers v. United States*, 272 U.S. 52 (1926), 115, 161. But in that

same case, Justice Louis Brandeis dissented, arguing that no congressional majority in 1789 had recognized that the Constitution bestowed the power (*Myers v. United States,* 285). Subsequent legal scholars have divided along these lines. Many have echoed Brandeis's claim; see Corwin, *President's Removal Power,* 12–24; Hart, *American Presidency in Action,* 201–214; Lessig and Sunstein, "President and the Administration," 22–27; Currie, *Constitution in Congress,* 40–41; Lynch, *Negotiating the Constitution,* 248–249n61; Bradley and Flaherty, "Executive Power Essentialism and Foreign Affairs," 658–664; John F. Manning, "Separation of Powers as Ordinary Interpretation," *Harvard Law Review* 124 (June 2011), 2030–2031. Others have forcefully argued the opposite; see Prakash, "New Light on the Decision of 1789"; Calabresi and Yoo, *Unitary Executive,* 35; Prakash, *Imperial from the Beginning,* 195–197; and, more tentatively advancing this conclusion, Alvis, Bailey, and Taylor, *Contested Removal Power,* 115–122.

67. Madison to Edmund Pendleton, June 21, 1789, *PJM,* 12:252–253; Madison to Johnston, June 21, 1789, *PJM,* 12:250, emphasis mine; Madison to Jefferson, June 30, 1789, *PJM,* 12:271, emphasis mine. Also see Madison to Randolph, May 31, 1789, *PJM,* 12:190; Madison to Coxe, June 24, 1789, *PJM,* 12:257.

68. Madison, June 17 and 18, 1789, *DHFFC,* 11:921, 987.

4. The Sacred Text

Epigraph: Edmund Randolph, Virginia Ratifying Convention, June 9, 1788, *DHRC,* 9:1085.

1. Thomas Sinnickson, Aug. 15, 1789, *DHFFC,* 11:1279. The literature is voluminous, but see especially Akhil Reed Amar, *The Bill of Rights: Creation and Reconstruction* (New Haven, CT: Yale University Press, 1998); Leonard W. Levy, *Origins of the Bill of Rights* (New Haven, CT: Yale University Press, 1999); Jürgen Heideking, *The Constitution before the Judgment Seat: The Prehistory and Ratification of the Constitution, 1787–1791,* ed. John P. Kaminski and Richard Leffler (Charlottesville: University of Virginia Press, 2012), ch. 7; Michael J. Klarman, *The Framers' Coup: The Making of the United States Constitution* (New York: Oxford University Press, 2016), ch. 7. For traditional narrative histories, see Robert A. Rutland, *The Birth of the Bill of Rights, 1776–1791,* 3rd ed. (1955; Boston: Northeastern University Press, 1991); Irving Brant, *The Bill of Rights: Its Origins and Meaning* (Indianapolis: Bobbs-Merrill, 1965); Bernard Schwartz, *The Great Rights of Mankind: A History of the American Bill of Rights* (New York: Oxford University Press, 1977); Carol Berkin, *The Bill of Rights: The Fight to Secure America's Liberties* (New York: Simon and Schuster, 2015). For a still-valuable overview of scholarly trends, see James H. Hutson, "The Birth of the Bill of Rights: The State of Current Scholarship," *Prologue* 20 (Fall 1988), 143–161.

2. George Mason, Sept. 12, 1787, *Records,* 2:587. Arguing persuasively that the first amendments were not called a "bill of rights" for nearly a century, see Pauline Maier, *Ratification: The People Debate the Constitution, 1787–1788* (New York: Simon and

Schuster, 2010), 459–464. On former Anti-Federalists' disillusionment with the first amendments, see Saul Cornell, *The Other Founders: Anti-Federalism and the Dissenting Tradition in America, 1788–1828* (Chapel Hill: University of North Carolina Press, 1999), 162–163; Klarman, *Framers' Coup,* 583–585. On how the federal amendments differed from previous declarations of rights, see Herbert Storing, "The Constitution and the Bill of Rights," in *How Does the Constitution Secure Rights?* ed. Robert Goldwin and William Schambra (Washington, DC: AEI Press, 1985), 123–127; Jack N. Rakove, *Declaring Rights: A Brief History with Documents* (Boston: Bedford, 1998), 191–192.

3. Denatus, *Virginia Independent Chronicle,* June 11, 1788, *DHRC,* 10:1602; *DHFFC,* 4:12–26; Richard Henry Lee to Patrick Henry, Sept. 27, 1789, *DHFFC,* 17:1625. Disputants sometimes differentiated between the two kinds of amendments, calling structural changes "alterations" and rights-based additions "bills" or "declarations of rights." But, throughout, "amendment" carried ambiguity; see *Creating,* ix–xi. Emphasizing the structural and majoritarian character of the first amendments, see Amar, *Bill of Rights,* introduction, part I; but complicating this singular emphasis, also see William Michael Treanor, "Taking Text Too Seriously: Modern Textualism, Original Meaning, and the Case of Amar's *Bill of Rights,*" *Michigan Law Review* 106 (Dec. 2007), 487–543. Some have suggested that adding a bill of rights was Anti-Federalists' core demand; see John P. Kaminski, "The Making of the Bill of Rights, 1787–1792," in *Contexts of the Bill of Rights,* ed. Stephen L. Schechter and Richard B. Bernstein (Albany: New York State Commission on the Bicentennial of the United States Constitution, 1990), 18–64; David E. Kyvig, *Explicit and Authentic Acts: Amending the U.S. Constitution, 1776–1995* (Lawrence: University Press of Kansas, 1995), 90–93, 98–99. But many others have stressed the largely structural character of proposed amendments; see Cornell, *Other Founders,* 31–34, 153–157, 158–163; *Creating,* ix–xi; Kenneth R. Bowling, "'A Tub to the Whale': The Founding Fathers and Adoption of the Federal Bill of Rights," *JER* 8 (Autumn 1988), 228–230; Treanor, "Taking Text Too Seriously," 540–541; Calvin H. Johnson, *Righteous Anger against the Wicked States: The Meaning of the Founders' Constitution* (New York: Cambridge University Press, 2005), 171–173; Heideking, *Constitution before the Judgment Seat,* 379–385. For an account suggesting they were evenly divided between the two demands, see Richard B. Bernstein with Jerome Angel, *Amending America: If We Love the Constitution So Much, Why Do We Keep Trying to Change It?* (New York: Times Books, 1993), 32–33.

4. Aedanus Burke, Aug. 15, 1789, *DHFFC,* 11:1278–1279. Also see John Page, Aug. 15, 1789, *DHFFC,* 11:1281; George Clymer to Richard Peters, June 8, 1789, *DHFFC,* 16:723; Peters to James Madison, July 5, 1789, *DHFFC,* 16:957–958; and, from the previous fall, Centinel XIX [Samuel Bryan], *Independent Gazetteer,* Oct. 7, 1788, *DHFFE,* 1:308. For more on the metaphor, see *Creating,* xv. Those who have interpreted the first amendments through the lens of the modern Bill of Rights often have been at a loss to understand the Anti-Federalists' logic; see Leonard W. Levy, *Original Intent and the Framers' Constitution* (New York: MacMillan, 1988), 169–172. For a subtler take

arguing that Anti-Federalists transformed from republican communitarians to individualist libertarians, see Michael Lienesch, "Reinterpreting Rights: Antifederalists and the Bill of Rights," in *The Bill of Rights: Government Proscribed*, ed. Ronald Hoffman and Peter J. Albert (Charlottesville: University of Virginia Press, 1997), 245–273. For persuasive rebuttals, see Saul Cornell, "Moving Beyond the Canon of Traditional Constitutional History: Anti-Federalists, the Bill of Rights, and the Promise of Post-Modern Historiography," *Law and History Review* 12 (Spring 1994), 1–28; Saul Cornell, "Mere Parchment Barriers? Antifederalists, the Bill of Rights, and the Question of Rights Consciousness," in Hoffman and Albert, *The Bill of Rights*, 175–208; Jud Campbell, "Republicanism and Natural Rights at the Founding," *Constitutional Commentary* 32 (Winter 2017), 85–112; Amar, *Bill of Rights*, xii–xiii, ch. 6. More generally, there has been a misguided tendency to paint the entire Founding generation as opposed to a modern notion of excessive state power, even though that generation's much different conception of power and liberty is not easily mapped onto the conceptual scheme implicit in such a formulation. For leading examples of this trend, see Richard A. Epstein, *The Classical Liberal Constitution: The Uncertain Quest for Limited Government* (Cambridge, MA: Harvard University Press, 2014), esp. 3–6; Randy E. Barnett, *Our Republican Constitution: Securing the Liberty and Sovereignty of We the People* (New York: Harper Collins, 2016), chs. 1–3. On the anachronism of modern efforts to distill Founding-era rights talk, see Richard Primus, *The American Language of Rights* (New York: Cambridge University Press, 1999), 123–126.

5. A large and growing literature has been devoted to the study of individual amendments, usually with an interest in elucidating their original meaning. See generally Amar, *Bill of Rights*, xi–xii. For examples, see generally the work of Leonard Levy, which paved much of the way—*Origins of the Bill of Rights* is the latest compilation of his related efforts. See, as well, Eugene W. Hickok Jr., *The Bill of Rights: Original Meaning and Current Understanding* (Charlottesville: University of Virginia Press, 1991); James H. Hutson, "The Bill of Rights and the American Revolutionary Experience," in *A Culture of Rights: The Bill of Rights in Philosophy, Politics, and Law—1791 and 1991*, ed. Michael J. Lacey and Knud Haakonssen (New York: Cambridge University Press, 1991), 87–97. For an overview detailing this approach, see Gaspare J. Saladino, "The Bill of Rights: A Bibliographic Essay," in Schechter and Bernstein, *Contexts of the Bill of Rights*, 82–98. On the dearth of rights talk in the original amendments debate, see Bowling, "'A Tub to the Whale,'" 224. On the advantages of thinking about the early amendments as a whole, see Jack N. Rakove, *Original Meanings: Politics and Ideas in the Making of the Constitution* (New York: Knopf, 1996), 289–290.

6. For important exceptions that, while considering the debate over how amendments were to be added only briefly, appreciate its importance, see Mary Sarah Bilder, *Madison's Hand: Revising the Constitutional Convention* (Cambridge, MA: Harvard University Press, 2015), 174–176; Kyvig, *Explicit and Authentic Acts*, 101–102. While most scholars have downplayed the debate's significance, some have gone so far as to claim

that it "was based on stylistic rather than substantive considerations"; see David P. Currie, *The Constitution in Congress: The Federalist Period, 1789–1801* (Chicago: University of Chicago Press, 1997), 114.

7. For more on amendments and ratification, see Maier, *Ratification*, 50–64, 192–198, 261–267, 291–309, 316–317, 378–393, 397–400, 430–434; Kyvig, *Explicit and Authentic Acts*, 71–72, 76–86; Klarman, *Framers' Coup*, 439–442, 468–476, 513–514, 554–555. On the second convention movement, see Cornell, *Other Founders*, 136–143; Maier, *Ratification*, 401–403, 425–429; Heideking, *Constitution before the Judgment Seat*, 385–394. On Federalists' fears of this movement, see Klarman, *Framers' Coup*, 530–539. For the New York circular letter, see *DHRC*, 23:2335–2336; and on its significance, see John P. Kaminski, *George Clinton: Yeoman Politician of the New Republic* (Madison: Madison House, 1993), 166–169; Maier, *Ratification*, 396–398, 425–426. North Carolina would ratify the Constitution in November 1789 and Rhode Island in May 1790.

8. Henry to William Grayson, Mar. 31, 1789, *DHFFC*, 15:168; Edward Carrington to Madison, May 12, 1789, *DHFFC*, 15:529; John Vining, June 8, 1789, *DHFFC*, 11:818; John Fenno to Joseph Ward, July 5, 1789, *DHFFC*, 16:947. Also see Pacificus [Noah Webster] to Madison, Aug. 14, 1789, *DHFFC*, 11:1310–1312. For Virginia's and New York's applications, see *Creating*, 235–238. On Federalists' interpretations of their electoral success, see Bowling, "'A Tub to the Whale,'" 223–224, 234–239; Heideking, *Constitution before the Judgment Seat*, 394–399.

9. Thomas Jefferson to Madison, Feb. 6, 1788, *PTJ*, 12:569; Madison to Jefferson, Oct. 17, 1788, *PJM*, 11:297. For Jefferson's recurring criticism, also see letters of Dec. 20, 1787; July 31, 1788; Nov. 18, 1788; Jan. 12, 1789; Mar. 15, 1789, *PTJ*, 12:438–442; 13:440–443; 14:187–190, 436–438, 659–662. Madison's change of mind has often been interpreted as political pragmatism; for example, see Bowling, "'A Tub to the Whale,'" 224, 231–234; Paul Finkelman, "James Madison and the Bill of Rights: A Reluctant Paternity," *Supreme Court Review* 9 (1990), 301–347; Stanley Elkins and Eric McKitrick, *The Age of Federalism, the Early American Republic, 1788–1800* (New York: Oxford University Press, 1993), 57–62; Gordon S. Wood, *Empire of Liberty: A History of the Early Republic, 1789–1815* (New York: Oxford University Press, 2009), 66–69; Jeff Broadwater, *James Madison: A Son of Virginia and Founder of a Nation* (Chapel Hill: University of North Carolina Press, 2012), 74–84. But some have stressed the principled foundations undergirding Madison's shift; see Rakove, *Original Meanings*, 330–336; Lance Banning, *The Sacred Fire of Liberty: James Madison and the Founding of the Federal Republic* (Ithaca, NY: Cornell University Press, 1995), 266–267, 279–290; Stuart Leibiger, "James Madison and Amendments to the Constitution, 1787–1789: 'Parchment Barrier,'" *Journal of Southern History* 59 (Aug. 1993), 441–468; Ralph Ketcham, *James Madison: A Biography* (1971; Charlottesville: University of Virginia Press, 1990), 288–292; Robert A. Goldwin, *From Parchment to Power: How James Madison Used the Bill of Rights to Save the Constitution* (Washington, DC: AEI Press, 1997); Richard Labunski, *James Madison and the Struggle for the Bill of Rights* (New York:

Oxford University Press, 2006), 192–194; Colleen A. Sheehan, *James Madison and the Spirit of Republican Government* (New York: Cambridge University Press, 2009), 108–109. For Madison's most thorough enumeration of his reasons, see Madison to Peters, Aug. 19, 1789, *PJM*, 12:346–347. On his frustrations with the final Constitution, see Madison to Jefferson, Oct. 24, 1787, *PJM*, 10:207–215. On his concerns about amendments that had been promised in several ratifying conventions, see Feb. 19 and July 24, 1788, *PJM*, 10:519; 11:196. Beyond branding them "parchment barriers," Madison also had long thought text-based rights provisions were unnecessary in a federal system of enumerated powers, he worried about denigrating rights not included, and he still believed that the state governments posed the greatest threat to liberty.

10. Robert Morris to Francis Hopkinson, Aug. 15, 1789, *DHFFC*, 16:1324. Also see Theodore Sedgwick to Benjamin Lincoln, July 19, 1789, *DHFFC*, 16:1075–1076. On the political context, see Labunski, *Madison and the Struggle for the Bill of Rights*, ch. 7; Banning, *Sacred Fire of Liberty*, 269–274; Bowling, "'A Tub to the Whale,'" 231–234; Maier, *Ratification*, 440–446; Klarman, *Framers' Coup*, 556–566. On why scholars have perhaps overstated the significance of this context, see Banning, *Sacred Fire of Liberty*, 279–281. It has long been assumed that Henry further leveraged his power in the legislature to draw Madison's electoral district in a highly unfavorable way, but for a counterview to this long-standing charge, see Thomas Rogers Hunter, "The First Gerrymander? Patrick Henry, James Madison, James Monroe, and Virginia's 1788 Congressional Districting," *Early American Studies* 9 (Fall 2011), 781–820.

11. Benjamin Goodhue, June 8, 1789, *DHFFC*, 11:813; Vining, June 8, 1789, *DHFFC*, 11:835; Roger Sherman, June 8, 1789, *DHFFC*, 11:834, 815; James Jackson, June 8, 1789, *DHFFC*, 11:827.

12. Burke, June 8, 1789, *DHFFC*, 11:813; Jackson, June 8, 1789, *DHFFC*, 11:813, 829; Elbridge Gerry, June 8, 1789, *DHFFC*, 11:830–831, 810; John Laurance, Aug. 13, 1789, *DHFFC*, 11:1219. Also see Samuel Livermore, June 8, 1789, *DHFFC*, 11:833.

13. Laurance, Aug. 13, 1789, *DHFFC*, 11:1219; Vining, June 8, 1789, *DHFFC*, 11:817; Jackson, June 8, 1789, *DHFFC*, 11:812, 813, 830. Also see Sherman, July 21, 1789, *DHFFC*, 11:1159.

14. Madison to Edmund Randolph, Nov. 2, 1788, *PJM*, 11:329; Madison to George Washington, Aug. 11, 1788, *PJM*, 11:230; Madison to Randolph, Aug. 22, 1788, *PJM*, 11:237; Madison to Jefferson, Dec. 8, 1788, *PJM*, 11:383; Madison, June 8, 1789, *DHFFC*, 11:820, 814; Madison to Jefferson, Mar. 29, 1789, *PJM*, 12:38. Echoing Madison's concerns, see Page, June 8, 1789, *DHFFC*, 11:816–817.

15. Madison, June 8, 1789, *DHFFC*, 11:821, 827; Samuel Johnston to Madison, July 8, 1789, *DHFFC*, 16:980. Between October 1787 and March 1789, Madison and Jefferson exchanged sixteen substantial letters. For more on this correspondence, see Rakove, *Declaring Rights*, ch. 12; Lance Banning, *Jefferson and Madison: Three Conversations from the Founding* (Madison: Madison House, 1995), ch. 1.

16. Madison, June 8, 1789, *DHFFC*, 11:820, 821, 823; Madison to Jefferson, Oct. 17, 1788, *PJM*, 11:297, 299. For Madison's full proposal for amendments presented on June 8, see *DHFFC*, 4:9–12. For Madison's acknowledgment of other Anti-Federalist criticisms, see Madison to Jefferson, Oct. 17, 1788, *PJM*, 11:297; and "Notes for Speech in Congress," June 8, 1789, *DHFFC*, 12:193, which identified three distinct areas of constitutional criticism.

17. Madison, Virginia Ratifying Convention, June 24, 1788, *DHRC*, 10:1507; Madison, June 8, 1789, *DHFFC*, 11:823. On Wilson's objections to a federal bill of rights, see Chapter 2.

18. Madison, June 8, 1789, *DHFFC*, 11:823, 822, 824.

19. Madison, June 8, 1789, *DHFFC*, 11:823, 822, 825. For an insightful analysis countering this enduring claim about judicial enforcement, see Jud Campbell, "Judicial Review and the Enumeration of Rights," *Georgetown Journal of Law and Public Policy* 15 (Summer 2017), 569–592. For those who have contended that Madison was highlighting judicial enforcement, see Leibiger, "James Madison and Amendments to the Constitution," 463–464; Amar, *Bill of Rights,* 129–130; Levy, *Origins of the Bill of Rights,* 259; Currie, *Constitution in Congress,* 112; Laurence Claus, "Protecting Rights from Rights: Enumeration, Disparagement, and the Ninth Amendment," *Notre Dame Law Review* 79 (Feb. 2004), 590, 609; Michael W. McConnell, "Natural Rights and the Ninth Amendment: How Does Lockean Legal Theory Assist in Interpretation?" *N.Y.U. Journal of Law and Liberty* 5 (2010), 19–20, 24, 28.

20. Madison, June 8, 1789, *DHFFC*, 11:823; Madison to Jefferson, Oct. 17, 1788, *PJM*, 11:298–299; "Notes for Speech in Congress," *PJM*, 12:193. For a similar take, see Rakove, *Original Meanings,* 332–333, 336; Sheehan, *James Madison and the Spirit of Republican Government,* 108–109. For a more skeptical view, see Jeremy D. Bailey, *James Madison and Constitutional Imperfection* (New York: Cambridge University Press, 2015), 79–88.

21. *DHFFC*, 3:84, 117, 124, 148, 4:9–12, 27–31. Whether amendments needed to be generated in the Committee of the Whole House or could be tackled by a smaller committee proved a consuming debate, further testifying to the deeply uncertain character of the task at hand; see *DHFFC*, 11:811, 818–819, 832–833, 834–836, 1158–1163.

22. Jefferson to Madison, July 31, 1788, *PTJ*, 13:442; Publius [Alexander Hamilton], "The Federalist 84," New York, May 28, 1788, *DHRC*, 18:127–135. Significantly, though, Anti-Federalists thought a distinct kind of addition was necessary only for the federal Constitution due to its unique flaws. As noted in Chapter 2, most often they conceived of the state constitutions and the state declarations of rights as extensions of one another.

23. Madison, June 8, 1789, *DHFFC*, 11:814, 820, 825. Also see Madison to Jefferson, May 27, 1789, *PJM*, 12:186.

24. See Madison's Resolution, June 8, 1789, *DHFFC*, 4:9–12; House Committee Report, July 28, 1789, *DHFFC*, 4:27–31.

25. Aug. 13, 1789, *DHFFC*, 11:1209. For Sherman's motion, see Aug. 13, 1789, *DHFFC*, 11:1221. The best illustration of Sherman's long-standing opposition to amendments was an essay he wrote shortly before Congress assembled; see Sherman, "A Citizen of New Haven," Mar. 24, 1789, *DHFFC*, 15:124–125. A draft proposal of amendments written in Sherman's hand was discovered several decades ago. Unlike Madison's proposal that emerged from the House select committee, the draft proposal put forward amendments as a stand-alone list to append the Constitution. It remains unclear when and why it was produced. Given Sherman's opposition both to amending and to a number of the provisions on the proposal (some of which differed from Madison's proposal), it is doubtful that it reflected his own thinking. It might well have been the work of other members of the committee who opposed Madison's preference for incorporation (thus suggesting opposition might have been registered prior to the August 13 debate). On the draft proposal and why Sherman was likely not the author, see Scott D. Gerber, "Roger Sherman and the Bill of Rights," *Polity* 28 (Summer 1996), 521–540. For the draft proposal itself, see *Creation*, 266–268.

26. "William Pierce: Character Sketches of Delegates to the Federal Convention," *Records*, 3:88–89; Jeremiah Wadsworth to Rufus King, June 3, 1787, *Records*, 3:34; *DHFFC*, 14:506–512.

27. Sherman, Aug. 13, 1789, *DHFFC*, 11:1221; Jackson, Aug. 13, 1789, *DHFFC*, 11:1228. Also see Thomas Hartley, Aug. 13, 1789, *DHFFC*, 11:1227.

28. Jackson, Aug. 13, 1789, *DHFFC*, 11:1229; Livermore, Aug. 13, 1789, *DHFFC*, 11:1223; Sherman, Aug. 13, 1789, *DHFFC*, 11:1230; Michael Jenifer Stone, Aug. 13, 1789, *DHFFC*, 11:1226; Jackson, Aug. 13, 1789, *DHFFC*, 11:1228–1229. For a refutation of Jackson's argument, see William Loughton Smith, Aug. 13, 1789, *DHFFC*, 11:1230.

29. Stone, Aug. 13, 1789, *DHFFC*, 11:1224. On how some constitutional disputants had earlier during ratification emphasized the importance of the Constitution's signers as authors, see Simon J. Gilhooley, "The Framers Themselves: Constitution Authorship during the Ratification," *American Political Thought* 2 (Spring 2013), 62–88.

30. Stone, Aug. 13, 1789, *DHFFC*, 11:1224–1225; Sherman, Aug. 13, 1789, *DHFFC*, 11:1221; Livermore, Aug. 13, 1789, *DHFFC*, 11:1223; Jackson, Aug. 13, 1789, *DHFFC*, 11:1229; Laurance, Aug. 13, 1789, *DHFFC*, 11:1226–1227. Also see Stone, Aug. 13, 1789, *DHFFC*, 11:1224; Livermore, Aug. 13, 1789, *DHFFC*, 11:1228.

31. Sherman, Aug. 13, 1789, *DHFFC*, 11:1229; Jackson, Aug. 13, 1789, *DHFFC*, 11:1228. Also see Stone, Aug. 13, 1789, *DHFFC*, 11:1224–1225; Livermore, Aug. 13, 1789, *DHFFC*, 11:1225; Laurance, Aug. 13, 1789, *DHFFC*, 11:1227.

32. Jackson, Aug. 13, 1789, *DHFFC*, 11:1228; Clymer, Aug. 13, 1789, *DHFFC*, 11:1224; Sherman, Aug. 13, 1789, *DHFFC*, 11:1229. Also see Stone, Aug. 13, 1789, *DHFFC*, 11:1224; Vining, Aug. 13, 1789, *DHFFC*, 11:1230; Sherman, Aug. 13, 1789, *DHFFC*, 11:1231.

33. Madison, Aug. 13, 1789, *DHFFC*, 11:1221. Intriguingly, right when he was first responding to Sherman's fundamental challenge, Madison claimed, "I am not, how-

ever, very solicitous about the form, provided the business is but well completed"; see Aug. 13, 1789, *DHFFC*, 11:1222. This aside should not be read, though, to mean that he was relatively indifferent toward the core issue under debate. Given everything else he argued, the more plausible reading is that he was taken aback—merely, to that point, having presumed rather than defended the logic of incorporation, he was coming to terms with its essential significance. Moreover, he stressed mainly that the business be completed properly, and everything else he said suggested this could not be done save the method of incorporation. To the extent that this statement expressed something meaningful, it was captured in the latter rather than the former sentiment.

34. Sherman, Aug. 13, 1789, *DHFFC*, 11:1221; W. Smith, Aug. 13, 1789, *DHFFC*, 11:1222; Madison, Aug. 13, 1789, *DHFFC*, 11:1221–1222; Vining, Aug. 13, 1789, *DHFFC*, 11:1223–1224.

35. Madison, Aug. 13, 1789, *DHFFC*, 11:1222; Gerry, Aug. 13, 1789, *DHFFC*, 11:1225–1226; W. Smith, Aug. 13, 1789, *DHFFC*, 11:1222; Vining, Aug. 13, 1789, *DHFFC*, 11:1223–1224. Also see Gerry Aug. 13, 1789, *DHFFC*, 11:1225–1226, 1231.

36. Page, Aug. 13, 1789, *DHFFC*, 11:1228; W. Smith, Aug. 13, 1789, *DHFFC*, 11:1222.

37. Madison, Aug. 13, 1789, *DHFFC*, 11:1221–1222; Gerry, Aug. 13, 1789, *DHFFC*, 11:1226.

38. Gerry, Aug. 13, 1789, *DHFFC*, 11:1225–1226; W. Smith, Aug. 13, 1789, *DHFFC*, 11:1222.

39. United States Constitution, Article V; Gerry, Aug. 13, 1789, *DHFFC*, 11:1231, 1225–1226; W. Smith, Aug. 13, 1789, *DHFFC*, 11:1230. Also see Gerry, Aug. 13, 1789, *DHFFC*, 11:1226.

40. Laurance, Aug. 13, 1789, *DHFFC*, 11:1226–1227; W. Smith, Aug. 13, 1789, *DHFFC*, 11:1222; Gerry, Aug. 13, 1789, *DHFFC*, 11:1226.

41. Gerry, Aug. 13, 1789, *DHFFC*, 11:1225–1226.

42. Madison to Alexander White, Aug. 24, 1789, *PJM*, 12:352. Madison's side won the initial vote held on August 13; see *DHFFC*, 11:1210, 1231. But the matter was revisited on August 19, when Sherman "renewed his motion," after which, as one reporter described it, "hereupon ensued a debate similar to what took place in the committee of the whole." But this time Sherman's side decisively prevailed; see *DHFFC*, 11:1308. For Sherman's warning, see *DHFFC*, 11:1231.

43. On the (far more studied) debates over the specific amendments, see Klarman, *Framers' Coup*, 576–590; Bowling, "'A Tub to the Whale,'" 241–246.

44. Madison to Randolph, June 15, 1789, *PJM*, 12:219; Madison, June 8, 1789, *DHFFC*, 11:820, 821. Also see Madison to Johnston, June 21, 1789, *PJM*, 12:249–250; as well as George Washington's first inaugural address (believed to be written by Madison), which, while describing amendments as "expedient," nonetheless urged Congress to "carefully avoid every alteration which might endanger the benefits of . . . effective Government" and instead to extend "reverence for the characteristic rights of freemen"; Washington, "First Inaugural Address," [Apr. 30, 1789], in *The Papers of*

George Washington: Presidential Series, ed. Donald Jackson, W. W. Abbot, Dorothy Twohig, Philander D. Chase, Theodore J. Crackel, and Jennifer E. Steenshorne, 19 vols. (Charlottesville: University of Virginia Press, 1987–2016), 2:176.

45. House Committee Report, July 28, 1789, *DHFFC,* 4:27–31. On how Madison changed some structural amendments into rights provisions, see Klarman, *Framers' Coup,* 578–579. Unlike the proposed protections for individual rights against state governments, the proposed amendment to the preamble did not survive the House debate.

46. Madison, Aug. 15, 1789, *DHFFC,* 11:1279; Burke, Aug. 15, 1789, *DHFFC,* 11:1278–1279, 1280. Also see Page, Aug. 15, 1789, *DHFFC,* 11:1281. Those who did not wish to see the Constitution changed, unlike former Anti-Federalists, similarly testified (albeit in private) about how insubstantial Madison's proposed amendments were; see Clymer to Tench Coxe, June 28, 1789, *DHFFC,* 16:874; Pierce Butler to James Iredell, Aug. 11, 1789, *DHFFC,* 16:1289. For a compilation of state-proposed amendments (from Massachusetts, South Carolina, New Hampshire, Virginia, and New York), see *DHFFC,* 4:12–26. Amendments were also proposed by minorities in the Pennsylvania ratifying convention, see "The Dissent of the Minority of the Convention," *DHRC,* 2:623–625; in the Maryland ratifying convention, see "To the People of Maryland," Annapolis *Maryland Gazette,* May 1, 1788, *DHRC,* 12:663–666; and, in lieu of approving the Constitution, by the first North Carolina ratifying convention, see *Debates,* 4:243–247.

47. Gerry, Aug. 15, 1789, *DHFFC,* 11:1281; Burke, Aug. 15, 1789, *DHFFC,* 11:1281–1282; Thomas Tudor Tucker, Aug. 18, 1789, *DHFFC,* 11:1297–1298. On Burke's personality and speaking style, see *DHFFC,* 14:837–838.

48. Madison to Peters, Aug. 19, 1789, *PJM,* 12:346; Tucker, Aug. 18, 1789, *DHFFC,* 11:1300; *DHFFC,* 3:160–162, 163–164; 4:31, 35–39; W. Smith to Edward Rutledge, Aug. 15, 1789, *DHFFC,* 16:1327; William Smith to Otho H. Williams, Aug. 17, 1789, *DHFFC,* 16:1338; Gerry to Samuel R. Gerry, June 30, 1790, *DHFFC,* 19:1970; Klarman, *Framers' Coup,* 582–583. Also see Gerry, Aug. 15, 1789, *DHFFC,* 11:1272–1273. The states whose proposed amendments called for the insertion of "expressly" to describe powers delegated were Massachusetts, South Carolina, and New Hampshire; see *DHFFC,* 4:12, 13, 14; and the minorities from both Pennsylvania and Maryland, see *DHRC,* 2:624, 12:663.

49. Livermore, Aug. 22, 1789, *DHFFC,* 11:1321; Tucker to St. George Tucker, Oct. 2, 1789, *DHFFC,* 17:1657; Lee to Henry, Sept. 14, 1789, *DHFFC,* 17:1542; Grayson to Henry, Sept. 29, 1789, *DHFFC,* 17:1641. Also see Mason to Samuel Griffin, Sept. 8, 1789, *DHFFC,* 17:1492; Lee and Grayson to Beverley Randolph, Sept. 28, 1789, *DHFFC,* 1635; and the three essays written by Samuel Bryan (as Centinel) that were published in Pennsylvania newspapers, "Centinel Revived," *Independent Gazeteer* (Philadelphia), Aug. 27, Aug. 29, and Sept. 9, 1789. On Tucker's penchant to ridicule Congress's activities in his correspondence, see *DHFFC,* 14:859.

50. For the final amendments, see *DHFFC,* 4:1–3; and for the versions the House submitted to the Senate, the Senate ultimately sent back, and the conference report

between the two, see *DHFFC*, 4:35–39, 45–48. For a good overview of Madison's successes and failures in the debate, see Banning, *Sacred Fire of Liberty*, 287–290. On the Senate's changes, about which little is known, see Rakove, *Declaring Rights*, 186–188. Little is known either about the state ratification process; see Kyvig, *Explicit and Authentic Acts*, 105–109; Bowling, "'A Tub to the Whale,'" 247–251; Heideking, *Constitution before the Judgment Seat*, 412–417; Klarman, *Framers' Coup*, 587–590. On why the amendments generated little attention in the states, see Kenneth R. Bowling, "Overshadowed by States' Rights: Ratification of the Bill of Rights," in Hoffman and Albert, *Bill of Rights*, 77–102. More is known about the debate over the amendments in Virginia, where significant opposition in the state legislature prevented ratification until 1791; see J. Gordon Hylton, "Virginia and the Ratification of the Bill of Rights," *University of Richmond Law Review* 25 (Spring 1991), 450–466.

51. For the Senate's revisions, see *DHFFC*, 4:45–47; Rakove, *Declaring Rights*, 188.

52. Madison to Jefferson, Oct. 17, 1788, *PJM*, 11:297; House Committee Report, July 28, 1789, *DHFFC*, 4:31; Articles of Confederation and Perpetual Union, Article II; Madison, Aug. 18, 1789, *DHFFC*, 11:1301. In his initial speech defending the project of amendments, Madison justified his proposed version of what became the Ninth Amendment on the grounds that it would weaken the meaning of enumeration; see Madison, June 8, 1789, *DHFFC*, 11:824–825. For a related take on what became the Ninth and Tenth Amendments, see Rakove, *Declaring Rights*, 193. After long being ignored by scholars, in the past few decades the Ninth Amendment has become a subject of concerted interest and fierce debate. Independent from the matter of Madison and textuality, most disagreement has turned on the original meaning of retained rights, including especially what Madison might have meant by that formulation—whether it referenced individual, majoritarian, or collective rights. Many have assumed it referenced individual natural rights; for a start see Randy E. Barnett, "James Madison's Ninth Amendment," in *The Rights Retained by the People: The History and Meaning of the Ninth Amendment*, ed. Randy E. Barnett, 2 vols. (Fairfax, VA: George Mason University Press, 1989), 1:1–49; Daniel A. Farber, *Retained by the People: The "Silent" Ninth Amendment and the Constitutional Rights Americans Don't Know They Have* (New York: Basic Books, 2007), chs. 2–4. For those who have argued that the amendment primarily sought to protect the people of the separate states' collective right to popular sovereignty, see Amar, *Bill of Rights*, ch. 6; Kurt T. Lash, *The Lost History of the Ninth Amendment* (New York: Oxford University Press, 2009), esp. chs. 2–4. But Founding-era Americans would have struggled to recognize the distinctions that supposedly so categorically differentiated these kinds of liberty.

53. Laurance, Aug. 13, 1789, *DHFFC*, 11:1226–1227.

54. Bilder, *Madison's Hand*, ch. 7 (on why he abandoned his notes), chs. 8–9 (on why he returned to them). Much of the discussion that follows in this chapter owes an enormous debt to Bilder's pathbreaking work. It is important also to look beyond Madison, though, to appreciate that his forgotten notes could seem relevant only once a

certain vision of the Constitution had come into focus, not merely a transformation in his mind but one that swept through the discursive community in which so much of his own constitutional reckoning took shape. In other words, Madison's own mental shift was embedded in, and thus largely determined by, a broader communal transformation otherwise taking shape. On how Madison ignored the debates that had surrounded American constitutional creation until 1789, see Jack N. Rakove, "The Original Intent of Original Understanding," *Constitutional Commentary* 13 (Fall 1996), 165–167.

55. Bilder, *Madison's Hand*, 182, and generally ch. 9. On the official records of the Constitutional Convention, see Mary Sarah Bilder, "How Bad Were the Official Records of the Federal Convention?" *George Washington Law Review* 80 (Nov. 2012), 1636–1640.

56. Bilder, *Madison's Hand*, 15–16, 193; *Documentary History of the Constitution of the United States, 1786–1870,* 5 vols. (Washington, DC: Department of State, 1894–1905), 3:339.

57. Jefferson to Madison, Sept. 6, 1789, *PTJ*, 15:392, 395–396.

58. Madison to Jefferson, Feb. 4, 1790, *PJM*, 13:19. On Madison's earlier engagement with these ideas, see Jonathan Gienapp, "How to Maintain a Constitution: The Virginia and Kentucky Resolutions and James Madison's Struggle with the Problem of Constitutional Maintenance," in *Nullification and Secession in Modern Constitutional Thought,* ed. Sanford Levinson (Lawrence: University Press of Kansas, 2016), 69–73. This famous exchange has been interpreted in these terms by a plethora of scholars. See especially Andrew Burstein and Nancy Isenberg, *Madison and Jefferson* (New York: Random House, 2010), 204–207; Adrienne Koch, *Jefferson and Madison: The Great Collaboration* (New York: Oxford University Press, 1950), 70–73; Jack N. Rakove, *Revolutionaries: A New History of the Invention of America* (Boston: Houghton Mifflin, 2010), 336–338, 388–390; Annette Gordon-Reed and Peter S. Onuf, *"Most Blessed of the Patriarchs": Thomas Jefferson and the Empire of the Imagination* (New York: Liveright, 2016), 279–280; Noah Feldman, *The Three Lives of James Madison: Genius, Partisan, President* (New York: Random House, 2017), 289–292. More broadly, many have juxtaposed Madison's and Jefferson's dueling commitments to constitutional veneration and revolution, respectively, to expose their intellectual differences; see Drew R. McCoy, *The Last of the Fathers: James Madison and the Republican Legacy* (New York: Cambridge University Press, 1989), 51–59, 77–83; Leibiger, "James Madison and Amendments," 468; Michael Zuckert, *The Natural Rights Republic: Studies in the Foundation of the American Political Tradition* (South Bend, IN: University of Notre Dame Press, 1996), 232–243; Gary Rosen, *American Compact: James Madison and the Problem of Founding* (Lawrence: University Press of Kansas, 1999), 126–141, 173–174; Richard K. Matthews, "James Madison's Political Theory: Hostage to Democracy Fortune," *Review of Politics* 67 (Winter 2005), 49–67; Sanford Levinson, *Our Undemocratic Constitution: Where the Constitution Goes Wrong (And*

How We the People Can Correct It) (New York: Oxford University Press, 2006), 16–20; Richard Beeman, *Plain, Honest Men: The Making of the American Constitution* (New York: Random House, 2009), 421–423; Greg Weiner, *Madison's Metronome: The Constitution, Majority Rule, and the Tempo of American Politics* (Lawrence: University Press of Kansas, 2012), 58–61. But some scholars have insisted that Madison's and Jefferson's views were closer in spirit; see Sheehan, *James Madison and the Spirit of Republican Government,* 134–143; Banning, *Sacred Fire of Liberty,* esp. 1–10, 370–376; Banning, *Jefferson and Madison,* ch. 2; Alan Gibson, "Veneration and Vigilance: James Madison and Public Opinion, 1785–1800," *Review of Politics* 67 (Jan. 2005), 5–35; Robert W. T. Martin, "James Madison and Popular Government: The Neglected Case of the 'Memorial,'" *Polity* 42 (Apr. 2010), 185–209; Bailey, *James Madison and Constitutional Imperfection,* 9–11, 18–22. For my own take, see Gienapp, "How to Maintain a Constitution."

59. Madison, "For the *National Gazette:* Charters," Jan. 18, 1792, *PJM,* 14:191–192.

5. The Rules of the Constitution

Epigraph: Fisher Ames, Feb. 3, 1791, *DHFFC,* 14:393.

1. Ames, Feb. 3, 1791, *DHFFC,* 14:392.

2. Ames, Feb. 3, 1791, *DHFFC,* 14:392; James Madison, Feb. 2, 1791, *DHFFC,* 14:372.

3. Ames, Feb. 3, 1791, *DHFFC,* 14:392, 397. On Ames's rhetorical abilities and political background, see *DHFFC,* 14:615–616.

4. On constitutional debates in Congress between contests over amendments and the bank, see David P. Currie, *The Constitution in Congress: The Federalist Period, 1789–1801* (Chicago: University of Chicago Press, 1997), ch. 2; Joseph M. Lynch, *Negotiating the Constitution: The Earliest Debates over Original Intent* (Ithaca, NY: Cornell University Press, 1999), 50–77. Congress gathered in the building that became known as Congress Hall. It was overshadowed by the nearby Pennsylvania State House, and congressmen found that it lacked the elegance of Federal Hall, their previous home in New York City; see *DHFFC,* 21:3.

5. See generally Stanley Elkins and Eric McKitrick, *The Age of Federalism, the Early American Republic, 1788–1800* (New York: Oxford University Press, 1993), 92–105.

6. Alexander Hamilton, "Report Relative to a Provision for the Support of Public Credit," Jan. 9, 1790, *PAH,* 6:65–168; Hamilton, "Final Version of the Second Report on the Further Provision Necessary for Establishing Public Credit (Report on a National Bank)," Dec. 14, 1790, *PAH,* 7:305–342.

7. Of the many works on Hamilton's financial program, I have relied most heavily on Max M. Edling, *A Hercules in the Cradle: War, Money, and the American State, 1783–1867* (Chicago: University of Chicago Press, 2014), chs. 2–3; Elkins and McKitrick, *Age*

of Federalism, 92–131; and the introductory notes to Hamilton's proposals, *PAH*, 6:51–65; 7:236–256. Also see E. James Ferguson, *The Power of the Purse: A History of American Public Finance, 1776–1790* (Chapel Hill: University of North Carolina Press, 1961), 289–325; Thomas K. McCraw, *The Founders and Finance: How Hamilton, Gallatin, and Other Immigrants Forged a New Economy* (Cambridge, MA: Harvard University Press, 2012), 87–109, 121–136, 357–365; Janet A. Riesman, "Money, Credit, and Federalist Political Economy," in *Beyond Confederation: Origins of the Constitution and American National Identity*, ed. Richard Beeman, Stephen Botein, and Edward C. Carter II (Chapel Hill: University of North Carolina Press, 1987), 128–161; Andrew Shankman, *Original Intents: Hamilton, Jefferson, Madison, and the American Founding* (New York: Oxford University Press, 2017), ch. 4.

8. Madison to Thomas Jefferson, July 10, 1791, *PJM*, 14:43; Jefferson to Edmund Pendleton, July 24, 1791, *PTJ*, 20:670 (this testimony came after the bank was chartered and sale of its stock had begun). On this opposition, see Lance Banning, *The Jeffersonian Persuasion: Evolution of a Party Ideology* (Ithaca, NY: Cornell University Press, 1978), ch. 5; Drew R. McCoy, *The Elusive Republic: Political Economy in Jeffersonian America* (Chapel Hill: University of North Carolina Press, 1980), ch. 5; John M. Murrin, "The Great Inversion, or Court Versus Country: A Comparison of the Revolution Settlements in England (1688–1721) and America (1776–1816)," in *Three British Revolutions: 1641, 1688, 1776*, ed. J. G. A. Pocock (Princeton, NJ: Princeton University Press, 1980), 368–453; Elkins and McKitrick, *Age of Federalism*, 18–29, 79–92, 133–152, 209–211. On the pivotal role debt played in this opposition worldview, see Herbert E. Sloan, *Principle and Interest: Thomas Jefferson and the Problem of Debt* (New York: Oxford University Press, 1995). By contrast, others have emphasized the opposition's commercial and capitalist impulses; for example, see Joyce Appleby, *Capitalism and the New Social Order: The Republican Vision of the 1790s* (New York: New York University Press, 1984); Joyce Appleby, *Liberalism and Republicanism in the Historical Imagination* (Cambridge, MA: Harvard University Press, 1992), esp. chs. 10, 12–13. But on why these interpretations were not so opposed, see Lance Banning, "Jeffersonian Ideology Revisited: Liberal and Classical Ideas in the New American Republic," *WMQ* 42 (Jan. 1986), 3–19.

9. James Jackson, Feb. 2, 1791, *DHFFC*, 14:376. On how the bank exacerbated divisions, see Elkins and McKitrick, *Age of Federalism*, 223–229. On how it was the tipping point specifically for Madison, see Lance Banning, *The Sacred Fire of Liberty: James Madison and the Founding of the Federal Republic* (Ithaca, NY: Cornell University Press, 1995), 324–325. On the importance of the capital's location, see Kenneth R. Bowling, *The Creation of Washington, DC: The Idea and Location of the American Capital* (Fairfax, VA: George Mason University Press, 1991).

10. "The Diary of William Maclay," Jan. 3, 1791, *DHFFC*, 9:355; Madison, Feb. 2, 1791, *DHFFC*, 14:369. On the bank bill's uncontroversial time in the Senate, see *DHFFC*, 1:522, 526, 528, 530–536, 551; 9:360. Evidence of Madison's preparation can be seen in his extensive notes on banks (first in various European countries and then in England);

see "Notes on Banks" and "Notes on the Bank of England," [Feb. 1, 1791], *PJM,* 13:364–369.

11. Madison, May 31, 1787, *Records,* 1:53, 60 (Robert Yates's Notes); Publius [Madison], "The Federalist 44," *New York Packet,* Jan. 25, 1788, *DHRC,* 15:471–473; Madison, Aug. 18, 1789, *DHFFC,* 11:1301.

12. Publius [Hamilton], "The Federalist 32–33," *New York Independent Journal,* Jan. 2, 1788, *DHRC,* 15:221–222; Publius [Hamilton], "The Federalist 25," *New York Packet,* Dec. 21, 1787, *DHRC,* 15:63. My analysis here is indebted to Lynch, *Negotiating the Constitution,* 33–37. For a valuable take on Hamilton's constitutionalism, arguing that he was less committed to unfettered national political authority than many have assumed, see Kate Elizabeth Brown, *Alexander Hamilton and the Development of American Law* (Lawrence: University Press of Kansas, 2017), 7–8, chs. 3–4.

13. Michael Jenifer Stone, Feb. 23, 1790, *DHFFC,* 12:510; Jackson, July 23, 1790, *DHFFC,* 13:1697; Madison, Apr. 22, 1790, *DHFFC,* 13:1175–1176; Elbridge Gerry, Feb. 23, 1790, *DHFFC,* 12:520–521; Lynch, *Negotiating the Constitution,* 73–77. On the House floor, Madison doubted whether the Convention had expected Congress to have the right to assume state debts. But Hamilton later claimed that he and Madison had explicitly discussed the issue in private during the Convention and that Madison had agreed with him that including an article in the Constitution would cause needless controversy since Congress would have the power to assume the debts regardless; see Hamilton to Edward Carrington, May 26, 1792, *PAH,* 11:428. Gerry and Sherman, both of whom had been delegates to the Convention, offered similar takes on what had been expected during the summer of 1787; see Gerry, Feb. 25, 1790, *DHFFC,* 12:575–576; Sherman, May 25, 1790, *DHFFC,* 13:420–421.

14. Ames, Feb. 3, 1791, *DHFFC,* 14:391–392. This point is entirely indebted to Richard Primus, "Enumerated Powers and the Bank Debate," *Michigan Law Review* (forthcoming, Dec. 2018). Madison had promised his father that the bank would be opposed in the House, but he did not indicate that the opposition would be constitutional in nature; see Madison to James Madison Sr., Jan. 23, 1791, *PJM,* 13:358. As Primus shows, in a letter focused on constitutionalism, Madison mentioned the bank without connecting the two subjects; see Madison to Edmund Pendleton, Jan. 2, 1791, *PJM,* 13:344. And there are only two examples of congressmen anticipating a constitutional challenge; see Pierce Butler to Jackson, Jan. 24, 1791, *DHFFC,* 21:515; Theodore Sedgwick to Peter Van Schaack, Jan. 30, 1791, *DHFFC,* 21:609.

15. Sedgwick, Feb. 4, 1791, *DHFFC,* 14:398–399; Stone, Feb. 5, 1791, *DHFFC,* 14:428; Madison, Feb. 8, 1791, *DHFFC,* 14:475. Also see William Loughton Smith, Feb. 5, 1791, *DHFFC,* 14:422; Gerry, Feb. 7, 1791, *DHFFC,* 14:458. For a defense of Madison's motivations as principled and consistent, see Banning, *Sacred Fire of Liberty,* 331–333. For a take acknowledging that Madison's commitments evolved but which situates them in his long-standing efforts to analyze republican politics, see Jack N. Rakove, *Original Meanings: Politics and Ideas in the Making of the Constitution*

(New York: Knopf, 1996), 350–355. For parallel takes on Smith's and Gerry's motives, see George C. Rogers Jr., *Evolution of a Federalist: William Loughton Smith of Charleston (1758–1812)* (Columbia: University of South Carolina Press, 1962), 193–241; George Athan Billias, *Elbridge Gerry: Founding Father and Republican Statesman* (New York: McGraw Hill, 1976), 236–244; *DHFFC*, 14:618–619, 621–622.

16. Stone, Feb. 5, 1791, *DHFFC*, 14:423. For those who have treated the debate's constitutional arguments as instruments of political and regional interests, see Benjamin Klubes, "The First Federal Congress and the First National Bank," *JER* 10 (Spring 1990), 19–41; Kenneth R. Bowling, "The Bank Bill, the Capital City, and President Washington," *Capitol Studies* 1 (Spring 1972), 59–71; James Roger Sharp, *American Politics in the Early Republic: The New Nation in Crisis* (New Haven, CT: Yale University Press, 1993), 38–39.

17. When the bank debate's constitutional arguments are not reduced to political interests, they are often understood as a dispute between strict and broad constitutional construction. See Elkins and McKitrick, *Age of Federalism*, 229–232; Currie, *Constitution in Congress*, 78–80; Lynch, *Negotiating the Constitution*, 77–90; Saul Cornell, *The Other Founders: Anti-Federalism and the Dissenting Tradition in America, 1788–1828* (Chapel Hill: University of North Carolina Press, 1999), 187–191. On why at least Madison's arguments cannot be reduced to this dichotomy, though, see Banning, *Sacred Fire of Liberty*, 331–332. While there is much to recommend this approach to the debates, given how deeply uncertain the Constitution still was, it is important also to realize that debates over how to interpret the Constitution were, accordingly, as much contests over the Constitution's fundamental character—and that is the emphasis here, how debates over meaning gave way to debates over constitutional ontology.

18. Sedgwick, Feb. 4, 1791, *DHFFC*, 14: 409; Gerry, Feb. 7, 1791, *DHFFC*, 14:453; Ames, Feb. 3, 1791, *DHFFC*, 14:391. Also see W. Smith, Feb. 5, 1791, *DHFFC*, 14:421. On the diverse usages of the phrase "necessary and proper" during this period, see John Mikhail, "The Necessary and Proper Clauses," *Georgetown Law Journal* 102 (Apr. 2014), 1055, 1108, 1115–1121.

19. Elias Boudinot, Feb. 5, 1791, *DHFFC*, 14:431–432; Ames, Feb. 3, 1791, *DHFFC*, 14:392, 393.

20. Sedgwick, Feb. 4, 1791, *DHFFC*, 14:400–401; Boudinot, Feb. 5, 1791, *DHFFC*, 14:438. Also see John Laurance, Feb. 4, 1791, *DHFFC*, 14:404; Boudinot, Feb. 5, 1791, *DHFFC*, 14:441. On Sedgwick's avowed commitment to the Hamiltonian vision, see *DHFFC*, 14:638–640.

21. Ames, Feb. 3, 1791, *DHFFC*, 14:397; Sedgwick, Feb. 4, 1791, *DHFFC*, 14:400; Gerry, Feb. 7, 1791, *DHFFC*, 14:457. Also see Ames, Feb. 3, 1791, *DHFFC*, 14:387–388; Laurance, Feb. 4, 1791, *DHFFC*, 14:413.

22. Sedgwick, Feb. 4, 1791, *DHFFC*, 14:399; Boudinot, Feb. 4, 1791, *DHFFC*, 14:436; Gerry, Feb. 7, 1791, *DHFFC*, 14:458; John Vining, Feb. 2, 1791, *DHFFC*, 14:378; Boudinot, Feb. 5, 1791, *DHFFC*, 14:438.

23. Vining, Feb. 2, 1791, *DHFFC*, 14:378; Laurance, Feb. 4, 1791, *DHFFC*, 14:403; Ames, Feb. 3, 1791, *DHFFC*, 14:393; United States Constitution, Tenth Amendment; Thomas Tudor Tucker, Aug. 18, 1789, *DHFFC*, 11:1300. On the Tenth Amendment, also see Ames, Feb. 3, 1791, *DHFFC*, 14:390; Gerry, Feb. 7, 1791, *DHFFC*, 14:458. On Laurance's connections to Hamilton, see *DHFFC*, 14:718–722.

24. Ames, Feb. 3, 1791, *DHFFC*, 14:395, 397; Gerry, Feb. 7, 1791, *DHFFC*, 14:458; Laurance, Feb. 4, 1791, *DHFFC*, 14:403–404; Boudinot, Feb. 5, 1791, *DHFFC*, 14:434.

25. Laurance, Feb. 4, 1791, *DHFFC*, 14:413; Gerry, Feb. 7, 1791, *DHFFC*, 14:454; United States Constitution, Preamble; Ames, Feb. 3, 1791, *DHFFC*, 14:397. Also see Boudinot, Feb. 4, 1791, *DHFFC*, 14:434.

26. Vining, Feb. 8, 1791, *DHFFC*, 14:472; Ames, Feb. 3, 1791, *DHFFC*, 14:389, 393; United States Constitution, Article I, Section 8; W. Smith, Feb. 5, 1791, *DHFFC*, 14:423. For a related discussion, see Primus, "Enumerated Powers and the Bank Debate." For the important background of Wilson's 1785 argument, see Mikhail, "Necessary and Proper Clauses," 1074–1078. On the importance of legal corporations as a category of thought at this time, see Mikhail, "Necessary and Proper Clauses," 1109–1114; and on how several prominent Founding-era leaders analogized the national government to a corporation and the Constitution to its corporate charter, see John Mikhail, "The Constitution and the Philosophy of Language: Entailment, Implicature, and Implied Powers," *University of Virginia Law Review* 101 (June 2015), 1082–1084, 1097–1103; David Ciepley, "Is the U.S. Government a Corporation? The Corporate Origins of Modern Constitutionalism," *American Political Science Review* 111 (May 2017), 418–435.

27. Laurance, Feb. 1 and 4, 1791, *DHFFC*, 14:364, 413; Vining, Feb. 2, 1791, *DHFFC*, 14:378; Gerry, Feb. 7, 1791, *DHFFC*, 14:460–461; Ames, Feb. 3, 1791, *DHFFC*, 14:386.

28. Laurance, Feb. 4, 1791, *DHFFC*, 14:403–404; Gerry, Feb. 7, 1791, *DHFFC*, 14:457. Also see Ames, Feb. 3, 1791, *DHFFC*, 14:393.

29. Ames, Feb. 3, 1791, *DHFFC*, 14:395; Vining, Feb. 8, 1791, *DHFFC*, 14:472; *DHFFC*, 14:537–539. Also see Ames, Feb. 3, 1791, *DHFFC*, 14:397; Laurance, Feb. 4, 1791, *DHFFC*, 14:403.

30. Sedgwick, Feb. 4, 1791, *DHFFC*, 14:400; Ames, Feb. 3, 1791, *DHFFC*, 14:393.

31. Ames, Feb. 3, 1791, *DHFFC*, 14:395.

32. "William Pierce: Character Sketches of Delegates to the Federal Convention," *Records*, 3:88; Gerry, Feb. 7, 1791, *DHFFC*, 14:453–454. Also see Boudinot, Feb. 5, 1791, *DHFFC*, 14:436–437. On Gerry's speaking style, see *DHFFC*, 14:621–622.

33. Sedgwick, Feb. 4, 1791, *DHFFC*, 14:399; W. Smith, Feb. 5, 1791, *DHFFC*, 14:430.

34. Ames, Feb. 3, 1791, *DHFFC*, 14:390; W. Smith, Feb. 5, 1791, *DHFFC*, 14:430; Gerry, Feb. 7, 1791, *DHFFC*, 14:457; Sedgwick, Feb. 4, 1791, *DHFFC*, 14:399; Gerry, Feb. 7, 1791, *DHFFC*, 14:458.

35. Ames, Feb. 3, 1791, *DHFFC*, 14:392. While keeping in mind crucial differences between these eighteenth-century claims and later ideas, nonetheless it is valuable to see how this specific argument in the bank debate bears a family resemblance to two

other famous ideas. First, it is akin to H. L. A. Hart's influential conception of primary rules and secondary rules and why the latter are needed to make the former operational; H. L. A. Hart, *The Concept of Law*, 3rd ed. (New York: Oxford University Press, 1961; 2012), esp. ch. 5. Next, in broad outlines it resembles Ludwig Wittgenstein's famous rule-following argument; Ludwig Wittgenstein, *Philosophical Investigations*, trans. G. E. M. Anscombe (New York: Macmillan, 1953), sect. 201.

36. Gerry, Feb. 7, 1791, *DHFFC*, 14:457–458. Also see Laurence, Feb. 4, 1791, *DHFFC*, 14:403. Gerry's point echoed the philosophy of language upon which Thomas Hobbes in part based his absolutist political program; see Philip Pettit, *Made with Words: Hobbes on Language, Mind, and Politics* (Princeton, NJ: Princeton University Press, 2008).

37. Ames, Feb. 3, 1791, *DHFFC*, 14:396; Laurance, Feb. 4, 1791, *DHFFC*, 14:414; Sedgwick, Feb. 4, 1791, *DHFFC*, 14:400. Also see Boudinot, Feb. 5, 1791, *DHFFC*, 14:434–435.

38. W. Smith, Feb. 5, 1791, *DHFFC*, 14:423; Boudinot, Feb. 5, 1791, *DHFFC*, 14:437; Ames, Feb. 3, 1791, *DHFFC*, 14:392. Also see Gerry, Feb. 7, 1791, *DHFFC*, 14:458–459; Vining, Feb. 8, 1791, *DHFFC*, 14:472.

39. Sedgwick, Feb. 4, 1791, *DHFFC*, 14:400; Vining, Feb. 2, 1791, *DHFFC*, 14:378.

40. Madison, Feb. 2, 1791, *DHFFC*, 14:372.

41. Madison, Feb. 2, 1791, *DHFFC*, 14:371; Edward Carrington to Madison, Dec. 25, 1790, *DHFFC*, 21:224; Giles, Feb. 7, 1791, *DHFFC*, 14:466; Stone, Feb. 5, 1791, *DHFFC*, 14:428. On Giles, see *DHFFC*, 14:895–896. On Giles's personality and style in Congress, see *DHFFC*, 14:896–898. On Stone's contributions to the First Congress, see *DHFFC*, 14:599–603.

42. Madison, Feb. 2, 1791, *DHFFC*, 14:371; Stone, Feb. 5, 1791, *DHFFC*, 14:425, 424; Giles, Feb. 7, 1791, *DHFFC*, 14:467. Also see Madison, Feb. 8, 1791, *DHFFC*, 14:474–475.

43. Stone, Feb. 5, 1791, *DHFFC*, 14:424; Madison, Feb. 2, 1791, *DHFFC*, 14:372.

44. Madison, Feb. 8, 1791, *DHFFC*, 14:474; Stone, Feb. 5, 1791, *DHFFC*, 14:425; Giles, Feb. 7, 1791, *DHFFC*, 14:464; Jackson, Feb. 4, 1791, *DHFFC*, 14:407.

45. Madison, Feb. 2, 1791, *DHFFC*, 14:375, 371. For Madison's 1789 arguments, see Chapter 4. For examples of bank supporters invoking Madison's prior understanding of what became the Tenth Amendment, see Laurance, Feb. 4, 1791, *DHFFC*, 14:403; Gerry, Feb. 7, 1791, *DHFFC*, 14:458. In advancing this understanding of the soon to be Ninth and Tenth Amendments, Madison was also attempting to assuage concerns over the proposed amendments in Virginia, where opposition in the state legislature had thwarted ratification up to that point; see Kurt T. Lash, *The Lost History of the Ninth Amendment* (New York: Oxford University Press, 2009), 39–42, 50–69.

46. Giles, Feb. 7, 1791, *DHFFC*, 14:468; Madison, Feb. 2, 1791, *DHFFC*, 14:375. Also see Giles, Feb. 2, 1791, *DHFFC*, 14:377. For a good elaboration on Madison's understanding of this point, see Jeremy D. Bailey, *James Madison and Constitutional Imperfection* (New York: Cambridge University Press, 2015), 102–104.

47. Jackson, Feb. 2, 1791, *DHFFC*, 14:376; Madison, Feb. 2, 1791, *DHFFC*, 14:370, 379. Also, teasing out the logic of Madison's argument, see Laurance, Feb. 4, 1791, *DHFFC*, 14:413. On the Bank of North America and Madison's original opposition to it, see Chapter 1.

48. Madison, Feb. 2, 1791, *DHFFC*, 14:375; Stone, Feb. 5, 1791, *DHFFC*, 14:426.

49. Stone, Feb. 5, 1791, *DHFFC*, 14:425, 429, 423; Jackson, Feb. 4, 1791, *DHFFC*, 14:405–406. Also see Giles, Feb. 7, 1791, *DHFFC*, 14:466.

50. Ames, Feb. 3, 1791, *DHFFC*, 14:392; Madison, Feb. 2, 1791, *DHFFC*, 14:372–373; Giles, Feb. 7, 1791, *DHFFC*, 14:463. Reinforcing Ames's point, see Laurance, Feb. 4, 1791, *DHFFC*, 14:403.

51. Madison, Feb. 2, 1791, *DHFFC*, 14:375, 369; Stone, Feb. 5, 1791, *DHFFC*, 14:429.

52. Others have highlighted such historical appeals, but often by downplaying them in the process. Some have done so by attributing these appeals to partisan maneuvering; see Klubes, "First Federal Congress and the First National Bank"; Lynch, *Negotiating the Constitution,* 80, 82, 85–86; Louis J. Sirico Jr., "Original Intent in the First Congress," *Missouri Law Review* 71 (Summer 2006), 700–701, 711–712, 717–720. Other scholars have considered these historical appeals insignificant compared with other kinds of interpretive moves; see H. Jefferson Powell, "The Original Understanding of Original Intent," *Harvard Law Review* 98 (Mar. 1985), 914–917; Banning *Sacred Fire of Liberty,* 326–327; Rakove, *Original Meanings,* 350–355. Still others have pointed to the bank debate as evidence that America's first political generation did not agree on the Constitution's original meaning; see Leonard W. Levy, *Original Intent and the Framers' Constitution* (New York: MacMillan, 1988), 7–10. While no doubt all to varying extents true, disputants' capacity to converge on common argumentative sources and methods was, in many ways, more important than the heterogeneity that such resources facilitated. Meanwhile, others have claimed that Madison's appeal to original intent was significant, but only because it revealed his long-standing commitments to popular sovereignty; see Colleen A. Sheehan, *James Madison and the Spirit of Republican Government* (New York: Cambridge University Press, 2009), 109–110. But whatever such appeals might have suggested about the consistency of Madison's principles, importantly they also began to signal a rupture in his constitutional imagination. These historical appeals must be appreciated as the novelty that they were. In a different, if related, vein, Lance Banning influentially argued that Madison, Jefferson, and their allies, without an ancient constitution to which to appeal, "made the Constitution old," venerating it as a fundamental standard against which Hamilton's transgressions could be judged; see Lance Banning, "Republican Ideology and the Triumph of the Constitution," *WMQ* 31 (Apr. 1974), 176–188. While a stimulating interpretation, importantly, nothing about conceiving of the Constitution in this way necessitated appealing to the events of its putative creation or imagining it as an archival object. Its antiquity easily

could have been understood and venerated in much the way the British constitution previously had been.

53. Madison, Feb. 2, 1791, *DHFFC*, 14:368, 374. It is unknown exactly which speeches Madison read, but for Federalist assurances along the lines that Madison described from the specified conventions, see *DHRC*, 2:454, 482, 496, 539, 9:1135, 10:1340; *Debates,* 4:141, 179, 182. I credit the editors of the *DHFFC* for these citations; see 14:374n9. To draw on these conventions, Madison likely would have relied on the following versions of published debates: Thomas Lloyd, *Debates of the Convention, of the State of Pennsylvania* (Philadelphia: Joseph James, 1788); *Debates and Other Proceedings of the Convention of Virginia,* 3 vols. (Petersburg, VA: Hunter and Prentis [vol. I], Prentis [vols. II–III], 1788–1789); *Proceedings and Debates of the Convention of North-Carolina* (Edenton, NC: Hodge and Wills, 1789).

54. Madison, Feb. 2, 1791, *DHFFC*, 14:375.

55. Ames, Feb. 3, 1791, *DHFFC*, 14:392; Ames to Timothy Dwight, Feb. 7, 1791, *DHFFC*, 21:720; Ames to George Richards Minot, Feb. 17, 1791, *DHFFC*, 21:858; Ames to Andrew Craigie, Feb. 2, 1791, *DHFFC*, 21:657; Madison, Feb. 2, 1791, *DHFFC*, 14:374.

56. Vining, Feb. 8, 1791, *DHFFC*, 14:471; Gerry, Feb. 7, 1791, *DHFFC*, 14:459–460. Also see Boudinot, Feb. 5, 1791, *DHFFC*, 14:436. On Gerry's strong rebuttal, also see Mary Sarah Bilder, "How Bad Were the Official Records of the Federal Convention?" *George Washington Law Review* 80 (Nov. 2012), 1669.

57. Gerry, Feb. 7, 1791, *DHFFC*, 14:460. The judges were James Wilson (Pennsylvania) and James Iredell (North Carolina), both of whom in 1791 were serving on the Supreme Court. On Gerry's experience at the Massachusetts convention, see *DHRC*, 6:1115–1116; and on complaints about the records of that convention, see *DHRC*, 6:1135–1136. Laurance cited proposed amendments from three state ratifying conventions (New Hampshire, Massachusetts, and New York) in an effort to prove that members of the conventions assumed Congress would have the power to establish companies with exclusive privileges; see Laurance, Feb. 4, 1791, *DHRC*, 14:404.

58. Boudinot, Feb. 4, 1791, *DHFFC*, 14:439; Jackson, Feb. 2, 1791, *DHFFC*, 14:376. On *Federalist* 44, see Chapter 2.

59. Boudinot, Feb. 5, 1791, *DHFFC*, 14:439; Publius [Madison], "The Federalist 44," *New York Packet,* Jan. 25, 1788, *DHRC*, 15:472. Boudinot also read from *Federalist* 23, Feb. 5, 1791, *DHRC*, 14:439; while Smith invoked Hamilton as interpretive authority, Feb. 5, 1791, *DHRC* 14:421. On Boudinot's personality, see *DHFFC*, 14:685.

60. None of the authors of the *Federalist* were yet well known, although rumors circulated widely. On public knowledge of the authorship, although primarily what was known in 1787–1788, see *DHRC*, 13:488–490.

61. *DHFFC*, 1:703–704. On Washington's obsession with precedent and its connection to the veto, see Joseph J. Ellis, *His Excellency: George Washington* (New York: Knopf, 2004), 188–240; Elkins and McKitrick, *Age of Federalism,* 34–64, 232–233. On Madison's attempts to persuade Washington, recounted later in life, see "Detached

Memoranda," 1819–1820, *PJM RS*, 1:603–604; and for the version of the veto Madison drafted, see "Draft Veto of the Bank Bill," Feb. 21, 1791, *PJM*, 13:395–396. On their friendship more generally, see Stuart Leibiger, *Founding Friendship: George Washington, James Madison, and the Creation of the American Republic* (Charlottesville: University of Virginia Press, 1999).

62. For a good discussion of the three opinions, which similarly grasps that their significance lay not in their arguments but in their broader constitutional assumptions, see H. Jefferson Powell, *A Community Built on Words: The Constitution in History and Politics* (Chicago: University of Chicago Press, 2002), 21–31. Whereas, Powell assumes that the disagreement turned on what kind of legal text the Constitution was, I see the disagreement over the Constitution's nature running much deeper. On the opinions, also see *DHFFC*, 21:766–769.

63. Edmund Randolph, "Opinion," Feb. 12, 1791, *DHFFC*, 21:769–777; Thomas Jefferson, "Opinion on the Constitutionality of the Bill for Establishing a National Bank," Feb. 15, 1791, *PTJ*, 19:276–279.

64. Randolph, "Opinion," *DHFFC*, 21:770.

65. Randolph, "Opinion," *DHFFC*, 21:771. On Randolph's arguments in the *Case of the Prisoners* and how he drew on them as a member of the Committee of Detail at the Federal Convention, see Chapter 1 and supporting notes.

66. Randolph, "Opinion," *DHFFC*, 21:771–772. For Randolph's arguments about constitutional interpretation in the state convention, see Edmund Randolph, Virginia Ratifying Convention, June 17, 1788, *DHRC*, 10:1347–1348. Although, at this earlier date, Randolph did suggest that the federal Constitution was distinct because its powers were enumerated.

67. Randolph, "Opinion," *DHFFC*, 21:776, 772.

68. Jefferson, "Opinion on the Constitutionality of the Residence Bill," July 15, 1790, *PTJ*, 17:195; Jefferson, "Opinion on the Constitutionality of the Bill for Establishing a National Bank," *PTJ*, 19:276, 279. On Jefferson's initially idiosyncratic relationship with the Constitution, see Mary Sarah Bilder, *Madison's Hand: Revising the Constitutional Convention* (Cambridge, MA: Harvard University Press, 2015), 202–205.

69. Jefferson, "Opinion on the Constitutionality of the Bill for Establishing a National Bank," *PTJ*, 19:277–278. This reading of Madison's notes was tendentious because most delegates who opposed the motion assumed that the federal government would already enjoy the power in question, making the addition of the power redundant; see Sept. 14, 1787, *Records*, 2:615–616. On Jefferson's use of Madison's notes, see Bilder, *Madison's Hand*, 205–208. Madison later complained that Washington should have known that the Convention had done this; see "Detached Memoranda," 1819–1820, *PJM RS*, 1:603–604, 605.

70. Hamilton, "Opinion on the Constitutionality of an Act to Establish a Bank," Feb. 23, 1791, *PAH*, 8:132, 106, 100.

71. Hamilton, "Opinion on the Constitutionality of an Act to Establish a Bank," *PAH*, 8:98, 100, 105, 102, 97.

72. Hamilton, "Opinion on the Constitutionality of an Act to Establish a Bank," *PAH*, 8:107.

73. Hamilton, "Opinion on the Constitutionality of an Act to Establish a Bank," *PAH*, 8:130.

74. For the bill, see *DHFFC*, 4:164–170.

75. Madison, Feb. 8, 1791, *DHFFC*, 14:476, 477.

76. Hamilton, "Report on the Subject of Manufactures," Dec. 5, 1791, *PAH*, 10:303; Madison to Henry Lee, Jan. 1, 1792, *PJM*, 14:180; Madison to Lee, Jan. 21, 1792, *PJM*, 14:194.

6. The "People's" Constitution

Epigraph: Hancock, "For the Aurora," *Aurora General Advertiser* (Philadelphia), Aug. 21, 1795, 3.

1. Uriah Tracy, Mar. 7, 1796, *AC*, 5:427; Albert Gallatin, Mar. 7, 1796, *AC*, 5:436; Edward Livingston, Mar. 7, 1796, *AC*, 5:427.

2. Livingston, Mar. 2, 1796, *AC*, 5:426.

3. Daniel Buck, Mar. 7, 1796, *AC*, 5:432–433; United States Constitution, Article II, Section 2.

4. Theodore Sedgwick, Mar. 11, 1796, *AC*, 5:514.

5. Sedgwick, Mar. 11, 1796, *AC*, 5:521. On how the Jay Treaty solidified partisan coalitions, see Joseph Charles, "The Jay Treaty: The Origins of the American Party System," *WMQ* 12 (Oct. 1955), 581–630; Jeffrey L. Pasley, *The First Presidential Contest: 1796 and the Founding of American Democracy* (Lawrence: University Press of Kansas, 2013), 101.

6. On the traumatic violence of the Revolutionary War, see Holger Hoock, *Scars of Independence: America's Violent Birth* (New York: Crown, 2017). On cultural separation from Britain, see John M. Murrin, "A Roof without Walls: The Dilemma of American National Identity," in *Beyond Confederation: Origins of the Constitution and American National Identity*, ed. Richard Beeman, Stephen Botein, and Edward C. Carter II (Chapel Hill: University of North Carolina Press, 1987), 333–348; Kariann Akemi Yokota, *Unbecoming British: How Revolutionary America Became a Postcolonial Nation* (New York: Oxford University Press, 2011). On discrimination efforts, see Stanley Elkins and Eric McKitrick, *The Age of Federalism, the Early American Republic, 1788–1800* (New York: Oxford University Press, 1993), 65–75, 223–225; Merrill D. Peterson, "Thomas Jefferson and Commercial Policy," *WMQ* 22 (Oct. 1965), 584–610.

7. Thomas Jefferson to Brissot de Warville, May 8, 1793, *PTJ*, 25:679. Hamilton's financial program relied on a stable revenue, which relied on the new federal impost, which was tied to the volume of international trade (and Britain was America's leading trading partner). Hamilton envisioned that American merchants would turn trading profits into investment capital. On this point, see Gautham Rao, *National Duties: Custom Houses and the Making of the American State* (Chicago: University of Chicago

Press, 2016), introduction, chs. 2–3; Max M. Edling, *A Hercules in the Cradle: War, Money, and the American State, 1783–1867* (Chicago: University of Chicago Press, 2014), ch. 2; Samuel Flagg Bemis, *Jay's Treaty: A Study in Commerce and Diplomacy,* 2nd ed. (New York: Macmillan, 1962), ch. 2. On Anglo-inspired state-building, see Elkins and McKitrick, *Age of Federalism,* 77–161; Richard H. Kohn, *The Federalists and the Creation of the Military Establishment in America, 1783–1802* (New York: Free Press, 1975). On fears of monarchism, see Joanne B. Freeman, *Affairs of Honor: National Politics in the Early Republic* (New Haven, CT: Yale University Press, 2001), 38–48; Lance Banning, *The Jeffersonian Persuasion: Evolution of a Party Ideology* (Ithaca, NY: Cornell University Press, 1978), 117–120; Gordon S. Wood, *Empire of Liberty: A History of the Early Republic, 1789–1815* (New York: Oxford University Press, 2009), ch. 2.

8. On the French Revolution in America, see Susan Dunn, *Sister Revolutions: French Lightning, American Light* (New York: Faber & Faber, 1999); Elkins and McKitrick, *Age of Federalism,* ch. 8; Wood, *Empire of Liberty,* ch. 5; James Roger Sharp, *American Politics in the Early Republic: The New Nation in Crisis* (New Haven, CT: Yale University Press, 1993), ch. 4; Pasley, *First Presidential Contest,* 63–82. On festive support, see David Waldstreicher, *In the Midst of Perpetual Fetes: The Making of American Nationalism, 1776–1820* (Chapel Hill: University of North Carolina Press, 1997), 112–117, 126–140; Simon P. Newman, *Parades and Politics of the Street: Festive Culture in the Early American Republic* (Philadelphia: University of Pennsylvania Press, 1997), ch. 4; Susan Branson, *These Fiery Frenchified Dames: Women and Political Culture in Early National Philadelphia* (Philadelphia: University of Pennsylvania Press, 2001), ch. 2; Heather Nathans, *Early American Theater from the Revolution to Thomas Jefferson: Into the Hands of the People* (New York: Cambridge University Press, 2003), 78–81. On how the French Revolution's violence polarized early republican America, see Rachel Hope Cleves, *The Reign of Terror in America: Visions of Violence from Anti-Jacobinism to Antislavery* (New York: Oxford University Press, 2009), chs. 1–3. On how the French Revolution affected American political assumptions, see Seth Cotlar, *Tom Paine's America: The Rise and Fall of Transatlantic Radicalism* (Charlottesville: University of Virginia Press, 2011), 5–6, 36–39, 49–55, 69–78; James T. Kloppenberg, *Towards Democracy: The Struggle for Self-Rule in European and American Thought* (New York: Oxford University Press, 2016), chs. 10–11; Matthew Rainbow Hale, "Regenerating the World: The French Revolution, Civic Festivals, and the Forging of Modern American Democracy, 1793–1795," *Journal of American History* 103 (Mar. 2017), 891–920. On the personal connections between France and the United States initiated by revolution, see Francois Furstenberg, *When the United States Spoke French: Five Refugees Who Shaped a Nation* (New York: Penguin Press, 2014).

9. Jeffrey L. Pasley, *"The Tyranny of Printers": Newspapers Politics in the Early American Republic* (Charlottesville: University of Virginia Press, 2001), ch. 3; "Jefferson, Freneau, and the Founding of the *National Gazette,*" *PTJ,* 20:718–754. On newspaper politics generally, see Pasley, *"Tyranny of Printers";* Marcus Daniel, *Scandal and Civility: Journalism and the Birth of American Democracy* (New York: Oxford University Press, 2009).

10. John Beckley to Madison, Sept. 10, 1792, *PJM*, 14:361; Catharine Maria Sedgwick, "A Reminiscence of Federalism," in *Tales and Sketches* (Philadelphia: Carey, Lea, and Blanchard, 1835), 23, 10; Fisher Ames to Dwight Foster, Jan. 4, 1796, *WFA*, 2:1128. On the Jeffersonian Republican opposition and its ideology, see Saul Cornell, *The Other Founders: Anti-Federalism and the Dissenting Tradition in America, 1788–1828* (Chapel Hill: University of North Carolina Press, 1999), chs. 5–7; Banning, *Jeffersonian Persuasion*, chs. 5–7; Joyce Appleby, *Capitalism and the New Social Order: The Republican Vision of the 1790s* (New York: New York University Press, 1984); Elkins and McKitrick, *Age of Federalism*, ch. 7; and Alfred F. Young, *The Democratic Republicans of New York, 1763–1797* (Chapel Hill: University of North Carolina Press, 1967), chs. 8–15. On Federalists' own ideology, see Elkins and McKitrick, *Age of Federalism*, 21–25; David Hackett Fischer, *The Revolution of American Conservatism: The Federalist Party in the Era of Jeffersonian Democracy* (New York: Harper and Row, 1956). On Federalists' and Republicans' cultivation of rival personas, see Alan Taylor, "From Fathers to Friends of the People: Political Personas in the Early Republic," *JER* 11 (Winter 1991), 465–491. Historians in the 1950s and 1960s emphasized the continuities between these early party associations and their modern counterparts; for example, see Richard Hofstadter, *The Idea of a Party System: The Rise of Legitimate Opposition in the United States, 1780–1840* (Berkeley: University of California Press, 1969); Joseph Charles, *The Origins of the American Party System* (New York: Harper and Row, 1956); William Nisbit Chambers, *Political Parties in a New Nation: The American Experience, 1776–1809* (New York: Oxford University Press, 1963). Subsequently, historians more sensitive to the workings of the eighteenth century have claimed that these parties were distinct from modern counterparts; see Ronald Formisano, "Federalists and Republicans: Parties, Yes—System, No," in Paul Kleppner et al., *The Evolution of American Electoral Systems* (Westport, CT: Greenwood Press, 1981), 33–76; Sharp, *American Politics in the Early Republic*, 42–43, 53, 58–59, 138–142, 157–159; Freeman, *Affairs of Honor*, xviii–xix, 8–9, 213–216, 286–287; Sean Wilentz, *The Rise of American Democracy: From Jefferson to Lincoln* (New York: Norton, 2005), 50–53. Having moved past the debate over whether early republican parties lived up to modern standards, historians now sensibly weigh the coherence of party association, how best to characterize it, and where best to find it. Those who have seen political ties in flux have tended to render associations in personal and elite terms, focusing on national leaders and their negotiations with one another. From this focus, they have concluded that politics were traditional in character; for example, see Freeman, *Affairs of Honor*. Those who have stressed the coherence of partisan affiliation have explored how leaders and voters were linked by stable patterns of ideology and emotion, focusing on the midlevel party brokers (like newspaper printers and state officials) who constructed many of the narratives that held them together and the cultural sites (like festivals and nominating meetings) in which they were played out. This focus has portrayed politics as more modern in character; see especially Pasley, *First Presidential Contest*; Alan Taylor, "'The Art of Hook &

Snivey': Political Culture in Upstate New York during the 1790s," *Journal of American History* 79 (Mar. 1993), 1371–1396; and, more generally, Jeffrey L. Pasley, Andrew W. Robertson, and David Waldstreicher, eds., *Beyond the Founders: New Approaches to the Political History of the Early Republic* (Chapel Hill: University of North Carolina Press, 2004). A complete picture of early republican politics, capturing all its contradictory imperatives and practices, benefits from both perspectives. On the founding generation's wariness of political parties, see Pasley, *First Presidential Contest*, 1–2; Elkins and McKitrick, *Age of Federalism*, 263–264; Alan Taylor, *William Cooper's Town: Power and Persuasion on the Frontier of the Early American Republic* (New York: Knopf, 1995), 229–235.

11. Jefferson to James Madison, July 7, 1793, *PTJ*, 26:444; Elkins and McKitrick, *Age of Federalism*, 335–341, 360–362.

12. [Alexander Hamilton], "Pacificus," No. 1, June 29, 1793, *PAH*, 15:42; [Madison], "Helvidius" No. 1, Aug. 24, 1793, *PJM*, 15:68–69, and on executive removal, 72; "Helvidius" No. 4, Sept. 14, 1793, *PJM*, 15:106, 108. My discussion here is indebted to David M. Golove and Daniel J. Hulsebosch, "A Civilized Nation: The Early American Constitution, the Law of Nations, and the Pursuit of International Recognition," *N.Y.U. Law Review* 85 (Oct. 2010), 1021–1022n348, 1035–1039.

13. Elkins and McKitrick, *Age of Federalism*, 375–406; Bemis, *Jay's Treaty*, chs. 6–9; Jerald A. Combs, *The Jay Treaty: Political Battleground of the Founding Fathers* (Berkeley: University of California Press, 1970), chs. 6–7; Sharp, *American Politics in the Early Republic*, 113–138; Joseph M. Fewster, "The Jay Treaty and British Ship Seizures: The Martinique Cases," *WMQ* 45 (July 1988), 426–452.

14. Elkins and McKitrick, *Age of Federalism*, 406–414; Bemis, *Jay's Treaty*, chs. 12–13; Combs, *Jay Treaty*, ch. 9. Jay was unable to secure certain demands: full neutrality rights for American ships, prohibitions on British military alliances with American Indians or military ships on the Great Lakes, or compensation for slaves taken by the British during the Revolution, although none were realistic possibilities.

15. Jefferson to James Monroe, Sept. 6, 1795, *PTJ*, 28:449; William Manning, *The Key of Liberty: The Life and Democratic Writings of William Manning, "A Laborer," 1747–1814*, ed. Michael Merrill and Sean Wilentz (Cambridge, MA: Harvard University Press, 1993), 150; William Munford, *Poems and Compositions in Prose on Several Occasions* (Richmond, VA: Samuel Pleasants, 1798), 166; [Anonymous], *Letters of Franklin, on the conduct of the executive, and the treaty negociated, by the chief justice of the United States with the Court of Great Britain* (Philadelphia: E. Osward, 1795), 20, 11. On initial opposition to the treaty, see Pasley, *First Presidential Contest*, 109–116.

16. *Aurora General Advertiser* (Philadelphia), June 22, 1795, 3; Daniel, *Scandal and Civility*, 136. Although the speeches in the Senate were not recorded, the general parameters of the debate can be tracked in *AC*, 4:853–863; also see Combs, *Jay Treaty*, 159–162. In the Senate, there were constitutional challenges to Article IX (which protected British property rights in the United States) and Article XV (which prevented either Britain or the United States from discriminating against the other's trade status). There

were also political objections to Article XII (which reopened American trade with the British Caribbean but on unfavorable terms), and the Senate refused to ratify that article. For more, see David P. Currie, *The Constitution in Congress: The Federalist Period, 1789–1801* (Chicago: University of Chicago Press, 1997), 210–211; Elkins and McKitrick, *Age of Federalism,* 418–420.

17. Todd Estes, *The Jay Treaty Debate, Public Opinion, and the Evolution of American Political Culture* (Amherst: University of Massachusetts Press, 2006), 71–78; Pasley, *First Presidential Contest,* 116–131; Paul A. Gilje, *The Road to Mobocracy: Popular Disorder in New York City, 1763–1834* (Chapel Hill: University of North Carolina Press, 1987), 100–104; Waldstreicher, *In the Midst of Perpetual Fetes,* 138–152; Daniel, *Scandal and Civility,* 137–138; Hope Cleves, *Reign of Terror in America,* 67–68. On public charges of unconstitutionality, see David M. Golove, "Treaty-Making and the Nation: The Historical Foundations of the Nationalist Conception of the Treaty Power," *Michigan Law Review* 98 (Mar. 2000), 1161–1168; Amanda C. Demmer, "Trick or Constitutional Treaty? The Jay Treaty and the Quarrel over the Diplomatic Separation of Powers," *JER* 35 (Winter 2015), 584–591. On Washington's struggle, see Combs, *Jay Treaty,* 164–170; Elkins and McKitrick, *Age of Federalism,* 422–431.

18. Madison, "For the *National Gazette:* Who Are the Best Keepers of the People's Liberties?" Dec. 20, 1792, *PJM,* 14:426; Jefferson to Madison, Mar. 27, 1796, *PTJ,* 29:51.

19. *Aurora General Advertiser* (Philadelphia), June 22, 1795, 3; Madison, "For the *National Gazette*: Who Are the Best Keepers of the People's Liberties?" 14:426. On the comparative openness of the ratification process, see Akhil Reed Amar, *America's Constitution: A Biography* (New York: Random House, 2005), 5–21; but for a skeptical take, see Michael J. Klarman, *The Framers' Coup: The Making of the United States Constitution* (New York: Oxford University Press, 2016), 409–412, 530–532, 618–619. Even if the ratification process fell short of the openness of state practices, that was only because they were more democratic and public than what was otherwise common at the time. On the democratization of American political culture following the Revolution, see Gordon S. Wood, *The Radicalism of the American Revolution* (New York: Knopf, 1992), chs. 13–16; and on how Republicans exploited these energies, see Taylor, "From Fathers to Friends of the People." On popular politics, see Pasley, Robertson, and Waldstreicher, *Beyond the Founders,* esp. introduction; Waldstreicher, *In the Midst of Perpetual Fetes;* Newman, *Parades and the Politics of the Street;* Cornell, *Other Founders,* 243–253. On publicity, see Cotlar, *Tom Paine's America,* ch. 1, 161–188; Michael Warner, *The Letters of the Republic: Publication and the Public Sphere in Eighteenth-Century America* (Cambridge, MA: Harvard University Press, 1990), 118–122; Christopher Grasso, *A Speaking Aristocracy: Transforming Public Discourse in Eighteenth-Century Connecticut* (Chapel Hill: University of North Carolina Press, 1999), ch. 6. On the Democratic-Republican societies, see Philip S. Foner, ed., *The Republican Societies, 1790–1800: A Documentary Sourcebook of Constitutions, Declarations, Addresses, Resolutions, and Toasts*

(Westport, CT: Greenwood Press, 1976), introduction; John L. Brooke, "Ancient Lodges and Self-Created Societies: Freemasonry and the Public Sphere in the Early Republic," in *Launching the "Extended Republic": The Federalist Era,* ed. Ronald Hoffman and Peter J. Albert (Charlottesville: University of Virginia Press, 1996), 309–316; Pasley, *First Presidential Contest,* 82–87; Wilentz, *Rise of American Democracy,* 40–42, 53–71; Elkins and McKitrick, *Age of Federalism,* 451–461.

20. Madison, "For the *National Gazette*—Public Opinion," [Dec. 19, 1791], *PJM,* 14:170; Buck, Mar. 7, 1796, *AC,* 5:435; Madison, "For the *National Gazette:* Charters," Jan. 18, 1792, *PJM,* 14:192. On public opinion, see Gordon S. Wood, "The Founders and Public Opinion," in *Revolutionary Characters: What Made the Founders Different* (New York: Penguin Press, 2006), 244–274; Estes, *Jay Treaty Debate,* esp. 1–13, 71–149; Mark G. Schmeller, *Invisible Sovereign: Imagining Public Opinion from the Revolution to Reconstruction* (Baltimore: The Johns Hopkins University Press, 2016), 47–54. On Madison and public opinion, above all see Colleen A. Sheehan, *James Madison and the Spirit of Republican Government* (New York: Cambridge University Press, 2009), chs. 3–5; Robert W. T. Martin, *Government by Dissent: Protest, Resistance, and Radical Democratic Thought in the Early American Republic* (New York: New York University Press, 2013), 130–139; and on his intellectual influences, see Colleen A. Sheehan, *The Mind of James Madison: The Legacy of Classical Republicanism* (New York: Cambridge University Press, 2015), ch. 3. On Madison's *National Gazette* essays (published between Nov. 1791 and Dec. 1792), see the introductory editorial note, *PJM,* 14:110–112. On the influential French context in which ideas about public opinion developed, see Keith Michael Baker, *Inventing the French Revolution: Essays on French Political Culture in the Eighteenth Century* (New York: Cambridge University Press, 1990), 167–199; Mona Ozouf, "'Public Opinion' at the End of the Old Regime," trans. Lydia C. Cochrane, *Journal of Modern History* 60, Supplement (1988), 1–21. On Federalists' rival understanding of the public's relationship to politics, see Cotlar, *Tom Paine's America,* 188–206; Hope Cleves, *Reign of Terror in America,* 32–52; Waldstreicher, *In the Midst of Perpetual Fetes,* 140–141; Schmeller, *Invisible Sovereign,* 64–69.

21. On the pamphlet debate that largely followed Washington's decision to sign the treaty, see Elkins and McKitrick, *Age of Federalism,* 432–436; Estes, *Jay Treaty Debate,* 78–94, ch. 4. The leading Republican authors were Robert R. Livingston, Alexander Dallas, and Brockholst Livingston, while the leading Federalist defenders were—in addition to Hamilton—Noah Webster, James Kent, and Rufus King. Robert Goodloe Harper and William Loughton Smith were among the congressmen who joined the debate. Federalists grew convinced that, thanks in part to their pamphleteering campaign, public anger had tempered, which then encouraged Washington finally to deliver the treaty to the House in March 1796; see Estes, *Jay Treaty Debate,* 94–103. On the public censure of Washington, see Pasley, *First Presidential Contest,* 133–145; Daniel, *Scandal and Civility,* 138–144; Estes, *Jay Treaty Debate,* 108–111. For a good discussion of

how the pamphlet debate focused on important constitutional issues, including especially the tensions between national treaty power and states' rights, see Golove,
"Treaty-Making and the Nation," 1164–1174.

22. Belisarius, No. II, "For the Aurora," *Aurora General Advertiser,* Sept. 15, 1795, 3;
Jefferson to Edward Rutledge, Nov. 30, 1795, *PTJ,* 28:542; William Branch Giles, Mar.
11, 1796, *AC,* 5:503; Manning, *Key of Liberty,* 150; Ames to Oliver Wolcott, Sept. 2, 1795,
WFA, 2:1115; Ames to Thomas Dwight, Dec. 30, 1795, *WFA,* 2:1125. Also see Jefferson to
James Monroe, Sept. 6, 1795, *PTJ,* 28:449; Robert R. Livingston to Madison, Nov. 16,
1795, *PJM,* 16:125–126. On the petitions that began flooding into the House of Representatives, see Estes, *Jay Treaty Debate,* ch. 5. The Virginia state legislature also drafted
constitutional amendments, the most important of which would have required House
approval on any treaty that interfered with the House's authority to legislate; see Thomas
J. Farnham, "The Virginia Amendments of 1795: An Episode in the Opposition to Jay's
Treaty," *Virginia Magazine of History and Biography* 75 (Jan. 1967), 75–88.

23. Madison to Jefferson, Nov. 16, 1794, *PJM,* 15:380; Ames to Dwight, Feb. 11,
1796, *WFA,* 2:1133; Gordon S. Wood, "Interests and Disinterestedness in the Making
of the Constitution," in *Beyond Confederation: Origins of the Constitution and American National Identity,* ed. Richard Beeman, Stephen Botein, and Edward C. Carter
II (Chapel Hill: University of North Carolina Press, 1987), 93–109; Roland M. Bau-
mann, "John Swanwick: Spokesman for 'Merchant Republicanism' in Philadelphia,
1790–98," *Pennsylvania Magazine of History and Biography* 97 (Apr. 1973), 131–182;
Taylor, *William Cooper's Town,* chs. 6–7, 275–277. On the development of partisan-
ship in Congress, see Raymond W. Smock, "The Institutional Development of the
House of Representatives, 1791–1801," in *The House and Senate in the 1790s: Petitioning,
Lobbying, and Institutional Development,* ed. Kenneth R. Bowling and Donald R.
Kennon (Athens: Ohio University Press, 2002), 321–336. On how the expanding fron-
tier was remaking American society and politics, see Taylor, *William Cooper's Town.*
On the Whiskey Rebellion and the radicalism of western Pennsylvania, see Thomas P.
Slaughter, *The Whiskey Rebellion: Frontier Rebellion to the American Revolution* (New
York: Oxford University Press, 1986); Terry Bouton, *Taming Democracy: "The People,"
the Founders, and the Troubled Ending of the American Revolution* (New York: Oxford
University Press, 2007), ch. 10; Andrew Shankman, *Crucible of Democracy: The Struggle
to Fuse Egalitarianism & Capitalism in Jeffersonian Pennsylvania* (Lawrence: University
Press of Kansas, 2004), 54–63.

24. John Swanwick, Mar. 8, 1796, *AC,* 5:449. Also see Gallatin, Mar. 7, 1796, *AC,*
5:436; Abraham Baldwin, Mar. 7 and 14, 1796, *AC,* 5:435, 541.

25. Gallatin, Mar. 7, 1796, *AC,* 5:436, 437; Combs, *Jay Treaty,* 174–176; Pasley, *First
Presidential Contest,* 146–148; Young, *Democratic Republicans of New York,* 420–421,
460–461; Livingston to R. Livingston, Dec. 24, 1795, *PJM,* 16:248n5. On Madison's
uneasiness over Livingston's tactic, see Madison to Jefferson, Mar. 6, 1796, *PJM,*

16:247; Ralph Ketcham, *James Madison: A Biography* (1971; Charlottesville: University of Virginia Press, 1990), 360–361. For Madison's unsuccessful attempt to weaken the resolution, see Madison, Mar. 7 and 8, 1796, *AC*, 5:438.

26. William Loughton Smith, Mar. 10, 1796, *AC*, 5:497; William Vans Murray, Mar. 7, 1796, *AC*, 5:429; Nathaniel Smith, Mar. 9, 1796, *AC*, 5:453. Also see Ezekiel Gilbert, Mar. 7, 1796, *AC*, 5:437; Robert Goodloe Harper, Mar. 9, 1796, *AC*, 5:458, 464; W. Smith, Mar. 8, 1796, *AC*, 5:440; Roger Griswold, Mar. 10, 1796, *AC*, 5:476; Sedgwick, Mar. 11, 1796, *AC*, 5:514; Samuel Lyman, Mar. 14, 1796, *AC*, 5:531; Theophilus Bradbury, Mar. 14, 1796, *AC*, 5:553; Benjamin Bourne, Mar. 15, 1796, *AC*, 5:573; James Hillhouse, Mar. 22, 1796, *AC*, 5:675.

27. Gallatin, Mar. 7, 1796, *AC*, 5:436; William Findley, Mar. 16, 1796, *AC*, 5:593; John Nicholas, Mar. 8, 1796, *AC*, 5:444; Giles, Mar. 11, 1796, *AC*, 5:501. Also see Livingston, Mar. 7, 1796, *AC*, 5:427; Baldwin, Mar. 7 and 14, 1796, *AC*, 5:435, 541; Swanwick, Mar. 8, 1796, *AC*, 5:449.

28. Nathaniel Freeman Jr., Mar. 16, 1796, *AC*, 5:584; Madison, Mar. 10, 1796, *AC*, 5:487; Madison to Jefferson, Mar. 13, 1796, *PJM*, 16:264. In the House debate, Republicans tended to retreat from the more extreme positions Republican writers had staked out during the public debate vis-à-vis the House's agency in making treaties; see Golove, "Treaty-Making and the Nation," 1174–1178. But House Republicans still insisted that the House was necessary to carry out commercial agreements like Jay's Treaty.

29. Joshua Coit, Mar. 22, 1796, *AC*, 5:654; John Williams, Mar. 21, 1796, *AC*, 5:645. Also see John Milledge, Mar. 21, 1796, *AC*, 5:650; Aaron Kitchell, Mar. 21, 1796, *AC*, 5:653; Hillhouse, Mar. 22, 1796, *AC*, 5:669. For an example of a Republican making this argument, see Livingston, Mar. 18, 1796, *AC*, 5:632.

30. Sedgwick, Mar. 11, 1796, *AC*, 5:530; William Cooper, Mar. 14, 1796, *AC*, 5:542; Gilbert, Mar. 23, 1796, *AC*, 5:680; Bourne, Mar. 15, 1796, *AC*, 5:575. Also see Chauncey Goodrich, Mar. 24, 1796, *AC*, 5:717, 719; Bourne, Mar. 15, 1796, *AC*, 5:574.

31. Murray, Mar. 23, 1796, *AC*, 5:703; James Holland, Mar. 14, 1796, *AC*, 5:544; Richard Brent, Mar. 15, 1796, *AC*, 5:584. Also see Hillhouse, Mar. 22, 1796, *AC*, 5:672.

32. Murray, Mar. 23, 1796, *AC*, 5:700; Cooper, Mar. 14, 1796, *AC*, 5:541–542; Coit, Mar. 22, 1796, *AC*, 5:659. Also see W. Smith, Mar. 7 and 8, 1796, *AC*, 5:439, 443; Sedgwick, Mar. 11, 1796, *AC*, 5:514–515, 518; S. Lyman, Mar. 14, 1796, *AC*, 5:530; Bourne, Mar. 15, 1796, *AC*, 5:573; Williams, Mar. 21, 1796, *AC*, 5:649.

33. Jeremiah Smith, Mar. 16, 1796, *AC*, 5:598; Tracy, Mar. 17, 1796, *AC*, 5:618; Hillhouse, Mar. 22, 1796, *AC*, 5:661; Griswold, Mar. 10, 1796, *AC*, 5:479. Also see N. Smith, Mar. 9, 1796, *AC*, 5:455–456; Harper, Mar. 9, 1796, *AC*, 5:463; Williams, Mar. 21, 1796, *AC*, 5:645; Buck, Mar. 24, 1796, *AC*, 5:709–710, 716.

34. Sedgwick, Mar. 11, 1796, *AC*, 5:515; Hillhouse, Mar. 22, 1796, *AC*, 5:668; Cooper, Mar. 14, 1796, *AC*, 5:542. Also see Griswold, Mar. 10, 1796, *AC*, 5:476; W. Smith, Mar. 11, 1796, *AC*, 5:500; John Reed, Mar. 17, 1796, *AC*, 5:610; Williams,

Mar. 21, 1796, *AC*, 5:643; Coit, Mar. 22, 1796, *AC*, 5:654; Hillhouse, Mar. 22, 1796, *AC*, 5:669.

35. Sedgwick, Mar. 11, 1796, *AC*, 5:514; Goodrich, Mar. 24, 1796, *AC*, 5:725; Murray, Mar. 23, 1796, *AC*, 5:685; Goodrich, Mar. 24, 1796, *AC*, 5:719; W. Smith, Mar. 8, 1796, *AC*, 5:443. Also see N. Smith, Mar. 9, 1796, *AC*, 5:455; S. Lyman, Mar. 14, 1796, *AC*, 5:532; Bradbury, Mar. 9, 1796, *AC*, 5:548, 553; Tracy, Mar. 17, 1796, *AC*, 5:613; Kitchell, Mar. 21, 1796, *AC*, 5:653; Buck, Mar. 24, 1796, *AC*, 5:710–711; Cooper, Mar. 24, 1796, *AC*, 5:747.

36. W. Smith, Mar. 8, 1796, *AC*, 5:443; S. Lyman, Mar. 14, 1796, *AC*, 5:531; Buck, Mar. 7, 1796, *AC*, 5:432; Harper, Mar. 9, 1796, *AC*, 5:462; Eric Robert Papenfuse, *The Evils of Necessity: Robert Goodloe Harper and the Moral Dilemma of Slavery* (Philadelphia: American Philosophical Society, 1997), 20–27; Michael L. Kennedy, "A French Jacobin Club in Charleston, South Carolina, 1792–1795," *The South Carolina Historical Magazine* 91 (Jan. 1990), 11. Also see Reed, Mar. 17, 1796, *AC*, 5:609. Murray, Mar. 23, 1796, *AC*, 5:702; Gilbert, Mar. 23, 1796, *AC*, 5:676; Enclosure [Draft of a Response to Concerns about the Jay Treaty], Hamilton to George Washington, Mar. 29, 1796, *PAH*, 20:101–102.

37. Hillhouse, Mar. 22, 1796, *AC*, 5:671; Isaac Smith, Mar. 18, 1796, *AC*, 5:627; Coit, Mar. 22, 1796, *AC*, 5:657; Ames to Dwight, Mar. 9, 1796, *WFA*, 2:1136–1137. Also see Bradbury, Mar. 9, 1796, *AC*, 5:549; Griswold, Mar. 10, 1796, *AC*, 5:476, 480; J. Smith, Mar. 16, 1796, *AC*, 5:596, 598.

38. Murray, Mar. 23, 1796, *AC*, 5:688, 692, 686, 698; Gilbert, Mar. 23, 1796, *AC*, 5:676; J. Smith, Mar. 16, 1796, *AC*, 5:597; Williams, Mar. 21, 1796, *AC*, 5:651; Cooper, Mar. 14, 1796, *AC*, 5:542. Also see Griswold, Mar. 10, 1796, *AC*, 5:479; Madison, Mar. 10, 1796, *AC*, 5:490; Gilbert, Mar. 23, 1796, *AC*, 5:676; Murray, Mar. 23, 1796, *AC*, 5:702.

39. Williams, Mar. 21, 1796, *AC*, 5:646. Also see Murray, Mar. 23, 1796, *AC*, 5:686.

40. Murray, Mar. 23, 1796, *AC*, 5:693, 692; W. Smith, Mar. 7, 1796, *AC*, 5:438. Also see Buck, Mar. 7, 1796, *AC*, 5:432; N. Smith, Mar. 9, 1796, *AC*, 5:454; Harper, Mar. 9, 1796, *AC*, 5:462; W. Smith, Mar. 24, 1796, *AC*, 5:747.

41. Cooper, Mar. 14, 1796, *AC*, 5:542; S. Lyman, Mar. 14, 1796, *AC*, 5:531. Also see Murray, Mar. 23, 1796, *AC*, 5:698, 699.

42. Baldwin, Mar. 14, 1796, *AC*, 5:537, 536.

43. Madison, Mar. 10, 1796, *AC*, 5:488, 494; Baldwin, Mar. 14, 1796, *AC*, 5:537; Gallatin, Mar. 24, 1796, *AC*, 5:726.

44. Jonathan Havens, Mar. 10, 1796, *AC*, 5:486; Madison, Mar. 10, 1796, *AC*, 5:487–488.

45. Gallatin, Mar. 9, 1796, *AC*, 5:466. On Gallatin's address, Jefferson reported, "I am enchanted with Mr. Gallatin's speech. . . . It is worthy of being printed at the end of the Federalist, as the only rational commentary on the part of the constitution to which it relates"; see Jefferson to Madison, Mar. 27, 1796, *PTJ*, 29:51.

46. Gallatin, Mar. 7, 1796, *AC*, 5:437; Findley, Mar. 16, 1796, *AC*, 5:590; W. Lyman, Mar. 16, 1796, *AC*, 5:603.

47. On how radical Republican arguments were vis-à-vis the treaty-making power, see Golove and Hulsebosch, "A Civilized Nation," 1044–1055.

48. Havens, Mar. 10, 1796, *AC*, 5:482; Findley, Mar. 16, 1796, *AC*, 5:591; Madison, Mar. 10, 1796, *AC*, 5:490. Also see Gallatin, Mar. 9, 1796, *AC*, 5:467; Holland, Mar. 14, 1796, *AC*, 5:545; Baldwin, Mar. 14, 1796, *AC*, 5:536–537; Brent, Mar. 15, 1796, *AC*, 5:578; W. Lyman, Mar. 16, 1796, *AC*, 5:602–603; Gallatin, Mar. 24, 1796, *AC*, 5:726.

49. Robert Rutherford, Mar. 14, 1796, *AC*, 5:555; John Page, Mar. 15, 1796, *AC*, 5:562; Holland, Mar. 14, 1796, *AC*, 5:547. Also see Nicholas, Mar. 8, 1796, *AC*, 5:445; Giles, Mar. 11, 1796, *AC*, 5:509; Gallatin, Mar. 24, 1796, *AC*, 5:740. Some Republicans even invoked the "necessary and proper" clause to argue that the president and Senate's treaty-making authority was subject to legislative regulation; see Findley, Mar. 16, 1796, *AC*, 5:590–591.

50. Gallatin, Mar. 9, 1796, *AC*, 5:466; Madison, Mar. 10, 1796, *AC*, 5:493; Findley, Mar. 16, 1796, *AC*, 5:589; Giles to Jefferson, Mar. 26, 1796, *PTJ*, 29:46. Also see Freeman, Mar. 16, 1796, *AC*, 5:590–591.

51. Swanwick, Mar. 8, 1796, *AC*, 5:450; Madison, Mar. 10, 1796, *AC*, 5:493; Gallatin, Mar. 9 and 10, 1796, *AC*, 5:472, 474. Also see Nicholas, Mar. 8, 1796, *AC*, 5:445; Holland, Mar. 14, 1796, *AC*, 5:545. On the prevalence of a certain perceived relationship between political liberty and will in the Anglo-American world at this time, see Quentin Skinner, *Liberty before Liberalism* (New York: Cambridge University Press, 1998); Eric Nelson, *The Royalist Revolution: Monarchy and the American Founding* (Cambridge, MA: Harvard University Press, 2014), 12–13, 71–75, 114–117.

52. Livingston, Mar. 18, 1796, *AC*, 5:631; Giles, Mar. 11, 1796, *AC*, 5:510; Gallatin, Mar. 24, 1796, *AC*, 5:738. Also see Holland, Mar. 14, 1796, *AC*, 5:545–546; Madison, Mar. 10, 1796, *AC*, 5:491.

53. Giles, Mar. 11, 1796, *AC*, 5:508; Gallatin, Mar. 9, 1796, *AC*, 5:468. Also see Baldwin, Mar. 14, 1796, *AC*, 5:536. Federalists insinuated that Republicans were, as William Branch Giles put it, "rebels and traitors against the constituted authorities"; see Giles to Jefferson, Mar. 26, 1796, *PTJ*, 29:46.

54. Giles, Mar. 11, 1796, *AC*, 5:503; W. Lyman, Mar. 16, 1796, *AC*, 5:603.

55. Page, Mar. 15, 1796, *AC*, 5:561, and generally 560–563; W. Lyman, Mar. 16, 1796, *AC*, 5:604; Brent, Mar. 15, 1796, *AC*, 5:583; Giles, Mar. 11, 1796, *AC*, 5:506; Gallatin, Mar. 9, 1796, *AC*, 5:466; Madison, Mar. 10, 1796, *AC*, 5:488, and generally 488–494; W. Lyman, Mar. 10, 1796, *AC*, 5:602–604; Livingston, Mar. 18, 1796, *AC*, 5:631–632. Also see Havens, Mar. 10, 1796, *AC*, 5:484, 486; Baldwin, Mar. 14, 1796, *AC*, 5:538; Holland, Mar. 14, 1796, *AC*, 5:543; Brent, Mar. 15, 1796, *AC*, 5:562, 577; Findley, Mar. 16, 1796, *AC*, 5:589–591; Samuel Smith, Mar. 17, 1796, *AC*, 5:623, 624; Gallatin, Mar. 24, 1796, *AC*, 5:738.

56. Madison, Mar. 10, 1796, *AC*, 5:488–489. Also see Gallatin, Mar. 9, 1796, *AC*, 5:466. Jefferson also invoked a similar interpretive rule; see Jefferson to Madison, Mar. 27, 1796, *PTJ*, 29:51.

57. Madison, Mar. 10, 1796, *AC*, 5:493–494; Murray, Mar. 7, 1796, *AC*, 5:429; United States Constitution, Article VI. Also see Sedgwick, Mar. 11, 1796, *AC*, 5:515; Hamilton to King, Mar. 16, 1796, *PAH*, 20:76–77; Enclosure [Draft of a Response to Concerns about the Jay Treaty], Hamilton to Washington, Mar. 29, 1796, *PAH*, 20:89–90, 98.

58. Sedgwick, Mar. 11, 1796, *AC*, 5:515–516; Bradbury, Mar. 14, 1796, *AC*, 5:549, and generally 548–553; J. Smith, Mar. 16, 1796, *AC*, 5:599. Also see Murray, Mar. 7 and 23, 1796, *AC*, 5:436–437, 685, 683; Griswold, Mar. 10, 1796, *AC*, 5:478; Cooper, Mar. 14, 1796, *AC*, 5:541. Federalists believed, like many who had designed the Constitution, that the supremacy clause had incorporated the self-executing treaty doctrine into the Constitution, a controversial principle that broke with standard practice in which treaties did not require legislative implementation; see Golove and Hulsebosch, "A Civilized Nation," 995–997, 1048–1049, 1052–1055.

59. Baldwin, Mar. 14, 1796, *AC*, 5:539. Also see Gallatin, Mar. 9, 1796, *AC*, 5:468; Brent, Mar. 15, 1796, *AC*, 5:576.

60. Gallatin, Mar. 9, 1796, *AC*, 5:468–469; Swanwick, Mar. 8, 1796, *AC*, 5:450; Madison, Mar. 10, 1796, *AC*, 5:488. Also see Giles, Mar. 11, 1796, *AC*, 5:506; Baldwin, Mar. 14, 1796, *AC*, 5:539; Findley, Mar. 16, 1796, *AC*, 5:592; Gilbert, Mar. 23, 1796, *AC*, 5:681.

61. Havens, Mar. 10, 1796, *AC*, 5:485; Madison, Mar. 10, 1796, *AC*, 5:489–490. Also see Gallatin, Mar. 9, 1796, *AC*, 5:473; Madison, Mar. 10, 1796, *AC*, 5:448; Giles, Mar. 11, 1796, *AC*, 5:506–507.

62. Gallatin, Mar. 24, 1796, *AC*, 5:742; Madison, Mar. 10, 1796, *AC*, 5:494; Gallatin, Mar. 9, 1796, *AC*, 5:469. Also see Giles, Mar. 11, 1796, *AC*, 5:506.

63. Giles, Mar. 11, 1796, *AC*, 5:509; Brent, Mar. 15, 1796, *AC*, 5:575; Havens, Mar. 10, 1796, *AC*, 5:482. Also see Gallatin, Mar. 9, 1796, *AC*, 5:468; Findley, Mar. 16, 1796, *AC*, 5:592–593.

64. W. Lyman, Mar. 16, 1796, *AC*, 5:607.

65. Baldwin, Mar. 7, 1796, *AC*, 5:435; Williams, Mar. 21, 1796, *AC*, 5:642; Rutherford, Mar. 14, 1796, *AC*, 5:555; John Heath, Mar. 8, 1796, *AC*, 5:448; Livingston, Mar. 20, 1796, *AC*, 5:639–640. Also see Baldwin, Mar. 8, 1796, *AC*, 5:533–534; Swanwick, Mar. 8, 1796, *AC*, 5:452; W. Smith, Mar. 10, 1796, *AC*, 5:496.

66. Freeman, Mar. 16, 1796, *AC*, 5:586; Gallatin, Mar. 9, 1796, *AC*, 5:474; S. Smith, Mar. 17, 1796, *AC*, 5:625–626; Kitchell, Mar. 21, 1796, *AC*, 5:653. Also see Giles, Mar. 11, 1796, *AC*, 5:511; Holland, Mar. 14, 1796, *AC*, 5:543–544; Rutherford, Mar. 14, 1796, *AC*, 5:555; Findley, Mar. 16, 1796, *AC*, 5:590; W. Lyman, Mar. 16, 1796, *AC*, 5:608; Livingston, Mar. 20, 1796, *AC*, 5:641. Some have influentially suggested that this connection had waned post-1787; see Gordon S. Wood, *The Creation of the American Republic, 1776–1787*, 2nd ed. (1969; Chapel Hill: University of North Carolina Press, 1998), chs. 9, 15. On how Republicans during the Jay Treaty debate stressed the "immediate representatives" of the people, see Daniel, *Scandal and Civility*, 135–136.

67. Sedgwick, Mar. 11, 1796, *AC*, 5:518; Griswold, Mar. 10, 1796, *AC*, 5:480; I. Smith, Mar. 18, 1796, *AC*, 5:627. Also see Buck, Mar. 7 and 24, 1796, *AC*, 5:433, 704; Tracy,

Mar. 21, 1796, *AC*, 5:619; Coit, Mar. 22, 1796, *AC*, 5:659; Hillhouse, Mar. 22, 1796, *AC*, 5:673; Gilbert, Mar. 23, 1796, *AC*, 5:679, 680; Murray, Mar. 23, 1796, *AC*, 5:697; Hamilton to W. Smith, Mar. 10, 1796, *PAH*, 20:72–73; Hamilton to Rufus King, Mar. 16, 1796, *PAH*, 20:77; Enclosure [Draft of a Response to Concerns about the Jay Treaty], Hamilton to Washington, Mar. 29, 1796, *PAH*, 20:93–99.

68. Harper, Mar. 9, 1796, *AC*, 5:464; Gilbert, Mar. 23, 1796, *AC*, 5:678; Williams, Mar. 21, 1796, *AC*, 5:644. Also see Buck, Mar. 7, 1796, *AC*, 5:433; Sedgwick, Mar. 11, 1796, *AC*, 5:515; S. Lyman, Mar. 14, 1796, *AC*, 5:530–531; Bradbury, Mar. 14, 1796, *AC*, 5:552; Harper, Mar. 24, 1796, *AC*, 5:709.

69. Goodrich, Mar. 24, 1796, *AC*, 5:720; Hillhouse, Mar. 22, 1796, *AC*, 5:672; Murray, Mar. 23, 1796, *AC*, 5:691, 696, and generally 689–697. Stressing that the purpose of constitutional exegesis was to minimize absurdity, also see Griswold, Mar. 10, 1796, *AC*, 5:478; Cooper, Mar. 14, 1796, *AC*, 5:541; J. Smith, Mar. 16, 1796, *AC*, 5:596; Milledge, Mar. 22, 1796, *AC*, 5:651; Gilbert, Mar. 23, 1796, *AC*, 5:681.

70. Gallatin, Mar. 9, 1796, *AC*, 5:469; Madison, Mar. 7, 1796, *AC*, 5:488.

7. The Apotheosis of the Fixed Constitution

Epigraph: James Madison to William Eustis, July 6, 1819, *PJM RS*, 1:479.

1. By the time House debate commenced, public opposition had somewhat diminished—in part because of an economic boom that was linked to the treaty—but it was still pronounced; see Stanley Elkins and Eric McKitrick, *The Age of Federalism, the Early American Republic, 1788–1800* (New York: Oxford University Press, 1993), 440–443.

2. There are only a smattering of examples of anybody questioning the applicability of historical appeals; see Theodore Sedgwick, Mar. 11, 1796, *AC*, 5:539; Joshua Coit, Mar. 22, 1796, *AC*, 5:657.

3. Sir Matthew Hale, *The History of the Common Law of England,* ed. Charles M. Gray (Chicago: University of Chicago Press, 1971), 40. For more, see Chapter 1.

4. James Holland, Mar. 14, 1796, *AC*, 5:547; John Page, Mar. 15, 1796, *AC*, 5:565; Abraham Baldwin, Mar. 14, 1796, *AC*, 5:533. Also see Richard Brent, Mar. 15, 1796, *AC*, 5:575.

5. Brent, Mar. 15, 1796, *AC*, 5:577; William Lyman, Mar. 16, 1796, *AC*, 5:603; William Loughton Smith, Mar. 10, 1706, *AC*, 5:495; Sedgwick, Mar. 11, 1796, *AC*, 5:523.

6. Edward Livingston, Mar. 18, 1796, *AC*, 5:633; Sedgwick, Mar. 10, 1796, *AC*, 5:526–527. Others have stressed how Federalists' and Republicans' use of history showed an abandonment of earlier commitments; see Joseph M. Lynch, *Negotiating the Constitution: The Earliest Debates over Original Intent* (Ithaca, NY: Cornell University Press, 1999), 150–160. But what is crucial is that they implicitly converged on the legitimacy of a certain mode of constitutional arbitration.

7. William Vans Murray, Mar. 23, 1796, *AC*, 5:701; Sedgwick, Mar. 11, 1796, *AC*, 5:524. On the impact of the publication of some ratifying convention debates, see Saul

Cornell, *The Other Founders: Anti-Federalism and the Dissenting Tradition in America, 1788–1828* (Chapel Hill: University of North Carolina Press, 1999), 228–229.

8. Murray, Mar. 23, 1796, *AC*, 5:701. On Washington's custody of the Convention record, see Mary Sarah Bilder, "How Bad Were the Official Records of the Federal Convention?" *George Washington Law Review* 80 (Nov. 2012), 1663–1665.

9. Sedgwick, Mar. 11, 1796, *AC*, 5:524. Ratifying convention debates were published in the following volumes: Thomas Lloyd, *Debates of the Convention, of the State of Pennsylvania* (Philadelphia: Joseph James, 1788); Benjamin Russell, *Debates, Resolutions and Other Proceedings, of the Convention of the Commonwealth of Massachusetts* (Boston: Adams and Nourse, 1788); *Debates and Other Proceedings of the Convention of Virginia*, 3 vols. (Petersburg, VA: Hunter and Prentis [vol. 1], Prentis [vols. 2–3], 1788–1789); *The Debates and Proceedings of the Convention of the State of New-York* (New York: Francis Childs, 1788); *Proceedings and Debates of the Convention of North-Carolina* (Edenton, NC: Hodge and Wills, 1789). For contemporaneous complaints about Lloyd's omissions from the Pennsylvania debates, see *DHRC*, 2:40–42. For complaints about revisions and additions to Russell's printed volume as well as its Federalist bias, see *DHRC*, 6:1135–1136. On Robertson's accuracy as note taker and the publishing of his rendition of the Virginia debates (first in late 1788), see *DHRC*, 9:902–906. Fuller accounts of the proceedings for the second half of the New York convention (July 1788) were published in Greenleaf's *New York Journal;* see *DHRC*, 19:lxix–lxx. William R. Davie and James Iredell (both Federalists who had attended the convention) had compiled what became the printed record of North Carolina's first convention from problematic notes taken by the man they had hired to do so but whose work had then disappointed them; see Pauline Maier, *Ratification: The People Debate the Constitution, 1787–1788* (New York: Simon and Schuster, 2010), 408–409. On the surviving record of the ratifying conventions, see *DHRC*, 2:324–325 (Pennsylvania); 3:126–127 (New Jersey); 3:212–213, 269 (Georgia); 3:333–336, 535–536 (Connecticut); 6:1128–1143 (Massachusetts); 9:901–906 (Virginia); 12:620–621 (Maryland); 19:lxviii–lxx (New York); 26:900–903 (Rhode Island); 27:303–304 (South Carolina); and 28:lxxi–lxxii (New Hampshire). Proceedings from the Delaware convention have been lost; see *DHRC*, 3:44–45, 105–106. Debate survives from only the first of North Carolina's two ratifying conventions (held in 1788 in Hillsborough and 1789 in Fayetteville); see Maier, *Ratification*, 408–409, 453. On the documentary record generally, see James H. Hutson, "The Creation of the Constitution: The Integrity of the Documentary Record," in *Interpreting the Constitution: The Debate over Original Intent*, ed. Jack N. Rakove (Boston: Northeastern University Press, 1990), 158–162; Leonard W. Levy, *Original Intent and the Framers' Constitution* (New York: MacMillan, 1988), 284–295.

10. James Madison, Apr. 6, 1796, *AC*, 5:777; Madison, Feb. 2, 1791, *DHFFC*, 14:374; Elbridge Gerry, Feb. 7, 1791, *DHFFC*, 14:460; Livingston, Mar. 18, 1796, *AC*, 5:635; Uriah Tracy, Mar. 17, 1796, *AC*, 5:617.

11. Murray, Mar. 23, 1796, *AC,* 5:701–702; Sedgwick, Mar. 11, 1796, *AC,* 5:524; W. Smith, Mar. 10, 1796, *AC,* 5:495.

12. Madison, Apr. 6, 1796, *AC,* 5:777, 778. The Davis volume was published as *The Ratifications of the New Federal Constitution, Together with the Amendments, Proposed by the Several States* (Richmond, VA: Augustine Davis, 1788). For more on this compilation, see *DHRC,* 10:1710. For more on all of these different kinds of evidence, see Jack N. Rakove, *Original Meanings: Politics and Ideas in the Making of the Constitution* (New York: Knopf, 1996), 9–18.

13. W. Smith, Mar. 10, 1796, *AC,* 5:495; Sedgwick, Mar. 11, 1796, *AC,* 5:522–523.

14. James Hillhouse, Mar. 22, 1796, *AC,* 5:666; Coit, Mar. 22, 1796, *AC,* 5:658.

15. Hillhouse, Mar. 22, 1796, *AC,* 5:666; Chauncey Goodrich, Mar. 24, 1796, *AC,* 5:719, 722; Ezekiel Gilbert, Mar. 23, 1796, *AC,* 5:679. Also see Theophilus Bradbury, Mar. 14, 1796, *AC,* 5:549; John Williams, Mar. 21, 1796, *AC,* 5:649.

16. Hillhouse, Mar. 22, 1796, *AC,* 5:666–667.

17. Williams, Mar. 21, 1796, *AC,* 5:649. On the creation of the Senate, see Rakove, *Original Meanings,* ch. 4; Michael J. Klarman, *The Framers' Coup: The Making of the United States Constitution* (New York: Oxford University Press, 2016), 169–212.

18. W. Smith, Mar. 10, 1796, *AC,* 5:495; Sedgwick, Mar. 11, 1796, *AC,* 5:523; Williams, Mar. 21, 1796, *AC,* 5:648. Also see Sedgwick, Mar. 11, 1796, *AC,* 5:522; Bradbury, Mar. 14, 1796, *AC,* 5:550. On Federalists' ironic use of Anti-Federalists' ratification arguments, which helped revive Anti-Federalist writings, see Cornell, *Other Founders,* 222–225. On Anti-Federalists' objections to the treaty-making power during ratification, see Klarman, *Framers' Coup,* 335–340.

19. Robert Goodloe Harper, Mar. 24, 1796, *AC,* 5:748.

20. Tracy, Mar. 17, 1796, *AC,* 5:619, and generally 619–621. Also see W. Smith, Mar. 8, 1796, *AC,* 5:451.

21. Williams, Mar. 21, 1796, *AC,* 5:648; John Reed, Mar. 17, 1796, *AC,* 5:616. Also see W. Smith, Mar. 10, 1796, *AC,* 5:495; Sedgwick, Mar. 11, 1796, *AC,* 5:524.

22. W. Smith, Mar. 10, 1796, *AC,* 5:495; Hillhouse, Mar. 22, 1796, *AC,* 5:668; Williams, Mar. 21, 1796, *AC,* 5:649. Also see Sedgwick, Mar. 11, 1796, *AC,* 5:526. For Virginia's recommended amendments—composed of a declaration of rights (twenty articles) and twenty structural alterations—see Virginia Ratifying Convention, June 27, 1788, *DHRC,* 10:1551–1556. The proposed change to treaty making came in the seventh of the twenty recommended structural alterations and, in addition to requiring the concurrence of two-thirds of all senators to ratify commercial treaties, it also required the concurrence of three-fourths of both houses of Congress to ratify treaties affecting the territorial claims of the United States; see *DHRC,* 10:1554.

23. W. Smith, Mar. 10, 1796, *AC,* 5:496. The Pennsylvania minority comprised twenty-one of the twenty-three delegates to the Pennsylvania ratifying convention who had voted against ratification. Angered not just by the Constitution's ratification but

as much by Federalists' heavy-handed tactics, this group published a lengthy diatribe three days after ratification; see "The Dissent of the Minority of the Convention," *DHRC*, 2:617–618. They included amendments because, when they submitted them to the Convention, Federalists had refused to consider them or even enter them into the record of official proceedings. The substance of their critique proved influential. For more, see Maier, *Ratification*, 115–122.

24. Sedgwick, Mar. 11, 1796, *AC*, 5:524; Benjamin Bourne, Mar. 15, 1796, *AC*, 5:567. On Bourne, see *DHFFC*, 14:820–822.

25. Sedgwick, Mar. 11, 1796, *AC*, 5:524–525; Bourne, Mar. 15, 1796, *AC*, 5:571; Sedgwick, Mar. 11, 1796, *AC*, 5:526. Also generally see Sedgwick, Mar. 11, 1796, *AC*, 5:525, 526; Bourne, Mar. 15, 1796, *AC*, 5:568, 570; Tracy, Mar. 17, 1796, *AC*, 5:616–617.

26. Sedgwick, Mar. 11, 1796, *AC*, 5:525; Bourne, Mar. 15, 1796, *AC*, 5:568; Williams, Mar. 21, 1796, *AC*, 5:645. Williams also referenced one of New York's proposed amendments, which stipulated that no treaty ought to be understood to abrogate any federal or state law; see Williams, Mar. 21, 1796, *AC*, 5:649. For New York's proposed amendments, see New York Ratifying Convention, July 26, 1788, *DHRC*, 23:2326–2334.

27. Sedgwick, Mar. 11, 1796, *AC*, 5:525–526, and generally 520–526. Also see Bradbury, Mar. 14, 1796, *AC*, 5:550–551. On the central importance of honor culture among early national congressmen, see Joanne B. Freeman, *Affairs of Honor: National Politics in the Early Republic* (New Haven, CT: Yale University Press, 2001).

28. Murray, Mar. 23, 1796, *AC*, 5:700–701; Bradbury, Mar. 14, 1796, *AC*, 5:551. Also see Coit, Mar. 22, 1796, *AC*, 5:657–658. The other House members who had been delegates to the Constitutional Convention were Nicholas Gilman (New Hampshire) and Jonathan Dayton (New Jersey).

29. Sedgwick, Mar. 11, 1796, *AC*, 5:526, 527, 524. Contending that Virginia's convention confirmed Sedgwick's reading, see Hillhouse, Mar. 22, 1796, *AC*, 5:667.

30. William Findley, Mar. 16, 1796, *AC*, 5:591. Also see Jonathan Havens, Mar. 10, 1796, *AC*, 5:487; W. Lyman, Mar. 16, 1796, *AC*, 5:604; Livingston, Mar. 18, 1796, *AC*, 5:635.

31. W. Lyman, Mar. 16, 1796, *AC*, 5:604. For examples of vaguer appeals to history, see Baldwin, Mar. 14, 1796, *AC*, 5:537; Holland, Mar. 14, 1796, *AC*, 5:543; Page, Mar. 15, 1796, *AC*, 5:558, 559. On Republicans' use of ratification materials, also see Cornell, *Other Founders*, 225–228.

32. Findley, Mar. 16, 1796, *AC*, 5:591–592.

33. Findley, Mar. 16, 1796, *AC*, 5:592. Findley relied upon personal memory for Pennsylvania's convention debates because the available record was so limited.

34. Brent, Mar. 15, 1796, *AC*, 5:582; William Branch Giles, Mar. 11, 1796, *AC*, 5:502.

35. Albert Gallatin, Mar. 24, 1796, *AC*, 5:734–735.

36. Gallatin, Mar. 24, 1796, *AC*, 5:734; Findley, Mar. 16, 1796, *AC*, 5:592; Gallatin, Mar. 24, 1796, *AC*, 5:735–736. Also see Brent, Mar. 15, 1796, *AC*, 5:580; Livingston, Mar. 18, 1796, *AC*, 5:635.

37. Samuel Smith, Mar. 17, 1796, *AC,* 5:625. Also see Brent, Mar. 15, 1796, *AC,* 5:578.

38. Brent, Mar. 15, 1796, *AC,* 5:579–580; Gallatin, Mar. 24, 1796, *AC,* 5:736.

39. Brent, Mar. 15, 1796, *AC,* 5:580; Holland, Mar. 14, 1796, *AC,* 5:546; Gallatin, Mar. 24, 1796, *AC,* 5:736.

40. Bourne, Mar. 15, 1796, *AC,* 5:567; W. Lyman, Mar. 16, 1796, *AC,* 5:608.

41. Gallatin, Mar. 24, 1796, *AC,* 5:737.

42. Mar. 24, 1796, *AC,* 5:759–760; Mar. 25, 1796, *AC,* 5:760. On how public criticism wounded Washington, see Jeffrey L. Pasley, *The First Presidential Contest: 1796 and the Founding of American Democracy* (Lawrence: University Press of Kansas, 2013), 145.

43. "Secretary of State: Convention Papers Received from President Washington," Mar. 19, 1796, *Records,* 3:370.

44. Camillus [Hamilton], "The Defence No. XXXVIII," Jan. 9, 1796, *PAH,* 20:22, 23. For more, see Bilder, "How Bad Were the Official Records of the Federal Convention?" 1674–1679.

45. George Washington's Speech, Mar. 30, 1796, *AC,* 5:760. For more on the drafting, see "Introductory Note: To George Washington," Mar. 7, 1796, *PAH,* 20:66. Hamilton drafted an extensive reply, but it arrived too late for Washington to make use of it; see *PAH,* 20:66; Alexander Hamilton to George Washington, Mar. 24, 1796, *PAH,* 20:81; Washington to Hamilton, Mar. 31, 1796, *PAH,* 20:103–105; and, for Hamilton's response, see Enclosure [Draft of a Response to Concerns about the Jay Treaty], Hamilton to Washington, Mar. 29, 1796, *PAH,* 20:86–103. Washington claimed that his response captured most of the principles Hamilton had highlighted if, intriguingly, "not the reason[ings]"—as Hamilton made no mention of the history of the Constitution's construction; see Washington to Hamilton, Mar. 31, 1796, *PAH,* 20:104.

46. Washington's Speech, Mar. 30, 1796, *AC,* 5:761. Washington reiterated this argument in strong terms in a private letter a month later; see Washington to Charles Carroll, May 1, 1796, *Founders Online,* National Archives, available at http://founders .archives.gov/documents/Washington/99-01-02-00480. Washington had earlier invoked the same claim and virtually the same "spirit of amity" phrasing in his cover letter from the Constitutional Convention; see the President of the Convention to the President of Congress, Sept. 17, 1787, *DHRC,* 1:305.

47. Washington's Speech, Mar. 30, 1796, *AC,* 5:761. For the vote on the treaty amendment as recorded in the Convention journal, see *Records,* 2:382–383. On Washington's response generally, see Todd Estes, *The Jay Treaty Debate, Public Opinion, and the Evolution of American Political Culture* (Amherst: University of Massachusetts Press, 2006), 155–157.

48. Thomas Blount, Mar. 31, 1796, *AC,* 5:762, 763; Giles, Mar. 31, 1796, *AC,* 5:762.

49. George Thatcher, Mar. 31, 1796, *AC,* 5:763; Samuel Sitgreaves, Mar. 31, 1796, *AC,* 5:763–764; Sedgwick, Mar. 31, 1796, *AC,* 5:763. Also see William Cooper, Mar. 31, 1796, *AC,* 5:764; John Kittera, Mar. 31, 1796, *AC,* 5:765.

50. Gallatin, Mar. 31, 1796, *AC,* 5:764; Findley, Mar. 31, 1796, *AC,* 5:768. Also see Jeremiah Crabb, Mar. 31, 1796, *AC,* 5:765–766. For the vote, see Mar. 31, 1796, *AC,* 5:768–769.

51. N. Smith, Apr. 6, 1796, *AC,* 5:769–771.

52. Blount, Apr. 6, 1796, *AC,* 5:771–772; Noble E. Cunningham Jr., *The Jeffersonian Republicans: The Formation of Party Organization, 1789–1801* (Chapel Hill: University of North Carolina Press, 1957), 82–83.

53. Madison to Jefferson, Apr. 4, 1796, *PJM,* 16:286; Camillus [Hamilton], "The Defence No. XXXVIII," Jan. 9, 1796, *PAH,* 20:22–23; Murray, Mar. 23, 1796, *AC,* 5:701.

54. Madison to Jefferson, Apr. 4, 1796, *PJM,* 16:286, 287; Fisher Ames to George Richards Minot, Apr. 2, 1796, *WFA,* 2:1140. This discussion is indebted to Bilder, "How Bad Were the Official Records of the Federal Convention?" 1674–1679. Later in life, Madison again complained about Washington's misreading of the Convention vote; see "Detached Memoranda," 1819–1820, *PJM RS,* 1:604. Madison did not expressly refuse to publish his notes at this time, nor did Jefferson or anybody else ask him to at this time, but Jefferson later pleaded with Madison to do just that; see Jefferson to Madison, Jan. 16, 1799, *PTJ,* 30:623. When Jefferson directly asked, Madison refused, not because (following his criticism of Washington) he deemed it inappropriate, but because he worried how his notes might be used and abused; see Madison to Jefferson, Feb. 8, 1799, *PJM,* 17:229. It stands to reason that he weighed similar considerations in 1796.

55. Madison, Apr. 6, 1796, *AC,* 5:772, 775.

56. Madison, Apr. 6, 1796, *AC,* 5:775. Madison also considered James Wilson's speech from the Pennsylvania ratifying convention that Gallatin had cited, the fact that three South Carolinians who had attended the Federal Convention had condemned the Jay Treaty, and the fact that a leader of Delaware's treaty opposition had been a member of the Federal Convention; see Madison, Apr. 6, 1796, *AC,* 5:775–776. For the relevant portion of Gerry's speech that Madison read, see Gerry, Feb. 7, 1791, *DHFFC,* 14:459–460.

57. Madison, Apr. 6, 1796, *AC,* 5:776. Madison was not the first to make this claim. Republicans had begun emphasizing the special authority of the ratifying conventions before Gallatin offered an even firmer defense of their interpretive value; see Gallatin, Mar. 24, 1796, *AC,* 5:733–734. Many have emphasized the importance of Madison's choice to imbue the ratifying conventions with such authority, especially since he had previously looked to the drafting Convention for guidance; see Rakove, *Original Meanings,* 361–365; Jack N. Rakove, "The Original Intent of Original Understanding," *Constitutional Commentary* 13 (Fall 1996); Drew R. McCoy, *The Last of the Fathers: James Madison and the Republican Legacy* (New York: Cambridge University Press, 1989), 75–79, 88–89, 96, 110, 127; Gary Rosen, *American Compact: James Madison and the Problem of Founding* (Lawrence: University Press of Kansas, 1999), 160–169. Jeremy Bailey has argued that, this speech withstanding, Madison ultimately privi-

leged the interpretive importance of the Constitutional Convention, which explains why he took the time to complete his Convention notes; see Jeremy D. Bailey, *James Madison and Constitutional Imperfection* (New York: Cambridge University Press, 2015), 149–170. Donald Dewey has argued that while Madison did indeed claim to privilege the ratifying conventions in this speech and elsewhere, he typically appealed to the Convention whenever he could; see Donald O. Dewey, "James Madison Helps Clio Interpret the Constitution," *American Journal of Legal History* 15 (Jan. 1971), 39–46. Bilder has appropriately highlighted Madison's political motivations for making this speech, thus questioning what it ultimately reveals about his interpretive commitments; see Bilder, "How Bad Were the Official Records of the Federal Convention?" 1677–1680. Later in life, in recounting the Jay Treaty episode, Madison reiterated his commitment to the preeminence of the ratifying conventions; see "Detached Memoranda," 1819–1820, *PJM RS,* 1:605. More important than whether Madison privileged the drafting or ratifying conventions, I think, was the fact that, irrespective of motive, he appealed to the historical record *at all.*

58. Madison, Apr. 6, 1796, *AC,* 5:777, 779. For evidence Madison had singled out Iredell's and Wilson's convention speeches, see "Notes for Speech in Congress," ca. Mar. 23–Apr. 2, 1796, *PJM,* 16:274. For evidence that Madison owned the Davis compilation, see Madison to Jefferson, Oct. 17, 1788, *PJM,* 11:297. In a letter written three decades later, Madison reported that while giving the 1796 speech he had in his possession records of the debates from the Massachusetts, New York, and North Carolina conventions and a pamphlet containing some speeches from Pennsylvania's convention; he also reported that he had previously possessed records of the Virginia debates; see Madison to Jonathan Elliott, Nov. 25, 1826, *Letters,* 3:544.

59. For the best discussion of this transformation, see Rakove, *Original Meanings,* 355–365.

60. Ames, Apr. 28, 1796, *AC,* 5:1240, 1254; Apr. 29 and Apr. 30, 1796, *AC,* 5:1280, 1291. For this portion of the debate, see Elkins and McKitrick, *Age of Federalism,* 445–449. On Federalists' campaign to earn popular support for the treaty, see Pasley, *First Presidential Contest,* 152–159; and for an excellent discussion of Ames's speech, see 162–172.

Epilogue

Epigraph: James Madison to Henry Lee, June 25, 1824, *PJM RS,* 3:339.

1. Noah Webster, *An American Dictionary of the English Language,* 2 vols. (New York: S. Converse, 1828); Samuel Johnson, *A Dictionary of the English Language,* 2 vols. (London: W. Strahan, 1755). On Webster's project, see Jill Lepore, *A Is for American: Letters and Other Characters in the Newly United States* (New York: Knopf, 2002), 3–7, 57–60.

2. Publius [James Madison], "The Federalist 37," New York *Daily Advertiser,* Jan. 11, 1788, *DHRC,* 15:346. On when Madison first received this distinctive moniker,

"father of the Constitution," see Noah Feldman, *The Three Lives of James Madison: Genius, Partisan, President* (New York: Random House, 2017), 625.

3. On the Virginia and Kentucky resolutions and Madison's role in shaping them, see Stanley Elkins and Eric McKitrick, *The Age of Federalism, the Early American Republic, 1788–1800* (New York: Oxford University Press, 1993), 694–726; James Roger Sharp, *American Politics in the Early Republic: The New Nation in Crisis* (New Haven, CT: Yale University Press, 1993), ch. 9; Saul Cornell, *The Other Founders: Anti-Federalism and the Dissenting Tradition in America, 1788–1828* (Chapel Hill: University of North Carolina Press, 1999), 230–245; Gordon S. Wood, *Empire of Liberty: A History of the Early Republic, 1789–1815* (New York: Oxford University Press, 2009), 247–271. On how Madison's engagement revealed core aspects of his constitutionalism, see Jonathan Gienapp, "How to Maintain a Constitution: The Virginia and Kentucky Resolutions and James Madison's Struggle with the Problem of Constitutional Maintenance," in *Nullification and Secession in Modern Constitutional Thought,* ed. Sanford Levinson (Lawrence: University Press of Kansas, 2016), 53–90. On Madison's constitutional thought during his tenure as secretary of state and then president, see Jeremy D. Bailey, *James Madison and Constitutional Imperfection* (New York: Cambridge University Press, 2015), ch. 6; and more generally see Feldman, *Three Lives of James Madison,* Book III.

4. On Madison's later years, see Drew R. McCoy, *The Last of the Fathers: James Madison and the Republican Legacy* (1971; New York: Cambridge University Press, 1989); Ralph Ketcham, *James Madison: A Biography* (Charlottesville: University of Virginia Press, 1990), ch. 22, esp. 628–644; Jack N. Rakove, *James Madison and the Creation of the American Republic* (New York: Longman, 1990), ch. 16.

5. Madison to Edward Livingston, Apr. 17, 1824, *PJM RS,* 3:266; Madison to Unknown, 1833, *WJM,* 9:528. Also see Madison to Robert S. Garnett, Feb. 11, 1824, *PJM RS,* 3:216; Madison to Joseph C. Cabell, Sept. 18, 1828, *WJM,* 9:322–324; Madison to Nicholas P. Trist, Feb. 15, 1830, *Letters,* 4:61; Madison to Daniel Webster, May 27, 1830, *Letters,* 4:85; Madison to James Robertson, Jr., Apr. 20, 1831, *Letters,* 4:171; Madison to Trist, Dec. 1831, *WJM,* 9:471–477.

6. Madison to Sherman Converse, Mar. 10, 1826, *Letters,* 3:519.

7. Madison to Converse, Mar. 10, 1826, *Letters,* 3:519; Madison to Henry Lee, June 25, 1824, *PJM RS,* 3:339; Madison to Trist, Mar. 2, 1827, *Letters,* 3:565.

8. Madison to Professor Davis (unsent), 1833, *Letters,* 4:249; Madison to Charles J. Ingersoll, June 25, 1831, *Letters,* 4:184.

9. Madison to Converse, Mar. 10, 1826, *Letters,* 3:519; Madison to Lee, June 25, 1824, *PJM RS,* 3:339. Also see Madison to Robertson Jr., Apr. 20, 1831, *Letters,* 4:171–172. Madison thus envisioned the Constitution's language and history as fundamentally intertwined. For the opposite claim, embedded in a valuable discussion, see Donald O. Dewey, "James Madison Helps Clio Interpret the Constitution," *American Journal of Legal History* 15 (Jan. 1971), 39–46. Madison also occasionally referenced the authority of "public sanction," in which doubtful meaning was clarified "through a

period of years," which helped square his seeming inconsistency on the constitutionality of chartering a national bank; see Madison to Cabell, Sept. 18, 1828, *WJM*, 9:334; Madison to Cabell, Oct. 30, 1828, *Letters*, 3:655–656; Madison to Martin L. Hurlbut, May 1830, *WJM*, 9:372; Madison to Charles E. Haynes, Feb. 25, 1831, *WJM*, 9:442–443; Madison to Ingersoll, June 25, 1831, *Letters*, 3:183–186; Madison to Trist, Dec. 1831, *WJM*, 9:476–477. Such references (though they surely represented a vital and competing strand of thought) nonetheless paled in comparison to his appeals to original meaning.

10. Madison to John Jackson, Dec. 28, 1821, *PJM RS*, 2:442; Madison, "A Sketch Never Finished nor Applied," ca. 1835, *WJM*, 2:410. For when Madison recounted what happened at the Federal Convention, see Madison to Jared Sparks, Apr. 8, 1831, *WJM*, 9:447–451; Madison to J. K. Paulding, Apr. 1831, *WJM*, 9:451–456; Madison to Sparks, Nov. 25, 1831, *WJM*, 9:464–468. For when Madison encouraged others' research into the 1780s, see Madison to William Cabell Rives, Dec. 20, 1828, *Letters*, 3:664; Madison to Edward Everett, Nov. 14, 1831, *Founders Online*, National Archives, available at http://founders.archives.gov/documents/Madison/99-02-02-2470; Madison to Everett, Jan. 5, 1832, *Founders Online*, National Archives, available at http://founders .archives.gov/documents/Madison/99-02-02-2501; Madison to Trist, Dec. 4, 1832, *Letters*, 4:227; Madison to Everett, Aug. 22, 1833, *Letters*, 4:307.

11. Madison to W. A. Duer, June 5, 1835, *WJM*, 9:557; Madison to Cabell, Feb. 2, 1829, *Letters*, 4:10; Madison to Jackson, Dec. 28, 1821, *PJM RS*, 2:441; Madison to Thomas Ritchie, Sept. 15, 1821, *PJM RS*, 2:381; Madison to Andrew Stevenson, Mar. 25, 1826, *Letters*, 3:522; "Madison's Will," Apr. 19, 1835, *WJM*, 9:549. For Madison's other criticism of the *Secret Proceedings*, see Madison to Joseph Gales, Aug. 26, 1821, *PJM RS*, 2:378; Madison to Thomas Cooper, Dec. 26, 1826, *Letters*, 3:545–546; Madison to Cabell, Feb. 2, 1829, *Letters*, 4:10–11; Jared Sparks, "Notes of a Visit to James Madison," Apr. 25, 1830, *Records*, 3:481; Madison to Trist, Dec. 1831, *WJM*, 9:474–475; Madison to Rives, Oct. 21, 1833, *Letters*, 4:310–311. For Madison's historical sensibilities, see Madison to William Eustis, July 6, 1819, *PJM RS*, 1:479; Madison to Edward Everett, Mar. 19, 1823, *PJM RS*, 3:17; Madison to Thomas S. Grimke, Jan. 17, 1829, *Founders Online*, National Archives, available at http://founders.archives.gov/documents /Madison/99-02-02-1672; Madison to John Tyler (unsent), 1833, *WJM*, 9:502–510; and generally see Jack N. Rakove, *Original Meanings: Politics and Ideas in the Making of the Constitution* (New York: Knopf, 1996), 1–2. For Madison's struggles with the timing of publication, see Madison to Jonathan Elliot, Nov. 15, 1826, *Founders Online*, National Archives, available at http://founders.archives.gov/documents/Madison/99-02-02 -0793; Madison to Samuel Harrison Smith, Feb. 2, 1827, *WJM*, 9:269–270; Madison to Elliot, Nov. 1, 1827, *Letters*, 3:598. For when Madison privileged the ratifying conventions, see "Detached Memoranda," c. 1819–1820, *PJM RS*, 2:605; Madison to Ritchie, Sept. 15, 1821, *PJM RS*, 2:381; Madison to Hurlbut, May 1830, *WJM*, 9:372; Madison to Trist, Dec. 1831, *WJM*, 9:477. For when Madison put the ratifying conventions on

equal footing with the Federal Convention, see Madison to Robert S. Garnett, Feb. 11, 1824, *PJM RS*, 3:216; Madison to Cabell, Sept. 18, 1828, *WJM*, 9:329–330, 332–333, 335; Madison to Andrew Stevenson, Nov. 27, 1830, *WJM*, 9:420–424; Madison to Charles Francis Adams, Oct. 12, 1835, *WJM*, 9:561–562. On the importance of other contemporaneous testimony from the ratification debates, see Madison to Thomas Jefferson, Feb. 8, 1825, *PJM RS*, 3:471; Madison to Trist, Mar. 1, 1829, *Founders Online,* National Archives, available at http://founders.archives.gov/documents/Madison/99-02-02-1720. On how scholars have disagreed on which moment of constitutional creation Madison privileged, see Chapter 6, n. 54. On Yates's notes, see Michael J. Klarman, *The Framers' Coup: The Making of the United States Constitution* (New York: Oxford University Press, 2016), 242–243. In 1808, distorted excerpts of Yates's notes were first published by Edmond-Charles Genêt (of French Revolutionary fame) in an attempt to help Vice President George Clinton seize the Democratic-Republican presidential nomination from Madison; see John P. Kaminski, *George Clinton: Yeoman Politician of the New Republic* (Madison: Madison House, 1993), 285. On the publication of the *Secret Proceedings,* see Mary Sarah Bilder, *Madison's Hand: Revising the Constitutional Convention* (Cambridge, MA: Harvard University Press, 2015), 226–227; Cornell, *Other Founders,* 288–294. On Madison's investment in a reliable history of the Founding, see Bailey, *Madison and Constitutional Imperfection,* 167–170. On Madison's struggle with publishing his notes and their eventual posthumous publication, see Bilder, *Madison's Hand,* 229–240.

12. Considerable energy has been devoted to the question of Madison's ideological consistency, especially whether his opposition to Hamiltonian nationalism in the 1790s and beyond marked a departure from the brand of constitutional reform he championed in the 1780s. Stressing rupture, see Marvin Meyers, ed., *The Mind of the Founder: Sources of the Political Thought of James Madison,* rev. ed. (Hanover, NH: University Press of New England, 1981), xxxiv–xliii; Elkins and McKitrick, *Age of Federalism,* 133–161, 233–235; Kevin R. Gutzman, "A Troublesome Legacy: James Madison and 'the Principles of '98,'" *JER* 15 (Winter 1995), 569–589; and most recently and emphatically Feldman, *Three Lives of Madison.* Stressing consistency, see Lance Banning, *The Sacred Fire of Liberty: James Madison and the Founding of the Federal Republic* (Ithaca, NY: Cornell University Press, 1995); Alan Gibson, "The Madisonian Madison and the Question of Consistency: The Significance and Challenge of Recent Research," *Review of Politics* 64 (Spring 2002), 311–339; Gordon S. Wood, "Is There a 'James Madison Problem'?" in *Revolutionary Characters: What Made the Founders Different* (New York: Penguin Press, 2006), 141–172; Michael Schwarz, "The Great Divergence Reconsidered: Hamilton, Madison, and U.S.-British Relations, 1783–89," *JER* 27 (Fall 2007), 407–436; Colleen A. Sheehan, *James Madison and the Spirit of Republican Government* (New York: Cambridge University Press, 2009); Alan Gibson, "Madison's 'Great Desideratum': Impartial Administration and the Extended Republic," *American Political Thought* 1 (Sept. 2012), 181–207; Robert W. T. Martin, *Government by Dissent: Protest,*

Resistance, and Radical Democratic Thought in the Early American Republic (New York: New York University Press, 2013), ch. 5; Bailey, *Madison and Constitutional Imperfection;* James T. Kloppenberg, *Towards Democracy: The Struggle for Self-Rule in European and American Thought* (New York: Oxford University Press, 2016), esp. 425–433 and supporting notes. For the heterodox take that Madison was consistently Hamiltonian, see Richard K. Matthews, *If Men Were Angels: James Madison and the Heartless Empire of Reason* (Lawrence: University Press of Kansas, 1995). For an intermediate take between the prevailing positions, see Jack N. Rakove, "The Madisonian Moment," *University of Chicago Law Review* 55 (Spring 1988), 473–505; and more generally, Rakove, *Original Meanings,* esp. chs. 2, 11. For a sophisticated take that argues that the Madison of the 1790s was the outlier, and the Madison of the 1780s and that of the 1820s were perfectly alike, see McCoy, *Last of the Fathers.* Whatever is concluded on this question, though, the transformation in Madison's constitutional imagination, though, was immense. While other crucial areas of his political and constitutional thinking may have remained steady, the mode through which he rendered the Constitution did not, and it is worth pondering the relationship between that imagination and related forms of his thought. The larger point is that something akin to Madison's constitutional transformation was widely experienced across the generation of which he was a part.

13. Jefferson to Samuel Kercheval, July 12, 1816, *PTJ RS,* 10:226; Jefferson to Wilson Cary Nicholas, Sept. 7, 1803, *PTJ,* 41:347; Jefferson to William Johnson, June 12, 1823, in *Thomas Jefferson: Writings,* ed. Merrill D. Peterson (New York: Library of America, 1984), 1475.

Acknowledgments

This book is about the often hidden ways in which the American Constitution was created. One of the great joys of completing this work is being able to reveal all that went into its creation, particularly by acknowledging the many people who helped along the way. This project began at Johns Hopkins University under the supervision of Philip Morgan. Phil was an unwaveringly supportive adviser who, in demanding the best out of me, sharpened my thinking and writing considerably. His infectious passion for all things early America continues to inspire me. Even though our research interests did not overlap, from the knowledge he brought to bear on my chosen subject, one never would have known. I will always appreciate the generosity and commitment he showed me, and I will always value his counsel and friendship.

At Hopkins my thinking was also molded by dedicated professors who taught me how to engage with the past creatively and rigorously. Michael Johnson's enthusiasm for history, like his knowledge of it, knows no limits, and he helped teach me how to ask thought-provoking questions. Angus Burgin arrived halfway through my graduate studies and became a stimulating interlocutor. David Bell, John Marshall, Toby Ditz, Lou Galambos, and Gabrielle Spiegel all refined my historical thinking in meaningful ways. Many of my graduate peers profoundly shaped me. Cole Jones, Craig Hollander, Claire Gherini, Nick Radburn, and Katherine Smoak were unfailing sources of intellectual and moral support. Several others left their mark on me as well, including especially Ian Beamish, Andrew Devereux, Katie Hemphill, Kat Maxson, Alex Orquiza, Justin Roberts, and Molly

Warsh. Thanks to all the participants in the Atlantic history seminar for engaging with my work and forming a vibrant scholarly community. Chance brought me in contact with Albert Beveridge III, and I am most grateful for that. Aside from becoming a dear friend, he has also proved a resolute champion of me and my work.

My passion for history and my desire to become a scholar were nourished while I was an undergraduate at Harvard University. I had the great pleasure to learn from, among others, James Kloppenberg, Eric Nelson, Laurel Thatcher Ulrich, James Hankins, Lisa McGirr, Thomas Bisson, and Michael McCormick, all of whom taught me how thinking historically involves far more than knowing what happened in the past. I was also encouraged by an uncommonly generous group of graduate students while there, including Philip Mead, Michael Bernath, Yonatan Eyal, Katherine Grandjean, Alison LaCroix, Daniel Sargent, and Daniel Wewers.

As this book took shape, I had the privilege of working in two splendid history departments. At the University of Mississippi, I received crucial support from the chair, Joseph Ward. I benefited from the guidance and friendship of many, including Mikaëla Adams, Jesse Cromwell, Oliver Dinius, Darren Grem, April Holm, Vivian Ibrahim, Zack Kagan Guthrie, Marc Lerner, Theresa Levitt, Antoinette Sutto, Jeff Watt, and Noell Wilson. My predecessor, Sheila Skemp, has been an unfailing advocate from the time we met. Special recognition is owed to John Ondrovcik and Jarod Roll for teaching me valuable tricks of the trade while sharpening my thinking in the process. Thanks as well to Jack Nowlin and Christopher Green for welcoming me into the law school and providing helpful feedback on my work.

I can think of no better place to have completed this book than Stanford University. The incredible collection of scholars, both within and beyond the history department, who share my interests have provided an incomparable set of interlocutors and scholarly mentors. Above all, Jack Rakove, Keith Baker, and Dan Edelstein have supported every facet of my intellectual development. Within the history department, Paula Findlen and Matthew Sommer have been supremely supportive chairs. My colleagues have been similarly welcoming and encouraging. Many of them offered me helpful assistance and advice, especially Jennifer Burns, James Campbell, Gordon Chang, David Como, J. P. Daughton, Zephyr Frank, Estelle Freedman, Fiona Griffiths, Allyson Hobbs, Yumi Moon, Tom Mullaney, Jessica Riskin, Richard Roberts, Aron Rodrigue, Priya Satia, Jun Uchida, Richard White, Kären Wigen, Caroline Winterer, and Mikael Wolfe.

Norman Naimark has ably and sympathetically served as my official department mentor. I am particularly grateful for the friendships I have developed with fellow junior faculty members, Rowan Dorin, Ana Minian, Kathryn Olivarius, Steven Press, and Ali Yaycioglu, and for the help each has given me on this project. Thanks to the uncommonly supportive department administrative staff for their essential assistance. Outside of the history department, my work has profited from interactions with Greg Ablavsky, Robert Gordon, Amalia Kessler, Michael McConnell, and Bernadette Meyler. I have learned so much about my fields of study from teaching such talented and curious students, undergraduate and graduate alike. Two of those terrific pupils, Elizabeth Lindqwister and Zachary Brown, contributed valuable research assistance toward the end of the project. A special thanks to Morgan Frank and Tasha Eccles for providing much-needed friendship and intellectual support during my initial time in Palo Alto.

Shortly after arriving in California, I was offered the incredible opportunity to present an earlier draft of this book in one of the Stanford Humanities Center's manuscript review workshops. Sincere thanks to Caroline Winterer for organizing the event and then offering such constructive feedback as a workshop participant, to Kelda Jamison for handling the logistics, and to the remarkable collection of scholars who took part and provided such invaluable suggestions for revisions: Daniel Hulsebosch, Mark Peterson, Sophia Rosenfeld, Greg Ablavsky, and Dan Edelstein. I am grateful to those individuals who generously invited me to present portions of my work at their institutions—Sanford Levinson, John Marshall, Stephen Griffin, Doug Smith, John Mikhail, and William Treanor—and to those who commented on my work at conferences, especially Jane Kamensky and Jeffrey Pasley. My work has benefited from engaged audiences at the Montpelier Roundtable on James Madison and the American Constitution, Stanford Law School, University of Texas School of Law, Johns Hopkins University, the New Horizons in Madison Scholarship Roundtable, and Georgetown Law, as well as at meetings of the Omohundro Institute of Early American History and Culture, the Consortium on the Revolutionary Era, the Organization of American Historians, the Society for U.S. Intellectual History, the American Society for Legal History, and the Society for Historians of the Early American Republic. I have also benefited from stimulating conversations with Jack Balkin, Tom Cutterham, Ned Foley, Francois Furstenberg, Aaron Hall, Larry Kramer, Lance Sorenson, Alex Statman, Mark Storslee, Bertrand Van Ruymbeke, Andrew Kalloch, Dan Margolskee, and Ian Nichols.

As anybody who works on Founding-era American constitutional and political history knows well, the kind of research we do would be unthinkable without the benefit of the monumental editorial work that has yielded so many indispensable documentary collections. For my own purposes, it would have been nearly impossible to complete this project without the help of the *Documentary History of the Ratification of the Constitution* and the *Documentary History of the First Federal Congress*. My deepest thanks to the editors and staffs of these projects for their superb work and immense contribution to scholarship.

Numerous individuals generously read and commented on all or much of this book. My friendship with Will Deringer extends back to our days as college roommates, and, as we have grown up together in the historical profession, he has been one of my most trusted readers and interlocutors. He has profoundly shaped many of the ideas found within these pages. Peter Onuf and David Waldstreicher each read an early draft in its entirety and offered countless suggestions for improvement. Both have remained unfalteringly supportive of the project. Daniel Rodgers engaged with the larger argument in his characteristically incisive and sympathetic way. Eric Nelson and Jud Campbell both read portions of the book and brought to bear their immense knowledge of the subject to help clarify my thinking. Evan Hepler-Smith helped sharpen my argumentation and organization through a careful reading of the early chapters. Keith Baker and Quentin Skinner—the two historians whose work on intellectual history has influenced me the most—each read the Introduction and provided not only penetrating advice but also crucial encouragement. At a late stage, John Mikhail and Richard Primus engaged with large parts of the manuscript and suggested important revisions. Two anonymous reviewers for Harvard University Press offered tremendously supportive feedback while helping me tighten my arguments. Michael Klarman read the whole book and productively challenged many of my claims. John Kaminski, whose knowledge of the making of the United States Constitution is matched by very few, read every word I wrote—including every footnote—and saved me from many interpretive and factual errors. Mary Bilder, whose work has immeasurably shaped me, devoted considerable time to my manuscript and helped improve it immensely. The same goes for Saul Cornell, whose careful reading and commentary pushed me in valuable new directions, whose legendary sense of humor kept me in check, and whose warmth and support fueled my confidence. Finally, my debt to Jack Rakove is incalculable. For many years now, he has been a resolute champion of my work, both underscoring its achievements and subjecting its weaknesses to trenchant critique. I have learned more than I can track from his immense knowledge of early American constitutionalism. Toward the end of the process, he generously found time to read the entire manuscript (yet again), not only sharpening its arguments but also enhancing its clarity by line editing every single chapter. I extend my deepest gratitude to each of these readers. The book is colossally better thanks to their assistance. Any errors that remain, of course, are attributable entirely to me.

Harvard University Press has proved an ideal home for this book. Joyce Seltzer has been a marvelous editor, believing in the project from the beginning, refining its focus, and skillfully shepherding it to completion. Many thanks as well to all members of the talented editorial team that greatly improved the final product. For expert proofreading of the final book, my thanks to Maggie Smith.

I am fortunate to have had such a caring family that values the importance of teaching and thinking. The grandparents I got to know, June Gienapp and Frank Kilian, taught me the importance of selflessness and hard work. My brother, Bill Gienapp, has long been my partner in crime and ever a source of the best brand of humor. My mother, Erica Gienapp, has supported me in every conceivable way. She taught me the right kind of values and always urged me to do things the right way. My father, William Gienapp, did not live to see me become a professional historian or to read this book, but I know how profoundly it bears his mark. For me, he long ago set the standard for historical excellence, and I have tried, no doubt in vain, to live up to his towering example. However successful I have been, I know my work is better for having tried and that, no matter what, he would have provided his steadfast encouragement.

My deepest gratitude is saved for Annie Twitty. Without her resolute love and support, this book would not have turned out as it did. No matter how incessantly the conversation veered toward the original Constitution, she never complained. More than merely humoring my excesses, she engaged with my work so often and with such insight that, by this point, there is not an idea contained in these pages that has escaped her influence. One of the best writers and editors I know, she waded through the entire manuscript—and in the case of some chapters, through multiple drafts—each time improving what I had to say beyond measure. On top of all that, she always has known when to encourage me, when to keep me honest with her sharp and clever wit, and when to pull me away from the early Constitution to enjoy the world beyond it. As with writing, so too in life. Without her companionship, things would simply not be as interesting, meaningful, or fun. With love, this book is for her.

Index

Baldwin, Abraham: appeals to history, 156, 291; on executive removal, 136, 138, 147–148, 151; member of First Congress, 14; member of Constitutional Convention, 136, 156, 304; on Jay Treaty, 271–272, 280, 282

Bank of North America, 50, 53, 218–219, 229–230

Bank of the United States, 206–208. *See also* National bank

Beckley, John, 253

Bedford, Gunning, 61, 66

Benson, Egbert, 127, 137, 139, 148, 155, 159–160

Bilder, Mary Sarah, 36–37, 198

Bill of rights, omission from United States Constitution: Anti-Federalists on, 98–102, 165; Federalists on, 99–100, 104–105; George Mason on, 99, 165; James Wilson on, 99–100; Madison on, 174. *See also* Amendments, first ten to United States Constitution; Declarations of rights

Bill of Rights. *See* Amendments, first ten to United States Constitution

Blackstone, William: *Commentaries on the Laws of England,* 27, 32, 118, 221, 303, 381n84; on common law, 26–27; context of writings, 118–119; rules of interpretation, 118, 121–123, 221

Bland, Theodorick, 134, 150, 226

Blount, Thomas, 313–314, 315–316

Bolingbroke, Henry St. John, Viscount, 27–28

Boudinot, Elias: appeals to history, 237–238; on executive removal, 126, 133, 135, 137, 140, 151, 160; on national bank, 214–217, 224, 237–238

Bourne, Benjamin, 302–303, 305, 310

Bowdoin, James, 40

Bradbury, Theophilus, 279, 304

Brandom, Robert, 9

Brent, Richard, 265, 277, 281, 291, 307, 308–309

British constitution: American colonies and, 23–24, 31, 73–74; consent, 28–29; criticism of, 47; custom, 26–28; descriptive versus prescriptive, 28, 33–34; emergence, 24–25; enforcement, 29–30; fixity of, 34–35, 101–102, 289; fundamental status of, 25, 32–33, 36; multiple constitutions under, 32; relationship to imperial constitution, 31; repugnancy and, 31, 36, 355n29; unwritten, 20–22, 270; written, 27, 36–37

British crown: British constitution and, 27–28, 32, 47; colonial charters and, 36; colonial judges and, 92; colonial struggle with, 14, 31; dispute with Parliament, 24–25, 28, 32, 87–88, 105; Jay Treaty and, 249, 303

British Empire, 31, 52

"Brutus": on constitutional permanence, 83–85; on imprecision of Constitution's language, 86, 89–90; 91; on problems of judicial interpretation, 93–95, 115, 122

Buck, Daniel, 249–250, 267

Burke, Aedanus, 14, 166, 192

Burke, Edmund, 29, 132, 289

Butler, Pierce, 60, 365n86, 405n14

Caldwell, David, 96

Capital, of the United States, 130–131, 205, 208

Carrington, Edward, 79, 169, 226

Case of the Prisoners, 52, 66, 239–240

"Cato," 82, 86

Centinel, 85, 86, 87, 90, 393n4, 400n49

Chancery, Court of, 93–94

Charter of Liberties and Privileges (New York), 51

Charters: as governing document of American colonies, 22, 32, 35, 51, 356n30; state constitutions and, 36–37, 51–52; United States Constitution and, 141–142, 201, 203, 229–230

Clinton, George, 82, 88, 431n11. *See also* "Cato"

Clymer, George, 152, 182–183

Coit, Joshua, 264, 266, 268, 298

Coke, Edward, 26, 118

Collin, Nicholas, 83

Colonies, British North American, 23–24, 31–32

Commentaries on the Laws of England, 27, 32, 118–119, 221, 303

Committee of Detail, 65–69, 72–73, 239, 364n82. *See also* Randolph, Edmund; Wilson, James

Committee of Style, 72–73, 366n91

Common law: applicability to United States, 108, 115, 118–120, 241; artificial reason of, 27–29; British constitution and, 26–30; colonial Americans' claim to, 32, 34; "common-law mind," 27; courts of, 26, 30; custom and, 26–27; opposition to Chancery, 93–94

Common Sense, 47. *See also* Paine, Thomas

Commonwealth v. Caton, 52. See also *Case of the Prisoners*

Confederation Congress. *See* Continental Congress

Congress, Federal: Anti-Federalists' fears of, 84,
87, 89–91, 97, 102; construction of at
Constitutional Convention, 59; discretion of
criticized, 143–144, 146–147, 203, 225–228,
230–232; discretion of defended, 129, 138–139,
141–142, 148, 174–175, 209–210, 223–224,
243–244, 251, 275–276, 278, 280, 285;
Federalists' faith in, 80–81, 106, 108–109, 112;
importance to development of the Constitution, 14–15; partisanship in, 16, 18, 211–213,
260–261; value as constitutional laboratory,
13–14
Considerations on the Bank of North America,
218
Constitution: meaning of word, 24–25, 325;
mechanical metaphors used to describe,
39–40, 61–62; uncertainty surrounding
meaning of term, 74
Constitution, United States: Article I,
Section 8; 88–92, 203, 215, 218; Article III,
92–95, 115–116; Article V, 80, 85, 146,
186–187; drafting of, 59–73; imagined as a
system, 61–62, 74, 81, 103–107, 129, 138,
141–142, 161–162, 184–185, 201, 216, 332;
taxing power, 76, 89–90, 192–193, 208–209,
214, 239; supremacy clause, 64, 278–281, 284;
treaty making, 249–251, 254–255, 263, 271.
See also Constitutional imagination; Implied
powers; "Necessary and proper" clause;
Preamble; Supremacy clause; Written
constitutionalism
Constitutional Convention: calling of, 5, 54–55;
Committee of Detail at, 65–69, 72–73, 239,
364n82; Committee of Style at, 72–73,
366n91; debates over enumeration at, 59–61,
100; debates over negative at, 63–65; historical
appeals to, 155–156, 234–235, 242, 297–299,
310, 312–313; historical appeals to, problems
with, 319–320, 331; language debated at,
57–58, 62–63, 68–70, 110–111; Madison's notes
from, 197–199, 242, 294, 311, 318–319, 330–331;
Madison's preparations for, 55–57; "necessary
and proper" clause devised and debated at,
67–68, 70, 213; official records of, 198, 311–312;
purpose of, 15, 58–59; secrecy of, 294;
supremacy clause devised at, 64
Constitutional conventions: drafting, 38;
ratifying, 38–39, 71, 75. *See also* Constitutional
Convention; Ratifying conventions
Constitutional imagination, 1–2, 4, 8, 10–12, 17,
326–327. *See also* "Archival" Constitution;
"Fixed" Constitution; "Imperfect" Constitu-

tion; "Indeterminate" Constitution; "Textual"
Constitution; "Unfinished" Constitution
Constitutional interpretation, 3, 5–6, 8–9, 51–52,
58, 185–186, 223–224, 239–240, 276–277,
284–285. *See also* Rules of interpretation
Continental Congress: Bank of North America
and, 219, 229; call for new state constitutions
by, 20; defense of American rights by, 32;
Hamilton's experience in, 205; Madison on,
49, 54–55, 59; replaced by First Federal
Congress, 130–131
Cooper, William, 261, 264–266, 269, 270
Corbin, Francis, 302, 303, 309
Corporate charter, Constitution imagined as, 5,
117, 218–219
Coxe, Tench, 79, 125, 161

Davie, William, 302, 424n9
Davis, Augustine, 297, 321
Dayton, Jonathan, 310, 426n28
Debates of the Convention, 294, 410n53, 424n9
Declaration of Independence, 2, 35, 51
Declaration of Rights of 1689, 27, 51
Declarations of rights: in British constitutional
tradition, 27, 98; in American colonies, 22, 51;
as part of state constitutions, 50–52, 98–99,
104, 174–175. *See also* Bill of Rights, omission
from United States Constitution
Declaratory Act, 87
Democratic-Republican societies, 258–259, 262,
268
"De Witt, John," 83, 87–88, 96, 102
Dickinson, John, 36, 61, 63, 79, 80, 112
"Dissent of the Minority of the Pennsylvania
Convention," 89, 301–302, 305–308,
425–426n23
Duane, James, 48

Ellsworth, Oliver, 14, 65, 71, 78, 109–110,
112–113, 132
English Civil War, 24, 28, 30
English constitution. *See* British constitution
Enumerated powers: Committee of Detail on,
65–68, 364–365n84; debates at Constitutional Convention over, 59–61, 69–70,
365–366n86; during amendments debate,
193, 395–396n9; during bank debate,
203–204, 215–217, 228–229, 233, 239–240,
243–244; during Jay Treaty debate, 273–274;
during ratification debates, 100–101; during
removal debate, 144
Equity, 51, 92–95, 119, 360n58

INDEX

www.ingramcontent.com/pod-product-compliance
Ingram Content Group UK Ltd.
Pitfield, Milton Keynes, MK11 3LW, UK
UKHW012232250525
458816UK00002B/8/J